HORACE FULLY PARSED

Word by Word

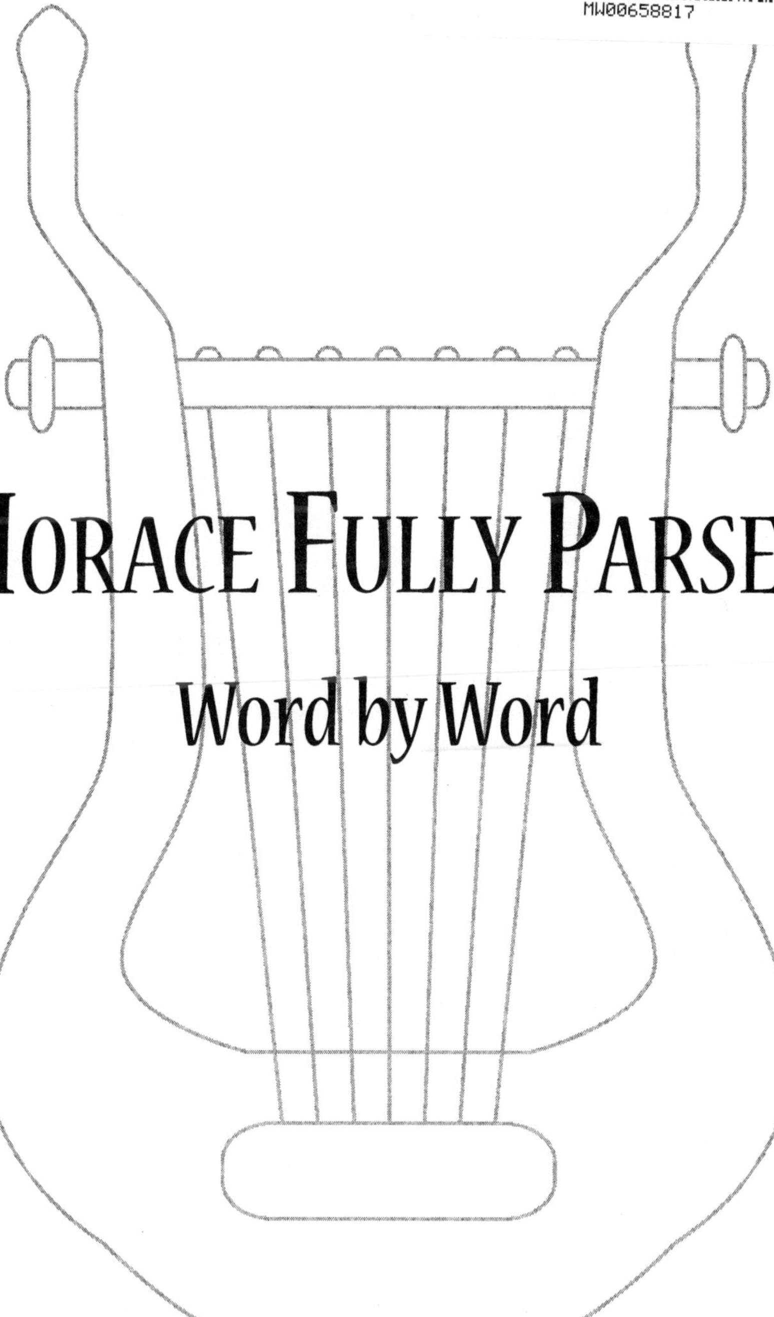

Editor
LeaAnn A. Osburn

Cover Design
Adam Phillip Velez

Horace Fully Parsed
"Word by Word"

Introduction
Thomas J. Sienkewicz

Printed in the United States of America
2003
by Bang Printing

BOLCHAZY-CARDUCCI PUBLISHERS, INC.
1000 Brown Street, Unit 101
Wauconda, Illinois 60084 U.S.A.
www.bolchazy.com

ISBN: 0-86516-552-1

Library of Congress Cataloging-in-Publication Data

Horace.
[Carmina. Book 1-2. English & Latin]
Horace fully parsed word by word : Books I and II of Horace Odes grammatically analyzed and literally translated / [introduction : Tom Sienkewicz].
p. cm.
Originally published: New York : Translation Pub. Co., 1917.
ISBN 0-86516-552-1 (alk. paper)
1. Laudatory poetry, Latin. 2. Horace--Translations into English. 3. Laudatory poetry, Latin--Translations into English. I. Title.
PA6393.C2 2003
874'.01--dc21

2003040100

Introduction

This book, originally published in 1917, was recently rediscovered by Dr. L.J.Bolchazy in a used bookstore. It appears to have been part of a series that included Caesar's *De Bello Gallico* I, Cicero's *Oratio in Catilinam* I, *De Amicitia* and *De Senectute*, Vergil's *Aeneid* I, and Xenophon's *Anabasis* I but no copies of other books in the series have been found so far, despite some effort by the publisher. I suspect that the unknown author of *Horace Fully Parsed, Odes Books I and II* was a high school Latin teacher who was well versed in Horace's poetry and committed to helping students to understand the grammar used in an ancient text. The pedagogical philosophy of the author is well described in the introduction to the original edition, which is not reprinted here. In this introduction D. S. Elbon, says that "unless a student can analyze and grammatically understand each sentence of the textbook he is reading, — regardless of his ability to express in English the general sense of the writing—it cannot be truly said that he is translating the book." Many aspects of the Latin classroom have changed in recent years, but Elbon's observation about the importance of grammatical analysis of the Latin sentence is in many ways as valid in 2002 as it was in 1917.

While the original audience of *Horace Fully Parsed* was the Latin student beginning to translate the *Odes* of Horace for the first time, few Latin students beginning the study of Horace in 2002 would know how to use this book or find it useful if they did. Rather, Bolchazy-Carducci Publishers is reprinting *Horace Fully Parsed* primarily as an aid for the beginning high school Latin teacher. Until the last quarter of the twentieth century, the typical high school Latin teacher had studied Latin for several years in high school and continued the language in college. Today, however, many high school Latin teachers begin their study of Latin only in college and have no more than three or four years of college Latin before they enter the Latin classroom and begin teaching authors like Horace. They often find themselves the only Latin teachers at their schools where they are expected to use the Advanced Placement curriculum even in their first year of teaching. Horace, of course, is an Advanced Placement author. A teacher in this situation needs all possible resources to teach such sophisticated and complex Latin poetry. *Horace Fully Parsed* will be of great help to these teachers.

Horace Fully Parsed contains a wealth of resources. The text of Horace's *Odes* appears at the top of the page. Elbon describes this text as "complete and accurate—well edited for school use." There is no apparatus criticus but this is not a detriment at this level. Occasionally the organization of the text offers some anomalies. For example, the author, along with other editors of Horace's *Odes* in this time period, indicates an elision between lines at *Ode* I.2.19-20 by placing the u- in *uxorius* at the end of line 19 and the rest of the word (-xorius) on the next line.

Although the traditional numeration by book, poem and line appears at the right hand side of the page, it is accompanied by a different numeration on the left, where the 1449 lines of poetry in these two books are numbered consecutively. A literal translation of the *Odes, Books I and II* is provided at the end of the book. In order to provide easy reference to the Latin verse while using this translation, the line numeration provided on the left-hand-side of the Latin text is repeated with this translation (but without the traditional line numeration at the right). Italics are used in the translation in order to indicate English words that do not have equivalents in the Latin version but that have been added to complete the sense. Given the many good English translations of Horace that have been produced since 1917, this literal translation, while quite accurate, is perhaps less useful than other parts of this book.

The most valuable elements of *Horace Fully Parsed* are unquestionably the line-by-line vocabulary and notes that appear below the text of the poem. Indeed, these notes are so extensive that only three or four lines of Latin appear on most pages of the book. The first note for each poem is metrical. The meter and types of feet used in the poem are identified by name and are illustrated with long and short marks, foot divisions, and information about caesura. Below this metrical information the author provides extensive grammatical, metrical, syntactical, cultural, mythological, and geographical information for each word, line by line. These notes follow the numerical system on the left-hand side of the Latin text.

Each word of the text is carefully parsed. For nouns case and number are followed by the nominative and genitive singular forms, the declension, gender and meaning(s) of the word. For adjectives case, number, gender, and words they modify are followed by all the adjective's nominative singular forms and the meaning(s) of the word. For verbs the entry begins with the person, number, tense, mood, and voice followed by the principal parts of the verb and the meaning(s) of the word. Especially useful are the macrons and short marks provided for those words with syllables long by nature.

In addition to this grammatical information, some notes provide cultural, mythological and geographical background and explanation. While this information is accurate, it often lacks contextual reference. For example, the note to *Ode* I.1.1 provides the full name of Maecenas, provides his genealogy, and identifies him as a Roman knight, friend of Augustus, critic and literary patron. The fact that Maecenas was Horace's patron, however, can only be deduced from the context of the poem.

Sometimes this background information is unnecessarily obscure. For example the note on *uxorius* (I.2.20) explains that the subject (the river Tiber) is uxorious because he was "influenced by his wife to avenge the death of Caesar, her descendant." It is not clear from the note that the husband is the river Tiber and that his wife, Ilia or Rhea Silvia, is the ancestor of Julius Caesar.

Generally detailed information on a word is provided only once. The second time a word appears the reader is referred back to the first occurrence by the numerical system on the left-hand side of the Latin text in parentheses. For example, for the word *Africum* all the grammatical information and the relationship of this wind to other Mediterranean winds is provided at I.1.15. When the word appears again at *Odes* I.3.12, the reader is told only that the word here is governed by *timuit* and is referred back to I.1.15 for all other information.

Once teachers are able to familiarize themselves with the unique aspects of this book they will find it an excellent reference for teaching Horace. With the *utile* provided by *Horace Fully Parsed* the *dulce* of Horace's *Odes* will be much more accessible.

THOMAS J. SIENKEWICZ
MONMOUTH, ILLINOIS
2002

EXPLANATORY NOTE

A careful method for facilitating a ready comparison of those words and phrases which the author has used that are parallel in their grammatical construction has been developed. It will be seen in the notes that after certain words a key number is printed within brackets. If the reader upon coming to such words will turn to the line of the corresponding number which is indicated by the figures in heavy type on the outer margin of each page, the translating of this new word may be more thoroughly appreciated through a direct comparison with another word or phrase of similar construction. The students' understanding and appreciation of the ancient language is thus strengthened by this method which first teaches the principles of the language, and then regularly points to the way in which these principles are applied.

Q. HORATII FLACCI

CARMINUM.

LIBER PRIMUS.

CARMEN I.—AD MÆCENATEM.

MÆCENAS atavis edite regibus,
O et præsidium et dulce decus meum:

METRE—*First or Lesser Asclepiad:*

– –	– ⏑ ⏑ –	– ⏑ ⏑ –	⏑ – or ⏑ ⏑
spondee	choriambus	choriambus	iambus or trochee

The cæsura after the first choriambus.

1. **Mæcenas,** voc. s.; fr. Mæcēnas, -atis, 3rd mas., *C. Clinius Mæcenas,* a Roman knight, descended on the mother's side from the Arretian gens of the Mæcenates, and on the father's side from that of the Clinii, a statesman, friend of Augustus, critic and patron of literature. **atavis,** abl. plu. after edite; fr. ătăvus, -i, 2nd mas., *a great-great-great-grandfather,* i.e., the fifth ancestor; the series being pater, avus, proavus, abavus, atavus; *an ancestor, forefather.* This is the abl. of origin jnd. to verbs and partcs. expressing or implying *descent, origination,* etc., *e.g.,* nasci, oriri, creatus, etc.; a special instance of the ablative of separation or ablative proper. **ēdĭte,** voc. mas. s. ag. w. Mæcēnas; fr. ēdĭtus, -a, -um, pf. pass. part. of ēdo, -dĕre, -dĭdi, -dĭtum, 3rd trans. (e or ex, 691; do, 65; see condo, 9). *To put forth* or *out, bring forth. To produce, beget, form* anything, esp. in editus. *To set forth, declare* a thing. *To produce, bring about, cause,* e.g., battles, etc. **rēgĭbus,** abl. plu. in app. to or used as an adj. ag. w. atavis; fr. rex, rēgis, 3rd mas., *ruler, king.* Of persons, animals, things, *head, chief, master, leader,* e.g., rivers, wine, etc. *A governor, preceptor* of youth (824). *A prince,* i.e., son of a king or chief. *A powerful, fortunate person,* etc.

2. **O,** interj. of joy, astonishment, desire, grief, etc. *O! Oh!* w. voc., acc., and (less freq.) nom.; folld. by utinam, si rare (ō or ŏ before an initial cons.). **et...et,** copulative or sociative conj., *and. Also,* esp. in et ille, et ipse, et nunc; et...et, *both...and.* **præsidium,** voc. s.; fr. præsĭdĭum, -ii, 2nd neut. (præ, *before;* sedeo, *to sit*). *A guarding, protecting,* hence *defence, aid, protection. Defence, assistance,* i.e., that which aids, protects. Of soldiers, *a convoy, escort; outpost, military station. A fortified place, post. Means of aid,* etc. Of persons, *a defence, protection, assistance,* w. dat. (889). **dulce,** voc. s. neut. ag. w. decus; from dulcis, -e, adj. (rt. in in-dul-geo, *to indulge*), *sweet. Agreeable, delightful, pleasant, dear.* **decus** voc. s. jnd. by et to praesidium; fr. dĕcus, dĕcŏris, 3rd neut., *ornament, embellishment, splendour, glory, honour, dignity. Moral dignity, virtue.* **meum,** voc. s. neut. ag. w. decus; fr. meus, mea, meum, voc. mī, used w. mas., fem., and neut. nouns; poss. pron. adj. of 1st. pers. *my, mine, belonging to me. In my own power, free, independent;* meum, -i, 2nd neut., *my affair; custom, duty,* etc.; mei, meorum, *my friends, relatives, followers,* etc.

Sunt quos curriculo pulverem Olympicum
Collegisse juvat, metaque fervidis
Evitata rotis palmaque nobilis

3. **Sunt,** 3rd plu. pres. ind.; fr. sum, esse, fui, etc. It is either the verb of being, *to be, exist* (as here), when it forms a complete predication; or the copulative verb *to be*, when it requires the addition of an adj., adv., etc. (called by Ken. a *complement*), to complete the predication. **quos,** mas. plu. ag. w. demonst. und. in sunt; acc. gov. by juvat; fr. qui, quæ, quod, gen. cujŭs, dat. cui; adj. relat. pron., *who, which, whom, that.* On qui w. subj., see 730. "Sunt qui" = "there are (those) who," used (*a*) w. subj. when qui is *final*, "sunt qui habeant," "*there are people to*," or = talis ut, *i.e.*, it is *consecutive*, "*there are* (*those*) *of such a character that*," this is more com., esp. in prose; (*b*) w. ind. when "sunt qui" is a new pron. like "nescio quis" in a definite categorical statement; this is more com. in Hor. (Wick.) **curriculo,** abl. sing.; fr. currĭcŭlum, -i, 2nd neut. (currus 342), *a race-ground, race-course. A running for a wager, race. A chariot;* fig., *career, course;* abl. instrum. if it here = *chariot*, local if it = *race-course.* **pulverem,** acc. s. gov. by collegisse; fr. pulvis, pulvĕris, 3rd mas., *dust, powder. Place of contest, arena, lists; a scene of action, field.* **Olympicum,** acc. mas. s. ag. w. pulverem; fr. Olympĭcus, -a, -um, adj., *Olympic, of Olympia,* a sacred region in Elis Pisatis, where the Olympic games were held.

4. **Collegisse,** pf. inf. act. subj. of juvat; fr. collĭgo, -lĭgĕre, -lēgi, -lectum, 3rd trans. (cum, 31; lĕgo, *to gather*), *to gather* or *assemble together. To contract, draw up. To compress, concentrate. To obtain, acquire. To put together* in the mind, *weigh, think upon.* The pf. is here aoristic, exp. *frequency* or *habit.* **juvat,** 3rd. sing. ind. pres. act.; fr. jŭvo, jŭvāre, jūvi, jūtum, 1st. irreg. trans. and intr., *to delight, please,* gov. acc. w. pers. or thing as subj. (23), or w. inf. esp. in 3rd sing., *it delights me, you,* etc., i.e., *I, you,* etc., *am delighted to. To help, aid.* Of things, *to profit, advantage, further, advance,* esp. in 3rd pers. w. inf. **metaque,** mēta, -æ, 1st fem. nom. s. subj. of evehit, (metior, *to measure*) a pillar with a conical top for marking a *measured* space. Three in a group were erected at each end of a Roman chariot-course, around them the charioteers had to drive seven times; *pillar, goal, end, boundary, limit.* -que; a copulative or sociative conj., *and;* always enclitic, *i.e.*, affixed to the word to which it belongs, genly. the first in the sentence [et joins things equally important; -que closely connects the second member as an appendage or supplement to the first, and often joins words which make up one idea; atque...ac (37, 131) adds something important, on which it lays greater stress, as an afterthought]. **fervidis,** abl. plu. fem. ag. w. rotis; fr. fervĭdus, -a, -um (ferveo, 348), *glowing, hot, burning, fiery* (1269). *Boiling, raging, furious* (242); fig., *hot, vehement, impetuous* (705).

5. **Evitata,** pf. pass. part. (causal) nom. fem. s. ag. w. meta; fr. ēvītō, -āre, -āvi, -atum (e or ex, 691; vito, 226), 1st trans., *to shun, avoid.* **rŏtis,** abl. plu. instrumental; fr. rŏta, -æ, 1st fem., *a wheel* of potter, chariot, etc. By synecdoche, *i.e.*, taking a part for the whole, *a chariot.* **palma,** -æ, 1st fem., nom. sing., jnd. by -que to meta; *the palm* of the hand. By synecdoche, *the hand; a palm-tree; date,* i.e., fruit of the palm-tree; *a palm-branch* or *wreath* with which a victor was ornamented, hence *victory, preeminence, superiority.* **nōbĭlis,** -e, adj., nom. fem. s. ag. w. palma (orig. *that can be known;* for gnobilis, fr. gnosco, nosco, 411), *well-known, famous renowned,* w. inf. (310). *Of noble birth,* i.e., born of a family whose members had held curule offices, opp. to "novus homo." *Of a noble kind: excellent.*

Terrarum dominos evehit ad Deos;
Hunc, si mobilium turba Quiritium
Certat tergeminis tollere honoribus;

6. **Terrarum,** gen. plu. after dominos; fr. terra, -æ, 1st fem., *the earth* opp. to heaven, sea, air, etc.; terra marique, *by land and sea. The land, ground, soil. A land, country, region, territory,* "orbis terrarum, less com. terræ;" *the globe, earth, world.* **dominos,** acc. plu.; fr. dŏmĭnus, -i, 2nd mas. (dŏmus, 117), *possessor, proprietor, owner. Lord, ruler, commander,* genly. w. odious notion, "terr. dom;" may be taken (*a*), in app. to deos; or (*b*), as gov. by evehit=quasi sint facti terrarum domini, *i.e.*, the very lords of the world; *i.e.*, in their own feeling and estimation. **evehit,** 3rd sing. ind. pres. act.; fr. ēvĕho, -vĕhere, -vexi, -vectum (e or ex, 691; vĕho, *to carry, convey*); 3rd trans., *to carry out,* or *forth;* pass. reflex., *to ride out,* or *forth, move out, move forth. To carry upwards, raise aloft.* **ad,** prep. gov. acc. Of place, *to* after vb. of motion; *at,* after a vb. not of motion; of time, *to* also exp. *point* of time, and time *within which.* It has several derived uses; esp. it exp. *purpose, e.g.*, ad limina custos; *a doorkeeper.* **deos,** acc. plu. gov. by ad.; fr. deus, dei, plu. nom. dei, dii and di, dat. and abl. deis, diis and dis (nom. di, dat. and abl. dis, in best MSS.), 2nd mas., *a god, deity.* In poets, sts. of a *female deity;* fig. of the highly distinguished and fortunate.

7. **Hunc,** acc. mas. s. gov. by juvat (und. fr. line 4); fr. hic, hæc, hoc, gen. hujus, dat. huic, demonst. emphatic pronom. adj., *this;* hic...ille, *the one...the other; the latter, the former;* hic ref. to what is nearer to the speaker's mind, though in the position of the words it is sometimes more remote. **si,** conditional or hypothetical conj., *if,* folld. by ind., pres. impf., pf. or plpf., or fut. simple or perfect, or by subj. pres. impf. or plpf. It has usu. the same tense in both protasis, *i.e.*, the clause which contains the condition, and the apodosis, *i.e.*, the principal sentence or conclusion. When the protasis has the ind. it may be assumed that both the condition and conclusion are real (sumptio dati), see 32, w. pf. ind. 9, w. fut. ind. 35. **mobilium,** gen. plu. mas. ag. w. Quiritium; fr. mōbĭlis, -e, adj. (for mŏvĭbilis; fr. mŏveo, 394), *that can be easily moved.* Of persons, *quick, nimble, active.* Of things, *rapid, fleet, swift* (198); fig., *that can be influenced, pliant, flexible; that can be excited, excitable,* genly. in bad sense, *changeable, uncertain.* **turba,** -æ, 1st fem., nom. subj. of certat; *turmoil, uproar, commotion, disturbance. Crowd, band, troop, number.* **Quiritium,** gen. after turba; fr. Quĭrītes, gen. -ĭum and -um, 3rd mas., orig., *the inhabitants of the Sabine town, Cures.* The Romans, after their union with the Sabines under Romulus, called themselves Quĭrites in a civil capacity only, hence it was a reproach to soldiers; sing. Quĭris, Quĭritis, 3rd mas., *an uninjured Roman citizen* (1043).

8. **Certat,** 3rd sing. pres. ind. act.; fr. certo, -are, -avi, -atum, 1st intr. (rt. in cer-tus, 212), *to fight, struggle, contend, combat;* fig., *to emulate, vie with,* esp. at law, w. inf. (genly. poet.) *to strive to do* something. **tergeminis,** abl. plu. mas. ag. w. honoribus; fr. tergĕmĭnus, -a, -um, adj. (=trigeminus; tres, *three;* geno, rt. of gigno, *to beget*), *born three at a birth. Threefold, triple, triform, e.g.*, Cerberus, Hecate, etc., here ref. to offices of curule ædile, prætor, consul; (alit.) *manifold, very great.* **tollere,** pres. inf. prolative (570) after certat; fr. tollo, -ere, 3rd trans. defective, borrows pf. sustuli, and sup. sublatum; fr. suffero (sub, 21; fero, 138), *to take up, lift up, raise, elevate. To take away, remove, bear off. To make away with, kill; to abolish, annul.* **honoribus,** abl. (of manner) plu.; fr. hŏnor or hŏnos,

Illum, si proprio condidit horreo,
Quidquid de Libycis verritur areis
Gaudentem patrios findere sarculo
Agros Attalicis conditionibus

hŏnōris, 3rd mas., *honour*, *repute*, in which one is held. *Official dignity*, *office*. *Recompense*, *reward*, given as a mark of honour. *Ornament*, *grace*, *charm*, *beauty*.

9. **Illum**, acc. mas. s. gov. by juvat (und. fr. 4); fr. ille, illa, illud, gen. illīus, dat. illi, etc.; demonst. emphatic pronom. adj. of 3rd pers.; *that*, sts.= *that well-known* or *celebrated*. As subst. *he*, *she*, *it*, and in oblique cases *him*, *her*. **si** (7), here w. pf. ind. in protasis, and pres. ind. (juvat) in apodosis. **proprio**, abl. neut. s. ag. w. horreo; fr. proprius, -a, -um, adj., *belonging to oneself alone*. *Special*, *peculiar*. *Suitable*, *proper*. *Lasting*, *permanent*=perpetuus. **condidit**, 3rd s. pf. ind. act.; fr. condo, -dĕre, -dĭdi, -dĭtum, 3rd irreg. trans. (cum, 31; do, 65; the compds. of which, exc. pessumdo, venumdo, circumdo, are of the 3rd conj.), *to bring*, *lay*, or *put together*. *To form by putting together*, *found*, *establish*. *To put away*, *store up*; *conceal*, *hide*. **horreo**, abl. local. s.; fr. horreum, -i, 2nd neut., a *storehouse* for grain, *granary*, *barn*.

10. **Quidquid**, neut. s. ag. w. demonst. und. after condidit, nom. to verritur; fr. quisquis (263). **de**, prep. gov. abl. Of place, *down from*; *from*, of source, origin, starting-point, abode. Of the whole fr. which something is taken, *from among*, *e.g.*, una de multis. Of material, *e.g.*, templum de marmore ponam, *i.e.*, *made of*. Of respect, *concerning*, *about*. Of cause, *for*, *from*, *e.g.*, multis de causis. Of manner, *according to*, *e.g.*, de more, *according to custom*. Of time, (*a*) *immediately after*, *e.g.*, de prandio; (*b*) *in the course of*, *e.g.*, de nocte, *by night*; de die, *by day*. **Libycis**, abl. plu. fem. ag. w. areis; fr. Lĭby̆cus, -a, -um, *Libyan*. **verritur**, 3rd s. pres. ind. pass.; fr. verro, -ĕre, verri, versum, 3rd trans., *to sweep up* or *together*. *To cleanse by sweeping*. *To sweep along*, *impel*. *To sweep* over the surface, *skim*. **areis**, abl. plu. gov. by de; fr. ārea, -æ, 1st fem. (akin to aresco, *to be dry*), *ground-plot*, *building-ground*, *site* for a house or near a house, *i.e.*, *court-yard*, *area*, or for recreation (250). *A threshing-floor*, an open space near the house among the ancients.

11. **Gaudentem**, acc. mas. s. pres. part. gov. by dimoveas; fr. gaudeo, -ēre, gāvisus sum, 2nd intrans. semi-depon. (see soleo, 184; audeo, 861), *to rejoice inwardly*, *be glad* respecting anything, *be pleased with*, *delight in* (diff. fr. lætor, 1399). In salutation=salvere (Hor.); partc. as subst., *the man who delights*. **patrios**, acc. plu. mas. ag. w. agros; fr. patrius, -a, -um, adj. (pater, 38), *of* or *belonging to one's father*, *paternal*. **findere**, pres. inf. act. (prolative, 570) after gaudentem; fr. findo, -ĕre, fĭdi, fissum, 3rd trans., *to cleave*, *split*, *separate*, *divide*. **sarculo**, abl. instrum. s.; fr. sarcŭlum, -i, 2nd neut. (sarco=sarrio, *to hoe*), *a light hoe*.

12. **Agros**, acc. plu. gov. by findere; fr. ager, agri, 2nd mas. (Eng. acre), *a field*, whether pasture, arable, nursery, etc. *Territory*, *district*, belonging to some community; agri, plu., *open fields*, opp. to town. **Attalicis**, abl. fem. plu. ag. w. conditionibus; fr. Attălĭcus, -a, -um, *of Attalus*, a wealthy king of Pergamus who left his riches to the Roman people. **conditionibus**, abl. plu. of means; fr. condĭtĭo, -ōnis (also condicio), 3rd fem. (condo, 9), *a putting together*, *setting up*. Of persons, *situation*, *condition*, *rank*, *circumstances*. Of things, *situation*, *nature*, *mode*, *manner*. *A marriage*, *match*. In business, *a settling of terms*, *stipulation*, *agreement*, *terms*. "Att. cond.," *by such terms as Attalus could offer*.

Nunquam dimoveas, ut trabe Cypria
Myrtoum pavidus nauta secet mare.
Luctantem Icariis fluctibus Africum
Mercator metuens otium et oppidi

13. **Nunquam** (ne, 41; unquam, 1070), adv., *at no time, never;* nunquam non, *always;* nunquam nisi, *never otherwise than, always. Not, in no way, by no means*=non or nullo modo.. **dimoveas**, 2nd sing. conj. (potential), pres.; fr. dīmŏvĕo, -ēre, -mōvi, -mōtum, 2nd trans. (dis-, 870; moveo, 394). When dis- prevails, *to move from one another, part asunder, separate* (567). Of a multitude or many things, *scatter, disperse.* When moveo prevails, *separate from, remove from* something; fig., *to entice from* the pursuit of a thing (here). **ut** or uti 413, (i.) a relative particle of manner; *how*, 233; (ii.) in exclamations; *how*, 279; (iii.) co-ordinate conj. in comparisons; *as*, 199, 299, 413; (iv.) a subordinative conj., (*a*) final, 388, 856; (*b*) consecutive, *i.e.*, introducing a consequence, followed by subj. pres. after pres. fut. and pf. incomplete, by subj. impf. or pf. after strictly historical (past) tenses. **trăbĕ**, abl. instrumental s.; fr. trabs, trăbis, 3rd fem., *a beam, a timber, a tall slender tree.* Of anything made of beams or timbers, esp. *a ship.* **Cypria**, abl. fem. s. ag. w. trabe; fr. Cyprĭus, -a, -um (Cyprus, 89), *Cyprian.*

14. **Myrtoum**, acc. neut. s. ag. w. mare; fr. Myrtōus, -a, -um, adj. (Myrtos, an island), a part of the Ægean Sea between Crete, Peloponnesus, and Eubœa. **păvidus**, -a, -um, adj. (păvĕo, *to fear, tremble*), nom. mas. s. ag. w. nauta; *trembling, quaking; fearful, alarmed, timid;* comp. pavĭdior, sup. adv. pavidissime. **nauta**, -æ, 1st fem. nom. s. in app. to sub. of secet, shrtnd. for nāvĭta, -æ (navis, 93), *a sailor, seaman.* **secet**, 3rd sing. subj. (after ut) pres. (after dimoveas); fr. sĕco, -āre, sĕcŭi, sectum, 1st irreg. trans., *to cut, cut off, cut up* (1369). *To scratch, tear, wound, hurt;* fig., *to divide, cleave, separate, e.g.*, a river through the fields. *To cut through, e.g.*, sail, fly, swim, *e.g.*, æthera, pontum. The sub. und. fr. gaudentem. **mare**, acc. s. gov. by secet; fr. măre, gen. măris, *the sea*, opp. to dry land.

15. **Luctantem**, acc. mas. s. pres. part. ag. w. Africum; fr. luctor, -ari, -atus sum, 1st depon. intrans., *to seize, lay hold of. To wrestle, strive, contend. To struggle, labour.* **Icariis**, dat. plu. mas. ag. w. fluctibus; fr. Icărĭus, -a, -um, adj., *Icarian;* Icărĭum, -ii, or w. mare, *the Icarian Sea* (Icarus, 1437), part of the Ægean, E. of Myrtoum, named from the island Icaria, W. of Samos. **fluctibus**, dat. plu. after trajective (873) luctantem; fr. fluctus, -us, 4th mas. (fluo, *to flow*), *a flow, flood, waving water, billow, surge* of the sea; fig., *turbulence, commotion.* **Africum**, acc. s. gov. by metuens; fr. Africus, -i, 2nd mas., *south-west wind;* Gk. *Lips*, blowing between Auster (1248) and Favonius (129), opp. to Volturnus.

16. **Mercator**, -oris, 3rd mas. (merces, 638), nom. sub. of laudat; *a trader, merchant,* esp. *wholesale*, opp. to caupo, *a retailer.* **metuens**, pres. part. act. nom. mas. s. ag. w. mercator; fr. mĕtŭo, -uĕre, -ui, -ūtum, 3rd trans. and intrans. (metus, 564), *to fear, dread, be afraid of*, w. a pers. or thing (924), as sub.; w. dat. *to fear for, on account of* (1089); w. inf. *to fear to;* w. ne and subj. *to fear that;* w. ut or ne non w. subj. *to fear that not* [as the effect of the idea of threatening evil; *timere*, of the effect of some external cause of terror]. The part. here temporal, *when, at the moment he fears.* **otium**, acc. s. governed by laudat; fr. ōtĭum, -ii, 2nd neut. *leisure, vacant time, freedom from business* (1281), *base inactivity, idle life. Rest, repose, quiet, peace.* **et** (2). **oppidi**, gen. s. after rura; fr. oppĭdum, -i, 2nd neut., *a town*, rarely of Rome, which was called urbs.

Laudat rura sui; mox reficit rates
Quassas indocilis pauperiem pati.
Est qui nec veteris pocula Massici
Nec partem solido demere de die

17. **Laudat,** 3rd s. pres. ind. act.; fr. laudo, -āre, -āvi, -ātum, 1st trans. (laus, 175), *to praise, extol. To praise,* as happy. *To pronounce, name, quote, e.g.,* certissimos auctores. **rura,** acc. plu. jnd. by et to otium; fr. rus, rūris, 3rd neut. (plu. only in nom. and acc.), *the country* (opp. to the city), *lands, fields. A country seat, farm, estate;* "otium et rura" =*rural retirement;* a case of hendiadys, *i.e.,* when two nouns jnd. by a conj. are used for a noun and a gen. case, or adj. and noun. **sui,** gen. s. neut. ag. w. oppidi; fr. suus, sua, suum, adj. of reflex. pron. sui (53), *his own, her own, its own;* most com. with some case of ipse; "sŭi, suorum," *one's followers, friends, people. One's own master* or *mistress, free, independent. Inclined* or *devoted to one, favorable, friendly* (opp. to alienus). **mox,** temporal adv. (ak. to moveo, 394), *all but present, soon, anon; directly, the next moment,* w. pres. or fut. Of more remote time, *soon, afterwards, then, in the next place.* **reficit,** 3rd s. pres. ind act.; fr. rĕfĭcĭo, -ĕre, -fēci, -fectum, 3rd trans. (re, 656; facio, 542), *to make again, make anew, restore, rebuild, repair, put into condition again. To get back again, recover, e.g.,* money. *To make strong again; reinvigorate, refresh,* physically or mentally, *e.g.,* equos, mentem. **rates,** acc. plu. gov. by reficit; fr. rătis, -is, 3rd fem., prop. *vessel* made of logs fastened together, *float, raft, bark, boat, vessel.*

18. **Quassas,** acc. plu. fem. ag. w. rates; fr. quassus, pf. pass. part. of quătĭo, quătĕre, no pf., quassum, 3rd trans., *to strike.* Of wind, *to agitate,* fig., *to move, touch, affect, excite* (425). *To plague, vex, harass. To beat, batter, shatter, break in pieces.* **indŏcĭlis,** -e, adj. nom. mas. s. ag. w. mercator (in, *not;* docilis, *teachable*), *difficult to be taught, unteachable;* w. inf. only poet. Of things *that cannot be taught, untaught, unlearned.* With gen. *unacquainted with, ignorant of.* **pauperiem,** acc. s. gov. by păti; fr. paupĕrĭes, -ei, 5th fem. (paupero, *to impoverish*), *an impoverishing, reducing to narrow circumstances. Poverty* (poet. and post-Aug. for paupertas, 327). **păti,** pres. inf. prolative (570) after indŏcĭlis; fr. pătĭor, păti, passus sum, 3rd depon. trans. and intrans., *to bear, support, suffer, endure. To allow, permit, let.*

19. **Est,** 3rd s. pres. ind.; fr. sum (3). **qui** (3), mas. s. ag. w. demonst. und. as subj. of est; nom. to spernit. **nec** or nĕque (used indifferently before vowels and consonants), disjunctive conj.=et non, *and not, also not;* neque (nec)...neque (nec); *neither...nor;* neque (nec) non (or necnon), *and also, and besides, and indeed,* emphatic. **vĕtĕris,** gen. neut. s. ag. w. Massici; fr. vĕtus, vĕtĕris, abl. vetere (rarely -i), nom. plu. vĕtĕres, neut. vĕtĕra, gen. vĕtĕrum, adj., *that has existed for a long time, aged, old, inveterate.* **pocula,** acc. plu. gov. by spernit; fr. pōcŭlum, -i, 2nd neut. (po- in po-tare, *to drink*), *a drinking vessel, cup, goblet, bowl. Drink, draught, potion. Drinking bout, carouse.* **Massici,** gen. s. after pocula; fr. Massicum, -i, 2nd neut., *Massic wine,* prop. neut. adj. (und. vinum); fr. Massicus, -a, -um, in mas. (und. mons), *Mt. Massicus,* a mt. in Campania celebrated for its excellent wine.

20. **Partem,** acc. s. gov. by demere; fr. pars, partis, 3rd fem., *part, piece, portion, share. Place, region* of the earth. *Character* on the stage. *Function, office, duty. Part, i.e.,* some out of many. *A party,* genly. in plu. **solido,** abl. mas. s. ag. with die; fr. sŏlĭdus, -a, -um, cont. soldus, -a, -um (in Hor.), (sŏlum, -i, *the floor, ground*), *firm, dense, compact, not hollow. Whole, com-*

21 Spernit, nunc viridi membra sub arbuto
22 Stratus, nunc ad aquæ lene caput sacræ.
23 Multos castra juvant et lituo tubæ
24 Permixtus sonitus bellaque matribus

plete, entire, opp. to what is scattered, divided, or in parts=integer; fig. *substantial, genuine, true, real. Firm, determined, e.g.*, mens (Hor.); here "solidus dies" =*the business part of the day*. **demere**, pres. inf. objective (570), jnd. by nec to pōcula; fr. dēmo, -ĕre, dempsi, 3rd trans. (de, 20; emo, *to buy*), *to take away* or *off, withdraw, remove*. **de** (10). **die**, abl. s. gov. by de; fr. dies, -ēi, also gen. dies, die, and dii, dat. also die, 5th mas. sts. fem. (esp. =*a set day*). *The civil day of twenty-four hours*, mas. less com. fem. (826), *a fixed day, appointed time* for anything, esp. fem. *A natural day, day* opp. to night. *Time, space of time, period*, mas. and fem. *Light of day, daylight*.

21. **Spernit**, 3rd s. pres. ind. act.; fr. sperno, spernĕre, sprēvi, sprētum, 3rd trans., *to despise, contemn, spurn*. **nunc**, temp. adv. *now, at present, at this time*, w. pres. impf. and pf. tenses. In antithesis, nunc...nunc, *now... now; sometimes...sometimes*. **viridi**, abl. mas. s. ag. w. arbuto; fr. vĭrĭdis, -e, adj. (vireo, 249) *green* (456). *Young, youthful, fresh, vigorous*. **membra**, acc. s. of medial obj. (1048); fr. membrum, -i, 2nd neut., *limb, member* of the body. *Part, portion*. **sub**, prep. gov. acc. (230) and abl., w. abl. of place, *under*, implying rest (470). Of time, *about, at the time of; in, during*. Of other relations, *beneath, under*. **arbuto**, abl. s. gov. by sub.; fr. arbŭtus, -i, 2nd fem. (ak. to arbor, 329), *the wild strawberry* or *arbute tree; its fruit*; arbutum, -i, 2nd neut., *the fruit, wild strawberry*, a very ancient food of men.

22. **Stratus**, nom. mas. s. pf. pass. (with middle sense) part. ag. w. qui: fr. sterno, -ĕre, strāvi, strātum, 3rd trans., *to spread out, spread abroad extend*; pass. reflex. and w. acc. of pers. pron., *to stretch oneself out. To spread flat, smooth. To bestrew, strew over. To throw down, overthrow, prostrate*. **nunc** (20). **ad** (6). **aquæ**, gen. s. after caput; fr. ăqua, -æ, 1st fem., *water* in its widest sense, as an element, rain, river, etc.; more restricted =mare, flumen, *river, stream*. **lene**, acc. neut. s. ag. w. caput; fr. lēnis, -e, adj., *soft, smooth. Moderate, gentle, not violent*; non lenis, *hard, difficult, inexorable* (589). Here ref. to *gentle murmuring* of the stream. **caput**, acc. s. gov. by ad; fr. căput, căpĭtis, 3rd neut., *the head*. By synecdoche, *the man, person, animal itself. The chief, head, leader, principal* of persons and things. Of things, *top, summit, end, extremity*. Of rivers, *origin, source. Life*, esp. *physical life* and *political life. Origin, source, e.g.*, of guilt. **sacræ**, gen. sing. fem. ag. w. aquæ; fr. sacer, sacra, sacrum, adj., *dedicated* or *consecrated to a divinity, holy, sacred* (477). *Holy, sacred, awful, venerable, e.g.*, silentium. In bad sense, *devoted to the deity for destruction, accursed, criminal, wicked; detestable, infamous*.

23. **Multos**, acc. plu. mas. gov. by juvant; fr. multus, -a, -um, adj. *much*, plu. *many*. **castra**, nom. plu. sub. of juvant; fr. castrum, -i, 2nd neut. (akin to casa, *a hut*), *any fortified place, castle, fortress*; plu. castra, -orum, prop. *several soldiers' tents together, a military camp, encampment*. **juvant**, 3rd plu. pres. ind. act.; from juvo (4). **et** (2). **lituo**, dat. s. after trajéctive (873) permixtus; fr. lĭtŭus, -i, 2nd mas., *a trumpet, clarion, cornet* slightly bent at the end like an augur's staff, emitting a shrill note, used by the cavalry; here=litui sonitus. **tubæ**, gen. s. after sonitus; fr. tŭba, -æ, 1st fem., *a trumpet* w. a straight tube, used by the infantry.

24. **Permixtus**, nom. mas. s. pf. pass. part. ag. w. sonitus; fr. per-

Detestata. Manet sub Jove frigido
Venator teneræ conjugis immemor,
Seu visa est catulis cerva fidelibus,
Seu rupit teretes Marsus aper plagas.

misceo, -ēre, -ui, -stum and -xtum, 2nd trans. (per, 114; misceo, 30), *to mingle thoroughly* or *together, intermingle.* Of persons, *to join* or *mix* people. *To confound, disturb, throw into confusion.* **sŏnĭtus**, -us, 4th mas., nom. s. jnd. by et to castra, (sono, 1218) *a noise, sound, din.* **bella**, nom. plu. jnd. by -que to sonitus; from bellum, -i, 2nd neut., orig., *a contest between two* (for duellum; fr. duo, *two*), *duel; war.* **-que** (4). **matribus**, dat. plu. (of agent, 524) w. detestata; fr. māter, -tris, 3rd fem., *a mother.* Of animals, *a dam, parent.* A title of honour given to priestesses, goddesses, etc. Of trees, *a parent stock. Producing source, origin.*

25. **Detestata**, nom. neut. plu. ag. w. bella; fr. detestatus, pf. part. of dētestor, -ari, -atus sum, 1st dep. (de, 10; testor, 660), *to call upon, invoke earnestly* a deity as a witness, (*a*) agst. a pers. or thing, *to curse, execrate, abominate; to imprecate,* acc. of thing; (*b*) to avert anything from some pers. or thing w. acc. of thing. Of persons, *to pray for the removal of* a thing, *deprecate;* here pass., *detested, abhorred.* **manet**, 3rd s. pres. ind. act.; fr. măneo, -ēre, mansi, mansum, 2nd irreg. intrans., *to stay, remain. Continue, last, endure. Be fixed, settled, implanted. Await* one, as fate, etc.; here, *he stays out.* **sub** (21). **Jove**, abl. s. gov. by sub; fr. Jūpĭter, gen. Jŏvis, acc. Jovem, dat. Jovi, *Jupiter,* son of Saturn; here=*the open air* (556). **frigido**, abl. s. mas. ag. with Jove; fr. frīgĭdus, -a, -um, adj. (frīgeo, *to be cold*), *cold, cool, chill;* fig., *without ardour* or *energy, indifferent, feeble.* Of things, *without force* or *point, flat, dull, trivial, e.g.*, joci, verba.

26. **Vēnātor**, -oris, 3rd mas. nom. sub. of manet (vēnor, *to hunt*), *a hunter.* **teneræ**, gen. s. fem. ag. w. conjugis; fr. tĕner, tĕnera, tĕnĕrum, adj., *soft, delicate, tender. Of tender age, young* (521); fig., *tender, soft* of poets, mind, etc. **conjugis**, gen. sing. (of matter, 910) after immemor; fr. conjunx, conjŭgis, 3rd com. (cum, 31; jungo, 134), *one joined to another,* usu. *a wife,* poet. *a husband.* **immemor**, gen. -mĕmŏris, adj., nom. mas. s. ag. w. venator (in, *not;* memor, 745), *unmindful, not thinking, forgetful of,* w. gen. or absol. (414).

27. **Seu** or sive (both equally used in poets), a disjunctive conditional particle, *or if*=vel si, genly. repeated with disjunct. sense predominant, *if.. or if; whether...or;* sts. instead of one sive (seu), aut, vel, or interrog. -ne or an are used. **visa est,** visa, nom. fem. s. pf. pass. part. ag. w. cerva; w. est (19) the combinate (1336) pf. pass. 3rd. s. ind.; fr. vĭdeo, -ēre, vīdi, vīsum, 2nd trans., *to see with the eyes;* of other senses, *perceive, observe. To see* w. the mind's eye, *mark, observe, understand. To look at, think, reflect upon. To take care, provide.* Pass. *to be looked upon* or *regarded. To seem, appear.* **cătūlis**, dat. of agent (524), plu. after visa est; fr. cătŭlus, -i, 2nd mas., diminutive of canis (*a dog*), *a young dog, whelp, puppy.* **cerva**, -æ, 1st fem. nom. sub. of visa est (cervus, 413), *a hind,* poet. for *deer* genly. **fidelibus**, dat. plu. mas. ag. w. catulis; fr. fĭdēlis, -e, adj. (fides, 153). Of living beings, *that may be trusted* or *relied on, trusty, faithful.* Of things, *to be depended on, sure, safe, strong, durable, e.g.*, navis, lorica.

28. **Seu** (27). **rupit**, 3rd s. pf. ind. act.; fr. rumpo, -ēre, rūpi, ruptum, 3rd trans., *to break, burst, tear, rend. To break asunder, burst in pieces, force open;* w. acc. pers. pron. or pass refl., *to burst, split oneself. To violate, destroy, annul,* e.g., edicta "rumpere vocem, gemitum," *to cause to burst forth, send forth, utter.* **teretes**, acc. plu. fem. ag. w. plagas; fr. tĕres,

Me doctarum hederæ præmia frontium
Dîs miscent superis; me gelidum nemus
Nympharumque leves cum Satyris chori

tĕrĕtis, adj., (*rubbed off; tero, to rub*) *rounded off, rounded, well turned round;* teretes suræ (989), *round, slender;* here, *of close twisted cord; not loose in texture,* i.e., *strong;* fig., *smooth, polished, elegant, e.g.*, oratio; comp. tĕretior, no sup. **Marsus**, -a, -um, adj., nom. masc. s. ag. w. aper; = Marsius, -a, -um, *of* or *belonging to the Marsi*, a people of Latium, on the Lacus Fucinus. **ăper**, apri, 2nd masc.; nom. s. subj. of rupit; *a wild boar.* **plagas**, acc. plu. gov. by rupit; fr. plăga, -æ, 1st fem., (ak. to plecto, *to plait, entwine*) *a hunting-net, snare, gin.*

29. **Me**, acc. s. gov. by (direct obj. of) miscent; fr. ego, gen. mei, dat. mĭhi. Plu. nos, nostrum, pron. subst. of 1st pers.; *I*, and in oblique cases, *me.* Plu. *we, us.* **doctarum**, gen. plu. fem. ag. w. frontium; fr. doctus, pf. pass. part. of dŏceo, -ēre, -ui, doctum, 2nd trans., (orig., *to show*, ak. to dico, 86) *to teach, instruct, form, show, tell;* aliquem aliquid, or obj. inf. **hederæ**, nom. plu. subj. of miscent; fr. hĕdĕra, -æ, 1st fem., *ivy*, sacred to Bacchus; from it garlands to crown poets were made (609). **præmia**, nom. plu. in. app. to hederæ; fr. præmium, -ii, 2nd neut., (præ, *beyond;* emo = accipio, *what is taken beyond* or *above others*) *profit derived from booty, booty* (poet.). *Advantage, prerogative. Distinction, reward, recompense.* **frontium**, gen. plu. after præmia; fr. frons, frontis, 3rd fem., *forehead, brow, front. Brow* as mirror of feelings. *Forepart, front, façade. Outside, exterior, external qualities.*

30. **Dis**, dat plu. after (remote obj. of) trajective (873) miscent; fr. deus (6). **miscent**, 3rd plu. pres. ind. act. fr. misceo, -ēre, miscui, mistum or mixtum, 2nd irreg. trans., *to mix, mingle, blend, intermingle;* reflex. or in pass., *to mingle oneself* with others. *To inflict on* one another wounds, etc. Of storms, *disturb, confound.* **superis**, dat. plu. mas. ag. with dis; fr. sŭpĕrus, -a, -um, adj., (super, 237) *above, upper, on high;* superi, -orum, *the gods above;* comp. superior, superl. supremus or summus; "dis miscent superis," i.e., *admit to happy dreamland* (W.). **me** (29), gov. by secernunt. **gelidum**, nom. neut. s. ag. w. nemus; fr. gĕlĭdus, -a, um, adj., (gelu, *frost*) *icy cold, very cold, icy, frosty* (290), fig., *cold, stiff* with old age, fright, etc.; meton. of death (1079). **nĕmus**, nĕmŏris, 3rd neut.; nom. s., one member of the comp. subj. (see 555) of secernunt; *feeding land* among woods, *a wood* with open glades or pastures for cattle. *A tree.*

31. **Nympharum**, gen. pl. after chori; fr. nympha, -æ, 1st fem., *a nymph* or demi-goddess, occupying sea, air, etc. *A bride.* **-que** (4). **leves**, nom, plu. mas. ag. w. chŏri; fr. lĕvis, -e, adj., *lightly moving* or *springing, swift, quick, nimble, fleet. Light in weight, without weight, unimportant, trivial, insignificant. Light-minded, capricious, fickle, inconsistent.* **cum**, prep. gov. abl., *with, together with, in connection with, along with*, of time, manner, intercourse, and rarely of instrument regarded as accompanying the actor. In comp. it appears as con- before all consons. except b, p, m, before which it is com-, and l, n, -r- with which -m is assimilated; co- before all vowels and h. **Sătyris**, abl. gov. by cum; fr. Sătȳri, -orum, 2nd mas. plu., *the Satyrs*, a kind of woodland deities like apes (1396). **chori**, nom. plu. jnd. by -que to nemus as subj. of secernunt; fr. chŏrus, -i, 2nd mas., (Gk.) *a dance in a ring, choral dance. Dancing and singing troop* or *band, choir;* any *multitude, band, troop.*

Secernunt populo, si neque tibias
Euterpe cohibet nec Polyhymnia
Lesboum refugit tendere barbiton.
Quod si me lyricis vatibus inseres,
Sublimi feriam sidera vertice.

32. **Secernunt,** 3rd plu. pres. ind. act. fr. sēcerno, -cernĕre, -crēvi, -crētum, 3rd trans., (se=*apart by itself;* cerno, *to separate, sift*) *to put apart, sunder, separate;* secretus, *separated,* fig., *disjoin, dissociate, distinguish, set aside,* w. acc. or abl. alone, *from* which. **populo,** abl. of separation, s. after secernunt; fr. pŏpŭlus, -i, 2nd mas., a *people, multitude, host, crowd, throng* [pōpŭlus, *a poplar*]. **si,** w. pres. ind. (7). **neque**=nec (19). **tibias,** acc. plu. gov. by cohibet; fr. tībia,-æ, 1st fem., *a pipe, flute,* made of bone; "tib. dextera," *treble;* "tib. sinistra," *bass;* the plu. is used of the double pipe, one of a higher pitch than the other.

33. **Euterpe,** -es, 1st. fem., (Gk.) subj. of cohibet; *Euterpe,* the muse of music. **cohibet,** 3rd s. pres. ind. act. fr. cŏhĭbeo, -ēre, -ui, -ĭtum, 2nd trans., (cum, 31; habeo, 641) *to hold together, contain, confine. To keep back, restrain, stop, repress, subdue. To contain, hold; e.g.,* universa natura omnes naturas cohibet. **nec** (32). **Polyhymnia,** -æ, 1st fem., (Gk.) subj. of refugit; one of the Muses.

34. **Lesboum,** acc. s. mas. ag. w. barbiton; fr. Lesbōus, -a, -um, adj. (Gk.), *Lesbian,* i.e., lyric like that of Alcæus and Sappho (623). **refugit,** 3rd s. pres. ind. act. fr. rĕfŭgio, -gĕre, -fūgi, -fŭgĭtum, 3rd trans. and intr., (re-, 659; fŭgio, 206) *to flee back, run away, escape.* Of places, *to recede* in the distance, *e.g.,* templum. Of the mind *to shrink from;* w. ad, *to take refuge in. To avoid, shun; e.g.,* anguem, here with inf. **tendere,** pres. inf. objective (570) act. after rĕfŭgit; fr. tendo, -ĕre, tĕtendi, tentum and tensum, 3rd irreg. trans. and intrans; *to stretch, stretch out, distend, extend. To direct. To direct oneself go, travel.* Of things, *to extend. To aim, strive, exert oneself, endeavour. To be directed* or *proceed, be inclined. To strive, contend.* **barbiton,** acc. s. gov. by tendere; fr. barbĭtos (Gk.), mas. and fem., only in nom., acc. and voc., *a lyre, lute,* voc. in 732.

35. **Quod,** conj.; orig. acc. neut. of reference, fr. qui (3); (*a*) *that, in that,* w. ind. or subj.; (*b*) *why, wherefore;* nihil est quod, etc., *there is no reason why,* etc.; (*c*) *as respects that;* quod scribis te venturum, *as to what you write;* (*d*) w. si, nisi, utinam, ne, ubi, quum, ut, it contrasts merely to connect sentences. *but, though.* With vbs. of perceiving and declaring=*that,* instead of an objective clause, *e.g.,* recordatus sum quod, etc., esp. after illud, *e.g.,* illud, mihi occurrit quod, etc. **si,** w. fut. ind. in protasis and apodosis (7). **me** (29), gov. by (direct obj. of) inseres. **lyricis,** dat. plu. mas. ag. w. vatibus; fr. lўrĭcus, -a, -um, adj., (Gk.) *of* or *belonging to the lute* or *lyre* (174), *lyric.* **vatibus,** dat plu. after trajective (173) inseres; fr. vātes, -is, 3rd mas. and fem., (ak. to for, fari, *to speak*) *foreteller, soothsayer, prophet;* fem. *a prophetess; a poet,* mas. (1427); *poetess,* fem. *a teacher.* **inseres,** 2nd s. fut. ind. act. fr. insĕro, -sĕrĕre, -sĕrŭi, -sertum, 3rd traject. trans., (873) (in, 76; sero, *to join,* or *bind together*) *to put, bring* or *introduce into; mingle* or *mix up with. To incorporate with, enrol among;* fig., *to engraft upon, implant.*

36. **Sublimi,** abl. mas. s. ag. w. vertice; fr. sublīmis, -e, adj., (sublevo, *to lift up*), *uplifted, lofty, exalted, elevated. Eminent, distinguished.* Of language, orators, etc., *sublime.* **feriam,** 1st sing. fut. ind. act. fr. fĕrio, -īre, no pf., no sup. (percussi, percussum, supply them), 4th trans., *to stripe, smite, beat, knock.*

CARMEN II.—AD AUGUSTUM CÆSAREM.

JAM satis terris nivis atque diræ
Grandinis misit Pater, et rubente
Dextera sacras jaculatus arces

cut, thrust. To kill by striking, *slaughter* for sacrifice. **sidera,** acc. plu. gov. by feriam; fr. sīdus, sidĕris, 3rd neut., *stars united in a figure, group of stars;* genly. plu.; metaph. *highest fame, fortune.* **vertice,** abl. instrum. sing. fr. vertex, vertĭcis, 3rd mas., (verto, 780) *whirl, eddy, whirlpool, vortex; whirlwind. Coil* of flame. *Top* or *crown* of head, *head, highest point, peak, summit.*

CARMEN II. METRE—*The lesser Sapphic.*

The first three are the Lesser Sapphic	– ◡ trochee	– – spondee	– ◡ ◡ dactyl	– ◡ trochee – ◡ or – – trochee or spondee
The fourth a Versus Adonius	– ◡ ◡ dactyl	– ◡̄ spondee or trochee.		

37. **Jam,** adv. of time marking the occurrence of some action or the existence of some condition as present in past, present, or future time. (*a*) Past, *at that time, at that very time.* Jam primum, primo, *then* or *in the very beginning* or *outset. Previously, ere now.* (*b*) *Present, at this time, now,* w. def. or indef. present. (*c*) *Already* of a future certainty (395); non jam, *not henceforth, not any longer.* **satis,** poet. sat, *enough;* (*a*) adjectivally, *sufficient, satisfactory;* e.g., satis est, sts. w. gen. as here; (*b*) adverbially, *enough, sufficiently.* Comp. sătĭus, *more satisfying,* i.e., *better, more serviceable;* here direct obj. of misit. **terris,** dat. pl. after (remote obj. of) traject. (873) misit; fr. terra (6). **nivis,** gen. sing. after satis; fr. nix, nĭvĭs, 3rd fem., *snow;* "capitis nives," *white hairs, hoary locks* (Hor.). **atque,** or (before consonants only) ac; copulative or sociative conj., *and also, and besides, and moreover;* it connects single words and whole clauses. In comparisons after adjs. or advs. denoting similarity or identity, *as, with;* after words denoting dissimilarity or difference, *than, to.* **diræ,** gen. fem. s. ag. w. grandinis; fr. dīrus, -a, -um, adj. prop. in augury, *ill-omened, ominous, boding, portentous. Dreadful, horrible, abominable;* it qualifies nivis and grandinis.

38. **Grandinis,** gen. s. jnd. by atque to nivis; fr. grando, 3rd fem., *hail, a hailstorm.* **misit,** 3rd sing. pf. ind. act. fr. mitto, -ere, mīsi, missum, 3rd irreg. trans., *to let go, suffer* or *allow to escape, release. To despatch, cause to go. To send* word, *announce. To yield, produce, put forth. To throw, cast, hurl* of weapons. *To omit* in speaking. *To dismiss* from the mind. **Pater,** patris, 3rd mas, (ak. to pasco, 723, *he who nourishes*) *father, sovereign;* plu. *forefathers. Senators.* **rubente,** abl. s. fem. pres. part. act. ag. w. dexterâ; fr. rŭbeo, -ēre, -ui, no sup., 2nd intr., *to be red* or *ruddy. To grow red, blush, colour up;* rubens as adj., *red, reddish.. Red with shame, blushing;* here *red* from the flames of the bolt hurled.

39. **Dextera,** abl. instrumental s. fr. dextĕra, -æ, 1st fem., also dextra, -æ, (prop. fem. of dexter, und. manus) *the right hand,* freq. sign of salutation, fidelity, etc. *The right side.* **sacras,** acc. plu. fem. ag. w. arces; fr. sacer (22). **jaculatus,** nom. mas. s. pf. part. fr. jăcŭlor, -āri, -ātus sum, 1st. dep. intr., *to hurl, fling, cast a javelin* Of language, *to attack;* w. in, and acc. or abl., trans., *to aim at, assail with a javelin, pierce with a javelin. To hurl, fling,* e.g., facem. *To throw, cast at,* w. acc. of thing aimed at; *to hit, smite* (rare). *To aim at, strive after.* **arces,** acc. plu. gov. by jaculatus; fr. arx, arcis, 3rd

Terruit Urbem,
Terruit gentes, grave ne rediret
Seculum Pyrrhæ nova monstra questæ,
Omne quum Proteus pecus egit altos

fem., *a castle, citadel, fortress. Height, summit. Defence, protection, refuge:* arces refers to the arx and temple of Jupiter, each on a summit of the Capitoline Hill.

40. **Terruit,** 3rd s. pf. ind. act. fr. terreo, -ēre, -ŭi, -ĭtum, 2nd trans., *to frighten, affright, alarm, terrify. To frighten away, drive away by fear. Deter by fear, scare from* an action. **urbem,** acc. s. gov. by terruit; fr. urbs, urbis, 3rd fem., (akin to orbis) *a walled town,* esp. of Rome.

41. **Terruit** (40), a case of anaphora (895). **gentes,** acc. pl. gov. by terruit; fr. gens, gentis, 3rd fem., *a begetting. That which is begotten. A house,* including several families united by a common name and certain religious rites. *A single descendant. Offspring, race. Nation, population.* **grave,** nom. neut. s. ag. w. sæculum; fr. grăvis, grăve, adj., *heavy, burdensome. Loaded, laden, burdened. Pregnant.* In bad sense, *troublesome, grievous, disagreeable.* In good sense, *weighty, important, of authority, great.* Of small thgs. *offensive.* **nē,** strengthening of nĕ (the primitive negative, *e.g.* nĕque), used, (i.) in prohibitions, 277; (ii.) final, 231; (iii.) after words denoting hindrance, *e.g.*, moneo, 483; (iv.) after words denoting fear, to express the wish that something may not take place, Eng. *that;* as in Eng. the particle depends on the idea of fearing, not wishing. So also after words denoting precaution, *e.g.*, caveo, folld. by subj. mood: tense accdg. to rules of words denoting the final cause. **rediret,** 3rd sing. impf. (after terruit) subj. (after nē) fr. rĕdĕo, -īre, -ĭi, -ĭtum, (re-, 659; eo, 51) irreg. intr., *to go* or *come back, turn back, turn round.* In speaking, *to recur to,* w. ad and acc. Of revenue, *to come in, proceed. To be brought to, reduced to, arrive at, attain to.*

42. **Sæculum,** -i, 2nd neut.; nom. s. subj. of rediret, (also sēclum) *the lifetime* of the human species, *a lifetime, generation,* 33⅓ years. *Human race living in a particular age, generation; the times. The utmost lifetime* of man, 100 years, *a century. An indefinitely long period, age.* **Pyrrhæ,** gen. after sæculum; fr. Pyrrha, -æ, 1st fem., dau. of Epimetheus and wife of Deucalion, famous for the deluge sent during his days, and as the founder of a new race of men. **nova,** acc. neut. pl. ag. w. monstra; fr. nōvus, -a, -um, adj., *fresh, young, that has lately occurred. Novel, strange, unheard of. Unused to, inexperienced. in;* superl. novissimus=extremus. Of order, succession, time, etc., *last, latest.* Of position or degree, *lowest* or *highest.* **monstra,** acc. pl. governed by questæ; fr. monstrum, -i, 2nd neut., (moneo, 484) *divine omen, intimation* of the will of the gods. *Evil* or *bad omen. Monster, monstrosity,* in size or character (857). *A terrible wonder, marvel.* **questæ,** gen. fem. s. pf. part. ag. w. Pyrrhæ; fr. quĕror, quĕri, questus sum, 3rd depon. trans., *to complain of, lament, bewail, utter plaintively;* also intrans.; querendus used=*to be complained of.*

43. **Omne,** acc. neut. s. ag. w. pecus; fr. omnis, omne, adj.; in sing., *all* of a class. *The whole* or *entire* of a thing; plu., *all, every.* **quum** (also written cum), a temporal conj., *when,* correl. to demonst. tum, of a point of time: (i.) w. ind. (*a*) when merely temporal, pres. fut. (simple or exact), or impf., even w. pf. and plpf. when time strongly marked; (*b*) when=quod in predications of emotion, *i.e.*, after dolet, angor, etc.; (ii.) w. subj. (*a*) when causal, *since,* exp. a conceived case; Fr. *puisque;* (*b*) when concessive, *although.* **Prōtēus,** gen. -ĕi and -ĕos (Gk.); mas. nom. s.,

Visere montes,
Piscium et summa genus hæsit ulmo,
Nota quæ sedes fuerat columbis,
Et superjectò pavidæ natarunt

subj. of egit; a sea-god, who often changed his form; he was in the service of Neptune, and kept his sea calves. **pecus,** acc. s. gov. by egit; fr. pecus, pĕcŏris, 3rd neut., genly. collective in sing., [pecus, pecudis, genly. = *a single head* of cattle] *the larger cattle, a herd;* also of goats, swine, sheep, etc.; even of birds, fishes, bees, etc. **egit,** 3rd sing. pf. ind. act. fr. ăgo, ăgĕre, ēgi, actum, 3rd irreg. trans., *to put in motion, move. To lead, drive, tend conduct. To impel, pursue.* It has many derivative and applied meanings. **altos,** acc. plu. mas. ag. w. montes; fr. altus, -a, -um, adj., (partc. of alo, *to nourish*) *grown great by nourishment. High,* seen from below. *Deep,* seen from above.

44. **Visere,** pres. inf. (prolative esp. purpose, 570) act. after egit; fr. vīso, -sĕre, vīsi, vīsum, 3rd trans. and intr., (intensive of video, 49) *to look at attentively, view, behold, survey. To go or come in order to look at, see to; look after. To go to see, to visit.* **montes,** acc. pl. gov. by visere; fr. mons, montis, 3rd mas., (mineo, *to jut, project,* rare) *mount, mountain. Towering mass, quantity.*

45. **Piscium,** gen. plu. after genus; fr. piscis, -is, 3rd mas, *a fish.* **et** (2). **summa,** abl. sing. fem. ag. w. ulmo; fr. summus, -a, -um, contr. for supremus, superl. of superus (30), *uppermost, highest.* As a partitive attribute, (*i.e.*, distinguishing one part of the thing with which it agrees from the other) *top of, highest part of.* Of time or order, *last, latest, final,* esp. *closing, dying* (364, 1331); *highest, greatest, utmost, extreme.* Of persons, *first, foremost, most distinguished.* Of things, *most important, weighty;* comp. superior. **gĕnus,** gĕnĕris, 3rd neut.; nom. sing. subj. of hæsit; *birth, descent, origin;* esp. *noble birth. A descendant, offspring. Descendants. Race, class, sort;* any *assemblage* of homogeneous persons or things. **hæsit,** 3rd sing. pf. ind. act. fr. hæreo, -ēre, hæsi, hæsum, 2nd intr., *to hang* or *hold fast, hang, stick, cleave, adhere, be fixed, set firm, remain fast* to anything, or in any manner, w. in, abl., etc. *To keep close to* a person, *join* or *attach oneself* to or *keep at* a thing. *To continue* in a place. *To come to a standstill, be embarrassed. To be suspended* or *retarded.* **ulmo,** abl. (local) s.; fr. ulmus, -i, 2nd fem., *an elm, an elm-tree* (1265).

46. **Nota,** nom. fem. s. ag. w. sedes; fr. nōtus, -a, -um, adj., *known,* generally in good sense; rarely *notorious* in a bad sense. **quæ,** fem. s. ag. w. ulmo, nom. to fuerat; fr. qui (3). **sēdes,** -is, 3rd fem., predic. after fuerat, in case of quæ, (sĕdeo, *to sit*) *a couch, chair, throne. Dwelling-place, habitation, abode. Foundation, bottom,* i.e., *that on which anything rests.* **fuerat,** 3rd sing. plpf. ind.; fr. sum (3). **columbis,** dat. (acquisitive or possessive) after fuerat; fr. cŏlumba, -æ, 1st fem., *a dove, pigeon* (854)

47. **Et** (2). **superjecto,** abl. s. neut. pf. pass. part. ag. w. æquore; fr. superjicio, -jĭcĕre, -jēci, -jectum, 3rd trans., (super, 237; jacio, *to throw*) *to throw; cast on, over,* or *upon. To strew, scatter above* or *upon. To spread, extend over, overwhelm.* **pavidæ,** nom. pl. fem. ag. w. damæ; fr. păvĭdus (14). **natarunt,** syncop. for nătāvērunt, 3rd pl. pf. ind. act.; fr. năto, -are, -avi, -atum, 1st intrans. intens., *to swim, float,* of things and living creatures. *To be driven about in sailing, be tossed.* Of fluids, *to swim, spread out.* Of fields, *to swim, overflow, be overflowed* w. anything. Of the eyes, the drunk, the dying, etc., *to swim,* i.e., *be unsteady.* Of the mind, *to fluctuate, waver.*

Æquore damæ.
Vidimus flavum Tiberim, retortis
Litore Etrusco violenter undis
Ire dejectum monumenta regis
Templaque Vestæ;

48. **Æquore,** abl. abs. (88) s. fr. æquor, -ŏris, 3rd neut., *an even, level surface, smooth surface, plain, sea.* **damæ,** nom. pl. subj. of natarunt; fr. dāma, -æ, 1st fem., *a fallow-deer, buck* or *doe.*

49. **Vidimus,** 1st pl. pf. ind. act. fr. vĭdeo (27). **flavum,** acc. mas. s. ag. w. Tiberim; fr. flāvus, -a, -um, adj. (ak. to furvus, fulvus), *golden yellow, reddish yellow, flaxen coloured.* **Tiberim,** acc. s. subj. of ire; fr. Tĭbĕris, also in poet. contr. Tībris or Tȳbris, -is or -ĭdis, 3rd mas., *R. Tiber,* fmly. called *Albula* (958). All names of rivers are mas. **retortis,** abl. pl. fem. ag. w. undis; fr. retortus, pf. pass. part. of rĕtorqueo, -ēre, -torsi, -tortum, 2nd trans., (re, 659; torqueo, *to twist*) *to twist* or *bend back, turn* or *cast back.* "Retortus," *repulsed;* pass. reflex., *to wheel round.*

50. **Litore,** abl. (of separation) s. fr lītus, lītŏris, 3rd neut., (perh. for lin-tus; fr. lino, *to overspread*) pass., *that which is overspread,* esp. by the sea, *sea-shore, sea-side, coast* [ripa, a *river's bank*]. **Etrusco,** abl. neut. sing. ag. w. litore; fr. Etruscus, -a, -um, adj., *Etruscan;* litus Etruscum; "the shore of the Etruscan sea," or "the right bank of the Tiber." **violenter,** adv.; fr. violens (1338), *impetuously, vehemently, furiously;* comp. violentius, superl. violentissime. **undis,** abl. absol. (88) fr. unda, -æ, 1st fem., *wave, billow, surge. Water, moisture, fluid.* Any *liquid.* A single *billow, stream.*

51. **Ire,** pres. inf. after vidimus; fr. eo, īre, īvi, ĭtum, irreg. intr., *to go* of every kind of motion. *Walk, ride, fly, move, pass. To go* as an enemy. Of time, *to pass by.* Of things and events, *to proceed, turn out, happen.* With sup. in -um, *to go* or *set about, prepare, be about to, e.g.,* it dormitum, *he goes for the purpose of sleeping,* i.e., *goes to bed.* **dejectum,** acc. supine; fr. dejĭcĭo, -jĭcĕre, jēci, -jectum, 3rd trans., (de, 10; jacio, *to throw*) *to throw down, cast down, precipitate;* milit., *to drive down, dislodge* an enemy; legal, *to turn out* of possession. *To bring down dead, kill, slay. To cast down* from the prospect of a thing, *prevent* from obtaining, *deprive, rob of.* The supines are cases of the -i declension. The accus. supine implies purpose after a verb of actual or implied motion; īre w. this sup.= *to set about doing* a thing. The impers. inf. iri w. this sup. is used to supply a pass. fm. for inf. fut., *e.g.,* facturum iri, *to be about to make.* **monumenta,** acc. plu. gov. by dejectum; fr. mŏnŭmentum, -ī, 2nd neut., (moneo, 484) *memorial, monument,* of any building erected to perpetuate the memory of a person or thing, here "*ancient building,*" or "*citadel,*" ref. to "Atrium Vestæ, residence of Pontifex Maximus, and the temple of Vesta near it. *Sepulchre, tomb. Written records,* fig., memorial *records, e.g.,* laudis. **regis,** gen. s. after monumenta, fr. rex (1), *i.e.,* Numa Pompilius.

52. **Templa,** acc. pl. jnd. by -que to monumenta; fr. templum, -i, 2nd neut., (like tempus, *a piece* or *portion cut off*) *an open place* marked out by the augur w. his staff. *A consecrated* or *sacred place, sanctuary. A place dedicated to some particular god, fane, shrine;* plu. here for sing. **-que** (4). **Vestæ,** gen. s. after templa; fr. Vesta, -æ, 1st fem. (i) = Ops, Cybele, Terra, wife of Cœlus, mother of Saturn; (ii.) granddaughter of Ops, dau. of Saturn, goddess of flocks, herds and the household in general.

53 Iliæ dum se nimium querenti
54 Jactat ultorem, vagus et sinistra
55 Labitur ripa Jove non probante u-

53. **Iliæ**, dat. (commodi) s. after jactat; fr. Īlia, -æ, 1st fem. a poet. name of Rhea Silvia, dau. of Numitor, mother of Romulus and Remus. **dum**, temporal conj., (i.) *while, while that, as long as*, w. ind. and pres. tense even of a past action or event, subj. in obliqua narratio. (ii.) In conditional relations restrictivé, *so long as, if so be that, if only*, w. subj., *e.g.*, oderint, dum metuant. (iii.) Of succession, *until, until that*, w. subj. or ind. as idea of aim or merely time prevails. **se**, acc. sing. gov. by jactat; fr. reflex. pron. of 3rd pers., gen. sui, dat. sibi, acc. and abl. se or sese, *self*, sing. and pl., and of all genders, sing. *himself, herself, itself*; plu. *themselves*. **nimium**, adv. w. querenti, (prop. neut. of nimius, -a, -um, adj., *too much, excessive*) *too much, too*; "non nimium," *not particularly Very much, exceedingly*; "nimium quantum" or "quam," *as much as may be, very much*. **querenti**, dat. s. fem. pres. part. ag. w. Iliæ; fr. queror (42).

54. **Jactat**, 3rd sing. pres. ind. act. fr. jacto, -are, -avi, -atum, 1st frequentative of jacio (*to throw*), trans. and intr., *to throw, fling, toss about, hurl, to toss to and fro, drive hither and thither*. Of speech, *to pour forth, utter*; "jactare se," *to conduct oneself in a conceited, haughty manner, vaunt, boast oneself*. **ultorem**, acc. sing. depend. predic. in appos. to se, after factitive jactat; fr. ultor, -ōris, 3rd mas., (ulciscor, *to avenge*) *a punisher, avenger, revenger*. *Factitive verbs* are those wh. contain the idea of making by deed, thought or word, *e.g.*, vbs. of thinking, naming, etc. The acc. after these verbs is followed by another acc. called the complemental or predicative acc., but instead of this acc. a prep. and its case are sts. used. These verbs in the pass., like the copulative sum (3), are vbs. of imperfect predication, *i.e.*, they require an adj. or subst. (sts. called a complement) to complete the predication. **văgus**, -a, -um, adj. nom. mas. sing. ag. w. amnis; *strolling about, roaming, roving, unfixed, unsettled*, of persons and things (671); of rivers (769); fig., *wandering, inconstant, doubtful, uncertain, vague. Fickle, uncertain*, in love, etc. **et** (2). **sinistra**, abl. fem. s. ag. w. ripâ; fr. sĭnister, -tra, -trum, adj., comp. sĭnisterior, no sup., *left, on the left hand* or *side; fig., awkward, wrong, perverse, improper. Unlucky, injurious, adverse, bad*; also, as the Romans faced the South in taking auguries and so had the E. on the left, *favourable, lucky, auspicious*, but also used in Gk. sense, *inauspicious*.

55. **Labitur**, 3rd s. ind. pres. fr. lābor, lābi, lapsus sum, 3rd depon., *to glide, move gently* either of horizontal motion or motion downwards. *To slip away, haste away, escape*. Of time, words, etc., *to flow smoothly onwards*. Of things, *to slip away* from one, *be gone, be lost. To fall down, commit a fault, make a mistake. To sink into misfortune; be deteriorated, grow weak*. Of an army, *to waver, be disordered*. **ripa**, abl. (of separation) s. after labitur; fr. rīpa, -æ, 1st fem., *bank* of a stream, sts. *shore* of the sea. **Jove** (25), abl. absol. (88). **non**, neg. adv., (for ne-unum, *not one*) *not*. In interrog. (405)=nonne (367); w. adjs. (485). **probante**, pres. part. act. abl. mas. s. ag. w. Jove; fr. prŏbo, -āre, -avi, -atum, 1st trans., (probus, *good, excellent*) *to try, test, examine* anything in respect of fitness, goodness, etc. (not in Cic. nor Cæs.). *To judge of as just, fit, good*, etc., *be satisfied with, approve of. To represent* a thing *as good, acceptable*, etc., *recommend. To make credible, show, prove, demonstrate* a thing to any one.

xorius amnis.
Audiet cives acuisse ferrum
Quo graves Persæ melius perirent,
Audiet pugnas vitio parentum
Rara juventus.
Quem vocet Divum populus ruentis

56. **Uxorius,** -a, -um, adj., nom. mas. s., ag. w. amnis (uxor, 455); *of or belonging to a wife, married. Excessively fond of one's wife, uxorious, i.e.*, influenced by his wife to avenge the death of Cæsar, her descendant. **amnis,** -is, 3rd mas., (rare fem.) abl. amne, (reg. in poets) often amni, (akin to ăqua, 22) *any deep flowing, rapid water, torrent, stream, large river* (chiefly poet.).

57. **Audiet,** 3rd s. fut. ind. act. fr. audio, -īre, -īvi, -itum, 4th trans., *to hear, perceive, understand by hearing. Listen to, attend to. Agree to, obey, heed.* **cives,** acc. plu. subj. of acuisse; fr. cīvis, -is, abl. usu. cive, also civi, 3rd com., *a citizen*, male or female. **acuisse,** pf. inf. act. after audiet; fr. ăcŭo, -uĕre, -ui, -ūtum, 3rd trans., (rt. ac- in ac-us, *needle*) *to make sharp* or *pointed, sharpen, whet.* Of the tongue, *to exercise, improve.* Metaph. of the mind, intellect, etc. *To spur, incite, drive one on. To excite, kindle, inflame, e.g.*, passion, etc. **ferrum,** acc. s. gov. by acuisse; fr. ferrum, -i, 2nd neut., (ak to fir-mus, *strong* metal) *iron*, of many things made of iron, esp. *sword, arms*, etc.

58. **Quo,** neut. s. ag. w. ferrum; abl. instrum. w. perirent; fr. qui (3). **graves,** nom. mas. plu. ag. w. Persæ; fr. gravis (41). **Persæ,** -arum, 1st mas.; nom. plu. subj. of perirent, here=*the Parthians* (504). **melius,** compar. adv. of bene (1050), prop. neut. of melior (209), *better*, i.e., *more properly.* **perirent,** 3rd plu. impf. conj.; fr. pereo, -īre, -ĭi, (-īvi), -ĭtum, intr. irreg. (per, 114; eo, 51), *to go, run through: To pass away, come to nothing, vanish; be destroyed, die* (class.). *To pine away w. love, be desperately in love* (636). *To be wasted, spent in vain, e.g.*, opera. *To be ruined, undone.* The conj. is potential, *might, would have perished.*

59. **Audiet** (57). **pugnas,** acc. plu. gov. by audiet; fr. pugna, -æ, 1st fem., (pug- rt. in pungo, *to prick*) *a fight man to man, fight between individuals* or *armies. Contest, action, engagement.* **vitio,** abl. s. (of cause w. rara); fr. vĭtĭum, -ii, 2nd neut. *A fault, defect, blemish, imperfection, vice*, physical or moral. *A crime, fault*, esp. a *defect* in the auspices. **parentum,** gen. plu. after vitio; fr. părens, -entis, gen. pl. -entum, and -entium, 3rd. mas. and fem. (pario, 892). Of persons and animals, a *parent, father, mother* (1197), *sire, dam*, plu. *parents*, i.e., *father and mother, grand-parents, progenitors, ancestors;* fig. *author, inventor, originator* (262), *founder* of a city; sts. an honorary epithet (297).

60. **Rara,** nom. fem. s. ag. w. juventus; fr. rārus, -a, -um, adj., *having wide interstices between the parts, of a loose texture, not thick* or *dense. Scattered about, wide apart. Few, rare, uncommon*, of things found in small numbers, or which rarely take place; here *thinned.* **jŭventus,** -ūtis, 3rd fem., nom. sing., subj. of audiet; *age of a juvenis* (77), *season of youth. Youthful age*, strictly fr. 17th to 45th or 46th year. *Young persons*, abstract for concrete.

61. **Quem,** acc. mas. s. ag. w. Divum; fr. qui or quis, quæ, quod or quid, acc. quem, quam, quod, gen. cūjus, dat. cui, plu. like relat. qui (3); interrog. pron. adj., *who? which?* The distinction drawn betw. "qui," as adjectival and "quis," as substantival can hardly be maintained. **vocet,** 3rd sing.

62 Imperî rebus? prece qua fatigent
63 Virgines sanctæ minus audientem
64 Carmina Vestam?
65 Cui dabit partes scelus expiandi

pres. conj. (dubitative) act.; from vŏco, -are, -avi, -atum, 1st trans. *to call together, summon. To call out aloud, proclaim, announce. To invoke, pray to* a deity. *To invite* as a guest, etc. *To name, denominate* w. a second acc. (79). *To call*, i.e., *bring, draw, put, set,* esp. w. in and acc. **Divum,** acc. s. gov. by vŏcet; fr. Dīvus, -i, 2nd mas., *a god;* prop. mas. of divus, -a, -um, adj., *of* or *belonging to* a deity (rare). **populus** (32), nom. sing. subj. of vocet. **ruentis,** gen. s. neut. pres. part. act. ag. w. imperi; fr. ruo, ruĕre, rui, rŭtum, 3rd intr., *to fall with violence, fall* or *rush down, tumble down, crumble. To hasten, hurry, rush;* trans., *to cast down, dash down. To cast up from the bottom, tear up, rake up.*

62. **Imperi**=imperii, gen. s. after rebus; fr. impĕrium, -ii, 2nd neut., (impero, *to command*) *a command, order. The right* or *power of command, authority, control,* esp. *supreme power, sovereignty, dominion.* Concr., *dominion, realm, empire* (here). Milit., *the chief command,* opp. to magistratus. *The Imperial Government.* **rebus,** *the fortunes,* dat. (commodi) pl. after vocet; fr. res, rei, 5th fem., *that which is spoken of* or *thought of, thing, object, being, matter, affair, event, circumstance, occurrence, condition. Something. Thing itself, reality, fact,* opp. to appearance. *Effects, property. Benefit, advantage, interest. Cause, reason, ground, account;* "res publica," *commonwealth.* **prece,** abl. (of means) s.; as if fr. prex, prĕcis, 3rd fem., obsol. in nom. and gen. sing. *A prayer, request, entreaty,* esp. to a deity. *A curse, imprecation.* **qua,** abl. s. fem. ag. w. prece; fr. qui (61). **fatigent,** 3rd pl., pres. conj. (dubitative) act.; fr. fătīgo, -are, -avi, -atum, 1st trans., *to employ to weariness, weary, tire, fatigue, vex, harass. To importune, plague, torment, vex;* "prece fatigare," *to importune.*

63. **Virgines,** nom. pl., subj. of fatigent; fr. virgo, virgĭnis, 3rd fem., (vireo, *to be fresh*) *maid, virgin, young woman, girl.* **sanctæ,** nom. pl. fem. ag. w. virgines; fr. sanctus, -a, -um, adj., (sancio, *to render sacred*) *rendered sacred, established as inviolable; venerable, august, divine. Pure, holy, innocent, just, pious* of persons. **minus,** adv. prop. neut. of minor (332), compar. of parve. *Less, not so much,* sts. *too little.* Of time, *less, not so long* or *much as;* here=non (55) w. audientem; sup. minime. **audientem,** acc. fem. s. pres. part. act. ag. w. Vestam; fr. audio (57). Caesar was her Pontifex Maximus.

64. **Carmina,** acc. pl. gov. by audientem; fr. carmen, -ĭnis, 3rd neut., (ak. to cano, 61) *a poem, poetry* of every kind, Hor. often uses it of *lyric poetry* only. *Poetic inscription. Response* of an oracle, *prophecy, prediction,* genly. in verse. *Tune, song, air,* vocal or instrumental. **Vestam,** acc. s. gov. by fatigent; fr. Vesta (52).

65. **Cui,** dat. s. after (remote obj. of) dabit; fr. quis or qui interrog. (61). **dabit,** 3rd s. fut. ind. act. fr. do, dare, dĕdi, dătum, 1st. irreg., *to give away, grant, concede, allow, permit, yield, resign, bestow, offer. To put, place, carry somewhere. To impute, attribute* anything to any one. *To announce, tell, communicate.* **partes,** acc. pl. gov. by (direct obj. of) dabit; fr. pars (20). **scelus,** acc. s. gov. by expiandi; fr. scĕlus, -ĕris, 3rd neut., *an evil deed, a wicked, heinous,* or *impious action, crime, sin, enormity;* here "*curse*" of civil war; concrete, *rascal, villain.* **expiandi,** gen. gerund. after partes; fr. expio, -are, -avi, -atum, 1st trans., (ex, 691; pio, *to atone for, expiate*) *to*

Jupiter ? Tandem venias precamur
Nube candentes humeros amictus
    Augur Apollo ;
Sive tu mavis, Erycina ridens,
Quam Jocus circum volat et Cupido ;

make complete satisfaction, amends, or *atonement for* a crime or criminal. *To purify* anything defiled w. crime, *atone for, expiate* (881). *To make amends for, make good.*

66. **Jupiter** (25), nom. subj. of dabit. **tandem** (tam, 194; and demonst. dem), *just so far.* Of time, *after so long, after a long time ; at last, at length, in the end, finally* of what takes place after long delay, w. jam, aliquando, denique, or alone. In interrog., *pray, pray now, then.* **venias,** 2nd s. subj. pres. act. fr. vĕnio, -īre, vēni, ventum, 4th irreg., *to come ;* pres. after pres. precamur, subj. as ut (final, 388) is und. after precamur. **precamur,** 1st pl. pres. ind. fr. prĕcor, -āri, -atus sum, 1st depon. intrans. and trans., *to ask, beg, pray, beseech, entreat, address entreaties to. To beg,* etc. *for* something ; w. acc. of pers and acc. of thing, *to beg, entreat, pray,* etc., some one *for* something.

67. **Nube,** abl. (instrumental w. amictus) s. fr. nūbes, -is, 3rd fem., nūbis, -is, mas. (rt. NUB, *to cover,* as in nubere, *to veil*). *That which covers, cloud, vapour, dark spot. Thick multitude, swarm.* **candentes,** acc. mas. s. pres. part. act. ag. w. humeros ; fr. căndeo, -ēre, -ui, no sup., 2nd intr., (ak. to canus, 132) *to be of glittering, brilliant whiteness, shine, glisten. To be glowing hot.* Partic. sts. in compar. and sup. candentior, candentissimus. **humeros,** acc. plu. of medial obj. (1048) w. amictus ; fr. hŭmĕrus, -i, 2nd mas., (the upper bone of the arm) in poet. for lacertus. *The upper part of the arm. Shoulder* of a man ; fig. in plu., *the shoulders.* **amictus,** pf. pass. part. nom. mas. s. ag. w. tu und. w. venias ; fr. ămĭcĭo, -īre, -ĭcŭi, or -ixi, -ictum, (am-, *round ;* jaceo, *to throw*), 4th trans., *to throw around, wrap about* of upper garments ; w. pers. pron. or pass. refl., *to throw one's garments about one, veil oneself. To veil around, clothe, cover, e.g.,* loca amicta nive.

68. **Augur,** voc. s. in app. to Apollo ; fr. augur, -ŭris, 3rd mas, *an augur, diviner, soothsayer ; one who foretells futurity, seer.* The augures were a college of priests at Rome, who foretold the future by observing lightning, flight of birds, etc. Here of Apollo as "god of augury." **Apollo,** -ĭnis, 3rd mas., here voc., son of Jupiter and Latona, twin brother of Diana ; the sun god, god of divination, archery, the healing art, poetry, music, etc.

69. **Sive,** =seu (27). **tu,** nom. subj. of mavis ; acc. and abl. te, gen. tui, dat. tibi, pl. nom. acc. and voc. vos, gen. vestrum and vestri, dat. and abl. vobis, 2nd pers. pron. s. *thou ;* plu. *you, ye.* **mavis.** 2nd s. pres. ind. fr. mālo, malle, mālui, irreg. (contr. fr. māvolo ; fr. magis, 603 ; volo, 104), *to choose rather, prefer ;* genly. w. obj. clause (rarely acc.), sts. folld. by quam in comparisons. **Erycīna,** voc. s. fr. Erўcīna, -æ, 1st. fem. prop. fem. of Erўcīnus, -a, -um, adj., *Ericynian,* i.e. of *Mt. Eryx,* i.e., *Venus,* who had a temple on Mt. Eryx in Sicily. **rīdens,** voc. fem. s. pres. part. act. ag. w. Erўcina ; fr. rīdeo, -ēre, rīsi, rīsum, 2nd intrans. and trans., *to laugh,* w. si. *To laugh pleasantly, smile on* w. ad aliquem, alicui. Of things, *to look cheerful* or *pleasant* (1030) w. dat. *To laugh over* anything w. acc. *To laugh at, ridicule* one. Und. venias, *mayest thou come,* here fr. prec. sentence.

70. **Quam,** fem. s. ag. w. Ericyna, acc. gov. by circum ; fr. qui (3). **Jŏcus,** -i, 2nd mas., nom. subj. of volat ; plu. also jŏca, jŏcorum ; *a jest, joke, sport, sportiveness,* in words s. and plu. (1417), *a cause for jesting,*

Sive neglectum genus et nepotes
Respicis auctor,
Heu nimis longo satiate ludo,
Quem juvat clamor galeæque leves,

subject of mirth; personified, *the god of sportive mirth.* **circum,** prep. gov. acc. (acc. fr. circus, *in a circle, ring*); *around, about,* both of an entire encompassing or surrounding, and of proximity only partially embracing, *in, into, around on the borders of* a stream (1313); adv. *around, round about.* **volat,** 3rd s. pres. ind. act. fr. vŏlo, -are, -avi, -atum, 1st intrans., *to fly, move swiftly* like a thing flying. *To speed, hasten away.* **Cŭpīdo,** -inis, 3rd mas. nom. jnd. by et to jocus; *Cupid* the god of love. On volat, see 555–6.

71. **Sive** (69), before this vel tu venias must be und. fr. above. **neglectum,** acc. neut. s. pf. pass. part. ag. w. genus; fr. neglĭgo, -ĭgere, -exi, -ectum, 3rd trans. and intrans., (nec, 19; lego, *to gather; not to gather*) trans., *to not heed, not attend to, not trouble oneself about, slight, neglect,* opp. to curare; intr., *be neglectful. To make light of, not to care for, take no notice of, despise, disregard, disdain. To look w. indifference upon* anything that takes place, etc., *pay no heed to,* w. obj. clause. *To pass over, overlook.* **genus,** acc. s. gov. by respicis; fr. genus (55). **nepōtes,** acc. pl. jnd. by et to genus; fr. nĕpos, -ōtis, 3rd mas. and fem. *A grandson, son's* or *daughter's son. A brother's* or *sister's son;* a *nephew. A descendant;* genus et nepotes = genus nepotum; a case of hendiadys (17)

72. **Respicis,** 2nd s. pres. ind. act. fr. respĭcĭo, -spĭcĕre, -spexi, -spectum, 3rd trans. and intrans., (re-, 659; spĕcĭo, obsol., *to look, look at*) *to look back* or *behind; turn one's eyes,* intrans. w. ad, in, etc., or trans. w. acc. of that on which; fig., *to look to,* i.e., *be centered in. To have regard for, regard, e.g.,* ad utilitatem. *To be mindful of, consider, e.g.,* of deities (here). **auctor,** -ōris, 3rd mas., sts. fem.; nom. s. in app. to tu und. in respicis, (augeo, *to cause to grow, increase*). Of parentage, *father, founder, progenitor,* here of Mars, father of Romulus and Remus. Of writings, *writer, author.* Of buildings, *founder, builder. One by whose influence, counsel, care,* etc., anything is done, *cause, occasion, contriver, instigator, counsellor, adviser, promoter. One who is considered a model, pattern, exemplar. One who searches into abstruse matters to teach them,* i.e., *expounder, exponent* (662).

73. **Heu,** an exclamation of grief or pain, *oh! ah! alas!* **nĭmis,** adv. modal, w. longo; *too much, over much, excessive, beyond measure;* w. neg. *not too much, not particularly, not very.* Alone, *beyond measure, exceedingly.* **longo,** abl. mas. s. ag. w. ludo; from longus, -a, -um, adj. Of size or space, *long, tall. Far off, remote, distant.* Of time, *of long duration* or *continuance. Occupying a long time, tedious. Remote, far off, distant.* Of persons, *prolix, tedious.* **satiate,** voc. s. mas. pf. pass. part.; fr. sătĭo, -are, -avi, -atum, 1st trans., (satis, 37) *to fill, satisfy, satiate* w. food, and fig., *saturate, impregnate, content, glut,* esp. in pf. part. *To overfill, cloy, disgust.* **ludo,** abl. s., (of cause) fr. lūdus, -i, 2nd mas., (luo = solvere, *that which causes relaxation*) *play, game, diversion, pastime.* Plu. esp. *public games, plays, spectacles* in honour of the gods, *stage plays.* Fig., *anything done without trouble, sport, child's play. A sport, jest, joke,* "ludum dare alicui," of persons, *to indulge one,* of things, *to give loose to. A place of exercise for body* or *mind, a school;* here "*game of war.*"

74. **Quem,** mas. s. ag. w. satiate; acc. gov. by juvat; fr. qui (3). **juvat** (4). **clāmor,** ōris, 3rd mas., nom. sing. subj. of juvat; (clāmo, *to call, cry out*) *a loud call, shout, cry* of men and animals. *A friendly call, acclamation,*

75 Acer et Mauri peditis cruentum
76 Vultus in hostem;
77 Sive mutata juvenem figura
78 Ales in terris imitaris almæ

applause. **galeæ,** nom. pl. jnd. by -que to clamor; fr. gălea, -æ, 1st fem., *a helmet,* usu. of leather; *headpiece,* also of bronze helmets. **-que** (4). **lēves,** nom. fem. pl. ag. w. galeæ; fr. lēvis, -e, adj., *smooth, smoothed, not rough* (1435). *Without hair, beardless, bald. Without wrinkles. Polished, bright, shining* (here), *fair, beauteous. Finely dressed, spruce, smart.*

75. **Acer,** acrĭs, acre, gen. acris, adj.; nom. mas. s. ag. w. vultus, (ac- rt. of aceo, *to be acid*) prop. *sharp, pointed, edged* of the senses and things affecting them. *Violent, vehement, strong, passionate, consuming.* Of intellectual qualities, *subtle, acute, sagacious, shrewd.* Of moral qualities, in good sense, *active, ardent, spirited, zealous;* in bad sense, *hot, fierce, severe, violent, hasty.* **Mauri,** gen. mas. s. ag. w. peditis; fr. Maurus, -a, -um, adj., *of or belonging to the Moors, Moorish, Mauritanian. African* (538, 1020). Mauri, -orum, 2nd mas., *the inhabitants of Mauretania.* **pĕditis,** gen. s. after vultus; fr. pĕdes, 3rd mas., (pes, 135) *one that goes on foot,* esp. *a foot-soldier,* sts. collective *foot-soldiery.* **cruentum,** acc. mas. s. ag. w. hostem; fr. crŭentus, -a, -um, adj., (cruor, 831) *bloody, blood-stained, bleeding. Attended* or *marked with blood, e.g.,* victoria. Of persons, *delighting in blood, cruel.*

76. **Vultus,** -us, 4th mas. nom. s. jnd. by et to galeæ, (volo, 104, *the expressing one's wish in one's countenance*) *expression of countenance, countenance, visage,* as to features, expression, etc. *The face.* **in,** prep. gov. acc. or abl. With acc. of place, *into, to, upon, against* implying motion; of direction, *towards* (922). Of time, *into; until, till, up to; for, e.g.,* in diem; in 1206, in horas, *hour by hour.* Of purpose, *for* (1144, 192). Of manner, *after* (828); here w. adj. acer. **hostem,** acc. s. gov. by in; fr. hostis, -is, 3rd com., *a stranger, foreigner. One who is entertained as a guest. An enemy* in arms or to one's country.

77. **Sive** (69). **mutata,** abl. fem. s. pf. pass. part. ag. w. figura; fr. mūto, -āre, āvi, -ātum, 1st trans., *to move, move away from* a place *to* a place (rare). *To alter, change* a thing. *To alter for the better, improve,* or *alter for the worse, spoil. To change* one thing *for* another, w. acc. of that taken in exchange, and abl. of that given, or vice versâ. *To leave* one place *for* another. *To interchange, barter* w. abl. of that for which exchange is made. Intrans., *alter, change, differ, be different.* **juvenem,** acc. s. gov. by imitaris; fr. jŭvĕnis, -is, adj. com.; compar. juvenior, more com. junior, *young, youthful;* as subst. 3rd com., *a young person,* male or female betw. 17 and 46, esp. *a young man* of the age of military service. **figura,** abl. absol. (824) s. fr. fĭgūra, -æ, 1st fem., *a form, shape,* of bodies; poet., *shade, ghost* of the dead; fig., a *quality, kind, species, nature, manner.*

78. **Ales,** -ĭtis, gen. plu. alĭtum and alituum, orig. adj., here nom. mas. s. ag. w. filius; (ala, 1345; eo, 51) *winged, quick, hasty, rapid;* subst. 3rd, *a bird,* com., or fem. of a female *bird;* mas., of a *winged* deity. *Augury, omen,* fem. **in** (76), w. abl. of place, implying rest, *in, within,* fig., *in the midst* of (941); of time, *in, at, during, in the course of* (443). In 467, *for, on account of.* **terris,** abl. plu. gov. by in; fr. terra (6). **imitaris,** 2nd s. ind. pres. fr. ĭmĭtor, -āri, -atus sum, 1st depon. intens., *to imitate, i.e.,* express by means of something similar, *express, copy, portray;* fig., *to copy after, seek to resemble, counterfeit* something (most frequ.); mutatus, sts. pass. since the act. imito

Filius Maiæ patiens vocari
            Cæsaris ultor:
Serus in cælum redeas diuque
Lætus intersis populo Quirini.
Neve te nostris vitiis iniquum
            Ocior aura

is used ante- and post-class. **almæ,** gen. s. fem. ag. w. Maiæ; fr. almus, -a, -um, adj., (alo, 550) *nourishing, nutritious,* esp. of patron deities of the earth, light, day, wine, etc. *Genial, refreshing. Kind, propitious, bountiful.*

79. **Filius,** -ii, 2nd mas., *a son,* nom. s. for voc. **Maiæ,** gen. s. after filius; fr. Maia or Maja, dau. of Atlas and Pleione, and mother of Mercury by Jupiter. **patiens** (194), nom. mas. s. pres. part. ag. w. filius. **vocari,** pres. inf. (prolative, 570) pass. after patiens; fr. voco (61).

80. **Cæsăris,** gen. s. after ultor; fr. Cæsar, 3rd mas., a cognomen of the gens Julia, of whom C. Julius was the most distinguished. After him all the emperors bore the name Cæsar, with the title Augustus, until, under Adrian, Augustus denoted the ruling emperor, Cæsar the heir to the throne. **ultor** (53), nom. s. in app. to tu und. in imitaris.

81. **Serus** (403), adverbial attribute (867), ag. w. tu und. in redeas. **in,** with acc. (76). **cælum,** acc. s. gov. by in; fr. cælum, -i, 2nd neut., *heaven, heavens; quarter* or *region of heaven. Climate, zone, region. Aerial region, air, sky. Atmosphere,* fig., *summit* of happiness, etc. **redeas,** 2nd sing. conj. (optative) pres. fr. redeo (41). **diu,** adv. of time (locative of dies=*a space of time;* so noctu, fr. nox), *a long time, very long time* without any comparison. *Long since, a great while ago.* Comp. diutius, sup. diutissime. **-que** (4).

82. **Lætus,** -a, -um, adj., nom. mas. s. adverbial attrib. (867), ag. w. tu und. in intersis; *feeling joy, rejoicing, joyous, delighted. Exhibiting joy, cheerful. Doing anything with joy, ready. Causing joy, pleasing, pleasant. Abundant, fertile, luxurious.* **intersis,** 2nd sing. pres. conj. (optative), jnd. by -que to redeas; fr. intersum, -esse, -fui, irreg. intr. (inter, 330; sum, 3). Of place, *to be between. To be present in* or *at,* esp. *to share in, assist in. To live among.* Of time, *to elapse between, intervene. To be different, to differ,* esp. in 3rd pers. impers. The 3rd pers. impers. also=*it is of importance to, interests,* w. gen. of person whom it interests, or if a pron. meâ, tuâ, suâ, etc.; ad w. acc. of that *in reference to* which. **populo,** dat. s. after intersis; fr. populus (32). **Quirini,** gen. s. after populo; fr. Quirīnus, -i (quiris, curis, a Sabine word=hasta, *spearman*), a prop. name of Romulus after his deification; populus Quirini=*Romans.*

83. **Neve** or neu (nē...ve, *and not, nor*), a sociative conj. used in joining a negative sentence to a prec. one where a command, purpose, etc., is implied, or to distribute such a sentence or thought into two or more coordinate clauses which are foreseen; neve...neve, *neither...nor, that neither...nor* [neque jns. negative categorical propositions]. **te,** acc. s. gov. by tollat; fr. tu (69). **nostris,** dat. plu. neut. ag. w. vitiis; fr. noster, -stra, -strum (nos, plu. of ego, 29), possessive adj., *our, our own, ours.* **vitiis,** dat. plu. after trajective iniquum (873); fr. vitium (59). **iniquum,** acc. mas. s. ag. w. te; fr. īnīquus (271), here "*intolerant of*" (W.).

84. **Ocior,** nom. fem. s. ag. w. aura; compar. adj.; neut. ocius; no positive; superl. ocissimus (ak. to acer, 75; acutus, 236), *swifter, fleeter* (1303, 1437). Of time (rarer), *quicker, sooner, earlier.* **aura,** -æ, 1st fem. nom. s. subj. of

Tollat. Hic magnos potius triumphos,
Hic ames dici pater atque princeps.
Neu sinas Medos equitare inultos,
Te duce, Cæsar.

tollat; *the air in gentle motion, gentle breeze, breath of air. Wind, blast. Breath, atmosphere, upper air.* Of things which influence bodies like a breath of air, *e.g.*, light, heat, sand, vapour, gleam, glitter.

85. **Tollat,** 3rd s. pres. conj. (optative) act. fr. tollo (8). **hīc,** adv. of place, *in this place, here,* opp. to illic. Of circumstances, *in this matter, on this occasion, in this particular, herein, here.* **magnos,** acc. plu. mas. ag. w. triumphos; fr. magnus (104). **potius,** neut. of pŏtior (1260), as adv., *rather, in preference.* **triumphos,** acc. plu. gov. by ames; fr. triumphus, -i, 2nd mas., *triumphal procession, triumph, i.e.,* solemn and magnificent entrance of a general into Rome after having obtained an important victory. *The shout of the multitude on the occasion,* fig., *a triumph, victory.*

86. **Hic** (85), anaphora (895). **ames,** 2nd s. pres. conj. (optative) act. fr. ămo, -are, -avi, -atum, 1st trans., *to love,* genly. in an honourable sense, sts. in Com. in a low sense; fig., *to be fond of, find pleasure in.* In 595, amat janua limen, *loves to remain shut, i.e.,* is always closed. With inf. *to be wont, accustomed to,* etc. (not here, but so in 950), genly. poet. and post-Aug. [amare is intuitive opp. to odisse; diligere, of love produced from regard, esteem, reverence, etc., *i.e.*, exercise of the reasoning powers]. **dici,** pres. inf. (objective 560) pass. after ames; fr. dīco, dīcĕre, dixi, dictum, 3rd trans., (rt. dic, akin to digitus, *a finger*) *to say, tell, mention, relate. Call, name. Appoint, fix upon.* **pater** (38), predicative after the factitive (54) dici. **atque** (37). **princeps,** -ĭpis, adj. com., (primus, 100; capio, 1388) here as subst.; nom. s. jnd. by atque to pater; *that takes the first place, first* in time or order, *most eminent, principal, superior,* etc.; as subst. *the first* on a list, *originator* of an action or opinion good or bad, *founder* of a family, etc. *Head, chief, leader.*

87. **Neu**=neve (83). **sinas,** 2nd sing. pres. conj. (optative) act. fr. sĭno, sĭnĕre, sīvi, sĭtum, 3rd irreg. trans., but rare with acc.; *to let, suffer, allow, permit.* **Medos,** acc. subj. of equitare; fr. Mēdi, -orum, 2nd mas. plu. *The Medes,* poet. for *Assyrians, Persians, Parthians* (see 629). **equitare,** pres. inf. act. after sinas; fr. ĕquĭto, -āre, -āvi, -ātum, 1st intens., trans. and intrans., (equus, 167) *to be a horseman, ride* (1116), *to gallop, e.g.,* of flame. *To ride through* a place. **inultos,** acc. mas. plu. ag. w. Medos; fr. inultus, -a, -um, adj. (in neg., ultus, partc. of ulciscor, *to avenge*). *Unavenged, for whom vengeance is not* or *has not been taken, who cannot take revenge. On which* or *whom vengeance is not inflicted, unpunished.* Meton., *unhurt, safe, secure, unmolested* (Hor.); "preces inultæ," *intreaties that obtain not satisfaction, unheard.*

88. **Te** abl. absolute s. fr. tu (69). **duce,** abl. s. in app. to te; fr. dux, dŭcis, 3rd com., *a leader, conductor, guide;* milit., *general, commander-in-chief;* fig., *chief, head,* etc. The ablative absolute or ablativus convenientiæ is the name given to the abl. of a subst. or pron. joined with another abl. of a participle, adjective or substantive; rarely a pronoun, which in construction is independent of the rest of the sentence and is equivalent to a clause of time (*when, since,* etc.), condition, concession (*though, although*) or cause. It is not used, as a rule, when a noun term for the partic. to agree with can be found in the principal sentence. **Cæsar** (80), voc. s.

CARMEN III.

AD NAVEM QUA VEHEBATUR VIRGILIUS ATHENAS PROFICISCENS.

Sic te diva potens Cypri,
  Sic fratres Helenæ, lucida sidera,
Ventorumque regat pater
  Obstrictis aliis præter Iapyga,

CARMEN III. METRE—*Second Asclepiad.*

First the Glyconic	– –	– ᴗ ᴗ	– ᴗ ⏓
	spondee	dactyl	dactyl or Cretic

Second. The Lesser Asclepiad as in Carm. I.

89. **Sic**, pronominal particle, *in this manner, in such a manner; so*=hoc, tali modo. *So much, to such a degree. Thus, so truly. On these conditions.* In comparisons answers to ut, quemadmodum, etc. In wishes and protestations it implies a condition, here "may you be safe only on condition that you preserve etc." (see 673). **te** (83), *i.e.*, the ship; gov. by regat. **diva**, -æ, 1st fem.; subj. of regat und. fr. 91; *a goddess*, prop. fem. of adj. dīvus, -a, -um, *of* or *belonging to a deity; metaph., godlike, divine*, of anything deified or of extraordinary excellence (rarely used as adj.); divus, -i, 2nd mas., *a God, deity* (161); divum, -i, 2nd neut., *the sky*, esp. sub divo, *under the open sky, in the open air* (489, 963). **pŏtens**, -ntis, adj.; partc. of possum (372); as adj., *having power over, lord, ruler of* (174). *Able, mighty, powerful.* **Cypri**, gen. s. after potens (164, 174; the objective gen., 749); fr. Cȳprus, -i, 2nd fem., island in the Mediterranean, celebrated for fertility, mines, etc., and the worship of Venus.

90. **Sic** (89). **fratres**, nom. plu. subj. of regant und.; fr. frāter, fratris, 3rd mas., *a brother*, sts., *a cousin*; fratres Helenæ, Castor and Pollux. **Helenæ**, gen. s. after fratres; fr. Helena, -æ, or Helene, -es (Gk.), dau. of Jupiter and Leda, sister of Castor and Pollux and Clytemnestra, wife of Menelaus, carried away by Paris to Troy, hence the cause of the Trojan war. **lucida**, nom. neut. plu. ag. w. sidera; fr. lūcĭdus, -a, -um, adj., (luceo, *to shine*) *shining, bright, brilliant, splendid, glittering, glistening, dazzling.* Of speech, orators, etc., *clear, lucid, luminous.* Adv., lucidum, *brilliantly, splendidly, dazzlingly* (1178). **sidera**, nom. plu. in app. to fratres; fr. sidus (36). This refers to St. Elmo's fire, certain electric lights said to play about the spars of a vessel after stormy weather in the Mediterranean, in which Roman sailors recognized the presence of Castor and Pollux, their guardian deities. Others explain it of the constellation Gemini.

91. **Ventorum**, gen. plu. after pater; fr. ventus, -i, 2nd mas., *wind*, used fig. of fortune, etc. **regat**, 3rd s. pres. conj. (optative) act. fr. rĕgo, regĕre, rexi, rectum, 3rd trans., *to rule, govern, sway, have the supremacy over, control. Guide, lead, conduct, direct. To set right, correct* one who has erred. *To keep straight, guide straight.* **pater** (38), *i.e.*, Æolus, subj. of regat; jnd. by -que (4) to fratres.

92. **Obstrictis**, pf. pass. part. abl. plu. mas. ag. w. aliis; fr. obstringo, -ngĕre, -nxi, -ctum, 3rd trans., (ob, exp. *persistence;* stringo, *to bind*) *to bind, fasten against* or *to. To fasten about* or *around, bind up*, fig., *to fetter, hamper, bind* w. debts, an oath, obligation, etc. **aliis**, abl. (absol., 824) plu. mas. ag. w. ventis und.; fr. ălĭus, ălĭa, ălĭud, gen. ălius, dat. ăli,

93 Navis, quæ tibi creditum
94 Debes Vergilium, finibus Atticis
95 Reddas incolumem, precor,
96 Et serves animæ dimidium meæ.
97 Illi robur et æs triplex

plu. reg.; *the other, other* of many [alter, *one* of two]; alius...alius, *the one...the other*, or alii...alii, *the one party...the other*, may be repeated in successive clauses without limit of number; here *all other* winds (W.). **præter,** prep. gov. acc. Of place, *past, by, before, along;* fig., *beyond, above, more than. Besides, in addition to, together with. Besides, except.* **Iapyga,** acc. s. gov. by præter; fr. Iāpyx, -ygis (Gk.), 3rd mas., a wind that blows in the S. of Italy, the N.N.W. of the Greeks.

93. **Navis,** voc. s. fr. nāvis, -is, 3rd fem., *a ship.* **quæ** (46), fem. sing. ag. w. navis; nom. subj. to debes. **tibi,** dat. s. (commodi) after creditum; fr. tu (69). **creditum,** acc. mas. s. pf. pass. part. ag. w. Vergilium; fr. crēdo (583).

94. **Debes,** 2nd s. pres. ind. act. fr. dēbeo, -ēre, -ui, -ĭtum, 2nd trans., (de, 10; habeo, 641, orig. *to have from* a person) trans., *to owe,* aliquid alicui. *To be bound to, under obligation to* something, *e.g.,* gratiam; with inf., *to be bound* to do something, *I ought, I must,* etc. Pass., *to be due* or *owing* (1039). Poet. and post-Aug. prose, of things to which by a law of fate or nature we are bound or destined, more com. in pass., *e.g.,* fatis debitus, *devoted to death;* "debere ludibrium alicui" (380), *to become the sport of any one. To have to thank one for,* i.e., *to owe,* e.g., vitam alicui. **Vergilium,** acc. s. gov. by dēbes; fr. Vergĭlĭus, -ii, P. Vergilius Maro, author of the Æneid. **finibus,** dat. plu. after (remote obj. of) reddas; fr. fīnis, -is, 3rd mas., (fem. only ante- and post-class. and poet.) *boundary, limit, border. Borders, territory* enclosed within bounds. *End. End of life, death. Extremity* of an ascending series, *highest degree, summit. Purpose, design, intention.* **Atticis,** dat. plu. mas. ag. w. finibus; fr. Attĭcus, -a, -um, *of* or *belonging to Attica* or *Athens.*

95. **Reddas,** 2nd s. pres. conj. (optative) act. fr. reddo (265). **incolumem,** acc. s. mas. pred. ag. w. Vergilium; fr. incŏlŭmis, -e; adj., (in, neg.; columis, obsol. adj.) *uninjured, unimpaired, in good condition; sound, entire, whole.* Comp. incolumior, superl. and adv. not found. **prĕcor** (66), 1st sing. pres. ind.

96. **Serves,** 2nd sing. pres. conj. (optative) act. jnd. by et to reddas; fr. servo, -are, -avi, -atum, 1st trans., *to save, deliver, keep unharmed, preserve, protect. To keep, lay up, reserve. Give heed, tend, watch, observe.* **animæ,** gen. s. after dimidium; fr. ănĭma, -æ, 1st fem., *that which blows, breathes, current of air* (an element). *Air inhaled, breath. Vital principle. Life* (physical). *Soul* separated from body. **dimidium,** acc. sing. gov. by serves; fr. dīmĭdĭum, -ii, 2nd neut., *the half,* prop. neut. of dimidius, -a, -um, adj., (dis-, 870; medius, 975) until Aug. age only used w. pars. **meæ,** gen. s. fem. ag. w. animæ; fr. meus (2).

97. **Illi,** dat. (acquisitive) mas. s. after erat; fr. ille (9). **rōbur,** rōbŏris, 3rd neut.; nom. subj. of erat; *an oak, trunk of an oak, oakwood,* also used of other trees. Of things made of oak or any other hard wood, *e.g., a bench, plough.* The lower part of the prison built by Servius Tullus at Rome so called (1211). *Hardness, strength, vigour, power, force.* In sing. and plu. *the strongest, most effective part* of anything, *e.g.,* militum, civium. **et** (2), conj. where we use a disjunctive. **æs,** æris, 3rd neut.; nom. s. jnd. by et to robur; plu. nom. and acc. æra, gen. ærum, dat. æribus (rare); any crude

98 Circa pectus erat, qui fragilem truci
99 Commisit pelago ratem
100 Primus nec timuit præcipitem Africum
101 Decertantem Aquilonibus
102 Nec tristes Hyadas nec rabiem Noti,

metal dug out of the earth exc. gold, esp. *copper* and *bronze;* then of statues, tables, money, etc. made of such metals. **triplex,** trĭplĭcis (abl. trĭplĭci) adj.; nom. neut. s. ag. w. æs; (tres; 956; plĭco, *to fold*) *threefold, triple.*

98. **Circa,** prep. w. acc. Of place, *about, around, on the side of. In the neighbourhood of,* less def. than "in" (997, 607); a later fm. than circum (70). **pectus,** acc. s. gov. by circa; fr. pectus, pectŏris, 3rd neut., *the breastbone* or *breast.* **erat,** 3rd s. impf. ind. fr. sum (3), see 555. Hor. often has sing. vb. where all the subjs. or subj. nearest it is in the sing. (74, 91, 580, etc.). **qui** (19), mas. s. ag. w. illi; nom. subj. of commisit. **fragilem,** acc. fem. s. ag. w. ratem; fr. frăgĭlis, -e, adj. (frango, 570), *easily broken, brittle, fragile,* fig., *weak, frail,* physically or mentally. **truci,** dat. s. neut. ag. w. pelago; fr. trux, trŭcĭs, adj., *wild, rough, hard, harsh, savage, fierce, grim, stern* of persons and things; no comp. or sup.

99. **Commisit,** 3rd s. pf. ind. act.; fr. committo, -ĕre, -mīsi, -missum, 3rd trans., (cum, 31; mitto, 38, *to cause to go together*) *to combine, join together, connect, unite. To set* or *bring together in a contest* or *fight,* men or animals. With prœlium, certamen, bellum, *to engage in a contest* or *battle. To celebrate* games. *To compare, put together. To place* a thing anywhere *for care, protection,* etc., *give, intrust, consign to. To practise, perpetrate* wrong, a crime, etc. **pelago,** dat. s. after (remote obj. of) commisit; fr. pĕlăgus, -i (Gk.), 2nd neut., no pl.; poet. and post-Aug. for mare=*sea.* **ratem,** acc. s. gov. by (direct obj. of) commisit; fr. ratis (17).

100. **Primus,** -a, -um, adj. nom. mas. s. adv. attribute (867), ag. w. qui; *first,* superl. of compar. prior, *former.* There is no positive adj. but positive seen in prep. præ, *before.* **nec** (19). **timuit,** 3rd s. perf. ind. act. jnd. by nec to commisit; fr. tĭmeo, -ēre, -ŭi, no sup., 2nd trans., *to fear, be afraid of, dread, apprehend.* Intrans., w. ut, ne, etc., *to be fearful, apprehensive.* **præcĭpitem,** acc. mas. s. ag. w. Africum; fr. præceps, -cĭpĭtis, adj. Of living beings, *headforemost, headlong.* Of persons, rushing *in headlong haste.* Of places running down suddenly in front, *downhill, steep, precipitous.* Of the sun, *declining.* Of a river, *swift, rapid, rushing, violent* (197); fig., *hasty, rash, inconsiderate. Inclined to* anything. Of time, dice, etc., *hazardous, critical.* **Africum** (15), gov. by timuit.

101. **Decertantem,** acc. mas. s. pres. part. act. ag. w. Africum; fr. decerto, -āre, -āvi, -ātum, 1st trans. and intrans. (de, exp. *fierceness, pertinacity;* certo, *to contend*), *to fight, contend earnestly* or *violently; fig. to contend, strive.* **Aquilonibus,** dat. plu. after decertantem; fr. Aquĭlo, Aquilōnis, 3rd mas., *the north wind.* Gk. *Boreas. The North. The north side.*

102. **Nec** (19). **tristes,** acc. plu. fem. ag. w. Hyadas; fr. tristis, -e, adj. (tero, *to rub; rubbed, worn*). Of living beings, *sad, sorrowful, mournful, dejected, melancholy, disconsolate.* Of taste, *harsh, disagreeable. Gloomy, peevish, ill-tempered, morose. Stern, harsh, severe.* **Hyădas,** acc. jnd. by nec to Africum; fr. Hȳădes, -um, 3rd. (Gk., *rainers*), a group of seven stars in the head of Taurus, called in pure Lat. sŭcŭlæ. **rabiem,** acc. s. jnd. by nec to Hyadas; fr. răbĭes, acc. -em, abl. -e (no other cases), 5th fem., *rage, madness. Any violent emotion, anger, fury, fierceness, eagerness.* **Noti,** gen. s. after rabiem; fr. Nŏtus, -i, 2nd mas., *south wind.*

Quo non arbiter Hadriæ
Major, tollere seu ponere vult freta.
Quem mortis timuit gradum,
Qui siccis oculis monstra natantia,
Qui vidit mare turgidum et

103. **Quo** (56), mas. s. ag. w. Noti, abl. (comparative) after major. This abl. (referred by some to the abl. of origin, by others to that of respect) is used for quam w. the nom. and acc. In comparing the other cases quam must be used, and sts. for clearness it is used with nom. and acc. **non** (55). **arbiter,** -tri, 2nd mas.; nom. subj. of est und. (ar=ad, bito=eo; *one who goes to something in order to see* or *hear it*). *Spectator, beholder, hearer, eye-witness.* Legal, *one who enquires into* a cause, *umpire, judge, arbiter;* fig., *a judge, umpire, one who can treat a thing according to his own will, master, lord of* (1065). **Hadriæ,** gen. s. after arbiter; fr. Hădria, -æ (Adria), 1st mas., *the Hadriatic Sea* (1246, 759). The town is fem.

104. **Măjor,** neut. majus; nom. mas. s. ag. w. arbiter; comp. adj.; fr. magnus, -a, -um, adj., superl. maximus (orig., *increased, become great, grown*). Of living beings and things, *great, large, extensive,* of weights, quantity, sound, etc. Of time, *long,* and of persons in ref. to time, *advanced in* age, esp. in comparative. Of degree or extent, *excessive, much.* Of value, consideration, etc., *high;* "magni or magno," *at a high price.* Of rank, estimation, etc., *of great importance* or *weight, weighty.* **tollere** (8), prolative (570) after vult. **seu** (27), here the first seu is omitted. **ponere,** pres. inf. act. jnd. by seu to tollere; fr. pōno, -ĕre, pŏsui, pŏsĭtum, 3rd trans., *to put* or *set down, place, set, lay;* here *to lay* by ceasing to blow. *To place, post, station. To set up, build, form, fashion. To set out, plant. To lay aside, put down* clothes, etc. *To bury, lay* in the grave. *To lay out, spread. To employ* time in any way. *To appoint, ordain, make* something. *To lay down, state, assert. To put away, dismiss. To forego, surrender.* Intrans. of winds, *abate, subside.* **vult,** 3rd. s. pres. ind. fr. vŏlo, velle, vŏlui, no sup. irreg. intrans. and trans., *to will, be willing, wish, desire, have a mind, be disposed, intend, purpose,* w. inf. or object. clause (633), w. ut and subj., very frequ. w. simple subj. *To suppose, be of opinion, think, say, maintain.* **freta,** acc. plu. gov. by ponere; fr. frĕtum, -i, 2nd neut., (ferveo, 348) *a strait, sound, channel. The sea* (poet.); fig. *straits, dangerous circumstances.*

105. **Quem** (61), ag. w. gradum. **mortis,** gen. s. after gradum; fr. mors, 3rd fem., *death.* **timuit** (100). **gradum,** acc. s. gov. by timuit; fr. grădus, -ūs, 4th mas., (gradior, *to walk*) *a step, pace;* milit., *station, position, ground* taken by a combatant; usu. in plu., *that on which one steps, stair, round* of a ladder, etc. *Degree* in relationship, rank, etc., "quem mortis gradum" = *death in what form?*

106. **Qui** (19), mas. s. ag. w. demonst. und. subj. of timuit; nom. to vidit. **siccis,** abl. plu. mas. ag. w. oculis; fr. siccus, -a, -um, adj., *dry;* siccæ carinæ, i.e., *standing dry.* Of weather, *without rain, e.g.,* dies (Hor.). *Dry, thirsty. Abstemious, temperate, sober* (471). *Firm, solid.* Of speech, *insipid, jejune.* **oculis,** abl. (instrumental) plu.; fr. ŏcŭlus, -i, 2nd mas., *eye. Bud.* **monstra** (42), gov. by vidit und. **natantia,** pres. part. act. acc. neut. plu. ag. w. monstra; fr. năto (47).

107. **Qui** (106), anaphora (895). **vidit,** 3rd. s. pf. ind. act.; fr. video (49). **mare** (14), gov. by vidit. **turgidum,** acc. neut. s. predic. ag. w. mare; fr. turgĭdus, -a, -um, adj. (turgeo, *to swell*), *swollen, inflated, distended, turgid.*

Infames scopulos Acroceraunia?
Nequicquam Deus abscidit
Prudens Oceano dissociabili
Terras, si tamen impiæ
Non tangenda rates transiliunt vada.
Audax omnia perpeti

108. **Infames,** acc. plu. mas. ag. w. scopulos; fr. infāmis, -e, adj., (in neg., fāma, 330), *of ill repute, ill spoken of, disreputable, notorious.* **scopulos,** acc. plu. gov. by vidit; fr. scŏpŭlus, -i, 2nd mas., orig., *a look-out place. Projecting point of rock, shelf, crag. Difficulty, danger, harm.* **Acroceraunia,** acc. in. app. to scopulos; fr. Acroceraunia, -orum, 2nd neut. (Gk. ἀκρός, *high;* κεραυνός, *a lightning flash*). A high mountain range betw. Macedonia and Epirus extending to a very rocky promontory in the sea.

109. **Nequicquam** (also -quidquam and best MSS. -quiquam); (ne-, 41: quīquam, adv. abl. of quisquam, 302). *Not in any way,* hence *in vain; to no purpose, fruitlessly.* **Deus** (6), nom. s. subj. of abscidit. **abscidit,** 3rd s. pf. ind. act. fr. abscindo, -dĕre, -scĭdi, -scissum, 3rd trans., (ab, 254; scindo, 475) *to bear off, away,* or *apart;* fig., *to rend away from one, deprive* one of. *To separate, part, divide.*

110. **Prudens,** -ntis, adj.; nom. mas. s. ag. w. Deus, (provĭdeo, *to see beforehand*) *foreseeing, foreknowing* (rare). *Knowing, skilled, experienced, versed, practised in,* w. gen. *Wise, discreet. Sagacious, sensible, intelligent, clever, judicious* (very com.); here "*in his prudence.*" **Oceano,** abl. (instrumental) s. fr. Ōcĕănus, -i, 2nd mas., *the great sea,* a body of water encompassing the land. *Ocean.* **dissociabili,** abl. (instrum.) s. mas. ag. w. Oceano; fr. dissŏcĭābĭlis, -e, adj., (dissocio, *to separate*) *separating, estranging, dividing.*

111. **Terras,** acc. plu. gov. by abscidit; fr. terra (6). **si,** w. pres. ind. (7, 32). **tamen** (lengthd. fm. of tam, *in so far as*), adversative qualifying conj., *nevertheless, for all that, however, yet, still,* placed where most emphatic to detract from the force of a condition or concession w. or without a corresp. particle, *e.g.,* quamvis, quamquam, etsi, licet, etc. Often jnd. w. other particles, *e.g.,* sed tamen, attamen, verumtamen, etc. **impiæ,** nom. fem. pl. ag. w. rates; fr. impius (906).

112. **Non** (55), w. tangenda. **tangenda,** acc. neut. plu. gerundive (639), ag. w. vada; fr. tango, -ĕre, tĕtĭgi, tactum, 3rd trans., *to touch. To take away, carry off. To taste, eat, drink. To reach, arrive at* a place. Of places, *to border on. To strike, beat. To take hold of, handle. To besprinkle, wash, smear.* Of mind or feelings, *touch, move, affect, impress.* Of speech, *to touch upon, refer to.* **transiliunt,** 3rd plu. pres. ind. act.; fr. transĭlĭo or (-ssil-), -ire, -ŭi or -īvi, -ultum, 4th trans., (trans, 228; salio, 1378) *to leap, jump* or *spring across, leap over, spring over;* intrans., *to go quickly, hasten, make haste, speed, pass rapidly;* fig., *skip over, pass over in silence, omit. To exceed, go beyond, transgress* (483). **rates,** nom. plu. subj. of transiliunt; fr. ratis (17). **vădа,** acc. plu. gov. by transiliunt; fr. vădum, -i, 2nd neut., (vado, *to go*) *shallow, ford, shoal. Body of water, sea, stream. Bottom of a piece of water, depths.*

113. **Audax,** audācis, adj.; nom. fem. s. ag. w. gens; (audeo, 861) in good sense, *bold, courageous, spirited.* In a bad sense (so usu.) *bold, audacious, rash, presumptuous.* **omnia,** acc. plu. neut. gov. by perpeti; fr. omnis

Gens humana ruit per vetitum nefas
Audax Iapeti genus
Ignem fraude mala gentibus intulit.
Post ignem ætheria domo

(43). **perpeti,** pres. inf. (prolative, 570) after audax; fr. perpĕtior, -pĕti, -pessus sum, 3rd dep. trans. and intrans., (per, 114; patior, 18) *to bear completely, thoroughly, steadfastly, firmly. To suffer with patience, endure; "to bear" and "to dare"* (W.).

114. **Gens** (41), nom. s. subj. of ruit. **humana,** nom. fem. s. ag. w. gens; fr. hūmānus, -a, -um, adj., (homo, 123) *of* or *belonging to man, human. Humane, philanthropic, kind, benevolent, polite. Of good education, well informed;* advs., humane and humaniter. **ruit,** 3rd s. pres. ind. act. fr. ruo (61). **per,** prep. gov. acc. Of place, of passage fr. one end to another, *all over, all along, throughout.* Of time, *throughout, during, for.* Of agency, *by means of, through.* Of manner or means, *by.* Of motive or cause, *through, on account of.* In prayers, oaths, etc., *by.* **vĕtĭtum,** acc. neut. s. pf. pass. part. ag. w. nefas; fr. vĕto, -āre, vĕtui, vĕtĭtum, 1st irreg. trans., *to prevent, hinder, forbid, not to allow* a thing to take place. **nefas,** neut. indecl. acc. s. gov. by per; (ne-, 41; fas, 486) *what is contrary to divine law, execrable, abominable;* an *impious, wicked deed, sin;* "fas nefasque," *right and wrong. An abominable person, monster. A horrible, monstrous thing.* In 592, an *impossibility;* "per vetitum nefas," *through sin, despite of prohibitions* (W.).

115. **Audax** (113), neut. ag. w. genus. **Iapeti,** gen. s. after genus; fr. Ĭăpĕtus, -i, 2nd mas., a giant, father of Atlas, Prometheus and Epimetheus. **genus** (45), subj. of intulit; here=filius, *i.e.*, Prometheus.

116. **Ignem,** acc. s. gov. by (direct obj. of) intulit; fr. ignis, -is, 3rd mas., *fire* (in s. and plu.). *Lightning,* etc. *Fire* or *glow* of passion, love, etc. *Brightness, splendour, lustre.* **fraude,** abl. (of manner) s. fr. fraus, fraudis, gen. plu. fraudium (Cic.), fraudum (Tac.), 3rd fem., *deceit, deception, guile, imposition, fraud;* plu. fraudes=*deceptions. A bad action, offence* (679). *A being deceived, delusion, error, mistake.* Legal *injury, detriment, damage;* "fraude mala," *unhappy fraud* (W.). **mala,** abl. s. fem. ag. w. fraude; fr. mălus, -a, -um, adj., (orig., *black, filthy*) *bad* in the widest sense, morally *evil, wicked; bad* of its kind. *Improper, low, injurious, mischievous. Unfortunate, calamitous. Betokening ill, ill-omened, unlucky;* mălum, -i, 2nd neut., *misfortune, punishment, calamity, adversity.* **gentibus,** dat. plu. after (remote obj. of) trajective (873) intulit; fr. gens (41). **intulit,** 3rd s. pf. ind. act. fr. infĕro, -ferre, -tŭli, illatum, irreg. trans. traj., (in, 76; fero, 138) *to carry, bring, put* or *throw into* or *to* a place, esp. *to bring to* a place for burial, *inter.* Milit., signa, arma, etc., inferre in hostem, *to attack;* "inferre bellum," *to wage war against. To bring forward, introduce, produce, cause,* etc.; *e.g.*, spem, injuriam, etc.

117. **Post,** prep. gov. acc. Of place, *behind.* Of time, *after, since;* esp. adv. of place, *behind, back, backwards.* Of time, *afterwards, after.* **ignem** (116), gov. by post. **ætherea,** abl. s. fem. ag. w. domo; fr. æthĕreus, -a, -um, adj., (æther, 1426) *of* or *belonging to the æther, ethereal. Pertaining to heaven, celestial. Belonging to the air, the upper world.* **domo,** abl. (of separation) s. after subductum; fr. dŏmus, 2nd and 4th fem. *A house, home, any building, abode;* gen. domi (Comedy only), elsewhere dŏmus, dat. domo and domui, abl. domo (Comedy only once or twice); plu. nom. domus, gen. domorum and domuum, dat. and abl. domibus, acc. domos, domus (rare).

Subductum macies et nova febrium
Terris incubuit cohors,
Semotique prius tarda necessitas
Leti corripuit gradum.
Expertus vacuum Dædalus aëra

118. **Subductum,** pf. pass. part. acc. mas. s. ag. w. ignem; fr. subduco, -cĕre, -xi, -ctum, 3rd trans., (sub, 21; duco, 133) *to draw from under* or *from below. To draw, pull up, raise up,* esp. a ship out of the water. *To draw away from, remove. To take away stealthily, steal away,* w. pers. pron. me, te, se, etc., *to draw oneself stealthily away;* "post ig. sub.," *after the stealing of fire.* **măcies,** -ei, 5th fem.; nom. s. subj. of incubuit; (măceo, *to be lean,* rare) of living beings, their bodies, etc., *leanness, thinness.* Of inanimate things, *meagreness, poorness;* here the result of the febres. **et** (2). **nŏva,** nom. fem. s. ag. w. cohors; fr. nŏvus (42). **febrium,** gen. plu. after cohors; fr. febris, -is, acc. s. febrem and febrim, abl. genly febri, 3rd fem. (transposed for ferbis, fr. ferveo, 348), *a fever.*

119. **Terris** (37), after incubuit. **incubuit,** 3rd s. (see 98, 555) pf. ind. act.; incumbo, -ĕre, -cŭbŭi, -cŭbĭtum, 3rd traject., *to lay oneself upon, lie, lean, recline upon* a thing; *fall upon, swoop down upon. Apply oneself attentively to, devote oneself to. Incline, be inclined, choose.* **cohors,** -rtis, 3rd fem.; nom. s. subj. of incubuit; (ak. to hortus; Eng. *garden*) *a place enclosed, court, enclosure,* esp. for cattle, *a cattle-yard. A multitude enclosed, fenced in,* hence *company* of soldiers. The tenth part of a Rom. legion. *Train, retinue* of a prætor. *Crowd, multitude, throng* (1414).

120. **Semoti,** gen. neut. s. pf. pass. partc. ag. w. leti; fr. sēmŏveo, -ēre, -mōvi, -mōtum, 2nd trans., (se-, exp. *apart, from;* moveo, 394) *to move apart, put aside, separate* (rare but class.); semotus, -a, -um, *remote, distant, far removed.* **-que** (4). **prius,** compar. adv. w. semoti, (prop. neut. of prior, 1086) *before, sooner. Formerly, heretofore.* **tarda,** nom. fem. s. ag. w. necessitas; fr. tardus, -a, -um, adj. Of motion or action, *slow, sluggish. Slow of apprehension, dull, heavy, stupid.* Of speech, *slow, measured, deliberate.* **nĕcessitas,** -atis, 3rd fem.; nom. s. subj. of corripuit; (necesse, *it is necessary*) *unavoidableness, inevitableness,* esp. *unalterable necessity, destiny. Necessary wants* or *requirements, interests. Unavoidable circumstances. The goddess Necessity* (793). *Want, need, poverty, embarrassment. Connection* betw. persons, natural or moral, *bond, friendship,* etc.; "necessitas leti," *the doom of death* (W.).

121. **Leti,** gen. s. after necessitas; fr. lētum, -i, 2nd neut., *dissolution, death.* **corripuit,** 3rd s. pf. ind. act. fr. corripio, -pĕre, -pui, -reptum, 3rd trans., (cum, 31; rapio, 489) *to seize, draw, pull on all sides* or *entirely. To seize upon violently. To carry off, rob, plunder. To sweep* or *carry away. Reproach, reprove.* **gradum** (105), gov. by corripuit.

122. **Expertus,** pf. partc. nom. mas. s. ag. w. Dædalus; w. est und. 3rd sing. pf. ind. (combinate, 1336); fr. expĕrior, -iri, -rtus sum, 4th depon., (ex, 691; perior, *to try,* obsol.) *to try thoroughly, try, prove, put to the test.* Pf. *to find* or *know by experience. To attempt to do, make trial of* a thing. **vacuum,** acc. mas. s. ag. w. aëra; fr. văcŭus, -a, -um, adj., (văco, *to be empty*) *empty, void, free, clear, without* something; w. abl. or gen. *free,* etc. *from.* Of mind, *disengaged* (158, 183), esp. *at leisure, unoccupied, idle* (729). Of a woman, *unmarried.* Of possessions, *without an occupant* or *master.* Of places, *open, accessible. Valueless, worthless, empty, vain*

Pennis non homini datis;
Perrupit Acheronta Herculeus labor.
Nil mortalibus ardui est;
Cælum ipsum petimus stultitia, neque
Per nostrum patimur scelus

(491)=vanus (post-Aug.). Of places, *resort of idlers*, e.g., Athenæ (Hor.). **Dædalus,** -i, Gk. acc. Dædolon, 2nd mas.; nom. subj. of expertus (est); a famous Athenian architect, father of Icarus, and builder of the Cretan labyrinth. Adj. (1437). **aēra,** acc. s. gov. by expertus (est); fr. āĕr, āĕris, 3rd mas. (Gk.); *the air*, prop. *the lower atmosphere* [æther, *the upper, pure air*]. Poet. *clouds, vapour, mist.* With an epithet, *state of the weather.*

123. **Pennis,** abl. (instrum.) pl. fr. penna, -æ, 1st fem. (ak. *to feather*), *feather* on the body of a winged creature, *a wing. A flying, flight.* **non** (55), w. datis. **homini,** dat. (commodi) s. after datis; fr. hŏmo, hŏmĭnis, 3rd com., (hŭmus, *the ground;* others connect it w. rt. fu=*being*) *a human being; man,* less com. *woman,* sts. *man* as a poor weak being opp. to vir. **datis,** pf. pass. part. abl. pl. fem. ag. w. pennis; fr. do (65).

124. **Perrupit,** 3rd s. pf. ind. act. fr. perrumpo, -ere, -rūpi, -ruptum, 3rd trans. and intrans. (per, 114; rumpo, 28) *to break through, force one's way through. To break down, overcome, e.g.,* leges. **Acheronta,** acc. s. gov. by perrupit; fr. Acheron, -ontis, 3rd mas. (also Gk. Acheros, -i, mas.), a riv. in the infernal regions, sts., *the infernal regions* (Gk., *stream of woe*). **Herculeus,** -a, -um, adj.; nom. mas. s. ag. w. labor; *of* or *belonging to Hercules* (1170). **lăbor,** -ōris, 3rd mas.; nom. s. subj. of perrupit; *labour, toil; exertion,* physical or mental. *Drudgery, hardship, fatigue, pain, peril.*

125. **Nil,** poet. for nihil (ne, *not;* hilum=filum, *not a thread,* i.e., *nothing*); subst., *nothing;* adv., *in no respect, not at all* (378); here subj. of est. **mortalibus,** dat. mas. plu. (acquisitive) after est; fr. mortālis, -e, adj. (mors, 105), *subject to death, liable to die;* as subst. mortālis, -is, 3rd mas., *a human being,* plu., *mankind. Perishable, transient. Human, earthly.* Of things, *done by men,* etc. **ardui,** gen. neut. s. (of thing measured) fr. arduus, -a, -um, adj., *steep;* arduum, -i, 2nd neut., *a steep place, height, summit* (1413); poet., *high, elevated, lofty;* fig., *difficult to reach, arduous, hard;* neut. as substantive (here). *Troublesome, unpleasant.* Of fortune, *inauspicious, difficult, e.g.,* res (251). **est** (19).

126. **Cælum** (81), gov. by petimus. **ipsum,** acc. neut. s. ag. w. cælum; fr. ipse, ipsa, ipsum; gen. ipsīus, dat. ipsi; plu. regular, a definitive pronominal adj.=*self, very, identical,* w. substs., esp. w. pron. subst., *e.g.,* ego, tu, etc., esp. sui reflexive. By itself used as a pron. of all three persons, but in oblique cases of 3rd pers. only, *one's own self, its own self. Himself, herself, itself.* It genly. implies a contrast with something else; sts.=*of himself, herself,* etc., *i.e.,* of his, her, etc., own accord. Used w. words of time, number, etc., to precisely define, *very, exactly, precisely, e.g.,* decem ipsos dies. **petimus,** 1st plu. pres. ind. act. fr. pĕto, -ĕre, pĕtīvi or pĕtĭi, pĕtītum, 3rd trans., *to attack, assault, assail. Aim at, thrust at. Direct one's course towards, go to, make for. To take hold of. To seek, demand, require. To beg, beseech. To strive after. To fetch.* **stultitia,** abl. (of manner) s. fr. stultĭtia, -æ, 1st. fem., (stultus, *foolish*) *folly, silliness, fatuity.* **nĕque** (19).

127. **Per** (114). **nostrum,** acc. neut. s. ag. w. scelus; fr. noster (83). **patimur,** 1st. plu. pres. ind. fr. patior (18). **scelus** (65), gov. by per.

Iracunda Jovem ponere fulmina.

CARMEN IV.—AD L. SESTIUM.

Solvitur acris hiems grata vice veris et Favoni,
Trahuntque siccas machinæ carinas.

128. **Iracunda,** acc. neut. plu. ag. w. fulmina; fr. īrācundus, -a, -um, adj. (ira, 429), of living beings, the mind, etc., *prone to anger, irritable, quick tempered.* Of things, *violent, furious, raging;* "ir. ful.," *bolts of his wrath;* epith. prop. of Jove himself (W.). **Jovem,** acc. s. subj. of ponere; fr. Jupiter (25). **ponere** (104), after patimur. **fulmina,** acc. plu. gov. by ponere; fr. fulmen, -ĭnis, 3rd neut., (fulgeo, 203) *lightning* that strikes or sets on fire, *lightning flash, thunderbolt* [fulgur, *the flash*]; metaph. of a crushing calamity, etc.

Carmen IV. Metre—*Archilochium Quartum.*

The first line, Archilochus Major	– ⏑ ⏑ or – –	– ⏑ ⏑ or – –	– ⏑ ⏑ or – –	– ⏑ ⏑ ‖	– ⏑	– ⏑	– ⏑ or – –
The second line, Iambic Trimeter Catalectic	⏑ – or – –	⏑ –	⏑ – or – –	⏑ –	⏑ –	⏑ or –	

129. **Solvitur,** 3rd s. pres. ind. pass. fr. solvŏ, -ĕre, -vi, sŏlūtum, 3rd trans., *to loose, loosen, untie, unbind. To relax. To destroy, break down. To solve, explain, unfold. To banish, disperse, dispel. To free, release, deliver. To pay* satisfaction, *discharge. To make powerless.* **acris,** nom. fem. s. ag. w. hiems; fr. acer (75). **hiems,** hiĕmis, 3rd fem., nom. s. subj. of solvitur; *the winter. Rainy, stormy weather. Storm, tempest,* fig. *tempest, violence.* **grata,** abl. fem. s. ag. w. vice; fr. grātus, -a, -um, adj., *enjoying favour, regarded, beloved. Entertaining favourable feelings, thankful, grateful. Beloved, dear, acceptable, pleasing. Thankworthy, deserving* or *procuring thanks.* In class. prose gratiosus, used of persons. **vice,** abl. s. of cause; fr. gen. vĭcis, no nom., acc. vĭcem. Plu. nom. acc. vĭces, dat. and abl. vĭcĭbus; 3rd fem., *change, interchange, alternation; alternate* or *reciprocal succession, vicissitude* (vicissitudo in class. prose); "invicem," *in turns; mutually. Reciprocal service, requital,* i.e., *remuneration* or *retaliation. Changes of fate, lot, fortune, misfortune* (680). *Position, place, duty, office, stead* of a person or thing, assumed by another, *e.g.,* cotis. **veris,** gen. s. after vice; fr. ver, veris, 2nd neut., *the spring.* **et** (2). **Favoni**=Favonii, gen. s. jnd. by et to veris; fr. Făvōnĭus, 2nd mas. (faveo, *to favour*)=Zephyrus; a spring wind which promoted vegetation.

130. **Trahunt,** 3rd plu. pres. ind. act. fr. trăho, -hĕre, -xi, -ctum, 3rd trans., *to draw, drag, drag along; trail. To contract, wrinkle, e.g.,* vultum. Of drink, *quaff. To lead in one's train, conduct slowly. To carry off, plunder. To spin, manufacture. To attract, allure. To ponder, deliberate.* Of time, *prolong, protract, spin out.* **-que** (4). **siccas,** acc. plu. fem. ag. w. carinas; fr. siccus (106). **machinæ,** nom. fem. plu. subj. of trahunt; fr. māchĭna, -æ, 1st fem. In good sense, *means, expedient, device, contrivance;* bad sense, *trick, artifice. A machine, engine,* for any purpose; here "*rollers.*" **carinas,** acc. plu. gov. by trahunt; fr. cărīna, -æ, 1st fem., *the bottom* of a ship, *keel.* By synecdoche, *ship, boat, vessel* (371, 784).

131 Ac neque jam stabulis gaudet pecus aut arator igni;
132 Nec prata canis albicant pruinis.
133 Jam Cytherea choros ducit Venus imminente Luna,
134 Junctæque Nymphis Gratiæ decentes
135 Alterno terram quatiunt pede, dum graves Cyclopum

131. **Ac** (37). **neque** (32). **jam** (37). **stabulis,** abl. (of cause) plu. fr. stăbŭlum, -i, 2nd neut., (sto, 233) orig. *standing place. Stall, stable, enclosure* for animals. **gaudet,** 3rd s. pres. ind. act. fr. gaudeo (11). **pecus** (43), nom. subj of gaudet. **aut,** coordinate disjunct. conj. *or; aut...aut, either...or;* vel or neque in the place of one aut is poetic. **ărātor,** -ōris, 3rd mas., nom. s. subj. of gaudet und. fr. prec. clause; (aro, *to plough*) *a ploughman. Husbandman, farmer*=agricola. **igni,** abl. (of cause) s. fr. ignis (116).

'132. **Nec** (32). **prata,** nom. plu. subj. of albicant; fr. prātum, -i, 2nd neut., *meadow,* rare *meadow-grass.* **canis,** abl. plu. fem. ag. w. pruinis; fr. cānus, -a, -um, adj., *gray, ash-coloured, hoary,* esp. of *gray* hair; here *white.* **albicant,** 3rd plu. pres. ind. act. fr. albĭco, -are, no pf., no sup., 1st intrans., (albus, 311) *to be white.* **pruinis,** abl. (of cause) plu. fr. prŭīna, -æ, 1st fem., (Gk., *what belongs to early morning*) *hoar-frost, rime. Snow.*

133. **Jam** (37). **Cytherea,** nom. fem. s. ag. w. Venus; fr. Cȳthĕrēus, -a, -um, adj., *of Cythera* (Cythera, -orum, 2nd neut.), an island (now Cerigo) celebrated for the worship of Venus. **choros,** acc. plu. gov. by ducit; fr. chorus (31). **ducit,** 3rd s. pres. ind. act. fr. dūco, -cĕre, -xi, -ctum, 3rd trans., *to lead, conduct, draw, bring forward. To cause to move. To produce, form, frame, fashion, shape. To derive* origin, etc. *To incite, induce. To protract, delay. To hold as* being, *deem, consider.* **Venus,** -ĕris, 3rd fem., nom. s. subj. of ducit; the goddess of love, here the companion of spring. **imminente,** abl. fem. s. pres. part. act. ag. w. Lunâ; fr. immĭneo, -ēre, no pf., no sup., (in, 76; mineo, *to jut, project*) *to project over* or *towards, bend* or *lean towards. To hang down over, overhang. To threaten* from nearness. *To strive eagerly after, be eager for.* **Luna,** abl. absol. (824) fr. Lūna, -æ, 1st fem., (luceo, *to shine*) *the moon. A month;* "imminente lunâ" =*by moonlight.*

134. **Junctæ,** pf. pass. part. nom. fem. plu. ag. w. Gratiæ; fr. jungo, -ngĕre, -nxi, -nctum, 3rd trans., *to join, unite, bind, fasten together. To yoke, connect, harness. To match.* **-que** (4). **Nymphis,** dat. plu. after traject. (873) junctæ; fr. Nympha (31). **Gratiæ,** -arum, 1st. fem. plu., nom. subj. of quatiunt; *the Graces:* Aglaia, Euphrosyne, Thalia, dau. of Jupiter and Eurynome (706). **decentes,** nom. plu. fem. ag. w. Gratiæ; fr. dĕcens, -ntis, adj., *seemly, becoming; proper, fit. Well shaped, well formed, noble* of corporeal fitness (482); prop. partc. of impers. vb. dĕcet, -cēre, -cuit, *it is, was fitting, suitable, proper.*

135. **Alterno,** abl. s. mas. ag. w. pede; fr. alternus, -a, -um, adj., (alter, 413) *one after another, by turns, alternate, reciprocal, interchangeable;* no comp. or sup. **terram,** acc. s. gov. by quatiunt; fr. terra (6). **quatiunt,** 3rd plu. pres. ind. act. fr. quatio (18). **pede,** abl. (instrumental) s. fr. pes, pĕdis, 3rd mas., *foot* of man or beast. Of birds, *claws, talons. Foot* of a table, mountain, etc. A rope attached to a sail for the purpose of setting it to the wind, *a sheet;* "alt. pede," *i.e.,* each falling in its due turn and time (W.). **dum** (53). **graves,** acc. fem. plu. ag. w. officinas; fr. gravis (41), *with ponderous forges* (W.). **Cyclopum,** gen. plu. after officinas; fr. Cyclops, -ōpis, (Gk., *the round eye*) *a Cyclops;* plu., Cyclōpes, -ōpum, a race of giants in Sicily, workmen of Vulcan.

Vulcanus ardens urit officinas.
Nunc decet aut viridi nitidum caput impedire myrto
Aut flore, terræ quem ferunt solutæ.
Nunc et in umbrosis Fauno decet immolare lucis,
Seu poscat agna sive malit hædo.

136. **Vulcanus,** -i, 2nd mas., nom. subj. of urit; the fire god, son of Jupiter and Juno. **ardens,** pres. part. act. nom. mas. s. ag. w. Vulcanus; fr. ardeo (975), here "*glowing in the blaze.*" **urit,** 3rd s. pres. ind. act. fr. ūro, ūrĕre, ussi, ustum, 3rd trans.; *to burn up, destroy by fire, scorch, parch, dry up. To cause a hot, burning pain, sting, pain acutely. To rub sore, gall, fret, chafe,* lit. and fig. *To pinch* w. cold. *To burn, consume* w. passion; here, "*makes fiery hot*" (W.). **officinas,** acc. plu. gov. by urit; fr. offĭcīna, -æ, 1st fem. (for opificina; fr. opifex, *a workman*). *A workshop, manufactory, laboratory.*

137. **Nunc** (21). **decet,** 3rd s. pres. ind. act. impers. (134). **aut** (131). **viridi** (21), fem. ag. w. myrto. **nitidum,** acc. neut. s. ag. w. caput; fr. nĭtĭdus (1183). **caput** (22), gov. by impedire. **impĕdire,** pres. inf. act. subj. of decet; fr. impĕdĭo, -īvi or -ii, -ītum, 4th trans., (in, 76; pes, 135, *to entangle the foot) to ensnare, shackle, hamper;* fig., *to embarrass.* Meton., *to clasp, encircle, embrace. To hinder, obstruct, impede, check.* **myrto,** abl. (instrum.) s. fr. myrtus, -i and -us, 2nd and 4th fem. and mas., collat. myrta, -æ, 1st fem., *a myrtle tree; a myrtle branch* or *wreath.*

138. **Aut** (131). **flore,** abl. s. jnd. by aut (131) to myrto; fr. flos, flōris, 3rd mas., *a blossom, flower* (1149); fig., *flower, crown, ornament* of anything. *Prime* of life. *The best part* or *kind* of a thing, *flower, bouquet.* **terræ,** nom. plu. subj. of ferunt; fr. terra (6). **quem** (74), mas. s. ag. w. flore, acc. gov. by ferunt. **ferunt** 3rd plu. pres. ind. act. fr. fĕro, ferre, tŭli, lātum, irreg. trans., *to bear, carry, bring; put in motion. To display to view, report, relate;* ferunt, *they say;* fertur, *it is said. To yield, produce* of earth, etc. **solutæ,** nom. fem. plu. pf. pass. part. ag. w. terræ; fr. solvo (129).

139. **Nunc** (21). **et** (2), *also.* **in** (78). **umbrosis,** abl. plu. mas. ag. w. lucis; fr. umbrōsus, -a, -um, adj., (umbra, 205) *full of shade, shady.* **Fauno,** dat. (commodi) s. after immolare; fr. Faunus, -i, 2nd mas., (faveo, *to favour*). Mythical son of Picus, grandson of Saturn, father of Latinus, king of Latium, tutelar deity of agriculture, shepherds, etc.; afterwds. identified w. Pan. **decet** (137). **immolare,** pres. inf. act. subj. of decet; fr. immŏlo, -āre, -avi, -atum, 1st trans., (in, 76; mola, *grains of spelt mixed with salt*). *To sprinkle a victim with mola salsa. To bring as an offering, offer, sacrifice.* Poet. still more general, *sacrifice, slay.* **lucis,** abl. plu. gov. by in; fr. lūcus, -i, 2nd mas., *an open wood, i.e.,* in which the trees are not crowded together; *a wooded parklike glade,* sacred to a deity; *a wood* in general.

140. **Seu** (27). **poscat,** 3rd s. pres. subj. (see 357) act. fr. posco, -scĕre, pŏposci, no sup., 3rd trans., *to ask for earnestly, beg, demand, request, desire* (implies demanding a thing in return for merit) w. two accs. (584). Pass. w. acc. of thing, *to be asked for* something; something *is demanded from* some one. In 729, *to be asked to sing.* Of things, *to require, need.* **agna,** abl. (instrumental) s. w. immolare und. after poscat; fr. agna, -æ, 1st fem., (agnus, -i, mas.) *a ewe lamb.* **sive** (6). **malit,** 3rd s. pres. subj. fr. malo (69). Subj. follows sive as it would the simple si. **hædo,** abl. (instrumental as agnâ) s. fr. hædus, -i, 2nd mas., *a young goat, kid.*

Pallida Mors æquo pulsat pede pauperum tabernas
Regumque turres. O beate Sesti,
Vitæ summa brevis spem nos vetat inchoare longam.
Jam te premet nox fabulæque Manes

141. **Pallida,** nom. fem. s. ag. w. mors; fr. pallĭdus, -a, -um, adj., (palleo, *to be pale) pale, pallid. Making pale, giving a pale appearance* **Mors** (105), nom. s. subj. of pulsat. **æquo,** abl. s., mas. ag. w. pede; fr. æquus -a, -um, adj. *that extends horizontally, plain, even, level, flat;* æquum, -i, 2d neut., *a level, plain. On a level with* something else. Of time and place, *favourable, advantageous.* Of persons and things, *kind, friendly. Equal* to another in any point. *Half* of things equally divided. *Fair, equitable* in conduct. Of things, *reasonable, fair.* Of the mind, *equal to* or *like itself, calm, composed, tranquil, unruffled* (941). **pulsat,** 3rd s. pres. ind. act. fr. pulso, -are, -avi, -atum, 1st trans. and intrans., intens. of pello (215), *to push, strike, beat* (838). *To strike against, touch, e.g.,* sidera; fig., *to set in motion, agitate, e.g.,* animos; here of *knocking* at the door **pede** (135), instrumental. **pauperum,** gen. plu. after tabernas; fr. pauper, -ĕris, adj., (fem. -ra, neut. -rum, rare) ak. to paucus (1145), *poor, that has only enough for moderate expenses;* as subs. (und. homo), *a poor person.* Of things, *scanty, small, meagre.* **tabernas,** acc. plu. gov. by pulsat; fr. tăberna, -æ, 1st fem., (orig., *hut made of boards) shed, booth, shop* (rare). *Workshop, stall, inn, tavern.*

142. **Regum,** gen. plu. after turres; fr. rex (1). **turres,** acc. plu. jnd. by -que to tabernas; fr. turris, -is, acc. s. -im, less com. -em, abl. -i or -e; 3rd fem., *a tower* (1127). *High building, castle, palace, citadel.* **O** (2). **beate,** voc. mas. s. ag. w. Sesti; fr. beatus, -a, -um, adj., (part. pass. of beo=*to make happy, make blest) happy, prosperous, fortunate. Opulent, wealthy.* Of inanimate things, *rich, abundant, excellent, magnificent.* **Sesti,** voc. s. fr. Sestius, -ii, 2nd mas., name of a Roman gens.

143. **Vitæ,** gen. s. after summa; fr. vīta, -æ, 1st fem., (vivo, 731) *life, way, mode of life. The living,* i.e., *mankind, the world.* **summa,** -æ, 1st fem., nom. s. subj. of vĕtat, (prop. fem. of summus; und. res, *that which is highest, most prominent* in anything) *the main thing, chief point, principal matter. Completion, perfection.* Of numbers, *amount, sum, sum total. The whole* opp. to a part. **brevis,** -e, adj., nom. fem. s. ag. w. summa; *short, little, of small extent,* of space or time. *Narrow* opp. to latus. Of height, *small.* Of length opp. to longus. *Shallow* opp. to profundus. *Concise* of things done or taking place in a short time. **spem,** acc. s. gov. by inchoare; fr. spes, spĕi, 5th fem., (spero, 159) *anticipation* of something desired, *i.e., hope;* rare of something not desired, *i.e., presentiment. That which is hoped for, in which hope is placed;* plu. sperum, spebus, post-class. **nos,** acc. plu. subj. of inchoare; fr. ego (29). **vetat,** 3rd s. ind. pres act. fr. veto (114). **inchoare,** pres. inf. act. after vetat; fr. inchŏo, -āre, -āvi, -atum, 1st trans., *to lay the foundation* of a thing, *begin, commence,* opp. to finishing; pf. pass. inchoatus, *incomplete, imperfect.* **longam,** acc. fem. s. ag. w. spem; fr. longus (73).

144. **Jam** (37). **te** (83), gov. by premet. **premet,** 3rd s. (see 98) fut. ind. act. fr. prĕmo, -ĕre, pressi, pressum, 3rd act., *to squeeze, rest heavily on. To press firmly* or *closely, press together, close. To cover, to press hard. to pursue closely.* **nox,** noctis, 3rd fem., nom. s. subj. of premet; *night,* Of nocturnal *noise, revelling. Dream, sleep. Death;* fig., *darkness, obscurity, blindness, gloom.* **fabulæ,** nom. plu. in app. to Manes; fr. fābŭla,

145 Et domus exilis Plutonia; quo simul mearis,
146 Nec regna vini sortiere talis,
147 Nec tenerum Lycidan mirabere, quo calet juventus
148 Nunc omnis et mox virgines tepebunt.

-æ, 1st fem., (fari, *to speak, say*) *narration, narrative, account, story*, esp. *a fiction, myth;* here "*the source of story.*" *Drama, play.* **Manes,** -ium, 3rd plu. mas.; nom. jnd. by et to nox, (rt. in immanis, 630; orig. *the worshipped, benevolent ones*) *deified souls of the departed, ghosts. Gods of the lower world*, so genly. w. Di (benevolent opp. to larvæ and lemures). *Shades, spirits* of the dead. *The lower world* (here).

145. **Domus** (117), nom. s. jnd. by et to Manes. **exīlis,** -e, adj., nom. fem. s. ag. w. domus, (contr. for exigilis; fr. exigo, 1223) *small, thin, slender, lank, meagre, unsubstantial* (here); some take it here as=*poor.* **Plutonia,** nom. fem. s. ag. w. domus; fr. Plūtōnius, -a, -um, adj., (Pluto, 1239) *of* or *belonging to Pluto*, the king of the lower world. **quo,** adv. orig. abl. of qui (3). i. Relative, of place, (*a*) *where*, rare; (*b*) *to which place, whither.* Of persons, *to whom;* (*c*) *in order that; so that, that;* quo ne= ut ne; (*d*) *for the reason that, because.* ii. Interrog., *to what end? wherefore? why?* iii. Indef., *to any place, anywhere,* after si (rare). **sĭmul,** (ak. to similis, 302) adv. *together, at once, at the same time, in company;* sts. w. et, -que, atque; simul...simul, *as well...as, both...and, partly...and partly;* simul atque (ac), simul ut, and sts. simul alone (so here) =*as soon as.* **mearis**=meāveris, syncop. fut. pf. (3rd fut.) 2nd s. fr. meo, -āre, -āvi, -atum, 1st intrans., *to go, pass;* rare of inanimate things. When temporal conjunctions have fut. pf. in the subordinate clause, and fut. simple in the principal clause, it is implied that the event or action expressed in the subordinate clause, is to precede that in the princ. clause.

146. **Nec** (19). **regna,** acc. plu. gov. by sortiere; fr. regnum, -i, 2nd neut., (rego, 91) *dominion, sovereignty, rule, authority, despotism. Kingly government. Territory over which one rules; a kingdom.* **vini,** gen. s. after regna; fr. vīnum, -i, 2nd neut., *wine* (282, 953). **sortiere,** 2nd s. fut. ind. fr. sortior, -īri, -ītus sum, 4th depon. intrans., (sors, 967) *to cast* or *draw lots;* trans. *to cast, draw lots for, fix, assign, appoint by lot.* Impf. tenses, *obtain, receive by lot*, e.g., provincias. *To share, divide, distribute* an action or labour, also *choose, select.* **talis,** abl. (instrumental) plu. fr. tālus, -i, 2nd mas., *the ankle, ankle-bone.* Of animals, *knuckle-bone. The heel* (Hor.). *A die*, orig. made of knuckle-bones rounded on two sides, marked only on the other four [tessaræ, cubes, marked on all six sides; four tali, three tesseræ, were used in playing].

147. **Tenerum,** acc. mas. s. ag. w. Lycidan; fr. tener (26). **Lycidan,** acc. s. gov. by mirabere; fr. Lўcĭdas, -æ (Gk.), 1st mas. **mirabere,** 2nd s. fut. ind. fr. mīror, -āri, -atus sum, 1st depon., (ak. to *smile*) *to admire, wonder, marvel, be astonished at.* **quo** (103), mas. s. ag. w. Lycidan, abl. (of cause) w. calet. **calet,** 3rd s. pres. ind. act. fr. căleo, -ēre, -ui, no sup., 2nd intrans., *to be warm* or *hot, glow. To glow in mind, be roused, warmed, inflamed. To be warmed, urged on* by zeal, etc. **juventus** (60), subj. of calet.

148. **Nunc** (21). **omnis** (43), nom. fem. s. ag. w. juventus. **et** (3). **mox** (17). **virgines** (63), subj. of tepebunt. **tepebunt,** 3rd plu. fut. ind. act. fr. tĕpeo, -ēre, no pf., no sup., 2nd intrans., *to be lukewarm, moderately warm, tepid* (rare). *To glow with love, be enamoured. To be cool, indifferent, without ardour* in love.

CARMEN V.—AD PYRRHAM.

149 Quis multa gracilis te puer in rosa
150 Perfusus liquidis urget odoribus,
151 Grato, Pyrrha, sub antro?
152 Cui flavam religas comam,
153 Simplex munditiis? Heu quoties fidem

Carmen V. Metre—*Fourth Asclepiad, which consists of four-line stanzas.*
Two of the lesser Asclepiad, as in Carm. I.
Third, the Pherecratic – ⏓ | – ⏑ ⏑ | – ⏓
Fourth, the Glyconic – – | – ⏑ ⏑ | – ⏑ ⏓

149. **Quis**, quæ, quid, nom. mas. s. ag. w. puer; interrog. pron. adj. and subst. (*a*) Direct, *what*, i.e., *what sort of?* subst., *who? which? what?* Quid (i.) w. gen. *what*, i.e., *what sort of?* (ii.) adv., *how? why? wherefore?* (*b*) Indirect, *who? what person?* **multa**, abl. fem. s. ag. w. rosa; fr. multus (23). **grăcĭlis**, -e, adj., nom. mas. s. ag. w. puer; *thin, small* in good or bad sense. *Slender, slim. Meagre, lean.* **te** (83), gov. by urget. **puer**, puĕri, 2nd com., nom. s. subj. of urget; *a child, boy* strictly till 17th year, afterwards of those much older. *Young girl. A son. Grown up youth, young man. Boy* for attendance, *servant, slave.* **in** (78). **rosa**, abl. s., gov. by in; fr. rŏsa, -æ, 1st fem., *a rose* (871), latest of spring flowers (831, 1154), here collect. "*a wreath*" or "*bed of roses.*"

150. **Perfusus**, nom. mas. s. pf. pass. part. ag. w. puer; fr. perfundo, -ere, -fūdi, -fūsum, 3rd trans., (per, 114; fundo, 711) *to wet, moisten, bedew, besprinkle thoroughly*, esp. *to wash, bathe* something. Pass., *to bathe, wash, sprinkle oneself*, etc.; fig., *to imbue, inspire with* anything. *To wet, moisten. To bestrew.* **liquidis**, abl. mas. plu. ag. w. odoribus; fr. lĭquĭdus, -a, -um, adj., (liqueo, 282) *flowing, fluid, liquid.* Of speech, *flowing, continuing uninterruptedly. Clear, calm, serene. Unmixed, unadulterated.* Of the voice, *clear* (575). **urget**, 3rd s. pres. ind. act. fr. urgeo (-gueo), -ēre, ursi, no sup., 2nd trans., *to press, push, drive, force, impel. Press upon, bear hard upon, beset closely. Weigh down, burden, oppress. Urge, solicit, ply* with argument. **odoribus**, abl. (instrumental) plu. w. perfusus; fr. ŏdor, -ōris, 3rd mas., *smell, scent, odour;* disagreeable *stench* or agreeable *scent. Inkling, presentiment;* concr. genly. in plu., *perfumes, perfumery.*

151. **Grato**, abl. neut. s. ag. w. antro; fr. gratus (129). **Pyrrha**, voc. s. fr. Pyrrha, -æ, 1st fem. **sub** (21). **antro** (915), gov. by sub.

152. **Cui** (65), dat. (commodi) after religas; *for whose sake.* **flavam**, acc. fem. s. ag. w. comam; fr. flavus (49). **religas**, 2nd s. pres. ind. act. fr. rĕlĭgo, -are, -avi, -atum, 1st trans., (re, 659; lĭgo, *to bind*) *to bind, fasten up, bind fast* (1164), esp. a ship to the shore. *To unbind* (poet. and post-Aug.). **comam**, acc. gov. by religas; fr. cŏma, -æ, 1st fem., *hair* of head, *mane* of animals; *leaves* of trees; *ears* of corn.

153. **Simplex**, -ĭcis, abl. -ici, sts. -ice, adj.; nom. fem. s. ag. w. tu und. in religas, (semel, 588; plico, *to fold*) *simple, plain, uncompounded, unmixed* (873), esp. morally *without dissimulation, open, guileless, sincere.* **munditiis**, abl. (of manner) plu. fr. mundĭtĭa, -æ, 1st fem., collat. mundities,

154 Mutatosque Deos flebit et aspera
155 Nigris æquora ventis
156 Emirabitur insolens,
157 Qui nunc te fruitur credulus aurea;
158 Qui semper vacuam, semper amabilem
159 Sperat nescius auræ

-ei, 5th fem., (condition of the mundus) *elegance, fineness. Neatness, niceness*, i.e., *scrupulous care* in dress. *Cleanliness, cleanness.* **Heu** (73). **quŏtĭes** (-ens), adv. *How often, how many times*, in exclamation or interrogation. *As often as.* **fĭdem,** acc. s. gov. by flebit; fr. fĭdes, -ei, 5th fem., *trust, faith, confidence* in a person or thing. *Trustworthiness, faithfulness, i.e.*, that which produces confidence. Of inanimate and abstract things, *credulity, truth, authority. A promise, engagement, word. A given promise of security* or *protection, guardian care;* und. mutatam fr. follg. line.

154. **Mutatos,** acc. mas. plu. ag. w. Deos; fr. mutatus (77). **Deos** (6), jnd. by -que to fidem, *i.e.*, the gods by whom she swore. **flebit,** 3rd s. fut. ind. act. fr. fleo, flēre, flēvi, flētum, 2nd (ak. to fluo and ploro) intrans. *to weep, cry;* trans. *to weep for, bewail, lament* a person or thing (602, 1109). *To sing* anything *mournfully.* **aspera,** acc. plu. neut. ag. w. æquora; fr. asper, -pĕra, -pĕrum, adj., *rough, uneven. Harsh, sour, bitter.* Of moral qualities, *unkind, cruel, fierce. Warlike.* Of things, *calamitous, cruel, troublesome;* here "*roughened.*"

155. **Nigris,** abl. plu. mas. ag. w. ventis; fr. nĭger, -gra, -grum, adj., *black, sable, dark, dusky.* **æquora,** acc. plu. gov. by emirabitur; fr. æquor (48). **ventis,** abl. (instrumental) plu. fr. ventus (91).

156. **Emirabitur,** 3rd s. fut. ind. fr. ēmīror, -ari, pf. not found, (ex, 691; miror, 147) *to wonder greatly at.* **insolens,** -ntis, adj.; nom. mas. s. ag. w. subj. of emirabitur, (in neg., soleo, 184) of persons, *contrary to custom, unaccustomed, not habituated, unused to.* Of things, *unusual* (rare). *Excessive, immoderate, too great* (943). *Haughty, arrogant, insolent.* Of things, *extravagant, lavish, profuse.*

157. **Qui** (19), mas. s. ag. w. subj. of emirabĭtur, nom. to sperat. **nunc** (21). **te** (88), after fruitur. **fruitur,** 3rd s. pres. ind. fr. fruor, frŭi, fruĭtus and fructus sum, 3rd depon., *to derive enjoyment from* a thing, *delight in, enjoy,* w. abl.; gerundive fruendus, used in class. prose; more restricted than utor. **crēdŭlus,** -a, -um, adj., nom. mas. s. ag. w. qui; (credo, 93) *that quickly* or *readily believes* a thing, *confiding;* w. dat. (284). Pass. *easily believed* (very rare). **aurea,** abl. s. fem. predic. ag. w. te; fr. aureus, -a, -um, adj., (aurum, 714) *of gold, golden. Beautiful, magnificent. Attractive, excellent. Gleaming like gold. Interwoven* or *ornamented with gold.*

158. **Qui** (157), nom. subj. of sperat. **sĕmper,** temp. adv., *ever, always, at all times, for ever.* **vacuam,** acc. fem. s. predic. ag. w. te und. (as subj. of futuram esse und. after sperat); fr. vacuus (122). **amabilem,** acc. fem. s. (constr. as vacuam) fr. ămābilis, -e, adj., (amo, 86) *deserving love, worthy of love, lovely.*

159. **Sperat,** 3rd s. pres. ind. act.; fr. spēro, -āre, -āvi, -atum, 1st trans., *to hope* (something desirable), *trust, expect, promise* or *flatter oneself;* w. inf. fut. less com. pres. and pf.; rarely of what is not desirable **nescius,** -a, -um, adj.; nom. mas. s. ag. w. qui, (nescio, 981) *unknowing, ignorant, unaware. Not knowing how, unable to* w. inf.; w. inf. pass. *not known,*

Fallacis. Miseri quibus
Intentata nites! Me tabula sacer
Votiva paries indicat uvida
Suspendisse potenti
Vestimenta maris Deo.

CARMEN VI.—AD AGRIPPAM.

SCRIBERIS Vario fortis et hostium

unknown (rare). **auræ,** gen. (objective, 749) s. after nescius; fr. aura (84); here metaph. of what is *fickle*, etc.

160. **Fallacis,** gen. s. fem. ag. w. auræ; fr. fallax, -ācis, adj., (fallo, 272) *deceitful, deceptive.* **Miseri,** nom. plu. mas. predic. ag. w. ii und. in sunt und.; fr. mĭser, mĭsera, mĭserum, (mæreo, 984) of persons, *wretched, unfortunate, miserable,* esp. *sick, ill, in pain.* Of things, *afflicting, sad, wretched. Excessive, extravagant,* e.g., amor. *Vile, worthless, poor.* **quibus,** mas. plu. ag. w. miseri, dat. (incommodi) after nites; fr. qui (3).

161. **Intentata,** nom. fem. s. ag. w. tu und. in nites; fr. intentatus, -a, -um, adj., (in, neg.; tento, 279) *untouched,* fig. *untried, unattempted.* **nites,** 2nd. s. ind. pres. act. fr. nĭteo, -ĕre, -ŭi, no sup., 2nd intrans. *to shine, look bright, glitter, glisten. To be sleek, glossy, look well, appear healthy, flourish, be brilliant* or *beautiful.* **me** (29), subj. of suspendisse. **tabula,** abl. (instrumental) s. fr. tăbŭla, -æ, 1st fem., *board, plank, writing, tablet. Letter, e.g.,* contract, account, list. *Will. Painted tablet, painting.* **sacer** (22), nom. mas. s. ag. w. paries.

162. **Votiva,** abl. fem. s. ag. w. tabula; fr. vōtīvus, -a, -um, adj., (vōtum, 1074) *pronounced by a vow, given according to a vow. Conformable to one's wish, longed for, desired.* **părĭes,** -ĕtis, 3rd mas., *wall* of a house, etc., dist. fr. that of a city. **indĭcat,** 3rd sing. pres. ind. act. fr. indĭco, -are, -avi, -atum, 1st trans., (in, 76; dĭco, *to dedicate*) *to make known, point out, show, declare. To intimate, briefly state* (not class.). *To give evidence against, inform against,* esp. in. a court, w. acc. *To put a price on* a thing. **uvida,** acc. neut. plu. ag. w. vestimenta; fr. ūvĭdus, -a, -um, adj., (uveo, *to be moist*) *moist, wet, damp, humid; fig. having freely drank* (1410).

163. **Suspendisse,** pf. inf. act. after indicat; fr. suspendo, -dĕre, -di, -sum, 3rd trans., (sub, 21; pendo, *to hang*) *to hang* one thing *beneath* another, *hang up. To choke by hanging, hang.* Of offerings, *dedicate. To make uncertain; doubtful. To stop, check, arrest.* **potenti,** dat. s. mas. ag. w. Deo; fr. potens (89).

164. **Vestimenta,** acc. plu. gov. by (direct obj. of) suspendisse; fr. vestīmentum, -ī, 2nd neut., (vestis, 476) *clothing, garment, vestment.* **maris,** gen. (objective) s. after potenti; fr. mare (14). **Deo,** *i.e.*, Neptune, dat. (commodi) s. after suspendisse; fr. deus (6).

CARMEN VI. METRE—*Third Asclepiad, consists of four-line stanzas.*

Three Lesser Asclepiad, as Carm. I.
Fourth, the Glyconic, as fourth line in Carm. V.

165. **Scrībĕris,** 2nd s. fut. ind. pass. fr. scrībo, -bĕre, -psi, -ptum, 3rd trans., orig. *to scratch, grave, engrave* w. a sharp point. *To write, draw,* etc. *To write down, compose, depict, draw up, communicate in writing, e.g.*,

Victor Mæonii carminis alite,
Quam rem cunque ferox navibus aut equis
    Miles te duce gesserit.
Nos, Agrippa, neque hæc dicere, nec gravem
Pelidæ stomachum cedere nescii,

carmina, etc. (178). The permissive fut. *I shall leave V. to write* (cf. 185, 518). **Vario,** abl. absol. (824) fr. Vărĭus, -ii, 2nd mas.; *L. Varius Rufus.* **fortis,** e, adj., nom. mas. s. predic. after scriberis, (fero, 138) *bearing* or *enduring much, strong, powerful, manly, brave. Firm, courageous.* **hostium,** gen. (objective) plu. after victor; fr. hostis (76).

166. **Victor,** -ōris, 3rd mas., nom. s. jnd. by et to fortis, *conqueror, vanquisher.* Adj., *conquering, vanquishing.* **Mæŏnii,** gen. neut. s. ag. w. carminis; fr. Mæŏnĭus, -a, -um, adj., *of* or *belonging to Mæonia, Lydian.* **carminis,** gen. (of quality) s. fr. carmen (64). **alite,** abl. s. in app. to Vario; fr. ales, subst. (78).

167. **Quam...cunque,** acc. fem. s. ag. w. rem; fr. quicunque (783). This separation is called tmesis (209). **rem,** acc. s. gov. by gesserit; fr. res, rei, 5th fem., *that which is spoken* or *thought of, thing, object. Matter, affair, event. Circumstance, occurrence, condition. The thing itself,* opp. to appearance, talk. *Effects, property, substance. Benefit, interest, weal. Cause, reason, ground,* "quamcunque rem," *every exploit which.* **ferox** (1005), nom. mas. s. ag. w. miles. **navibus,** abl. (instrumental) pl. fr. navis (93). **aut** (131). **equis,** abl. plu. jnd. by aut to navibus; fr. equus, -i, 2nd mas., *a horse.*

168. **Miles,** -ĭtis, 3rd mas.; nom. s. subj. of gesserit; *a soldier,* used esp. of foot soldiers opp. to equites, and of common soldiers opp. to the general. Collective *the soldiery, armies, forces.* **te duce** (88). **gesserit,** 3rd s. fut. pf. act. fr. gĕro, -ĕre, gessi, gestum, 3rd trans., *to bear, carry, have about one. Bring forth, produce. Have, entertain, cherish;* w. reflex. pron. *deport, behave, conduct oneself. Administer, manage, rule, govern, conduct, carry on, wage* (see 145).

169. **Nos** (143), nom. subj. of conamur (173). **Agrippa,** voc. s. fr. Agrippa, -æ, 1st mas., *M. Vipsanius Agrippa.* **neque**. **nec** (19, 32). **hæc,** acc. plu. neut. gov. by dicere; fr. hic (7). **dicere,** pres. inf. (prolative, 570) after conamur; fr. dico (85). **gravem,** acc. mas. s. ag. w. stomachum; fr. gravis (41).

170. **Pelidæ,** gen. s. after stomachum; fr. Pēlīdes, -æ (Gk.), 1st mas., *son of Peleus, i.e.,* Achilles. **stomachum,** acc. s. jnd. by nec to hæc; fr. stŏmăchus, -i, 2nd mas., *gullet, alimentary canal.* Meton., *the stomach;* fig. (in good sense) *taste, liking* (very rare); in bad sense, *distaste, disliking* to anything, hence *displeasure, irritation, chagrin.* **cedere,** pres. inf. act. prolative after nescii; fr. cēdo, cēdĕre, cessi, cessum, 3rd intrans. and trans., *to go,* i.e., *be in motion, move, go along* (poet. rare, in prose incedo). *To go from* some place, *remove, withdraw, go away from;* fig. *to succeed, prosper, have some result, turn out, happen. To pass away, vanish, disappear.* Of men, *to die.* Of time, etc., *vanish;* w. dat. *to go out of the way of, yield* to one's superiority, *give precedence to, submit to. To be inferior to. To comply with the wishes of,* i.e., *yield to. To fall to one's lot* or *share, accrue;* cedere aliquid alicui, *to concede, grant, give up, permit something to some one.* **nescii,** gen. s. mas. ag. w. Pelidæ; fr. nescius (159).

171 Nec cursus duplicis per mare Ulixei,
172 Nec sævam Pelopis domum
173 Conamur, tenues grandia, dum pudor
174 Imbellisque lyræ Musa potens vetat
175 Laudes egregii Cæsaris et tuas

171. **Cursus,** acc. plu. jnd. by nec to stomachum; fr. cursus, -us, 4th mas., (curro, 684) *quick motion, running, course, march, voyage, journey. Course, progress, direction.* **duplicis,** gen. s. mas. ag. w. Ulyxei; fr. duplex, duplicis, multiplicative numeral adj., *twofold, double. Split, divided, double. Both*=ambo, uterque of things in pairs. *Thick, strong, stout;* here *wily.* **per** (114). **mare** (14), gov. by per. **Ulixei,** gen. s. after cursus; fr. Ulixes, gen. Ulixĕi or Ulixei (trisyll.) 3rd mas. Prop. name for Gk. Odysseus, king of Ithaca, husb. of Penelope, father of Telemachus.

172. **Sævam,** acc. fem. s. ag. w. domum; fr. sævus, -a, -um, adj.; *roused to fierceness* [ferus, *naturally fierce, savage*] *cruel. Severe, dire* of persons and things. **Pĕlŏpis,** gen. s. after domum; fr. Pĕlops, -ŏpis, 3rd mas., son of Tantalus, father of Atreus and Thyestes, grandfather of Agamemnon and Menelaus (655). **domum,** acc. s. jnd. by nec to cursus; fr. domus (117).

173. **Conamur,** 1st plu. pres. ind. fr. cōnor, -ari, -ātus sum, 1st depon., *to undertake, attempt, try, venture* w. acc. and inf. or absol. **tenues,** nom. mas. plu. ag. w. nos; fr. tĕnŭis, -e, adj., (orig. *stretched out, drawn out;* fr. tendo, 34) *thin, fine, slim, slender, lank, narrow, close* (749, 1425). *Slight, trifling, poor, mean, e.g.,* oppidum. Of persons, *of small means, poor;* fig. *fine, nice, delicate, e.g.,* oratio. *Weak, trifling, insignificant, mean, low, e.g.,* res, spes, etc. *Of lower rank, lower orders, e.g.,* homines. **grandia,** acc. plu. neut. in app. to cursus, domum, etc.; fr. grandis, -e, adj. Of things (most com.) *grown, big, large, full, great, abundant.* Of persons, *grown up, big, tall; aged, old,* absol. or w. natu, ævo, etc.; fig., *strong, powerful* (1324), munus (887). Of style, *high, lofty, sublime.* **dum** (53). **pŭdor,** -ōris, 3rd mas., nom. s. subj. of vetat; (pudeo, 809) *a sense of shame, shamefacedness, shyness, modesty, good manners, propriety* [pudor generic, pudicitia particular]. *A cause for shame, disgrace* (not Cic.).

174. **Imbellis,** gen. fem. s. ag. w. lyræ; fr. imbellis, -e, adj., (in neg. bellum, 24) *unwarlike, not fit for war, peaceful, fond of peace.* Of persons and things, *weak, powerless* (399) here. **lyræ,** gen. s. after potens; fr. lўra, -æ (Gk.), 1st fem., *a lute, lyre,* a stringed instrument, acc. to fable invented by Mercury and presented to Apollo (262). *Lyric poetry, song* (here). **Musa,** -æ, 1st fem., jnd. by -que to pudor. *Muse,* one of the goddesses of poetry. *A song, poem.* **potens** (89), ag. w. Musa. **vetat** (143).

175. **Laudes,** acc. plu. gov. by deterere; fr. laus, laudis, 3rd fem., *praise, commendation, good report. A thing* or *deed deserving praise, noble* or *glorious deed.* Of things, *value, repute, estimation, worth.* **egregii,** gen. s. mas. ag. w. Cæsaris; fr. ēgrĕgius, -a, -um, adj., (e, 877; grex, 590) *excellent, eminent, surpassing, extraordinary, peerless.* Of rank and consequence, *distinguished, illustrious, honourable.* **Cæsaris** (80), after laudes. **tuas,** acc. plu. fem. ag. w. laudes; fr. tuus (205). It is jnd. by et to Cæsaris as the pron. adj. is genly. used instead of the subjective (749) gen. of corresp. pron. subst.

Culpa deterere ingenî.
Quis Martem tunica tectum adamantina
Digne scripserit? aut pulvere Troico
Nigrum Merionen? aut ope Palladis
Tydiden Superis parem?
Nos convivia, nos prælia virginum

176. **Culpa,** abl. (of cause) s. fr. culpa, -æ, 1st fem., *crime, fault, defect, failure* (as a state worthy of punishment), esp. *unchastity.* **dētĕrĕre,** pres. inf. (objective, 570) after vetat; fr. dētĕro, -tĕrere, -trīvi, -trītum, 3rd intrans., (de, 10; tero, *to rub, wear by rubbing*) *to rub away, wear away* or *out; fig., to diminish in force, weaken, lessen, impair. To thrash out* grain. **ingeni**=ingenii, gen. s. after culpâ; fr. ingĕnium, -ii, 2nd neut., (in, 78; geno rt. of gigno, *to implant, beget*) of things, *innate, natural quality; nature, character, e.g.,* arvorum. Of persons, *natural disposition, temper, mode of thinking, character, bent, inclination. Natural capacity, talent, capacity, genius* (1361).

177. **Quis** (149), subj. of scripserit. **Martem,** acc. s. gov. by scripserit; fr. Mars, Martis, 3rd mas., *Mars,* father of Romulus, and primogenitor of the Roman people, god of war, husbandry, shepherds, etc. **tŭnĭca,** abl. (instrumental) s. w. tectum; fr. tŭnĭca, -æ, 1st fem., *tunic,* undergarment worn by Roman men and women. Meton., *coating, skin, tegument, husk, peel.* **tectum,** acc. mas. s. pf. pass. part. ag. w. Martem; fr. tĕgo, -gĕre, -xi, -ctum, 3rd trans., *to cover, hide, conceal* (rare). *To shelter, protect, defend,* sts. w. ab *from* what. *To cover over, bury, enclose; fig. cloke, hide. To protect, guard, e.g.,* leges. **adamantina,** abl. fem. s. ag. w. tunica; fr. ădămantĭnus, -a, -um, adj., (adamas, -antis, Gk. *hard steel*) *adamantine; fig. extremely hard, firm, inflexible.*

178. **Digne,** adv., (dignus, 644) *worthily, fitly, becomingly;* compar. in Hor., sup. not found. **scripserit,** 3rd s. fut. pf. act. fr. scribo (165). The fut. pf. exp. "who will be held to have succeeded in his poem?" (M.). **aut** (131). **pulvere,** abl. (instrumental w. nigrum) s. fr. pulvis (3). **Troico,** abl. mas. s. ag. w. pulvere; fr. Trōĭcus, -a, -um, adj., (Tros, Trois) *of* or *belonging to Troy.*

179. **Nigrum,** acc. mas. s. ag. w. Merionen; fr. niger (155). **Merionen,** acc. s. jnd. by aut to Martem; fr. Mērĭŏnēs, -æ (Gk.), 1st mas., a charioteer of Idomeneus, who piloted his ships from Crete to Troy (410). **ope,** abl. (of means) s. fr. ops, only used in three cases in sing., gen. opis, acc. opem, abl. ope (nom. Ops, only found as the name of a goddess); plu. opes, opum, reg.; 3rd fem. In sing. (rare) *aid, help, support, assistance;* plu. *power, might, strength, ability. Property, substance, wealth.* **Palladis,** gen. s. after ope; fr. Pallas, gen. -dis or dos, Gk. for Minerva.

180. **Tydiden,** acc. s. jnd. by aut to Merionen; fr. Tȳdīdes, -æ (Gk. patronymic), 1st mas., *son of Tydeus, i.e.,* Diomede. These words fluctuate betw. 1st and 3rd decl. in Latin. **Superis** (30), as subs. after trajective (873) parem. **parem,** acc. mas. s. ag. w. Tydiden; fr. păr, păris, adj., abl. pări and păre, gen. plu. părŭm, *equal* of another person or thing of the same nature. *Equally divided, e.g.,* annus. *Equal* in station, rank or age; as subst. par, păris, 3rd mas., *a counterpart, equal, match for,* w. dat. or cum w. abl., *mate, companion. A pair.*

181. **Nos,** subj. of cantamus (183). **convivia,** acc. plu. gov. by cantamus; fr. convīvium, -ii, 2nd neut., (cum, 31; vivo, 731) *a living together, a meal in company, feast, banquet.* **prælia,** acc. plu. gov. by cantamus;

Sectis in juvenes unguibus acrium
Cantamus vacui sive quid urimur,
Non præter solitum leves.

CARMEN VII.—AD L. MUNATIUM PLANCUM.

LAUDABUNT alii claram Rhodon aut Mytilenen,
Aut Epheson bimarisve Corinthi

fr. prælium, -ii, 2nd neut., *a battle, combat. Contest, strife;* poet. and post-Aug. *a foe, warrior, combatant.* **virginum,** gen. plu. after prælia; fr. virgo (63).

182. **Sectis,** *pared, i.e.,* not likely to hurt or *cut to a point*; abl. plu. mas. pf. pass. part. ag. w. unguibus; fr. sĕco (14). **in** (76), w. acrium. **juvenes,** acc. plu. gov. by in; fr. juvenis (77). **unguibus,** abl. (instrumental) plu. fr. unguis, -is, 3rd mas., *a nail* of a person's finger or toe. Of animals, *talon, claw, hoof* (1416). **acrium,** gen. plu. fem. ag. w. virginum; fr. acer (75).

183. **Cantamus,** 1st. plu. pres. ind. act. fr. canto, -are, -avi, -atum, 1st trans. and intrans., intens. of cano (261), *to produce with energy melodious sounds. To make* a person or thing *the subject of a song, play,* or *poem. To praise in song, sing of* (1403, 1111). Trans., *to represent in acting, e.g.,* fabulam (of an actor). **vacui,** nom. mas. plu. ag. w. nos; fr. văcuus (122). **sive** (69), first sive omitted (194). **quid,** acc. neut. s. as adv. fr. quis, neut. quid, indef. pron., *any one, anything. Some one, something,* used esp. after si, nisi, ne [dist. fr. quis, quid, interrog. 149]. **urimur,** 1st plu. pres. ind. pass. fr. uro (136).

184. **Non** (54). **præter** (92). **solitum,** acc. s. neut. gov. by præter; fr. sŏlĭtus, -a, -um, (pf. partc. of soleo, *to be accustomed, be wont,* semi-depon. passive) *which one is used to, which usually happens, wonted, accustomed;* solitum, -i, 2nd neut., *that which is customary, usual thing.* **leves** (31), mas. ag. w. nos; non...leves, "*light hearted much after my wont,*" *i.e.*, whether in love or not, always given to light and fanciful themes (Wick.).

CARMEN VII. METRE.—*Alcmanian, a couplet,* see Carm. xxviii.

1st. A Dactylic Hexameter } – ⏑ ⏑ | – ⏑ ⏑ | – ⏑ ⏑ | – ⏑ ⏑ | – ⏑ ⏑ | – ⏑

2nd. Four last feet of a Hexameter or a Dactylic Tetrameter Catalectic } – ⏑ ⏑ | – ⏑ ⏑ | – ⏑ ⏑ | – ⏑

185. **Laudabunt,** 3rd plu. fut. (165) ind. act. fr. laudo (17). **alii,** nom. mas. plu. subj. of laudabunt; fr. alius (92). **claram,** acc. fem. s. ag. w. Rhodon; fr. clārus, -a, -um, adj.; of hearing, *clear, loud, distinct.* Of sight, *clear, bright, shining, light, brilliant;* mentally, *clear, distinct, manifest, plain;* morally, *brilliant, celebrated, glorious* (here), esp. epithet of illustrious men, *e.g.,* consuls, pontiffs; some tr. here, *sunny.* **Rhodon,** acc. s. gov. by laudabunt; fr. Rhŏdos (rare -us), -i, 2nd fem.; an island on S.W. of Asia Minor, its people distinguished for navigation, rhetoric, etc. **aut** (131). **Mytilenen,** acc. s. jnd. by aut to Rhodon; fr. Mȳtĭlene, -es (Mĭtyl-), 1st fem., used also in plu. Mytilenæ, -arum, capital city of Lesbos, birthplace of Pittacus, Alcæus, etc.

186. **Epheson,** acc. s. jnd. by aut to Mytilenen; fr. Ephĕsos (-us), -i, 2nd fem., commercial city of Ionia, where was a temple of Diana. **bimaris,** gen.

Mœnia, vel Baccho Thebas vel Apolline Delphos
Insignes aut Thessala Tempe.
Sunt, quibus unum opus est intactæ Palladis urbem
Carmine perpetuo celebrare, et
Undique decerptam fronti præponere olivam.

s. fem. ag. w. Corinthi; fr. bĭmăris, -e, adj., (bis, *twice*; mare, 14) *lying between two seas.* **-ve,** disjunctive or alternative conj., *i.e.*, it connects sentences, but disconnects their meaning; *or,* like -ne (961), and -que (4), an enclitic. **Corinthi,** gen. s. after mœnia; fr. Cŏrinthus, -i (or -os, acc. -on), 2nd fem., city on the isthmus so called.

187. **Mœnia,** acc. jnd. by -ve to Epheson; fr. mœnia, -ium, 3rd plu., *defensive walls, bulwarks, fortifications. Fortified city.* **vel,** disjunctive or alternative conj. (184), ak. to volo (104). It leaves the preference to be decided by the subjective opinion or choice [*aut* opposes absolutely and objectively), *or;* vel potius, *or rather,* corrects what has been said: vel...vel, *either...or,* sts. repeated several times. It sts. implies a climax, *or even; or indeed; or...itself, even, indeed, surely, certainly,* w. substs., adjs., vbs., prons. With superls., esp. the highest possible degree, *the very, the utmost, the most... possible, e.g.,* vel minimus, maximus. **Baccho,** abl. (of manner) w. insignes; fr. Bacchus, -i, 2nd mas., the god of wine, also called Liber (*deliverer*), son of Jupiter and Semele, dau. of Cadmus. **Thebas,** acc. jnd. by vel to mœnia; fr. Thebæ, -arum, 1st fem. pl. *Thebes,* capital of Bœotia; adj. (494). **Apolline,** abl. (constr. like Baccho); fr. Apollo (68). **Delphos,** acc. jnd. by vel to Thebas; fr. Delphi, -orum, 2nd mas., where was the oracle of Apollo.

188. **Insignes,** acc. mas. plu. ag. w. Delphos; fr. insignis, -e, adj., (signum, 203) *that has a mark upon it, distinguished by a mark. Remarkable, noted, distinguished, eminent.* **aut** (131). **Thessala,** acc. plu. neut. ag. w. Tempe; fr. Thessălus, -a, -um, adj., *of* or *belonging to Thessaly* (978, 271, 645), also Thessălĭus and Thessălĭcus. **Tempe** (Gk.), neut. plu. indecl. (here acc. jnd. by aut to Delphos), a valley in Thessaly through which ran the Peneus (529).

189. **Sunt** (3). **quibus** (160), possessive (acquisitive) after est. **unum,** nom. neut. s. ag. w. opus; fr. ūnus, -a, -um, gen. unīus, dat. uni, cardinal num. adj., *one;* when used in the sing. without other numerals it=*singularly, especially.* Its plu. is used w. substs. wh. have no singular. **opus,** -ĕris, 3rd neut.; nom. s. predic. after est; *work, labour. Result of labour, work, building, fortification. Book. Work of art. Workmanship, skill, skilfulness. Deed, action, performance.* **est** (19). **intactæ,** gen. s. fem. ag. w. Palladis; fr. intactus (811), *virgin.* **Palladis** (179), after urbem. **urbem** (40), gov. by celebrare.

190. **Carmine,** abl. (of means) s. fr. carmen (64). **perpetuo,** abl. s. neut. ag. w. carmine; fr. perpĕtuus, -a, -um, adj., (perpes, -petis, *extending through*) *continuous,* or *continued throughout, uninterrupted, e.g.,* agmen. Of time, *whole, entire, e.g.,* dies. Of things, *lasting* through a time, *constant, perpetual, continuing uninterruptedly, e.g.,* cura; "carmine perpetuo," *a continuous poem,* containing all the myths, etc. about Athens, or *unceasing song* (W.). **celebrare,** pres. inf. act. subj. of est; fr. celebro (286).

191. **Undique,** indef. adv., (unde, 291; -que, 4) *whencesoever, from all parts* or *sides, on all sides, everywhere;* here *from every one.* **decerptam,** acc. fem. s. pf. pass. part. ag. w. olivam; fr. decerpo, -pĕre, -psi, -ptum, 3rd trans., (de, 10; carpo, 284) *to pluck away, pull off, gather. To take away, detract*

192 Plurimus in Junonis honorem
193 Aptum dicet equis Argos ditesque Mycenas.
194 Me nec tam patiens Lacedæmon
195 Nec tam Larissæ percussit campus opimæ,

from, *e.g.*, de gravitate. **fronti,** dat. s. after præponere; fr. frons (29). **præponere,** pres. inf. act. jnd. by et to celebrare; fr. præpōno, -ĕre, -pŏsuī, -pŏsĭtum, 3rd trans. traject., (præ, *before;* pono, 104) *to put before, place first. To set over* as chief, *give the charge of to, e.g.*, aliquem provinciæ. *To set before* or *above, prefer.* **olivam,** acc. s. gov. by (direct obj. of) præponere; fr. ŏlīva, -æ, 1st fem., *an olive, olive-tree. Olive-branch;* undique... olivam, *i.e.*, to seek fame by writing on a well-known theme (W.).

192. **Plurimus,** -a, -um, nom. mas. s., (used as subst.) subj. of decet; superl. adj. s. of multus (23); *very many a one,* sing., for plu. **in** (76), of purpose. **Junōnis,** gen. (objective) s. after honorem; fr. Juno, dau. of Saturn, sister and wife of Jupiter. **honorem,** acc. s. gov. by in; fr. honor (8).

193. **Aptum,** acc. neut. s. ag. w. Argos; fr. aptus, -a, -um, adj., (apio or capio, *to take*) *joined, fastened;* fig. *dependent, depending,* w. ex, etc. *Joined together, adhering together. Endowed, furnished with. Suited, fit, appropriate, suitable for,* w. ad, in and acc., qui and subj. *Fit, suitable, apposite,* w. lar (327). **dicet,** 3rd s. fut. ind. act. fr. dico (85). **equis,** dat. plu. after traject. aptum; fr. equus (167). **Argos,** acc. (Gk.) gov. by dicet; fr. Argos. neut. (in nom. and acc. only); collat. Argi, -orum, 2nd mas., the capital of Argolis, sacred to Juno. **dites,** acc. fem. plu. ag. w. Mycenas; fr. dis, neut. dite, poet. and post-Aug. for dives, gen. divitis, abl. divite, rarer -ti, neut. plu. not found (class. and frequ. only in nom. and acc.). Of persons, *rich.* Of things, *sumptuous, magnificent, costly, precious.* Comp. divitior, most com. in prose and poet., exc. Hor., who uses ditior, sup. divitissimus, good prose, ditissimus, genly poet. and post-Aug. **-que** (4). **Mycenas,** acc. jnd. by -que to Argos; fr. Mȳcēnæ, -arum, 1st fem. plu. (collat. Mȳcēna, -æ, Mycĕne, -es), city in Argolis of which Agamemnon was king.

194. **Me** (29), gov. by percussit. **nec** (19). **tam,** adv. orig. acc., fr. same rt. as talis (like quam, jam, palam). (i.) Correlative demonst. particle of comparison, *so far, in so far,* folld by quam; w. adjs., advs., vbs., rarely substs. and prons., also folld. by ut, qui, quasi, w. subjunctive. (ii.) In absolute expressions, *so, so very, to such a high degree,* w. adjs., advs., vbs., rarely substs. With superls.=*the, so much the; all the;* rare w. comparative. *So very, so exceedingly.* Non tam...quam; *not so much as, less than.* **patiens,** -entis, adj.; nom. fem. s. ag. w. Lacedæmon, (prop. part. pres. of patior, 18) *suffering, allowing, permitting, bearing, e.g.*, terram. Of disposition, *patient,* meton., *firm, unyielding, resolute.* Of things, *hard.* **Lacedæmon,** -ŏnis, Gk. acc. -ona, 3rd fem., nom. subj. of percussit; *Lacedæmon* or *Sparta.*

195. **Nec** (19). **tam** (194). **Larissæ,** gen. s. after campus; fr. Lārissa, -æ, 1st fem., city of Thessaly on the Peneus. **percussit,** 3rd s. pf. ind. act. fr. percŭtio, -cŭtĕre, -cussi, -cussum, 3rd trans., (per, 114; quatio, 18) *to strike, thrust, pierce through. To slay, kill. To strike, beat, hit, smite very much.* Of misfortunes, *to shock, affect deeply, move, astound* (class.). *To impress* (here). *To deceive, impose upon.* **campus,** -i, 2nd mas., nom. s. subj. to percussit; *even, flat place, plain, field* (998, 553), esp. Campus Martius (250), poet. *any level surface, e.g.*, the sea, w. natantes, liquentes; fig. of any *open space* for action, *field, theatre.* **opimæ,** gen. fem. s. ag. w. Larissæ; fr. ŏpīmus, -a, um, adj. (opes, 179), *having opes,* i.e., *rich, abundant, copious, sumptuous. Noble, splendid. Enriched, rich. Enriching,*

196 Quam domus Albuneæ resonantis
197 Et præceps Anio ac Tiburni lucus et uda
198 Mobilibus pomaria rivis.
199 Albus ut obscuro deterget nubila cœlo
200 Sæpe Notus neque parturit imbres

gainful; meton., *honourable, high, exalted, e.g.*, triumphus (Hor.). Of animals, etc., *fat, plump.* Of a country, *fertile* (711); w. gen., *abounding in.*

196. **Quam,** (orig. acc. of qui, 3); (i.) Correl. adv., used in comparisons, *as*, w. tam; with superl. and a corresp. tam, *by how much the more...the more;* tam magis...quam magis, *the more...the more.* Often w. comparatives or words of comparison after alius, aliter, etc., in correlations of unlikeness. (ii.) Without correl. word, *in what manner, how, how much, as much as, e.g.*, quam quisque potest, *as much as each one can.* It augments superls., esp. superl. with possum, "quam possunt mollissime," *as gently as possible.* **domus** (145), jnd. by quam to campus. **Albuneæ,** gen. s. after domus; fr. Albŭnea, -æ, the last of the Sibyls. This refers to a temple at Tibur, which re-echoed from a cataract close by. **resonantis,** gen. s. fem. pres. part. act. ag. w. Albuneæ; fr. resŏno, -are, -āvi, sup. not found, 1st intrans. There is an ante-class. collat. fm. of 3rd conj., (re, 659; sono, 1218) *to send a sound back, ring back, resound, re-echo,* lit. and fig.; trans., *give back the sound of, re-echo with* anything.

197. **Præceps** (100), nom. mas. s. ag. w. Anio. **Anio,** Aniēnis, etc., all through class. age; Aug. and post-Aug. have gen. Aniōnis, and collat. Aniēnus, -i; a tributary of the Tiber, wh. rises in the Apennines, and has a cataract at Tibur. **Tiburni,** gen. s. after lucus; fr. Tiburnus, 2nd mas., an Argive, he gave his name to an ancient town of Latium on both sides the Anio (Tivoli), see 478. **lucus** (139), nom. mas. s. jnd. by ac (131) to Anio. **uda,** nom. neut. plu. ag. w. pomaria; fr. ūdus, -a, -um, adj., (uveo, obsol.=*to be wet*) *wet, moist, humid* (735, 999, 1063).

198. **Mobilibus,** abl. plu. mas. ag. w. rīvis; fr. mobilis (7). **pomaria,** nom. plu. jnd. by et to lucus; fr. pŏmārium, -ii, 2nd neut., (pomum, *an apple*) *a fruit garden, orchard. Store room for fruit;* orig. neut. of adj. pomarius, -a, -um, *belonging to fruit trees.* **rivis,** abl. (instrumental) plu. w. uda; fr. rīvus, -i, 2nd mas., *small stream of water, brook* (695); fig., fortunæ (Hor.); meton., artificial *water-course, gutter, channel. A stream* of anything liquid, *e.g.*, lactis (1403).

199. **Albus** (311), nom. mas. s. predic. ag. w. Notus, *a bright fresh wind* (M.). **ut** (13), here a comparative conj. (229). **obscuro,** abl. neut. s. ag. w. cælo; fr. obscūrus, -a, -um, adj., *covered over by anything, dark, dusky, obscure. Invisiblé, unseen, indistinct, unintelligible. Unknown, e.g.*, nomen. Of rank, birth, *ignoble, low.* Of character, *close, reserved.* **deterget,** 3rd s. pres. ind. act. fr. detergeo, -gēre, -si, -sum, 2nd trans., (de, 10; tergeo, *to rub off, wipe off, wipe dry*) *to wipe away, drive away, remove;* meton., *cleanse by wiping, cleanse, clean. To strip off, break in pieces, e.g.*, remos. **nubila,** acc. plu. gov. by deterget; fr. nūbĭlum, -i, 2nd neut., (prop. as neut. of nūbĭlus, -a, -um, *overcast, lowering*) *a clouded sky, cloudy weather;* plu. nubila, -orum, *clouds.* **cælo,** abl. (of separation) s. after deterget; fr. cælum (81).

200. **Sæpe** (215). **Notus** (102), nom. subj. of deterget. **neque** (32). **parturit,** 3rd s. pres. ind. act. fr. partūrio, -īre, -īvi or -ĭi, -ītum, 4th trans. desiderative, *to desire to bring forth, be in travail* or *labour;* fig., *be big*

Perpetuos, sic tu sapiens finire memento
Tristitiam vitæque labores
Molli, Plance, mero, seu te fulgentia signis
Castra tenent seu densa tenebit

with, pregnant with, brood over. Meditate, purpose; meton., *to yield, generate.* **imbres,** acc. plu. gov. by parturit; fr. imber, -bris, 3rd mas., *a heavy, violent rain. Shower of rain, pelting* or *pouring rain* (class.); meton., *rain-cloud, storm, cloud.*

201. **Perpetuos,** acc. plu. mas. ag. w. imbres; fr. perpetuus (190). **sic** (89). **tu** (69), subj. of memento. **sapiens,** -ntis (abl. s. sts. -e, and gen. plu. -tum), adj., nom. mas. s. ag. as adv. attribute (867) w. tu; *wise, knowing, sensible, discreet, judicious. Of nice taste* (Hor.). Philosoph. *wise, sage;* adv. sapienter. **finire,** pres. inf. act. prolative (570) after memento; fr. fīnio, -īre, -ivi or -ĭi, ītum, 4th trans., (finis, 94) *to limit, bound, enclose within boundaries* (class.). *To set bounds to, restrain, check*=definio. *To determine, fix, appoint, assign. To finish, terminate* (496). Pass., *to come to an end* or *close*, esp. of speaking. **memento,** 3rd s. imper. fr. memini, defective of the class Præteritiva, *i.e.*, whose fms. in use are expressed by the pf.; imper. mĕmento, -tote, fut. pf. meminero, plpf. memineram, (redup. of rt. men-, seen in mens, mentior, etc.) *to remember, recollect, think of. To bear in mind, not to have forgotten;* w. gen., *be mindful of* or *about. Mention* (rare but class.).

202. **Tristitiam,** acc. s. gov. by finire; fr. tristĭtia, -æ, 1st fem., (tristis, 102) *sadness, mournfulness, sorrow, grief. Gloominess, dejection. Moroseness, sternness, harshness.* **vitæ** (143), after labores. **labores,** acc. plu. jnd. by -que to tristitiam; fr. labor (124).

203. **Molli,** abl. neut. s. ag. w. mero; fr. mollis, -e, adj., (moveo, 394) *that may* or *can be moved, pliant, flexible. Soft, tender, delicate. Gentle.* Of weather, atmosphere, *calm, temperate.* Of wine, *mild, mellow. Powerless, relaxed, feeble. Pliant, yielding.* Of age, *delicate, youthful, effeminate, unmanly, weak. Not difficult, easy. Agreeable, gentle, pleasant, e.g.,* senectus. Of music, poetry, etc., *gentle, touching.* **Plance,** voc. s. fr. Plancus, -i, *L. Munatius Plancus,* Cos. B.C. 42. **mero,** abl. (instrumental) s. fr. mĕrum, -i, 2nd neut., *pure, unmixed, unadulterated wine;* prop. neut. of mĕrus, -a, -um, adj., *unadulterated, unmixed.* **seu** (27). **te** (83), gov. by tenent. **fulgentia,** nom. neut. plu. pres. part. act. ag. w. castra; fr. fulgeo, -gēre, -si, no sup., 2nd intrans., (collat. 3rd ante- and post-class., ak. to flagro, 605; flamma, 423) *to flash, lighten;* meton., *glitter, gleam, glisten, shine* (1283, 1179); fig. of oratory, virtue, etc. **signis,** abl. (instrumental) plu. w. fulgentia; fr. signum, -i, 2nd neut., *mark, token, sign;* milit., *standard, ensign,* sts. including sts. opposed to aquila (standard of the whole army), as ensign of a cohort, maniple, etc. *Signal, watchword, password* given by a wind instrument. *Prognostic, symptom* of anything. *Work of art, statue, picture,* etc. *Device* on a seal, ring, etc., *signet. Sign* in the heavens, *constellation.*

204. **Castra** (23), subj. of tenent. **tenent,** 3rd plu. pres. ind. act. fr. tĕneo, -ēre, -ŭi, tentum, 2nd trans., *to hold, keep, have in hand. Possess, hold fast, occupy. Watch, guard. Hold back, hinder, restrain.* **seu** (27). **densa,** nom. fem. s. ag. w. umbra; fr. densus, -a, -um, adj., *thick, dense, i.e.,* consisting of parts crowded together (1054, 1224). Of the parts themselves so crowded, *thick, set close.* With abl., *thickly set, full of. Quickly succeeding* in time, *e.g.,* plagæ (Hor.). **tenebit,** 3rd s. fut. ind. act. fr. teneo (204).

Tiburis umbra tui. Teucer Salamina patremque
    Quum fugeret, tamen uda Lyæo
Tempora populea fertur vinxisse corona,
    Sic tristes affatus amicos:
"Quo nos cunque feret melior fortuna parente

205. **Tībŭris,** gen. s. after umbra; fr. Tībur (1021), abl. -i and -e; see 197. **umbra,** -æ, 1st fem., nom. s. subj. of tenebit; *shade, shadow. Ghost* of a dead person. *Shady place. That which gives shade* or *shadow, e.g.,* a tree. *Uninvited guest* (Hor.). **tui,** gen. mas. s. ag. w. Tiburis; fr. tuus, tua, tuum, pron. possess. adj. of 2nd pers. (tu, 69), *thy, thine; your, yours;* pregnant *favourable, auspicious, right, proper for you;* sts. = obj. gen. tui, *e.g.,* odio tuo. **Teucer,** -cri, 2nd mas., nom. subj. of fertur (207), son of Telamon, king of Salamis, who founded a new Salamis in Cyprus, when his father would not receive him on his return from Troy. **Salamina,** acc. (Gk.) s. gov. by fugeret; fr. Salamis, -is, (collat. Lat. fm. Salamīna, -æ), *Salamis,* island in the Saronic Gulf (Coluri), adj. (407). **patrem,** acc. s. jnd. by -que to Salamina; fr. pater (38).

206. **Quum** (43). **fugeret,** 3rd s. impf. ind. act. fr. fŭgio, fŭgĕre, fūgi, fŭgĭtum, 3rd intrans. and trans., *to flee, fly, take to flight, run away,* esp. *to become an exile.* Of things, *to pass quickly, speed, hasten away* (314). *To hasten from sight, vanish, disappear, e.g.,* vires (931), ætas (283); trans., *to flee from, shun, seek to avoid* (548), esp. one's country (1300); fig., very com., *e.g.,* ignominiam. With obj. clause (245, 990). *To escape, e.g.,* Acheronta (668), a poetic inversion; cum fugeret, *when he was starting.* **tamen** (111). **uda** (197), acc. ag. w. tempora. **Lyæo,** abl. (instrumental) w. uda; fr. Lyæus, -i (luo, Gk. *to relax*). *Relaxer. Unbinder. Deliverer from care,* surname of Bacchus; meton., *wine* (here).

207. **Tempora,** acc. gov. by vinxisse; fr. tempora, -um, 3rd neut. plu., (sing. tempus, -oris, rare) *temples* of the head; meton., *face, visage,* genly. **pōpŭlea,** abl. fem. s. ag. w. coronâ; fr. pōpŭleus, -a, -um, adj., (pōpŭlus, -i, *a poplar*) *of* or *belonging to poplars, poplar* (sacred to Hercules). **fertur,** *is said;* 3rd s. ind. pres. pass. fr. fero (138). **vinxisse,** pf. inf. (prolative, 570) act. after fertur; fr. vincio, -cīre, vinxi, vinctum, 4th trans., *to bind, wind about. Encircle, clasp, surround, fetter, tie. To secure firmly, attach to* one; fig., *confine, restrain.* **corona,** abl. (instrumental) s. fr. cŏrōna, -æ, 1st fem., *a garland, wreath, crown.* Of things in the shape of a crown, *assembly, crowd, multitude,* esp. of besiegers around a place.

208. **Sic** (89). **tristes** (102), mas. ag. w. amicos. **affatus,** pf. part. nom. mas. s. ag. w. Teucer (205); fr. affor, -fāri, -fātus, 1st depon. trans., (ad, 6; for, *to speak, say*) *to speak* or *say to, address, accost; address* a deity in prayer, *implore, beseech.* Pres. -fatur, -famur, -famini; impf. -fabar, pf. -fata est, imper. -fare, plpf. -fatus esset, inf. -fari, partc. -fatus, are found. **amicos,** acc. plu. gov. by affatus; fr. ămīcus, -i, 2nd mas., *a friend;* publicly *a friend of the state* [every socius was amicus, but not vice versâ]; amicus, -a, -um, adj., *loving, friendly, favourable, kind.*

209. **Quo-cunque,** adv. (prop. abl. s. neut. of quicunque, 167); see quo (145), *to whatsoever place, whithersoever.* **nos** (143), gov. by feret. **feret,** 3rd s. fut. ind. act. fr. fero (138). **melior** (58), nom. fem. s. ag. w. fortuna. **fortuna,** -æ, 1st fem., nom. s. subj. of feret, (lengthened fr. fors, 246) *chance, luck, fame, fortune. Goddess of fate. Good* or *ill luck* acc. to context; sts. w. secunda, adversa. *Condition, circumstances, lot;* plu. (less

Ibimus, o socii comitesque!
Nil desperandum Teucro duce et auspice Teucro
Certus enim promisit Apollo,
Ambiguam tellure nova Salamina futuram
O fortes pejoraque passi

com. sing.) *possessions, goods.* **parente,** abl. of comparison (103) after melior; fr. parens (59).

210. **Ibimus,** 1st plu. fut. ind. fr. eo (51). **o** (2). **socii,** voc. plu. fr. sŏcĭus, -ii, 2nd mas., *fellow, partner, ally, confederate.* **comites,** voc. plu. jnd. by -que to socii; fr. cŏmes, -ĭtis, 3rd com., (cum, 31; eo, 51) *one who goes with another, associate, comrade,* esp. *overseer, guardian, tutor, teacher;* more com. *a suite, retinue* of friends, relatives, scholars, etc., who accompanied magistrates and private men; fig., of things.

211. **Nil** (125), subj. of est und. **desperandum,** nom. neut. s. predic. ag. w. nil; fr. desperandus, -a, -um, gerundive (639) of despēro, -are, -avi, -atum, 1st intrans. and trans., (de, 10; spero, 159) *to have no hope of, despair of. To give up hope* or *expectation of.* Cæs. only uses in part. pf. **Teucro,** abl. (absol. 824) fr. Teucer (205). **duce** (88), in app. to Teucro. **et** (2). **auspice,** abl. s. in app. to Teucro; fr. auspex, -ĭcis, 3rd com., (avis, 389; specio, obsol. *to look at*), *bird inspector, bird seer, i.e.,* one who predicts fr. observations of flight, singing, etc. of birds, *diviner, foreboder.* Meton., *author, founder. Director. Aider. Protector, favourer,* etc.

212. **Certus,** -a, -um, adj.; nom. mas. s. adv. attribute (867) ag. w. Apollo; (cerno, *to perceive*), *fixed, determined. About which there is no doubt, established, settled* of external qualities. *Certain, sure, to be depended on* of internal moral qualities. *Made certain, sure;* sts. like quidam = *a certain one.* **enim,** a causal conj. It originally strengthened and then proved and explained a statement already made; (*a*) *truly, certainly, to be sure, indeed;* like equidem, certe, vero. Enimvero, *yes indeed, yes truly,* placed first in a sentence; (*b*) gives the grounds of a prec. assertion; sts. the reason which is given, must be mentally supplied, esp. in "quid enim?" *For instance, namely,* to explain a prec. assertion. **promisit,** 3rd s. pf. ind. act. fr. promitto, -ĕre, -mīsi, -missum, 3rd trans. and intrans., (pro, *forward;* mitto, 38) *to let go forward, send* or *put forth, let hang down, let grow, e.g.,* of hair; fig., *to promise, hold out, cause to expect, give promise of;* intrans., *to make a promise, promise, vow* to a deity. **Apollo** (68), subj. of promisit.

213. **Ambiguam,** acc. fem. s. predic. after futuram, ag. w. Salamina; fr. ambĭgŭus, -a, -um, adj., (ambi, *around;* ago, 43) *drifting* or *moving to both sides, wavering, uncertain. Wavering, uncertain, doubtful.* Of speech, *obscure, dark.* Of moral conduct, *not to be relied on, uncertain; e.g.,* fides; here *like named, second.* **tellure,** abl. (of cause) s. fr. tellus, -ūris, 3rd fem., poet. *the earth* opp. to other planets or the sea, *the globe. Land, ground* even personified. *A region, district.* **nova,** abl. s. fem. ag. w. tellure; fr. nŏvus (42). **Salamina** (205), subj. of futuram (esse). **futuram,** acc. fem. s. ag. w. Salamina; fr. fŭtūrus, fut. partc. fr. sum; with esse (pres. inf. of sum) und. it is the periphrastic (542) fut. inf. after promisit.

214. **O** (2). **fortes,** voc. mas. plu. ag. w. viri; fr. fortis (165). **pejōra,** acc. neut. plu. gov. by passi; fr. pĕjor, comp. adj. of mălus, -a, -um, adj. (orig. *black*), opp. to bonus (581). Morally *evil, wicked, bad. Bad* of its kind, *not good. Improper, low. Destructive, injurious. Unfortunate, calamitous;* malum, -i, 2nd neut., *misfortune, hurt, injury; punishment,*

Mecum sæpe viri, nunc vino pellite curas;
    Cras ingens iterabimus æquor."

CARMEN VIII.—AD LYDIAM.

LYDIA, dic, per omnes
    Te Deos oro, Sybarin cur properes amando

severity. Betokening or *foreboding ill, ill omened* (389). Of appearance, *ugly; misshapen, e.g.*, crus. **passi,** voc. mas. plu. pf. part. jnd. by -que to fortes; fr. patior (18).

215. **Mecum,** me, abl. s. fr. ego (29), gov. by cum (31), wh. here enclitic, so w. te, se, nobis, etc. **sæpe,** temp. adv., *oft, oftentimes, many times, frequently.* Comp. sæpius often absolute, sup. sæpissime, "sæpe numero" strengthens the main idea. **viri,** voc. plu. fr. vĭr, vĭri, 2nd mas., *a man* distinguished from woman. *Husband*=maritus. *Hero, soldier* [more honourable than homo, wh.=*man* opp. to *beast*]. **nunc** (21). **vino,** abl. (instrumental) s. fr. vinum (146). **pellite,** 2nd plu., pres. imper. act. fr. pello, -ĕre, pĕpŭli, pulsum, 3rd trans., *to cause to go, thrust, turn out* or *away, expel* w. ex, ab esp. *to banish,* fig. (930); milit., *rout, put to flight. To beat* the earth, *knock* at a door. *To move, affect, impress.* **curas,** acc. plu. gov. by pellite; fr. cūra, -æ, 1st fem., (quæro, 245) *trouble* physical or mental, bestowed on something, *attention, pains. Care, guardianship* of a thing. *Management, charge, office. Anxiety, concern, trouble, grief.*

216. **Cras,** adv., *to-morrow,* sts. indecl. subst.; *for the future, in future* (245). **ingens,** acc. neut. s. ag. w. æquor; fr. ingens, -gentis, adj., (in, neg; gens, 41) *of immoderate size, huge, vast, prodigious, enormous. Remarkable, distinguished.* **iterabimus,** 1st plu. fut. ind. act. fr. ĭtĕro, -are, -avi, -atum, 1st trans., (iterum, 374) *to do* or *go over* a thing *again,* or *the second time, repeat;* fig., *to tell over again, rehearse.* In 1404, *to sing over and over again;* here, *to make a new voyage;* iterare cursum, *retrace one's course, sail back again* (764). **æquor,** acc. s. gov. by iterabimus; fr. æquor (48)

CARMEN VIII. METRE—*Greater Sapphic.*

1st Aristophanic } – ⏑ ⏑ – | ⏑ – | ⏓ or – ⏑ ⏑ | – ⏑ | – ⏓

2nd Greater Sapphic } – ⏑ | – – | – ⏑ ⏑ – | – ⏑ ⏑ | – | ⏑ – | ⏓

or

– ⏑ | – – | – ⏑ ⏑ | – || – ⏑ ⏑ | – ⏑ | – ⏓

217. **Lydia,** voc. s. fr. Lȳdia, -æ, 1st fem. **dic,** 2nd s. imper. pres. apocopated colloquially fr. dico (85); so fac fr. făcio. **per** (113), here, in intreaties. **omnes,** acc. plu. mas. ag. w. Deos; fr omnis (43).

218. **Te** (83), gov. by oro. **Deos** (6), gov. by per. **oro** (710), 1st s. pres. ind. act. **Sybarin,** acc. (Gk.) s. gov. by perdere; fr. Sȳbăris, -is, 3rd mas., fictitious name. **cur** (old quor), abl. contr. fr. quare (acc. to some for cui rei), interrog. and relat, *for what reason, why, to what purpose.* **properes,** 2nd s. pres. subj. act. fr. prŏpĕro, -are, -avi, -atum, 1st trans., *to hasten, quicken, accelerate, make* or *do with haste;* intrans., *to make haste, hasten, be quick.* It is pres. after dic; subjunct. in indirect quest. after cur. **amando,** gerund. (639) ablative (of means) fr. amo (86).

Perdere; cur apricum
　　Oderit campum, patiens pulveris atque solis?
Cur neque militaris
　　Inter æquales equitat, Gallica nec lupatis
Temperat ora frenis?

219. **Perdere,** pres. inf. (prolative) after properes; fr. perdo, -dĕre, -dĭdi, -dĭtum, 3rd trans., (per, 114; do, 65; acc. to others fr. Gk. πέρθω) *to make away with, destroy, ruin;* morally *ruin, corrupt* (here). *To throw away, waste, spend needlessly. To lose utterly.* **apricum,** acc. s. mas. ag. w. campum; fr. āprīcus, -a, -um, adj., (contr. for apericus; fr. aperio, *to open*) *uncovered,* esp. *lying open to the sun, sunny. Fond of sunshine* (619).

220. **Oderit,** pf. (as pres.) subj. (in indirect quest.) fr. odi (869). **campum,** acc. s. gov. by oderit; fr. campus (195); here, the Campus Martius. **patiens** (79), nom. mas. s. ag. w. subj. (Sybaris) of oderit, here, *capable of bearing.* **pulveris,** gen. (objective) sing. after patiens; fr. pulvis (3). **atque** (37). **solis,** gen. s. jnd. by atque to pulveris; fr. sol, sōlis, 3rd mas., *the sun; Apollo. Sunshine, sunlight, warmth of sun. Sunny place. Day.*

221. **Cur** (218). **neque** (32). **militaris,** -e, adj., nom. mas. s. ag. w. subj. (Sybaris) of equitat; (miles, 168) *of* or *belonging to a soldier, the soldiers, military;* here, militaris, -is, 3rd mas., *soldier, military person. For the use of soldiers, e.g.,* signa; militaris ætas, *military age, i.e.,* fr. 17th to 46th year. *Of* or *relating to war, e.g.,* res.

222. **Inter,** prep. gov. acc, (in- and adv. termin. -ter, which seen in Eng. *under*). Of space, *between* two or more points; *through the midst of; into the midst of; in the midst of,* according to sense of verb. Of time, either *between* two points of time or two events, or *during, in the course of* a certain time or event, esp. w. gerunds or gerundive, *e.g.,* inter ludendum. Of an order, class, rank or number, *among* which any one or anything appears. Of distribution, *among.* Of choice, difference, etc., *between;* inter se, vos, etc., *among themselves,* etc., i.e., *mutually, reciprocally.* **æquales,** acc. plu. mas. (as subst.) gov. by inter; fr. æquālis, -e, adj. Of dimension, *of corresponding length, extent, size,* etc., w. dat., absol., or as subst. w. gen. *Plain, smooth* of surface. Of abstract things, *equal in degree, of corresponding value.* Of persons, *resembling,* esp. *of same age; contemporary with.* Subst. *a compeer.* Of things, *coexistent with.* **equitat,** 3rd sing. pres. ind. (because quest. is direct) act. fr. equito (87). **Gallica,** acc. neut. plu. ag. w. ora; fr. Gallicus, -a, -um, adj., (Gallus, *a Gaul*) *of* or *belonging to the Gauls.* **nec** (19). **lupatis,** abl. neut. plu. ag. w. frenis; fr. lŭpātus, -a, um, adj., *provided* or *furnished with wolves teeth, i.e.,* with iron spikes, etc., shaped like the teeth of a wolf, genly. lupati or lupata, -orum, subst., *a curb of jagged spikes.*

223. **Temperat,** 3rd. s. pres. ind. act. fr. tempĕro, -are, -avi, -atum, 1st trans., (tempus, 660) *to divide* or *proportion duly, mingle in due proportion. Qualify, temper. Rule, govern, manage, order;* intrans., *restrain oneself, forbear, abstain. Be moderate, temperate.* **ora,** acc. plu. gov. by temperat; fr. os, ōris, 3rd neut., *mouth, face, countenance. Face, front,* indicating modesty or impudence. *Opening, entrance. Source* of a stream. "Gallica ora" =ora Gallicorum equorum. **frenis,** abl. (instrumental) plu. fr. frēnum, -i, more com. in plu. frēna, -orum (and heterog. freni, -orum), 2nd neut. in s., neut. and mas. in plu., *a bridle* including bit, head-piece and reins. **Meton.,** *a curb, restraint,* so plu. *limit, hindrance, check.*

Cur timet flavum Tiberim tangere? Cur olivum
Sanguine viperino
Cautius vitat neque jam livida gestat armis
Brachia, sæpe disco,
Sæpe trans finem jaculo nobilis expedito?
Quid latet, ut marinæ

224. **Cur** (218). **timet,** 3rd s. pres. ind. act fr. timeo (100). **flavum Tiberim** (49), gov. by tangere. **tangere,** pres. inf. (objective, 570) after timet; fr. tango, -ĕre, tĕtĭgi, tactum, 3rd trans., *to touch. Take away, carry off. Taste, eat, drink, To reach, arrive at* a place. Of places, *border on. To strike, beat,* merely poet. *To handle, take hold of.* Of feelings, mind, etc., *touch, move, affect.* Of speech, *mention, refer to.* **olivum,** acc. s. gov. by vitat; fr. olĭvum, -i, 2nd neut., (oliva, 91) *oil,* poet. and post-class. prose for oleum.

225. **Sanguine,** abl. (comparative, 103) s. after cautius; fr. sanguis, sanguĭnis, 3rd mas., only s., *blood. Consanguinity, descent, race, stock, family. Descendant, offspring. Vigour, strength, force. life.* **viperino,** abl. s. mas. ag. w. sanguine; fr. vīpĕrīnus, -a, -um, adj., *of a viper, serpent* or *snake* (1411).

226. **Cautius,** neut. compar. (used as adv. of caute) of cautus, -a, -um, adj., (caveo, 380) *careful, wary, provident. Sly, artful, cunning* (Hor.). Pass. *made safe;* fig., *secure, safe, e.g.,* urbes; adv., caute; (i.) *cautiously, carefully;* (ii.) *with security, with safety.* **vitat,** 3rd s. ind. pres. act. fr. vīto, -are, -avi, -atum, 1st trans. and intrans., *to shun, seek to escape, avoid, evade.* **neque** (32). **jam** (37). **livida,** acc. neut plu. predic. ag. w. brachia; fr. līvidus, -a, -um, adj., (liveo, *to be of a lead colour*) *of a leaden colour, bluish, blue* (1002), esp. fr. beating, bruising, etc., *black and blue;* here, w. the cæstus. *Looking black, envious, despiteful.* **armis,** abl. (instrumental) fr. arma, -orum, 2nd neut. plu. only (so bellaria, crepundia, cibaria, etc.), *body armour,* genly. defensive, also offensive [used only in close combat, opp. to tela]; *war implements, utensils;* here of quoit and javelin. **gestat,** 3rd s. pres. ind. act. fr. gesto, -are, -avi, -atum, 1st trans. (intens. of gero, 168); *to bear, carry, have* (795). Pass. *to be carried about, take the air* in a litter.

227. **Brachia,** acc. plu. gov. by gestat; fr. brachium (1182). **sæpe** (200). **disco,** abl. (of manner) s. w. nobilis; fr. discus, -i, 2nd mas. (Gk.), a round plate of stone or metal thrown from a player's hand.

228. **Sæpe** (200). **trans,** prep. gov. acc., *across, over, beyond, on the other side of,* w. vbs. of motion or rest. **finem,** acc. s. gov. by trans; fr finis (94). **jaculo,** abl. (of means) s. fr. jăcŭlum, -i, 2nd neut., *a missile, dart, javelin* (538); prop. neut. (und. telum) of jăcŭlus, -a, -um, adj., (jacio, *to throw*) *that is* or *may be thrown, cast, hurled.* **nobilis** (5), mas. ag. w. subj. (Sybaris) of gestat. **expedito,** abl. neut. s. pf. pass. part. ag. w. jaculo; fr. expĕdio, -īre, -īvi or -ii, -ītum, 4th trans., (ex, 691; pes, 135) *to extricate, disentangle, let loose;* pass. refl., *extricate oneself, get clear through. Deliver, release, Put in order, arrange.* Of speech, *disclose, narrate;* aliquid expedit, *is serviceable, profitable, advantageous. To fetch out, bring forward. To procure, make ready;* expedito goes w. disco and jaculo; here, *to send clear beyond* (W.).

229. **Quid,** neut. of quis (65, 149) as interrog. adv., *Why?* **latet,** 3rd s. pres. ind. act. fr. lăteo, -ēre, lătŭi, no sup., 2nd intrans., *to be,* or *lie hid, be concealed, buried in obscurity. To lurk, have a secret place. Be in*

Filium dicunt Thetidis sub lacrimosa Trojæ
Funera, ne virilis
Cultus in cædem et Lycias proriperet catervas?

CARMEN IX.—AD THALIARCHUM.

VIDES, ut alta stet nive candidum

safety, be sheltered. Escape notice, be unknown, intrans. or w. acc. **ut,** compar. (193). **marinæ,** gen. s. fem. ag. w.. Thetidis; fr. mărīnus, -a, -um, adj., (mare, 14) *of or belonging to the sea, sea.*

230. **Filium,** acc. subj. of latuisse und. fr. latet; fr. filius (79). **dicunt.** 3rd plu. pres. ind. act. fr. dico (85). **Thĕtĭdis,** gen. s. after filium; fr. Thĕtĭs, gen. -ĭdis or ĭdos (Gk.), abl. Thĕtĭdi and Thĕti, a sea nymph, mother of Achilles. **sub** (21), here w. acc. Of place, *under, below, beneath,* with verbs of motion. Of lofty objects to the foot of which or near which a thing comes, extends, etc., *close to, up to, towards.* Of time, *before, towards, about* (251). *After, immediately after, just upon.* **lacrimosa,** acc. plu. neut. ag. w. funera; fr. lăcrĭmōsus, -a, -um (lacrima, 1039), *abounding in tears, weeping much.* Physically, *causing tears, e.g.,* cepa (*onion*). *Mournful, e.g.,* bellum (533). **Trojæ,** gen. s. after funera; fr. Troja or Trōia, -æ, 1st fem., *Troy,* noted city of Phrygia.

231. **Funera,** acc. plu. gov. by sub; fr. fūnus, -ĕris, 3rd neut., *funeral procession, funeral rites, burial, funeral. Destruction, fall. Death,* esp. *violent death. Murder* (mostly poet.). **ne** (41), of neg. purpose. **virilis,** -e, adj., nom. mas. s. ag. w. vultus (vir, 215), *of or belonging to a man.* Of sex, *male, masculine. Manly, full grown, arrived at the age of manhood, e.g.,* toga, assumed at the age of sixteen. Of quality, *manly, manful, firm, vigorous, bold, spirited, e.g.,* animus.

232. **Cultus,** -us, 4th mas., nom. s. subj. of proriperet, (colo, 797) prop., *a labouring at, labour, care, cultivation.* Meton., *manner* or *style of living, refinement of life.* In good sense, *culture, civilization* (258). In bad sense, *luxury, wantonness,* esp. (concr.) *clothing, splendid dress* (here). *An educating, nursing, regard paid to* anything. *Honouring, reverence, e.g.,* deorum. *Improvement, refinement, e.g.,* animi. **in** (76, 81). **cædem,** acc. s. gov. by in; fr. cædes, -is, 3rd fem., (cædo, *to kill*) *a cutting* or *lopping off* (rare), *a casting down in death, slaughtering, murder,* sts. of animals sacrificed. **Lycias,** acc. fem. plu. ag. w. catervas; fr. Lўcius, -a, -um, adj., *Lycian.* **proriperet,** 3rd s. impf. subj. act. fr. prorĭpio, -rĭpĕre -rĭpui, -reptum, 3rd trans., (pro, *forward;* rapio, 489) *to snatch, drag, hurry forth.* With acc. of pers. pron., *to rush forth, hasten, hurry forth* or *away;* here pers. pron. omitted. It is subj. after ne final, impf. after pf. inf. lituisse und. **catervas,** acc. plu. jnd. by et to cædem; fr. căterva, -æ, 1st fem., *crowd, troop, band* of men, sing. and plu. Of soldiers, *company, troop,* esp. of barbarians opp. to Rom. legions. Of animals, *a flock,* "Lycias catervas," *i.e.,* followers of Sarpedon and Glaucus.

CARMEN IX. METRE.—*Alcaic.*

1st and 2nd. Greater Alcaic ⏓ – | ⏑ – | – || – ⏑ ⏑ | – ⏑ ⏓
3rd. Archilochian ⏓ – | ⏑ – | – – | ⏑ – | ⏓
4th. Lesser Alcaic – ⏑ ⏑ | – ⏑ ⏑ | – ⏑ | – ⏓

233. **Vides,** 2nd s. ind. pres. act. fr. video (49). **ut** (13), *how,* relative.

234 Soracte, nec jam sustineant onus
235 Silvæ laborantes, geluque
236 Flumina constiterint acuto.
237 Dissolve frigus, ligna super foco

alta, abl. fem. s. ag. w. nive; fr. altus (43). **stet,** 3rd s. pres. subj. act. fr. sto, stāre, stĕti, stătum, 1st irreg., intrans., *to stand still,* opp. to sitting or walking. *To stand firm* or *immovable, last, remain, continue. To tarry, linger* anywhere. Milit., *to stand in the ranks, stand one's ground.* Of ships, *to ride at anchor. To stand up, bristle with, be thick with.* Of a play, *to stand,* i.e., *please, take.* Of price, *to stand one in, cost;* pres. after vides; subj. in dependent clause after ut. **nive,** abl. (instrumental) s. w. candidum; fr. nix (37). **candidum,** nom. neut. s. predicative ag. w. Soracte; fr. candĭdus, -a, -um, adj., (candeo, 67) *glistening, dazzling, white, clear, bright,* opp. to niger (*glistening black*). Of a god or deified man (487). Of personal beauty, *fair, beautiful* (353); fig., *pure, clear, serene, clean, upright, frank, guileless,* etc., of character, disposition, etc. Of circumstances, *happy, prosperous, fortunate.*

234. **Soracte,** -is, 3rd neut. (collat. Soractis, -is, 3rd mas.), nom. subj. of stet, a high mountain on which was a temple of Apollo. **nec jam**=neque jam (226). **sustineant,** 3rd plu. pres. subj. act. fr. sustĭneo, -ēre, -ui, -tentum, 2nd trans., (sub, 21; teneo, 204) *to hold upright, uphold, bear up, support. To keep back, stay, hold in, restrain;* fig., *to uphold, maintain, e.g.,* causam publicam. *To bear, undergo, endure, withstand;* constr. as stet. **onus,** acc. s. gov. by sustineant; fr. ŏnus, -ĕris, 3rd neut., *a load, burden* of goods. *Baggage, lading, freight;* fig., *weight, charge, trouble.*

235. **Silvæ,** nom. plu. subj. of sustineant; fr. silva, -æ, 1st fem., *wood, forest, woodland, plantation, orchard, grove;* plu. *trees.* **laborantes,** nom. plu. fem. pres. part. act. ag. w. silvæ; fr. lăbōro, -are, -avi, -atum, 1st trans. and intrans., (labor, 124) *to toil, labour, work, take pains, exert oneself* physically or mentally. *To be fatigued, be troubled,* w. abl. etc.; *to be sick, be in pain. To act* or *move with difficulty, struggle, make efforts. To be anxious, very concerned;* milit., *to be hard pressed, be in great danger;* trans., (poet. and post-Aug.) *to make, produce with labour; bestow labour on.* **gelu,** abl. (instrumental) s. fr. gĕlu, -us, 4th neut., *icy coldness, frost, cold;* fig., *chill* of death, old age, etc. **-que** (4).

236. **Flumina,** nom. plu. subj. of constitĕrint; fr. flūmen, -ĭnis, 3rd neut., (fluo, *to flow*) *flood, stream, flowing water, river,* so fig. of other things *flowing in streams.* **constiterint,** 3rd plu. pf. subj. act.; fr. consto, -stāre, -stĭti, -stĭtum, 1st irreg. intrans., *to stand with* another. *Agree with, be consistent with.* Of facts, *to be established,* esp. constat, *it is allowed. To exist, be extant. To consist in* or *of, be composed of;* here "*are congealed.*" Subj. in depend. clause; pf. of what happened before the time of the main verb vides. **acuto,** abl. neut. s. ag. w. gelu; fr. ăcūtus, -a, -um, adj., (acuo, 57) *sharpened, made pointed. Sharply affecting the senses, sharp, piercing, acute* (of voice, etc.). *Clear sighted, intelligent.*

237. **Dissolve,** 2nd s. imper. pres. act. fr. dissolvo, -ĕre, -vi, -sŏlūtum, 3rd trans., (dis, 870; solvo, 129) *to loosen asunder, disunite, separate, dissolve, destroy.* Mercantile, *pay, discharge, settle, e.g.,* debts. Pass. (reflex.) *to free oneself. To abolish, abrogate, annul, destroy* (here). **frigus,** acc. s. gov. by dissolve; fr. frīgus, frīgŏris, 3rd neut., *cold, coldness. Cold weather, winter. Coldness of death, death. Shudder. Coolness* in demeanour, *indifference.* **ligna,** acc. plu. gov. by reponens; fr. lignum, -i, 2nd neut.

Large reponens, atque benignius
Deprome quadrimum Sabina,
O Thaliarche, merum diota.
Permitte Divis cetera, qui simul
Stravere ventos æquore fervido
Deprœliantes, nec cupressi

wood, firewood [materia, *timber for building*]. **super,** prep. gov. acc. and abl. With abl. of place or situation, *over, on top of, upon* (290). Of time, *during, in.* Of respect, reference, *upon, about, concerning, respecting* (rare in Cic. not in Cæs.). **foco,** abl. s. gov. by super; fr. fŏcus, -i, 2nd mas., (fŏveo, *to warm*) *a fireplace, hearth,* on which were placed in little niches the household gods (Lares) for whom a fire was kept up. *The house, family. An altar.*

238. **Large,** adv. of largus (1365), *abundantly, plentifully, bountifully.* Meton., *to a great degree, very much.* **reponens,** nom. mas. s. pres. part. (gerundial exp. manner) act. ag. w. tu und. in dissolve; fr. repōno, -pōnĕre, -pŏsui, -pŏsĭtum; pf. pass. repostus, metri. grat. in all hexameters, (re, 659; pono, 104) *to put back again, i.e.,* in its former place, *replace, restore.* Of virtue, *requite, return.* *To lay aside* or *away* for preservation, *store up, preserve, reserve* (273). *To lay aside, put away. To substitute* one thing *for* another. *To lay, place, put, set* a thing anywhere. *To count, reckon, e.g.,* in numero deorum. **atque** (37). **benignius,** compar. of benigne (benignus, 463), *in a friendly manner, kindly.* Meton., *abundantly, liberally, generously, willingly.* "Benigne facis" or "benigne" in thanking for something taken or refused. *You are very good. No, I thank you.*

239. **Deprome,** 2nd s. pres. imper. act. fr. depromo, -mĕre, -mpsi, -mptum, 3rd trans., (de, 10; promo, 774) *to draw out* or *forth. To bring, fetch from* a place (841); used of *bringing* wine from the store or "*drawing* it *off*" from a large vessel (W.). **quadrimum,** acc. neut. s. ag. w. merum; fr. qŭadrīmus, -a, -um, adj., (quatuor, *four*) *four years old.* **Sabina,** abl. fem. s. ag. w. diotâ; fr. Sābīnus, -a, -um, adj., *of the Sabines,* an ancient Italian people, part of whom, as early as Romulus, joined with the Romans under the name Quirites.

240. **O** (2). **Thaliarche,** voc. s. fr. Thălĭarchus, -i, fictitious name. **merum,** acc. s. gov. by deprome; fr. merum (203). **diota,** abl. (of separation) s. fr. dĭōta, -æ, 1st fem. (Gk.), *a two-handled vessel.*

241. **Permitte,** 2nd s. pres. imper. act. fr. permitto, -mittere, -mīsi, -missum, 3rd trans., (per, 114; mitto, 38) *to let through, suffer to pass through. To let go, let loose;* w. pers. pron., *to rush* or *spring, spread. To give up, yield, let go. To entrust, surrender, submit. To grant, allow, grant the choice of.* **Divis,** dat. plu. after (indirect obj. of) permitte; fr. Dīvus (61). **cetera,** acc. neut. plu. gov. by (direct obj. of) permitte; fr. cētĕrus, -a, -um, adj. s., very rare and never in nom., (akin to iterum, 374) *the other, i.e.,* that which exists besides, comes to, or can be added to what is already named of a like kind with it, *the other part;* plu. *the rest, the others* [reliquus, *what remains* of an obj.]. **qui** (3), mas. plu. ag. w. Divis, nom. subj. of stravere. **simul**=simulac (145).

242. **Stravere,** 3rd. plu. pf. ind. act. fr. sterno (22). **ventos,** acc. plu. gov. by stravere; fr. ventus (91). **æquore** (48), local. **fervido,** abl. neut. s. ag. w. æquore; fr. fervidus (4).

243. **Deprœliantes,** acc. plu. mas. ag. w. ventos; fr. deprœlians, -antis, *warring, violent,* pres. part. of obsol. deprœlior (de 10, exp. persistence;

244 Nec veteres agitantur orni.
245 Quid sit futurum cras, fuge quærere, et
246 Quem Fors dierum cunque dabit, lucro
247 Appone, nec dulces amores
248 Sperne peur neque tu choreas,
249 Donec virenti canities abest

prœlium, 181). **nec** (19). **cupressi,** nom. plu. subj. of agitantur; fr. cŭpressus, -i (nom. plu. also cўpărissi), abl. -o and -u, acc. plu. -os and -us. *The cypress* sacred to Pluto, used at funerals (1255).

244. **Veteres,** nom. fem. plu. ag. w. orni; fr. vetus (19). **agitantur,** 3rd plu. pres. ind. pass. fr. ăgĭto, -are, -avi, -atum, 1st trans. intens., (ago, 43) *to put* a thing *in motion, drive, impel, e.g.,* cattle, esp. of *violent motion,* caused by wind, etc. *To disturb, hunt, pursue* animals, etc.; fig., *rouse, excite, to drive* to some state, *e.g.,* in furias. *To assail* w. reproach, scoffs, etc., *mock. To occupy oneself with, be engaged in. Keep, celebrate.* Of life, time, etc., *to spend, to live.* With in mente, animo, etc., *to turn over,* also *to plot, devise, intend.* **orni,** nom. plu. subj. of agitantur; fr. ornus, -i, 2nd fem., *the wild mountain ash.*

245. **Quid,** nom. neut. s. subj. of sit; fr. quis (65). **sit,** 3rd. s. pres. subj. fr. sum (13). **futurum,** nom. neut. s. predic. ag. w. quid; fr. futurus (213); futurum sit, the fut. subj. (periphrastic, 542) of sum, subj. in indirect question. **cras** (216). **fuge,** 2nd s. imper. pres. act. fr. fugio (216). **quærere,** pres. inf. (objective) act. after fuge; fr. quæro (orig. quæso), -ĕre, quæsīvi or quæsii, -sītum, 3rd trans., *to seek* or *search for* a thing, esp. something missing, *to miss. To seek,* i.e., *think over, meditate, aim at, plan* a thing. *To get, obtain, procure. To seek to learn from* any one, *ask, enquire. To examine judicially, investigate* a thing. **et** (2).

246. **Quem...cunque,** acc. mas. s. ag. w. diem (und. fr. dierum), gov. by (direct obj. of) appone; fr. quicunque (167). **fors,** fortis, 3rd fem., nom. s. subj. of dabit; (fero, 138) *chance, hap, luck, hazard* (as appellative only nom. and acc.). *Goddess of chance;* fors used=fors sit, *it might occur, perhaps, perchance;* forte, *by chance, casually, accidentally,* usu. in conditional and causal sentences after si, nisi, ne. **dierum,** gen. (of thing distributed after quamcunque) plu. fr. dies (20). **dabit** (65). **lucro,** dat. s. after (indirect obj. of) appone; fr. lucrum, -i, 2nd neut., (luo, *to pay*) *gain, profit, advantage;* ponere, deputare in lucro, *to count as gain.*

247. **Appone,** 2nd s. imper. pres. act. fr. appōno, -ĕre, -pŏsui, -pŏsĭtum, 3rd trans., (ad, 6; pono 104) *to put, place, set beside* or *near* a person or thing. Of food, *to set before* one. *To put on* or *upon, apply. To appoint, assign* a person to any subject. *To put* a thing *down as, regard, deem, e.g.,* aliquid alicui rei (here). *To add to.* **nec** (19). **dulces,** acc. plu. mas. ag. w. amores; fr. dulcis (2). **amores,** acc. plu. gov. by sperne; fr. ămor, -ōris, 3rd mas., (amo, 86) *love* in good or bad sense. Of men or animals, *eager desire,' longing for. An object beloved* or *exciting desire;* "lucro appone," *set down as gain.*

248. **Sperne,** 2nd s. pres. imper. act. fr. sperno (21). **puer** (141), *whilst a boy,* in app. to tu und. in sperne. **neque** (32). **tu** (69), subj. of sperne und. **choreas,** acc. plu. gov. by sperne und. fr. chŏrēa, -æ, 1st fem., *a dance in a ring, dance* (genly. plu., 1417).

249. **Donec,** adv., denotes the relation of two actions to each other as regards time, (*a*) contemporaneously, *while, as long as, all the time that,* w. ind.

Morosa. Nunc et campus et areæ
  Lenesque sub noctem susurri
    Composita repetantur hora,
Nunc et latentis proditor intimo
Gratus puellæ risus ab angulo

pres., impf., pf., fut.; tense in both clauses usu. the same, (*b*) in immediate succession, so that with the commencement of one action the other ceases *till, until*, w. ind. in oratio recta of a simple fact, w. subj. pres. or impf. where purpose, expectation, etc. involved. **virenti,** dat. mas. s. pres. part. act. ag. w. tibi und. after abest; fr. vĭreo, -ēre, no pf., no sup., 2nd intrans., *to be green, verdant*; fig., *to be fresh, lively, vigorous, flourish, bloom.* **cānĭties,** -ei, 5th fem., acc. -em, abl. -e (no other cases found), *grayish or grayish white colour, hoariness*; concr. *gray hair, old age* (here, and 1148). **abest** (796).

250. **Morosa,** nom. fem. s. ag. w. canities; fr. mōrōsus, -a, -um, adj., (abounding in mos, 260, *self will*) good sense, *full of resolute attention, fastidious, scrupulous, careful*; bad sense, *self willed, wayward, capricious, fretful, sour.* **nunc** (21). **et...et** (2). **campus** (195), one member of subj. of repetantur. **areæ,** nom. plu. jnd. by et to campus; fr. area (10), here *open spaces*, esp. round temples (W.).

251. **Lenes,** nom. plu. mas. ag. w. susurri; fr. lenis (22). **sub** (230). **noctem,** acc. s. gov. by sub; fr. nox (144). **susurri,** nom. plu. jnd. by -que to areæ; fr. sŭsurrus, -i, 2nd mas., *a low gentle noise, humming, murmuring, muttering, whispering*, etc.

252. **Compositâ,** abl. fem. s. pf. pass. part. ag. w. horâ; fr. compōno, -pōnere, -pŏsui, -pŏsĭtum, 3rd irreg. trans., (cum, 31; pono, 104) *to put together into a whole, join together, unite, connect, form,* i.e., *make by joining together. To put in order, set right, adjust, arrange. To put something in order for laying by,* i.e., *keep, preserve, lay up. To compose, write, contrive* something, *feign, invent. To agree together, settle. To compose, calm. To adjust* one thing *to* another; *match against, bring into contact with, compare with.* **repetantur,** 3rd plu. pres. conj. (hortative) pass. fr. rĕpĕto, -ĕre, -īvi, or -ii, -ītum, 3rd trans., (re-, 659; peto, 126) *to seek again, go back to, return to, revisit, To fetch back, take back. To undertake again, resume, renew. To repeat* an action, speech, etc. (here). In discourse, *deduce, derive. To demand back again, e.g.,* fr. the enemy. **hora,** abl. (temporal) s. fr. hōra, -æ, 1st fem., (Gk.) *an hour* of varying length acc. to time of the year, there being 12 between sunrise and sunset; "hora natalis" (1339), *the hour of one's birth;* "in horam or horas" (1206), poet. *time, time of year, season* (1312).

253. **Nunc** (21). **et** (139), *also.* **latentis,** gen. fem. s. pres. part. act. ag. w. puellæ; fr. lateo (229). **prodĭtor,** -ōris, 3rd mas. s. in app. to risus, (prōdo, 1075) *betrayer, traitor, treacherous, betraying* (here). **intimo,** abl. mas. s. ag. w. angulo; fr. intĭmus, -a, -um, superl. adj., comp. intĕrior, (intra, 1115), *innermost, inmost*; as a part. attrib. *innermost part of* a thing; fig., *deepest, excessive, intense, immense.* Of mind, feelings, counsels, etc., *inmost, most secret; most deeply seated, most profound.* Of persons, *most intimate, closely related* or *attached.*

254. **Gratus** (129), nom. mas. s. ag. w. risus. **puellæ,** gen. s. after risus; fr. puella, 1st fem., *a female child, girl, maiden, lass* (1013), esp. *daughter. Sweetheart, mistress. Young wife.* **risus,** -us, 4th mas., nom. subj. of repetatur und. fr. prec.; (rideo, 69) *a laughing, laughter, laugh.* **ab** (a before consonants), prep. gov. abl. Of place, motion *from,* distance

255 Pignusque depretum lacertis
256 Aut digito male pertinaci.

CARMEN X.—AD MERCURIUM.

257 MERCURI, facunde nepos Atlantis,
258 Qui feros cultus hominum recentum
259 Voce formasti catus et decoræ

from; position, *in regard to, on the side of.* Of time, *from.* Of rank, *after.* Of separation, origin, etc., *from.* Of the agent after pass. and intrans. vbs., *by.* Of respect, *to, in front of, on the side of.* **angulo,** abl. s. gov. by ab.; fr. angŭlus, -i, 2nd mas., *angle, corner, e.g.,* occulorum. *A secret place, nook, lurking place* (1030).

255. **Pignus,** -ŏris and -ĕris, 3rd neut.; nom. s. jnd. by -que to risus, (pango, *to fasten*) orig., *that which binds* or *fastens. Pledge, gage, pawn, security, mortgage;* fig., *pledge, token, assurance, proof. Object of a wager, wager, stake.* **dereptum,** nom. neut. s. pf. pass. part. ag. w. pignus; fr. dērĭpio, -rĭpere, -rĭpŭi, -reptum, 3rd trans., (de, 10; rapio, 489) *to tear off, tear away, pull down.* **lacertis,** abl. (of separation) plu. after dereptum; fr. lăcertus, -i, 2nd mas., prop. *the upper part of the arm,* then *the arm. Muscular power, vigour, might* [brachium, *forearm* between elbow and wrist].

256. **Aut** (131). **digĭto,** abl. s. jnd. by aut to lacertis; fr. dĭgĭtus, -i, 2nd mas., (dic- rt. in dico, *that which points*) *a finger, a toe.* **mălĕ,** adv. of mālus (116), *badly, wickedly, in an evil way. Not well;* (*a*) intensifies anything bad in itself, *exceedingly, very much, e.g.,* male odi; (*b*) gives a contrary meaning to words having per se a good force, *un-, -not, mis-, e.g.,* male fidus. *Injuriously, hurtfully, mischievously. Unfortunately, adversely, calamitously;* here, *faintly* resisting or *wickedly, i.e.,* coquettishly, *i.e.,* so as to invite the violence. **pertinaci,** abl. mas. s. ag. w. digito; fr. pertĭnax, -ācis, adj., (per, 114; tenax, verb. adj. ak to teneo, 204) *that holds very fast, that clings very firmly, very tenacious.* Of duration, *that lasts, continues for a very long time;* good sense, *firm, steadfast, persevering;* bad sense, *obstinate, stubborn.*

CARMEN X. METRE—*Lesser Sapphic,* as in Carm. II.

257. **Mercuri,** voc. s. fr. Mercŭrĭus, -ii, 2nd mas., (merx, *gain*) son of Jupiter and Maia, god of eloquence, gain, merchandise, traders, and thieves, etc. **facunde,** voc. mas. s. ag. w. nepos; fr. făcundus, -a, -um, adj., (fari, *to speak*) *speaking with ease, eloquent* (post-Aug. chiefly). **nepos,** voc. s. in app. to Mercuri; fr. nepos (71). **Atlantis,** gen. s. after nepos; fr. Atlas, -antis, 3rd mas., a king of Mauretania, son of Jupiter and Clymene, lover of astronomy, said to have been changed by Perseus with the aid of Medusa's head into Mt. Atlas in Africa.

258. **Qui** (19), mas. s. 2nd pers. ag. w. Mercuri; nom. subj. to formasti. **feros,** acc. plu. mas. ag. w. cultus; fr. fĕrus, -a, -um, adj., *wild,* of animals and plants. Of places, *uncultivated;* fig., *rude, savage, barbarous, cruel* (1165). **cultus,** acc. plu. gov. by formasti; fr. cultus (232). **hominum,** gen. plu. after cultus; fr. homo (123). **recentum,** gen. plu. mas. ag. w. hominum; fr. recens (806); here, "*newly created*" (W.).

259. **Voce,** abl. (instrumental) s. fr. vox, vōcis, 3rd fem., (voco, 61) *a voice, sound, tone, cry, call;* meton., *what is uttered by the voice, word, say-*

More palæstræ,
Te canam, magni Jovis et Deorum
Nuntium curvæque lyræ parentem,
Callidum, quidquid placuit, jocoso

ing, speech, sentence, proverb, s. and plu. (937). *Speech, language* in general=sermo; here, *by the gift of language.* **formasti,** 2nd s. pf. ind. act., syncopated for formavisti; fr. formo, -are, -avi, -atum, 1st trans., (forma, 755) *to shape, fashion,* esp. in a fig. sense, *dispose, regulate, direct, compose.* **cătus,** -a, -um, adj., nom. mas. s. ag. w. tu und. in formasti; (Sabine for acūtus), *operating acutely on the hearing, clear-sounding.* Of intellectual objects; (*a*) good sense, *clear sighted, intelligent, sagacious, wise,* opp. to stultus; (*b*) bad sense, *sly, cunning, artful*=callidus. **et** (2). **decoræ,** gen. s. fem. ag. palæstræ; fr. dĕcōrus, -a, -um, adj., (decor, 1146) *that befits a person, is becoming, suitable* to him. *Becoming, fitting, seemly, proper. Decorated, ornamented, adorned, beautiful, handsome,* here, *grace-giving* (W.).

260. **More,** abl. (of means) s. fr. mos, mōris, 3rd mas., *will* of a person. *Self-will, humour, caprice. Usage, custom, practice, rule;* more, in more, ad morem, *in* or *after the manner of.* Plu. morally, *character, conduct, manners, behaviour. Law, precept, rule. Quality, nature, properties, e.g.,* cæli (Verg.). **palæstræ,** gen. s. after more; fr. pălæstra, -æ, 1st fem., *wrestling school, place for gymnastic exercises. Wrestling* in the palæstra. *Exercise of wrestling. Exercise in the School of Rhetoric.*

261. **Te** (83), gov. by canam. **canam,** 1st s. fut. ind. act. fr căno, -ere, cĕcĭni, sup. and fut. part. not used, 3rd trans., *to utter melodious notes, sing, play. To make some one* the subject *of singing, playing,* etc. *To rehearse, recite,* w. cogn. acc. of song. *To predict, prophesy.* **magni,** gen. s. mas. ag. w. Jovis; fr. magnus (85). **Jovis,** gen. s. after nuntium; fr. Jupiter (25). **Deorum,** gen. plu. jnd. by et to Jovis; fr. Deus (16).

262. **Nuntium,** acc. s. in app. to te; fr. nuntius, -ii, 2nd mas., (novus, 42) *a bearer of intelligence or news, messenger;* meton., *message, news, tidings. Command, injunction;* neut. nuntium, -ii, *a thing that brings tidings.* **curvæ,** gen. s. fem. ag. w. lyræ; fr. curvus, -a, -um, adj., *crooked, curved, bent* (merely poet); fig., moral sense, *not straightforward, not right* (Hor.). **lyræ** (174), after parentem. **parentem,** acc. s. jnd. by -que to nuntium; fr. parens (59).

263. **Callidum,** acc. mas. s. ag. w. te; fr. callĭdus, -a, -um, adj., (calleo, *to be skilled*) *that is taught, used by experience* and *practice, shrewd, expert, worldly wise, skilled. Ingenious, dexterous, skilful* (class.); bad sense, *crafty, cunning, artful, sly.* Of things, *well wrought, cunning, artful.* **quidquid** (10), gov. by condere und. w. placuit; fr. quisquis, neut. quod-quod, quicquid, quidquid, acc. quemquem; abl. quoquo, *e.g.,* w. tempore, modo; fem. quâquâ; plu. quiqui; pron. indef., *whatever, whatsoever* (1201). With gen. distributive (901); neut. as adv., *how much soever;* subst. mas. *whoever, whosoever, every one who, all who;* neut. *whatever thing;* as subst. mas. *any one whatever;* neut. *anything whatever.* **placuit,** 3rd s. pf. ind. (impers.), fr. plăcĕo, -cēre, pf. plăcŭi and placitus sum, sup. placĭtum, 2nd intrans., (intr. of placo, *to appease*) *to be pleasing* or *agreeable, be welcome* or *acceptable, find favour, give satisfaction;* placet or placitum est w. dat., *e.g.,* mihi, tibi, sibi=*I, thou,* etc., *am of opinion,* etc.; polit., *to be resolved upon, determined, willed, ordered.* **jocoso,** abl. s. neut. ag. w. furto; fr. jŏcōsus, -a, -um, adj., (jocus, 70) *full of joking, humorous, facetious, sportive.*

Condere furto.
Te, boves olim nisi reddidisses
Per dolum amotas, puerum minaci
Voce dum terret, viduus pharetra
Risit Apollo.
Quin et Atridas duce te superbos

264. **Condere,** pres. inf. (prolative, 570) after callidum; fr. condo, -dĕre, -dĭdi, -dĭtum, 3rd trans. irreg., (cum, 31; do, 55) *to bring, lay, put together. To set up, join together, form by putting together, establish. To put away, lay by, store up. To compose, write. To conceal.* **furto,** abl. (of means) s. fr. furtum, -i, 2nd neut., (furor, *to steal*) act. *theft;* pass. *a stolen thing;* meton., *secret action, trick, crafty deceit. Stolen, secret love,* merely plu.

265. **Te** (85), gov. by terret. **boves,** acc. plu. gov. by reddidisses; fr. bōs, bōvis, gen. plu. boum (rarely bovum), dat. plu. bobus, much more com. būbus 3rd com. genly mas., (*lowing, bellowing*), *an ox* or *cow.* **olim** (olle, old fm. of ille, 9), adv. of time, *at that time,* hence; (i.) past, *some time ago, formerly. In time past, once,* here=when a boy. Of future, *at some time* or *other; in time to come, hereafter;* "nunc...olim," *now...hereafter* (1133). (ii.) *Now for a long time, this good while, long ago* (post-Aug.). In interrog. and conditional clauses, *at any time, ever.* Of something that is *wont* to take place, *at times, sometimes, ofttimes.* **nisi,** conj. (ni=ne, not; si, 7), *if not, unless.* After interrog. and neg. or w. neg. follg., *except, save only.* After nihil aliud, quid aliud, *save, but, than;* nisi si, *except if, unless;* nisi quod, *except that;* "nisi forte," *except perhaps.* **reddidisses,** 2nd s. plpf. subj. act. fr. reddo, -ere, -dĭdi, -dĭtum, 3rd irreg. trans., (re-, 659; do, 65) *to give back, restore, return;* meton., *to give up, hand over, e.g.,* a letter. *To render, yield, give, pay. To surrender, e.g.,* vitam. Of sound, *to yield, put forth. To grant, bestow, e.g.,* veniam. *To repeat, declare, report, narrate. To return in answer, e.g.,* voces. *To represent, imitate, express, e.g.,* vultum. W. two accs., *to render, cause* a thing *to be* something. The plpf. subj. in oratio obliqua, where the fut. pf. would be in oratio recta. Apollo would have said, "nisi reddideris," the apodosis being implied in minaci.

266. **Per** (114). **dolum,** acc. s. gov. by per; fr. dolus (130). **amotas,** acc. plu. fem pf. pass. part. ag. w. boves; fr. āmŏveo, -ēre, -mōvi, -mōtum, 2nd trans., (a or ab, 254; moveo, 394) *to remove from* a place, *remove,* etc.; w. acc. pers. pron., *take oneself off, retire;* fig., *to get rid off.* **puerum,** acc. s. in app. to te; fr. puer (149). **minaci,** abl. s. fem. ag. w. voce; fr. mĭnax, -acis, adj., (minor, 673) *projecting, jutting out, overhanging* (poet.). *Full of threats* or *menaces.*

267. **Voce** (259), of means. **dum** (53). **terret,** 3rd s. ind. pres. act. fr. terreo (40); here, *is trying to terrify,* historical present. **viduus,** -a, -um, adj., nom. mas. s. ag. w. Apollo, (vid- rt. in di-vid-o, 399) *deprived, bereft of, without* anything, *bereaved. Widowed, i.e.,* without husband or wife; vĭdŭa, -æ, 1st fem., *a widow* or *unmarried, single girl.* Of trees, *without vines* (Hor.). **pharetra,** abl. (of separation) s. after vĭdŭus; fr. phăretra, -æ, 1st fem., *a quiver.*

268. **Risit,** 3rd s. perf. ind. act. fr. rideo (69) "viduus risit," *laughed to find himself robbed* (W.). **Apollo** (68), subj. of risit.

269. **Quin** (qui, old abl. of rel. pron.; -ne=non), conj. (i.) Relative, (*a*)=qui non, *that not, but that,* after words exp. doubt or ignorance; facere non possum quin, *I cannot but;* (*b*)=qui, quæ, quod non. (ii.) Corroborative,

Ilio dives Priamus relicto
Thessalosque ignes et iniqua Trojæ
Castra fefellit.
Tu pias lætis animas reponis
Sedibus virgaque levem coërces

but, indeed, really, of a truth; quin etaim or immo, *yea indeed, yea rather.* (iii.) Interrogative or hortatory, *why not? wherefore not?* w. ind. or imper. rare w. subj. **et** (139). **Atridas,** acc. plu. gov. by fefellit; fr. Atrīdes, -æ, 1st mas., (Gk. patronymic) a male descendant of Atreus, here Agamemnon and Menelaus. **duce te** (88). **superbos,** acc. plu. mas. ag. w. Atridas; fr. sŭperbus, -a, -um, adj., (super, 237) *that is* or *thinks himself above* others; *haughty, proud, arrogant, insolent;* in good sense, *excellent, distinguished, splendid.*

270. **Ilio,** abl. absol. (824) s. fr. Ilium, -ii, 2nd neut.; poet. for Troy. **dives** (193), nom. mas. s. ag. w. Priamus, ref. to the presents he was taking with him. **Priamus,** -i, s. nom. subj. of fefellit; *Priam* son of Laomedon, king of Troy, father of Hector. **relicto,** abl. neut. s. pf. pass. part. ag. w. Ilio; fr. relinquo, -quĕre, relīqui, relictum, 3rd trans., (re-, 659; linquo, *to leave*) *to leave behind* by removing one's self; lit. and fig., esp. *to leave behind* at death. *To bequeath, leave as a legacy. To leave remaining, let remain* (1262). With two accs. *to leave behind, allow to be* in a particular state. *To go away from* (here), esp. *leave in the lurch, forsake, give up* (1050); fig., *neglect. To resign, relinquish.*

271. **Thessalos,** acc. plu. mas. ag. w. ignes; fr. Thessalus (188). **ignes,** acc. plu. jnd. by -que to Atridas; fr. ignis (116). **iniqua,** acc. neut. plu. ag. w. castra; fr. inīquus, -a, -um, adj., (in neg. æquus, 141) *uneven, not level, steep. Not equal to* a required standard, *too great* or *too small.* Of place, *unfavourable.* Of time, *inconvenient.* Of feelings, etc., *unkind, hostile.* Of circumstances, *hapless, unpropitious. Unfair, unjust* (1025). *Not calm, not composed, discontented.* **Trojæ,** dat. s. after traject. (873) iniqua; fr. Troja (230).

272. **Castra,** acc. plu. gov. by fefellit; fr. castrum (23). **fefellit,** 3rd s. pf. ind. act. fr. fallo, -ĕre, fefelli, falsum, 3rd trans., *to deceive, trick, dupe, cheat;* me fallit, *I am mistaken. To imitate deceitfully* (rare). *To swear falsely by* (Hor.). *To be concealed from, escape the notice of;* genly. impers. fallit me, *it is unknown to me* (genly. with negs. or neg. interrogs.). *To beguile, lighten, cause to pass away imperceptibly* of time or anything disagreeable.

273. **Tu** (69), subj. of reponis. **pias,** acc. plu. fem. ag. w. animas; fr. pius, pia, pium, adj., *pious, devout,* in ref. to gods. *Affectionate, dutiful, tender, kind,* in ref. to parents. *Legal, patriotic,* in ref. to country. *Benevolent, kind, gentle.* Of things, *sacred, holy.* Comp. magis pius, superl. piissimus, used by Antony, condemned by Cic., frequ. post-Aug. **lætis,** abl. plu. fem. ag. w. sedibus; fr. lætus (82). **animas,** acc. plu. gov. by reponis; fr. anima (96). **reponis,** 2nd s. pres. ind. act. fr. repono (238). This refers to Mercury's functions as conductor of the dead, "*place in their distant home*" (M.).

274. **Sedibus,** abl. plu. (local) w. reponis; fr. sedes (46). **virga,** abl. (instrumental) s. fr. virga, -æ, 1st fem., (vireo, 249) a slender *green branch, twig, sprout, switch, rod,* esp. rods in the fasces used for flogging. **levem,** acc. fem. s. ag. w. turbam; fr. levis (31). **coerces,** 2nd s. pres. ind. act. jnd. by -que to reponis; fr. coerceo, -ēre, -ŭi, -ĭtum, 2nd trans., (cum, 31;

Aurea turbam, superis Deorum
Gratus et imis.

CARMEN XI.—AD LEUCONOEN.

Tu ne quæsieris, scire nefas, quem mihi, quem tibi
Finem Dî dederint, Leuconoë, nec Babylonios
Tentaris numeros. Ut melius, quidquid erit, pati!

arceo, *to shut up, enclose*) *to enclose* something *wholly, hold together, surround by enclosing* (1411). *To restrain, confine, hold in confinement* (1390). Of speech, *to keep within limits, confine, restrain.* Of persons, faults, passions, etc., *check, curb, restrain.*

275. **Aurea** (157), ag. w. virga. **turbam,** acc. s. gov. by coerces; fr. turba (7); "levis turba," *shadowy throng,* distinct from piæ animæ (W.). **superis** (30), after trajective (873) gratus. **Deorum** (261), distributive after superis.

276. **Gratus** (254), ag. w. tu. **imis,** dat plu. mas. jnd. by et to superis; fr. īmus, -a, -um, contr. for infĭmus, superl. adj., *nethermost, deepest, lowest;* compar. infĕrior, posit. infĕrus only in "inferum mare." The posit. prep. is infra, cf. summus, intimus, etc.

CARMEN XI. METRE—*Second Asclepiad.*

– – | – ∪ ∪ – | – ∪ ∪ – | – ∪ ∪ – | ∪ ⏓

277. **Tu** (69), subj. of quæsieris. **ne** (41), here in prohibitions. **quæsieris,** 2nd s. pf. conj. act. fr. quæro (245), more usu. than pres. conj. or imperat. in prohibitions in 2nd pers. **scire,** pres. inf. act. subj. to est und.; fr. scio, scīre, scīvi or scii, sup. scītum, 4th trans. and intrans., *to know,* (in its widest sense) *understand, perceive. To have knowledge* or *skill in* anything=intelligo, sentio, video. **nefas** (114), predicative. **quem** (61), ag. w. finem. **mihi,** dat. s. fr. ego (29). **tibi** (93); both after (dat. commodi, indirect obj. of) dederint.

278. **Finem** (238), gov. by (direct obj. of) dederint. **Di,** nom. plu. subj. of dederint; fr. deus (6). **dederint,** 3rd plu. pf. subj. act. fr. do, (65) pf. of time, antecedent to quæsieris; subj. in indirect question. **Leuconoë,** voc. (Gk.), a fictitious name. **nec** (19). **Babylonios,** acc. plu. mas. ag. w. numeros; fr. Băbȳlōnĭus, -a, -um, adj., *pertaining to Babylon;* here= *Chaldean, i.e.,* of astrology.

279. **Tentaris,** syncopated for tentaveris, 2nd s. pf. conj. act. jnd. by nec to quæsieris; fr. tento (-mpt-) -āre, -āvi, -ātum, 1st trans., (intensive of tendo, 34) *to handle, touch, feel* a thing. *To try the strength of, make an attempt on,* i.e., *attack, assail. To prove, put to the test. To attempt, essay* a course of action, etc. *To try to influence, e.g.,* by prayers. *To try* in a friendly or hostile way. *To tamper with. To excite, disquiet, disturb.* **numeros,** acc. plu. gov. by tentaris; fr. nŭmĕrus, -i, 2nd mas., *a number. A body, collection, mass* of persons or things; sts. with access. notion of greatness, *great number;* numeri, *mathematics, astronomy, tables, calculations;* fig., *place, rank, position, estimation* (934). *A part* of a whole *number.* Music and poetry, *a measure, number, rhythm, time, harmony.* **Ut** (13), in exclamations. *How!* **melius** (58), here nom. neut. predic. ag. w pati; "ut melius," *how much better.* **quidquid** (10), subj. of erit. **erit,** 3rd s. fut. ind. fr. sum (3). **pati** (18), subjective.

Seu plures hiemes seu tribuit Jupiter ultimam,
Quæ nunc oppositis debilitat pumicibus mare
Tyrrhenum, sapias, vina liques et spatio brevi
Spem longam reseces. Dum loquimur, fugerit invida

280. **Seu...seu** (27). **plures,** acc. plu. fem. ag. w. hiemes; fr. plus, gen. pluris, compar. adj. of multus (23). **hiemes,** acc. plu. gov. by tribuit; fr. hiems (129). **tribuit,** 3rd s. pf. ind. act. fr. trĭbuo, -ŭere, -ŭi, -ūtum, 3rd trans., (to give to a tribus) *to assign, impart, bestow, give,* aliquid alicui; fig., *grant, give, show, pay, render. To yield, give up, concede, e.g.,* aliquid voluptati. *To ascribe, attribute* a thing to a person or thing as cause. With in and acc., *to divide, distribute.* **Jupiter** (66), subj. of tribuit. **ultimam,** acc. fem. s. dependent predicate or complemental acc., ag. w. hanc und. after tribuit; fr. ultimus, -a, -um, adj. (superl. fr. posit. ulter, *that is beyond,* found only in adv. ultro and ultra). Of space, *the most distant, most remote* (820, 1356, 1442), esp. as partitive attribute *the farthest, most distant part* of a thing. Of time or order of succession, *the remotest, earliest, oldest, first. Last, latest.* Of rank, *the highest* or *lowest* condition. *The utmost, extreme, highest.*

281. **Quæ** (46), fem. s. ag. w. hanc und. after tribuit; nom. subj. to debilitat. **nunc** (21). **oppositis,** abl. plu. mas. pf. pass. part. ag. w. pumicibus; fr. oppono, -ĕre, -pŏsŭi, -pŏsĭtum, 3rd trans., (ob, *over against;* pono, 104), *to set* or *place against, before* or *opposite;* esp. milit., *to station* troops against. *To bring forward, adduce, allege* as accusation, proof, threat, etc. *To oppose* by way of comparison. *To expose to,* aliquid alicui. **dēbĭlĭtat,** 3rd s. pres. ind. act. fr. dēbĭlĭto, -are, -avi, -atum, 1st trans., (debĭlis, *enfeebled*) *to lame, maim, cripple, weaken;* here *breaks the force of, i.e.,* beats the waves on the rocks till they are tired; fig., *enervate, crush.* **pumicibus,** abl. (instrumental) plu. fr. pūmex, -ĭcis, 3rd mas., *a pumice stone* used for smoothing books, etc.; meton., *soft stone, porous rock* of any kind. **mare** (14), gov. by debilitat.

282. **Tyrrhenum,** acc. neut. s. ag. w. mare; fr. Tyrrhēnus, -a, -um, adj., *Etruscan* or *Tuscan.* **sapias,** 2nd s. conj. (hortative introd. apodosis after seu) act. fr. săpĭo, sapĕre, pf. sapīvi or -ii, no sup., 3rd intrans. Of eatables and drinkables, *to taste, savour, e.g.,* oleum male sapit; trans., *to have a taste* or *flavour* of, w. acc.; fig., *to have good taste, i.e.,* discernment. *To be sensible, discreet, prudent, wise* (genly. in pass.), trans., *to know, understand* a thing. **vina,** acc. plu. gov. by liques; fr. vinum (146). **liques,** 2nd s. pres. conj. (hortative) fr. lĭquo, -are, -avi, -atum, 1st trans., *to make liquid, melt, dissolve;* meton., *strain, filter, clarify.* **et** (2). **spatio,** abl. (of means) s. fr. spătĭum, -ii, 2nd neut., (pateo, *to lie open*) *room, space,* esp. *distance, interval* (limited). *Size, bulk. An open space* for walking, racing, etc., *promenade, race-course.* Of time, *interval, period,* (here) esp. of time in which to do anything, *leisure, opportunity,* w. gen. of gerund or ad w. acc. gerund. *Path, course, race-track.* **brevi,** abl. neut. s. ag. w. spatio; fr. brevis (143); spatio brevi, *by the thought of the little span of* (W.).

283. **Spem** (143), gov. by reseces. **longam** (143), ag. w. spem. **reseces,** 2nd. s. pres. conj. act. ind. by et to liques; fr. rĕsĕco, -āre, -cui, -ctum, 1st trans. irreg., (re-, 659; seco, 14) *to cut loose, cut off. To curtail, check, restrain.* **dum** (53). **loquimur,** 1st plu. pres. ind. fr. lŏquor, lŏqui, lŏcūtus sum, 3rd dep. trans., *to speak, talk* in ordinary colloquial language, *say, tell, utter, mention, name. To speak of, talk about.* **fugerit,** 3rd s. fut. pf. fr. fugio (206), more

284 Ætas. Carpe diem quam minimum credula postero.

CARMEN XII.—AD AUGUSTUM.

285 Quem virum aut heroa lyra vel acri
286 Tibia sumis celebrare, Clio?

emphatic than fut. simple. **invida,** nom. fem. s. ag. w. ætas; fr. invĭdus, -a, -um, adj., (invideo, 615) *envious;* w. obj. gen. of person or thing, *envious of.*

284. **Ætas,** -ātis, 3rd fem.; nom. s. subj. of fugerit; (contr. for ævitas, fr. ævum, 329) *the period of life, lifetime,* esp. *life* of man. *A space of time, age, generation. The time* or *period of life* for *the man himself,* or *the age* fr. *the people living* in it. **carpe,** 2nd s. imper. pres. act. fr. carpo, -pĕre, -psi, -ptum, 3rd trans., *to pick, pluck off, crop, gather, cull* of plants, flowers, etc. Of animals, *to take as nourishment, crop, graze on;* poet., *tear off, tear away. To cull, enjoy, make use of, live upon. To gnaw with envious tooth, carp at, slander. To deprive of strength, weaken, wear away, consume.* With viam, iter or def. local subst., *to tread, pass over, navigate, sail over,* etc. **diem,** acc. s. gov. by carpe; fr. dies (20). **quam,** adv., (acc. fem. of qui, 3) *in what manner, how much, as much as;* quam cupiunt laudari! esp. augmentative w. superl. and possum or superl. alone, *e.g.,* quam mollissime, or w. possunt, "*as gently as they can.*" In comparisons *as,* w. or without corresp. tam. With superl. and follg. tam, *by how much the more...the more;* alius...quam, *other ..than;* aliter .quam, *otherwise...than.* **minimum,** neut. s. used as adv. fr. mĭnĭmus, -a, -um, superl. of parvus (1293), *very little, very slightly, not at all;* non minimum, *chiefly, particularly, especially.* **credula,** nom. fem. s. ag. w. tu und. in carpe; fr. credulus (157). **postero,** dat. mas. s. ag. w. diei und. after credula (trajective, 873), fr. postĕrus, -a, -um, adj., *coming after, following, next, ensuing, future;* comp. posterior, -ius, *that comes* or *follows after, next* in time or place. *Latter, later, e.g.,* cogitationes, *after thoughts;* superl. postumus and postrēmus, *the hindmost, the last;* also used esp. of the youngest child born after the father's death.

CARM. XII METRE—*The Lesser Sapphic.* (Carmen II.).

285. **Quem** (61), ag. w virum. **virum,** acc. s. gov. by sumis; fr. vir (215). **aut** (131). **heroa,** acc. s. jnd. by aut to virum; fr. hēros, -ōis, (Gk.) 3rd mas., *a demigod, hero.* **lyra,** abl. (instrumental) s. w. celebrare; fr. lyra (174). **vel** (187). **acri,** abl. s. fem. ag. w. tibia; fr. acer (75).

286. **Tibia,** abl. (instrumental) s, fr. tibia (32). **sumis,** 2nd. s. ind. pres. act. fr. sūmo, -ĕre, sumpsi, sumptum, 3rd trans., (sub, 21; emo, *to buy*) *to take, take up, lay hold of, assume,* esp. *take by choice, assume, select. To take* as one's own, *appropriate to oneself, assume, arrogate. To take* for some purpose, i.e., *use, employ, spend. To take for granted, assume, maintain, affirm. To bring forward, cite, mention* as proof. *To take as a purchase, buy.* **celebrare,** pres. inf. (prolative, exp. purpose, 570) after sumis; fr. cĕlĕbro, -are, -avi, -atum, 1st trans., (celeber, 1184) *to resort, go in great numbers, frequent. To do* something *frequently* or *in numbers, engage in, say, use, employ, repeat* (class.). *To fill up* with something, *e.g.,* ripas carmine. *To solemnise, keep* a festival, *e.g.,* festos dies. *To honour, praise, celebrate the praises of* in song. *To make known, publish.* **Clio,** us (Gk.), fem., voc. s., the Muse of History.

287 Quem Deum? Cujus recinet jocosa
288 Nomen imago
289 Aut in umbrosis Heliconis oris
290 Aut super Pindo, gelidove in Hæmo?
291 Unde vocalem temere insecutæ
292 Orphea silvæ

287. **Quem** (61), ag. w. Deum. **Deum,** acc. s. gov. by sumis und.; fr. Deus (6) **cujus,** mas. s. ag. w. Deum, gen. after nomen; fr. qui (3). **recinet,** 3rd s. fut. ind. act. fr. recĭno, -ĕre, no pf., no sup., 3rd trans. and intrans., (re, 659; cano, 261) *to sing again,* hence *to resound, re-echo, set forth again. To repeat. To praise, celebrate in song.* **jocosa,** nom. sing. fem. ag. w. imago; fr. jocosŭs (263); jŏcosa imago, "*mocking echo*" (M.).

288. **Nomen,** acc. s. gov. by recinet; fr. nōmen, -ĭnis, 3rd neut., (nosco, 511) *a name, appellation,* esp. the middle name which every freeborn Roman had, which distinguished one gens. fr. another. *Race, family, i.e.,* those who have a particular name. *A nation, people. A bond, note, demand, claim, debt. Fame, reputation, renown. Pretext, pretence, excuse. Account, reason.* **ĭmāgo,** -ĭnis, 3rd fem.; nom. s. subj. to recinet (rt. in imitor, 78; s-im-ilis, 302) *an imitation, copy* of a thing. *Imitation, likeness,* e.g., *picture, statue. Apparition, ghost, phantom. Image* or *likeness* of a thing in the mind, *conception, idea. A mere form, image,* opp. to reality. *Reverberation, echo* of a sound.

289. **Aut** (131). **in** (75). **umbrosis** (139), fem. ag. w. oris. **Hĕlĭconis,** gen. s. after oris; fr. Hĕlĭcon, 3rd mas., a mountain in Bœotia, sacred to Apollo and the Muses. **oris,** abl. plu. gov. by in; fr. ōra, -æ, 1st fem., *extremity* of a thing. *Border, edge, limit, coast, sea-coast. Region, country* (616).

290. **Aut** (131). **super** (537). **Pindo,** abl. s. gov. by super; fr. Pindus, -i, 3rd mas., lofty mountain in Thessaly on the borders of Macedonia and Epirus. **gelido,** abl. s. mas. ag. w. Hæmo; fr. gelidus (30). **-ve** (186). **in** (78). **Hæmo,** abl. s. gov. by in; fr. Hæmus, -i, (Gk. Hæmos, -i) 2nd mas., high range of mountains in Thrace (The Great Balkan).

291. **Unde,** adv. (for cunde; fr. qui, 3; cf. inde, fr. is). Of place, *from which place, where,* relat. correl. w. inde, ibi, eo. Interrog., *whence?* Of persons or things, *from whom, from which,* as origin, cause, etc., so as interrog. Poet. and post-class prose=unde unde, *whencesoever, from wherever*=undecunque. **vocalem,** acc. mas. s. ag. w. Orphea; fr. vōcālis, -e, adj., (vox, 259) *that utters a voice, sounding, sonorous, speaking. Crying, singing, vocal.* **tĕmĕre,** ante-class. collat. tĕmĕriter, (temno, *to despise*) *by chance, at random, without design, fortuitously. Rashly, heedlessly, thoughtlessly* (1154); here, *blindly, spell bound* (M.) or *pell mell* (W.). **insecutæ,** pf. part. nom. fem. plu. ag. w. silvæ; w. sunt und., 3rd plu. pf. combinate (1336) fr. insĕquor, -sĕqui, -sĕcūtus sum, 3rd depon., (in, 76; sequor, 402) *to follow after* or *close upon,* esp. *press, harass* an enemy. In time, *to succeed, come after. To follow upon, attend upon, e.g.,* suspicio insequitur. Of order, succession, *to succeed, come after. To assail, attack, To condemn, reprove. censure.*

292. **Orphea,** acc. s. (Gk.) gov. by insecutæ; fr. Orpheus (dissyll.), gen. Orphei, Gk. dat. Orpheo., voc. Orpheu; mythic singer of Thrace, son of Oagrus and Calliope, husb. of Eurydice. **silvæ** (135), subj. of insecutæ (sunt).

293 Arte materna rapidos morantem
294 Fluminum lapsus celeresque ventos,
295 Blandum et auritas fidibus canoris
296 Ducere quercus.
297 Quid prius dicam solitis parentis

293. **Arte,** abl. (of means) s. fr. ars, artis, 3rd fem.; (fr. Gk. rt. ar-, *the fitting, joining,* etc., or fr. aro, *to plough*). *Skill* in any work. Any physical or mental *activity* as far as it is practically exhibited, *profession, art. Science, knowledge, i.e.,* theory at the basis of any science or art. *The knowledge, workmanship, skill* employed in working on any subject. Concrete *work of art.* Morally, *the character* of a man in so far as made known by his actions, *manner of acting, habit, practice, i.e.,* a vox media, *virtue* or *vice,* acc. to context. In bad sense, *cunning, artifice, fraud.* **materna,** abl. fem. s. ag. w. arte; fr. māternus, -a, -um, adj., (mater, 24) *of* or *belonging to a mother, maternal,* ref. to Calliope. **rapidos,** acc. plu. mas. ag. w. lapsus; fr. răpĭdus, -a, -um, adj., (rapio, 489) *tearing away, seizing. Fierce, consuming* of fire, heat, etc. *Tearing* or *hurrying along, swift, quick, rapid.* **morantem,** acc. mas. s. pres. part. ag. w. Orphea; fr. mŏror, -ari, -atus sum, 1st dep. intrans., *to tarry, stay, delay, linger, loiter, wait. To stay* or *remain on a visit;* trans., *to detain, cause to wait, hinder, check, obstruct. To let pass, not regard* or *value.* With quominus, *hesitate about, raise an obstacle to;* non moror=*I do not care about,* or *I raise no objection.*

294. **Fluminum,** gen. plu. after lapsus; fr. flumen (236). **lapsus,** acc. plu. gov. by morantem; fr. lapsus, -us, 4th mas., (labor, 55). Of horizontal motion, *a gliding, gliding along, moving along* with gentle or easy motion. Of motion downwards, *a gliding downwards,* also of *gliding* upwards. Of earth, *slipping,* fig., *a falling into misfortune;* fluminum lapsus,=flumina rapide labentia. **celeres,** acc. plu. mas. ag. w. ventos; fr. cĕler, cĕlĕris, celere, adj., *swift, fleet, quick,* w. idea of energy, struggle, power. Superl. cĕlerrĭmus. **ventos** (242), jnd. by -que to lapsus.

295. **Blandum,** acc. mas. s. jnd. by et to morantem; fr. blandus, -a, -um, adj., *of smooth tongue, flattering, fawning, caressing.* Of things, *friendly, kind, pleasant, agreeable, enticing, alluring, charming.* **et** (139). **auritas,** acc. plu. fem. ag. w. quercus; fr. aurītus, -a, -um, adj., (auris, 642) *having large ears, long-eared;* fig., *attentive, listening,* of persons and things. **fidibus,** abl. (instrumental) plu. fr. fĭdes, sing. 584; (more frequently, and in class. only plu.) fĭdes, fidium, 3rd fem., *a gut, string* of a musical instrument; meton., *a stringed instrument, lute, cithern, guitar* (817). **canoris,** abl. plu. fem., ag. w. fidibus; fr. cănōrus, -a, -um, adj., (canor, -oris, *melody, tone*) *of* or *pertaining to melody, melodious, euphonious,* (trans. and intrans.) of men, animals, instruments, etc. (1439).

266. **Ducere,** pres. act. inf. (prolative) after blandum; fr. duco (133). **quercus,** acc. plu. gov. by ducere; fr. quercus, -us, 4th fem., *an oak, oak-tree,* esp. Italian or esculent *oak-tree,* sacred to Jupiter.

297. **Quid** (295), acc gov. by dicam. **prius,** neut. (as adv.) of prior, gen. prioris. Compar. adj., fr. obsol. pris, (whence primus, pridem, pridie) *former, previous,* often=*first. Better, superior, more excellent* or *important;* priores, -um, 3rd mas., *forefathers, ancestors, the ancients.* **dicam,** 1st sing. fut. ind. act. fr. dico (36). **solitis,** abl. plu. fem., ag. w. laudibus; fr. sŏlĭtus (184). **parentis,** gen. s. after laudibus; fr. parens (59).

Laudibus, qui res hominum ac Deorum,
Qui mare ac terras variisque mundum
Temperat horis?
Unde nil majus generatur ipso,
Nec viget quidquam simile aut secundum:
Proximos illi tamen occupavit
Pallas honores.

298. **Laudibus,** abl. (of comparison, 103) plu. fr. laus (175). **qui** (19), mas. s. ag. w. parentis, nom. subj. to temperat. **res,** acc. plu. gov. by temperat; fr. res (167). **hominum** (258), after res. **ac** (131). **Deorum** (261), jnd. by ac to hominum.

299. **Qui** (298). **mare** (14), gov. by temperat. **ac** (131). **terras** (111), jnd. by ac. to mare. **variis,** abl. plu. fem. ag. w. horis; fr. vărius, -a, -um, adj., *diverse, different, manifold, changing, varying;* cœlum varium = *diversified with stars* (1004). *Changing, various* of fortune, etc. **mundum,** acc. s. jnd. by -que to terras; fr mundus, -i, 2nd mas. (rarer mundum, -i, 2nd neut.). Act., *that which adorns, adornment, decoration, dress* of a female. Pass., *the thing adorned, the universe,* esp. *the expanse of heaven. The world, the earth,* i.e., *the inhabitants of earth, mankind* (poet.).

300. **Temperat** (223). **horis,** abl. (instrumental) plu. fr. hora (252), here *the seasons* (W.).

301. **Unde** (291), *from whom,* relat. ref. to parentis. **nil** (125), subj. of generatur. **majus,** nom. neut. s. ag. w. nil; fr. major (194). **generatur,** 3rd s. ind. pres. pass. fr. gĕnĕro, -are, -avi, -atum, 1st trans., (genus, 45) *to beget, procreate, engender, produce* (551); in pass., also *to spring, descend from;* fig., esp. of the mind, *create, produce.* **ipso,** abl. mas. (ref. to Jupiter) s. of thing compared (103), fr. ipse (129).

302. **Nec** (19). **viget,** 3rd s. ind. pres. act. fr. vĭgeo, -ēre, no pf., no sup., 2nd intrans., *to be lively* or *vigorous, thrive, flourish, bloom.* **quidquam,** nom. neut. s. subj. of vigĕt; fr. quisquam, fem. quæquam, (quisquam ante-class.) neut. quicquam. Subst. mas., *any one;* neut., *anything,* used in negat. or virtually negat. sentences; nec quisquam, *not any one.* **simile,** nom. neut. s. ag. w. quidquam; fr. sĭmĭlis, -e, adj., *of a common* or *corresponding nature, like, resembling,* absol. or w. gen. (Plaut., Ter.) or dat., (Verg., Hor., Ovid). Cic. and contemporaries use gen. of a god, man, or beast, very rarely dat.; gen. and dat. of a thing. Livy and later writers use dat. quite as often of both; a pers. pron. is always in gen. **aut** (131). **secundum,** nom. neut. s. jnd. by aut to simile; fr. sĕcundus, -a, -um, adj., (sĕquor, 402) *following* in time or order. *Next, second* in rank or value. Of wind or water, *favourable, fair,* i.e., *following* the vessel. *Prosperous, fortunate.*

303. **Proximos,** acc. mas. plu. ag. w. honores; fr. proximus (1375). **illi** (97), *i.e.,* Jupiter, after traject. (873) proximos. This is for illius honoribus, a common Brachyology. **tamen** (111). **occupavit,** 3rd s. pf. ind. act. fr. occŭpo, -āre, āvi, -ātum, 1st trans., (ob, exp. *occupation of space in front;* capio, 1388) *to take, seize, lay hold of, occupy,* esp. *to hold possession of* by force. Of localities, *to reach, enter. To fill up* with anything. *To fall upon, attack. To anticipate, be the first to do,* w. inf., (1192) *to be beforehand with, anticipate a* person. *To come upon unexpectedly, surprise. To outstrip, get before. To take up, busy, employ.*

304. **Pallas** (179), nom. subj. of occupavit. **honores,** acc. plu. gov. by occupavit; fr. honor (8).

Prœliis audax, neque te silebo,
Liber, et sævis inimica Virgo
Belluis, nec te metuende certa
    Phœbe sagitta.
Dicam et Alciden puerosque Ledæ,
Hunc equis, illum superare pugnis
Nobilem; quorum simul alba nautis

305. **Prœliis,** abl. (of manner) plu. w. audax; fr. prælium (181). **audax** (113), voc. sg. w. Liber. **neque** (32). **te** (83), gov. by silebo. **silebo,** 1st s. fut. ind. act. fr. sĭleō, -ēre, sĭlui, no sup., 2nd intrans., *to be noiseless, still, silent* (not in Cæs.). *To be inactive, cease, rest* (of things); trans., *to be silent about* (stronger than taceo).

306. **Liber,** voc. s. fr. Līber, Līběri, 2nd mas., (fr. liber, *free*, as *freeing* from care, or liber, *a child*, as son of Semele or Ceres) old Italian deity, who presided over planting and fructification; later applied to Bacchus; meton., *wine*. **et** (2). **sævis,** dat. plu. fem. ag. w. belluis; fr. sævus (172). **inimica,** voc. s. fem. ag. w. virgo; fr. ĭnĭmīcus, -a, -um, adj., (in, neg.; amicus, 208). Of persons, *unfriendly, hostile, unsocial;* subst., inimīcus, -i, 2nd mas., *a private enemy, foe* [private opp. to hostis, *public enemy*]. Of things, *hurtful, injurious, e.g.*, imber (Hor.). **Virgo** (63), voc. s., *i.e.*, Diana.

307. **Belluis,** dat. plu. after traject. inimica; fr. bellua, -æ, 1st fem., prop. fem. adj., (und. bestia) *a beast* of large size and ferocious; *monster, e.g.*, elephant, wild boar, etc. (1226), sts. of small or tame animals; fig., *a monster* **nec te** (305). **metuende,** voc. mas, s. gerundive (639) ag. w. Phœbe; fr. metuo, (16). **certa,** abl. fem. s. ag. w. sagitta; fr. certus (212).

308. **Phœbe,** voc.‸s. fr. Phœbus, -i, 2nd mas., (*the radiant*) poet., name for Apollo. **sagitta,** abl. (of cause) s. fr. sagitta, -æ, 1st fem., *an arrow, shaft, bolt.*

309. **Dicam** (227). **et** (139). **Alciden,** acc. gov. by dicam; fr. Alcīdes, -æ, (Gk.) mas., *grandson of Alceus, i.e.*, Hercules. **pueros,** acc. plu. jnd. by -que to Alciden; fr. puer (139). **Ledæ,** gen. s. after pueros; fr. Leda, -æ, 1st fem., (Gk. Lede, -es) dau. of Thestius and wife of Tyndaris, mother of Pollux and Helen, Castor and Clytemnestra.

310. **Hunc** (7), *i.e.*, Castor. **illum** (9), *i.e.*, Pollux; these are in app. to and distribute pueros. **equis** (167), instrum. w. superare. **superare,** pres. inf. (prolative nearly=superando) act. after nobilem; fr. sŭpěro, -āre, -āvi, -atum, 1st trans., (superus, 30) *to go over, overstep, surmount. To overcome, surpass;* fig., *to go past* or *beyond, exceed in size*, etc., *outstrip* in any quality. *To subdue, conquer, vanquish;* intrans., *to have the upper hand, be superior. To be in excess, be superfluous, abound. To be left over, remain, survive.* **pugnis,** abl. (instrumental) plu. fr. pugnus, -i, 2nd mas., (rt. pug-, whence pungo, *to prick*) *the striking thing, a fist*, here *boxing.*

311. **Nobilem,** acc. mas. s. ag. w. hunc, illum; fr. nobĭlis (5). **quorum,** mas. plu. ag. w. hunc, illum, gen. after stella; fr. qui (3). **simul** (145). **alba,** nom. fem. s. ag. w. stella; fr. albus, -a, -um, adj., *white* (199), prop., *dead-white*, not shining, opp. to ater (*lustreless black*); cf. candidus (233); fig., *favourable, lucky*, here of the twin star Castor, favourable as bringing fair weather to sailors. *Pale* from sickness, care, etc. (931). Of the wind, *making clear, dispelling the clouds*, i.e., *dry*. **nautis,** dat. plu. (commodi) after refulsit; fr. nauta (14).

312 Stella refulsit,
313 Defluit saxis agitatus humor,
314 Concidunt venti, fugiuntque nubes,
315 Et minax — quod sic voluere —, ponto
316 Unda recumbit.
317 Romulum post hos prius, an quietum

312. **Stella**, -æ, 1st fem., (akin to *strew*) *the strewer of light, star, comet.* **refulsit**, 3rd s. pf. ind. act. fr. refulgeo, -ēre, -fulsi, no sup., 2nd intrans., (re, 659; fulgeo, 203) *to flash back, reflect a shining light. To shine bright, glitter, glisten.*

313. **Defluit**, 3rd s. ind. pres. act. fr. defluo, -ere, -fluxi, -fluctum, 3rd intrans., (de, 10; fluo, *to flow*) *to flow, flow down, come, proceed.* Of things not liquid, *to move down gently* or *gradually, glide down, descend, slip. To cease flowing, vanish.* **saxis**, abl. (of separation) plu. after defluit; fr. saxum, -i, 2nd neut., *a large rough stone, detached fragment of rock, rock*, esp. Tarpeian *rock.* **agitatus**, pf. pass. part. nom. mas. s. ag. w. humor; fr. agito (244). **hūmor**, -ōris, 3rd mas.; nom. s. subj. of defluit; *liquid, fluid* of any kind, here of the sea, of tears (350).

314. **Concidunt**, 3rd plu. pres. ind. act. fr. concĭdo, -cĭdĕre, -cĭdi, no sup., 3rd intrans., (cum, 31; cado, 977) *to fall utterly, fall to the ground, tumble down. To fall* in death, a swoon, battle. Of victims, *to be slaughtered, slain, fall*; fig., *to lose strength, value*, etc. *To be overthrown, prostrated, decay, perish, go to ruin.* Of wind, *to abate, subside.* **venti**, nom. plu. subj. of concidunt; fr. ventus (91). **fugiunt**, 3rd plu. pres. ind. act. fr. fŭgio (206). **-que** (4), jns. two clauses here. **nubes**, nom. plu. subj. of fugiunt; fr. nubes (67).

315. **Et** (2). **minax** (266), nom. fem. s. ag. w. unda. **quod** (35), *because.* **sic** (89). **vŏlŭere**, 3rd plu. pf. ind. fr. volo (104). Castor and Pollux are the subj. **ponto**, abl. (local) s. fr. pontus, -i, 2nd mas., *the sea, deep. Deep sea.*

316. **Unda** (50), nom. s. subj. of recumbit. **recumbit**, 3rd s. pres. ind. act. fr. recumbo, -ĕre, -cŭbŭi, no sup., 3rd intrans. Of persons, *to lay oneself back again, lie down again, lie down. To recline at table* (post-Aug.). Of inanimate things, *to fall, sink down* (poet. and post-Aug.).

317. **Romulum**, acc. s. gov. by memorem; fr. Rŏmŭlus, -i, 2nd mas. *Romulus*, brother of Remus, founder of Rome. **post** (117). **hos**, acc. plu. mas. gov. by post; fr. hic (317), ref. to Castor and Pollux. **prius** (120). **an**, a particle which (i.) introduces the second half of a disjunctive interrogation or phrase implying doubt, *or, whether*; sts. *or rather, or on the contrary*; sts. the first question has to be supplied, then an begins the whole interrog. esp. in Cic., but it never introduces an interrog. unless a prec. one is expressed or implied. (ii.) In disjunctive sentences expresses doubt, *e.g.*, dubito, dubium, or incertum est. As the opinion of the speaker usually inclines in such sentences to the assertion of the second clause, *haud* scio an, nescio an, etc. = *I might assert, I almost think.* If the objective clause is negative it must contain non, nemo, nullus, etc., *i.e.*, negatives, *e.g.*, haud scio annon = *I almost think not*, i.e., *probably not*; but in later Latin the former mode of expression is put for the latter. **quietum**, acc. neut. s. ag. w. regnum; fr. quiētus, -a, -um, adj., (quiesco, *to rest*) *at rest, calm, quiet. Enjoying rest, keeping quiet. Taking no part in war, peaceful, neutral.* Of the mind, *free from* ambition, etc.

Pompilî regnum memorem, an superbos
Tarquinî fasces, dubito, an Catonis
Nobile letum.
Regulum et Scauros animaque magnæ
Prodigum Paullum superante Pœno
Gratus insigni referam Camena

318. **Pompili,** gen s. after regnum; fr. Pompĭlius, -ii, 2nd mas., *i.e.,* Numa Pompilius, second king of Rome. **regnum,** acc. s. jnd. by an to Romulum; fr. regnum (146). **memorem,** 1st sing. pres. (after dubito) subj. (in indirect question); fr. mĕmŏro, -āre, -avi, -atum, 1st trans. and intrans., (mĕmor, 356) *to make mindful of, remind. To mention, recount, relate, tell of.* **an** (317). **superbos,** acc. plu. mas. ag. w. fasces; fr. sŭperbus, -a, -um, adj., (super, 237) *that is* or *thinks himself above* others, *haughty, proud. Arrogant, insolent.* In good sense, *excellent, distinguished, splendid, magnificent.*

319. **Tarquini,** gen. s. after fasces; fr. Tarquĭnius, -ii, 2nd mas., (und. civis or homo), *Tarquinius,* the fifth king of Rome, who came fr. Tarquinii, and his descendants, esp. the last (here). **fasces,** acc. plu. jnd. by an to regnum; fr. fascis, -is, 3rd mas., (rt. fad; Eng., *bind*) *a bundle, packet, parcel* (so rare) esp. plu. fasces, a bundle of rods and an axe carried by the lictors before a chief magistrate, with which criminals were scourged and beheaded, then=*any high office,* esp. *consulship.* **dŭbito,** -are, -avi, -atum, 1st trans. and intrans., (duo, *two*) *to vibrate from one side to another, to and fro,* in one's opinions or in coming to a conclusion, esp. in negations and neg. interrogations, *e.g.,* non dubito, haud dubito, etc. *To waver in one's opinion, hesitate, doubt,* absol., or w. de, or acc. in class. prose only of pron., with relat. interrog. and clauses; w. quin, *e.g.,* non dubito quin, *I don't doubt but that;* w. inf. only (post-class). *To be uncertain, doubtful, e.g.,* fortuna dubitat. *To waver* in coming to a conclusion, *be irresolute, hesitate,* w. inf. genly. neg. **Catonis,** gen. s. after letum; fr. Căto, 3rd mas., *M. Porcius Cato* the Younger (Uticensis), Cæsar's enemy, who committed suicide at Utica, after the battle of Pharsalia.

320. **Nobile,** acc. neut. s. ag. w. letum; fr. nobĭlis (5). **letum,** acc. s. jnd. by an to fasces; fr. letum (121).

321. **Regulum,** acc. s. gov. by referam; fr. Rēgŭlus, -i, *Marcus Atilius Regulus,* taken prisoner by the Carthaginians in the Punic war. **et** (2). **Scauros,** acc. plu. jnd. by et to Regulum; fr. Scaurus (having large, bulging ankles), cognomen of Gens Æmilia and Aurelia, here esp. M. Æmilius Scaurus, cos. B.C. 115–107, censor B.C. 109. **animæ** (96), after prodigum. The objective gen. (749). **magnæ,** gen. fem. s. ag. w. animæ; fr. magnus (85).

322. **Prodigum,** acc. mas. s. ag. w. Paullum; fr. prōdĭgus, -a, -um, adj., (prodigo, *to drive forth, squander*) *wasteful, lavish, profuse;* lit. and fig. (492). *Rich, abounding in* anything, w. gen. (Hor.). **Paullum,** acc. s. jnd. by -que to Scauros; fr. Paullus, -i, *L. Æmilius Paullus,* cos. who perished at Cannæ, B.C. 216. **superante,** pres. part. (temporal) act. abl. mas. s. ag. w. Pœno; fr. supero (310). **Pœno,** abl. absol. (824); fr. Pœnus, -i, *the Carthaginian, i.e.,* Hannibal.

323. **Gratus** (254), ag. w. ego und. in referam. **insigni,** abl. s. fem. ag. w. Camenâ; fr. insignis (188). **referam,** 1st sing. fut. ind. act. fr. rĕfĕro, -ferre, -tŭli, -lātum, irreg. trans., (re, 659; fero, 138) *to bear, carry, draw*

Fabriciumque.
Hunc et incomptis Curium capillis
Utilem bello tulit et Camillum
Sæva paupertas et avitus apto
Cum lare fundus.
Crescit occulto velut arbor ævo

or *bring back*. *Convey by speech* or *writing, repeat, recite*. *To rejoin, answer, reply*. **Camena**, abl. (of means) s. fr. Cămēna, -æ, 1st fem., (contr. for Cammena or Carmena; fr. cano, 261) pure Lat. perhaps Ital. for Musa (174), *a Muse* (1318), meton., *poetry* (here).

324. **Fabricium**, acc. s. jnd. by -que to Paullum; fr. Fabrĭcius, -ii, 2nd mas. *C. Fabricius Luscinus*, cos. B.C. 282–278, who led the Romans against Pyrrhus; famous for frugality.

325. **Hunc** (7), *i.e.*, Fabricius, gov. by tulit. **incomptis**, abl. plu. mas. ag. w. capillis; fr. incomptus, -a, -um, adj., (in, neg.; comptus, 1163), *unadorned, inelegant, artless, rude*; here=*ancient*; the first barber came to Rome from Sicily, B.C. 300. **Curium**, acc. s. jnd. by et to hunc; fr. Cŭrĭus, -ii, 2nd mas. *Marcus Curius Dentatus*, conqueror of Samnites, Sabines, Lucanians, and Pyrrhus. **capillis**, abl. (of quality, 916) fr. căpillus, -i, 2nd mas., (caput, 22) *the hair*, genly. of head, less com. of *beard*, rare of animals, class. in sing. only, but plu. is very com. later.

326. **Utilem**, acc. mas. s. ag. w. Curium; fr. ūtĭlis, -e, adj., (utor, 936) *useful, serviceable, fit, suitable, profitable, advantageous*, w. dat.; superl. utilissimus and utillimus. **bello**, dat. s. after trajective utilem; fr. bellum (24). **tulit**, 3rd s. pf. ind. act. fr. fero (138). **Camillum**, acc. s. jnd. by et to Curium; fr. Camillus, -i, 2nd mas, *M. Furius Camillus*, who conquered Veii and delivered Rome from the Gauls.

327. **Sæva**, nom. fem. s. ag. w. paupertas; fr. sævus (172). **paupertas**, -ātis, 3rd fem.; nom. s. subj. of tulit; (pauper, 141) *poverty, small means, moderate circumstances*; sts.=egestas, *need, want, indigence*. **ăvītus**, -a, -um, adj.; nom. mas. s. ag. w. fundus; (avus, 1) *of* or *belonging to a grandfather, derived from a grandfather*; meton., *ancestral, very old, ancient*, *e.g.*, mĕrum. **apto**, abl. s. mas. ag. w. Lare; fr. aptus (193), here, *suited to* his poverty, i.e., *small*.

328. **Cum** (31). **Lare**, abl. s. gov. by cum; fr. Lār, Lăris, genly. plu. Lăres, Lărium, and Lărum, (*the bright*, or *shining ones*). The domestic deities of the Roman household, whose images were placed near the hearth or in a small chapel in the house (Lararium), introduced from Etruria; meton., *a hearth, dwelling, home* (genly. sing., rare plu.). **fundus**, -i, 2nd mas., (ak. to fŏdio, *to dig*). *The bottom* of anything, of the ground. *A piece of land* with all that stands upon it, *farm, estate*.

329. **Crescit**, 3rd sing. pres. ind. act. fr. cresco, -ĕre, crēvi, crētum, 3rd intrans. Of things not existing before, *to come forth, grow, arise, spring, be born, become visible, appear* (genly. poet.); pf. part. cretus, *sprung, descended, born from*. Of things existing, *to rise in height, grow, grow up, thrive, increase*; so fig. of distinction, honour, courage, etc., i.e., *be promoted, advanced, prosper, attain honour*. *To increase in number*, *e.g.*, amici. **occulto**, abl. neut. s., ag. w. ævo; fr. occultus, -a, -um, pf. pass. part. of occŭlo, -cŭlere, -cŭlui, -cultum, 3rd trans., (ob, exp. *occupation of space in front*; colo, ak. to celo, *to hide*) *to cover over*, very rare. *To cover up, hide, conceal*. **vĕlŭt** or vĕlŭti, (vel, 187; ut, 13). Comparative

330 Fama Marcelli, micat inter omnes
331 Julium sidus velut inter ignes
332 Luna minores.
333 Gentis humanæ pater atque custos
334 Orte Saturno, tibi cura magni
335 Cæsaris fatis data : tu secundo

conj., *even as, just as, like as,* correl. with follg. sic, ita; (i.) introd. comparison, veluti quum, etc., *as when,* etc. *As, like as, as it were,* introd. figurative expression; (ii.) introd. an example of a general propn., *as for instance, for example;* (iii.) velut si, rarely velut alone, introd. hypoth. compar. clause, *just as if, as though.* **arbor,** -ŏris, 3rd fem.; nom. s. jnd. by velut to fama; *a tree.* Of things made of wood, e.g., *mast, oar, ship,* etc. **ævo,** abl. (temporal) s. fr. ævum, -i, 2nd neut., ævus, -i, 2nd mas., (Plaut. and Lucr.) *duration of life, lifetime, life, age;* (Eng. *ever*). *Old age*=ætas; meton., *an age, generation* (1105). *Never ending time, eternity;* in ævum, *for ever;* occulto ævo, "*in the unmarked lapse of time*" (W.).

330. **Fama,** -æ, 1st fem.; nom. s. subj. of crescit; (for, *to speak*) *that which people say, the common talk, report, saying, tradition,* genly. in sing. *Public opinion,* i.e., *the voice of the many.* Objectively, *the fame, character, reputation* which a man has either in general or particular, *a good* or *bad reputation,* rarely latter, rarely plu. **Marcelli,** gen. s. after fama; fr. Marcellus, -i, 2nd mas., (diminutive of Marcus) a Roman family name in the plebeian gens Claudia; esp. M. Claudius Marcellus, taker of Syracuse, B.C. 212. **micat,** 3rd s. ind. pres. act. fr. mĭco, -āre, -ui, no sup., 1st irreg. intrans., *to move to and fro with a quick, tremulous motion, beat, palpitate* of veins, etc. *To twitch. To twinkle, flash.* **inter** (222). **omnes,** acc. plu. mas., (*i.e.*, all other heroes) gov. by inter; fr. omnis (43).

331. **Julium,** nom. neut. s. ag. w. sidus; fr. Julius, -a, -um, adj., *Julian,* name of a Roman gens. **sidus** (36), nom. s. subj. of micat, "Julium sidus," ref. to the comet visible at Rome for seven days after the murder of Julius Cæsar; here for the *greatness of the Julian house.* **velut** (329). **inter** (330). **ignes** (271), gov. by inter.

332. **Luna** (133), nom. s. jnd. by velut to sidus. **minores,** acc. plu. mas. ag. w. ignes; fr. minor (63), compar. of parvus (1293)

333. **Gentis,** gen. s. after pater; fr. gens (41). **humanæ,** gen. s. fem. ag. w. gentis; fr. humanus (114). **pater** (38), voc. s. **atque** (37). **custos** (677), voc. s. jnd. by atque to pater.

334. **Orte,** voc. s. mas. ag. w. pater; fr. ortus, pf. partc. of ŏrĭor, ŏrīri, ortus sum, fut. partc. ŏrĭtūrus, 4th dep. intrans. irreg. some of its forms being of the 3rd conj., *e.g.*, pres. ind. ŏrĕris, ŏrĭtur, etc., *to stir, bestir oneself, rise.* Of heavenly bodies, *to arise, become visible, appear.* Of persons, *to have one's origin from, be born.* Of things, *to grow up, grow forth.* Of streams, *to take their rise. To originate, proceed from.* **Saturno,** abl. (of origin) s. after ortus; fr. Sāturnus, -i, (sero, *to sow*) *the Sower,* the most ancient king of Latium, god of agriculture and civilization, hence identified with Gk. Kronos. **tibi** (93), after data (est). **cura** (215), nom. s. subj. of data (est.) **magni** (261), ag. w. Cæsaris.

335. **Cæsaris** (80), objective after cura. **fatis,** abl. (of means) plu. fr. fātum, -i, 2nd neut., (for, *to speak*), *prophetic declaration, oracle, prediction. What has been inevitably decreed, destiny. Bad fortune, ill luck, calamity.* **data,** nom. fem. s. pf. pass. part. ag. w. cura; fr. do (65); with est und.

336 Cæsare regnes.
337 Ille, seu Parthos Latio imminentes
338 Egerit justo domitos triumpho
339 Sive subjectos Orientis oræ
340 Seras et Indos,
341 Te minor latum reget æquus orbem;

3rd s. pf. pass., (combinate, 1336). **tu** (69), subj. of regnes. **secundo,** abl s. mas. ag. w. Cæsare; fr. secundus (302). Cæsare secundo, *with Cæsar as thy vicegerent* (W.).

336. **Cæsare,** abl. absolute (824) fr. Cæsar (80). **regnes,** 2nd s. pres. conj. (optative) fr. regno, -are, -avi, -atum, 1st intrans. and trans., *to be lord, rule, reign, govern* (good sense). *To tyrannise, domineer. To have royal power, be king. To hold sway, have the mastery.*

337. **Ille** (9), *i.e.*, Cæsar; nom. mas. s. subj. of reget. **seu** (27). **Parthos,** acc. gov. by egerit; fr. Parthi, -orum, 2nd mas. plu., a Scythian people in N.E. of passes of the Caspian, and S. of Hyrcania, skilful archers; adj., Parthus, -a, -um. **Latio,** dat. s. after traject. imminentes; fr. Latium (786). **imminentes,** acc. plu. mas. pres. part. ag. w. Parthos; fr. immineo (337).

338. **Egerit,** 3rd s. fut. pf. act. fr. ago (44), see 590. **justo,** abl. s. mas. ag. w. triumpho; fr. justus, -a, -um, adj., (jus, 680) *that acts in accordance with the principles of law* or *justice, just, upright,* etc. Of things, *according to principles of natural laws,* i.e., *equitable,* or civil law, i.e., *legitimate, legal. Recognised by the law, rightful, e.g.,* materfamilias. *Rightfully belonging, due* to a person, *e.g.,* justa, -orum, *dues. Proper, right, what ought to be;* plus justo, *more than is right.* Milit., *regular, pitched* of a battle. Of a victory, *perfect,* here *well earned* (W.). Of an army, *having the full number;* justus miles, *a soldier of the regular army.* **domitos,** acc. plu. mas. pf. pass. part. ag. w. Parthos; fr. dŏmo, -āre, dŏmŭi, dŏmĭtum, 1st irreg. trans., (ak., *to tame*) *to tame, break. To subdue, vanquish, overcome* (1170). Of Venus, (638) "domare uvam prælo," *to press* (517). Of abstract objs. and subjs. (925) **triumpho,** abl. (of means) s. fr. triumphus (85).

339. **Sive** (69). **subjectos,** acc. plu. mas. ag. w. Seras; fr. subjectus, -a, -um, adj., *subjected, subject.* Of places, *lying under* or *near, bordering on, neighbouring;* orig. pf. pass. part. of subjĭcĭo, -jĭcĕre, -jēci, -jectum, 3rd trans. traject., (sub, 21; jacio, *to throw*) *to throw, lay, place under.* **Orientis,** gen. s. after oræ; fr. Oriens, -ntis, 3rd mas., (prop. pres. part. of orior 334) *the rising sun. The East* (opp. to Occidens). *The Eastern parts of the world.* **oræ,** dat. s. after traject. subjectos; fr. ora (289).

340. **Seras,** acc. plu. jnd. by sive to Parthos; fr. Sēres, gen. Serum, 3rd mas., people in the E. of Asia (mod. Chinese). Adj. Sērĭcus, -a, -um, *of* or *belonging to the Seres* (693). **Indos,** acc. jnd. by et to Seras; fr. Indi, -orum, *the Indians.*

341. **Te** (88), abl. of comparison after minor. **minor** (63, 332), nom. mas. s. ag. w. Cæsar, und. subj. of reget; te minor, *while he gives precedence to thee.* **latum,** acc. mas. s. ag. w. orbem; fr. lātus, -a, -um, adj., *broad, wide. Extensive, extended.* Of the voice, *expanding, spreading, wide, full.* Of speech, *copious, diffusive, full, rich.* **reget,** 3rd s. fut. ind. act. fr. rego (91). **æquus** (141), nom. mas. s. ag. w. Cæsar, und. subj. of reget. **orbem,** acc. s. gov. by reget; fr. orbis, -is, 3rd mas., *a circle, ring, round, orbit;*

342 Tu gravi curru quaties Olympum,
343 Tu parum castis inimica mittes
344 Fulmina lucis.

CARMEN XIII.—AD LYDIAM.

345 QUUM tu, Lydia, Telephi
346 Cervicem roseam, cerea Telephi
347 Laudas brachia, væ meum
348 Fervens difficili bile tumet jecur.

applied to many things of a circular shape, sts. w. and sts. without terrarum or terræ, *the circle* or *orb of the earth, world. Rotation, round, circuit.*

342. **Tu** (69), subj. of quaties. **gravi,** abl. s. mas. ag. w. curru; fr. gravis (41). **curru,** abl. (instrumental) s. fr. currus, -us, 4th mas., (curro, 684) *a chariot, car.* **quaties,** 2nd s. fut. ind. act. fr. quatio (18). **Olympum,** acc. s. gov. by quaties; fr. Olympus, -i, 2nd mas. *Olympus,* name of several mountains; the highest, on the borders of Macedonia and Thessaly, was regarded as the abode of the gods; *Heaven.*

343. **Tu** (69), subj. of mittes. **părum,** adv., (akin to parvus, 1293) *too little, not enough,* opp. to satis, nimium; (*a*) w. vbs. parum habere, *to deem not enough* or *insufficient.* (*b*) w. advs. parum diu. (*c*) w. gen., as a subst., genly. subj., rarely obj. *Not particularly, very little, not,* w. vbs. and adjs. **castis,** dat. plu. mas. ag. w. lucis; fr. castus, -a, -um, adj.; morally *pure, unpolluted, spotless, chaste, continent.* Religiously *pure, holy, sacred.* **inimica,** acc. plu. neut. ag. w. fulmina; fr. inimicus (306). **mittes,** 3rd s. fut. ind. act. fr. mitto (38).

344. **Fulmina** (128), gov. by (direct obj. of) mittes. **lucis,** dat. plu. after (remote obj. of) mittes; fr. lucus (139).

CARMEN XIII. METRE.—*Lesser Asclepiad.* (Carmen III.)

345. **Quum** (43). **tu** (69), subj. of laudas. **Lydia,** voc. (217). **Telephi,** gen. s. after cervicem; fr. Telephus, -i, an ideal character.

346. **Cervicem,** acc. s. gov. by laudas; fr. cervix, cervīcis, 3rd fem., (rt. cer-, *head;* veho, *to carry*) *the neck,* including the back of the neck, *the nape,* genly. in plu. in class. age. **roseam,** acc. fem. s. ag. w. cervicem; fr. rŏseus, -a, -um, adj., (rosa, 149) *of roses, rose. Rose-coloured, rosy.* Of things, *blooming* w. youth, *ruddy, lustrous.* **cerea,** acc. neut. plu. ag. w. brachia; fr. cēreus, -a, -um, adj., (cera, *wax*) *waxen, of wax. Wax-coloured* (here), or *pliant, soft as wax.* **Telephi** (345), after brachia.

347. **Laudas,** 2nd s. ind. pres. act. fr. laudo (17). **brachia** (227), gov. by laudas. **væ,** exclamation of pain or dread, *ah! alas!* With dat. like our wo! væ victis, Brennus's exclamation. **meum** (2), ag. w. jecur.

348. **Fervens,** nom. neut. s. pres. part. act. ag. w. jecur; fr. ferveo, -vēre, -bui, no sup., 2nd intrans., also fervo, -vĕre, -vi, no sup., 3rd intrans., (latter ante- and post-class. and in class. poets, *e.g.,* Verg.; Hor. uses ferveo only), *to be hot.* Of liquids, *to be in a boiling state, boil;* fig., *burn, glow, be heated, rage, rave, be agitated. To eagerly desire.* Of wine, *to ferment, boil up, brim, foam.* Of living creatures, *to be crowded, crowd in numbers,*

Tunc nec mens mihi nec color
Certa sede manent, humor et in genas
Furtim labitur arguens
Quam lentis penitus macerer ignibus.

swarm forth. **difficili,** abl. fem. s. ag. w. bile*;* fr. diffĭcĭlis, -e, adj., (dis-, 870; facilis, 297) *not easy* to do, bear, etc., *hard, difficult to treat, troublesome* (very com.). Of character, *hard to manage* or *please, obstinate, morose, wrathful.* **bile,** abl. (of means) s. fr. bīlis, -is, abl. bīli, late bile, (ak. to fel, *gall*). *Bile, the bilious fluid* [fel, the bladder in which it is contained]; fig., *anger, wrath, choler, ire, spleen, displeasure.* **tumet,** 3rd s. ind. pres. act. fr. tŭmeo, -ēre, -ui, no sup., 2nd intrans., *to swell, be swollen, puffed out, inflated;* fig., of passionate excitement, *be excited, violent, ready to burst forth. To be turgid, pompous, bombastic.* **jĕcur,** jĕcŏris, jĕcĭnoris, and jăcĕnoris, 3rd neut. *The liver,* thought to be the seat of passions, affections, etc.

349. **Tunc,** temp. adv. (i.) coinciding with another pt. of time, *then, at the time,* correl. to quum, absol. of a def. period in past time. (ii.) following a point of time, *thereupon, hereupon, then.* Quid tunc? *What then?* (iii.) used in enumerating a series of facts or arguments, *again, furthermore, besides, in the next place.* (iv.) tunc...tunc, correl., *first...then. Now...now. As well as. Both...and;* quum...tunc, in a climax, *both...and especially; not only simply* or *merely...but especially.* **nec...nec** (19). **mens,** mentis, 3rd fem.; nom. s. one member in composite subj. (555); of manent, *mind* as origin of thought; *faculty* of thought, *understanding, intellect. Reason, intellectual powers. Feelings, disposition. Idea, thought.* **mihi** (277), possessive after manent. **color,** cŏlōris, 3rd mas.; nom. s. jnd. by nec to mens as subj. of manent; *colour, i.e.,* the natural *colour* of man, *complexion, hue* (971). *Beauty,* pregn. sense; fig., *external quality, state, condition, position, outward appearance. A brilliant quality, splendour* (917).

353. **Certa** (307), ag. w. sede. **sede,** abl. (local) s. fr. sedes (46). **manent,** 3rd plu. pres. ind. act. fr. maneo (25). **humor** (313), nom. s. subj. of labitur. **et** (2). **in** (81). **genas,** acc. plu. gov. by in; fr. gĕna, -æ, 1st fem. more frequ. in plu.; *the upper part of the face* from the cheek bones to the eyelids; hence genly. *a cheek,* plu. *cheeks,* poet. *the eyes.*

351. **Furtim,** adv., (furor, *to steal*) by *stealth, secretly, privily.* **lăbitur** (55). **arguens,** nom. mas. s. pres. part. act. ag. w. humor; fr. argŭo, -ŭere, ŭi, -ūtum, 3rd trans., *to make clear, bright,* etc. *To assert, show, prove, make known, declare.* Pass. reflex., *to make oneself known, betray oneself* (Hor.). *To accuse, inform against, charge,* w. gen. or de w. abl. of charge; w. inf. after pass. verbs, *e.g.,* arguitur esse. Of things, *to accuse, censure.*

352. **Quam** (284), *how,* w. lentis. **lentis,** abl. plu. mas. ag. w. ignibus; fr. lentus, a, -um, adj., *embracing, clinging to, adhesive, tenacious. Pliant, bending, yielding* as what embraces is elastic. *Tough, hard* as pliant things. *Slow, sluggish, immovable, inactive. Lingering, lazy, e.g.,* in speaking, *i.e., drawling. Lasting* or *continuing long.* Of character, *easy, calm, indifferent, phlegmatic.* **pĕnĭtus,** adj., (pen, -it, in Penates, 983) *from within, from inside. Deeply, far within, into the inmost part. From the inmost depths* or *recesses, deeply, thoroughly, completely.* **macerer,** 1st s. pres. subj. pass. fr. măcĕro, -are, -āvi, -atum, 1st trans., *to steep, soak. To soften by soaking, make soft* or *tender;* fig., *to weaken, waste away, wear out* (here). *To fret, vex, torment* w. acc. It is pres. after labitur; subj. in subordinate clause after arguens. **ignibus,** abl. (instrumental) plu. fr. ignis (116).

353 Uror, seu tibi candidos
354 Turparunt humeros immodicæ mero
355 Rixæ, sive puer furens
356 Impressit memorem dente labris notam.
357 Non, si me satis audias,
358 Speres perpetuum dulcia barbare
359 Lædentem oscula, quæ Venus

353. **Uror,** 1st s. pres. ind. pass. fr. uro (136). **seu,** folld. by sive (27). **tibi** (93), incommodi after turparunt; or possessive after humeros; fr. candĭdus (233).

354. **Turparunt,** syncopated for turpaverunt; 3rd plu. pf. ind. act. fr. turpo, -are, -avi, -atum, 1st trans., (turpis, 727) *to make ugly* or *unsightly, soil, defile, pollute, disfigure.* **humeros** (67), gov, by turparunt. **immodicæ,** nom. fem. plu. ag. w. rixæ; fr. immŏdĭcus, -a, -um, adj., (in, neg.; mŏdĭcus, 483) *beyond bounds,* or *measure, excessive, unrestrained, unruly.* **mero** (203) instrumental w. immodicæ.

355. **Rixæ,** nom. plu. subj. of turparunt; fr. rixa, -æ, 1st fem., *a quarrel, brawl, dispute, contest, strife* (628). *Battle, contest* (very rare). **sive** (69). **puer** (149), subj. of impressit. **furens,** nom. mas. s. pres. part. act. ag. w. puer; fr. fŭro., -ĕre, fŭrui, no sup., 3rd intrans., *to rage, rave. To be mad, furious, violent.*

356. **Impressit,** 3rd s. pf. ind. act. fr. imprĭmo, -prĭmĕre, -pressi, -pressum, 3rd trans. traject., (in, 70; premo, 144) *to press* or *thrust into. To form, make* by *pressing into, e.g.,* sulcus impressus altius. *To press upon, impress* (440). *To make by pressing upon, imprint, stamp, mark* (here); fig., *to impress* on the mind, etc. **memorem,** acc. fem. s. ag. w. notam, fr. mĕmor, mĕmŏris, adj.; gen. plu. memorum, found only once (in Verg.); no neut. nom. or acc., (memini, 201) *mindful, unforgetting, unsleeping,* etc. **dente,** abl. (instrumental) s. fr. dens, dentis, 3rd mas., *a tooth.* Of things like a tooth, *e.g., share, coulter* of a plough; *fluke* of an anchor, etc.; fig., of *envy, ill will,* w. invidus, ater (Hor.). **labris,** dat. plu. after (remote obj. of) trajective impressit; fr. labrum, -i, 2nd neut., *a lip;* meton., *the edge* of anything, *e.g.,* fountain, vessel, cask. *A basin, vat, vessel* for holding any liquid. **notam,** acc. s. gov. by (direct obj. of) impressit; fr. nŏta, -æ, 1st fem., (nosco, 411) *a mark, sign, note, e.g.,* of letters, stereographic signs, or on a jar denoting the quality of the wine (948). *Brand, mark, mole* on the body (Hor.); fig., *a sign, token,* esp. "censoria," *i.e.,* condemnation pronounced on any one by the censor; then *mark* of infamy, ignominy, reproach, etc. *A letter, epistle, inscription* (Hor.).

357. **Non,** w. speres. **si** (7), here w. pres. subj., in protasis and apodosis. **me** (29), gov. by audias. **satis** (37). **audias,** 2nd s. pres. subj. act. in protasis, fr. audio (57).

358. **Speres,** 2nd s. subj. pres. act. in apodosis; fr. spero (159). **perpetuum,** acc. mas. s. predicative after fore und. ag. w. lædentem; fr. perpĕtŭus (190), *constant* (W.). **dulcia,** acc. neut. s. ag. w. oscula; fr. dulcis (2). **barbăre,** adv. of barbarus (626), *rudely, ignorantly, in an uncultivated way. Roughly, cruelly.*

359. **Lædentem,** acc. mas. s. pres. part. act., (as subst.) subj. of fore und.; fr. lædo, -ĕre, læsi, læsum, 3rd trans. irreg.; *to strike forcibly, hurt, pain, injure, damage. To annoy, grieve, violate.* **oscula,** acc. plu. gov. by

360 Quinta parte sui nectaris imbuit.
361 Felices ter et amplius,
362 Quos irrupta tenet copula, nec malis
363 Divulsus querimoniis
364 Suprema citius solvet amor die.

lædentem; fr. oscŭlum, -i, 2nd neut., (diminutive of os, oris, 223) *a little mouth, pretty mouth, sweet mouth. Kiss.* **quæ**, neut. plu. ag. w. oscula; acc. gov. by imbuit; fr. qui (3). **Venus** (133), subj. of imbuit.

360. **Quinta**, abl. fem. s. ag. w. parte; fr. quintus, -a, -um, num. adj. ordin., (quinque, *five*) *fifth.* **parte**, abl. (instrumental) s. fr. pars (20). **sui** (17), ag. w. nectaris. **nectaris**, gen. s. after parte; fr. nectar, -ăris, 3rd neut., *nectar*, drink of the gods. Then used of anything sweet, pleasant, *e.g.*, honey, milk. **imbuit**, 3rd s. pf. ind. act. fr. imbuo, -bŭĕre, -bŭi, -būtum, 3rd trans., (in, 76; BU, rt. of bibo, 518) *to wet, moisten, soak, steep, saturate;* fig., *to fill, taint, infect, imbue*, esp. in partc. imbutus, *e.g.*, religione, superstitione. *To inspire, impress early, accustom, inure, initiate, instruct*, esp. w. pf. partc. *To do a thing for the first time, prove, e.g.*, bellum sanguine.

361. **Felices**, nom. mas. plu. predic. ag. w. demonst. antec. to quos; fr. fēlix, -īcis, adj., (rt. feo, as in femina, 398) *fruitful, fruit-bearing* (not in Cic.). *That brings good luck, of good omen, auspicious, favourable, propitious* (chiefly poet.). Pass. *lucky, happy, fortunate* (prose and poetry). **ter**, num. adv., *thrice*, often expressing a high degree. **et** (2). **amplius**, neut. sing. compar. fr. amplus (1239) used as compar. of ampliter, *amply, splendidly, magnificently;* compar. *more, longer, further*, usu. of time and number. Often w. non, haud, nihil, ne, nec, etc.; sts.=insuper, præterea, *besides, further, e.g.*, nihil dico amplius. It may be followed by a compar. abl. or a nom. gen. acc. or abl. as a mere adverbial modification of number or extent of time, the case to which it is attached being the same as it would be if amplius were not used.

362. **Quos** (3), mas. plu. ag. w. demonst. und. as subj. to felices; acc. gov. by tenet. **irrupta**, nom. fem. s. ag. w. copula; fr. irruptus, -a, -um, adj., (in, neg.; rumpo, 28) *unbroken, firm, unsevered.* **tenet**, 3rd s. pres. ind. act. fr. teneo (204). **cōpula**, -æ, 1st fem.; nom. s. subj. of tenet, (cum, 31; ap- rt. of Gk. apto, *to fasten*) *that which joins* or *binds together; rope, band*, fig. of love. **nec** (19). **malis**, abl. plu. fem. ag. w. querimoniis; fr. malus (116).

363. **Divulsus**, pf. pass. partc. nom. mas. s. ag. w. amor; fr. divello, -ĕre, -velli, -vulsum (vols-) 3rd trans., (dis, 870; vello, *to pluck*) *to rend asunder, tear in pieces, separate violently. To tear away, separate, remove from* (835). **quĕrimoniis**, abl. (instrumental) plu. fr. quĕrĭmōnia, -æ, 1st fem., (queror, 42) *a complaint.*

364. **Suprema**, abl. s. fem. ag. w. die; fr. supremus=summus (45). **cĭtius**, compar. of cĭto, *quickly*, adv. of cĭtus, -a, -um, adj., *put in motion, swift, rapid.* **solvet**, 3rd s. fut. ind. act. fr. solvo (129). **amor** (247), nom. s. subj. of solvet. **die** (20), abl. of comparison (103) after citius; suprema citius die=citius quam suprema dies.

CARMEN XIV.—AD REM PUBLICAM

O NAVIS, referent in mare te novi
Fluctus. O quid agis? Fortiter occupa
  Portum. Nonne vides, ut
    Nudum remigio latus
Et malus celeri saucius Africo
Antennæque gemant ac sine funibus

CARMEN XIV. METRE.—*The Fifth Asclepiad.* (Carmen V.).

365. **O** (2). **navis** (93), *i.e.*, the vessel of the state. **referent,** 3rd plu. fut. ind. act. fr. refero (323). **in** (81). **mare** (14), gov. by in. **te** (83), gov. by referent. **novi,** nom. mas. plu. ag. w. fluctus; fr. novus (42).

366. **Fluctus,** nom. plu. subj. of referent; fr. fluctus (15). **O** (2). **quid** (297), gov. by agis. **agis,** 2nd sing. pres. ind. act. fr. ago (43). **fortiter,** adv. of fortis (165), *strongly, powerfully, vigorously,* rare; fig., *boldly, intrepidly, manfully;* comp. fortius, superl. fortissime. **occupa,** 2nd sing. pres. imper. act. fr. occupo (303), *i.e.,* gain the harbour before these waves prevent you.

367. **Portum,** acc. s. gov. by occupa; fr. portus, -us, 4th mas., (akin to porta, *gate) an approaching, entering, thing approached. Harbour, haven, port. Place of refuge, asylum, retreat.* **nonne,** interrog. adv., (non, 55; ne, 961) direct *not?* indirect *if not, whether not,* used when an affirmative answer is expected. **vides ut** (233).

368. **Nudum,** nom. neut. s. ag. w. latus; predic. after sit und.; fr. nūdus, -a, -um, adj., *naked, bare, uncovered. Without clothes.* Of things, *naked. bare of, stripped of.* Of trees, *leafless. Bare, mere, pure, simple, alone, only, e.g.,* nuda ira Cæsaris. **remigio,** abl. (of separation) s. after nudum; fr. rēmĭgium, -ii, 2nd neut., (remigo, *to row) a rowing,* abstr. for concr. of the parts of the vessel belonging to the rowing, *the oars. The oarsmen, rowers.* **lătus,** -ĕris, 3rd neut.; nom. s. subj. of sit und.; *side, flank. Lungs. Lateral surface* of a thing, opp. to frons and tergum. *Flank* of an army.

369. **Et** (2) **mālus,** -i, 2nd mas. subj. of sit und., *an apple tree;* meton., *a mast* of a ship. **celeri,** abl. sing. mas. ag. w. Africo; fr. celer (294) **saucius,** -a, -um, adj., nom. s. mas. predic. ag. w. malus; *wounded, hurt;* meton., *smitten, injured, enfeebled, ill, sick, distempered.* Of drunkards, *sick,* etc. Of things, *injured. Smitten by love;* fig., *wounded, offended, e.g.,* of mind, etc. **Africo,** abl. (instrumental) s. fr. Africus (15).

370. **Antennæ,** nom. plu. subj. of gemant; fr. antenna, -æ, 1st fem., (ἀνατείνω, *to stretch out) a sailyard;* meton., *a sail.* **-que** (4). **gemant,** 3rd plu. pres. subj. in subordinate clause after vides; fr. gĕmo, gĕmere, gĕmŭi, gemitum, 3rd trans. and intrans., *to sigh, groan,* class. of persons and beasts. Of things, *to groan, creak.* With acc. *sigh over, bemoan, bewail.* **ac** (131) **sine,** prep. gov. abl., *without;* non sine=*with* (orig. fm. seen in se-, (before vowels sēd-) which is used in compds., *e.g.,* secedo, secerno, segrego, sēditio, and exp. *separation, removal from;* see 120). **funibus,** abl. plu. gov. by sine; fr. fūnis, -is, 3rd mas. (for fud-nis, rt. of fundo, 711; as filum for fidlum, ak. to Eng. *band) a rope, line, cord;* here ropes passing round the hull to prevent the timbers starting (W.).

371 Vix durare carinæ
372 Possint imperiosius
373 Æquor? Non tibi sunt integra lintea,
374 Non Dî, quos iterum pressa voces malo.
375 Quamvis Pontica pinus,

371. **Vix**, adv. modal, (perh. rt. vig-, *with effort, with difficulty*) *with much ado, scarcely, barely.* Of time, *hardly, scarcely;* followed by quum, it denotes the immediate sequence of one thing upon another, *e.g.*, vix hoc imperavit quum; sts. strengthd. by dum, *viz.*, vixdum. **durare**, pres. inf. (prolative, 570) after possint; fr. dūro, -are, -avi, -atum, (not in Cic.) 1st trans., (durus, 479) *to make hard, harden. To make hardy* or *callous, inure. To dull, blunt, render insensible* (post-Aug.); intrans., *to grow hard, be hardened* or *inured to* troubles. *To be patient, wait, persevere, hold out, continue in existence, last.* **carinæ**, nom. plu. subj. of possint; fr. cărīna, -æ, (130). The plu. for sing. = the keel and all that belongs it. Bentl. takes it in a plu. sense "other ships about you can't hold without anchors" (W.).

372. **Possint**, 3rd plu. pres. subj. (as gemant, 370) fr. possum, posse, pŏtŭi, irreg. intrans., (potis, neut. pote, *able, capable;* sum, 3) *to be able, have power, I (thou, he,* etc.) *can. To be able, have influence* or *avail, e.g.*, of money, etc. **imperiosius**, acc. neut. s. ag. w. æquor; fr. imperiosior, compar. of impĕrĭōsus, -a, -um, adj., (imperium, 62) *possessed of command, mighty, powerful,* sibi imperiosus, "*having dominion over himself*" (Hor.); badsense, *domineering, tyrannical,* here "*too tyrannous*" (W.).

373. **Æquor** (216), gov. by durare. **non** (55). **tibi** (93), possessive after lintea. **sunt** (3) copula. **integra**, nom. neut. plu. predic. ag. w. lintea; fr. intĕger, -gra, -grum, adj., (in, neg.; tango, 224) *untouched, unharmed, uninjured, sound. Whole, undiminished* (1328). *Undefiled, spotless, pure, e.g.*, fontes (618). *In its original* or *natural state; new, fresh,* esp. de integro. *Unimpaired in health* or *strength, vigorous.* Of troops, *remaining in line* or *array.* Of time, *whole, entire, e.g.*, dies (Hor.). *Unaffected* by prejudice or love (990); mens (726), *sound, uninjured;* morally, *upright, honest, pure* (537). *Untouched,* i.e., *not entered upon, undecided, undetermined, e.g.*, res. **lintea**, nom. plu. subj. of sunt; fr. linteum, -i, 2nd neut., *a linen cloth, linen;* meton., *towel, napkin, sail;* linteus, -a, -um, adj., (linum, -i, 2nd neut., *flax; linen cloth, a garment*) *made of linen.*

374. **Non** (55). **Di** (278), subj. of sunt integri und. This is a case of zeugma or ellipsis (429). The reference is to images carried in ships. **quos** (3), mas. plu. ag. w. Di; acc. gov. by voces. **iterum**, adv., (is demonst. and compar. affix -ter-, in alter, uter, etc.). *Beyond this, besides, further* (rare). Of order or succession, *next, in the second place, afterwards. Anew, afresh, the second time;* iterum atque iterum, iterum iterum, *over and over again, repeatedly.* In enumerations w. other adverbs, *a second time, the second time, again.* **pressa**, abl. fem. s. pf. pass. part. ag. w. malo; fr. premo (144). **voces**, 2nd s. subj. pres. act. fr. voco (61). The subj. in relat. clause exp. purpose, *that you may invoke, for you to invoke.* **malo**, abl. absol. (88) s. fr. malus (369), "pressa malo" equiv. to a temporal clause.

375. **Quamvis**, concessive conj., *although, albeit,* usu. w. subj. mood and rarely in neg. clauses; rarely in this sense w. adjs. and partcs. *As much as you will, ever so; as much as possible, very much, exceedingly, e.g.*, quam multi, *very many;* quam audacter. **Pontica**, nom. fem. s. ag. w. pinus;

376 Silvæ filia nobilis,
377 Jactes et genus et nomen inutile,
378 Nil pictis timidus navita puppibus
379 Fidit. Tu, nisi ventis
380 Debes ludibrium, cave.
381 Nuper sollicitum quæ mihi tædium,

fr. Pontĭcus, -a, -um, adj., *of Pontus, a province in Asia Minor.* **pīnus,** -i and -us, 2nd and 4th fem.; nom. s. in app. to tu und. in jactes; *a pine, pine tree, fir tree,* used of a ship, boat, oar, etc. made of pine.

376. **Silvæ,** gen. s. after filia; fr. silva (235). **filia,** -æ, 1st fem.; nom. s. in app. to pinus; *a daughter* (421), here *offshoot, offspring,* dat. and abl. plu. filiis and filiabus. **nobilis,** gen. fem. s. ag w. silvæ; fr. nobilis (5).

377. **Jactes,** 2nd s. pres. subj. (after quamvis) fr. jacto (54). **et... et** (2). **genus** (71), gov. by jactes. **nomen** (288), jnd. by et to genus. **inutile,** acc. neut. s. ag. w. nomen; fr. ĭnūtĭlis, -e, adj., (in, neg.; utilis, 326) *of no use, useless, unprofitable,* w. dat. or ad w. acc., *to* or *for* whom or which; meton., *hurtful, injurious, noxious.*

378. **Nil** (125), here as adv. **pictis,** dat. fem. plu. ag. w. puppibus; fr. pictus, -a, -um, adj., *painted; hence unreal, empty, vain. Coloured, variegated,* pf. pass. part. fr. pingo, -gĕre, -nxi, -ctum, 3rd trans., *to represent pictorially* w. pencil or needle. **tĭmidus,** -a, -um, adj.; nom. mas. s. ag. w. navita; (timeo, 100) *fearful, afraid, fainthearted, cowardly;* here "*in his fear.*" **navita,** -æ, 1st mas.=nauta (14), nom. subj. of fidit. **puppibus,** dat. plu. after traject. fidit; fr. puppis, -is, acc. -im, rarely -em, *the underpart of a ship, stern, poop,* where the helm was. By synecdoche, *a ship.*

379. **Fidit,** 3rd s. ind. pres. act. fr. fīdo, -ĕre, fisus sum, 3rd semi-depon., *to trust, confide in* a person or thing (rare). In verb form genly. poet. but class. in part. pres.; w. dat. more com. abl. **tu** (69), subj. of cave. **nisi** (265), here w. pres. ind. **ventis,** dat. plu. after (remote obj. of) traject, debes; fr. ventus (91).

380. **Debes** (94). **ludibrium,** acc. s. gov. by (direct obj. of) debes; fr. ludĭbrĭum, -ii, 2nd neut., (ludo, 730) *a mock, mockery, derision. A laughing stock, butt, jest. A scoff. A sport, e.g.,* ludibrio esse alicui. **cave,** 2nd s. imperat. pres. fr. căveo, -ēre, cāvi, cautum, 2nd trans. and intrans.; imper. căvē or căvĕ, (orig. *to guard* or *protect*) *to be on one's guard* for oneself or, more rarely, for another. With and without sibi, *to take heed, beware, guard against, avoid,* w. ab, *e.g.* ab homine; w. ne and subj., *take heed that, guard against.* The imperat. is used w. subj. without ne or ut. With acc., *to guard against, e.g.,* canem, hence cavendus, caveri, cautus (1206), sts. w. inf. "cavere ab aliquo," *to make oneself secure, procure bail* or *security from;* with acc. of thing and dat., *to keep* something *from, e.g.,* scabiem pecori; nisi cave, *unless thou art doomed to be the sport of the winds, beware, i.e.,* if it is any good warning thee.

381. **Nuper,** adv., (novus, 42) *newly, lately, recently, not long ago, in modern times.* **sollicitum,** nom. neut. s. ag. w. tædium; fr. sollĭcitus, -a, -um, adj., (sollus=totus, *whole;* cieo, *to stir up*), *wholly,* i.e., *violently tossed up, stirred up, moved, agitated* (rare). *Disturbed, disquieted, anxious* in mind. Of things, *full of anxiety, troubled, e.g.,* amor, animus; *causing uneasiness, e.g.,* amor. **quæ** (46), fem. s. ag. w. navis, nom. to fuisti und. **tædium,** -ii, 2nd neut.; nom. s. predic. after fuisti und. Subjectively

Nunc desiderium curaque non levis,
  Interfusa nitentes
    Vites æquora Cycladas.

CARMEN XV.—NEREI VATICINIUM DE EXCIDIO TROJÆ.

Pastor quum traheret per freta navibus
Idæis Helenen perfidus hospitam,
Ingrato celeres obruit otio
  Ventos, ut caneret fera

weariness, irksomeness, tediousness, disgust (not frequ. till post-Aug., perhaps not in Cic. and Cæs.); sollicitum tædium=sollicitudo, *care.* Objectively, *a disgusting* or *loathsome thing, nuisance* (Pliny.)

382. **Nunc** (21). **dēsīdĕrium,** -ii, 2nd neut.; nom. s. predic. after es und. (dēsīdero, *to long for*), *a longing, ardent desire* for a thing not possessed. *Grief, regret* for the absence or loss of a thing, sts. not implying regret for what is lost or impossible. *Want, need, necessity.* **cura** (334), jnd. by -que to desiderium. **non** (56). **levis** (31), nom. fem. s. ag. w. cura.

383. **Interfusa,** acc. neut. plu. pf. pass. part. ag. w. æquora; fr. interfundo, -ĕre, -fūdi, -fūsum, 3rd trans., (inter, 330; fundo, 711) *to pour between,* hence pass. (reflex.) of water, *to spread itself between, flow between. To scatter at intervals.* **nitentes,** acc. plu. fem. pres. part. act. ag. w. Cycladas; fr. niteo (161).

384. **Vites,** 2nd s. conj. (optative) pres. act. fr. vito (226). **æquora** (155), gov. by vites. **Cycladas,** acc. gov. by interfusa; fr. Cyclădes, -um, 3rd fem.; islands lying in a circle around Delos.

Carmen XV. Metre.—*Third Asclepiad.* (Carmen VI.).

385. **Pastor,** -ōris, 3rd mas.; nom. s. subj. of trăheret; (pasco, 723). *A feeder, keeper, maintainer;* meton., *feeder of cattle, shepherd.* ref. to Paris. **quum** (206). **trahĕret,** 3rd s. impf. subjunct. (after quum) act. fr. traho (130). **per** (114). **freta** (104), gov. by per. **navibus** (167), instrumental.

386. **Idæis,** abl. plu. fem. ag. w. navibus; fr. Idæus, -a, -um, adj., *of* or *belonging to Mt. Ida;* here *Trojan.* **Helenen,** acc. s. gov. by traheret; fr. Helene, -es (Gk.); see 90. **perfĭdus,** -a, -um, adj.; nom. mas. s. ag. w. pastor; (per, 114; fides, 153) *that breaks his promises, faithless, false, treacherous.* Of things, *treacherous, unsafe, dangerous.* **hospitam,** acc. s. in app. to Helenen; fr. hospĭta, -æ, 1st fem. of hospes, -ĭtis, 3rd mas., *a sojourner, visitor, guest, friend. He who treats another as his guest, a host;* here hospita=*hostess. Stranger, foreigner,* opp. to a native (not in fm. hospĭta). Hospes in post-Aug. poets, hospita in fem. sing. and neut. plu. as adj.=*hospitable. Strange, foreign, e.g.,* terra, æquora (Verg.).

387. **Ingrato,** abl. neut. s. ag. w. otio; fr. ingrātus, -a, -um, adj., (in, neg.; gratus, *pleasing, agreeable*). Of things, *unpleasant, disagreeable,* here to the winds as being enforced. *That do not repay trouble bestowed upon them.* Of persons, *unthankful, ungrateful.* **celeres** (294), ag. w. ventos. **obruit,** 3rd s. pf. ind. act. fr. obruo (670). **otio,** abl. (of means) s. fr. otium (16).

388. **Ventos** (242), gov. by obruit. **ut,** final (13). **caneret,** 3rd s. impf. (after pf. obruit) subj. (after ut) act. fr. cano (261) **fera,** acc. plu. neut. ag. w. fata; fr. ferus (258).

389 Nereus fata: "Mala ducis avi domum,
390 Quam multo repetet Græcia milite,
391 Conjurata tuas rumpere nuptias
392 Et regnum Priami vetus.
393 Heu heu! quantus equis, quantus adest viris
394 Sudor! quanta moves funera Dardanæ

389. **Nereus,** (dissyll.) gen. Nērei and Nēreos, (Gk.) mas.; subj. of obruit. Son of Oceanus and Tethys, a sea-god, husband of Doris and father of the Nereids. **fata,** acc. plu. gov. by caneret; fr. fatum (335). **mala,** abl. fem. s. ag. w. avi; fr. malus (214). **ducis,** 2nd s. ind. pres. act. fr. duco (133). **avi,** abl. (instrumental) s. fr. ăvis, -is, abl. s. -i and e (-i most com. in relig. sense), 3rd fem., *a bird*, collect. *the winged race, feathered tribe. A sign, omen, portent*=omen. **domum** (172). The acc. of place whither is chiefly used when the place is a town or small island (sts. as by poets, more extensively), also when expressed by domum (*home*), rus (*into the country*). Ken. 125.

390. **Quam** (70), fem. s. ag. w. eam und. after ducis; acc. gov. by repetet. **multo,** abl. mas. s. ag. w. milite; fr. multus (23). **repetet,** 3rd s. fut. ind. act. fr. repeto (252). **Græcia,** -æ, 1st fem.; nom. subj. of repetet, *Greece*. **milite,** abl. (instrumental) s. fr. miles (168).

391. **Conjurata,** nom. fem. s. pf. pass. part. ag. w. Græcia; fr. conjūro, -are, -avi, -atum, 1st trans. and intrans., *to swear together* or *in common with; to combine under an oath;* in good sense *to form a confederacy*, part. pf. pass. reflex. as here; bad sense, *form a conspiracy, plot, conspire;* fig., *to combine together, become united, e.g.*, rates. **tuas** (175), w. nuptias. **rumpere,** pres. inf. act. after conjurata; fr rumpo (28). Here by zeugma used of nuptias and regnum. **nuptias,** acc. gov. by rumpere; fr. nuptiæ, -arum, 1st fem. plu., (nubo, 1090) *the state*, or *condition of the nupta. Marriage, wedding, nuptials.*

392. **Regnum** (318), jnd. by et to nuptias. **Priami,** gen. s. after regnum; fr. Priamus (270). **vetus,** neut. acc. s. ag. w. regnum; fr. vetus (19).

393. **Heu** (73). **quantus,** -a, -um, pronominal adj.; nom. mas. s. ag. w. sudor; (i.) interrog., *How great?* used in exclamations; (ii.) correl. to tantus; tantus..quantus, *as great...as; such ..as; as much ..as*, tantus often omitted; quanti, of price, *How high? How dear?* **equis** (193), after adest. **adest,** 3rd sing. pres. ind. fr. adsum, adesse, adfui (aff.); impf. subj. adforem, -es, -et, irreg. intrans., *to be at* or *near* or *by* a person or place; *to be present.* Of things, *to be at hand, e.g.*, tempestas. *To be present* in order to aid, *stand by, support, defend;* ad esse animo or animis, *to be present in mind, i.e.*, with attention, interest, sympathy. *To give attention to* something, *perceive*, or *be present with courage, be fearless, courageous. To appear, approach.* **viris,** dat. plu. after adest; fr. vir (215).

394. **Sūdor,** -ōris, 3rd mas.; nom. s. subj. of adest; (sudo, *to sweat*) *sweat, perspiration;* meton., *any liquid, moisture, e.g.*, maris; fig. *toil, severe labour, fatigue.* **quanta,** acc. neut. plu. ag. w. funera; fr. quantus (393). The plu. is unusual and implies magnitude and number (W.). **moves,** 2nd s. ind. pres. act. fr. mŏveo, -ēre, -mōvi, mōtum, 2nd trans. irreg., *to move, set in motion, shake, agitate;* pass., *to dance. To remove, expel*, etc. *To affect, influence. To excite, occasion, produce, bring forth, cause to begin;* fig., *to rouse, agitate, disturb.* **funera** (231), gov. by moves. **Dardanæ,**

Genti! Jam galeam Pallas et ægida
Currusque et rabiem parat.
Nequicquam Veneris præsidio ferox
Pectes cæsariem, grataque feminis
Imbelli cithara carmina divides;
Nequicquam thalamo graves
Hastas et calami spicula Gnosii

dat. s. fem. ag. w. genti; fr. Dardănus, -a, -um, adj.=Dardanius, *Dardanian, Trojan.*

395. **Genti,** dat. (incommodi) s. after moves; fr. gens (41). **jam** (37). **galeam,** acc. s. gov. by parat; fr. galea (74). **Pallas** (304), nom. subj. of parat. **ægida,** acc. s. jnd. by et to galeam; fr. ægis, -ĭdis, 3rd fem., *the Ægis,* shield of Jupiter, here of Pallas.

396. **Currus,** acc. plu. jnd. by -que to ægida; fr. currus (342). **rabiem** (102), jnd. by et to currus. **parat,** 3rd s. pres. ind. act. fr. păro, -āre, -āvi, -ātum, 1st trans., (ak. to fero, 138) *to make* or *get ready, prepare, furnish, provide;* pass. (reflex.) or w. acc. of pers. pron., *to prepare oneself* or *make oneself ready. To procure, get, acquire, obtain. To prepare oneself* to do something, *determine, resolve.*

397. **Nequicquam** (109). **Veneris,** gen. s. after præsidio; fr. Venus (133). **præsidio,** abl. (of cause with ferox) s. fr. præsidium (2). **ferox** (167), ag. w. tu und. in pectes.

398. **Pectes,** 3rd s. fut. ind. act. fr. pecto, -ĕre, pexi, pexum and pectĭtum, 3rd trans., *to comb,* w. persons or their hair as objects. **cæsariem,** acc. s. gov. by pectes; fr. cæsaries, -ei, 5th fem., *the hair* of the head of man or women (genly. poet., only sing.), very rarely of the beard. **grata,** acc. plu. neut. ag. w. carmina; fr. gratus (129). **-que** (4), jns. two clauses here. **feminis,** dat. plu. after (remote obj. of) divides; fr. fēmĭna, -æ, 1st fem., (FEO, rt. *to bring forth, produce*) *a female, woman* used of animals and plants also.

399. **Imbelli,** abl. s. fem. ag. w. cithara; fr. imbellis (174). **cithara,** abl. (instrumental) s. fr. cĭthăra, -æ, 1st fem. (Gk.), *a cithara* or *cithern,* frequ. in the poets, though not in Hor. *Music* of the cithara. *Art of playing* on the cithara. **carmina** (64), gov. by divides. **divides,** 2nd s. fut. ind. act. fr. divido (1143); "carmina divides," *i.e.* sing to one and another (see 822).

400. **Nequicquam** (109). **thalamo,** abl. (local) s. fr. thălămus, -i, 2nd mas., (Gk.) *a sleeping room, bedchamber* (poet.). *Marriage bed, bridal bed,* often sing. and plu. *Dwelling place, residence, habitation, e.g.,* of bees, etc. **graves** (135), ag. w. hastas.

401. **Hastas,** acc. plu. gov. by vitabis; fr. hasta, -æ, 1st fem., *spear, lance pike, javelin,* esp. a *spear* stuck in the ground at public auctions or where the tribunals of the centurions were held, *e.g.,* venire sub hasta, *to be sold by auction.* **calami,** gen. s. after spicula; fr. călămus, -i, 2nd mas., (Gk.) *a reed, cane* (=pure Lat. arundo). Of things made of reed, e.g., *pen; pipe; arrow* (here). Of things of the shape of a reed, *stalk, stem, blade.* **spicula,** acc. plu. jnd. by et to hastas; fr. spīcŭlum, -i, 2nd neut., (spicum, *a point*) diminutive. *A little* sharp *point* or *sting,* esp. of a missile weapon. By synecdoche, *a dart, arrow.* **Gnosii,** gen. s. mas. ag. w. calami; fr. Gnōsius, -a, -um, adj., *belonging to Gnōsus* (Cnossus), the ancient capital of Crete; hence *Cretan.*

Vitabis strepitumque et celerem sequi
Ajacem; tamen heu serus adulteros
Crines pulvere collines.
Non Laërtiaden, exitium tuæ
Genti, non Pylium Nestora respicis?
Urgent impavidi te Salaminius
Teucer et Sthenelus sciens

402. **Vitabis,** 2nd s. fut. ind. act. fr. vito (226). **strepitum,** acc. s. jnd. by -que to spicula; fr. strĕpĭtus, -us, 4th mas., (strepo, *to make a noise*) *a clashing, crashing, rushing, rattling, clanking, rumbling,* etc., rarely of a measured, regular sound, *e.g.*, of cithara. **celerem,** acc. mas. s. ag. w. Ajacem; fr. celer (294). **sequi,** pres. inf. (prolative, 570) after celerem; fr. sĕquor, sĕqui, sĕcūtus sum, 3rd depon., *to follow, come or go after, attend. To chase, pursue. To succeed, come after,* i.e., *follow* in time or order. *To result, ensue,* • *To follow* as a leader, *accede, conform to.* *To strive for, aim at.*

403. **Ajacem,** acc. s. jnd. by et to strepitum; fr. Ājax, Ajācis, 3rd mas., son of Oïleus, king of Locri. **tamen** (111). **heu** (73). **serus,** -a, -um, adj.; nom. mas. s. ag. as adv. attribute (867) w. tu und in collines. Of a thing or person that is *late;* serum, -i, 2nd neut., (und. tempus) *a late time, late hour.* Of a person who does a thing or a thing taking place *late, i.e.,* at a late time or season (81). Pregn. *too late;* serum est w. subj. cláuse, *it is too late.* **adulteros,** acc. plu. mas. ag. w. crines; fr. ădulter, -ĕra, -ĕrum, adj.; (ad, 6; alter, 413) *of or belonging to an adulterer, i.e.,* one who approaches another criminally. *Unchaste,* here *finely-dressed* as of an adulterer; as subst. mas., *adulterer, paramour* (753, 835); fem., *an adulteress.*

404. **Crines,** acc. plu. gov. by collines; fr. crinis (1187). **pulvere** (178), instrumental w. collines. **collines,** 2nd s. fut. ind. act. fr. collĭno, -lĭnĕre, -lēvi, -lĭtum, 3rd trans., (cum, 31; lino, 511) *to besmear, cover over, defile, pollute* (not class. prose). *To contaminate, defile.*

405. **Non** (55), here in a question. **Laertiaden,** acc. s. gov. by respicis; fr. Laërtĭădes, -æ (Gk.), mas., *son of Laertes,* king of Ithaca and father of Ulysses. **exitium,** acc. s. in app. to Laertĭăden; fr. exĭtium, -ii, 2nd neut., (exeo, 967) *a going out, egress. A going to nought, ruin, destruction, hurt, mischief,* in sing. and plu. **tuæ,** dat. s. fem. ag. w. genti; fr. tuus (175).

406. **Genti** (395), after traject. exitium. **non** (405). **Pylium,** acc. mas. s. ag. w. Nestora; fr. Pўlĭus, -a, -um, adj., *of Pylos,* i.e., *Triphylia.* **Nestora,** acc. s. gov. by respicis; fr. Nestor, -ŏris, 3rd mas., king of Pylos, famous among the heroes before Troy for wisdom and eloquence, and who lived through three generations (1105), hence prov. "Nestoris ætas," *a long life.* **respicis** (72).

407. **Urgent,** 3rd plu. pres. ind. act. fr. urgeo (150). **impavidi,** nom. mas. plu. ag. w. Teucer et Sthenelus; fr. impăvĭdus, -a, -um, adj.; (in, neg.; pavidus, 14) *fearless, undaunted, intrepid* (chiefly post-Aug., not Cic. nor Cæs.). **te** (83), gov. by urgent. **Salaminius,** -a, -um, adj.; nom. mas. s. ag. w. Teucer; *belonging to the island of Salamis* (213).

408. **Teucer** (205), one member of comp. subj. of urgent. **Sthĕnĕlus,** -i, 2nd mas., nom. s. jnd. by et to Teucer; one of the Epigoni, charioteer of Diomede, shut up in the wooden horse. **sciens,** nom. mas. s. pres. part. act. ag. w. Sthenelus; fr. scio (277).

Pugnæ, sive opus est imperitare equis,
Non auriga piger. Merionen quoque
Nosces. Ecce furit te reperire atrox
  Tydides melior patre;
Quem tu cervus uti vallis in altera

409. **Pugnæ**, gen. (objective, 749) s. after sciens; fr. pugna (59). This is the gen. of the matter. **sive** (62). **opus**, nom. predic. after est; neut. word only used in nom. and acc.; (orig. *that which is, or must be followed up*) *what is needful, need, necessity;* opus est, *it is necessary;* person needing is put in dat., *e.g.*, mihi, tibi, etc. *I, thou,* etc., *need;* the thing needed is in nom. as subj. to which opus est or sunt is predic., or in abl. esp. of pf. partc., *e.g.*, consulto, rarely sup. in -u, rarely in genitive. It is also used rarely w. inf. *It is good, useful, serviceable, expedient*=expedit, *juvat.* **est** (19). **imperitare**, pres. inf. act. subject to est; fr. impĕrĭto, -are, -avi, -atum, 1st trans. and intrans.; (intens. of impero, *to command*) *to command, govern, rule* (not in Cic. nor Cæs.); genly. intrans. w. dat. or absol. **equis** (193), after traject. imperitare.

410. **Non** (55), w. piger. **auriga**, -æ, 1st com.; nom. s. in app. to Sthenelus, (aurea or oreæ, *headstall* or *bit*) *charioteer, driver,* esp. *one who contended in the chariot race.* **piger**, -gra, -grum, adj.; nom. mas. s. ag. w. auriga; (piget, *it grieves*) *reluctant, unwilling, averse* (very rare). *Backward, slow, dull, lazy, indolent,* of persons and things, *e.g.*, "campus impiger," *unfruitful* (553). **Merionem** (179), gov. by nosces. **quoque**, an intensive sociative conjunction like etiam; *also, even,* an emphatic -que (4). It follows the word it qualifies.

411. **Nosces**, 2nd sing. fut. ind. act. fr. nosco, -scĕre, nōvi, nōtum (old fm. gnosco). Many of its forms are syncopated, *e.g.*, nosti, noram, etc.; 3rd inceptive trans. In the pres. and its derivatives, *to acquire* or *obtain a knowledge, become acquainted with, come to know,* act. and pass. Perf. and derivatives, *to have acquired a knowledge of, know.* In pres. also *to examine, consider.* Pres. rare for pf. *To recognise, acknowledge, allow, admit, e.g.*, a reason as an excuse. **ecce**, demonst. pron. points out an obj. emphatically. *Lo! See! Behold!* esp. denoting that something is present. Fr. *voici,* and often announcing something unexpected. It is a redoubled -ce, wh. appears in ce-do, ceu, hicce, as ci- in huccine, as c in hic, sic, as ec- before k sound, *e.g.*, ecquis. **furit**, 3rd s. ind. pres. act. fr. furo (355). **te** (83), gov. by reperire. **reperire**, pres. inf. (prolative exp. purpose, 570) after furit; fr. rĕpĕrio, -īre, rĕpĕri, rĕpertum, 4th trans., (re, 659; pario, 892, orig. *to produce again*) *to find, meet with* by search or accident, fig., *to find out, discover;* trans., *to find, discover, perceive, learn* a person or thing to be of such a kind or in such a state; so in pass., *to be found to be,* etc., with predic. noun or inf. *To hit upon, invent, devise, discover*=invenire. **atrox**, atrōcis, adj.; nom. mas. s. ag. w. Tydides, (ater, 661) *disagreeable to behold, highly repulsive, horrid, hideous.* Of persons, *savage, fierce, cruel, morose, stern.* Of things, *cruel, terrible, raging, perilous;* in a good sense, *firm, unyielding* (900).

412. **Tydides** (179), nom. s. subj. of furit. **melior** (209), mas. ag. w. Tydides. **patre**, abl. (of comparison, 103) s. after melior; fr. pater (38).

413. **Quem** (74), mas. s. ag. w. Tydides; acc. gov. by fugies. **tu** (69), subj. of fugies. **cervus**, -i, 2nd mas.; jnd. by uti to tu as subj. of fugit und. (cer- rt. in cerebrum, cornu, orig. *the horned one*) *stag, deer.* **uti**=ut, comparat. (199). **vallis**, gen. s. after parte; fr. valles or vallis, -is, 3rd fem., *a valley,*

414 Visum parte lupum graminis immemor
415 Sublimi fugies mollis anhelitu,
416 Non hoc pollicitus tuæ.
417 Iracunda diem proferet Ilio
418 Matronisque Phrygum classis Achilleï;
419 Post certas hiemes uret Achaïcus
420 Ignis Iliacas domos."

vale. **in** (78). **altera,** abl. fem. sing. ag. w. parte; fr. alter, altĕra, alterum, gen. alterīus (sts. -ĭus in poetry) (rt. al- in alius, -ter is compar. radical element). *One, another;* in plu. w. words used only in plu. or used in the sense of a whole in plu., *e.g.,* literæ; alter...alter, *the one...the other.* As a numeral=secundus, *the second, next;* so with ordinals, *e.g.,* altero vicesimo die, *on the 22nd day;* unus et alter=(i.) *two;* (ii.) *this* or *that, several. A second, i.e.,* a similar one, *e.g.,* alter ego, *a second self.*

414. **Visum,** acc. s. mas. pf. pass. part. ag. w. lupum; fr. video (49). **parte** (360), gov. by in. **lupum,** acc. s. gov. by fugit und.; fr. lŭpus, -i, 2nd mas., *a wolf;* lupus Martialis, sacred to Mars (457). **graminis,** gen. objective (of material, 409) s. after immemor; fr. grāmen, -ĭnis, 3rd neut., *grass, a blade of grass,* meton., *a plant, herb.* **immemor** (26), ag. with cervus.

415. **Sublimi** (36), mas. ag. w. anhelitu. The breath is "stopped midway," can't get down, but stays at the entrance of the lungs (W.). **fugies,** 2nd s. fut. ind. act. fr. fugio (206). **mollis** (203), nom. mas. s. ag. w. tu. **anhelitu,** abl. (of manner) s. fr. ănhēlĭtus, -us, 4th mas., *a difficulty of breathing, panting, puffing* (=post-class. anhelatio). *A breathing, breath;* anhelitum ducere =*to pant* or *breathe.* Rare of things, *exhalation, evaporation, vapour.*

416. **Non** (55). **hoc,** acc. s. neut. gov. by (direct obj. of) pollicitus; fr. hic (7). **pollicitus,** pf. part. nom. mas. s. ag. w. tu; fr. pollĭceor, -lĭcēri, -lĭcĭtus sum, 2nd depon. trans. and intrans., (po- rt. in possum, 372; -lĭceor, *to bid,* or *offer largely* or *very much*); trans., *to hold forth, offer;* intrans. with pres. inf. *to make a promise, promise.* **tuæ** (405), ag. w. uxori und. after (*i.e.,* remote obj. of) pollicitus.

417. **Iracunda,** nom. fem. s. ag. w. classis; fr. iracundus (128). **diem** (284), gov. by proferet, *the day of doom.* **proferet,** 3rd s. fut. ind. act. fr. profĕro, -ferre, -tŭli, -lātum, irreg. trans., (pro, *forward;* fero, 138) *to carry, bring out, bring forth* (class.), esp. *to extend, stretch. To enlarge, e.g.,* castra. Of plants, *to produce. To put off, adjourn* (here). *To make known, produce in public, invent, discover. To quote, cite, mention* (class.). *To prolong, e.g.,* vitam. **Ilio** (270), dat. (commodi) after proferet.

418. **Matronis,** dat. plu. jnd. by -que to Ilio; fr. matrōna, -æ, 1st fem., (mater, 24) *a married woman, wife, matron. Lady, woman of rank,* a title of social dignity. *Virtuous woman, wife.* **Phrygum,** gen. after matronis; fr. Phrÿges, 3rd mas. plu. (sing. Phryx, -ÿgis), people of Asia Minor known for stupidity, insolence, and skill in embroidering in gold. **classis,** -is, abl. -e or -i, 3rd fem., *a people as assembled together, class. Forces. Force* of the land army (very old use). *Fleet* including troops in it. **Achilleï,** gen. s. after classis; fr. Achillĕus, gen. -ĕŏs, dat. -ĕi (Gk.). The Lat. form is Achilles, gen. -is, acc. -em, voc. -e, *Achilles.*

419. **Post** (117). **certas,** acc. plu. fem. ag. w. hiemes; fr. certus (212). **hiemes** (280), gov. by post. **uret,** 3rd s. fut. ind. act. fr. uro (136). **Achaïcus,** -a, -um (Gk.), nom. mas. s. ag. w. ignis. *Achæan, Grecian* (in poet. usu. Achæus).

420. **Ignis** (116), nom. s. subj. of uret. **Iliăcas,** acc. plu. fem. ag. w.

CARMEN XVI.—PALINODIA AD AMICAM.

421 O MATRE pulchra filia pulchrior,
422 Quem criminosis cunque voles modum
423 Pones iambis, sive flamma
424 Sive mari libet Hadriano.
425 Non Dindymene, non adytis quatit
426 Mentem sacerdotum incola Pythius,

domos; fr. Īlĭăcus, -a, -um, adj., *belonging to Ilium, Trojan.* **domos,** acc. plu. gov. by uret; fr. domus (117).

CARMEN XVI. METRE—*Alcaic.* (Carmen ix.)

421. **O** (2). **matre,** abl. of comparison (103) after pulchrior; fr. mater (24). **pulchra,** abl. fem. s. ag. w. matre; fr. pulcher, -chra, -chrum, adj., (polio, *to polish*) *beautiful, beauteous;* in a moral sense, *fine, excellent, honourable, noble;* comp. pulchrior, superl. pulcherrimus. **filia** (379), voc. **pulchrior,** voc. fem. s. compar. adj. ag. w. filia; fr. pulcher (421).

422. **Quemcunque** (246); ag. w. modum. **criminosis,** dat. mas. plu. ag. w. iambis; fr. crīmĭnōsus, -a, -um, adj., (crimen, *charge, accusation*) *full of reproaches, criminating, calumniating, slanderous.* **voles,** 2nd s. fut. ind. act. fr. volo (104). **modum,** acc. s. gov. by (direct obj. of) pones; fr. mŏdus, -i, 2nd mas., (ak. to metior, *to measure*) *a measure,* i.e., *standard by which anything is measured. Measurement, extent, size, amount, number, quality.* Of words, *rhythm, time, quantity, notes, melody, strains, metre, poems, verses. Moderation, proper measure. Bounds, limits, restriction, end. Way, manner, method, mode,* esp. modo, in-modum, ad-modum, *after the manner.* With gen. of pron., *a sort, kind, e.g.,* cujusmodi, istiusmodi, cujusdam modi.

423. **Pones,** 2nd s. fut. ind. act. fr. pono (104), the permissive future (165). **iambis,** dat. plu. after (remote obj. of) pones; fr. iambus, -i, 2nd mas., *an Iambic foot, Iambic poetry* or *poem.* **sive** (69). **flamma,** abl. (instrum.) s. fr. flamma, -æ, 1st fem., (rt. in flagrare, 605) *blazing fire. Blaze, flame* of passion, etc.

424. **Sive** (69). **mari,** abl. s. jnd. by sive to flammâ; fr. mare (14). **libet,** 3rd s. ind. pres. act. fr. lĭbeo, ēre, -ui, -ĭtum, 2nd intrans., (rt. lub-, *to be desirable*) *to please* very rare except in inf. and 3rd s. used either impers., *it is pleasing, is agreeable,* or w. neut. pron., inf., or a clause as subj. It has dat. tibi, etc., to whom; "ut lubet," colloq. mark of assent; und. here, "ponere modum," as subject. **Hadriano,** abl. neut. s. ag. w. mari; fr. Hădrĭānus, -a, -um, adj. = Hadriātĭcus or Hadrĭacŭs. *Belonging to Hadria.*

425. **Non** (55). **Dindymene,** -es (Gk), 1st fem.; nom. subj. of quatit; *Cybele,* so called because worshipped at Dindymus, a mt. in Mysia, near Cyzicum, sacred to her. **adytis,** abl. (local) plu. fr. ădўtum, -i, 2nd neut. (Gk., *not to be entered*), *the sanctuary* of a temple wh. only priests entered and from wh. oracles were delivered. **quatit,** 3rd s. pres. ind. act. fr. quatio (18).

426. **Mentem,** acc. s. gov. by quatit; fr. mens (349). **sacerdotum,** gen. plu. after mentem; fr. săcerdos, -ōtis, 3rd com., (sacer, 22; do, 65, *one giving sacred things*) *a priest* or *priestess.* **incŏla,** -æ, 1st mas.; nom. subj. of quatit; (incolo, *to inhabit*) *inhabitant* of a place, *a resident. Foreign resident,* so of animals and inanimate things. Of winds, *native* (Hor.).

Non Liber æque, non acuta
Sic geminant Corybantes æra,
Tristes ut iræ, quas neque Noricus
Deterret ensis nec mare naufragum
Nec sævus ignis nec tremendo
Jupiter ipse ruens tumultu.

Pȳthĭus, -a, -um, adj.; nom. mas. s. ag. w. incola (Gk.); *Delphic;* fr. Pȳthō, -ūs, fem.; former name of Delphi and its environs.

427. **Non** (55). **Liber** (306), sub. of quatit. **æque,** adv. of æquus, (141) *equally, just as, e.g.,* æque longæ; fig., *in like manner, equally, just so*=ex æquo, pariter; æque...ac, or atque, *as., as, as much as;* æque ac si, *just as if, altogether. Justly, with equity* (rare). **acuta,** acc. neut. plu. ag. w. æra; fr. ăcūtus (236).

428. **Sic** (201). **geminant,** 3rd plu. pres. ind. act. fr. gĕmĭno, -are, -avi, -atum, 1st trans. and intrans., *to double,* esp. pf. partc. geminatus, *e.g.,* plausus; meton., *to pair, join, unite* two things together; here=*to strike together.* **Corybantes,** -ium, 3rd mas.; subj. of geminant; the priests of Cybele or Ops, whose religious service consisted in noisy music and wild armed dances, originally employed by them to conceal from Saturn the birth of Corybas (κόρη, *i.e.,* sine patre natus), son of Cybele or Proserpine. They were also called Curetes. **æra,** acc. plu. gov. by geminant; fr. æs (97).

429. **Tristes,** nom. plu. fem. ag. w. iræ; fr. tristis (102). **ut,** compar. (199). **iræ,** nom. plu. subj. of quatiunt und.; fr. īra, -æ, 1st fem., *anger, wrath, fury.* Of things, *rage, violence, fury.* The plu., *bursts of passion* (W.). This is a case of ellipsis or zeugma, which is of several kinds; (i.) when merely another form of a word already expressed has to be supplied, *e.g.,* here quatiunt fr. quatit above; (ii.) when a word with a different sense has to be supplied from a prec. word, or a different sense of the prec. word as in 392; sts. an affirmative verb is supplied fr. a prec. negative one. This latter is more strictly zeugma. **quas,** fem. plu. ag. w. iræ; acc. gov. by deterret; fr. qui (3). **neque** (32). **Nōrĭcus,** -a, -um, adj.; nom. mas. s. ag. w. ensis; *belonging to Noricum,* a country betw. Danube and Alps.

430. **Deterret,** 3rd s. ind. pres. act. fr. dēterreo, -ēre, -ŭi, -ĭtum, 2nd trans. and intrans., (de, 10; terreo, 40) *to frighten from* anything, *deter, discourage from, hinder* (class.) w. abl. or abl w. ab, or quin w. subj., of that from *what,* sts. *to avert, e.g.,* a censoribus. **ensis,** -is, 3rd mas.; nom. s. subj. of deterret; *a sword,* poet., in pure Latin gladius. **nec** (19). **mare** (14), nom. s. jnd. by nec to ensis. **naufragum,** nom. neut. s. ag. w. mare; fr. naufrăgus,-a, -um, adj., (navis, 93; frango, 570) *that suffered shipwreck, wrecked. Causing shipwreck* (here); fig., *ruined* (Cic.).

431. **Sævus** (172), nom. mas. s. ag. w. ignis. **ignis** (420), jnd. by nec to mare. **tremendo,** abl. mas. s. ag. w. tumultu; fr. trĕmendus, gerundive (639) of tremo, (568) *that is to be trembled at,* hence *fearful, dreadful, frightful, formidable.*

432. **Jupiter** (66), jnd. by nec to ignis. **ipse** (126), nom. mas. s. ag. w. Jupiter. **ruens** (61), nom. mas. s. ag. w. Jupiter. **tumultu,** abl. (of manner) s. fr. tŭmultus, -us, 4th mas., (tumeo, 348) *a swelling* of the sea (rare). *Disturbance, disquietude* of mind or feelings; milit., *a sudden* or *impending civil war, insurrection, sedition, rebellion. Uproar, commotion, disturbance* of any kind; here, *roar* of thunder.

Fertur Prometheus, addere principi
Limo coactus particulam undique
Desectam, et insani leonis
Vim stomacho apposuisse nostro.
Iræ Thyesten exitio gravi
Stravere et altis urbibus ultimæ

433. **Fertur** (207). **Prŏmētheus,** (trisyll.) -ĕi and -ĕos, Gk., mas.; nom. s. subj. of fertur; (*Forethinker*) son of Iapetus and Clymene, brother of Epimetheus, father of Deucalion, who formed men of clay and animated them by fire stolen from heaven. **addere,** pres. inf. (prolative) act. after coactus; fr. addo, -dĕre, -dĭdi, -dĭtum, 3rd trans. traject., (ad, 6; do, 65) *to put, place near* a person or thing, alĭquem or aliquid alicui rei, *to add to, give, bestow, impart. To join* or *annex to, augment. To add* a new thought to what goes before. **principi,** dat. mas. s. ag. w. limo; fr. princeps (86), *primeval.*

434. **Limo,** dat. s. after (indirect obj. of) addere; fr. līmus, -i, 2nd mas., (rt. in liquor, 711) *thing liquefied, loosened, slime, mud.* **coactus,** pf. pass. part., nom. mas. s. ag. w. Prometheus; fr. cōgo, cōgĕre, cŏēgi, cŏactum, 3rd trans., (cum, 31; ago, 43) *to draw together* into one point, *collect, bring,* or *urge together, e.g.,* of *assembling* the Senate. Of liquids, *to condense, curdle, To contract* into a narrow place, *e.g.,* agmen cogere=*to bring together the rear. To urge on to* any action, *force, compel, constrain, e.g.,* absol., or w. acc. and inf., ut w. subj., ad w. gerund or two accs. In pass. sts. w. one acc. or inf., *e.g.,* aliquid cogor. **partĭcŭlam,** acc. s. gov. by (direct obj. of) addere; fr. partĭcŭla, -æ, 1st fem., (diminutive of pars, 20) *a small part, little piece, particle* (673). **undique** (191), w. desectam; *from every animal.*

435. **Desectam,** pf. pass. part. acc. fem. s. ag. w. particulam; fr. desĕco, -sĕcāre, -sĕcui, -sectum, 1st trans., (de, 10; seco, 14) *to cut off.* **et** (2), here= etiam, *even.* **insani,** gen. mas. s. ag. w. leonis; fr. insānus, -a, -um, adj., (in, neg.; sanus, 1066) prop. *unsound* in mind, *mad, insane;* fig., *outrageous, violent, furious, excessive. Acting like a madman, raving, foolish, silly.* Of things, *furious, excessive, immense.* Advs., insanum, insane, insaniter. **leonis,** gen. s. after vim; fr. leo, 3rd mas., (Gk.) *a lion.*

436. **Vim,** acc. s. gov. by (direct obj. of) apposuisse; fr. vis, gen. vis, acc. vim, but gen. and dat. s. are extremely rare; plu. vires, virium, viribus, etc. 3rd fem., *strength* physical or mental, *force, vigour, power, energy, virtue* of, persons or things. Plu. most frequ. of physical (esp. hostile) *strength, force, violence;* meton., *quantity, number, abundance* in sing. Plu. *military forces, troops;* fig., *moral strength, power, force, vigour.* Of things, *e.g.,* words, *force, notion, meaning, sense, import, nature, essence.* **stomacho,** dat. s. after (remote obj. of) apposuisse; fr. stomachus (170). **apposuisse,** pf. inf. (prolative) act. after fertur; fr. appono (247). **nostro,** dat. s. mas. ag. w. stomacho; fr. noster (83).

437. **Iræ** (429), subj. of stravere. **Thyesten,** acc. s. gov. by stravere; fr. Thȳestes, -æ, 1st mas. (Gk.), son of Pelops, brother of Atreus (who set before him for food the flesh of his own son), father of Ægistheus. **exitio,** abl. (of manner) s. fr. exitium (405). **gravi** (342), neut. ag. w. exitio.

438. **Stravere** (224). **altis,** dat. fem. plu. ag. w. urbibus; fr. altus (43). **urbibus,** dat. (acquisitive or incommodi) plu. after stetere; fr. urbs (40). **ultimæ,** nom. fem. plu. ag. w. causæ; fr. ultimus (280), *the farthest off, i.e.,* the first link of the chain.

439 Stetere causæ, cur perirent
440 Funditus imprimeretque muris
441 Hostile aratrum exercitus insolens.
442 Compesce mentem ; me quoque pectoris
443 Tentavit in dulci juventa
444 Fervor et in celeres iambos
445 Misit furentem. Nunc ego mitibus
446 Mutare quæro tristia, dum mihi

439. **Stetēre,** 3rd plu. pf. ind. act. fr. sto (233). **causæ,** nom. plu. predic. after stetere; fr. causa, -æ (ss), 1st fem., *that on account* of or *through which a thing takes place, cause, reason. Motive, occasion. Condition, state, situation,* (ak. to caveo, 380, *the guarding* or *protecting thing;* or cura, 215, *the thing in question*). **cur** (218). **perirent** (58), impf. after stetere; subjunct. after cur in indirect question.

440. **Funditus,** adv., (fundus, 328) *from the very bottom, from the foundation* (class.); fig., *utterly, entirely, totally, completely.* **imprimeret,** 3rd s. impf. subj. act. jnd. by -que to perirent; fr. imprimo (356). **muris,** dat. s. after (remote obj. of) imprimeret; fr. mūrus, -i, 2nd mas., *a wall* of a city, *wall* for protecting, *wall* of a private dwelling.

441. **Hostīle,** acc. neut. s. ag. w. aratrum; fr. hostīlis, -e, adj., (hostis, 76) *belonging to an enemy. Usual with* or *proper to an enemy.* **aratrum,** acc. s. gov. by (direct obj. of) imprimeret; fr. ărātrum, -i, 2nd neut. (Gk.), *a plough.* **exercitus,** -us, 4th mas.; nom. s. subj. of imprimeret; (exerceo, *to exercise*) milit., *a trained* or *disciplined body of men, an army,* esp. *a land army,* opp. to *a naval force* or *fleet,* or of *infantry* opp. to *cavalry.* Poet., *any multitude, flock.* **insolens** (156), ag. w. exercitus.

442. **Compesce,** 2nd s. imper. pres. act. fr. compesco, -ĕre, -uī, no sup., 3rd trans., (compes, *a fetter, shackle*) *to fasten together, confine, hold in check, repress, curb* (genly. poet.); fig., *to repress, suppress* (1447). **mentem** (426), gov. by compesce. **me** (29), gov. by tentavit. **quoque** (410). **pectoris,** gen. s. after fervor; fr. pectus (98).

443. **Tentavit,** 3rd s. pf. ind. act. fr. tento (279). **in,** w. abl. of time (78). **dulci,** abl. fem. s. ag. w. juventa; fr. dulcis (2). **juventa,** abl. s. gov. by in; fr. jŭventa, -æ, 1st fem., (not Cic.) *the age of one who is juvenis, youthful age,* of human beings and animals.

444. **Fervor,** -ōris, 3rd mas.; nom. s. subj. of tentavit; (ferveo, 348) *a raging heat, violent heat, raging, burning,* fig., *heat, vehemence, ardour.* **et** (2). **in** (76). **celeres** (294), ag. w. iambos; *hasty, impetuous.* **iambos,** acc. plu. gov. by in; fr. iambus (423).

445. **Misit** (38). **furentem,** acc. mas. s. ag. w. me; fr. furens (355). **nunc** (21). **ego** (29), nom. s. subj. of quæro. **mitibus,** abl. (of price) neut. plu. (as subst.) fr. mītis, -e, adj., of fruits, *arrived at full maturity, mellow, ripe.* Of character, nature, etc., *mild, gentle, free from harshness.* Of human beings and animals, *tame, gentle.* Of things, *softened.* Of speech, *mellow, pleasing, agreeable.* Of the soul, *mellow, fruitful* (478). Of wine, *free from harshness* or *roughness.*

446. **Mutare,** pres. inf. (objective) act. after quæro; fr. muto (77), here, *to give in exchange.* **quæro** (245), 1st s. pres. ind. act. **tristia,** acc. neut. plu. gov. by mutare; fr. tristis (102). **dum** (53), here *provided that* w. subj. pres. **mihi** (277), after trajective amicos.

Fias recantatis amica
  Opprobriis animumque reddas.

CARMEN XVII.—AD TYNDARIDEM.

Velox amœnum sæpe Lucretilem
Mutat Lycæo Faunus, et igneam
  Defendit æstatem capellis

447. **Fias,** 2nd s. subj. pres. fr. fio, fīs, fĭt, 3rd plu. fīunt, inf. fĭeri, fut. s. fiam, -es, etc. reg., impf. fīebam, -as, reg. Conj. pres. fīam, -as, etc., reg.; impf. fĭerem, -es, reg. Defective quasi-pass. vb. used as the pass. of facio in pres. stem tenses. Supine stem tenses fr. factus; its fut. inf. fore or futurus esse and fut. partc. futurus are formed as fr. sum (3, fio, for fu-i-o, being a strengthd. fm. of fu-), *to be made, become, come into existence.* **recantatis,** pf. pass. part. abl. neut. plu. ag. w. opprobriis; fr. recanto, -āre, no pf., no sup., 1st intens. trans. and intrans., (re, 659; canto, 183) *to sound back, re-echo* (Mart.). *To chant back,* i.e., *recall, recant, revoke.* **amica,** nom. fem. s. predic. ag. w. tu und. in fias; fr. amicus (208).

448. **Opprobriis,** abl. absol. (824) plu. fr. opprŏbrium, -ii, 2nd neut., (opprobro, *to taunt, reproach*) *a reproaching,* hence *a reproach, scandal, disgrace, dishonour* (not Cic. nor Cæs.). Of speech, *taunt, abuse, abusive word.* Of persons or things, *causing scandal* (1196). **animum,** acc. s. gov. by reddas; fr. ănĭmus, -i, 2nd mas., *the rational soul* or *intellectual principle of life in man,* (i.) *soul* as seat of will, emotion, thought, etc., *will, desire, purpose;* (ii.) *soul* as seat of feeling, *heart, feeling, sentiment. Courage, spirit;* (iii.) *thinking faculty, mind, intellect,* also of special powers of the mind [animus=*power, activity, rational soul;* anima, *animal spirit, life*]. **reddas** (95), jnd. by que to fias.

CARMEN XVII. METRE—*Alcaic.* (Carmen IX.)

449. **Vēlox,** -ōcis, adj.; nom. mas. s. ag. w. Faunus (perh. velum, *a sailing under sails*) *swift, fleet, quick, rapid, speedy.* **amœnum,** acc. mas. s. ag. w. Lucretilem; fr. ămœnus, -a, -um, adj., (acc. to some for amosinus; fr. amor, 247) *pleasant, delightful, charming,* usu. to the sense of sight, *e.g.,* of a landscape; post-Aug. of other things, *e,g.,* vita, animus. **sæpe** (200). **Lucretilem,** acc. s. gov. by mutat; fr. Lūcrĕtilis, -is, 3rd mas., a mt. in the Sabine territory.

450. **Mutat,** 3rd s. pres. ind. act. fr. muto (77); here, *to take in exchange.* **Lycæo,** abl. (of price) s. fr. Lўcæus, -i, 2nd mas., a mt. in Arcadia, where Jupiter and Pan were worshipped. The thing *taken* in exchange is more usu. in abl. (442), but 1187 as here. **Faunus** (139), nom. s. subj. of mutat; here identified w. Gk. Pan. **et** (2). **igneam,** acc. fem. s. ag. w. æstatem; fr. igneus, -a, -um, adj., (ignis, 116) *of fire, on fire, fiery, burning* (1333); fig., *glowing, ardent, vehement;* here *hot, scorching.*

451. **Defendit,** 3rd s. ind. pres. act. fr. dēfendo, -dĕre, -di, -sum, 3rd trans., (de, 10; -fendo, whence offendo, infensus) *to ward off* anything inimical, *repel, avert, keep off,* aliquid aliquo; meton., like prohibere w. acc. of that from which anything is warded. *To guard, protect* (com.), esp. aliquid or aliquem ab aliquâ re or aliquo. *To support, maintain, bring forward, allege in defence,* chiefly in Cic., *e.g.,* quod defendit. **æstatem,** acc. s.

452 Usque meis pluviosque ventos.
453 Impune tutum per nemus arbutos
454 Quærunt latentes et thyma deviæ
455 Olentis uxores mariti,
456 Nec virides metuunt colubras,
457 Nec Martiales Hædiliæ lupos,

gov. by defendit; fr. æstas, -ātis, 3rd fem., (ak. to æstus, 466) *the summer season*, fr. Mar. 22nd to Sept. 22nd, more restrictedly *the three months* fr. entrance of the sun into Cancer to the autumnal equinox; sts. in historians *a year*, as war was carried on only in the summer. *Fair weather, summer air.* **capellis,** abl. (of separation) plu. after defendit; fr. căpella, -æ, 1st fem., (diminutive of caper, *a goat*) *a she-goat.*

452. **Usque,** adv., (like uspiam, usquam, akin to quo, -que) *all the way, right on, continuously, without stop, constantly, incessantly.* Of place w. ab, ex, de, in, (w. acc.); sts. w. advs. istim, quaque. With acc. of place, *whither, as far as,* only of towns till post-Aug., *e.g.*, usque Romam. Of time, *all the while from* or *to* a period, *as long as, until* w. ab. ad; w. advs. inde, adhuc, eo, quaque, dum, adeo. Of other relations, *even up to, until, e.g.*, usque ad necem; so usque eo, ut, etc. **meis,** abl. fem. plu. ag. w. capellis; fr. meus (2). **pluvios,** acc. mas. plu. ag. w. ventos; fr. plŭvius, -a, -um, adj., (pluo, *to rain*) *causing* or *bringing rain. Rain, e.g.*, aqua, arcus. **ventos** (242), jnd. by -que to æstatem.

453. **Impune,** adv. of impunis, (in, neg.; punio, *to punish*) *without punishment, without fear of punishment, without harm, with impunity. Without loss* or *danger, securely, safely* (723). **tutum,** acc. neut. s. ag. w. nemus; fr. tūtus, -a, -um, adj., (orig., *well guarded;* fr. tueor, 461) *safe, secure, out of danger,* "diadema tutum," *that cannot be taken away* (937), "tutæ aures," *faithful* (642); fig., *watchful, cautious, careful, prudent* (post-Aug.). **per** (114). **nemus,** acc. s. gov. by per; fr. nemus (30). **arbutos,** acc. plu. gov. by quærunt; fr. arbutus (21); the kids fed on its leaves.

454. **Quærunt,** 3rd plu. pres. ind. act. fr. quæro (245). **latentes,** acc. plu. fem. pres. part. act. ag. w. arbutos; fr. lateo (229) **thyma,** acc. plu. jnd. by et to arbutos; fr. thȳmum, -i, 2nd neut., *thyme.* **deviæ,** nom. plu. fem. ag. w. uxores; fr. dēvius, -a, -um, adj., (dē, 10; via, 664) *apart* or *removed from the way, that lies out of the high road;* fig. *erroneous, foolish, eccentric. Retired, remote, sequestered, e.g.*, gens. *Wandering from the way,* or *in remote spots* (here).

455. **Olentis,** gen. mas. s. pres. part. act. ag. w. mariti; fr. ŏleo, -ēre, ŏlui, no sup., 2nd, collat. ŏlo, ŏlĕre, 3rd intrans., *to emit a smell, smell; fig., to have a scent* or *savour, e.g.*, nihil olet ex Academia; trans., *to smell of, have* or *emit a smell of,* etc.; fig., *to indicate, betray.* **uxores,** nom. plu. subj. of quærunt; fr. uxor, -ōris, 3rd fem., *a wife, spouse, consort.* Of animals, *a mate.* **mariti,** gen. s. after uxores; fr. mărītus, -i, 2nd mas., (mas. *a male*) *a married man, husband.* Of animals, *mate;* meton., *lover, suitor, wooer.*

456. **Nec** (13). **virīdes,** acc. fem. plu. ag. w. colubras; fr. viridis (21). **metuunt,** 3rd plu. pres. ind. act. fr. metuŏ (16) **colubras,** acc. plu. gov. by metuunt; fr. cŏlŭbra, -æ, 1st fem., cŏlŭber, -bri, 2nd mas., *a serpent.*

457. **Nec** (19). **Martiāles,** acc. plu. mas. ag. w lupos; fr. Martiālis, -e, adj., *sacred to Mars. Dedicated* or *in honour of Mars, e.g.*, ludi. *Named after Mars.* **Hædīliæ,** gen. s. after lupos; fr. Hædīlĭa, -æ, 1st fem., *a hill,*

Utcunque dulci, Tyndari, fistula
  Valles et Usticæ cubantis
    Levia personuere saxa.
Di me tuentur, Dis pietas mea
Et Musa cordi est. Hic tibi copia
  Manabit ad plenum benigno

or valley near Horace's Sabine villa. **lupos,** acc. plu. jnd. by nec to colubras; fr. lupus (414).

458. **Utcunque,** adv., (ut, *how*, and indef. affix -cunque, *ever*) *in whatever way, however, howsoever. At whatever time, whenever, as soon as* =quandocunque (799, 1331). **dulci** (443), ag. w. fistŭla. **Tyndari,** voc. s. fr. Tyndăris, -ĭdis, 3rd fem. **fistula,** abl. (instrum.) s. fr. fistŭla, -æ, 1st fem., (findo, 11) anything internally or externally of a tubular form, *a water-pipe. Hollow reed, stalk, reed, pipe;* used of many things of like shape.

459. **Valles,** nom. plu. subj. of personuere; fr. vallis (413). **Urticæ,** gen. s. after saxa; fr. Urtīca, -æ, 1st fem., a small hill in the Sabine country near Horace's villa. **cubantis,** gen. s. fem. pres. part. act. ag. w. Urticæ; fr. cŭbo, -āre, -bui, -ĭtum, 1st intrans. Of living beings, *to lie in a recumbent posture, lie on one's bed, lie,* esp. *to lie asleep. To recline at table. To keep one's bed through sickness.* Of places, *to be in an oblique, slanting direction,* (very rare); here cubans=*sloping*, but others translate it "*low lying,*" making Urtica a valley.

460. **Levia,** nom. plu. neut. ag. w. saxa; fr. levis (74). **personuēre,** 3rd plu. pf. ind. act. fr. persŏno, -āre, -ui, -ĭtum, 1st intrans., (per, 114; sono, *to sound*), *to sound through and through. To resound, make a sound* on a musical instrument, *sound, play;* trans., *to fill with a sound* or *noise, make resound. To cry out, call out, proclaim aloud.* **saxa,** nom. plu. subj. of personuere; fr. saxum (313).

461. **Di** (278), subj. of tuentur. **me** (29), gov. by tuentur. **tuentur,** 3rd plu. pres. ind. fr. tueor, tŭēri, tuĭtus sum, 2nd; collat. tŭor 3rd (rare), depon. trans. (tutus, 453 sts. as partc.), orig., *to see, look, gaze upon, watch, view,* hence *see* or *look to, defend, protect. To look at, gaze at, behold, watch, view, regard, consider, examine* (only poet.). *To care for. To keep up, uphold, maintain, support. To guard, preserve, protect.* **Dis** (30), dat. after trajective expression (872) est cordi. **pietas,** -ātis, 3rd fem.; nom. s. subj. of est; (pius, 273) *dutiful conduct, tenderness and goodness of heart* towards gods, parents, kinsmen, friends and country; *piety, dutiful affection, love, loyalty, patriotism.* **mea,** nom. fem. s. ag. w. pietas; fr. meus (2).

462. **Musa** (174), jnd. by et to pietas. **cordi,** dat. s. after est; fr. cor, cordis, 3rd neut., *heart* as seat of feelings, emotions, etc. By synecdoche, *a person.* This is the predicative dat. of purpose; so odio esse alicui, *to be hateful to another;* vitio vertere alicui, *to impute as a fault to another;* so subsidio venire alicui, etc. It is usu. found w. a second dat. of the recipient. **est** (19). **Hic** (85). **tibi** (93), commodi after manabit. **cōpia,** -æ, 1st fem.; nom. s. subj. of manabit; (cum, 31; ops, 179) *ability, power, might, means* of doing. *Fulness, copiousness;* personified, *Goddess of plenty;* s. and plu., *wealth, riches, possessions;* milit., plu., less. com. s., *forces, troops.*

463. **Manabit,** 3rd s. fut. ind. act. fr. māno, -are, -avi, -atum, 1st intrans. and trans., *to flow, run, trickle, drop, distil* (1094). Of things not liquid, *to flow, arise, proceed, spring, take* or *have their origin, emanate from, origi-*

464 Ruris honorum opulenta cornu.
465 Hic in reducta valle Caniculæ
466 Vitabis æstus et fide Teïa
467 Dices laborantes in uno
468 Penelopen vitreamque Circen.

nate from. To diffuse, extend itself, spread, etc. Rare trans., *to cause to flow forth, drop, distil* (Hor.). **ad** (6). **plenum,** acc. neut. s. gov. by ad; fr. plēnus, -a, -um, adj., (-pleo, *to make full,* whence compleo, expleo, suppleo) *filled, full,* esp. of bodily size, *full, stout, portly, plump* (class.); meton., *filled, sated, e.g.,* w. love. *Full packed, loaded, e.g.,* of bees; ad plenum, *to the full. Entire, complete, whole, e.g.,* gaudia. Of the voice, *full, clear, loud. Abundant, much, e.g.,* pecunia. Of age, *ripe, mature, complete.* With gen., *full of.* **benigno,** abl. s. neut. ag. w. cornu; fr. bĕnignus, -a, -um, adj. (fr. bonus, 531; cf. malignus, privignus) prop. of persons, *good, kind, friendly, pleasing, favourable, mild.* Of actions, *beneficent, obliging. That gives* or *imparts freely, liberal, bountiful.* Of things, *favourable, pleasant, abundant, fertile, rich* (mostly poet. and post-Aug., 1362).

464. **Ruris,** gen. s. after honorum; fr. rus (17). **honorum,** gen. (of abundance, 882) plu. after opulenta; fr. honor (8); ruris honores=omnia quibus honestatur rus, *i.e.,* flowers, fruits, etc. **opulenta,** nom. fem. s. ag. w. copia; fr. ŏpŭlentus, -a, -um, adj., (opes, 179) *rich, wealthy, opulent, fine, splendid. Respectable, influential, noble;* adv. opulente and opulenter. **cornu,** abl. s. of source whence; fr. cornu, gen. cornūs, 4th neut., *a horn.* Cornu Copiæ, *horn* of goddess Plenty placed among the constellations; symbol of fertility and abundance. Of things like horn in substance, *e.g., hoof, tooth* of an elephant, *ivory,* or like it in shape, *e.g., bow, bugle, horn, trumpet;* also as symbol of power, strength, etc.

465. **Hic** (85). **in** (78), w. abl. local. **reducta,** abl. fem. s. ag. w. valle; fr. rĕductus, -a, -um, (prop. pf. pass. part. of reduco, 1131) *drawn back, withdrawn,* i.e., *running among the hills.* Of place, *retired, remote, lonely, distant.* **valle,** abl. s. gov. by in; fr. vallis (413). **caniculæ,** gen. s. after æstus; fr. cănīcŭla, -æ, 1st fem., (diminutive of canis, *a dog*) *a little dog* or *bitch.* The heat-bringing dog-star in the month of the constellation Canis.

466. **Vitabis** (402). **æstus,** acc. plu. gov. by vitabis; fr. æstus, -ūs, 4th mas., orig. *a burning, heat, warmth, glowing* or *scorching heat. Passionate commotion* of mind, *fire, glow, ardour* of passion, *excitement. Waving* or *rolling motion* of a flame. Of the sea, *undulating, heaving, agitated motion, swell, surge, waves, tide. Vacillating* or *irresolute state of mind, anxiety, embarrassment.* **et** (2). **fide,** abl. (instrum.) s. fr. fides (295). **Teia,** abl. fem. s. ag. w. fide; fr. Tēĭus, -a, -um, adj. *Of Teos* (Teos or Tĕus) a town in Ionia, birthplace of Anacreon, hence *Anacreontic.*

467. **Dices,** 2nd s. fut. ind. act. jnd. by et to vitabis; fr. dico (86). **laborantes** (235), ag. w. Penelopen and Circen. **in** (78). **uno,** abl. mas. s. gov. by in; fr. unus (189), "laborantes in uno," *wearying themselves for love of the same man, i.e.,* Ulysses (W.).

468. **Penelopen,** acc. gov. by dices; fr. Pēnĕlŏpe,-es (Gk.), and Pēnĕlŏpa, -æ, 1st fem., dau. of Icarius and Peribœa, wife of Ulysses, mother of Telemachus. **vitream,** acc. fem. s. ag. w. Circen; fr. vĭtreus, -a, -um, adj., (vitrum, *glass*) *of glass, glassy, vitreous;* meton., *like glass, glassy* in colour or transparency, *clear, bright, shining;* here *glittering, brilliant, beautiful,* with idea of *deceptive* also. **Circen,** acc. s. jnd. by -que to Penelopen; fr.

Hic innocentis pocula Lesbii
Duces sub umbra; nec Semeleius
  Cum Marte confundet Thyoneus
    Prœlia, nec metues protervum
Suspecta Cyrum, ne male dispari
Incontinentes injiciat manus

Circe, -es, 1st fem. (Gk.), also gen. Circæ, acc. Circam, abl. Circa, daughter of the Sun and Persa or Perseis, sister of Œetes, a sea nymph, celebrated for magic arts, dwelt after her flight from Colchis near prom. of Circeii in Latium.

469. **Hic** (85). **innocentis,** gen. neut. s. ag. w. Lesbii; fr. innocens, -ntis; adj., (in, neg.; noceo, 678) prop. *that does not harm, inoffensive;* here of a *light* wine; fig., *blameless, guiltless,* esp. *disinterested, upright, e.g.,* vir. **pocula** (19), gov. by duces. **Lesbii,** gen. after pocula; fr. Lesbium, -ii, 2nd neut. prop. neut. of Lesbius, -a, -um; adj. (623, 733), und. vinum, *Lesbian wine.*

470. **Duces,** 2nd s. fut. ind. act. fr. duco (133), here *to quaff, drink.* **sub** (21), here w. abl. local. **umbra,** abl. s. gov. by sub; fr. umbra (205). **nec** (19). **Sĕmĕlēïus,** -a, -um, or Sĕmĕlēus, -a, -um, adj.; nom. mas. s. ag. w. Thyoneus; *of Sĕmĕle,* daughter of Cadmus, and mother of Bacchus by Jupiter.

471. **Cum** (31). **Marte,** abl. s. gov. by cum; fr. Mars (177). **confundet,** 3rd sing. fut. ind. act. fr. confundo, -dĕre, -fūdi, -fūsum, 3rd trans., (cum, 31; fundo, 711) prop. *to pour together;* meton., *to mix, mingle, blend. To mix in disorder* or *confusion;* fig., *to unite, combine, e.g.,* vera cum falsis, and here. Of mind, *to perplex, confound, disconcert,* (mostly post - Aug. perh. not Cic.). *To pour out, empty completely.* **Thyōneus,** -ĕi, 2nd mas.; nom. s. subj. of confundet. *The son of Thyone* (=Semele) *i.e., Bacchus.*

472. **Prœlia** (181), gov. by confundet. **nec** (19). **metues,** 2nd s. fut. ind. act. fr. metuo (16). **protervum,** acc. mas. s. ag. w. Cyrum; fr. prŏtervus, -a, -um, adj., (protero, *to beat down before*) *trampling* on things, *violent, vehement* (614); fig., *forward, bold, pert, wanton; impudent* (class., genly. milder than prŏcax and petulans).

473. **Suspecta,** nom. fem. s. ag. w. tu und. in metues; fr. suspectus, -a, -um, adj., (suspicio, *to suspect*) *mistrusted, that excites mistrust* or *suspicion;* act., *entertaining suspicion* (not class.); comp. suspectior. **Cyrum,** acc. s. gov. by metues; fr. Cȳrus, -i, 2nd mas. **ne** (41). **male** (256), increases the force of dispari. **dispari,** dat. fem. s. ag. w. tibi und. after injiciat; fr. dispar, -păris, adj., (dis, 870; par, 180) *unequal* in certain qualities; hence *dissimilar, different;* lit. and fig., *not a match for.*

474. **Incontinentes,** acc. fem. plu. ag. w. manus; fr. incontĭnens, -ntis, adj., (in, neg.; contineo, 1374) *not containing, not retaining* (class. not Cic.). *Incontinent, immoderate, intemperate, violent.* **injiciat,** 3rd s. pres. (after metues) subjunct. (after ne) fr. injĭcĭo, -jĭcĕre, -jēci, -jectum, 3rd trans., (in, 76; jacio, *to throw*) *to throw, cast into,* esp. *throw oneself anywhere,* fig., *to bring into, inspire, cause, e.g.,* metum alicui. *To cast* or *throw in* or *upon* a person or thing, esp. "injĭcĕre manum alicui," *to seize* as one's property; fig., *to exercise power over. To throw out a hint, casually mention, suggest.* **manus,** acc. plu. gov. by (direct obj. of) injiciat; fr. mănus, -us, 4th fem., *a hand. Force, violence. Handiwork, workmanship;* manus extrema, ultima, *the finishing stroke. Armed force, corps. Power.*

Et scindat hærentem coronam
Crinibus immeritamque vestem.

CARMEN XVIII.—AD QUINTILIUM VARUM.

Nullam, Vare, sacra vite prius severis arborem
Circa mite solum Tiburis et mœnia Catili.
Siccis omnia nam dura Deus proposuit neque

475. **Scindat,** 3rd s. pres. subj. act. jnd. by et to injiciat; fr. scindo (161). **hærentem,** acc. fem. s. pres. part. act. ag. w. coronam; fr. hæreo (45). **coronam,** acc. s. gov. by scindat; fr. cŏrōna, -æ, 1st fem., *a garland, wreath, crown;* sub corona vendere, *to sell captives as slaves,* since they were crowned as an animal for sacrifice. The northern *crown* (Ariadne), a constellation. Of things in shape of a *crown, circle* of men, *assembly, crowd, multitude, e.g.,* judicial or of besiegers, etc.

476. **Crinibus,** dat. plu. after trajective (873) hærentem; fr. crinis (404). **immeritam,** acc. fem. s. ag. w. vestem; fr. immĕrĭtus, -a, -um, adj., (in, neg.; mereor, *to deserve*) *that has not deserved* anything, *guiltless* (678). Pass. *that is not deserved, undeserved, unmerited.* **vestem,** acc. s. jnd. by -que to coronam; fr. vestis (800).

Carmen XVIII. Metre—*Fifth* or *Greater Asclepiad.* (Carmen xi.)

477. **Nullam,** acc. fem. s. ag. w. arborem; fr. nullus, -a, -um, gen. nullīus, dat. nulli, pronominal adj. (ne, 41; ullus, 169). *Not any, none, no;* sts.=non. *Of no account* or *moment, insignificant, trifling.* **Vare,** voc. s. fr. Varus, -i, a Roman cognomen, esp. in the Gens Quintilia. **sacra,** abl. fem. s. ag. w. vite; fr. sacer (22), *i.e.,* given by Bacchus. **vite,** abl. comparative (103) s. after prius; fr. vītis, -is, 3rd fem., (vieo, *to bind;* orig. *that which binds* or *winds about*) *a vine, grape vine;* meton., *a vine-branch.* A centurion's staff made of a vine branch. **prius** (120). **sĕvĕris,** 2nd sing. pf. (277) conjunctive (hortative) act. fr. sĕro, sĕrĕre, sēvi, sătum, 3rd trans. Of persons, *to beget, bring forth, produce,* esp. in part. pf. *begotten, sprung forth;* satus, *a son;* sata, *a daughter;* meton., *to sow, plant;* fig., *produce, occasion, excite, e.g.,* quarrels. *To found, establish, e.g.,* laws. *To spread abroad, scatter, e.g.,* rumours. **arborem,** acc. s. gov. by severis; fr. arbor (329).

478. **Circa** (98). **mite,** acc. neut. s. ag. w. solum; fr. mītis (445). **solum,** acc. s. gov. by circa; fr. sŏlum, -i, 2nd neut., (ak. to sedeo, *to sit,* orig. *that on which anything is placed*) *the lowest part* of a thing, *floor, pavement* of a room, etc. *Bottom* of a ditch. *Foundation of* a building *Ground, earth, land, soil,* sts. *country, region. Foundation* or *groundwork* of which anything is made. **Tiburis,** gen. s. after solum; fr. Tibur, an ancient town of Latium on both sides of the Anio (now Tivoli). **mœnia** (187), jnd. by et to solum. **Catili,** gen. s. after mœnia; fr. Cātĭlus (usu. Cātillus), -i, 2nd mas., brother of Tiburtus, with whom he built Tibur.

479. **Siccis,** dat. plu. mas. after (remote obj. of) proposuit; fr. siccus (106). **omnia,** acc. neut. plu. (as subst.) gov. by proposuit; fr. omnis (43). **nam,** conj. (*a*) introduces a confirmation or declaration of a statement already made, either first or after a word; (*b*) used in adversative or concessive transitions, *but, on the contrary. Yet, indeed, to be sure,* ref. to a

480 Mordaces aliter diffugiunt sollicitudines.
481 Quis post vina gravem militiam aut pauperiem crepat?
482 Quis non te potius, Bacche pater, teque, decens Venus?

prop. to be understood; (*c*) emphasises an interrog., affixed to a pron. or coming after a word in good prose; ante-class and poet. also placed first. **dura,** acc. neut. plu. ag. w. omnia, after factitive (54) proposuit; fr. dūrus, -a, -um, adj., *hard* as affecting sense of feeling, *harsh* of taste. *Uncultivated, raw, rough, rude. Hardy, vigorous, strong. Stern, unyielding, unfeeling.* Of things, *hard, severe, toilsome, troublesome, disagreeable, unfortunate, difficult.* **proposuit,** 3rd s. pf. ind. act. fr. propōno, -pōnĕre, -pŏsui, -pŏsĭtum, 3rd trans., (pro, *forward*; pono, 104) *to put, place, lay* or *set forth* or *out; hang out, expose to view, display;* fig. *to set forth, report, declare, represent, say;* in good sense *offer, propose* as a reward; in bad sense *threaten, denounce. To lay before* one as an example, or a thing to be pursued, etc. *To put forth, state beforehand. To purpose, e.g.*, propositum est mihi w. ut or inf., *I purpose.* **neque** (32).

480. **Mordaces,** nom. fem. plu. ag. w. sollicitudines; fr. mordax, -ācis, adj., (mordeo, *to bite*) *prone to biting, e.g.*, of dog; meton., *taking fast hold of, tenacious, e.g.*, clasp. Of a sword, *cutting deeply.* Of flavour, *sharp, pungent;* fig., *annoying, tormenting, painful* (here). *Snarling, captious, e.g.*, Cynics. **ălĭter,** adv. of ălius (92); (i.) denotes opposition to what is said in its own clause, *in another manner*, often in negatives. (ii.) = alioquin, *in any other case, else.* (iii.) *in a contrary manner, e.g.*, dis aliter visum. (iv.) in relations of inequality, aliter...atque, ac, quam, *otherwise...than;* esp. haud or non aliter quam, *just as if;* so w. quam si, quam quam, haud aliter nisi or quam ut "*on no other condition except*" or "*than that.*" **diffugiunt,** 3rd plu. pres. ind. act. fr. diffŭgio, -fŭgĕre, fūgi, no sup., 3rd intrans., (dis, 873; fugio, 206) *to flee in different directions, disperse, be scattered about* (802). Of things, *to depart, escape.* **sollicitudines,** nom. plu., subj. of diffugiunt; fr. sollĭcĭtūdo, -ĭnis, 3rd fem., (sollicitus, 381) *uneasiness of mind, care, disgust, anxiety,* in sing. and plu.

481. **Quis** (149), subj. of crepat. **post** (117). **vina** (282), gov. by post. **gravem** (169), fem. ag. w. militiam. **militiam,** acc. s. gov. by crepat; fr. mīlĭtia, -æ, 1st fem., (mīlĭto, *to serve as a soldier*) *military service,* domi militiæque, *at home and in the field, abroad.* Abstr. for concr., *the troops, military force. Service, employment, office* of any laborious even civil employment (class.). **aut** (131). **pauperiem** (18), jnd. by aut to militiam. **crepat,** 3rd s. pres. ind. act. fr. crĕpo, -āre, crĕpŭi, crĕpĭtum, 1st irreg. (ak. *to creak*), intrans., *to rattle, creak, rustle, clatter;* trans., *to make* something *sound, e.g.*, aëra. In 1346, lætum crepuit sonum = *to raise, make,* cogn. acc.; fig., *to make a great ado about, grumble, prate about,* etc.

482. **Quis** (149), subj. of crepat und. fr. prec. by zeugma. **non** (15). **te** (83), gov. by crepat. **potius** (85). **Bacche,** voc. s. of Bacchus, -i, 2nd mas., son of Jupiter and the Theban Semele, god of wine, hence called Liber, Lyæus (1399). Poets wore crowns of ivy, which was sacred to him; he was worshipped esp. in Thrace and Macedonia, esp. in Mt. Edon (1067); his horns alluded to (1422). **pater** (38), voc. in app. to Bacche. **te,** jnd. by -que to prec. te. **decens** (134), voc. fem. s. ag. w. Venus. **Venus** (133), voc.

483 At, ne quis modici transiliat munera Liberi,
484 Centaurea monet cum Lapithis rixa super mero
485 Debellata, monet Sithoniis non levis Evius,
486 Quum fas atque nefas exiguo fine libidinum

483. **At** (old fm. as retained by poets and Cicero's letters), adversative conj. It joins to a prec. idea a new and different one, *and indeed*, either, (*a*) a clause directly opp. to prec. one, *but indeed, on the contrary*, class.; (*b*) a clause containing something simply different from, but not entirely opposed to, what has been said, like autem. *But yet, on the other hand, moreover*, [sed also adds a new limitation]; *e.g.*, 671, in passing to an admonition. Often it adds an objection which one assumes as likely to be made, *but it may be objected, but one may say;* at enim introd. a reason for an objection, *but certainly, but it should be noted.* **ne** (41), final. **quis** (183), nom. mas. s., subj. of transiliat. **modici**, gen. mas. s. ag. w. Liberi; fr. mŏdĭcus, -a, -um, adj., (modus, 422) of *moderate size, observing due limits* or *bounds*, of size, length, extent, degree, etc. Of character, *modest, moderate, temperate* (Tac. and Sall.) meton. Of things, *small, not large* in amount, *trifling, slight* in degree, *few* in number, *unfrequent, rare*, etc.; here "*that loves moderation*," properly an epithet of the draught (W.). **transiliat**, 3rd s. subj. (after ne) pres. (after monet) act. fr. transilio (112). **munera**, acc. plu. gov. by transiliat; fr. mūnus, -ĕris, 3rd neut., *an office, place, post, function, employment, duty. A work. Service, favour*, esp. last *service* to the dead, *i.e., burial. A present, gift. A public show, exhibition, spectacle*, esp. of gladiators given to the people by the magistrates in gratitude for their election. **Liberi**, gen. s. after munera; fr. Liber (306). To overpass the bounty of Liber=to take more than he gives.

484. **Centaurea**, nom. fem. s. ag. w. rixa; fr. Centaurēus, -a, -um, adj., *pertaining to the Centaurs.* **monet**, 3rd s. ind. pres. act. fr. mŏneo, ēre, -ŭi, -ĭtum, 2nd trans. and intrans., (ak. to mens, *to cause*, or *make to think*) *to bring* something *to one's recollection, put in mind of*, w. acc. of pers. and gen. or abl. w. de of thing; also w. acc. of pron., *e.g.*, illud me; meton., *to admonish, advise, warn*, aliquem w. acc. neut. pron., or ut, ne w. subj. or subj. alone; intrans., *to give an admonition* or *warning. To instruct, teach, inform* (poet.) *To foretell, predict.* **cum** (31). **Lapithis**, abl. plu. gov. by cum; fr. Lăpĭtha, -æ, 1st com., Lăpĭthes, -æ, mas. Plu. Lăpĭthæ, -arum, mas., a Thessalian people dwelling near Olympus and Pindus. Their combat with the Centaurs at the marriage of their king Peirithous was celebrated. **rixa** (355), nom. s. subj. of monet. **super** (237), here either local, "*over* the spilt wine," or "*after*." **mero** (203), gov. by super.

485. **Debellata**, pf. pass. part., nom. fem. s. ag. w. rixa; fr. dēbello, -āre, -avi, -ātum, 1st intrans. and trans., (de, 10; bellum, 24) *to conclude a war, bring a war to an end*, genly. impers. *To war out completely, fight it out. To conquer completely, vanquish* or *utterly subdue.* **monet** (484), anaphora. **Sithoniis**, dat. after traject. levis; fr. Sīthŏnĭi, -orum, 2nd mas., a Thracian people, dwelling in Chalcidice. **non** (55), jnd. as one word w. levis. **lĕvis** (382), mas., ag. w. Evius. **Evius** (1157), nom. s., subj. of monet.

486. **Quum** (345). **fas**, indecl. noun; acc. gov. by decernunt; (fari, *to speak, that which is spoken*) *that which is right in the sight of God* [jus, *human law*]. *That which is right* by law, equity, custom, permission, *right, justice, equity. Lawful, fit, permitted, a pious duty.* **atque** (37). **nefas** (114), acc. jnd. by atque to fas. **exiguo**, abl. s. mas. ag. w. fine; fr. exĭguus, -a, -um, adj., (exigo, *to weigh out*, hence orig. either *exactly measured*, opp. to *abundant, beyond measure*, or *protractus, exilis*) *scanty*

487 Discernunt avidi. Non ego te, candide Bassareu,
488 Invitum quatiam nec variis obsita frondibus
489 Sub divum rapiam. Sæva tene cum Berecynthio
490 Cornu tympana, quæ subsequitur cæcus Amor sui,

in measure or number, *small, little, petty, short, poor, mean* (1116). **fine,** abl. (of means) s. fr. finis (94). **libidinum,** gen. plu. after fine; fr. lĭbīdo, -ĭnis, 3rd fem., (libet, 424) *desire, eagerness, longing, fancy, inclination,* esp. *unlawful desire, passion, caprice, wantonness, sensual desire.* Plu. in Cic. of *voluptuous, obscene representations* in painting and sculpture.

487. **Discernunt,** 3rd plu. pres. ind. act. fr. discerno, -cernĕre, -crēvi, -crētum, 3rd trans., (dis, 870; cerno, *to perceive*) *to separate, set apart, e.g.,* telas; part. pf. pass. discretus (1215). *To separate* things *according to their different qualities,* i.e., *distinguish, discern.* **avidi,** nom. plu. mas. ag. w. subj. of discernunt; fr. ăvĭdus, -a, -um, adj., (aveo, *to long for*) *longing eagerly for* something, *desiring, eager, greedy,* esp. *greedy of gain, avaricious, covetous*=avarus (917). *Desirous of food, voracious, gluttonous.* In Lucret., of space, *wide, large, vast;* "cum...avidi," *i.e.,* when the only distinction they place between right and wrong is that they desire the thing or not (W). **non** (55), w. quatiam. **ego** (445), subj. of quatiam. **te** (83), gov. by quatiam. **candide,** voc. mas. s. ag. w. Bassareu; fr. candidus (233); here "*ever fair and young,*" of the beauty of divine youth. **Bassareu,** voc. s. fr. Bassăreus, gen. -ei, 2nd mas. (Gk. bassara, a *fox-skin* clothing of the Bacchantes), a title of Bacchus.

488. **Invitum,** acc. mas. s. ag. w. te; fr. invītus, -a, -um, adj., (in, neg.; -vitus said to be akin to volo; cf. vis, fr. volis) *that does not will, unwilling, against one's will, reluctant;* adv. attribute (com.), *unwillingly, reluctantly,* ag. w. subject, genly. in nom., rarely acc. before inf. of things. **quatiam,** 1st s. fut. ind. act. fr. quatio (18); properly ref. to the thyrsus. **nec** (19). **variis** (299), ag. w. frondibus. **obsita,** acc. neut plu. gov. by rapiam; fr. obsĭtus, pf. pass. part. of obsĕro, -sĕrĕre, -sēvi, -sĭtum, 3rd trans., (ob, 329; sero, *to sow*) *to sow* or *plant. To sow* or *plant over* w. anything; obsitus, *overgrown, overrun, covered* or *filled w. trees.* **frondibus,** abl. (instrum.) plu. fr. frons, -ndis, 3rd fem., *leaves, a leafy branch, green bough, foliage* (class. sing. and plu.). Poet., *a garland made of leafy boughs, leafy chaplet.*

489. **Sub** (21, 230), here of place w. acc. **divum,** acc. s. gov. by sub; fr. dīvum, -i, 2nd neut., (prop. neut. of divus, -a, -um, 89) *the open air;* sub divum, *into the light* (W.). **rapiam,** 1st s. fut. ind. act. fr. răpio, răpĕre, răpui, raptum, 3rd trans., *to seize, carry off, snatch, tear, drag, hurry away. To carry off by force, seize, rob, plunder. To strongly attract, transport, captivate.* **sæva,** acc. neut. plu. ag. w. tympana; fr. sævus (172). **tene,** 2nd s. imper. pres. act. fr. teneo (204), *silence, i.e.,* do not excite us too much, addressed to Bacchus (W.). **cum** (31). **Berecynthio,** abl. neut. s. ag. w. cornu; fr. Bĕrĕcynthĭus, -a, -um, adj., *of* or *pertaining to Berecynthus,* a mt. in Phrygia, sacred to Cybele, on the river Sangarius; hence, *pertaining to Cybele.* This horn was also used in the Bacchic worship.

490. **Cornu** (464), gov. by cum. **tympana,** acc. plu. gov. by tene; fr. tympănum, -i, 2nd neut., *a drum, timbrel, tambourine.* **quæ** (359), neut. plu. ag. w. tympana, acc. gov. by subsequitur. **subsequitur,** 3rd s. pres. ind. fr. subsĕquor, -sĕqui, -sĕcūtus sum, 3rd depon., prop. *to follow close after, succeed, follow immediately;* fig., *to follow after mentally* or *in opinion, conform oneself to, comply with.* **cæcus,** -a, -um, adj.; nom. mas. s. ag. w. Amor; *having no light, devoid of light, not seeing, blind. Blinded*

Et tollens vacuum plus nimio Gloria verticem,
Arcanique Fides prodiga perlucidior vitro.

CARMEN XIX.—DE GLYCERA.

Mater sæva Cupidinum
Thebanæque jubet me Semeles puer
Et lasciva Licentia

mentally or morally. Pass., *that cannot be seen* or *known, invisible, hidden, secret. Dark, obscure, e.g.,* nox. *Uncertain, doubtful, e.g.,* expectatio. **Amor** (364), personified; subj. of subsequitur. **sui** (53), gen. (objective) s. after Amor.

491. **Tollens,** nom. fem. s. pres. part. act. ag. w. gloria; fr. tollo (8). **vacuum** (122), ag. w. verticem. **plūs,** adv., *more;* w. vbs., w. quam or compar. adv.; plus aut minus, plus minusve, *more or less,* i.e., *about;* plus quam or plus, *more than, beyond. Too much, overmuch.* **nimio,** abl. (of measure) neut. s. fr. nimius (53); nimio plus, *by a great deal too much.* **gloria,** -æ, 1st fem.; jnd. by et to Amor; (ak. to clarus, cluo; lit., *rumour, fame*) *glory, fame, renown.* Plur.=gloriose facta, *glorious deeds* (Cic.); meton., *thirst* or *passion for glory, ambition, vainglory* (here), *pride, vaunting, boasting.* **verticem,** acc. s. gov. by tollens; fr. vertex (36).

492. **Arcani,** gen. (objective of matter) neut. s. (as subst.) fr. arcānus, -a, -um, adj., (arca, *a shut up box*) *that keeps a secret, trusty. Secret, hidden, concealed, private,* esp. of things sacred and incommunicable; arcanum, -i, 2nd neut., *a secret, mystery.* **Fides** (153), personified, nom. s. jnd. by -que to gloria. **prodiga,** nom. fem. s. ag. w. Fides; fr. prodigus (322); "*Faith that blabs out her secret,*" an oxymoron (W.). **perlucidior,** nom. fem. s. compar. adj. ag. w. Fides; fr. perlūcĭdus, -a, -um, adj., (pelluceo=perluceo, *to shine through*) *transparent, pellucid;* meton., *very brilliant, glistening, resplendent.* **vitro,** abl. (comparative, 103) s. fr. vĭtrum, -i, 2nd mas., (video, 40) *glass.*

Carmen XIX. Metre.—*The Second Asclepiad.* (Carmen. iii.)

493. **Mater** (24), nom. s, subj. of jubet. **sæva** (237), ag. w. mater; "*imperious*" (W.). **Cupidinum,** gen. plu. after mater; fr. Cupido (70).

494 **Thebanæ,** gen. s. fem. ag. w. Semeles; fr. Thebānus, (Thebæ, 187) *Theban.* **jubet,** 3rd s. ind. pres. act. fr. jŭbeo, -ēre, jussi, jussum, 2nd irreg. trans. and intrans., *to order, command, bid. To order* one to do something or that something be done, w. inf., rare w. ut or subj. alone; sts. w. acc. of pers. or thing; esp. *to wish, desire, entreat, request, bid;* politically, *to ratify, propose, sanction. To appoint* a person to an office, *order, decree* that a person be something. **me** (29), subj. of reddere. **Semeles,** gen. s. after puer; fr. Sĕmĕle (see 470); collat. Lat. form Sĕmĕla, -æ, 1st fem. **puer** (149), jnd. by -que to mater.

495. **Lasciva,** nom. fem. s. ag. w. Licentia; fr. lascīvus, -a, -um, adj., *tricky, playful, frolicsome, sportive;* meton., *wanton, petulant, saucy, impudent. Lewd, wanton, voluptuous.* In 836, *luxuriant,* or perh. *closely clinging,* as in wantonness; fig. *sportive, playful* (1147); adv. lascive, lasciviter. **Licentia,** -æ, 1st fem.; nom. s. jnd. by et to puer; (licet, *it is permitted*) *freedom, liberty, acting according to one's own will or pleasure,* esp. *liberty* which one assumes, *boldness, presumption. Lawlessness, uncurbed state.*

Finitis animum reddere amoribus.
Urit me Glyceræ nitor
Splendentis Pario marmore purius;
Urit grata protervitas
Et vultus nimium lubricus aspici,
In me tota ruens Venus

496. **Finitis,** dat. mas. plu. pf. pass. part. ag. w. amoribus; fr. finio (201). **animum** (448), gov. by (direct obj. of) reddere. **reddere,** pres. inf. (prolative) after jubet; fr. reddo (95); "animum reddere," *to give my heart to.* **amoribus,** dat. plu. after (remote obj. of) reddere; fr. amor (247).

497. **Urit** (136). **me** (29), gov. by urit. **Glyceræ,** gen. s. after nitor; fr. Glўcĕra, 1st fem. **nĭtor,** -ōris, 3rd mas.; nom. s. subj. of urit; (niteo, 161) *a being bright, splendour, lustre. Sleekness, plumpness, good looks, beauty* (here). Of speech, *elegance, grace.*

498. **Splendentis,** gen. s. fem. pres. part. act. ag. w. Glyceræ; fr. splendeo, -ēre, -ui, no sup.; 2nd intrans., *to shine, be bright, gleam, glisten;* fig., *to be illustrious* (genly. poet., only once in Cic., then fig.). **Pario,** abl. neut. s. ag. w. marmore; fr. Părius, -a, -um, *of Păros,* one of the Cyclades, famed for white marble; birthplace of Archilochus. **marmore,** abl. comparative after purius; fr. marmor, -ŏris, 3rd neut., (mare doubled) *the water* of the sea. *Marble,* fr. its white glistening, *a piece of wrought marble, e.g.,* statue (1369). **purius,** compar. of pūre (class.), or pūriter (ante-class. and poet.), adv., (purus, 537) *purely* or *cleanly, in a pure, clean way* or *manner;* fig., *without evil* or *fault, chastely. Obviously,* w. apparere (Hor.). *Clearly, brightly, brilliantly* (here). *Perfectly, fully, entirely, e.g.,* tranquillare (Hor.).

499. **Urit** (136). **grata,** nom. fem. s. ag. w. protervitas; fr. gratus (129). **prŏtervitas,** -ātis, 3rd fem.; nom. s. subj. of urit; (protervus, 427) *pertness, sauciness, boldness, impudence. Forwardness, wantonness* (here).

500. **Vultus** (76), jnd. by et to protervitas. **nimium** (53), w. lubricus. **lubrĭcus,** -a, -um, adj.; nom. mas. s. ag. w. vultus; (luo, *belonging to what is made loose*) prop. of the ground, *slippery, causing to slip,* opp. to what is solid and so affords a firm standing-place. *Smooth,* and so *slippery, e.g.,* unguis. *Slimy, e.g.,* conchylea; fig., *uncertain, hazardous, critical, dangerous, e.g.,* ætas; "lubricus aspici," *dangerous to look upon,* on account of beauty; lubricum, -i, 2nd neut., *a slippery, loose place;* fig., *a critical position. Deceitfulness, slipperiness.* **aspici,** pres. inf. (prolative after lubricus) pass. fr. aspicio, -ĕre, -spexi, -spectum, 3rd trans., (ad, 6; specio, *to behold,* obsol.) *to look upon* some one or something, or somewhere, *behold, look at, see. To look at* in order to examine, *survey, inspect,* genly. *to behold. To reflect upon, weigh, consider, ponder;* esp. aspice, *see! behold! To look admiringly upon. To obtain a view of, descry.* Of places, *to command a view of, look towards;* "vultus...adspici," a face to look on which is to step from your resolve (W.).

501. **In** (81). **me** (29), gov. by in. **tota,** nom. fem. s. ag. as adv. attribute (867) w. Venus; fr. tōtus, -a, -um, gen., tōtīus, dat. tōti, adj., *all. The whole, entire, total;* adv. attrib., *altogether, wholly, entirely;* [tota in urbe, *in different parts of the whole city,* tota urbe, *over the whole city*]. **ruens** (432), fem. ag. w. Venus. **Venus** (133), subj. of deseruit.

502 Cyprum deseruit, nec patitur Scythas
503 Et versis animosum equis
504 Parthum dicere, nec quæ nihil attinent.
505 Hic vivum mihi cæspitem, hic
506 Verbenas, pueri, ponite thuraque
507 Bimi cum patera meri:

502. **Cyprum,** acc. s. gov. by deseruit; fr. Cyprus (89). **deseruit,** 3rd s. pf. ind. act. fr. dēsĕro, -erĕre, -ĕrui, -ertum, 3rd trans., (de, 10; sero, *to join, to connect*), *to leave in the lurch, fail, forsake, give up, abandon.* It denotes a cowardly running away, often jnd. w. prodere. **nec** (19). **patitur,** 3rd s. pres. ind. fr. patior (18). **Scythas,** acc. gov. by dicere; fr. Scythæ, -arum, 1st mas., *the Scythians,* general designation of the nomadic tribes in N. Europe and Asia beyond the Black Sea (785); sing. Scythes (Gk.). The Scythians, Parthians, and Spaniards, were those over whom Augustus gained victories.

503. **Versis,** abl. mas. plu. pf. pass. part. ag. w. equis; fr. verto, -ĕre, verti, versum, 3rd trans., *to turn, turn round* or *about. To overturn, turn upside down, overthrow*=everto. **animosum,** acc. mas. s. ag. w. Parthum; fr. ănĭmōsus, -a, -um, adj., (animus, 448) *full of courage, bold, spirited, undaunted* (1137). *Proud* on account of something. **equis** (167), absolute.

504. **Parthum,** acc. s. jnd. by et to Scythas; fr. Parthus, -i, *a Parthian;* plu. Parthi, -orum, m., *Parthians* (see 58). **dicere** (169), after patitur. **nec** (19), jns. demonst. und. (ea) as antecedent to quæ to Scythas. **quæ** (359), neut. plu. ag. w. demonst. und.; nom. to attinent. **nihil**=nil (125), adv. **attinent,** 3rd plu. pres. ind. act. fr. attĭneo, -tĭnēre, -tinui, -tentum, 2nd trans., *to hold* a person or thing *near, bring close to. To keep, lay hold of, hold fast. To possess, occupy, e.g.,* ripam Danubii. *To hold back, retain, detain, hinder;* intrans. in fig. sense only, 3rd s. with or without a subject or inf., *it belongs to, concerns, relates, pertains* or *appertains to, is of consequence to, is useful, avails,* w. ad and acc., rarely acc. alone; "quæ... attinent," aught which does not tell of love (M.).

505. **Hic** (85). **vivum,** acc. mas. s. ag. w. cæspitem; fr. vīvus, -a, -um, adj. Of living beings, *alive, living, that has life.* Of things, *natural, unwrought.* **mihi** (277), dat. commodi after ponite. **cæspitem,** acc. s. gov. by ponite; fr. cæspes, -ĭtis, 3rd mas., (cædo, *to cut*) *a turf, sod* cut out for mounds, tombs, etc. *Altar of turf* (here). *A grassy field, green field.* **hic,** anaphora (895).

506. **Verbenas,** acc. gov. by ponite; fr. verbēnæ, -arum, 1st fem. plu.; all green things, *boughs* or *branches* of laurel, olive, or any sacred boughs, and even grass used in sacrifices, etc. **pueri,** voc. plu. fr. puer (149). **ponite,** 2nd plu. imper. pres. act. fr. pono (104). **thura,** acc. plu. jnd. by -que to verbenas; fr. thus, thūris, 3rd neut., (tus, turis) *incense, frankincense* (817).

507. **Bimi,** gen. neut. s. ag. w. vini; fr. bīmus, -a, -um, adj., *two years old, of two years, continuing two years;* prob. *last year's wine* used till the wine of the year was ready. **cum** (31). **patera,** abl. s. gov. by cum; fr. pătĕra, -æ, 1st fem., (pateo, *to lie open*) *a broad flat dish* or *saucer,* esp. used in libations, offerings, etc. *Saucer, bowl.* **meri,** gen. s. after paterâ; fr. merum (203).

Mactata veniet lenior hostia.

CARMEN XX.—AD MÆCENATEM.

VILE potabis modicis Sabinum
Cantharis, Græca quod ego ipse testa
Conditum levi, datus in theatro

508. **Mactata,** abl. fem. s. pf. pass. part. ag. w. hostiâ; fr. macto, -āre, -avi, -atum, 1st trans., (obsol. mago ak. to mactus). Relig., *to venerate, worship, honour* a deity by means of something; meton., *to slaughter* in sacrifice, *immolate* a victim; then fig., *to sacrifice, offer up, e.g.,* perfidŏs. *To kill, slay* genly. *To overthrow, ruin, destroy. To afflict, punish* with anything, *pursue with punishment,* etc. **veniet,** 3rd s. fut. ind. act. fr. venio (66). **lenior,** nom. fem. s. compar. adj. ag. as adv. attribute w. subj. (Venus) of veniet; fr. lenis (22). **hostia,** abl. abs. s. fr. hostia, -æ, 1st fem., (hostio, *to strike*) *a victim, sacrifice;* hostiâ mactatâ=quum hostia mactata erit. The overpowering "afflatus" of a god was a sign of disfavour to be mitigated by reverence (W.).

CARMEN XX. METRE—*The Lesser Sapphic.* (Carmen ii.)

509. **Vile,** acc. neut. s. ag. w. Sabinum; fr. vilis, -e, adj., *of small price* or *value. Purchased at a low rate, cheap;* vili, abl. neut., *at a low rate;* meton., *of trifling value, mean, common, worthless. Found in great abundance, common, e.g.,* poma; here *of simple make* or *material* (W.). **potabis,** 2nd s. fut. ind. act. fr. pōto, -āre, -āvi, -ātum or pōtum; 1st trans., *to drink* (ante-class. and post-Aug.); "potare flumen," *i.e., to dwell near* it. Of things, as subjects, *to drink up, suck* or *draw in, absorb;* intrans., *to drink, tope, tipple.* **modicis,** abl. plu. mas. ag. w. cantharis; fr. mŏdĭcus (483). **Sabinum,** acc. s. gov. by potabis; fr. Săbīnum, -i, 2nd neut. (und. vinum, 239), *Sabine wine* or (und. prædium) *a Sabine estate.*

510. **Cantharis,** abl. (instrum.) plu. fr. canthărus, -i, 2nd mas.; prop. a large wide-bellied *drinking vessel* with handles, *tankard, pot,* esp. of Bacchus and his followers. **Græca,** abl. fem. s. ag. w. testâ; fr. Græcus, -a, -um, adj., *of* or *belonging to the Greeks. Grecian.* **quod,** neut. s. ag w. Sabinum; acc. gov. by levi; fr. qui (3). **ego** (445), subj. of levi. **ipse** (432), ag. w. ego. **testa,** abl. (instrum. w. conditum) s. fr. testa, -æ, 1st fem., (ak. to tesqua, torreo, *the dried thing) piece of burned clay, brick, tile. Piece of baked earthenware, earthen pot, pitcher, jug, mug. A lamp.* Meton., *a broken piece of earthenware; sherd, potsherd. Shell* of a shell fish or some testaceous animal, *a shell fish.* "Græca testâ," *i.e.,* which still kept some of the fragrance of the Chian or Sabine which it had held (W.).

511. **Conditum,** acc. neut. s. pf. pass. part. ag. w. Sabinum; fr. condo (264). **levi,** 1st sing. pf. ind. act. fr. lĭno, -ĕre, līvi, or lēvi, lĭtum, 3rd trans., (not class., lĭnĭo, līvi, lītum, 4th trans.), *to besmear, anoint, spread* or *rub over;* here *besmear over* with pitch. "Conditum levi," *stored and sealed* (W.). *To spread, apply* unguents, *overlay, overlap. To besmear, befoul;* fig., *disparage* (Hor). **datus** (123), nom. mas. s. ag. w. plausus; w. esset und. the combinate plpf. subj. pass. after quum. **in** (78). **theatro,** abl. s. gov. by in; fr. theātrum, -i, 2nd neut. (Gk.), *a playhouse, open space for exhibiting martial games. Spectators assembled. Theatrical audience. Place of exhibition, theatre for any public performance.*

512 Quum tibi plausus,
513 Care Mæcenas eques, ut paterni
514 Fluminis ripæ, simul et jocosa
515 Redderet laudes tibi Vaticani
516 Montis imago.
517 Cæcubum et prælo domitam Caleno
518 Tu bibes uvam: mea nec Falernæ

512. **Quum** (43). **tibi** (93), dat. commodi after datus (esset). **plausus**, -us, 4th mas.; nom. s. subj. of datus (esset); later collat. plausus, -i, 2nd mas., (plaudo, *to clap*) *a clapping sound, noise arising from clapping* or *beating together* of two bodies. *Clapping* of hands *in approbation, applause.*

513. **Care**, voc. mas. s. ag. w. Mæcenas; fr. cārus, -a, -um, adj., *dear, precious, valued. Dear, costly.* **Mæcēnas** (1). **eques**, -ĭtis, 3rd mas., voc. s. in app. to Mæcenas; (equus, 167; eo, 51) *a horseman, rider;* meton. *a horse-soldier, trooper*, opp. to pedes. Collective, *horse-soldiers.* Equites for eques, *the order of Knights.* **ut** (13), consecutive. **paterni**, gen. s. neut. ag. w. fluminis; fr. pāternus, -a, -um, adj., (pater, 38) *of* or *belonging to a father, pertaining* or *relating to a father, affecting a father, obtained from a father.* Of feeling, etc., *such as a father has* or *ought to have, fatherly* (922). *Of one's native country* (here). It refers to Mæcenas' Etrurian origin, as the Tiber is called by Hor. the "Tuscus alveus."

514. **Fluminis**, gen. s. after ripæ; fr. flumen (286). **ripæ**, nom. plu. subj. of redderent und. fr. follg. clause; fr. ripa (55). **simul** (145). **et** (2). **jocosa**, nom. fem. s. ag. w. imago; fr. jocosus (263).

515. **Redderet**, 3rd. s. impf. subj. act. fr. reddo (95), subj. after ut, impf. after datus (esset). **laudes** (175), gov. by redderet. **tibi** (63), commodi after redderet. **Vaticani**, gen. mas. s. ag. w. montis; fr. Vātīcānus, -a, -um, adj. (here -ĭc), *Vatican* on W. bank of the Tiber.

516. **Montis**, gen. s. after imago; fr. mons (44). **imago** (288), subj. of redderet.

517. **Cæcubum**, acc. s. gov. by bibes; fr. Cæcŭbum, -i, 2nd neut., *Cæcuban wine;* neut. (und. vinum) fr. Cæcŭbus, -a, -um, *Cæcuban, i.e.*, from a marshy place in S. Latium, distinguished for wine. **prælo**, abl. (instrum.) s. fr. prælum, -i, (prel-) 2nd neut., (premo, 144) *a press beam* for pressing grapes, olives, etc., *wine-press, oil-press.* **domitam**, acc. fem. s. ag. w. uvam; fr. domitus (338). **Caleno**, abl. neut. s. ag. w. prælo; fr. Călēnus, -a, -um, adj., *of Cales, Calenian* (717); a town in S. Campania, celebrated for its wine.

518. **Tu** (69), subj. of bibes. **bibes**, 2nd s. fut. (permissive) ind. act. fr. bĭbo, bĭbĕre, bĭbi, no sup., 3rd trans., *to drink from natural thirst. To inhale, breathe in, suck in, absorb.* So of inanimate things *e.g.* meadows, sword, etc. [poto, *to drink* from some strong love, *drink much, drink to excess*, but potus and potatus are used to supply the wanting partcs. of bibo]; here, *you may drink at home.* **uvam**, acc. s. gov. by bibes; fr. ūva, -æ, 1st fem., *a grape berry* (1002), *a cluster* or *bunch of grapes, a vine.* **mea**, acc. plu. neut. ag. w. pocula; fr. meus (2). **nec** (19). **Falernæ**, nom. fem. plu. ag. w. vites; fr. Fălernus, -a, -um, adj., *of the Falernian territory* (1035), which was at the foot of Mt. Massicus.

Temperant vites neque Formiani
Pocula colles.

CARMEN XXI.—IN DIANAM ET APOLLINEM.

DIANAM teneræ dicite virgines,
Intonsum, pueri, dicite Cynthium,
Latonamque supremo
Dilectam penitus Jovi.
Vos lætam fluviis et nemorum coma,
Quæcunque aut gelido prominet Algido,

519. **Temperant,** 3rd. plu. pres. ind. act. fr. tempero (223). **vites,** nom. plu. subj. of temperant; fr. vitis (477). **neque** (32). **Formiani,** nom. plu. mas. ag. w. colles; fr. Formĭānus, -a, -um, adj., *belonging to Formiæ,* a very ancient city of Latium on the borders of Campania (Mola di Gaeta).

520. **Pocula** (19), gov. by temperant. **colles,** nom. plu. jnd. by neque to vites; fr. collis, -is, 3rd mas., abl. colle, gen. plu. collium, (ak. to celsus, 1126) *high ground, hill.*

CARMEN XXI. METRE—*Fourth Asclepiadean.* (Carmen v.)

521. **Dianam,** acc. s. gov. by dicite; fr. Dīāna, -æ, 1st fem., orig. an Italian deity, aftwds. identified w. Gk. Artemis, dau. of Jupiter and Latona, sister of Apollo, virgin moon-goddess (Luna). **teneræ,** voc. plu. fem. ag. w. virgines; fr. tener (26). **dicite,** 2nd plu. pres. imper. act. fr. dico (86). **virgines,** voc. plu. subj. of dicite; fr. virgo (63).

522. **Intonsum,** acc. mas. s. ag. w. Cynthium; fr. intonsus, -a, -um, adj., (in, neg.; tondeo, *to shear, shave*) *unshorn. Unshorn, bearded,* esp. of the ancient Romans, who neither cut their hair nor shaved their beards. **pueri** (506), voc. subj. of dicite und. **Cynthium,** acc. s. gov. by dicite; fr. Cynthius, -ii, 2nd mas., *Apollo.* Cynthia, -æ, 1st fem., *Diana.* They were so named fr. *Cynthus,* a mt. in Delos, their birthplace.

523. **Latonam,** acc. s. jnd. by -que to Cynthium; fr. Lātōna, -æ, 1st fem., Gk. Lēto, -us, fem., dau. of the Titan Cœus and Phœbe, mother of Apollo and Diana. **supremo,** dat. mas. s. ag. w. Jovi; fr. supremus (364).

524. **Dilectam,** acc. fem. s. ag. w. Latonam; fr. dilectus (986). **penitus** (352). **Jovi,** dat. s. after dilectam; fr. Jupiter (25). In poetry the dat. is used of the agent after pass. verbs, where in prose a or ab with the abl. would be required.

525. **Vos,** voc. plu. subj. of dicite und.; fr. tu (69). **lætam,** acc. fem. s. ag. w. Latonam und.; fr. lætus (82). **fluviis,** abl. (of cause w. lætam) plu. fr. flŭvius, -ii, 2nd mas., (fluo, *to flow*) *a river,* much less com. than flumen. *Running water, stream.* **nemorum,** gen. plu. after comâ; fr. nemus (30). **coma,** abl. s. jnd. by et to fluviis; fr. coma (152).

526. **Quæcunque,** fem. s. ag. w. coma; nom. to prominet; fr. quicunque (167). **aut** (131). **gelido,** dat. s. mas. ag. w. Algido; fr. gelidus (30). **prominet,** 3rd s. ind. pres. act. fr. prōmĭneo, -ēre, -ui, no sup., 2nd intr. traject., (pro, *forward;* mĭneo, *to jut, project*) *to jut out, be prominent, overhang, project,* not Cic. nor Cæs. **Algido,** dat. s. after prominet; fr. Algĭdus, -i, 2nd mas.; (und. mons) mt. near Rome, sacred to Diana,

527 Nigris aut Erymanthi
528 Silvis aut viridis Cragi;
529 Vos Tempe totidem tollite laudibus
530 Natalemque, mares, Dedon Apollinis
531 Insignemque pharetra
532 Fraternaque humerum lyra.
533 Hic bellum lacrimosum, hic miseram famem
534 Pestemque a populo et principe Cæsare in

527. **Nigris**, dat. plu. fem. ag. w. silvis; fr. niger (155), *i.e.*, black w. pines, holm oaks, etc. This refers only to Erymanthus, not to Cragus, whose woods are "green" (W.). **Erymanthi**, gen. s. after silvis; fr. Ĕrȳmanthus, -i, 2nd mas., a chain of mountains in Arcadia, on the borders of Elis, where Hercules slew the Erymanthian boar.

528. **Silvis**, dat. plu. jnd. by aut (527) to Algido; fr. silva (235). **viridis**, gen. s. mas. ag. w. Cragi; fr. viridis (21). **Cragi**, gen. s. jnd. by aut to Erymanthi; fr. Crăgus, -i, 2nd mas., a promontory in Lycia, w. the rocky valley Chimæra.

529. **Vos** (525), subj. of tollite. **Tempe** (188), gov. by tollite; here Apollo purified himself after the murder of Pytho (W.). **totidem**, indecl. adj. w. laudibus; (tot, *so many*; dem, demonst. affix, cf. tantundem), *just so many, just as many*; totidem...quot, *just so many...as*. **tollite**, 2nd plu. pres. imper. act. fr. tollo (8). **laudibus** (298), of means w. tollite.

530. **Natalem**, acc. s. in app. to Delon; fr. nātalis, -is, 3rd mas., *a birth-place* or (und. dies), *the day on which one is born. A birthday, i.e.*, day commemorating one's birth. Of circumstances, *anniversary*; plu. natales, -ium (und. homines), *family connections*; hence, *family, lineage, those from whom one is descended* or *with whom one is connected by birth*; adj., natalis, -e, *of* or *belonging to one's birth, natal* (1339). Of a god, *presiding over one's birth.* Of places, *native.* Of time, *belonging to the periodical return of the date of one's birth.* **mares**, voc. plu. mas. fr. măs, măris, 3rd mas., (ak. to Mars, 177) *the male*, opp. to female. Of men, gods, animals and trees. Adj., măs, w. neut. măre, *of the male sex. Grown up to manhood, e.g.*, Curii (Hor.). *Brave, courageous.* **Delon**, acc. s. jnd. by -que to Tempe; fr. Dēlos, -i, acc. Delum or Delon (Gk.), a small island in the Ægean Sea, one of the Cyclades, birthplace of Apollo and Diana. **Apollinis**, gen. s. after natalem; fr. Apollo (68).

531. **Insignem**, acc. mas. s. ag. w. humerum; fr. insignis (118). **pharetra** (267), of means w. insignem.

532. **Fraterna**, abl. fem. s. ag. w. lyrâ; fr. frāternus, -a, -um, adj., (frater, 90) *brotherly*, here because "given by his brother Mercury;" meton., *closely connected, friendly.* **humerum**, acc. s. jnd. by -que (531) to Delon; fr. humerus (67). **lyra** (285), jnd. by -que to pharetrâ.

533. **Hic**, *i.e.*, Apollo; nom. mas. s. subj. of aget. **bellum**, acc. s. gov. by aget; fr. bellum (24). **lacrimosum**, acc. neut. s. ag. w. bellum; fr. lacrimosus (230). **hic**, anaphora. **miseram**, acc. fem. s. ag. w. famem; fr. miser (160). **famem**, acc. s. gov. by aget; fr. fămes, -is, 3rd fem., *hunger. Famine. Violent longing for anything. Greediness, greed*=sitis.

534. **Pestem**, acc. s. jnd. by -que to famem; fr. pestis, -is, 3rd fem., (perdo, *to destroy*) *a deadly* esp. infectious or contagious *disease, plague,*

Persas atque Britannos
Vestra motus aget prece.

CARMEN XXII.—AD ARISTIUM FUSCUM.

INTEGER vitæ scelerisque purus
Non eget Mauris jaculis neque arcu
Nec venenatis gravida sagittis,
Fusce, pharetra,

pestilence. Noxious atmosphere, unhealthy weather. Destruction, ruin, death. A pest, curse, bane of a thing or person. **a** (254). **populo** (32), gov. by a. **principe,** abl. s. in app. to Cæsare; fr. princeps (86). **Cæsare** (336), jnd. by et to populo. **in** (76), here in hostile sense.

535. **Persas,** acc. gov. by in; fr. Persæ (58). **atque** (37). **Britannos,** acc. jnd. by atque to Persas; fr. Brĭtanni, -orum, 2nd mas., *the Britons.*

536. **Vestra,** abl. s. fem. ag. w. prece; fr. vester, vestra, vestrum, poss. pron. adj. of 2nd plur., (vos, 525) *your, yours.* **motus,** nom. mas. s. pf. pass. part. ag. w. hic; fr. moveo (394). **aget,** 3rd s. fut. ind. act. fr. ago (43). **prece** (62), instrum. w. motus.

CARMEN XXII. METRE—*The Lesser Sapphic.* (Carmen ii.)

537. **Integer** (373), nom. mas. s. (as subst.) subj. of eget. **vitæ** (143), gen. after integer. A gen. often thus states the object to which an adj. or partc. refers in Hor., Verg. and Tac., *e.g.*, fessi rerum, lassi maris, etc., esp. w. gen. animi (M.). So Eng. idiom *wearied of, tired of, impatient of.* **sceleris,** gen. s. after purus; fr. scelus (65). Greek gen. where Latin idiom would have the ablative (W.). **pūrus,** -a, -um, adj., nom. mas. s. jnd. by -que to integer; prop., *clean from dirt* or *filth, undefiled,* lit. and fig., esp. of animal passions, *chaste, pure, spotless.* Of style, *faultless, unexceptionable. In a natural state, plain, naked, unadorned, unadulterated, unsophisticated. Clear, cleared from* anything, *e.g.* sol purus, *cleared from clouds;* adverbs, pure and puriter.

538. **Non** (55). **eget,** 3rd s. pres. ind. act. fr. ĕgeo, -ēre, -ui, no sup., 2nd intrans., *to be in need of; suffer need. To lack, need, want* anything, w. abl. or gen. *To be without, be destitute of. To do without, bear the want of. To desire, wish for.* **Mauris,** abl. plu. neut. ag. w. jaculis; fr. Maurus (75). **jaculis,** abl. plu. after eget; fr. jaculum (228). **neque** (32). **arcu,** abl. s. jnd. by neque to jaculis; fr. arcus (694).

539. **Venenatis,** abl. plu. fem. ag. w. sagittis; fr. vĕnēnātus, -a, -um, adj., (venenum, 646) *provided* or *furnished with poison, poisoned,* i.e., *steeped, dipped in poison. Harmful, biting, e.g.,* jocus. **gravida,** abl. s. fem. ag. w. pharetra; fr. grăvĭdus, -a, -um, adj., (grăvo, *to load, burden*) *burdened, loaded,* hence *pregnant* w. young. *Laden, filled, full.* **sagittis,** abl. (instrumental) plu. w. gravidâ; fr. sagitta (308).

540. **Fusce,** voc. s. fr. Fuscus, -i, a Roman cognomen. Aristius Fuscus was a learned historian, poet and grammarian. **pharetra** (267), after eget. Transitive vbs. of endowing, enriching, feeding, etc., or despoiling, emptying, stripping, etc, intransitive vbs. of abounding, overflowing, etc., or being devoid, being destitute of, etc., and adjs. of abundance and want, take an ablative of the matter.

541 Sive per Syrtes iter æstuosas
542 Sive facturus per inhospitalem
543 Caucasum vel quæ loca fabulosus
544 Lambit Hydaspes.
545 Namque me silva lupus in Sabina,
546 Dum meam canto Lalagen et ultra

541. **Sive** (69). **per** (114). **Syrtes,** acc. gov. by per; fr. Syrtes, -is, genly. plu. Syrtium; 3rd fem., a sandbank in the sea, esp. on the north coast of Africa; Syrtis Major near Cyrenaica, now Sitra; Syrtis Minor near Byzacene, now Cabes. **iter,** acc. s. gov. by facturūs; fr. ĭter, ĭtĭnĕris, 3rd neut., (eo, 51) *a going, walking* or *proceeding onwards. Journey.* Of troops, *a march. Flight, course, way. Voyage* over water. As a measure of distance, *journey, march. Road, way. Passage, roadway, leave of going;* fig., *a course, method, path.* **æstuosas,** acc. plu. fem. ag. w. Syrtes; fr. æstŭōsus, -a, -um, adj., (æstus, 466) *full of heat, very hot, burning hot.* This may refer either to the hot sandy coast that borders the Syrtes, or the boiling surf of the bay (W.).

542. **Facturus,** nom. mas. s. fut. part. act. ag. w. tu und.; w. es und. 2nd s. ind. of the periphrastic future; fr. făcio, -ĕre, fēci, factum, 3rd trans. irreg., *to make, prepare, produce, bring to pass, perform, do, effect. To esteem, regard* a person as such. *Make much of. To feign, assert, represent* a thing in any way. *To sacrifice, perform a religious rite;* pass. supplied in pres. and fut. tenses by fio (447), *to become, happen.* **inhospitalem,** acc. mas. s. ag. w. Caucasum; fr. inhospĭtālis, -is, adj., (in, neg.; hospĭtālis, fr. hospes, 386, *hospitable*) *inhospitable.*

543. **Caucasum,** acc. s. gov. by per; fr. Caucăsus, -i, 2nd mas. (Gk. acc. -on), a chain of rough mountains, inhabited by wild tribes in Asia betw. the Black and Caspian Seas. **vel** (187). **quæ** (359), neut. plu. ag. w. loca; acc. gov. by lambit. **loca,** acc. plu. strictly gov. by per, but placed in rel. clause; fr. lŏcus, -i, 2nd mas., *a place;* plu. heterogeneous, neut. loca, *places* properly speaking; loci, *places* metaphorically, *i.e., topics, places* in books, etc. **fābŭlosus,** -a, -um, adj.; nom. mas. s. ag. w. Hydaspes; (fabula, 144) *fabulous, i.e.,* with its storied dangers (W.).

544. **Lambit,** 3rd s. ind. pres. act. fr. lambo, -bĕre, -bi, -bĭtum, 3rd trans., (ak. to labrum, 356) *to lick;* here, *wash, bathe, lave.* Of fire, *to seize upon, lay hold of.* **Hydaspes,** -is, 3rd mas.; nom. s. subj. of lambit; a river of the Punjaub (*Jelum*).

545. **Namque** (nam, 479; -que, 4), an emphatic confirmative particle, *for indeed, for truly, for* (often before a vowel, and in Cic. and Cæs. it always, like nam, begins a propn., but in Livy, Terence, etc., often after a word). **me** (29), gov. by fugit (548). **silva,** abl. s. gov. by in; fr. silva (235). **lupus** (414), nom. s. subj. of fugit. **in** (78). **Sabina** (239), ag. w. silva.

546. **Dum** (53). **meam,** acc. fem. s. ag. w. Lalagen; fr. meus (2). **canto** (183), 1st s. pres. ind. act. **Lalagen,** acc. s. gov. by canto; fr. Lălăge, -es, 1st fem. (Gk.), a girl. **ultra,** (i.) adv. Of place, *beyond, farther,* very rare, *farther on.* Of time, *further, later, longer, more.* Of degree, *beyond, more,* sts. folld. by quam, *e.g.,* ultra quam satis est. Comp. ulterius, super. ultime, *to the last degree* (rare and non-class.); (ii.) prep. w. acc. Of place, *beyond, past, on the farther side of.* Of time, *beyond, past, longer than.* Of number, measure, degree, *over, above, more than.*

Terminos curis vagor expeditis,
Fugit inermem,
Quale portentum neque militaris
Daunias latis alit æsculetis,
Nec Jubæ tellus generat, leonum
Arida nutrix.
Pone me pigris ubi nulla campis

547. **Terminos**, acc. plu. gov. by ultra; fr. termĭnus, -i, 2nd mas., *a boundary line, boundary, limit* (1376); fig., *an end, term.* Personified, *the god who presided over boundaries;* ultra terminos, *i.e.*, beyond the limits of his own farm (W). **curis**, abl. absol. fr. cura (215). **văgor**, -āri, -ātus sum, 1st dep. intrans. and trans., 1st s. ind. pres.; *to wander about, ramble, rove,* genly. *to wander, roam;* fig. of a rumour, etc. **expeditis**, abl. absolute plu. fem. ag. w. curis; fr. expeditus (228).

548. **Fugit**, 3rd s. pf. ind. act. fr. fugio (206). **inermem**, acc. mas. s. ag. w. me; fr. inermis, -e, adj., (in, neg.; arma, 226) *without defensive weapons, unarmed.*

549. **Quale**, nom. neut. s. ag. w. portentum; fr. quālis, -e, pron. adj.; (i.) interrog., *how constituted, of what sort* or *nature, what kind of?* (ii.) relative w. correl. talis or not; *such...as.* In this case it follows the same rules as qui when placed betw. two cases (exp. or und.) of the same person or thing, *e.g.*, non sum qualis eram. If used to compare two different nouns, it agrees in number, gender and case w. the latter, while its demonstrative (talis) agrees with the former, *e.g.*, talis erat, qualem te esse video; (iii.) in quotations and citations, *as for instance, as for example;* (iv.) adv.=qualiter, *just as.* **portentum**, -i, 2nd neut.; nom. s. in app. to lupus, (portendo, *to point out, indicate*) prop. *a sign, token, omen. Monster, monstrosity. Strange tale, monstrous story.* **neque** (32). **militaris** (221), fem. ag. w. Daunias; *nurse of soldiers.*

550. **Daunias**, -ădis, 3rd fem.; nom. s. subj. of alit; *the province of Daunias;* meton., *Appulia.* Daunias was a mythic king of part of Appulia, ancestor of Turnus, son-in-law of Diomede. **latis**, abl. plu. neut. ag. w. æsculetis; fr. lātus, -a, -um, adj., *broad, wide. Extensive, extended.* Of the voice, *expanded, spreading wide, full.* Of speech, *copious, diffusive, full, rich.* **alit**, 3rd s. pres. ind. act. fr. ălo, ălĕre, ălŭi, ălĭtum and altum (altus class., part. pf.; alitus, post-Aug., to distinguish fr. adj. altus), 3rd trans., *to nourish, support, sustain, maintain;* fig., *cherish, support, foster.* **æsculetis**, abl. (local) plu. fr. æscŭlētum, -i, 2nd neut., *a forest* of winter or Italian oaks, genly. *an oak forest*

551. **Nec** (19). **Jubæ**, gen. s. after tellus; fr. Jŭba, -æ, 1st mas., king of Numidia, who defeated Cæsar's legate Curio, and committed suicide after the battle of Thapsus. **tellus** (213), nom. s. subj. of generat. **generat**, 3rd s. ind. pres. act. fr. genero (301). **leonum**, gen. plu. after nutrix; fr. leo (435).

552. **Arida**, nom. fem. s. ag. w. nutrix; fr. ārĭdus, -a, -um, adj., (areo, *to be dry*) *dry, parched, arid. Making dry, drying up. Dry, crackling* of sound. *Shrivelled.* **nutrix**, -īcis, 3rd fem.; nom. s. in app. to tellus. Of living beings, *a nurse.* Of country, *a rearer, breeder.*

553. **Pone**, 2nd s. imper. pres. act. fr. pono (194). **me** (29), gov. by pone. **pigris**, abl. plu. mas. ag. w. campis; fr. piger (410); here of the dull dead-

554 Arbor æstiva recreatur aura,
555 Quod latus mundi nebulæ malusque
556 Jupiter urget;
557 Pone sub curru nimium propinqui
558 Solis in terra domibus negata:
559 Dulce ridentem Lalagen amabo.
560 Dulce loquentem.

ness of winter. **ubi**, adv., (*a*) relat.; (i.) local, *in which place, where* ref. to antec. subst. or adv.; correl. to ibi; (ii.) temporal, *when, whenever* w. primum, simul, etc.; (iii.) ref. to persons and things, *in which, with which, by which*. (*b*) interrog, *where? when?* (*c*) temporal=quum, *when* (886). In 1225, *considering that, when*. **nulla**, nom. fem. s. ag. w. arbor; fr. nullus (477). **campis**, abl. (local) plu. fr. campus (195).

554. **Arbor** (329), subj. of recreatur. **æstiva**, abl. s. fem. ag. w. aurâ; fr. æstīvus, -a, -um, adj., (æstas, 451) *of summer, as in summer, summer-like, summer*. **recreatur**, 3rd s. pres. ind. pass. fr. recreo, -āre, -āvi, -ātum, 1st trans., (re, 659; creo, *to create*) *to make anew, remake, reproduce, restore* (very rare); fig., *to restore to a good condition, revive, recruit, invigorate* bodily or mentally. Pass. (reflex.) or act. w. pers. pron., *to become refreshed, revived, recruited*, etc. *To revive, recover oneself*. **aura**, abl. (of means) s. fr. aura (84). "Nulla...aura," *i.e.*, There is no tree to be woke to life again by the breeze of summer (W.).

555. **Quod** (510), neut. s. ag. w. latus; acc. gov. by urget. **latus** (368), wd. be strictly abl. in app. to campis, but being in the relative clause is, as usual in Latin, attracted into the case of the relative (543). **mundi**, gen. s. after latus; fr. mundus (299). **nebulæ**, nom. plu. subj. jnd. by -que to Jupiter; fr. nĕbŭla, -æ, 1st fem., *a mist, vapour*. Of smoke, dust, etc., *a cloud, exhalation, smoke*. *Any mistlike substance, vapour, darkness, obscurity*. **malus**, -a, -um, adj.; nom. mas. s. ag. w. Jupiter; see pejora (214).

556. **Jupiter** (66), subj. of urget: here for *climate*. **urget** (150). On the number see 98.

557. **Pone** (553). **sub** (470, 21). **curru** (342), gov. by sub. **nimium** (53), w. propinqui. **propinqui**, gen. s. mas. ag. w. solis; fr. prŏpinquus, -a, -um, adj., (prope, 651). Of place, *near, neighbouring*. Of time, *close at hand, not far off* (rare). Of resemblance or meaning, *similar, like*. Of relationship or connection, *kindred, related*.

558. **Solis** (220), after curru. **in** (78). **terra**, abl. s. gov. by in; fr. terra (6). **domibus**, dat. plu. after traject. negata; fr. domus (117). **negata**. abl. fem. s. pf. pass. part. ag. w. terrâ; fr. nĕgo, -āre, -avi, -atum, 1st trans. and intrans., *to say no. To deny, give* or *make a denial. To refuse* to a person, *i.e., refuse* to do; trans., *to deny* a thing. *To affirm, maintain* that a thing is *not*, w. inf. Pass. negor, *I am denied* to be, *i.e.*, persons *deny* that *I am*. "Domibus negata," *unfit for human habitation* (W.).

559. **Dulce**, adv. of dulcis (2), *sweetly, pleasantly*. **ridentem**, acc. fem. s. ag. w. Lalagen; fr. ridens (69). **Lalagen** (546), gov. by amabo. **amabo**, 1st sing. fut. ind. act. fr. amo (86).

560. **Loquentem**, acc. fem. s. pres. part. ag. w. Lalagen; fr. loquor (283).

CARMEN XXIII.—AD CHLOEN.

VITAS hinnuleo me similis, Chloë,
Quærenti pavidam montibus aviis
  Matrem non sine vano
    Aurarum et silüæ metu
Nam seu mobilibus veris inhorruit
Adventus foliis seu virides rubum
  Dimovere lacertæ,
    Et corde et genibus tremit.

CARMEN **XXIII.** METRE—*The Fourth Asclepiad.* (Carmen v.)

561. **Vitas,** 2nd s. ind. pres. act. fr. vito (226). **hinnuleo,** dat. s. after similis; fr. hinnŭleus, -i, 2nd mas., (hinnio, *to neigh, whinny*) *a young fawn.* **me** (29), gov. by vitas. **similis** (302), nom. fem. s. ag. w. tu und. in vitas. **Chloe,** voc. (Gk.) fr. Chloe, -es, 1st fem.

562. **Quærenti,** dat. mas. s. pres. part. act. ag. w. hinnuleo; fr. quæro (245). **pavidam,** acc. fem. s. ag. w. matrem; fr. pavidus (14). **montibus,** abl. (local) plu. fr. mons (44). **aviis,** abl. plu. mas. ag. w. montibus; fr. āvĭus, -a, -um, adj., (a, 254; via, 664) *that is* or *goes out of the way, remote from the way, untrodden, unfrequented, Wandering, erring.*

563. **Matrem,** acc. s. gov. by quærenti; fr. mater (24). **non** (55). **sine** (370). **vano,** abl. s. mas. ag. w. metu; fr. vānus, -a, -um, adj., (perh. for vac-anus; fr. vaco, *to be without*) *that contains nothing, empty, void, vacant* (rare, not Cic.), *e.g.*, vana imago, *shade of the dead* (Hor.). *Empty* as to purport or rêsult, *idle, null, groundless, fruitless, vain.*

564. **Aurarum,** gen. plu. after metu; fr. aura (84). **silüæ**=silvæ (376), jnd. by et to aurarum. **metu,** abl. s. gov. by sine; fr. mĕtus, -us, 4th mas., *fear, dread, apprehension. Religious awe, holy fear.*

565. **Nam** (479). **seu** (27). **mobilibus** (198), neut. ag. w. foliis. **veris** (129), after adventus. **inhorruit,** 3rd sing. pf. ind. act. fr. inhorreo, -ēre, -ŭi, no sup., 2nd intrans. and trans., *to stand on end* or *erect, bristle* of ears of côrn. *To have a tremulous motion, quiver, e.g.,* unda. *To tremble, shake* w. cold, etc.

566. **Adventus,** -us, 4th mas.; nom. s. subj. of inhorruit; (advenio, *to come to*) *a coming to* a person or thing, *a drawing near* of an uncompleted action. *An arrival, being present,* a completed action. **foliis,** abl. local plu. after inhorruit; fr. fŏlium, -ii, 2nd neut., *a leaf* of a tree. **seu** (27). **virides,** nom. plu. fem. ag. w. lacertæ; fr. viridis (21). **rubum,** acc. s. gov. by dimovere; fr. rŭbus, -i, 2nd mas., (rubeo, 38) *a bramble bush, a blackberry bush,*

567. **Dimovere,** 3rd plu. pf. ind. act. fr. dimoveo (13). **lacertæ,** nom. plu. subj of dimovere; fr. lăcerta, -æ, 1st fem., collat. lăcertus, -i, 2nd mas., *a lizard.*

568. **et...et** (2). **corde,** abl. (instrumental) s. fr. cor (462). **genibus,** abl. plu. jnd. by et to corde; fr. genu (320). **tremit,** 3rd s. pres. ind. act. ag. w. hinnuleus; fr. trĕmo, -ĕre, -ui, no sup., 3rd intrans. irreg., (ak. to terreo, 40) *to shake, quake, quiver, tremble;* trans., *to tremble at.*

569 Atqui non ego te tigris ut aspera
570 Gætulusve leo frangere persequor:
571 Tandem desine matrem
572 Tempestiva sequi viro.

569. **Atqui,** emphatically and closely connects an adversative assertion with what precedes, *but, yet, notwithstanding, however, but now, but nevertheless, and yet*, sts. it merely adds a confirmatory thought, *indeed, certainly, by all means.* **non** (55). **ego** (445), subj. of persequor. **te** (83), gov. by persequor. **tigris,** gen. tigris or tigrĭdis, 3rd com. (in prose mas., in poet. usu. fem.); nom. s. jnd. by ut to ego; (Pers., *an arrow*, hence the River so called), *a tiger.* **ut,** comparative (199). **aspera,** nom. fem. s. ag. w. tigris; fr. asper (154), *angry.*

570. **Gætulus,** -a, -um, adj.; nom. mas. s. ag. w. leo; *of* or *belonging to the Gætulians* (14, 39), a people in N.W. of Africa, S. of Mauri and Numidæ (mod. Morocco). **-ve** (186). **leo** (435), nom. s. jnd. by ve to tigris. **frangere,** pres. inf. (prolative, exp. purpose) act. after persequor; fr. frango, -gĕre, frēgi, fractum; 3rd trans., *to break, break in pieces, shiver. To break down, subdue. To weaken, diminish. To violate. To soften, move, touch. To break up small, grind, bruise;* here of *crushing* betw. the teeth. The inf. is a verb governing cases and having tense-forms, and also a neut. subst. having cases dependent upon it. It is used, (i.) as subj. esp. of an impers. verb; rarely as complement; (ii.) as object sts. even w. prep., *e.g.*, inter dare et accipere; (iii.) prolative or complementary, orig. joined to verbs whose idea was not complete without such a definition of their scope, *e.g.*, verbs expressing power, duty, inclination, purpose, effort, beginning, etc., or their negatives, also verbs expressing to allow or influence another to do or abstain from a thing; but it was soon extended to supply the place of a subordinate clause or substantival form of the verb after other verbs. In 44, 286, 570, 615, it expresses purpose. After participles or adjectives, this inf. names the action in reference to which the adj. or partc. is applicable (113), whether the adj. or partc. is incomplete in itself, *e.g.*, præsens tollere, or complete, *e.g.*, blandum ducere (see Wickham's Hor., App. II.). **persĕquor,** -sĕqui, -sĕcūtus, and -sĕquūtus sum, 3rd trans. and intrans.; in good sense, *to follow perseveringly, follow after, continue to follow;* in hostile sense, *chase, pursue;* meton., *to come upon, overtake;* fig., *to follow perseveringly, pursue, e.g.*, artes. *To hunt after, strive after. To obtain. To imitate* a person or thing as a guide or pattern. *To pursue, proceed against* in law, *to prosecute, to revenge, take revenge for, e.g.*, injurias. *To follow up* w. action, *execute, perform, accomplish. To follow out* in speech or writing, *relate, describe, e.g.*, res Hannibalis.

571. **Tandem** (66). **dēsĭne,** 2nd s. imper. pres. act. fr. desĭno, -ĕre, -sīvi or -sĭi, -sĭtum, 3rd trans. and intrans., (de, 10; sino, 87) *to leave off, give over, cease, desist,* opp. to cœpi, genly. w. inf. Pass. chiefly in perf. tenses, *e.g.*, desitum est disputare (quite Cic.); intrans., *to cease, stop, end, close* (genly. post-Aug.); imper. w. gen. (1109). **matrem** (563), gov. by sequi.

572. **Tempestiva,** nom. fem. s. ag. w. tu und. in desine; fr. tempestīvus, -a, -um, adj., (tempestas, *proper time, season*) *of* or *belonging to the right time; done* or *happening at the proper time, seasonable, fitting, appropriate;* esp. *seasonable, ripe, e.g.*, pinus. Pregn., *that which takes place in good time* or *season, early, betimes, e.g.*, convivia. No superl. **sequi** (402), prolative after desine. **viro,** dat. s. after trajective (873) tempestiva; fr. vir (215).

CARMEN XXIV.—AD VIRGILIUM.

573 Quis desiderio sit pudor aut modus
574 Tam cari capitis? Præcipe lugubres
575 Cantus, Melpomene, cui liquidam pater
576 Vocem cum cithara dedit.
577 Ergo Quintilium perpetuus sopor
578 Urget! cui Pudor et Justitiæ soror

Carmen XXIV Metre—*The Third Asclepiad.* (Carmen vi.)

573. **Quis** (149), ag. w. pudor. **desiderio,** dat. (acquisitive) s. after sit; fr. desīdĕrium (382). **sit** (245). The dubitative conjunctive. **pudor** (173), subj. of sit. **aut** (131) **modus** (422), jnd. by aut to pudor.

574. **Tam** (194). **cari,** gen. s. neut. ag. w. capitis; fr. cārus (513). **capitis,** gen. (objective) after desiderium; fr. caput (22). **præcipe,** 2nd s. imper. pres. act. fr. præcĭpĭo, -cĭpĕre, -cēpi, -ceptum, 3rd trans. and intrans., (præ, *before;* capio, 1388) *to take, get* or *receive beforehand;* milit., *to seize beforehand, preoccupy;* fig., *to obtain in advance, anticipate, e.g.,* animo victoriam. *To give* or *lay down rules about* a thing. *To give information* about anything, *e.g.,* aliquid alicui. *To give orders about* w. acc. *To teach, instruct in* w. acc. (here). *To enjoin, direct, bid,* w. inf., ut, ne, w. subj., w. acc. and dat., aliquid alicui, etc. **lugubres,** acc. plu. mas. ag. w. cantus; fr. lūgŭbris, -e, adj., *that causes mourning, disastrous, e.g.,* bellum (909). *Of* or *belonging to mourning, e.g.,* dress. *Doleful, plaintive, e.g.,* vox. Adv. lugubre and lugubrĭter.

575. **Cantus,** acc. plu. gov. by præcipe; fr. cantus, -us, 4th mas., (cano, 261) *tone, sound, melody. Singing, song* (freq. and class.); meton., *an incantation.* **Melpomene,** -es, 1st fem. (Gk.) voc.; Muse of tragic and lyric poetry. **cui,** fem. s. ag. w. Melpomene; dat. after dedit; fr. qui (3). **liquidam,** acc. fem. s. ag. w. vocem; fr. liquidus (150). **pater** (38), subj of dedit.

576. **Vocem,** acc. s. gov. by dedit; fr. vox (259). **cum** (31). **cithara** (399), gov. by cum. **dedit,** 3rd s. pf. ind. act. fr. do (65).

577. **Ergō,** adv., *proceeding from, in consequence of;* (i.) w. gen., *on account of, in consequence of,* so causâ, gratiâ; (ii.) =cujus rei ergo, *consequently, accordingly, therefore, then;* (iii.) illative, *therefore, consequently:* indicating a conclusion forced on the speaker to his surprise (W.); (iv.) in consecutive interrog., cur ergo, *why then?* (v.) w. imperats., *then, now,* date ergo; (vi.) like igitur in resuming an interrupted train of thought, *as I was saying, I say then, well then.* **Quintilium,** acc. s. gov. by urget; fr. Quintĭlĭus, -ii, 2nd mas.; name of a Roman gens., here a poet of Cremona and friend of Horace; kinsman of Vergil, died B.C. 24. **perpetuus** (190), nom. mas. s. ag. w. sopor; *broken by no waking* (W.) **sŏpor,** -oris, 3rd mas.; nom. s. subj. of urget; *sleep,* genly. poet. and post-Aug., sts. of *death* (here); rare of *laziness, indifference,* a *sleeping dose.*

578. **Urget** (150), *lies heavy on* (W.) **cui** (575), mas. s. ag. w. Quintilium, dat. after traject. parem **pudor** (173), personified subj. of inveniet. **Justitiæ,** gen. s. after soror; fr. Justĭtĭa, -æ, 1st fem., (justus, 338) *Justice, uprightness, upright conduct. Conduct in accordance with the Civil* or the

579 Incorrupta Fides nudaque Veritas
580 Quando ullum inveniet parem?
581 Multis ille bonis flebilis occidit,
582 Nulli flebilior quam tibi, Vergili.
583 Tu frustra pius heu non ita creditum

Divine law. Justice personified (here). *Mildness, clemency, gentleness.* **soror,** -ōris, 3rd fem; in app. to Fides; *a sister.*

579. **Incorrupta,** nom. fem. s. ag. w. Fides; fr. incorruptus, -a, -um, adj., (in, neg.; corruptus, *corrupted*) *unspoiled, uninjured, uninterrupted* (class.), fig., *pure, e.g.,* virgo; *unbribed* of a witness. Of abstract things, *unadulterated.* **Fides** (492), jnd. by et to pudor. **nuda,** nom. fem. s. ag. w. Veritas; fr. nudus (368). **Vēritas,** -ātis, 3rd fem., (vērus, 663) nom. s. jnd. by -que to Fides. *Truth, truthfulness, verity. The true* or *real nature, reality.*

580. **Quando,** adv. (i.) interrog., *at what time, when?* (ii.) relat., *at what time, when.* (iii.) indef., *at what time soever, at any time soever;* (iv.) temp. conj., *when;* (v.) introducing an adverbial causal clause, *since because,* genly. w. ind., rarely subj. unless suboblique. **ullum,** acc. mas. s. gov. by inveniet; fr. ullus, -a, -um, gen. ullīus, dat. ulli, pron. adj., (for un-ulus, dimin. of unus, 189), *any one,* genly. in neg. declarations or interrogations implying a neg. answer; also in conditional clauses; very rarely in purely affirm. clauses. **inveniet,** 3rd s. fut. ind. act. fr. invĕnio, -īre, -vēni, -ventum, 3rd trans. and intrans., (in, 76; venio, 66) *to come upon, light upon, find, hit upon, meet with, stumble upon* or *by chance,* fig., *to meet with. To get, gain, earn, e.g.,* veniam. *To procure, e.g.,* money. *To find out by seeking, discover. To find out by meditation, devise, invent. To contrive* how to do a thing, w. quomodo for inf. *To detect, discover, e.g.,* conjurationem. *To ascertain* w. objective clause, ne, an, etc. With double acc. or acc. and adj., *to find out* a person *to be* something. *To effect, bring about, e.g.,* salutem. *To perceive, understand, e.g.,* quid agam; observe sing. verb after several subjects (98). **parem** (180), ag. w. ullum.

581. **Multis,** dat. plu. mas. ag. w. bonis; fr. multus (23). **ille** (337), *i.e.,* Quintilius; subj. of occidit. **bonis,** dat. (of agent, 524) plu. mas. (as subst.) after flebilis; fr. bŏnus, -a, -um, adj., *good* of every kind of physical, moral, and intellectual goodness. *Beautiful, pleasant, fit, suitable, right. Wealthy;* bona=*riches, goods. Fit, able, excellent. Skilful. Noble, virtuous. Considerable, high, of good family, of high rank. Favourable, propitious, kind.* **flēbĭlis,** -e, adj.; nom. mas. s. ag. w. ille; pass., *to be wept over, lamented, lamentable;* act., *weeping, tearful, doleful,* class. (1100). **occidit,** 3rd s. pf. ind. act. fr. occĭdo, -cĭdĕre, -cĭdi, -casum, 3rd intrans., (ob, 329; cado, 977), *to fall down, fall.* Of heavenly bodies, *go down, set.* Of persons, *fall, perish, die.* Of plants, *wither away;* fig., *be ruined, lost, perish.*

582. **Nulli,** dat. of agent (524) mas. after flebilior; fr. nullus (477). **flebilior,** nom. mas. s. compar. adj. ag. w. ille; fr. flebilis (581). **quam** (284), comparative. **tibi** (93), jnd. by quam to nulli. **Vergili,** voc. of Vergilius (94).

583. **Tu** (69), subj. of poscis. **frustra,** w. pius; adv., (rt. in fraus, *deceit,* w. demonst. suffix, -terus; lit., *with deceit*) *in a deceived manner, in a state of deception. Without effect, in vain. To no purpose,* in ref. to aim. *Without reason* or *cause, groundlessly,* ref. to reason. **pius** (273), nom. mas. s. ag. w. tu. **heu** (73). **non** (55). **ita,** adv., (*a*) *in this way* or

584 Poscis Quintilium Deos.
585 Quod si Threïcio blandius Orpheo
586 Auditam moderere arboribus fidem,
587 Non vanæ redeat sanguis imagini,
588 Quam virga semel horrida,
589 Non lenis precibus fata recludere,

manner, as already stated or *commanded.* In replies, *just so, yes. On this account, therefore, for this reason,* ita w. conjunctive (optative), folld. by ut, *on these terms* or *conditions that,* implying that if what is stated is not the case, then a wish that the reverse of what is implied by the verb may take place; *e.g.* ita me Di ament ut, etc. (*b*) *In the following way* or *manner. On the following conditions* or *terms.* Ut or sicut...ita, *as...also* in comparison. Ita...ut, *in such a state* or *condition. as.* Of degree or extent, *to such an extent* or *degree, so very much, excessively, thoroughly.* **creditum** (93), ag. w. Quintilium; fr. crēdo, -ĕre, -dĭdi, -dĭtum, 3rd intrans. and trans., *to put faith, trust* or *confidence in,* w. dat. *To trust one in his declarations, believe one* w. dat. pers. or acc. neut. pron. With ref. to an object already mentioned, *to believe* a thing, *admit as true, suppose, think,* etc. *To commit* or *entrust* to one for safe keeping, *consign* to one's care, aliquid alicui. *To put* something *on loan, lend;* non ita creditum, *i.e.,* whom thou hast entrusted to the gods, not expecting to be thus bereft of him

584. **Poscis,** 2nd s. ind. pres. act. fr. posco (140). **Quintilium** (577), contained or internal obj. of poscis. **Deos** (6), attained or external obj. of poscis. Certain verbs of teaching, asking, concealing, sts. take one acc. (contained) of the matter; the other (attained) of the person. Ken. 130.

585. **Quod si** (35), si as in (357). **Threïcio,** abl. s. mas. ag. w. Orpheo; fr. Threĭcius, -a, -um, adj., *of* or *belonging to Thrace, Thracian;* also Thracius, Thracus and Thracicus. **blandius,** neut. s. compar. of blandus (295) as comp. of blande; *flatteringly, soothingly, courteously.* **Orpheo,** abl. (comparative) after blandius; fr. Orpheus (292).

586. **Auditam,** acc. fem. s. pf. pass. part. ag. w. fidem; fr. audio (57). **moderere,** 2nd s. pres. subj. (in protasis) fr. mŏdĕror, -āri, -ātus sum, 1st depon. intrans., *to appoint a measure* or *standard* (rare); fig., *to set bounds* or *limits to, restrict* (class.) w. dat.; trans., *to manage, rule, direct, govern* (most com.). **arboribus,** dat. of agent (524) plu. after auditam; fr. arbor (329). **fidem,** acc. s. gov. by moderere; fr. fides (295).

587. **Non** (55). **vanæ,** dat. s. fem. ag. w. imagini; fr. vanus (563). **redeat,** 3rd s. pres. subj. (in apodosis) fr. redeo (41). **sanguis** (225), nom. s. subj. of redeat. **imagini,** dat. (acquisitive) s. after redeat; fr. imago (288); "vana imago" *the shadowy form* (M.).

588. **Quam** (70), fem. s. ag. w. imagini; acc. gov. by (direct obj. of) compulerit. **virga** (274), instrum. w. compulerit. **sĕmel,** num. adv., *once, a single time;* semel atque iterum, *time and again,* i.e., *repeatedly. Once for all.* Of what occurs but *once.* In a series of numbers=*primum, primo, the first time, first,* folld. by iterum, etc. **horrida,** abl. fem. s. ag. w. virga; fr. horrĭdus, -a, -um, adj., (horreo, *to bristle*) *standing on end, sticking out, shaggy, rough, prickly. Rude, wild, savage,* i.e., *rough* in character. *Blunt, stern, unpolished, uncouth. Producing terror* or *horror, terrible, frightful.*

589. **Non** (55), w. lenis. **lenis** (22), nom. mas. s. ag. w. Mercurius. **precibus,** dat. plu. after recludere; fr. obsol. prex (62); *in answer to* (W.). **fata** (389), gov. by recludere. **recludere,** pres. inf. (prolative) act. after

590 Nigro compulerit Mercurius gregi.
591 Durum: sed levius fit patientia.
592 Quidquid corrigere est nefas.

CARMEN XXV.—AD LYDIAM.

593 Parcius junctas quatiunt fenestras
594 Ictibus crebris juvenes protervi,

lenĭs; fr. reclūdo, -ĕre, -clūsi, -clūsum, 3rd trans., (re, 659; claudo, *to shut*) *to unclose, lay* or *throw open, disclose, reveal. To unloose, let loose;* "fata recludere," to open the door of fate (W.).

590. **Nigro,** dat. mas. s. ag. w. gregi; fr. niger (145) **compulerit,** 3rd sing. fut. pf. act. fr. compello, -pellĕre, -pŭli, -pulsum, 3rd trans., (cum, 31; pello, 215) *to drive together* or *in a body* to a place. *To assemble, gather, collect. To force together, narrow. To drive, force, urge, move, impel.* When of two future actions one will commence after the other is completed, the verb exp. the former will be in the simple fut., that exp. the latter in fut. pf. **Mercurius** (257), nom. subj..of compulerit. **gregi,** dat. s. after (remote obj. of) compulerit; fr. grex, grĕgis, 3rd mas. Of animals, *a flock, herd, swarm, drove.* Of persons, *company, society, troop, band, crowd* (845).

591. **Durum,** nom. neut. s. predic. after est und.; fr. durus (479). **sed,** a particle of limitation, excĕption, or correction, *but, yet,* esp. used in transition to another subject. After negative clauses to indicate that the assertion does not hold good at all, but that something else does, or that it is not exclusively true, but something else is true in addition, *but on the contrary, but even;* non modo (solum, etc.)...sed or sed etiam (solum), etc., *not only, not merely...but also, but even.* **lĕvius,** nom. neut. s. predic. after fit; ag. w. quidquid...nefas; fr. levis (31). **fit,** 3rd s. ind. pres. fr. fio (447). **patientia,** abl. (of means) s. fr. pătĭentia, -æ, 1st fem., (patior, 18) *the act of bearing, suffering* or *enduring, patience, forbearance, indulgence.* In bad sense, *indolence, want of spirit* (rare)

592. **Quidquid** (263), neut. s. ag. w. demonst. und., acc. gov. by corrigere. **corrigere,** inf. pres. act. subj. of est; fr. corrĭgo, -ĕre, -rexi, -rectum, 3rd trans., (cum, 31; rego, 91) *to make straight, set right, bring into order. To improve, amend, correct, make better,* esp. *to correct* in oral or written discourse. **est** (19). **nĕfas** (277), predic. after est.

Carmen XXV. Metre—*The Lesser Sapphic.* (Carmen ii).

593. **Parcius,** comp. of parce (1090), adv. of parcus (761); *sparingly, moderately, cautiously.* Of time, *seldom, rarely.* In good sense, *thriftily, frugally, economically.* In bad sense, *niggardly, penuriously.* **junctas,** acc. fem. plu. ag. w. fenestras; fr. junctus (134), *i.e., closed for the night* (W.). **quatiunt** (135). **fenestras,** acc. plu. gov. by quatiunt; fr. fĕnestra, -æ, 1st fem., *an opening* in the wall to admit the light, *a window;* fenestræ bifores, windows w. two leaves or doors opening from top to bottom (as French windows now), when closed called junctæ, when open patulæ.

594. **Ictibus,** abl. (of means) plu. fr. ictus, -us, 4th mas., (ico, *to strike*) *a blow, stroke, hit, stab, thrust.* Poet. of the *rays* of the sun (1270), fig. of fortunes, etc., *strokes.* **crebris,** abl. mas. plu. ag. w. ictibus; fr. creber, crebra, crebrum, adj., (ak. to cresco, 329) *made to increase, existing* or *taking*

595 Nec tibi somnos adimunt, amatque
596 Janua limen,
597 Quæ prius multum facilis movebat
598 Cardines. Audis minus et minus jam:
599 "Me tuo longas pereunte noctes,
600 Lydia, dormis?"
601 Invicem mæchos anus arrogantes

place in a multitude, following close upon one another, thick, pressed together, frequent, numerous. That is furnished with or *produces abundantly, crowded with,* w. abl. of abundance (540). **juvenes,** nom. plu. subj. of quatiunt; fr. juvenis (77). **protervi,** nom. plu. mas. ag. w. juvenes; fr. protervus (472).

595. **Nec** (19). **tibi** (93), incommodi after (remote obj. of) adimunt. **somnos,** acc. plu. gov. by (direct obj. of) adimunt; fr. somnus, -i, 2nd mas., *sleep.* Personified son of Erĕbus and Nox; with longus, æger, frigidus = *death.* **adimunt,** 3rd plu. pres. ind. act. jnd. by nec. to quatiunt; fr. adĭmo, -ĭmere, -ēmi, -emptum, 3rd trans., (ad, 6; emo, *to buy*) *to take* a thing to oneself; hence w. exclusive ref. to the pers. fr. whom a thing is taken, *to take away* a thing from some one, *to deprive of;* in good sense, *to free from, e.g.,* metum; in bad sense, *deprive of, e.g.,* alicui vitam. **amat,** 3rd s. pres. ind. act. fr. amo (86), *cleaves to.* **-que** (4), here unites clauses.

596. **Jānua,** -æ, 1st fem.; nom. s. subj. of amat; (Janus) *the outer street-door* of profane buildings, rare of a temple; any *entrance* to a domain, abode, country; fig., *access, entrance* (Cic.). **limen,** acc. s. gov. by amat; fr. līmen, -ĭnis, 3rd neut., (fr. lĭgo, *to bind*) *connecting timber* or *support* of a doorway, *lintel, headpiece* above; *sill, threshold, footpiece* below. *Door, doorway, entrance. House, dwelling, abode. Barrier* in a racecourse. *Beginning, commencement. End, termination.*

597. **Quæ** (46), fem. s. ag. w. janua; nom. to movebat. **prius** (120). **multum,** neut. of multus (23), as adv., *much, greatly, very much* w. vbs. *Very* w. adjs. in posit. (here w. facilis); with adjs. in comp., *much, far. Often, frequently* (rarer). **facilis,** -e, adj.; nom. fem. s. ag. as adv. attribute (867) w. janua; (facio, 542) *easy to do, easy, without difficulty,* w. ad. and gerund.; w. sup. in -u; rarely w. inf. *Suitable, proper,* w. dat. Of persons, *ready, quick, easy, good-natured, compliant. Willing, yielding, courteous, affable;* adv. facile and faciliter. **movebat,** 3rd s. impf. ind. act. fr. mŏveo (394).

598. **Cardines,** acc. plu. gov. by movebat; fr. cardo (449). **audis,** 2nd s. ind. pres. act. fr. audio (57). **minus et minus** (63). **jam** (37).

599. **Me,** abl. absol. s. fr. ego (29). **tuo,** abl. s. mas. ag. w. me; fr. tuus (175). **longas,** acc. fem. plu. ag. w. noctes; fr. longus (73). **pereunte,** abl. mas. s. pres. part. ag. w. me; fr. pereo (58). **noctes,** acc. plu. of duration of time; fr. nox (144).

600. **Lydia,** voc. s. fr. Lydia, -æ, 1st fem. **dormis,** 2nd s. ind. pres. act. fr. dormio, -īre, -īvi or -ii, -ītum, 4th intrans., (Eng., *dream*) *to sleep;* poet. in pass. *to be slept through, e.g.,* nox; fig., *to rest, be at ease, be inactive.*

601. **Invicem,** sts. separated by tmesis; (in, 76; vicem, 129) *by turn, in turn, one after another, alternately,* esp. *in its turn. Mutually, reciprocally.* Of persons, *in one's place* or *room, in the place of.* **mæchos,** acc. plu. gov. by flebis; fr. mæchus, -i, 2nd mas. (Gk.), *a fornicator, adulterer.* **anus,**

602 Flebis in solo levis angiportu
603 Thracio bacchante magis sub inter-
604 lunia vento;
605 Quum tibi flagrans amor et libido,
606 Quæ solet matres furiare equorum,
607 Sæviet circa jecur ulcerosum,

-us, 4th fem.; nom. in app. to tu und. in flebis; (ak. to ante, *before*) *an old woman* married or unmarried, genly in contempt; sts. in honourable sense. **arrogantes,** acc. plu. mas. ag. w. mæchos; fr. arrŏgans, -ntis, adj., *appropriating to oneself* something not one's own. Of character, *assuming, presumptuous, haughty;* orig. pres. part. of arrogo, (ad, 6; rogo, 1281) *to appropriate* to oneself that which does not belong to one.

602. **Flebis,** 2nd s. fut. ind. act. fr. fleo (154), *you shall weep over* or *on account of.* **in** (78). **solo,** abl. mas. s. ag. w. angĭportu; fr. sōlus, -a, -um, gen. solīus, dat. soli, pronominal adj., *alone, only, single, sole. Alone, lonely, deserted, i.e.,* without friends, relatives, etc. Of places, *solitary, deserted, unfrequented.* **levis** (382), ag. w. tu und. in flebis; here *despised, of no value.* **angiportu,** abl. s. gov. by in; fr. angĭportus, -us, 4th mas., and angĭportum, -i, 2nd neut., (ango, Gk., *to straiten;* portus, 367) *a narrow street, lane* or *alley.*

603. **Thracio,** abl. s. mas. ag. w. vento; fr. Thrăcĭus, -a, -um=Thrēĭcius (585). **bacchante,** abl. s. mas. pres. part. ag. w. vento; fr. bacchor, -ari, -atus sum, 1st dep., *to celebrate the festival of Bacchus* (482). *To revel, rage, rave, rant* like the Bacchæ. Of every kind of mental excitement (1067). *To run about in a wild, raving* or *wanton manner.* **magis,** comp. adv., *in a higher degree, more completely, more;* (*a*) when the second term of the comparison is added w. vbs., substs., prons., adjs., advs., esp. w. adjs. and advbs. that do not admit the comparative termn.; (*b*) when the second term is not added, often strengthnd. by etiam, multo, eo, tanto, quo, etc.; magis magisque, magis et magis, *more and more.* Non (neque) magis quam, exp. perfect equality betw. two enunciations; if affirm., *no more than, just as much as;* if negat., *no more than, just as little as.* **sub** (230).

604. **Interlunia,** acc. plu. gov. by sub; fr. interlunium, -ii, 2nd neut., (interlunis, *at new moon*) *the change of the moon, time of new moon,* class., not Cic. nor Cæs. **vento,** abl. absol. s. fr. ventus (91).

605. **Quum** (43), here w. fut. indicative. **tibi** (93), incommodi after sæviet. **flagrans,** nom. mas. s. pres. part. act. ag. w. amor; fr. flagro, -āre, -avi, -atum, (ak. to fulgeo, *to shine*) *to flame, blaze, burn, be on fire. To be inflamed* (good or bad sense), *blaze, glow, burn. To be violently excited, stirred, provoked. To be annoyed at* anything, *suffer from;* pres. partc., flagrans. Of colour, *glittering, shining, e.g.,* rosæ, *blushing. Glowing* w. passion, *violent, vehement, eager.* **amor** (364), subj. of sæviet. **libido** (486), nom. s. jnd. by et to amor.

606. **Quæ** (46), fem. s. ag. w. libido; nom. to solet. **solet,** 3rd s. ind. pres. fr. sŏleo, -ēre, solĭtus sum, 2nd semi-depon., *to use, be wont, be accustomed,* used absol. or w. inf. act. or pass. **matres,** acc. plu. gov. by furiare; fr. mater (24). **furiare,** pres. inf. (prolative, 570)) act. after solet; fr. fŭrio, -āre, -avi, -atum, 1st trans., (furiæ, *rage, madness*) *to drive mad, madden, enrage, infuriate* (poet). **equorum,** gen. plu. after matres; fr. equus (167).

607. **Sæviet,** 3rd s. fut. ind. act. fr. sævio, -īre, sævĭ, sævītum, 4th intrans., (sævus, 172) *to be fierce, furious, rage, vent one's rage. To be made violent,*

608 Non sine questu,
609 Læta quod pubes hedera virente
610 Gaudeat pulla magis atque myrto,
611 Aridas frondes hiemis sodali
612 Dedicet Hebro.

CARMEN XXVI.—AD MUSAM DE ÆLIO LAMIA.

613 Musis amicus tristitiam et metus
614 Tradam protervis in mare Creticum

angry. **circa** (98). **jecur** (348), gov. by circa. **ulcerosum,** acc. neut. s. ag. w. jecur; fr. ulcĕrosus, -a, -um, adj., (ulcus, *a sore, ulcer*) *full of sores;* here *wounded* in love.

608. **Non sine** (55, 370). **questu,** abl. s. gov. by sine; fr. questus, -us, 4th mas., (queror, 42) *a complaining;* hence *complaint* (class.). *An accusation* (poet.).

609. **Læta,** nom. fem. s. ag. w. pubes; fr. lætus (82). **quod** (35, 315). **pubes,** -is, 3rd fem.; nom. s. subj. of gaudeat; *the signs of manhood, i.e.,* the hair which appears on the body at the age of puberty. Of persons, *grown-up males, men, young men.* **hedera,** abl. (of cause w. gaudeat) s. fr. hedera (29). **virente,** abl. fem. s. ag. w. hederâ; fr. virens (249).

610. **Gaudeat,** 3rd s. subj. pres. act. fr. gaudeo (11), subj. because virtually subolique after quod. **pulla,** abl. fem. s. ag. w. myrto; fr. pullus, -a, -um, adj., *blackish, grey, dusky;* here "*dark green,*" often of the clothes of the poor, mourning, etc; hence *sad, sorrowful* (poet.). **magis** (603). **atque** (37). **myrto** (137), abl. jnd. by atque to hederâ.

611. **Aridas,** acc. plu. fem. ag. w. frondes; fr. aridus (552). **frondes,** acc. plu. gov. by (direct obj. of) dedicet; fr. frons (418). **hiemis,** gen. s. after sodali; fr. hiems (129). **sodali,** dat. s. in app. to Hebro; fr. sŏdālis, -is, abl. -i, 3rd mas., (sedeo, *to sit*) *a mate, fellow, intimate, comrade, crony, boon companion,* (1045), sts. *accomplice, participator* in what is bad.

612. **Dedicet,** 3rd s. pres. conj. act., construction same as gaudeat; fr. dēdĭco,-āre, -āvi, -atum, 1st trans., traj., (de, 10; dĭco, *to consecrate, devote*) *to give out tidings* or *notice;* hence *affirm, declare, announce* (ante and post-class.). Relig., *to adjudge* a thing *from* oneself to the deity; hence *dedicate, consecrate* a thing *to* a deity or deified person; sts. w. deity to whom anything has been consecrated as obj. (709). *To devote to* any purpose, *consecrate* to any use. **Hebro,** dat. s. after (indirect obj. of) dedicet; fr. Hebrus, -i, 2nd mas., a river in Thrace (now Marizza), which rises in Mt. Hæmus and falls into the Ægean Sea; "dedicet Hebro=throw away" (W.)

CARMEN XXVI. METRE—*The Alcaic.* (Carmen ix.)

613. **Musis,** dat. plu. after trajective amicus; fr. musa (174). **amicus** (208), nom. s. in app. to ego und. in tradam. **tristitiam** (202), gov. by tradam. **metus,** acc. plu. jnd by et to tristitiam; fr. mĕtŭs (564).

614. **Tradam,** 1st s. fut. ind. act. fr. trādo (also written transdo, so most freq. in Cæs.), -dĕre, -dĭdi. -dĭtum, 3rd trans., traj., (trans, 228; do, 65) *to go across or over;* hence *to give up, hand over, deliver, transmit, surrender* (979).

Portare ventis, queis sub Arcto
Rex gelidæ metuatur oræ,
Quid Tiridaten terreat, unice
Securus. O, quæ fontibus integris
Gaudes, apricos necte flores,
Necte meo Lamiæ coronam,

To entrust for protection, etc. *To give up treacherously, betray;* fig., *to hand over, surrender;* here w. inf., *to bequeath. To hand down* to posterity by written narrative, *relate, recount. To deliver* by teaching, *propose, propound, teach* anything. **protervis,** dat. plu. mas. ag. w. ventis; fr. protervus (472); here, *at play.* **in** (81). **mare** (14), gov. by in. **Crēticum,** acc. neut. s. ag. w. mare; fr. Crētĭcus, -a, -um, adj., *of Crete* (Candia), celebrated in ancient times for fertility.

615. **Portare,** pres. inf. (prolative exp. purpose, 570) after tradam; fr. porto, -āre, -āvi, -ātum, 1st trans., (intens. of fero, 138) *to bear, carry along, convey* anything heavy; fig., *to carry, bring* (genly. poet. not Cic.). **ventis** (379), of remote obj. after tradam. **queis**=quibus (160), mas. plu dat. of agent after metuatur. **sub** (21). **Arcto,** abl. s. gov. by sub; fr. Arctos, (rare Arctus), acc. Arcton; nom. plu. Arctoe (Gk.). *The Great* and *Little Bear, Ursa Major* and *Minor. The North Pole.*

616. **Rex** (1), nom. s. subj. of metuatur. **gelidæ,** gen. s. fem. ag. w. oræ; fr. gelidus (30). **metuatur,** 3rd. s. pres. subj. pass. fr. metuo (16). The subj. after quis in indirect question. **oræ,** gen. s. after rex; fr. ora (289).

617. **Quid** (245), subj. of terreat. **Tiridaten,** acc. s. gov. by terreat; fr. Tiridates, -æ (Gk.), 1st mas.; name of several kings of Armenia. **terreat,** 3rd sing. pres. subj. act.; fr. terreo (40); subj. in indirect question. **unice,** adv., (unicus, unus, 189) *alone, solely, singularly, especially, in an extraordinary degree,* here "*utterly* regardless."

618. **Securus,** -a, -um, adj.; nom. mas. s. ag. w. ego und. in tradam; (se=sine, 370; cura, 215), in good sense *careless, untroubled, fearless, composed;* w. gen. or relat. clause, *about* what. Of inanimate things, *safe, serene, cheerful, untroubled, e.g.,* sleep (poet. and post-Aug.). Of a thing or place, *free from danger, safe.* **O** (2). **quæ** (46), fem. s. 2nd pers. ag. w. Pimplea; nom. subj. of gaudes. **fontibus,** abl. plu. of cause, after gaudes; fr. fons, fontis, 3rd mas., (akin to fundo, 711), *that which pours itself forth, spring, fountain. Fountain-head, source, origin.* **integris,** abl. mas. plu. ag. w. fontibus; fr. integer (373).

619. **Gaudes,** 2nd sing. ind. pres. act. fr. gaudeo (11). **apricos,** acc. plu. mas. ag. w. flores; fr. apricus (219). **necte,** 2nd s. imper. pres. act. fr. necto, -tĕre, nexui and nexi, nexum, 3rd trans., *to bind together, tie, fasten. To keep in fetters* or *prison. To tie* or *bind together* (here). *To entwine, clasp in each other. To make by joining together, weave, plait, work. To forge, make anything of links* (689). *To affix, attach* one thing *to* another, *e.g.,* ex alio alia nectere. *To fasten together, connect, unite, e.g.,* verba, caussas. *To devise, contrive, e.g.,* moras, dolos. **flores,** acc. plu. gov. by necte; fr. flos (138).

620. **Meo,** dat. s. mas. ag. w. Lamiæ; fr. meus (2). **Lamiæ,** dat. commodi after necte; fr. Lămia, -æ, 1st mas., cognomen in the Gens. Ælia (Lamus, founder of Formiæ). **coronam** (475), gov. by necte.

621 Pimplea dulcis! Nil sine te mei
622 Prosunt honores; hunc fidibus novis,
623 Hunc Lesbio sacrare plectro
624 Teque tuasque decet sorores.

CARMEN XXVII.—AD SODALES.

625 Natis in usum lætitiæ scyphis
626 Pugnare Thracum est: tollite barbarum

621. **Pimplea,** voc. s. fr. Pimplea, -æ, 1st fem., *a muse;* prop. fem. (und. puella); fr. Pimplēus, -a, -um, adj., of *Pimpla,* a hill and fountain in Pieria, sacred to the Muses. **dulcis,** voc. s. ag. w. Pimplea; fr. dulcis (2). **nil** (378) adv. **sine** (370). **te** (88), gov. by sine. **mei,** nom. mas. plu. ag. w. honores; fr. meus (2).

622. **Prosunt,** 3rd plu. pres. ind. fr. prōsum, prōfui, prodesse, irreg. traj., (pro, *for, in behalf of;* sum, 3) *to be for* or *in behalf of, benefit, be of use, profit* (652). **honores** (304), nom. subj. of prosunt. **hunc** (7), *i.e.,* Lamia, gov. by sacrare; mei honores, *honours that I can give* (W.). **fidibus** (295) instrum. w. sacrare. **novis,** abl. fem. plu. ag. w. fidibus; fr. novus (42).

623. **Hunc,** anaphora. **Lesbio,** abl. neut. s. ag. w. plectro; fr. Lesbius, -a, -um, adj., *of* or *belonging to Lesbos,* an island in the Ægean Sea off the coast of Troy and Mysia: Lesbius civis (733), *Alcæus.* Lesbium, -ii, 2nd neut. (und. vinum), *Lesbian wine:* here Lesbium plectrum = *Alcaics.* **sacrare,** pres. inf. act. subj. of decet; fr. săcro, -āre, -avi, -atum, 1st trans., (sacer, 22) *to declare, set apart as sacred, consecrate, devote* to a deity. *To devote* or *doom to destruction, declare accursed. To hallow, consecrate. To render imperishable, immortalise, canonize* (Hor. rare). **plectro,** abl. instrumental s. fr. plectrum, -i, 2nd neut. (Gk.), *a thing to strike with, a little stick* w. which the player struck the chords of a stringed instrument, *quill. Lyre, lute, lyric poem, lyric poetry, lyric strain* (916, 1219, 624). **te** (83), gov. by decet. **que.. que** (4), *both and.* **tuas** (175), ag. w. sorores. **decet** (137). **sorores,** acc. plu. jnd. by -que to te; fr. soror (578).

Carmen XXVII Metre—*The Alcaic.* (Carmen ix.)

625. **Natis,** abl. plu. mas. pf part. ag. w scyphis; fr. nascor (679). **in,** exp. purpose (192). **usum,** acc s. gov. by in, fr. ūsus, -ūs, 4th mas., (utor, *to use*) *using* a thing, *application, employment. Good intercourse, familiarity, intimacy. Constant use, practice, experience. Profit, advantage, utility, usefulness. Occasion, need, want, necessity,* usus est, w. dat. pers., abl. thing, *there is need of, one needs. A fit occasion* or *opportunity.* **lætitiæ,** gen. s. after usum; fr lætĭtia, -æ, 1st fem., (lætus, 82) *joy, joyousness, excessive delight* [stronger than gaudium]. Of lands, *luxuriousness, richness.* **scyphis,** abl. (instrum.) plu. fr. scȳphus, -i, 2nd mas., (Gk.) *a cup, goblet.*

626. **Pugnare,** pres. inf. act. subj. of est; fr. pugno, -āre, -āvi, -ātum, 1st intrans., *to fight* either singly or in armies, *to give battle, engage, contend;* fig., *to contend, conflict, disagree, oppose, contradict.* Of arguments, etc., *to exert oneself* for anything, w. ne, ut, and subj. **Thracum,** gen. plu. after est; fr. Thrax, Thrācis, adj.; *of* or *belonging to Thrace, Thracian* (1408); subst., (und. vir) *a Thracian.* This is the possessive gen. and may be supposed to depend on a suppressed notion, *e.g.,* token, nature, function,

Morem verecundumque Bacchum
Sanguineis prohibete rixis.
Vino et lucernis Medus acinaces
Immane quantum discrepat; impium
Lenite clamorem, sodales,
Et cubito remanete presso.

duty, part, etc. **tollite** (529). **barbarum,** acc. mas. s. ag. w. morem; fr. barbărus; -a, -um, adj., (Gk.) orig. *stammering* (ak. to balbus), *foreign, strange,* opp. to Greek or Roman (690). *Uncultivated, ignorant, rude. Wild, savage, cruel* (here). Compar. very rare. Superl. not found.

627. **Morem,** acc. s. gov. by tollite; fr. mos (260). **verecundum,** acc. mas. s. ag. w. Bacchum; fr. vĕrĕcundus, -a, -um, adj., (vereor, *to feel reverence*) *feeling much awe* or *reverence. For which awe is felt, worthy of awe* (post-class.). Of persons, *feeling much shame* at anything, *shamefaced, modest, diffident.* Of things, *betokening modesty, e.g.,* colour. *a blush.* **Bacchum,** acc. s. gov. by prohibete; fr. Bacchus (482).

628. **Sanguineis,** abl. fem. plu. ag. w. rixis; fr. sanguĭneus, -a, -um, adj.; (sanguis, 225) *of blood, consisting of blood. Blood-coloured, blood-red* (poet. and post-Aug.). **prohibete,** 2nd plu. pres. imper. act. fr. prohĭbeo, -ēre, -ŭi, -ĭtum, 2nd trans., (pro, *forward, in front;* habeo, 641) *to hold in front, before* one. *To hold back, restrain, check. To hinder, ward off* a thing. *To forbid, prohibit* a thing. *To protect from,* w. acc. of thing protected, and a or ab of that *from* which. **rixis,** abl. plu. of separation, fr. rixa (355).

629. **Vino,** dat. s. after traject. discrepat; fr. vinum (146). **lucernis,** dat. plu. jnd. by et to vino; fr. lŭcerna, -æ, 1st fem., (lūceo, *to shine*) *a lamp, oil-lamp;* "vinum et lucernæ," *evening entertainment.* **Medus,** -a, -um, adj.; nom. mas. s. ag. w. acinaces; (Medi, poet. for Persians, Assyrians, etc. 87, 1286), *Median, Assyrian.* **ăcīnăces,** -is, 3rd mas. (Pers.); nom. s. subj. of discrepat; a short straight *sword* or *sabre* of the Persians, Medians, Scythians, worn on the right side of the body.

630. **Immane,** neut. s. of immanis, -e, adj., (in intens. magnus, 85) *monstrous in size, immense, huge, vast,* genly. of things.; fig., *monstrous in character, inhuman, fierce, savage, wild;* "immane quantum" is a parenthetical sentence in wh. immane is predicative, *how much is immense,* i.e., *how exceedingly, how wonderfully.* **discrepat,** 3rd sing. ind. pres. act.; fr. discrĕpo, -are, -ŭi, no sup., 1st intrans., (dis, 870; crepo, 481), *to differ in sound, sound discordantly* (Cic.). *To disagree, be different, vary;* discrepat, impers., *there is a difference of opinion* about. **impium,** acc. mas. s. ag. w. clamorem; fr. impius (111), here "offending Bacchus" (W.).

631. **Lenite,** 2nd plu. pres. imp. act. fr. lēnio, -ire, -īvi or -ĭi, -ītum, 4th trans., (lenis, 22) *to make soft;* meton., *to moderate, render gentle, appease, pacify, e.g.,* stomachum. *To make gentle* in character, *appease, quiet.* **clamorem,** acc. s. gov. by lenite; fr. clamor (74). **sodales,** voc. plu. fr. sodalis, subst. (611).

632. **Cubito,** abl. (absolute) s. fr. cŭbĭtum, -i, 2nd neut., (cubo, 459) *the elbow,* serving for leaning upon. **remanete,** 2nd plu. pres. imper. act. fr. rĕmăneo, -ēre, -mansi, no sup., 2nd intrans., (re, 659; maneo, 25) *to remain behind, stay, continue, abide, endure.* With adj. as predic., *to continue, remain in a certain state.* **presso,** abl. neut. s. ag. w. cubito; fr. pressus (374). "Cubito...presso," *with the left arm deep in the cushions of the sofa* (W.).

633 Vultis severi me quoque sumere
634 Partem Falerni? dicat Opuntiæ
635 Frater Megillæ, quo beatus
636 Vulnere, qua pereat sagitta.
637 Cessat voluntas? Non alia bibam
638 Mercede. Quæ te cunque domat Venus.
639 Non erubescendis adurit

633. **Vultis,** 2nd plu. ind. pres. fr. volo (104). **severi,** gen. neut. s. ag. w. Falerni; fr. sĕvērus, -a, -um, adj., orig. *respected.* Of persons in a good sense, *serious, grave, strict, austere,* esp. *sober, temperate* in character, behaviour, etc. Of things *severe, austere;* here *rough, sharp.* Of feelings, opinions, laws, judgments, etc., style (885). *Bad, dreadful* (795). **me** (29), subj. of sumere. **quoque** (410). **sumere,** pres. inf. (prolative) act. after vultis; fr. sumo (286).

634. **Partem** (20), gov. by sumere. **Falerni,** gen. s. after partem; fr. Falernum (518). **dicat,** 3rd s. pres. conj. (optative) act. fr. dico (86). **Opuntiæ,** gen. s. fem. ag. w. Megillæ; fr. Opuntius, -a, -um, *of Opus,* a town of Locris in Greece.

635. **Frater** (90), nom. s. subj. of dicat. **Megillæ,** gen. s. after frater; fr. Megilla, 1st, a Gk. name. **quo,** abl. s. neut. ag. w. vulnere; fr. quis (65). **beatus** (142), nom. s. mas. predic. after sit und., here "*blest.*"

636. **Vulnere,** abl. instrum. s. w. beatus; fr. vulnus (voln-), -ĕris, 3rd neut. Of living beings, *a wound.* Of things, *hole, cut, incision, notch;* fig., of love, pain, grief. **qua** (62), w. sagitta. **pereat,** 3rd s. pres. subj. fr. pereo (58), subj. in indirect question. **sagitta** (308), instrum. w. pereat.

637. **Cessat,** 3rd s. pres. ind. act. fr. cesso, -are, -āvi, -atum, 1st intrans., (intens. of cedo, 170) *to stand back much, be remiss* in anything, *delay, loiter, cease from, stop, give over. To be inactive, idle, at leisure.* Of things, *to be unused, idle.* Of land, *be uncultivated. Not to be at hand* or *present* (here). *To depart from the right way, mistake, err.* **voluntas,** -atis, 3rd fem.; nom. s. subj. of cessat; (volo, 104) *will, free will, choice, desire, inclination. Goodwill, affection, favour,* w. erga, in, etc.; "cessat voluntas," *falters thy will.* **non** (55). **alia,** abl. s. fem. ag. w. mercede; fr. alius (92). **bibam,** 1st s. fut. ind. act. fr. bibo (518).

638. **Mercede,** abl. (of condition) s. fr. merces, -cēdis, 3rd fem., (merx, 720; cedo, 170) *what comes as gain;* good sense, *pay, wages, salary, fee, reward;* bad sense, *punishment, detriment, injury, disadvantage;* here *terms, condition;* meton., *rent, revenue, income,* as fr. a tenant, in plural. **quæ...cunque** (526), ag. w. Venus. **te** (83), gov. by domat. **domat,** 3rd s. ind. pres. act. fr. domo (358). **Venus** (133), subj. of domat.

639. **Non** (55). **erubescendis,** abl. plu. mas. ag. w. ignibus; fr. ērŭbescendus, -a, -um, *to be ashamed of;* gerundive of ērŭbesco, -cĕre, -cui, no sup., 3rd inceptive, (e, 691; rubeo, 38) intrans., *to grow red, redden. To blush up with shame, feel ashamed;* trans., *to feel shame about.* The gerundive is a participial adj., neither act. nor pass. exclusively, *e.g.,* bibendus, *proper for drinking;* (i.) its oblique cases in -di, -do, -dum, called gerunds, supply the gen., dat. and abl. and accus. of the act. inf. verb-noun; (ii.) its neut. w. the inf. or 3rd sing. forms of sum becomes a verb impersonal, exp. *duty, meetness;* (iii.) used as an adj. it exp. *necessity, duty, meetness,* either as attribute or complement. In the case of trans. verbs in-

640 Ignibus ingenuoque semper
641 Amore peccas. Quidquid habes, age,
642 Depone tutis auribus. Ah miser,
643 Quanta laborabas Charybdi,
644 Digne puer meliore flamma!
645 Quæ saga, quis te solvere Thessalis

stead of the gerunds gov. an accus., the object is put in the case in which the gerund would have been, and the gerundive is put in agreement with it. This is gerundial attraction, *e.g.*, not "colendi virtutem," but "colendæ virtutis." **adurit,** 3rd s. ind. pres. act. fr. ădūro, -ūrĕre, -ussi, -ustum, 3rd trans., (ad, 6; ūro, 136) *to burn*, pass. reflex., *to burn oneself. To burn up, destroy, consume by fire. To scorch* in cooking, fig. of love, *burn, waste, consume* (here). Of cold, frost, *to nip, freeze*,. Of sun, *to scorch, parch up.*

640. **Ignibus** (352), instrum. w. adurit. **ingenuo,** abl. s. mas. ag. w. amore; fr. ingĕnŭus, -a, -um, adj., (in, 78; gigno, *to beget*) *native, not foreign, e.g.*, fontes; fig., *inborn, innate. Free-born*, esp. of parents who have never been slaves. *That is worthy of a freedman, generous, candid, frank* (here). **que** (4), after a negative has an adversative force, *but*, so 1173, 1428. **semper** (158).

641. **Amore,** abl. (of manner) s. fr. amor (247). **peccas,** 2nd s. ind. pres. act. fr. pecco, -āre, -avi, -atum, 1st intrans., *to miss, mistake* anything, *do amiss, transgress, commit a fault*, w. acc. pron.; de w. abl., *in what respect*; w. in or erga, and acc., *towards* whom. **quidquid** (263), gov. by hăbes. **habes,** 2nd s. ind. pres. act. fr. hăbeo, -ēre, -ui, -ĭtum, 2nd trans., *to have* in the widest sense, *hold, keep, cherish, possess, entertain.* With two accs., *to keep* one *as, regard* one *as, consider as. To have in one's mind, know, be acquainted with. To do, perform, cause, prepare, e.g.*, ludos, iter, delectum. **age,** 2nd s. imper. pres. act. fr. ago (43), used almost as an exclamation.

642. **depone,** 2nd sing. imper. pres. act. fr. dēpōno, -pōnĕre, -pŏsui, -pŏsĭtum, 3rd trans., (de, 10; pono, 104) *to lay, place, set down. To deposit*, esp. *to entrust to the keeping of*, w. apud, etc. *To lay as a wager, stake. To resign, give up, get rid of.* **tutis,** dat. fem. plu. ag. w. auribus; fr. tutus (453). **auribus,** dat. plu. after traject. depone; fr. auris, -is, 3rd fem., *the ear*; depone tutis auribus, *i.e.*, whisper it to me if you won't tell it to the company. **ah,** exclamation of pain, grief, indignation, reproach, etc. **miseri** (163), voc. s. mas.

643. **Quanta,** abl. s. fem. ag. w. Charybdi; fr. quantus (393). **laborabas,** 2nd s. impf. ind. act. fr. laboro (235). The impf. ref. to time before the revelation, see 840. **Charybdi,** abl. local s. fr. Chărybdis, -is, acc. -in or -im, abl. -i, 3rd fem., dangerous whirlpool betw. Italy and Sicily, opp. Scylla; hence used of anything dangerous.

644. **Digne,** voc. mas. s. ag. w. puer; fr. dignus, -a, -um, adj., (rt. dic-, *pointed out*). In good or bad sense, *worthy, deserving.* Of things, *fit, becoming, proper*, w. abl., with relat. clause (not in Aug. poets), or absol. the thing *of which* being und. (1257) fr. context. **puer** (149), voc. s. **meliore,** abl. fem. s. ag. w. flamma; fr. melior (58, 209). **flamma** (423), after digne. The abl. of matter.

645. **Quæ,** nom. fem. s. ag. w. saga; fr. quis (65). **săga,** -æ, 1st fem.; nom. s. subj. of pŏterit; *female diviner, wise woman, fortune-teller*; fem. (und. mulier) of sāgus, -a, -um, adj., (ak. to sāgio, *to perceive quickly* or *acutely*) *presaging, prophetic* (post-Aug.). **quis** (149), ag. w. magus. **te**

646 Magus venenis, quis poterit Deus?
647 Vix illigatum te triformi
648 Pegasus expediet Chimæra.

CARMEN XXVIII.—ARCHYTAS.

649 *Nauta.* TE maris et terræ numeroque carentis arenæ
650 Mensorem cohibent, Archyta,

(83), gov. by solvere. **solvere,** pres. inf. (prolative) after poterit; fr. solvo (129). **Thessalis,** abl. neut. plu. ag. w. venenis; fr. Thessalus (188).

646. **Magus,** -i, 2nd mas.; nom. s. subj. of poterit; *magician, learned man* among the Persians; măga, -æ, 1st fem., *an enchantress.* **venenis,** abl. (of means) plu. fr. vĕnēnum, -i, 2nd neut., *any liquid that powerfully affects* or *changes the condition of the body, potion, drug, juice,* esp. bad, *poison. A magical potion, charm* (1200); good sense, *colouring, dye, paint.* **quis** (149), ag. w. Deus. **poterit,** 3rd s. fut. ind. fr. possum (372). **Deus** (109), subj. of poterit.

647 **Vix** (371). **illigatum,** acc. mas. s. pf. pass. partc. ag. w. te; fr. illĭgo, -āre, -āvi, -atum, 1st trans., (in, 76; lĭgo, *to bind*) *to bind* or *tie on, fasten,* esp., *entangle, impede;* fig., *attach, connect, e.g.,* verba, sententiam. *To oblige, hold bound,* or in bad sense, *encumber.* **te** (83), gov. by expediet. **triformi,** abl. fem. s. ag. w. Chimæra; fr. trĭformis, -e, adj., (tres, *three;* forma, 755) *having three forms, shapes* or *natures, threefold, triple.* Diana, also called Luna and Hecate.

648. **Pēgăsus,** -i, 2nd mas.; nom. s. subj. of expediet; the winged horse of the Muses, with whose aid Bellerophon destroyed the Chimæra. **expediet,** 3rd s. fut. ind. act. fr. expedio (228). **Chimæra,** abl. (of means w. illigatum) s. fr. Chĭmæra, -æ, 1st fem., (Gk., *a goat*) a fabulous monster in Lycia slain by Bellerophon (1333), prob. the fable arose fr. a burning mountain of that name.

CARMEN XXVIII. METRE.—*The Alcmanian.* (Carmen viii.)

Irregular in having a spondee in 5th foot of the Hexameter, v. 21, and in 3rd foot of Tetrameter, v. 2.

649. **Nauta** (14). This is a dialogue between a sailor and Archytas. **Te** (84), gov. by cohibent. **maris** (164), after mensorem. **terræ,** gen. s. jnd. by et to maris; fr. terra (6). **numero,** abl. s. after carentis, exp. want; fr. numerus (279). **carentis,** gen. fem. s. pres. part. act. ag. w. arenæ; fr. căreo, -ēre, -ui, -ĭtum, -ĭturus, 2nd intrans., *to be without, free from, devoid of* (912), carere morte (1080), *to be immortal. To deprive oneself of* a thing, *not to use.* Of places, *to keep away from, be absent from, e.g.,* foro, senatu. *To want, desire* something (728). **arenæ,** gen. s. fem. jnd. by -que to terræ; fr. ărēna, -æ, 1st fem., (areo, *to be dry*) *sand, sandy-place, desert. Seashore, beach, strand. Place of combat strewed with sand* in the amphitheatre, *arena.*

650. **Mensorem,** acc. s. in app. to te; fr. mensor, -ōris, 3rd mas., (metior, *to measure*) *a measurer* of land, *land surveyor. Measurer* for partition, *divider, distributor;* fig., *one who calculates, weighs in the mind.* **cohibent,** 3rd plu. pres. ind. act. fr. cohĭbeo (33), "*confine, keep you quiet*" (aliter), *restrain you, i.e.,* keep you from crossing in Charon's boat, then "munere," must=the want of a little dust. **Archyta,** voc. s. fr. Archȳtas, -æ, (Gk.) 1st mas., a Pythagorean philosopher of Tarentum, and friend of Plato.

Pulveris exigui prope litus parva Matinum
Munera, nec quidquam tibi prodest
Aërias tentasse domos animoque rotundum
Percurrisse polum morituro.
Archytas. Occidit et Pelopis genitor conviva Deorum,
Tithonusque remotus in auras

651. **Pulveris** (220), after munera. Descriptive gen. **exigui,** gen. mas. s. ag. w. pulveris; fr. exiguus (486). **prope,** adv. Of place, *near;* "prope a," *near to, hard by.* Of time, prope quum quando, ut, *the time is near, not far off when.* Of degree, *nearly, almost.* Prep. w. acc., *near by,* rare of time and figuratively *e.g.,* prope metum; comp. propius, superl. proxime. **litus,** acc. s. gov. by prope; fr. litus (50). **parva,** nom. plu. neut. ag. w. munera; fr. parvus, -a, -um, adj. Of size or space, *small, little;* of quantity, degree, amount, number, *small, little, few;* neut. as subst., *a small amount* (1293). Of sounds, *low.* Of time, *brief, of short duration.* Of persons, *little, youthful, young.* Of degree or extent, *slight, little.* Of value, consideration, *low, slight.* Of rank or estimation, *humble, mean* of persons, *unimportant, trifling* of things. Of power, ability, character, *mean, humble;* compar. minor (332), superl. minimus (284). **Matinum,** acc. s. neut. ag. w. litus; fr. Mătīnus, -a, -um, adj., *Matinian,* place doubtful, prob. in Appulia: acc. to some near Tarentum.

652. **Munera** (483), nom. subj. of cohibent. **nec** (19). **quidquam,** neut. s. as adv. w. prodest; fr. quisquam (302). **tibi** (93), after prodest. **prodest,** 3rd s. ind. pres. fr. prosum (622).

653. **Aërias,** acc. plu. fem. ag. w. domos; fr. āĕrĭus -a, -um, more rare āĕrĕus (Gk.), adj., *of the air, found in the air. Rising high in the air, lofty, high* of mountains, trees, etc.; "domi," *the heavens.* **tentasse,** syncop. for tentavisse; pf. inf. act. subj. of prodest; fr. tento (279); "tentasse" as well as "percurrisse," is qualified by animo. **domos** (420), gov. by tentasse. **animo,** abl. (of means) s. fr. animus (448). **rotundum,** acc. mas. s. ag. w. polum; fr. rŏtundus, -a, -um, adj., (rota, 5) *wheel-shaped,* i.e., *round, circular, spherical.* Of speech, *well turned, smooth, polished, elegant;* fig. of a man, "teres atque rotundus."

654. **Percurrisse,** pf. inf. act. jnd by -que to tentasse; fr. percurro, -ĕre, -cŭcurri or -curri, -cursum, 3rd trans. and intrans., (per, 114; curro, 684) *to run through, hasten through, traverse,* fig., *to run over.* In speaking, *mention cursorily. To run over* in the mind or with the eye, *scan briefly;* intrans., *to run along to* anything. **polum,** acc. s. gov. by percurrisse; fr. pŏlus, -i, 2nd mas., *the end of an axis, a pole. The North pole. Polar star. The heavens.* **morituro,** dat. mas. s. fut. part. ag. w. tibi; fr. mŏrior, mŏri, mortuus sum, 3rd dep. intrans., *to die.* Of things, *to pass away, vanish;* meton., *to be on the point of perishing* fr. hunger, love, etc. Of plants, fire, comets, *die away, wither, perish.*

655. **Occidit** (581). **et** (2), *too, also.* **Pelopis** (172), after genitor. **genitor,** -ōris, 3rd mas.; nom. s. subj. of occidit; (gigno, *to beget*) *a begetter, father, sire.* **conviva,** -æ, 1st mas. or fem.; nom. s. in app. to genitor; (cum, 31; vivo, 731) *one who lives with* another, *table-companion, guest.* **Deorum** (261), after conviva.

656. **Tithonus,** -i, 2nd mas.; nom. jnd. by -que to genitor; *Tithonus,* son of Laomedon, spouse of Aurora, endowed with immortality, but changed into a cicada after reaching extreme old age (1310). **remotus,** pf. pass.

Et Jovis arcanis Minos admissus habentque
  Tartara Panthoiden iterum Orco
Demissum, quamvis clipeo Trojana refixo
  Tempora testatus nihil ultra

part. nom. mas. s. ag. w. Tithonus; fr. rĕmŏveo, -ēre, -mōvi, -mōtum, 2nd trans., (re, 659; moveo, 394) *to move back, draw back. Take away, set aside. Remove.* **in** (81). **auras,** gov. by in; fr. aura (84), "remotus in auras," borne aloft to heaven by Aurora.

657. **Jovis** (261), after arcanis. **arcanis,** dat. plu. neut. (as subst.) after admissus; fr. arcanus (492). **Mīnos,** -ois (Gk.), nom. s. jnd. by et to Tithonus; son of Zeus and Europa, king of Crete, made after his death a judge in the infernal regions. **admissus,** pf. pass. part. nom. mas. s. ag. w. Minos; fr. admitto, -ĕre, -mīsi, -missum, 3rd trans., (ad, 6; mitto, 38) *to allow* a person or thing *to go* or *come to* a place. Of a horse, *to give the rein to;* fig., *to grant admission to, e.g.,* jocos, mentionem. *To let* a thing *be done* or *come to pass. To grant* an unlawful act, *admittance* to oneself, *commit,* expresses moral liability incurred freely, freq. w. in se, te, etc. **habent,** 3rd plu. pres. ind. act. fr. habeo (641). **-que** (4), jns. this w. prec. clause.

658. **Tartara,** -orum, 2nd neut. plu.; nom. subj. of habent; heteroclite sing. Tartarus, -i, acc. s. -on (Gk.), *the infernal regions. Tartarus*=prose, Inferi. **Panthoiden,** acc. s. gov. by habent; fr. Panthōĭdes, -æ, 1st mas. (Gk. patronymic), son of Panthūs or Panthŏus, -i, 2nd mas., voc. Panthu, i.e., *Euphorbus,* ref. to Pythagoras, who maintained that his soul animated Euphorbus during the Trojan war, which he proved by recognising Euphorbus's shield at Argos. **iterum** (374). **Orco,** dat. after traject. demissum; fr. Orcus, -i, 2nd mas., (Gk., ak. to urgeo, 150) *that which hems in. The lower world,* abode of the dead. *The god of the infernal regions, i.e.,* Pluto. *Death.*

659. **Demissum,** pf. pass. part. acc. mas. s. ag. w. Panthoiden; fr. demitto, -ĕre, -mīsi, -missum, 3rd trans., (de, 10; mitto, 38) *to let* or *allow to go down, lower, let fall;* w. pers. pron. or pass. reflex., *to let oneself down, stoop, descend. To let* any person or thing *settle* anywhere. *To send down, cause to come down;* demissus, -a, -um, com. as adj.; *lying low,* of places, Of persons, *downcast, dejected. Lowly, humble, unassuming.* **quamvis** (375). **clipeo,** abl. absol. s. fr. clĭpeus, -i, 2nd mas., sts. -um, -i, 2nd neut., *a shield,* round, of brass. **Trojana,** acc. neut. plu. ag. w. tempora; fr. Trōjānus, -a, -um, adj., (Trōja, 230) *of* or *from Troy.* **refixo,** abl. s. mas. pf. pass. part. ag. w. clipeo; fr. rĕfigo, -ĕre, -xi, -xum, 3rd trans., (figo, *to fix*) *to unfix, unfasten, unloose, pull down* or *off,* esp. *to take down* the table of laws suspended in public, *i.e.,* annul, abrogate, "clipeo refixo,"=*by taking down the shield.* In composition the insep. particle, re-, red-, expresses (*a*) *backward action, e.g.,* resideo, *to set back.* (*b*) *Away, removal, e.g.,* removeo; resigno, *unseal,* so here. (*c*) *Against,* implying *resistance, e.g.,* reluctor, *struggle against.* (*d*) *Repeated action, e.g.,* renovo, *to make anew.*

660. **Tempora,** acc. plu. gov. by testatus; fr. tempus, -ŏris, 3rd neut., *a portion* or *period of time, a time, time* genly. *The fitting, proper time, opportunity. State of the times, position, state, condition,* i.e., *time* in its moral aspect; plu., *the times, circumstances.* **testatus,** pf. part. nom. mas. s. ag. w. subj. (Pythagoras) of concesserat; fr. testor, -āri, -atus sum, 1st depon. trans., (testis, *a witness*) *to bear witness to* (907), *give evidence of* (testificor is Ciceronian); meton., *to make known, declare, demonstrate,*

661 Nervos atque cutem morti concesserat atræ,
662 Judice te non sordidus auctor
663 Naturæ verique. Sed omnes una manet nox
664 Et calcanda semel via leti.
665 Dant alios Furiæ torvo spectacula Marti;

assert, aver (class. and frequ.), esp. to *make a will. To call upon, invoke* a person or thing *as witness:* testatus sts. pass., as collat. testo, is sts. found. **nihil** (125), here acc. gov. by concesserat. **ultra** (546).

661. **Nervos,** acc. plu. gov. by ultra; fr. nervus, -i, 2nd mas., prop. *sinew, tendon, nerve. String* of a musical instrument, *bow. Fetter, prison;* fig., *nerve, vigour, force, strength, e.g.,* belli, so of style, etc. **atque** (37). **cutem,** acc. s. jnd. by atque to nervos; fr. cŭtis, -is, 3rd fem., (rt.=*to cover, hide*) *the skin.* **morti,** dat. s. after (remote obj. of) concesserat; fr. mors (105). **concesserat,** 3rd s. plpf. ind. act. fr. concēdo, -ĕre, -cessi, -cessum, 3rd traj., (cum, 31; cedo, 170) intrans. *to depart, withdraw, remove oneself from,* w. abl. or abl. w. ab, ex, etc., of place, *whence;* w. ad, in, etc., of place, *whither.* With dat., *to yield, submit to, comply with one's wishes,* etc., *assent to;* "concedere in," *to assent, agree to go* or *pass over to* anything; trans., *to grant, concede, allow, consign* something over to, *vouchsafe,* aliquid alicui rei. Concesserat is qualified by "test. Troj. temp.," and that again by "clip. ref.," plucking down his shield, and bearing witness to the wars of Troy as a proof that he had yielded, etc. (M.) *To desist from, give up, forgive, pardon*=condono, *e.g.,* petitionem alicui. **atræ,** dat. s. fem. ag. w. morti; fr. ater, atra, atrum, adj., *black, coal-black, sable. Gloomy, sad, dismal. Unfortunate.*

662. **Judice,** abl. absol.(88) s. in app. to te; fr. jūdex, -ĭcis, 3rd mas., (judico, *to judge*) *a judge. One who gives* or *pronounces an opinion. Umpire.* **non** (55). **Sordidus,** -a, -um, adj.; nom. mas. s. ag. w. auctor; (sordes, *dirt*) *unclean, foul, filthy, sordid, squalid* (1380). Of persons, *low, base, mean* in birth, condition, etc. Of things, *humble, small, paltry.* Of character, *vile, despicable, disgraceful. Mean, niggardly* (1296). **auctor** (72), in app. to subj. (Pythagoras) of concesserat; *master, teacher.*

663. **Naturæ,** gen. s. after auctor; fr. nātūra, -æ, 1st fem., (nascor, 625) *birth* (very rare). *Natural constitution* or *property* of a thing. *Nature* in its varied senses. **veri,** gen. s. neut. (as subst.) jnd. by -que to naturæ; fr. vērus, -a, -um, adj., *true, real, actual, genuine.* Neut. as subst., *truth, reality, fact. Consonant with reason* or *good morals,* i.e., *right, proper, fitting, suitable, just. Speaking truth* (rare). **sed** (591), adversative to the last clause (W.). **omnes** (217), gov. by manet. **una,** nom. fem. s. ag. w. nox; fr. unus (189). **manet** (25). **nox** (144), subj. of manet.

664. **Calcanda,** nom. fem. s. ag. w. via; fr. calcandus, -a, -um, gerundive of calco, -āre, -āvi, -ātum, 1st trans., (calx, *the heel*) *to tread, tread upon* something, *tread under foot. To trample upon, oppress;* hence *scorn, despise, contemn.* Of objects in space, *to tread, go upon, pass over* (here). *To press in, press close* or *firm;* und. est (19) here. The partc. in -dus like that in -urus may be combined w. all the tenses of the verb sum (conjugatio periphrastica gerundivi), expressing *must be,* etc. **semel** (588). **via,** -æ, 1st fem.; nom. s. subj. of calcanda (est); *a way* in most general sense, *highway, march, path, street. Passage* through which anything passes. *Way,* i.e., *road, journey. Method, mode, manner, fashion. Right way, mode,* etc. **leti** (121), after via.

665. **Dant,** 3rd plu. pres. ind. act. fr. do (65). **alios,** acc. plu. mas.

666 Exitio est avidum mare nautis;
667 Mixta senum ac juvenum densentur funera, nullum
668 Sæva caput Proserpina fugit.
669 Me quoque devexi rapidus comes Orionis
670 Illyricis Notus obruit undis.

gov. by dant; tr. alius (92), *some.* **Furiæ**, -arum, 1st plu.; nom. subj. of dant (furo, -ere, -ui, *to rage, rave*) *violent passion, rage, madness.* *The furies*, i.e., *tormenting, avenging spirits.* **torvo,** dat. s. mas. ag. w. Marti; fr. torvus, -a, -um, adj., of eyes, *staring, piercing, keen, stern.* Of character, nature, *wild, gloomy, fierce, savage.* **Spectacula,** acc. plu. depend. predicate (or oblique complement) after factitive dant (54, 903), in app. to alios; fr. spectācŭlum, -i, 2nd neut., (specto, 940) *a show, sight, spectacle,* esp. in the theatre, of gladiators, etc.; meton., *place where plays are performed.* **Marti,** dat. after (remote obj. of) dant; fr. Mars (177).

666. **Exitio,** dat. s. after est; fr. exitium (405); see cordi, 462. **est** (19). **avidum,** nom. neut. s. ag. w. mare; fr. avĭdus (487). **mare** (430), nom. to est. **nautis** (311), of recipient after est. Acc. to Dillenburger Archytas's answer begins with this line.

667. **Mixta,** nom. neut. plu. ag. w. funera; fr. mixtus, pf. pass. part. of misceo (30). **senum,** gen. plu. after funera; fr. sĕnex, sĕnis, adj.; nom. and acc. of neut. plu. in posit. and of neut. sing. in compar. not found; compar. sĕnior, *advanced in years;* as subst., *an old man,* rare of *an old woman* (1106). Sĕnĭor, -ōris, *an elder, elderly person,* sts. esp. in poets=senex, *an aged person.* **ac** (131). **juvenum,** gen. plu. jnd. by ac to senum; fr. juvenis (77). **densentur,** 3rd plu. pres. ind. pass. fr. denseo, -ēre, no pf., sup. densētum, 2nd trans. collat. denso, -are, -avi, 1st, (densus, 204) *to make thick* or *dense, press together;* in Quint. of style, *condense.* **funera,** nom. plu. subj. of densentur; fr. funus (231). **nullum,** acc. neut. s. ag. w. caput; fr. nullus (477).

668. **Sæva** (327), ag. w. Proserpina. **caput** (22), gov. by fugit. **Proserpina,** -æ, 1st fem.; nom. s. subj. of fugit; dau. of Ceres and Jupiter, and wife of Pluto. *The lower world.* **fugit,** 3rd s. pf. ind. act. fr. fugio (206). The pf. is aoristic of what is common, usual. This is poet. for "nullum caput Proserpinam fugit," none could die till Proserpine had cut a lock of hair from his head.

669. **Me** (29), gov. by obruit. **quoque** (410). **devexi,** gen. s. mas. ag. w. Orionis; fr. devexus, -a, -um, -adj. Of place, *inclining downwards, sloping, shelving;* fig., *turning from their course, setting, declining* (here); deveho, *to carry down.* **rapidus** (293), nom. mas. s. ag. w. comes. **comes** (210), nom. s. in app. to Notus. **Orionis,** gen. s. after comes; fr. Ŏrīon, -ōnis and -ŏnis, 3rd mas., a constellation attended w. storms at its rising and setting (in November). He was originally a hunter who offered violence to Diana.

670. **Illyricis,** abl. plu. fem. ag. w. undis; fr. Illўrĭcus, -a, -um, adj. *Of the Illyrians,* a people who occupied modern Dalmatia and Albania, here for the Adriatic generally. **Notus** (200), subj. of obruit. **obruit** (387), 3rd s. pf. ind. act. fr. obruo, -rŭere, -rŭi, -rŭitum, 3rd, (ob, 329; ruo, 61) intrans., *to fall with violence, go to ruin* (very rare); trans., *to overthrow, overwhelm.* *To cover* with earth, *bury.* *To overwhelm* with water. *To conceal, abolish, consign to oblivion.* *To oppress with, e.g.,* debt. *To surpass, obscure, eclipse.* **undis** (50), instrum.

At tu, nauta, vagæ ne parce malignus arenæ
  Ossibus et capiti inhumato
Particulam dare. Sic, quodcunque minabitur Eurus
  Fluctibus Hesperiis, Venusinæ
Plectantur silvæ te sospite, multaque merces,
  Unde potest, tibi defluat æquo
Ab Jove Neptunoque sacri custode Tarenti.

671. **At** (483). **tu** (69), subj. of parce. **nauta** (14), voc. **vagæ,** gen. s. fem. ag. w. arenæ; fr. vagus (54). **ne** (41), here w. imper. in prohibitions. **parce,** 2nd s. imper. pres. act. fr. parce, -ĕre, pĕperci, (parsi, ante-class. and post-Aug.) sup. parsĭtum and parsum, fut. part. parsurus, 3rd intrans. and trans., *to act sparingly, spare* a thing w. dat. *To preserve by sparing, use carefully, not to injure. To abstain from doing* an action, *forbear, let alone,* w. dat. or inf. **malignus,** -a, -um, adj.; nom. mas. s. ag. as adv. attribute (867) w. tu und. in parce; (fr. maligenus opp. to benignus) *of an evil nature, ill disposed, wicked, malicious, envious* (1319). *Stingy, niggardly. Scanty, petty, small, e.g.,* ignis: "ne parce malignus," *grudge not churlishly.* **arenæ** (649), after particulam.

672. **Ossibus,** dat plu. after (indirect obj. of) dare; fr. os, ossis, 3rd neut., *a bone.* **capiti,** dat. s. jnd by et to ossibus; fr. caput (22). **inhumato,** dat. neut. s. ag. w. capiti; fr. inhŭmātus, -a, -um, adj., (in, neg.; humo, *to bury*) *not interred, not buried.*

673. **Particulam** (434) gov. by (direct obj. of) dare. **dare,** pres. inf. (prolative) after parce; fr. do (65). **sic,** *i.e.,* if you do as I ask (W.), in wishes (89). **quodcunque,** acc. neut. s. gov. by (direct obj. of) minabitur; fr. quicunque (167). **minabitur,** 3rd s. fut. ind. fr. minor (1088). **Eurus,** -i, 2nd mas.; nom. s. subj. of minabitur; *south-east wind;* also called Volturnus, opp. to Zephyrus, *the East.*

674. **Fluctibus** (15), after (indirect obj. of) minabitur. **Hesperiis,** dat. plu. mas. ag. w. fluctibus; fr. Hespĕrius, -a, -um, adj., (Hesperus, *the evening star*), *of* or *situated towards the west, western, Hesperian;* "rex," *atlas* or *Hesperus* (1340), *Italian* (here and 908). **Venusinæ,** nom. fem. plu. ag. w. silvæ; fr. Vĕnŭsīnus, -a, -um, adj., *of* or *belonging to Venusia,* a town on the borders of Apulia and Lucania, birthplace of Horace.

675. **Plectantur,** 3rd plu. pres. conj. (optative) pass. fr. plecto, -ĕre, no pf., no sup., 3rd trans., *to strike, punish with blows,* genly. in pass., *to be punished.* Of wind, *to lash* (here). **silvæ** (235), subj. of plectantur. **te** (88), abl. absol. **sospite,** abl. mas. s. ag. w. te; fr. sospes, -ĭtis, adj.; collat. fem., sospĭta, -æ, act., *saving, delivering;* meton., *favouring, auspicious* (rare). Pass., *saved, unhurt, uninjured* (820, 849). **multa,** nom. fem. s. ag. w. merces; fr. multus (23). **-que,** jns. this clause w. preceding. **merces** (638), nom. s. subj. of defluat; "multa merces," *i.e.,* a rich reward for your humanity.

676. **Unde** (291), relat. ref. to Jove Neptunoque. **potest,** 3rd s. ind. pres. fr. possum (372), ag. w. merces. **tibi** (93), commodi after defluat. **defluat,** 3rd sing. conj. (optative) act. fr. defluo (313). **æquo** (141), ag. w. Jove.

677. **Ab** (254). **Jove** (25), gov. by ab. He as god of hospitality presided over duties to strangers. **Neptuno,** abl. s. jnd. by -que to Jove; fr. Neptūnus, -i, 2nd mas., *Neptune,* god of the sea, brother of Jupiter. He

678 Negligis immeritis nocituram
679 Postmodo te natis fraudem committere? Fors et
680 Debita jura vicesque superbæ
681 Te maneant ipsum: precibus non linquar inultis,
682 Teque piacula nulla resolvent.
683 Quamquam festinas, non est mora longa; licebit

was tutelary god of Tarentum, of which Archytas was a citizen. **sacri,** gen. neut. s. ag. w. Tarenti; fr. sacer (22). **custode,** abl. s. in app. to Neptuno; fr. custos, -ōdis, 3rd mas., (cubo, *to cover*) *guard, watch, overseer, defender,* friendly or hostile. **Tarenti,** gen. s. after custode; fr. Tarentum, -i, 2nd neut., or Tarentus, -i, 2nd mas., town in lower Italy, founded by Spartan Parthenians.

678. **Negligis,** 2nd sing. ind. pres. act. fr. negligo (71), *art thou careless about,* etc.? **immeritis,** dat. mas. plu. ag. w. natis; fr. immĕrĭtus (476). **nocituram,** acc. fem. s. fut. part. ag. w. fraudem; fr. nŏceo, -cēre, -cŭi, -cĭtum, 2nd intrans., *to harm, hurt, injure,* absol. or w. dat.; trans. w. acc., non-class.

679. **Postmodo,** adv., (post, 117; modo, *lately*) *afterwards, presently, shortly.* **te,** either (88) abl. of origin after natis; or (83) acc. subj. of committere. **natis,** dat. plu. mas. after traject. nocituram; fr. nātus, -a, -um, pf. partc. (used as subst.) fr. nascor (987), *born, made, destined by nature* for anything, w. dat., or ad or in w. acc. Of persons, *designed, intended* w. ad, or in of things (625). *Constituted by nature* in a certain way. Of compositions, *written, composed.* Of age, natus w. acc., *e.g.*, decem annos, *old, of the age of;* natus, -i, 2nd mas., *a son, boy, male-child;* plu., *children, offspring.* **fraudem,** acc. s. gov. by committere; fr. fraus (116). **committere,** pres. inf. (objective), act. after negligis; fr. committo (99). **Fors** (246), one member in comp. subj. of maneant. Others take "fors et," *perchance also* (M.), folld. by subjunct. maneant.

680. **Debita,** pf. pass. part. nom. neut. plu. ag. w. jura; fr. debeo (94). **jura,** nom. plu. jnd. by et to Fors; fr. jus (1069). **vices,** nom. plu. jnd. by -que to jura; fr. vicis (129). **superbæ,** nom. fem. plu. ag. w. vices; fr. superbus (318). "Vices superbæ," *a return of contumely* (W.).

681. **Te** (83), gov. by maneant. **maneant,** 3rd plu. conj. (optative) act. fr. maneo (25). **ipsum,** acc. mas. s. ag. w. te; fr. ipse (126). **precibus,** abl. absol. plu. fr. prex (62). **non** (55). **linquar,** 1st sing. fut. ind. pass. fr. linquo, -ĕre, līqui, lictum, 3rd trans., *to leave, quit, forsake, depart from. To let alone, abandon, give up.* **inultis,** abl. fem. plu. ag. w. precibus; fr. inultus, -a, -um, adj., (in, neg.; ultus, partc. of ulciscor, *to avenge*) *for whom vengeance is not* or *has not been taken, who cannot take revenge, on whom vengeance is not inflicted, unpunished;* meton., *unhurt, safe, secure, unmolested,* here *unheard, without satisfaction.*

682. **Te** (83), gov. by resolvent. **-que** (4). **piacula,** nom. plu. subj. of resolvent; fr. pĭācŭlum, -i, 2nd neut., (pio, *to appease*) *a sin offering, propitiatory sacrifice, expiation, atonement* for anything, *punishment. That which requires expiation, sin, crime, guilt.* **nulla,** nom. neut. plu. ag. w. piacula; fr. nullus (477). **resolvent,** 3rd plu. fut. ind. act. fr. rĕsolvo, -ĕre, -solvi, -sŏlūtum, 3rd trans., (re-, 659; solvo, 129) *to loosen, untie, unfasten;* fig., *release,* here. *To open,* e.g., *a prison, mouth,* etc. *To unnerve, enfeeble* the body. *To set free* fr. care, etc.

683. **Quamquam,** concessive conj., *though, although, albeit,* genly. w.

684 Injecto ter pulvere curras.

CARMEN XXIX.—AD ICCIUM.

685 Icci, beatis nunc Arabum invides
686 Gazis et acrem militiam paras
687 Non ante devictis Sabææ
688 Regibus horribilique Medo

ind., with subj. only when the general idea requires it. Used to introduce objections made by the speaker himself, *although, notwithstanding, nevertheless.* **festinas,** 2nd sing. pres. ind. act. fr. festīno, -āre, -āvi, -ātum, 1st intrans., *to make haste, be quick,* trans., *to make haste with, hurry, accelerate* a thing, *e.g.,* pœnas. **non** (55). **est** (19). **mora,** -æ, 1st fem., nom. s. subj. of est und., *a delay, a short space of time.* **longa,** nom. fem. s. ag. w. mora; fr. longus (73). **licebit,** 3rd sing. fut. ind. fr. impers. licet; pf. lĭcuit and lĭcĭtum est, *it is, was,* etc., *allowable* or *permitted,* w. subjective inf. or subjunct. (genly. without ut), or neut. pron. of what is allowed; dat. of person *to whom;* licet w. subjunct. also=quamquam, quamvis, *albeit, although.* The personal fms., lĭceo, -cēre, -cŭi, very rare.

684. **Injecto,** abl. mas. s. pf. pass. part. ag. w. pulvere; fr. injicio (474). **ter** (361). **pulvere** (178), absol. **curras,** 2nd sing. pres. subj. act. after licebit (ut omitted); fr. curro, -ĕre, cŭcurri, cursum, 3rd intrans., *to run, move quickly, hasten* on horse, foot, ship, etc.; w. cognate acc. iter. Of things, poet. (1005). Of time, *pass quickly.*

Carmen XXIX.—Ad Iccium. Metre.—*Alcaic.* (Carmen ix).

685. **Icci,** voc. s. fr. Iccius, -ii, 2nd mas. **beatis,** dat. plu. fem. ag. w. gazis; fr. beatus (142). **nunc** (21), emphatic *now* after being so differently disposed. **Arabum,** gen. plu. after gazis; fr. Arabs, Arăbis, Gk., acc. plu. -bas, *of Arabia;* subst., *an Arab;* plur., *Arabians.* **invides,** 2nd sing. ind. pres. act. fr. invĭdeo, -ēre, -vīdi, -visum, 2nd intrans., (in, 76; video, 49) *to look towards* (very rare). *To regard spitefully* or *maliciously, look upon with an evil eye;* meton., *to feel envy, be envious,* absol. or w. dat.; pass. only impers., *e.g.,* mihi invidetur. *To be vexed, annoyed, feel regret at* w. dat. *To begrudge* one anything. *Take away, deny* one anything through envy, w. acc. of thing, dat. pers. *To hinder* one doing w. inf. or ne w. subj. *To be unwilling, reluctant* w. inf. or ut w. subj. *To scorn, spurn, despise* (866).

686. **Gazis,** dat. plu. after invides; fr. gaza, -æ, 1st fem., *a treasure, riches, wealth,* a Persian word. **acrem,** acc. fem. s. ag. w. militiam; fr. acer (75). **militiam** (481), gov. by paras. **paras,** 2nd s. ind. pres. act. fr. paro (396).

687. **Non** (55). **ante,** adv., *before, formerly.* Prep. gov. acc., *before* of place, time, order, and circumstance. **devictis,** dat. plu. mas. pf. pass. part. ag. w. regibus; fr. dēvinco, -cĕre, -vīci, -victum, 3rd trans., (de, 10; vinco, 830) *to conquer completely, overcome, subdue.* **Sabææ,** gen. s. after regibus; fr. Săbæa, 1st fem., (prop. fem. of Săbæus, -a, -um, adj., *of Saba*) *the Sabæan territory, i.e.,* Arabia Felix, of which Săba was the chief town.

688. **Regibus,** plu. dat. (incommodi) after paras; fr. rex (1). **horribili,** dat. s. mas. ag. w. Medo; fr. horrĭbĭlis, -e, adj., (horreo, *to be in dread of*) bad sense, *terrible, dreadful, fearful, horrible;* good sense, *astonishing, amaz-*

689 Nectis catenas? Quæ tibi virginum
690 Sponso necato barbara serviet?
691 Puer quis ex aula capillis
692 Ad cyathum statuetur unctis,
693 Doctus sagittas tendere Sericas
694 Arcu paterno? Quis neget arduis

ing, tremendous. **-que,** jns. nectis to paras. **Medo,** dat. s. incom. after nectis; fr. Medus (87).

689. **Nectis,** 2nd s. ind. pres. act. fr. necto (619). **catenas,** acc. plu. gov. by (direct obj. of) nectis; fr. cătēna, -æ, 1st fem. (etym. dub.) prop., *chain, fetter;* fig., *barrier, restraint, check.* **quæ** (645), subj. of serviet. **tibi** (93), after serviet. **virginum** (181), of thing distributed after quæ. The expression is a mixture of "quæ virgo barbara" or "quæ virginum barbararum."

690. **Sponso,** abl. absol. s. fr. sponsus, -i, 2nd mas., (spondeo, *to betroth*) *a betrothed, bridegroom. Wooer, suitor.* **necato,** pf. pass. part. abl. mas. s. ag. w. sponso; fr nĕco, -āre, -āvi, -ātum, 1st trans., *to kill, slay, put to death,* usu. without a weapon, by hunger, etc. **barbara,** nom. fem. s. ag. w. quæ; fr. barbărus (626). **serviet,** 3rd s. fut. ind. act. fr. servio, -īre, -īvi or -ii, -itum, 4th intrans., (servus, *a slave*) *to be a servant* or *slave, be in service* (class.); fig., *be devoted to, subject to. To serve for,* i.e., *be fit* or *useful for. To comply with, gratify, humour, accommodate. To have respect* or *regard for.*

691. **Puer quis** (149), subj. of statuetur. **ex,** or e, prep. gov. abl. Of place, *out of, from, on.* Of time, *from, since.* Of origin, *from, of.* Of transition, *from, after.* Of partition, *of.* Of cause, *from, for, by.* Of manner in adv. phrases, *e.g.*, ex improviso, *unexpectedly.* **aula,** abl. s. gov. by ex; fr. aula, -æ, 1st fem., *a court, fore-court. Inner court* of a house=atrium. *Palace, castle of a noble, royal court.* "Puer ex aula," *a page from the court.* **capillis** (325), abl. absol. exp. manner.

692. **Ad** (6). **cyathum,** acc. s. gov. by ad; fr. cyăthus, -i, 2nd mas., *a ladle* by which the wine was transferred from the mixing bowl into the drinking cup; "ad cyathum," *to fill our cup* (M.). **statuetur,** 3rd s. fut. ind. pass. fr. stătuo, -ŭĕre, -ŭi, -ūtum, 3rd trans., (causative of sto, 233) *to put, place, set.* Milit., *to draw up in station* or *position. To set up, rear, build. To set down for certain* in one's mind, *think, believe, suppose. To appoint* one as something, w. predicative accus. (903). *To lay down as fixed* or *settled, dispose, decide, conclude, determine.* **unctis,** abl. plu. mas. ag. w. capillis; fr. unctus, -a, -um, *anointed. Rich, luxurious, sumptuous. Greasy, dirty. e.g.*, manus, aquæ; pf. pass. partic. of ungo, -gere, -xi, -ctum, 3rd trans., *to anoint, besmear, stain* (881).

693. **Doctus** (29), nom. mas. s. ag. w. puer. **sagittas,** acc. plu. gov. by tendere; fr. sagitta (308). **tendere** (34), prolative after doctus. **Sericas,** acc. plu. fem. ag. w. sagittas; fr. Sērĭcus, -a, -um, adj., (Seres, 340) *of* or *belonging to the Seres. Silken, e.g.*, toga. Sērĭcum, -i, 2nd neut., *silk.*

694. **Arcu** (538), instrum. fr. arcus, -ūs, 4th mas., abl. plu. only post-class., *a bow* for shooting; meton., *the rainbow;* poet. and post-Aug. of any thing bowed, arched or curved, *e.g.*, waves, bent trees, etc. **paterno,** abl. mas. s. ag. w. arcu; fr. paternus (513); "doctus...paterno," *i.e.*, a boy of high family. **quis** (149), subj. of neget. **neget,** 3rd s. conj. (dubitative); pres. act. fr. nego (558). **arduis,** dat. or abl. mas. plu. ag. w. montibus; fr. arduus (125).

695 Pronos relabi posse rivos
696 Montibus et Tiberim reverti,
697 Quum tu coëmptos undique nobilis
698 Libros Panæti, Socraticam et domum
699 Mutare loricis Iberis,
700 Pollicitus meliora, tendis?

CARMEN XXX.—AD VENEREM.

701 O Venus, regina Cnidi Paphique,

695. **Pronos,** acc. plu. mas. ag. w. rivos; fr. prōnus, -a, -um, adj., (pro, *before*). Of living beings, *bent, inclined forwards, hanging, stooping down.* Of things, *bending downwards, going downwards*; here, "flowing down." Of heavenly bodies, etc., *setting, sinking, declining; fig., inclined, disposed towards,* esp. w. ad, in, etc. **relabi,** pres. inf. prolative after posse; fr. relā-bor, -lābi, -lapsus sum, 3rd dep. intrans., (re-, 659; labor, 55) *to slide* or *glide back; sink* or *fall back. To go* or *come back with a swift, easy* motion*;* fig., *to relapse, return.* **posse,** pres. inf. after neget; fr. possum (372).. **rivos,** acc. plu. subj. of posse; fr. rivus (198).

696. **Montibus** (562), absol. w. arduis (604); cf. adverso, secundo flumine. Others consider it the dat. after relabi. **et** (2). **Tiberim** (49), subj. of reverti. **reverti,** pres. inf. jnd. by et to relabi; fr. revertor, -verti, -versus sum, 3rd dep. intrans., (re-, 659; verto, 780) *to turn back, turn about, return,* esp. *to revert to* a theme after digression. The perf. fms. except in reversus are fr. act., viz., reverti, -tisse, -teram, but act. not used in pres. fms.

697. **Quum** (43). **tu** (69), subj. of tendis. **coëmptos,** acc. mas. pl. pf. pass. part. ag. w. libros; fr. cŏĕmo, -ĕre, -ēmi, -emptum, 3rd trans., (cum, 31; emo, *to buy*) *to purchase together, buy up.* **undique** (191). **nobilis,** gen. mas. s. ag. w. Panæti; fr. nobilis (5).

698. **Libros,** acc. plu. gov. by mutare; fr. lībĕr, -bri, 2nd mas., *the inner bark* or *rind* of a tree. *Book, work, treatise,* orig. written on the bark of a tree. *Part of a book, e.g.,* primus, secundus, tertius. **Panæti,** gen. s. after libros; fr. Panætius, -ii or -i, a Stoic of Rhodes, friend of Scipio Africanus Jun. (B.C. 140): he wrote against Plato's Phædon. **Socraticam,** acc. fem. s. ag. w. domum; fr. Sŏcrătĭcus, -a, -um, adj., *of* or *belonging to Socrates.* **domum** (172), jnd. by et to libros: here of a *school* of philosophy.

699. **Mutare** (446), after tendis. **loricis,** dat. plu. after mutare; fr. lōrīca, -æ, 1st fem., *cuirass, corslet* made of leather thongs (loræ). **Iberis,** dat. plu. fem. ag. w. loricis; fr. Ībērus, -a, -um, adj., (Iberes, 1444) *of* or *belonging to the Iberes* or *Spaniards.*

700. **Pollicitus** (416), ag. w. tu. **meliora,** acc. neut. plu. gov. by pollicitus; fr. melior (58). **tendis,** 2nd sing. ind. pres. act.; fr. tendo (34); here *to purpose, aim.*

Carmen XXX.—Ad Venerem. Metre.—*Lesser Sapphic.* (Carmen ii.)

701. **O** (2). **Venus** (482). **regina,** voc. s. in app. to Venus; fr. rē-gīna, -æ, 1st fem., *queen, goddess, princess, lady, mistress.* **Cnidi,** gen. s. after regina; fr. Cnĭdus, -i, or Gnidos, -i, 2nd fem.; Doric city in Caria, celebrated for Praxiteles' statue of Venus. **Paphi,** gen. s. jnd. by -que to

702 Sperne dilectam Cypron et vocantis
703 Thure te multo Glyceræ decoram
704 Transfer in ædem.
705 Fervidus tecum puer et solutis
706 Gratiæ zonis properentque Nymphæ
707 Et parum comis sine te Juventas
708 Mercuriusque.

CARMEN XXXI.—AD APOLLINEM.

709 QUID dedicatum poscit Apollinem

Cnĭdi; fr. Păphos, -i, or Paphus, -i, 2nd fem.; city in Cyprus, with a celebrated temple to Venus.

702. **Sperne** (248). **dilectam** (524), ag. w. Cypron. **Cypron,** Gk.= Cyprum (502), gov. by sperne. **vocantis,** pres. part. act. gen. fem s ag. w. Glyceræ; fr. vŏco (61).

703. **Thure,** abl. (instrum.) s. fr. thus (506). **te** (83), gov. by vocantis. **multo,** abl. neut. s. ag. w. thure; fr. multus (23). **Glyceræ,** gen. after ædem; fr. Glўcĕra, -æ, 1st fem. **decoram,** acc. fem. s. ag. w. ædem; fr. decorus (259).

704. **Transfer,** 2nd sing. pres. imper. act. fr. transfĕro, -ferre, -tŭli, -lātum, irreg. trans., (trans, 228; fero, 138) *to carry* or *bring across, carry or bear over, transport. To transcribe, copy,* i.e., *transfer* by writing. *To translate* from one language into another. *To postpone, put off.* **in** (81). **ædem,** acc. s. gov. by in; fr. ædes and ædis, gen. ædis, 3rd fem., *a temple, sanctuary* of the gods; prop., one undivided edifice: plu. in this sense only of several temples w. sacræ, divinæ, deorum, etc, Plur. usu. *a dwelling* for man (very rare in sing. in this sense); here ref. to a little shrine or "sacrarium," or the whole house is called a temple.

705. **Fervidus** (4), nom. mas. s. ag. w. puer. **tecum,** te (88), gov. by cum, here enclitic; cf. mecum (215). **puer** (149), one member in comp. subj. of properent. **solutis,** abl. plu. fem. ag. w. zonis; fr. solutus (138).

706. **Gratiæ** (134), jnd. by et to puer. **zonis,** abl. absol. plu. fr. zōna, -æ (Gk.), 1st fem., *a belt, girdle, zone,* worn by unmarried women; *girdle* for holding money, *money-belt.* **properent,** 3rd plu. conj. (hortative) pres. fr. prŏpĕro, -āre, -āvi, -atum, 1st trans., *to hasten, accelerate, quicken, make* or *do with haste,* intrans., *to make haste, hasten, be quick.* **-que** (4), unusually placed. **Nymphæ,** nom. plu. jnd. by -que to Gratiæ; fr. Nympha (31).

707. **Parum** (343) with comis. **comis,** -e, adj.; nom. s. fem. ag. w. Juventas. Of persons, *courteous, affable, kind, obliging, friendly.* **sine** (370). **te** (88), gov. by sine. **Juventas,** -ātis, 3rd fem.; nom. s. jnd. by et to Nymphæ (1146). *The goddess of youth,* i.e., *Hebe.*

708. **Mercurius** (590), jnd. by -que to Juventas.

CARMEN XXXI.—AD APOLLINEM. METRE.—*Alcaic.* (Carmen ix.)

709. **Quid** (297), acc. of contained obj. after poscit; see 584. **dedicatum,** acc. mas. s. pf. pass. part. ag. w. Apollinem; fr. dēdĭco (612).

Vates? quid orat de patera novum
  Fundens liquorem? Non opimæ
    Sardiniæ segetes feraces,
Non æstuosæ grata Calabriæ
Armenta, non aurum aut ebur Indicum,
  Non rura, quæ Liris quieta
    Mordet aqua taciturnus amnis.

The god is identified with his temple. **poscit,** 3rd sing. ind. pres. act. fr. posco (140). **Apollinem,** acc. s. gov. by poscit; fr. Apollo (68).

710. **Vates** (35), nom. s. subj. of poscit. **quid** (297), gov. by orat. **orat,** 3rd s. pres. ind. act. fr. ōro, -are, -avi, -atum, 1st trans. and intrans., (os, *mouth*), *to speak* (ante-class. and poet.). *To treat, argue, plead* as ambassador, advocate, suppliant. *To pray, beg, beseech,* w. acc. of thing asked or ut w. subj. or inf. **de** (10). **patera** (507), gov. by de; fr. pătĕra, -æ, 1st fem., (păteo, *to be open, to spread out*) a broad flat *dish* or *saucer* used esp. in offering a libation. **novum,** acc. mas. s. ag. w. liquorem; fr. nŏvus (42).

711. **Fundens,** pres. part. act. nom. mas. s. ag. w. vates; fr. fundo, -ĕre, fūdi, fūsum, 3rd trans., *to pour, pour out, shed. To pour forth, extend, display, e.g.,* vitam. Of speech, *to utter.* Of things not liquid, *pour forth abundantly, scatter, hurl. To bring forth, produce, bear abundantly. To throw to the ground, prostrate.* **liquorem,** acc. s. gov. by fundens; fr. lĭquor, -ōris, 3rd mas., (lĭqueo, 282) *a being liquid, fluidness, liquidity;* meton., *a fluid, liquid. e.g.,* honey. **non** (55): **opimæ** (195), ag. w. Sardiniæ.

712. **Sardiniæ,** gen. after segetes; fr. Sardĭnia, 1st fem., *island of Sardinia.* **segetes,** acc. plu. gov. by poscit; fr. sĕges, sĕgĕtis, 3rd fem., (sero, *to sow*) *the thing* or *place sown, corn-field. Standing corn, growing corn, crop* in a field. Of a multitude of things crowded together, *crop.* **feraces,** acc. fem. plu. ag. w. segetes; fr. fĕrax, -ācis, adj., (fero, 138) *bearing,* hence, *fruitful, fertile.*

713. **Non** (55). **æstuosæ,** gen. s. fem. ag. w. Calabriæ; fr. æstuosus (541). **grata** (398), ag. w. armenta; "*pleasant*" to own or to see (W). **Calabriæ,** gen. after armenta; fr. Călabria, -æ, 1st fem., country in Lower Italy from Tarentum to the promontory of Iapygium.

714. **Armenta,** acc. plu. gov. by poscit; fr. armentum, -i, 2nd neut., (aro, *to plough*) *cattle for ploughing;* meton., *drove, herd* of any large animals. **non** (55). **aurum,** acc. s. gov. by poscit; fr. aurum, -i, 2nd neut., *gold. Colour* or *lustre of gold.* Of things made of gold, *goblet, chain, ring, coined gold.* **aut** (131). **ebur,** acc. s. jnd. by aut to aurum; fr. ĕbur, ĕbŏris, 3rd neut., *ivory;* also of thing *made of ivory.* **Indicum,** acc. neut. s. ag. w. ebur; fr. Indĭcus, -a, -um, adj. *Of India.*

715. **Rura** (17), gov. by poscit. **quæ** (359), neut. plu. ag. w. rura; acc. gov. by mordet. **Liris,** -is, 3rd mas.; nom. s. subj. of mordet; a river between Latium and Campania. **quieta,** abl. s. fem. ag. w. aquâ; fr. quietus (317).

716. **Mordet,** 3rd s. ind. pres. act. fr. mordeo, -ēre, mŏmordi, morsum, 2nd trans. and intrans., prop., *to bite,* esp. *eat, devour, consume. To take fast hold of, catch fast, grip. To bite into, eat into, force a way into* (here); fig., *attack, hurt, annoy, mortify, pain,* esp. *carp at, express ill will at,*

717 Premant Calena falce quibus dedit
718 Fortuna vitem; dives et aureis
719 Mercator exsiccet culullis
720 Vina Syra reparata merce,
721 Dîs carus ipsis, quippe ter et quater
722 Anno revisens æquor Atlanticum

criticise, satirise. **aqua,** abl. s. (instrum.) fr. aqua (22). **tăcĭturnus,** -a, -um, adj.; nom. mas. s. ag. w. amnis; (tăcitus, *silent*). Of persons, *not talkative, of few words.* Of things, *quiet, still, silent, noiseless.* **amnis** (56), in app. to Liris.

717. **Premant,** 3rd plu. pres. conj. (hortative) act. fr. premo (144), here *to keep short, prune*=reprimand, check their luxuriance (W.). **Calena,** abl. s. fem. ag. w. falce; fr. Calenus (517). **falce,** abl. (instrum.) s. fr. falx, falcis, 3rd fem., *a sickle, reaping hook, scythe.* Milit., a sickle-shaped instrument for pulling down walls. **quibus** (160), mas. plu. ag. w. demonst. und. subj. of premant; dat. after dedit. **dedit** (576).

718. **Fortuna** (209), subj. of dedit. **vitem,** acc. s. gov. by dedit and premant; fr. vites (477). **dives** (270), ag. w.-mercator. **et** (2). **aureis,** abl. plu. mas. ag. w. cul̆ullis; fr. aureus (157).

719. **Mercator** (16), subj. of exsiccet. **exsiccet,** 3rd sing. conj. (hortative) act. fr. exsicco, -are, -avi, -atum, 1st trans., (ex, 691; sicco, 803), *to dry up, make quite dry. To drain dry, empty* a bottle. **culullis,** abl. plu. of separation, after exsiccet; fr. cŭlullus, -i, 2nd mas. (dim of culeus), orig. a sacrificial *vessel* for liquids (used in the service of Vesta), afterwards *drinking-vessel, cup, bowl.*

720. **Vina** (282), gov. by exsiccet. **Sȳra,** abl. fem. s. ag. w. merce; fr. Sȳrus, -a, -um, adj., *of Syria.* **reparata,** acc. neut. plu. pf. pass. part. ag. w. vina; fr. rĕpăro, -āre, -avi, -ātum, 1st trans., (re-, 659; paro, 396) *to get, acquire* or *procure again. To recover, retrieve, restore; retrieve, renew, e.g.*, bellum; mercantile to *procure by exchange, purchase, attain with* something. In 860, *to seek to arrive at.* Like reficere, *to refresh, recruit, e.g.*, animos. **merce,** abl. instrum. sing. fr. merx, mercis, 3rd fem., (mereo, *to gain*) *that which gains, goods, wares, commodities.* "Syrâ reparata merce," *obtained by bartering Syrian wares.*

721. **Dis** (30), after traject. carus. **carus** (513), nom. mas. s. ag. w. mercator. **ipsis,** dat plu. mas. ag. w. Dis; fr. ipse (126). **quippe** (quia -pe), corroborative particle; like nempe (nam -pe), *surely, certainly, to be sure, by all means.* Ironically, *indeed, forsooth, because forsooth;* introduces a reason w. irony or indignation. Also jnd. w. causal particles, *e.g.*, enim, etenim, *since in fact, inasmuch as;* with qui, quæ, quod, *as one in fact who, since in fact I,* etc. **ter** (361). **et** (2), *or.* **quăter,** num. adv., *four times.*

722. **Anno,** abl. (of time) s. fr. annus, -i, 2nd mas., *a year:* at first ten months, but fr. time of Numa twelve; meton., *part of the year, season.* **revisens,** pres. part. act. nom. mas. s. jnd. by quippe to carus; fr. rĕvīso, -ĕre, no pf., no sup., 3rd trans., (re-, 659; viso, 44): *to look back* on a thing. *Come back* or *look back to see. To pay a visit again* (non-class.). *To go* or *come to see again, revisit.* **æquor** (216), gov. by revisens. **Atlanticum,** acc. neut. s. ag. w. æquor; fr. Atlantĭcus, -a, -um, adj., (Atlas, 257) *of* or *belonging to Mt. Atlas;* "mare Atlanticum," *the Atlantic Ocean;* adj., also Atlanteus.

723 Impune. Me pascunt olivæ,
724 Me cichorea levesque malvæ.
725 Frui paratis et valido mihi,
726 Latoë, dones et precor integra
727 Cum mente nec turpem senectam
728 Degere nec cithara carentem.

CARMEN XXXII.—AD LYRAM.

729 Poscimur. Si quid vacui sub umbra

723. **Impune** (453). **me** (29), gov. by pascunt. **pascunt,** 3rd. plu. pres. ind act. fr. pasco, -ĕre, -pāvi, pastum, 3rd trans. and intrans., *to nourish, maintain, support by food, feed. To feast, gratify. To cherish, let grow, maintain, support.* Pass. reflex., *to feed, graze, browse.* **olivæ,** nom. plu. subj. of pascunt; fr. oliva (191).

724. **Me** (29), gov. by pascunt und. **cichorea,** nom. plu. subj. of pascunt; fr. cĭchŏrēum, -i, (or cĭchŏrĭum), 2nd neut., (92) *chicory, succory, endive.* **leves,** nom. fem. plu. ag. w. malvæ; fr. levis (31), *digestible.* **malvæ,** nom. plu. jnd. by -que to cichorea; fr. malva, -æ, 1st fem., *mallows.*

725. **Frui,** pres. inf. direct obj. of dones; fr. fruor (157). **paratis,** abl. neut. plu. pf. pass. part. after frui; fr. paro (396), *my acquisitions.* The abl. of matter, originally instrumental. **et** (2), folld. by et in next line, *both...and;* jns. valido to integrâ mente. **valido,** dat. mas. s. ag. w. mihi; fr. vălĭdus, -a, -um, adj., (valeo, 772) *strong, stout, powerful,* not in Cæs. and very rare in Cic. *Well in body, healthy, sound;* fig., *mighty, powerful.* **mihi,** dat. s. after (remote obj. of) dones; fr. ego (29).

726. **Latoë,** voc. s. mas. fr. Lātōus, -i, 2nd mas., (prop. adj.=Latonius, und. filius, deus, puer). *The Latoan god,* i. e., Apollo, son of Latōna (Lāto) **dones,** 2nd s. conj. (hortative) act. fr. dōno, āre, -āvi, ātum, 1st trans., (donum, *a gift*) *to give* one something as a present, *bestow, present. To grant, vouchsafe,* aliquid alicui. *To remit, forgive* a debt, obligation, etc; *pardon* an offence or offender for another's sake. With acc. pers. abl. thing, *to present* one with anything. **precor** (95) parenthetic. **integra,** abl. s. fem. ag. w. mente; fr. integer (373).

727. **Cum** (31). **mente,** abl. s. gov. by cum; fr. mens (349). **nec** (19). **turpem,** acc. fem s. ag. w. senectam; fr. turpis, -e, adj., prop. *ugly, unsightly, unseemly, filthy, nasty* (845); fig., *shameful, infamous, scandalous.* **senectam,** acc. s. gov. by degere; fr. sĕnecta, -æ, 1st fem., (senex, 667) *old age, senility* (1022, 1235); prop. fem. (und. ætas) of adj., sĕnectus, -a, -um, (poet.). Cic. uses senectus.

728. **Degere,** pres. inf. act. jnd. by nec (727) to frui; fr. dēgo, -ĕre, dēgi, no sup., 3rd trans., (de, 10; ago, 43) *to drive away, remove. To spread, pass* w. acc. *To live* absol. (not com. till post-Aug.). **nec** (19). **cithara** (399), after carentem. **carentem,** acc. fem. s. jnd. by nec to turpem; fr. carens (649).

Carmen XXXII. Ad Lyram. Metre.—*Lesser Sapphic.* (Carmen ii.)

729. **Poscimur,** 1st plu. pres. ind. pass. fr. posco (140). **si** (7), folld. by imperat. in apodosis. **quid** (183), acc. gov. by lusimus. **vacui** (183), ag. w. nos und. in lusimus; *in hour of leisure.* **sub umbra** (470).

730 Lusimus tecum, quod et hunc in annum
731 Vivat et plures, age dic Latinum,
732 Barbite, carmen,
733 Lesbio primum modulate civi;
734 Qui ferox bello tamen inter arma
735 Sive jactatam religarat udo
736 Litore navim,
737 Liberum et Musas Veneremque et illi

730. **Lusimus,** 1st plu. pf. ind. act. fr. lūdo, -ĕre, lūsi, lūsum, 3rd intrans. and trans., *to sport, play, frisk, frolic* for relaxation or amusement or games of chance. Of things, *to play, be tossed about, e.g.*, a boat on the water; trans., *to play at, perform the game of*, w. acc. of game. Of composition, *to utter in sport, pour forth in a playful mood. To make fun of, jeer, banter* a person, *deride, deceive, delude.* **tecum** (705). **quod,** neut. s. ag. w. carmen; nom. subj. to vivat; fr. qui (3). The relative is followed by the subj. mood (i.) when it introduces a purpose; (ii.) when it introduces a consequence; (iii.) when it introduces a *cause* or *reason, since, in that he;* (iv.) when it refers indefinitely to a class and not to special individuals. **et...et** (2). **hunc** (7), ag. w. annum. **in,** w. acc. (76), here of time. **annum,** gov. by in; fr. annus (722).

731. **Vivat,** 3rd sing. pres. subj. act.; fr. vīvo, -ĕre, vixi, victum, 3rd intrans., *to live, be alive, have life. Live well, live at ease, enjoy life.* Of things, *to last, endure, remain. To live on* anything, *support life* with. *To pass one's life, dwell, live* in any employment or manner: pres after pf. lusimus; subj. after quod exp. purpose. **plures** (280), mas. ag. w. annos und. jnd. by et tc hunc annum. **age** (641). **dic** (217). **Latinum,** acc. neut. s. ag. w. carmen; fr. Lătinus, -a, -um, adj., *Latin.*

732. **Barbite,** voc. s. fr. barbiton (34). **carmen,** acc. s. gov. by dic; fr. carmen (64).

733. **Lesbio,** dat. mas. s. ag. w. civi; fr. Lesbius (623). **primum,** neut. of primus (100), used as adv., *first.* **modulate,** voc. mas. s. ag. w. barbite; fr. mŏdŭlātus, -a, -um, partc. (used passively) of mŏdŭlor, -āri, -ātus, 1st dep., trans, *to measure according to a standard* (mŏdŭlus). *To measure, calculate, regulate, keep in time. To bring within the rules* of rhythm, harmony, etc. *To play* on an instrument, *sing. To play* anything on an instrument; intrans., *to regulate, fix as a rule, ordain;* mŏdŭlatus, *played, played upon.* Of songs, *sung.* **civi,** dat. s. of agent after modulate; fr. civis (57), *i.e.*, Alcæus.

734. **Qui** (12), mas. s. ag. w. civi; nom. to canebat (738). **ferox** (167), ag. w. qui=*though brave.* **bello,** abl. of manner w. ferox; fr. bellum (24). **tamen** (111). **inter** (330). **arma,** acc. plu. gov. by inter; fr. arma (226).

735. **Sive** (27), the sive omitted before "inter arma." **jactatam,** acc. fem. s. pf. pass. part. ag. w. navem; fr. jacto (54). **religarat,** syncopated for religaverat; 3rd sing. plpf. ind. act. fr. rĕl go (152); here *to moor* a ship. **udo,** abl. s. neut. ag. w. litore; fr. udus (197).

736. **Litore** (50), local. **navim,** acc. s. gov. by religarat; fr. navis (93).

737. **Liberum,** acc. s. gov. by canebat; fr. Liber (306). **Musas,** acc. plu. jnd. by et to Liberum; fr. Musa (174). **Venerem,** acc. jnd. by -que to Musas; fr. Venus (133). **illi,** *i.e.*, Venus; fem. (97) after hærentem.

738 Semper hærentem puerum canebat
739 Et Lycum nigris oculis nigroque
740 Crine decorum.
741 O decus Phœbi et dapibus supremi
742 Grata testudo Jovis, o laborum
743 Dulce lenimen, mihi cunque salve
744 Rite vocanti.

CARMEN XXXIII.—AD ALBIUM TIBULLUM.

745 Albi, ne doleas plus nimio memor

738. **Semper** (158). **hærentem** (475), mas. ag. w. puerum. **puerum** (266), gov. by canebat. **canebat**, 3rd sing. impf. ind. act. fr. cano (261).

739. **Lycum**, acc. s. jnd. by et to puerum; fr. Lўcus, -i, 2nd mas. **nigris** (155), ag. w. oculis. **oculis** (106), abl. of means w. decorum. **nigro**, abl. mas. s. ag. w. crine; fr. niger (155)

740. **Crine**, abl. s. jnd. by -que to oculis; fr. crinis (404). **decorum**, acc. mas. s. ag. w. Lycum; fr. decorus (259).

741. **O decus** (2), in app. to testudo. **Phœbi**, gen. s. after decus; fr. Phœbus (308). **et** (2). **dapibus**, dat. plu. after traject. grata; fr. daps, dăpis, 3rd fem., no gen. plur., *a solemn religious banquet, sacrificial feast. Rich feast, magnificent banquet.* **supremi**, gen. mas. s. ag. w. Jovis; fr. supremus (364).

742. **Grata** (499), voc. ag. w. testudo. **testūdo**, -ĭnis, 3rd fem. voc. s.; *a tortoise, tortoise-shell* used for overlaying or veneering. Any stringed instrument of an arched shape, *lyre, lute, cithern. Any arch, vault, vaulted nave*, esp. a military contrivance for protecting soldiers. **Jovis** (261), after dapibus. **O** (2). **laborum**, gen. plu. after lenimen; fr. labor (124).

743. **Dulce** (2), ag. w. lenimen. **lēnīmen**, -ĭnis, 3rd neut., voc. sing.; (lēnio, 631) *soother, mitigator. Mitigation, alleviation.* **mihi** (277), commodi after salve. **cunque**, adv., (quum, 43; -que, 4) generalises relative adjs. and particles, *e.g.*, quicunque, quotiescunque, etc.; Eng., *-ever*, very rarely used, as here, w. the temporal participle as a temp. particle=cumcunque; "cunque vocanti"=quandocunque te vocavero. **salve**, 2nd s. imper. pres. act. fr. salvĕo, -ēre, no pf., no sup., 2nd intrans., *to be well, be in good health* (not used as a personal verb); chiefly in salutation, salve, -eto, salvere jubeo, *Good day! Welcome!* sts.=Vale, *Good bye! Farewell!*

744. **Ritĕ**, adv., (old abl. for ritu as reversely noctu for nocte, diu for die) *according to religious ceremonies* or *observances;* pregn., *with due religious observances* or *rites;* meton., *in a proper, just manner, duly, rightly, fitly, well. In the usual manner* or *fashion, according to custom.* **vocanti**, dat. mas. s. ag. w. mihi; fr. vocans (702).

Carmen XXXIII. Metre.—*Third Asclepiad.* (Carmen vi.)

745. **Albi**, voc. s. fr. Albius, -ii, 2nd mas., *Albius Tibullus*, a Roman elegiac poet. **ne** (41), prohibitive w. pres. conj. **doleas**, 2nd s. pres. conj. (hortative) act. fr. dŏleo, -ēre, -ui, 2nd trans. and intrans., *to feel pain. To grieve over, deplore. To lament, be sorry for. To resent.* **plus nimio** (491). **memor** (650), nom. mas. s. ag. w. tu und. in doleas.

Immitis Glyceræ, neu miserabiles
Decantes elegos, cur tibi junior
    Læsa præniteat fide.
Insignem tenui fronte Lycorida
Cyri torret amor: Cyrus in asperam
Declinat Pholoën; sed prius Apulis
    Jungentur capreæ lupis,
Quam turpi Pholoë peccet adultero.

746. **Immitis,** gen. s. fem. ag. w Glyceræ; fr. immītis, -e, adj., (in, neg.; mitis, 445). Of fruits, *not soft* or *mellow, harsh, rough* (1002); meton., *rough, rude, harsh, severe, stern, savage, inexorable.* **Glyceræ,** gen. s. after memor; fr. Glȳcĕra. **neu** (87, 83). **miserabiles,** acc. plu. mas. ag. w. elegos; fr. mĭsĕrābĭlis, -e, adj., (miseror, *to pity*) *worthy* or *deserving of pity, pitiable, deplorable, lamentable.*

747. **Decantes,** 2nd s. conj. act. jnd. by neu to doleas; fr. dēcanto, -are, -avi, -atum, 1st trans., (de, 10; canto, 183) *to sing, chant* a thing, *repeat in a sing-song way. To repeat, say over and over again,* esp., though not always, of something trite, absurd. **ĕlĕgos,** acc. gov. by decantes; fr. ĕlĕgi, -ōrum, 2nd mas., no sing.; *elegiac verses, an elegy.* **cur** (218), here interrog. introducing the question which he is always asking. **tibi** (93), after traject. præniteat. **jūnior,** contr. for juvenior; nom. mas. s. compar. adj., subj. of præniteat; fr. juvenis (77).

748. **Læsa,** abl. fem. s. pf. pass. part. ag. w. fide; fr. lædo (359). **præniteat,** 3rd s. pres. subj. fr. prænĭteo, -ēre, -ui, no sup., 2nd intrans., (præ, *before, beyond;* niteo, 161) *to shine, glitter much* or *brightly. To be more attractive* w. dat. **fide,** abl. absol. s. fr. fides (153).

749. **Insignem** (531), fem. ag. w. Lycorida. **tenui,** abl. s. fem. ag. w. fronte; fr. tenuis (173). **fronte,** abl. (of manner) s. w. insignem; fr. frons (29). **Lycorida,** acc. gov. by torret; fr. Lȳcōris, -ĭdis, 3rd fem.

750. **Cyri,** gen. (objective) after amor. The objective gen. usu. depends on words containing the transitive force of verbs from wh. they are derived, rendered in Eng. by *for, towards,* etc., not genly. *of.* **torret,** 3rd sing. ind. pres. act. fr. torreo, -ēre, -ui, tostum, 2nd trans., *to dry* or *burn* by fire or sun, *scorch, parch, roast, bake, dress* food, etc.; fig. of love, passion, etc. **amor** (364), subj. of torret. **Cyrus,** nom. subj. of declinat. **in** (76), w. acc. *towards.* **asperam,** acc. fem. s. predicative ag. w. Pholoën; fr. asper (154).

751. **Declinat,** 3rd s. ind. pres. act. fr. declīno, -āre, -āvi, -ātum, (de, 10; clino, Gk.) trans., *to bend off from* the right path, *turn aside, turn away* (class. not Cæs.); intrans. in fig. sense; meton., w. acc. of thing from which, *avoid, shun.* **Pholoën,** ac. s. gov. by in; fr. Pholoē, -es, 1st fem. (Gk.). **sed** (591). **prius** (130). **Apulis,** dat. plu. mas. ag. w. lupis; fr. Āpŭlus, -a, -um, adj., (also -pp-). *Of Apulia,* province in Lower Italy, north of Calabria.

752. **Jungentur,** 3rd plu. fut. ind. pass. fr. jungo (134). **capreæ,** nom. plu. subj. of jungentur; fr. căprea, -æ, 1st fem., *a wild she-goat, roe, roe-buck.* **lupis,** dat. plu. after traject. jungentur; fr. lupus (414).

753. **Quam,** compar. (284, 582) w. prius. **turpi,** dat. mas. s. ag. w. adultero; fr. turpis (727). **Pholoë** (751), subj. of peccet. **peccet,** 3rd s. pres. conj. (potential) fr. pecco (641) **adultero,** dat. (commodi) s. after peccet; fr. adulter, subst. (403).

754 Sic visum Veneri, cui placet impares
755 Formas atque animos sub juga aënea
756 Sævo mittere cum joco.
757 Ipsum me melior quum peteret Venus,
758 Grata detinuit compede Myrtale
759 Libertina fretis acrior Hadriæ
760 Curvantis Calabros sinus.

754. **Sic** (89, 315). **visum,** nom. neut. s. ag. w. the idea contained in prec. lines; pf. pass. part. fr. video (49); w. est. und., 3rd s. pf. combinate ind., "*it seemed good.*" **Veneri,** dat. s. after traject. visum; fr. Venus (133). **cui** (575), fem. s. ag. w. Veneri; dat. after placet. **placet,** 3rd s. ind. pres. act. fr. placeo (263). **impares,** acc. plu. fem. ag. w. formas; fr. impar, -păris, adj., (in, neg.; par, 180) *uneven, unequal, dissimilar* in size, number, quality, esp. *smaller than, unequal to, inferior to, not a match for.* Of things, *e.g.*, pugna, *beyond one's strength, for which one is no match.*

755. **Formas,** acc. plu. gov. by mittere; fr. forma, -æ, 1st fem., (fero, 138) *form* in widest sense, more general than figura, facies; *contour, figure, shape,* etc.; pregnant *a fine form, beauty* (974); fig., *shape, form, nature, manner, kind, e.g.*, dicendi. **atque** (37). **animos,** acc. plu. jnd. by atque to formas; fr. animus (448). **sub** (489). **juga,** acc. plu. gov. by sub; fr. jŭgum, -i, 2nd neut. (jungo, 134). Of draught animals, *yoke, pair, team,* esp. *a yoke* formed by a spear fastened to the top of two other spears under which an enemy was made to pass. *Height, summit of* a mountain; fig., *yoke, bond* of affection, love, etc. (993). *Slavery, subjection, misfortune* (804). **ænea,** acc. neut. plu. ag. w. juga; fr. ænĕus, -a, -um, adj., (ăhēneus) *made of bronze* or *copper* (æs, 97).

756. **Sævo,** abl. mas. s. ag. w. joco; fr. sævus (172). **mittere,** pres. inf. act. subj. of placet; fr. mitto (38). **cum** (31). **joco,** abl. s. gov. by cum; fr. jocus (70).

757. **Ipsum** (681), ag. w. me. **me** (29), gov. by peteret. **melior** (209), ag. w. Venus. **quum,** as in 206. **peteret,** 3rd s. impf. subj. act. fr. peto (126). **Venus** (133), subj. of peteret.

758. **Grata** (129), ag. w. compede. **detinuit,** 3rd s. pf. ind. act. fr. detĭneo, -ēre, -ui, -tentum, 2nd trans., (de, 10; teneo, 204) *to hold off, keep back, detain,* etc. *To hold thoroughly* or *firmly, occupy, engage.* **compĕde,** abl. (instrum.) s. fr. compes, -pĕdis, plu. gen. genly. compedium; not used in nom. and dat. sing., 3rd fem., (cum, 21; pes, 31) a wooden *fetter* or *shackle for the feet;* fig., *fetter, bond, chain* of love, etc. **Myrtale,** -es, 1st fem., (Gk.) nom. subj. of detinuit.

759. **Libertina,** -æ, 1st fem.; nom. s. in app. to Myrtale, *a freedwoman,* prop. fem. (und. mulier) of lībertīnus, -a, -um, adj., *belonging to a freedman,* opp. to ingenuus (640); libĕrtinus, -i, 2nd mas., *a freedman* (in respect of his condition; libertus, liberta, in respect of manumitter); meton., fr. Aug. to Sueton., *son of a freedman.* **fretis,** abl. of comparison, plu. after acrior; fr. frĕtum (104). **acrior,** nom. fem. s. compar. adj. fr. acris (129), ag. w. libertina; *more passionate.* **Hadriæ** (103), after fretis.

760. **Curvantis,** gen. s. mas. pres. part. act. ag. w. Hadriæ; fr. curvo, -are, -avi, -atum, 1st trans., (curvus, 262) *to bend, bow, curve, crook.* **Calabros,** acc. plu. mas. ag. w. sinus; fr. Călăber, -bra, -brum, adj., *of Calabria* (713). **sinus,** acc. plu. gov. by curvantis; fr. sĭnus, -us, 4th mas., *a bent sur-*

CARMEN XXXIV.—AD SE IPSUM.

761 PARCUS Deorum cultor et infrequens
762 Insanientis dum sapientiæ
763 Consultus erro, nunc retrorsum
764 Vela dare atque iterare cursus
765 Cogor relictos: namque Diespiter,
766 Igni corusco nubila dividens

face, raised or *depressed curve; fold* or *hollow* formed by anything; hanging *fold* of the upper part of the toga. *Bosom* of a garment. *Purse* carried therein. *Bosom*=love, protection, asylum. *Interior, inmost part* of a thing. *Hiding-place, bay, bight, gulf;* "that breaks into curving bays the Calabrian shore;" sinus is acc. of result rather than of object (W.).

CARMEN XXXIV. METRE.—*Alcaic.* (Carmen ix.)

761. **Parcus**, -a, -am, adj.; nom. mas. s. ag. w. cultor; *spare, scant, little, small;* meton., *sparing, scanty, moderate* in anything, esp. expenditure either in a good or bad sense; adv., parce, parciter. **Deorum** (261), after cultor. **cultor**, -ōris, 3rd mas.; nom. s. in app. to ego und. in cogor; (colo, 797) *an inhabitant, dweller, worker, cultivator,* esp. of the land, *husbandman. Fosterer, supporter. Worshipper, reverencer.* **infrequens**, -ntis, adj.; nom. mas. s. jnd. by et to parcus (in, neg.; frequens, 790). Of persons, etc., *that is not often in* a place or *seldom does a thing.* Of things, *not often happening, seldom used;* meton., *not numerous, few, small, thin in numbers.* Of places, *not full, not filled.*

762. **Insanientis**, gen. fem. s. pres. part. act. ag. w. sapientiæ; fr. insānio, -īre, -īvi or -ii, -ītum, 4th intrans., (insanus, 435) *to be senseless, without reason, mad, insane;* meton., *to act like a madman, rage, rave.* **dum** (53). **sapientiæ**, gen. (objective, 749) s. after consultus; fr. săpientia, -æ, 1st fem., (sapiens, 201) *good sense, discernment, discretion, prudence,* esp. *wisdom,* also of special departments of knowledge, *e.g., practical wisdom, knowledge of the world, philosophy,* esp. Epicurean, of which Hor. was once a follower. *Statesmanship, policy;* "insana sapientia," *witless, wisdom,* a case of oxymoron, a figure more com. in Gk. than Latin.

763. **Consultus**, -a, -um, adj.; nom. mas. s. ag. w. ego und. in erro; (consulo, 890) pass., *well-considered, weighed, deliberated upon;* act., *knowing, skilled in,* esp. in ref. to law, *e.g.*, juris consultis or consultus alone, *a lawyer.* **erro**, -are, -avi, -atum, 1st intrans., 1st s. ind. pres. act. *to wander, wander about, wander up and down. Wander from the right path, err, stray.* **nunc** (21). **rĕtrorsum** (retro, 801), adv., *back, backwards;* in other relations, *in return, in reversed order;* also rĕtrosus and retroversum.

764. **Vela**, acc. plu. gov. by dare; fr. vēlum, -i, 2nd neut., (veho, *to carry*) *a sail,* usu. in plu. **dare** (673), prolat. after cogor. **atque** (37). **iterare**, pres. inf. act. jnd. by atque to dare; fr. itero (216). **cursus** (171), gov. by iterare, *to steer again* in the course I had deserted, *i.e.*, to return to my old ways of thought (W.).

765. **Cogor**, 1st sing. ind. pres. pass. fr. cogo (434). **relictos**, acc, plu. mas. ag. w. cursus; fr. relictus (271). **namque** (545). **Diespiter**, -tris, 3rd mas.; nom. sing. subj. of egit; (Dies, Umbrian for Dis; pater, 38), *Jupiter.*

766. **Igni** (131), instrum. w. dividens. **corusco**, abl. mas. s. ag. w.

767 Plerumque, per purum tonantes
768 Egit equos volucremque currum;
769 Quo bruta tellus et vaga flumina,
770 Quo Styx et invisi horrida Tænari
771 Sedes Atlanteusque finis
772 Concutitur. Valet ima summis

igni; fr. cŏruscus, -a, -um, adj., (corusco, *to vibrate, shake*), *in waving motion, waving, vibrating, tremulous. Flashing, gleaming, glittering* **nubila** (199), gov. by dividens. **dividens,** nom. mas. s. pres. part. act. ag. w. Diespiter; fr. divido (399).

767. **Plerumque,** adv. w. dividens; (orig. neut. of plerusque, *a larger* or *greater part of;* plu., *very many*), *for the most part, mostly, commonly, very often;* post-Aug less emphatic, *often, commonly.* **per** (114). **purum,** acc. neut. (as subst.) gov. by per; fr. purus (537), *cloudless.* **tonantes,** acc. mas. plu. pres. part. act. ag. w. equos; fr. tŏno, -āre, tŏnui, tŏnĭtum, 1st irreg. intrans. and trans., *to thunder;* "tonat," *it thunders. To make a thundering noise, roar, rattle, crash;* trans., *to thunder forth* anything, *say with a thundering noise.*

768. **Egit** (43). **equos,** acc. plu. gov. by egit; fr. equus (167). **volucrem,** acc. s. mas. ag. w. currum; fr. vŏlŭcris, -e, adj.; (volo, 70) *flying, winged. Swift, rapid. Passing by quickly, fleeting;* volucris, -is, 3rd fem., *a bird.* **currum,** acc. s. jnd. by -que to equos; fr. currus (342).

769. **Quo** (58), neut., ag. w. notion contained in "egit...currum," abl. of cause. **bruta,** nom. fem. s. ag. w tellus; fr. brūtus, -a, -um, adj. prop., *heavy, unwieldy, unmoveable* (rare); fig., *dull, stupid, insensible, irrational.* **tellus** (551), subj. of concutitur. **vaga,** nom. neut. plu. ag. w. flumina; fr. vagus (54). **flumina** (236), jnd. by et to tellus.

770. **Quo** (769). **Styx,** Stȳgis or Stȳgos (Gk.), 3rd fem.; nom. s. subj. of concutitur; (*hated* or *detested thing*) a river in the infernal regions by which the gods swore; meton., *the infernal regions;* adj. Stȳgius, -a, -um, (i.) *of* or *belonging to the Styx;* (ii.) *of* or *belonging to the Lower World;* (iii.) *deadly, fatal, pernicious.* **invisi,** gen. s. mas. or neut. ag. w. Tænari; fr. invīsus, -a, -um, adj., (invideo, 685) *hated, detested. Hateful, detestable.* **horrida,** nom. fem. s. ag. w. sedes; fr. horridus (588). **Tænari,** gen. s. after sedes; fr. Tænărum, -i, 2nd neut., or Tænărus, -i, 2nd mas., promontory and town in Laconia, where was a temple of Neptune, and fabled entrance to the infernal regions.

771. **Sedes** (46), jnd. by et to Styx. **Atlanteus,** -a, -um=Atlanticus (722); nom. mas. s. ag. w. finis. **finis** (94), nom. mas. s. jnd. by -que to sedes.

772. **Concutitur,** 3rd s. ind. pres. pass. fr. concŭtio, -cŭtĕre, -cussi, -cussum, 3rd trans., (cum, 31; quatio, 18) *to shake violently, shake, agitate. To injure the power of, impair, cause to totter, distract, shatter.* Of persons, *to agitate terribly, put in fear, alarm, terror, anxiety.* **valet,** 3rd s. ind. pres. act. fr. văleo, -ēre, -ŭi, -ĭtum, 2nd intrans., *to be strong, stout* or *vigorous.* Of the body, *to be well in health, be hale.* In leavetaking, "vale, valeas," *farewell;* "vale, valeas," "valeat," *be off with you,* etc., exp. dismissal. *To have strength* or *power,* w. inf. or ad. w. ref. to what. Of prayers, *to prevail.* With apud, etc., *to have moral force* or *influence with.* Of things, *to have weight, be of service. To be effective* in speaking. Of money value, *to be of the value, be worth.* Of words, *to mean, signify.* **ima,** acc. neut. plu. gov. by mutare; fr.

773 Mutare et insignem attenuat Deus
774 Obscura promens; hinc apicem rapax
775 Fortuna cum stridore acuto
776 Sustulit, hic posuisse gaudet.

CARMEN XXXV.—AD FORTUNAM.

777 O Diva, gratum quæ regis Antium,
778 Præsens vel imo tollere de gradu

imus (276). **summis**, abl. neut. plu. w. mutare; fr. summus (45); see 446.

773. **Mutare** (446), prolative after valet. **insignem** (531), gov. by attenuat. **attenuat**, 3rd s. ind. pres. act. fr. attĕnuo, -are, -avi, -atum, 1st trans., (ad, 6; tenuo, *to make thin*) *to make very thin, lessen*; fig., *to weaken, reduce, impair, lower, lessen.* **Deus** (109), subj. of attenuat.

774. **Obscura**, acc. neut. plu. gov. by promens; fr. obscurus (199). **promens**, nom. mas. s. pres. part. act. ag. w. Deus; fr. prōmo, -ĕre, prompsi, promptum, 3rd trans., (pro, *forth, forward;* emo, *to buy*) *to take, give, bring out* or *forth, produce;* fig., *to draw forth*, esp. *bring to light, disclose. Utter, express, relate.* **hinc**, adv. Of place, *from this place, hence. From this side, on this side, here.* Of time, *from this time, from this, after this.* Of persons and things, *from this source, from this cause.* **apicem**, acc. s. gov. by sustulit; fr. ăpex, apĭcis, 3rd fem., *extreme end* of a thing, *point, summit, projecting point* of trees, mountains, etc. *The pointed piece of wood* on the cap of the Flamines. *The cap* itself. Any *hat, cap, crown. The highest ornament, crown.* **răpax**, -ācis, adj., nom. fem. s. ag. w. Fortuna; (rapio, 489). Of living beings, *grasping, greedy of plunder.* Of things, *ravenous, e.g.*, Orcus (1382). Of floods, etc., *sweeping. Grasping eagerly, prone to grasp at.*

775. **Fortuna** (209), subj. of sustulit. **cum** (31). **stridore**, abl. s. gov. by cum; fr. strīdor, -ōris, 3rd mas., (strideo, *to creak*) *creaking, hissing, buzzing, whistling.*

776. **Sustulit**, 3rd s. pf. ind. act. fr. tollo (8). The pf. is used for the pres. in the case of an act frequently repeated or customary. **hic** (85). **posuisse**, pf. inf. act. after gaudet; fr. pono (104); see collegisse (4). **gaudet** (131).

Carmen XXXV. Metre—*Alcaic.* (Carmen ix.)

777. **O** (2). **Diva** (89), voc. s. **gratum**, acc. neut. sing. ag. w. Antium; fr. gratus (129), und. tibi, *to thee.* **quæ** (46), fem. s. 2nd pers. ag. w. Diva; nom. subj. of regis. **regis**, 2nd s. ind. pres. act. fr. rego (91). **Antium**, acc. s. gov. by regis; fr. Antium, -ii, 2nd neut., a town in Latium, with a temple of Fortune, on the sea-coast (Anzio).

778. **Præsens**, -entis, adj.; voc. fem. s. ag. w. diva; abl. sing. of persons usu. in -e, of things in -i, (præ, *before;* sum, 3, of which pres. partc. not used in simple) *that is before one, in sight, in person;* "in præsens," *for the present. That happens* or *is done immediately, prompt, ready, direct. That operates immediately, efficacious.* Of character, *collected, resolute. Aiding, favouring, propitious.* **vel** (187). **imo**, abl. mas. s. ag. w. gradu; fr. sumi (276). **tollere** (8), prolative after præsens, which is not elsewhere found w. an infinitive. **de** (10). **gradu**, abl. s. gov. by de; fr. gradus (105).

Mortale corpus vel superbos
Vertere funeribus triumphos,
Te pauper ambit sollicita prece
Ruris colonus, te dominam æquoris,
Quicunque Bithyna lacessit
Carpathium pelagus carina.
Te Dacus asper, te profugi Scythæ,
Urbesque gentesque et Latium ferox

779. **Mortale,** acc. neut. s. ag. w. corpus; fr. mortalis (125). **corpus,** acc. s. gov. by tollere; fr. corpus (70). **superbos** (318), ag. w. triumphos.

780. **Vertere,** pres. inf. act. jnd. by vel to tollere; fr. verto (503). **funeribus,** abl. (of manner) plu. w. vertere; fr. funus (231). **triumphos** (85), gov. by vertere.

781. **Te** (83), gov. by ambit. **pauper** (141), nom. mas. s. ag. w. colonus. **ambit,** 3rd s. ind. pres. act. fr. ambio, -īre, -īvi and -ii, -ītum, 4th intrans. and trans., (ambi, *around;* eo, 51) impf. ambībat and ambiebat, otherwise reg., *to go round* or *about* a thing, *surround, encompass;* polit., *to canvass* persons for votes. *To entreat, solicit, court* a person. *To strive for, seek to gain* a thing. **sollicita,** abl. s. fem. ag. w. prece; fr. sollicitus (381). **prĕce** (62), of means.

782. **Ruris** (464), after colonus. **cŏlōnus,** -i, 2nd mas.; nom. s. subj. of ambit, (colo, 797) *an inhabitant of a colonial town, colonist. Husbandman, farmer.* **te,** anaphora. **dominam,** acc. s. in app. to te; fr. dŏmĭna, -æ, 1st fem., (abl. plu., -is) *mistress* of a family, ref. to domestics. *Mistress, lady.* In endearment, *wife, sweetheart.* Of abstract things, *mistress, ruler.* **æquoris,** gen. s. after dominam; fr. æquor (48).

783. **Quicunque** (167), quæcunque, quodcunque; nom. mas. s. subj. of lacessit, indef. relat. pron., *whoever, whatever, whosoever, everyone who, everything that. All who, all that;* Quodcunque w. gen., *however, whatever much. Each, every possible, each, every, all, e.g.,* quocunque modo. **Bithyna,** abl. s. fem. ag. w. carinâ; fr. Bīthȳnus, -a, -um, -adj. *Of Bithynia,* in Asia Minor, where the Romans carried on considerable trade. **lacessit,** 3rd s. ind. pres. act. fr. lăcesso, -ĕre, -īvi or ĭi, or -i, -ītum, 3rd trans. intens., (rt. lac-, *to bite*) *to bite eagerly, mangle* (rarely). *To attack, assail. To strike repeatedly. Keep dashing against.* Of inanimate things, *fall upon, strike, smite;* here *to chafe, tempt;* fig., *to attack, harass,* esp. the senses; *to exasperate, enrage. To stimulate* by exasperating. *To importune* (1364).

784. **Carpathium,** acc. neut. s. ag. w. pelagus; fr. Carpăthius, -a, -um, adj., *of Carpathos,* an island in the Ægean Sea betw. Crete and Rhodes (Scarpanto). **pelagus,** acc. s. gov. by lacessit; fr. pelagus (99). **carina,** abl. (instrum.) s. fr. carina (130).

785. **Te** (83), gov. by metuunt. **Dacus,** -i, 2nd mas., nom. s. subj. to metuit und. fr. metuunt (788). *The Dacian;* plu., *the Dacians,* a very warlike people of Upper Hungary, Transylvania, Moldavia, Wallachia, Bessarabia. **asper** (154), nom. mas. s. ag. w. Dacus. **profugi,** nom. mas. plu. ag. w. Scythæ; fr. prŏfŭgus, -a, -um, adj., (profugio, *to flee before* or *from*) *that flies* or *has fled, fugitive, roaming, wandering. Banished, exile.* **Scythæ** (502), nom. subj. of metuunt.

786. **Urbes,** nom. plu. jnd. by -que to Scythæ; fr. urbs (40). **gentes,** nom. plu. jnd. by -que to urbes; fr. gens (41). **Lătium,** -ii, 2nd neut.;

787 Regumque matres barbarorum et
788 Purpurei metuunt tyranni,
789 Injurioso ne pede proruas
790 Stantem columnam neu populus frequens
791 Ad arma cessantes, ad arma
792 Concitet imperiumque frangat.
793 Te semper anteit sæva Necessitas,

nom. s. jnd. by et to gentes; a country in Italy in which was Rome. **ferox** (167), neut. ag. w. Latium.

787. **Regum** (142), after matres. **matres,** nom. plu. jnd. by -que to Latium; fr. mater (24). **barbarorum,** gen. plu. mas. ag. w. regum; fr. barbarus (626).

788. **Purpurei,** nom. mas. plu. ag. w. tyranni; fr. purpŭreus, -a, -um, adj., *purple-coloured* of very different shades, *e.g., red, reddish, violet, brownish, blackish. Clothed in purple*=purpuratus (here). *Brilliant, bright, shining, beautiful.* **metuunt** (456). **tyranni,** nom. plu. jnd. by et to matres; fr. tÿrannus, -i, 2nd mas., (Gk.), *monarch, ruler, sovereign, king;* in 1340, of a constellation influencing the ocean. *A cruel tyrant, despot.*

789. **Injurioso,** abl. mas. s. ag. w. pede; fr. injūriosus, -a, -um, adj., (injuria, *injury*) *acting unjustly, injurious, wrongful, contumelious;* meton., *hurtful, noxious.* **ne** (41), after vbs. of fearing. **pede** (135), instrum. **proruas,** 2nd s. subj. pres. act. fr. proruo, -ŭĕre, -ui, -ŭtum, (pro, *forth, forward;* ruo, 61) intrans., *to fall forward, tumble down. To rush forward* or *onwards;* trans., *to cast down in front, hurl down* or *forwards, overthrow, overturn.* Subj. after ne; pres. after metuunt.

790. **Stantem,** acc. fem. s. pres. partc. ag. w. columnam; fr. sto (233). **columnam,** acc. s. gov. by proruas; fr. cŏlumna, -æ, 1st fem., (collat. fms. are columen, culmen) *that which is high, mountain top, summit* or *peak. Highest part* or *top* of an object. *Column, support, pillar;* here metaph., *stability.* **neu** (83, 87). **populus** (61), subj. of concitet. **frĕquens,** -entis, adj., nom. mas. s. ag. w. populus, *that repeatedly takes place, often, frequent.* Of persons, *often in a place, often doing* a thing. Of abstract things, *frequent, repeated, common.* Of a multitude, *gathering in crowds, crowding.* Of places, *filled, crowded, much frequented, stocked.*

791. **Ad** (6). **arma** (734), gov. by ad; "ad arma" is the actual cry (W.). **cessantes,** acc. mas. plu. pres. part. act. gov. by concitet; fr. cesso (637).

792. **Concitet,** 3rd s. pres. subj. act. jnd. by neu (790) to proruas; fr. concĭto, -are, -avi, -atum, 1st trans., intens. of concieo; *to set in violent motion, stir up, incite, excite;* fig., *to rouse, urge, impel* one to any act or feeling, etc., *influence, move strongly* w. ad, in adversus. With acc. of thing, *rouse, excite, produce, occasion, e.g.,* invidiam. **imperium,** acc. s. gov. by frangat; fr. imperium (62). **frangat,** 3rd s. pres. subj. act. jnd. by -que to concitet; fr. frango (570).

793. **Te** (83), gov. by anteit. **semper** (158). **anteit,** 3rd s. ind. pres. fr. anteeo, anteire, -īvi or -ii, no sup., intrans. irreg., (sts. -ei one syll., sts. we find antīre, antito), (ante, 687; eo, 51) *to go before, precede* in space. *To anticipate, precede* in time, *to hinder, prevent.* Of degree, *to excel* w. abl. wherein. **sæva** (327), ag. w. Necessitas. **Necessitas** (120), personified subj. of anteit.

Clavos trabales et cuneos manu
Gestans aëna, nec severus
Uncus abest liquidumque plumbum.
Te Spes et albo rara Fides colit
Velata panno nec comitem abnegat,
Utcunque mutata potentes
Veste domos inimica linquis.

794. **Clavos,** acc. plu. gov. by gestans; fr. clāvus, -i, 2nd mas., (like clavis, fr. rt. clu- in claudo, *to shut*) *a nail, peg, plug,* esp. that driven annually on the ides of Sept. into the temple of Jupiter to mark the year, an attribute of necessity, as a type of firmness she drives it into the wall with a hammer. *A rudder. A purple stripe* on the tunica, broad (latus) among senators, narrow among equites. **trabales,** acc. plu. mas. ag. w. clavos; fr. trăbālis, -e, adj., (trabs, 13) *of* or *belonging to beams;* "trabalis clavus," *a spike;* meton., *beam-like, stout as a beam.* **cuneos,** acc. plu. jnd. by et to clavos; fr. cŭneus, -i, 2nd mas., *a wedge. Troops drawn up for battle in a wedge form. The wedge form division of the rows of seats in the theatre.* **manu,** abl. (instrum.) s. fr. manus (474)

795. **Gestans,** pres. part. act. nom. fem. s. ag. w. Necessitas; fr. gesto (226). **aëna,** abl. s. fem. ag. w. manu; fr. ăēnus, -a, -um, adj., (trisyll.) or ahenus, -a, -um, adj., (rare); poet. for prose æneus, -a, -um, adj. (755), though Hor. uses latter oftener than former; (æs, 97) *of copper* or *bronze; here invincible.* **nec** (19). **severus** (633), nom. mas. s. ag. w. uncus.

796. **Uncus,** -i, 2nd mas.; nom. s. subj. of abest; *a hook, barb,* esp. hook by which condemned criminals were dragged to the Tiber; *a clamp* used to join blocks of stone. **abest** (249), 3rd s. ind. pres. fr. absum, -esse, abfui, abfuturus (sts. afui, afuturus), (ab, 254; sum, 3) *to be away from* a place or person, *be absent* or *distant;* fig., *to be removed from* a thing w. â or ut w. subj. *To be free from* anything. *To be different from* in quality, *inferior to. To be disinclined to, e.g.,* a consilio. Of things, =desum, *to be wanting* (249). **liquidum,** nom. neut. s. ag. w. plumbum; fr. liquidus (150); here *molten.* **plumbum,** -i, 2nd neut.; nom. s. jnd. by -que to uncus; *lead* (sts. plumbum nigrum, but plumbum album=*tin.*). *Leaden ball* or *bullet. Leaden pipe.*

797. **Te** (83), gov. by colit. **Spes** (143), nom. s. subj. of colit. **albo,** abl. mas. s. ag. w. panno; fr. albus (199). **rara** (60), ag. w. Fides; *rarely found* (W.). **Fides** (492), jnd. by et to Spes. **colit,** 3rd s. ind. pres. act. fr. cŏlo, cŏlĕre, cŏlŭi, cultum; 3rd trans., *to abide, dwell in, inhabit. Cultivate, till. Bestow care on, care for. Dress, clothe, adorn.*

798. **Velata,** nom. fem. s. pf. pass. partc. ag. w. Fides; fr. vēlo, -are, -avi, -atum, 1st trans., (velum, 764) *to cover, cover* or *wrap up, envelope, veil;* fig., *hide, conceal.* **panno,** abl. (instrum.) s. fr. pannus, -i, 2nd mas., collat. pannum, -i, 2nd neut., (pannus, *the thread* wound upon the bobbin in a shuttle) genly. *cloth, garment,* esp. of worn clothes, *rags, tatters.* **nec** (19). **comitem,** acc. s. predic. in app. to se und., gov. by abnegat; fr. comes (210). **abnegat,** 3rd s. ind. pres. act. jnd. by nec to colit; fr. abnĕgo, -are, -avi, -atum, 1st trans., (ab, 254; nego, 694) *to deny, refuse* (poet.); "comitem abnegat," denies thee a companion, *i.e.,* herself.

799. **Utcunque** (458). **mutata** (77), ag. w. veste. **potentes,** acc. fem. plu. ag. w. domos; fr. potens (89).

800. **Veste,** abl. (absol.) s. fr. vestis, -is, 3rd fem., *covering for* the body, *garment, vestment, robe, clothing, attire* (ante-Aug. only sing.); "mutare

801 At vulgus infidum et meretrix retro
802 Perjura cedit; diffugiunt cadis
803 Cum fæce siccatis amici
804 Ferre jugum pariter dolosi.
805 Serves iturum Cæsarem in ultimos
806 Orbis Britannos et juvenum recens
807 Examen Eois timendum

vestem," *to put on mourning;* meton., *carpet, curtain, tapestry,* etc. **domos** (420), gov. by linquis. **inimica** (306), nom. ag. as adv. attribute w. tu und. in linquis. **linquis,** 2nd s. ind. pres. act. fr. linquo (681).

801. **At** (483). **vulgus,** -i, 2nd neut. rarely mas.; nom. s. subj. of cedit; *great mass, multitude, people, public. Mass, crowd, throng, multitude* of persons or animals. *Mob, rabble, populace, vulgar,* implying contempt. **infidum,** nom. neut. s. ag. w. vulgus; fr. infīdus, -a, -um, adj., (in, neg.; fidus, *faithful*) *not to be trusted, faithless, treacherous, false.* **mĕrĕtrix,** -īcis, 3rd fem.; gen. plu., -cum and -cium, (mereo, *to gain*) *a harlot, courtesan.* **rĕtro,** adv., (re-, 659; -tro, cf. citro, intro, ultro) *backwards, back, on the back side, behind.* Of tendency, direction, etc., w. vbs of motion, *e.g.*, redire, regredi, fig. of time, *back, before, formerly., e.g.*, quodcunque retro est, *i.e.*, *is past.* Of other relations, *behind, in return, on the contrary, on the other hand;* retrorsus and retrovérsus are the only compds. that are not post-Aug.

802. **Perjura,** nom. fem. s. ag. w. meretrix; fr. perjūrus, -a, -um, adj., (perjuro, *to swear falsely*) *one who breaks his oath, perjured.* Plaut., *one who lies with an oath.* **cedit,** 3rd s. ind. pres. act. fr. cedo (170). **diffugiunt** (480). **cadis,** abl. (absol.) plu. fr. cădus, -i, 2nd mas., a large earthen vessel for holding liquids, *bottle, jug, jar, wine-jar.*

803. **Cum** (31), w. diffugiunt. **fæce,** abl. s. gov. by cum; fr. fæx, fæcis, 3rd fem., *grounds, sediment, lees, dregs,* prop. of liquids; fig., of the people, etc. **siccatis,** pf. pass. part. abl. mas. plu. ag. w. cadis; fr. sicco, -are, -avi, -atum, 1st trans., (siccus, 106) *to make dry, dry up. To drain* milk. Of soil, marshes, etc., *to dry, dry up.* Of goblets, etc., *drain, empty.* **amici,** nom. plu. subj. of diffugiunt; fr. amicus (208).

804. **Ferre,** pres. inf. (prolative) after dolosi; fr. fero (138). **jugum,** acc. s. gov. by ferre; fr. jŭgum (755). **pariter,** adv. w. ferre; (par, 180) *equally, in an equal* or *like manner,* w. cum, ut, atque (ac), -que or dative. Like simul, of equality in time or association, *at the same time, together with,* w. cum, atque, etc.; pariter...pariter, *as soon as.* **dolosi,** nom. mas. plu. ag. w. amici; fr. dŏlōsus, -a, -um, adj., (dolus, 266) *crafty, cunning, deceitful* (884); here *not honest enough, not loyal enough,* folld. by prolat. inf. dep. on the positive notion it (dolosus) denies (W.).

805. **Serves** (96). **iturum,** fut. part. acc. mas. s. ag. w. Cæsarem; fr. eo (51). **Cæsarem,** acc. s. gov. by serves; fr. Cæsar (80). **in** (81). **ultimos,** acc. plu. mas. ag. w. Britannos; fr. ultimus (280).

806. **Orbis,** gen. (of thing distributed) s. after ultimos; fr. orbis (341). **Britannos** (535), gov. by in. **juvenum** (667), after examen. **recens,** acc. neut. s. ag. w. examen; fr. rĕcens, -ntis, adj.; (abl. -nti, sts. poet. -nte, gen. plu. -ntium; but in 258, -ntum) *that has not long existed, fresh, young, recent* (opp. to vetus, difft. fr. novus), w. ab, *immediately after, fresh from. Fresh in strength, not exhausted by fatigue, vigorous.*

807. **Examen,** acc. s. jnd. by et to Britannos; fr. exāmen, -ĭnis, 3rd neut.,

808 Partibus Oceanoque rubro.
809 Eheu cicatrıcum et sceleris pudet
810 Fratrumque. Quid nos dura refugimus
811 Ætas? quid intactum nefasti
812 Liquimus? unde manum juventus
813 Metu Deorum continuit? quibus

(ex, 691, ago, 43) *a multitude issuing* or *flying forth, swarm*, orig. of bees, meton., *crowd, shoal, swarm.* **Eois,** dat. plu. fem. ag. w. partibus; fr. Eōus, -a, -um, adj.; (ēōs, *the morning*, Gk.), *belonging to the morning Of the East. Eastern.* **timendum,** acc. neut. s. ag. w. examen; fr. tĭmendus, gerundive of tĭmeo (100)

808. **Partibus,** dat. (of the agent) plu. after gerundive timendum; fr. pars (20). **Oceano** (110), dat. jnd. by -que to partibus. **rubro,** dat. s. mas. ag. w. Oceano; fr. rŭber, -bra, -brum, adj.; (rubeo, 38) *red, ruddy.* "Rubrum mare," *the Arabıan and Persian Gulfs.*

809. **Eheu** (sts. ēheu, epic and lyric, when some write heu, heu), exclamation of pain, *ah! alas!* **cicatricum,** gen. plu. after pudet; fr cĭcātrıx, -īcis, 3rd fem., *a scar; fig., a healed wound, sore, e.g.*, reipublicæ. **sceleris** (537), jnd. by et to cicatricum. **pudet,** 3rd sing. ind. pres. act. fr. pŭdeo, -ēre, pŭdui, 3rd s. puduit and pŭdĭtum est, no sup., 2nd intrans. and trans. Personal intrans., *to be ashamed, feel shame* (rare). Trans. of things or w. subj. inf., *to bring shame to, be a cause of shame to.* Impers., pudet, puduit or puditum est, *it is, was a shame to. It causes* or *brings*, etc., *shame to, e.g.*, aliquem alicujus rei.

810. **Fratrum,** gen. plu. jnd. by -que to sceleris; fr. frater (90). Cicatricum, sceleris, fratrum, a kind of hendiadys (17), the object of shame is the guilt of civil war, "the scars" are its memorials, "the brothers," its aggravation (W.). **quid** (297), gov. by refugimus. **nos** (169), subj. of refugimus. **dura,** nom. fem. s. ag. w. ætas; fr. durus (479). **refugimus,** 1st plu. perf. ind. act.; fr. refugio (34)

811. **Ætas** (284), in appos. to nos. **quid** (297), gov. by liquimus. **intactum,** acc. neut. s. predic. ag. w. quid; fr. intactus, -a, -um, adj.; (in, neg.; tango, 224) *untouched*, esp *unharmed, uninjured, safe, not spoiled.* Of cattle, *unyoked.* Of maidens, *undefiled.* Of garments, *unpolluted, pure; fig., free from, exempt from. Not treated of* in song, etc. **nefasti,** nom. plu. mas. ag. w. nos; fr. nĕfastus, -a, -um, adj.; (nĕ, 961; fastus) prop. opp. to fastus. Of days on which judgment cannot be pronounced nor assemblies of the people held; meton., *wicked, infamous, execrable, abominable, unlucky, inauspicious* (1193); nĕfastum, -i, 2nd neut., (und. facinus) *an impiety, wicked* or *impious deed.*

812. **Liquimus,** 1st plu. pf. ind. act. fr. linquo (681). **unde** (291), interrog. *from what?* **manum,** acc. s. gov. by continuit; fr. manus (474). **juventus** (60), subj. of continuit

813. **Metu** (564), of cause w. continuit. **Deorum** (261), after metu. **continuit,** 3rd s. pf. ind. act. fr. contĭneo, -ēre, -ŭi, -tentum, 2nd trans. (cum, 31; teneo, 204) *to hold* something *on all sides* or *in all its parts, keep together.* Pass. of places, *to be surrounded, encompassed. To preserve, retain* w. accessory idea of quiet, permanence, *e.g.*, rempublicam, exercitum. *To hinder, keep still, restrain, repress, enclose, fig., hold back, repress, subdue* (here). *To comprehend* something in itself, "contineri aliquâ re, *to be composed of, consist in.* **quibus,** dat. plu. fem. ag. w. arıs; fr. quis (65).

Pepercit aris? O utinam nova
    Incude diffingas retusum in
        Massagetas Arabasque ferrum.

CARMEN XXXVI.—IN HONOREM PLOTII NUMIDÆ.

ET thure et fidibus juvat
    Placare et vituli sanguine debito
Custodes Numidæ Deos,
    Qui nunc Hesperia sospes ab ultima

814. **Pepercit,** 3rd s. pf. ind. act. fr. parco (671). **aris,** dat. plu. after pepercit; fr. āra, -æ, 1st fem., *elevation* of wood, stone, earth, etc. Of a sepulchre, monument, esp. *altar, protection, refuge, shelter.* **O** (2). **utinam,** adv. of wishing, *Oh that! I wish that! Would that!* negat. w. ne or non; nec...nec. With conj. (opt.) pres. a possible wish. With conj. impf. an impracticable wish. With conj. plupf. a bygone possibility. **nova** (213), ag. w. incude.

815. **Incude,** abl. (instrum.) s. fr. incus, -ūdis, 3rd fem., (in, -cudo, *to strike upon*) *an anvil.* **diffingas,** 2nd s. pres. conj. (opt.) act. fr. diffingo, -ĕre, no pf., no sup., 3rd trans., (dis, -870; fingo, *to fashion, make*) *to form differently, make anew,* here *for a different purpose; remodel, change, alter.* **retusum,** acc. neut. s. ag. w. ferrum; fr. retūsus, -a, -um, *blunted, dull,* pf. pass. partc. of retundo, -ĕre, -tŭdi -tūsum, (retunsus, Plaut.) *to beat, pound back* anything sharp, *blunt, dull; fig., deaden, weaken, restrain, check.* **in,** hostile (534), w. diffingas.

816. **Massagetas,** acc. gov. by in; fr. Massăgĕtæ, -arum, 1st fem., a Scythian people on the E. of the Caspian (mod. Sungaria and Mongolia). **Arabas,** acc. jnd. by -que to Massagetas; fr. Arabes (685). **ferrum** (57), gov. by diffingas.

CARMEN XXXVI. METRE—*The Second Asclepiad.* (Carmen iii.)

817. **Et...et** (2). **thure** (703), instrum. w. placare. **fidibus** (295), jnd. by et to thure. **juvat** (4).

818. **Placare,** pres. inf. act. subj. of juvat; fr. plāco, -āvi, -atum, 1st (trans. of placeo, *to please*) *to make cheerful. To quiet, calm, soothe, assuage. To reconcile, cause to be at peace,* often "*to secure the favour of,*" not implying previous displeasure (W.). **vituli,** gen. s. after sanguine; fr. vĭtŭlus, -i, 2nd mas., *a bull-calf;* vitula, -æ, 1st fem., *a cow-calf.* **sanguine** (225), jnd. by et to fidibus. **debito,** abl. mas. s. ag. w. sanguine; fr. debitus (680); "*due*" whether actually vowed or not (W.).

819. **Custodes,** acc. plu. in app. to Deos; fr. custos (333). **Nŭmĭdæ,** gen. s. after custodes; fr. Nŭmĭda, -æ, 1st mas., cognomen of Gens Plautia or Plotia. This Numida is supposed to have returned from the Cantabrian war w. Augustus, B.C. 25. **Deos** (6), gov. by placare.

820. **Qui** (19), mas. s. ag. w. Numidæ; nom. subj. of dividet (822). **nunc** (21). **Hesperia,** abl. s. gov. by ab; fr. Hesperia (908); here "*the West,*" *i.e.*, Spanish countries. **sospes** (675), mas. s. as adv. attrib. ag. w.

821 Caris multa sodalibus,
822 Nulli plura tamen dividit oscula
823 Quam dulci Lamiæ, memor
824 Actæ non alio rege puertiæ
825 Mutatæque simul togæ.
826 Cressa ne careat pulchra dies nota,
827 Neu promptæ modus amphoræ,
828 Neu morem in Salium sit requies pedum,

qui. **ab** (254), w. sospes. **ultima,** abl. fem. s. ag. w. Hesperia; fr ultimus (280).

821. **Caris,** dat. plu. mas. ag. w. sodalibus; fr. carus (513). **multa,** acc. plu. neut. ag. w. oscula; fr. multus (23). **sodalibus,** dat. (commodi) plu. after (remote obj. of) dividit; fr. sodalis (611), subst.

822. **Nulli** (582), constr. as sodalibus. **plura,** acc. neut. plu. ag. w. oscula; fr. plus (280). **tamen** (111). **dividit,** 3rd s. pres. ind. act. fr. divido (399). **oscula** (359), gov. by (direct obj. of) dividit.

823. **Quam** (582). **dulci,** dat. mas. s. ag. w. Lamiæ; fr. dulcis (2). **Lamiæ** (620), jnd. by quam to nulli. **memor** (745), ag. w. qui (820).

824. **Actæ,** gen. s. fem. ag. w. puertiæ; fr. actus, pf. pass. partc. of ago (43). **non** (55). **alio,** abl. s. mas. ag. w. rege; fr. alius (92). **rege,** abl. (absol. 88) s. fr. rex; here, "*tutor*" or "*schoolmaster*" (very rare use). **puertiæ,** gen. (of matter) s. after memor; fr. puertia, -æ, 1st fem. = pueritia, (puer, 149) *boyhood, childhood, youth.*

825. **Mutatæ,** gen. s. fem. ag. w. togæ; fr. mutatus (77). **simul** (145). **togæ,** gen. s. jnd. by -que to puertiæ; fr. tŏga, -æ, 1st fem., (tego, 177) *garment, covering,* only ante-class. and rare. The outer garment, long, broad and flowing of a Roman citizen in time of peace, hence sts. *peace;* "prætexta," that of magistrates and freeborn children, ornamented with purple; "pura" or "virilis," the unornamented one of the youth who had laid aside the prætexta, which was done at the age of fifteen.

826. **Cressa,** abl. s. ag. w. notâ; fr. Cressa, -æ, fem. of Cres, Cretis; *Cretan, i.e.,* made w. Cretan earth or chalk, *i.e., favourable, lucky,* opp. to carbo. **ne** (745). **careat,** 3rd s. prês. conj. (prohibitive) fr. căreo (649). **pulchra,** nom. fem. s. ag. w. dies; fr. pulcher (421). **dies** (20), nom. s. subj. of careat. **nota,** abl. s. after careat; fr. nota (356).

827. **Neu** (87). **promptæ,** gen. s. fem. pf. pass. part. predic. ag. w. amphoræ; fr. promo (774). **modus** (573), subj. of sit. **amphoræ,** gen. s. after modus; fr. amphŏra, 1st fem., a large oblong vessel w. a handle on each side of the neck, sts. without these handles, for holding oil, wine, honey, etc.

828. **Neu** (87). **morem** (627), gov. by in. **in** (76), *according to.* **Salium** = Saliorum, poet. gen. after morem; fr. Sălii, 2nd mas. (salio, *to leap*). *The leapers,* a college of priests dedicated by Numa to Mars, who armed and bearing the ancilia made processions about Rome, with dances, etc., in the early part of March. Some think that this is the acc. mas. s. fr. Salius, -a, -um, adj. ag. w. morem; *Salian.* **sit** (245), hortative. **rĕquies,** -ētis, 3rd fem.; nom. s. subj. of sit; (re, 659; quiesco, *to rest*) *after rest,* i.e., *repose from* or *after* labour, etc., *relaxation, respite, recreation;* poet. = quies, *rest, repose;* sing. acc. -ētem and -iem, no dat., voc. -ies, abl. -iete and -ie. No plu. **pedum,** gen. plu. after requies; fr. pes (135).

Neu multi Damalis meri
  Bassum Threïcia vincat amystide,
Neu desint epulis rosæ
  Neu vivax apium neu breve lilium.
Omnes in Damalin putres
  Deponent oculos, nec Damalis novo
Divelletur adultero
  Lascivis hederis ambitiosior.

829. **Neu** (87). **multi**, gen. s. neut. ag. w. meri; fr. multus (23). **Dămălis**, -is, 3rd fem.; nom. sing. subj. of vincat. **meri** (507), gen. of quality, a species of descriptive gen. by which, like the abl. of quality, one subst. (in Latin, always w. an epithet) is joined to another for the purpose of describing it in some particular.

830. **Bassum**, acc. s. gov. by vincat; fr. Bassus, -i, 2nd mas. **Threïcia**, abl. fem. s. ag. w. amystide; fr. Thrēĭcius (830). **vincat**, 3rd s. pres. conj. (hortative) act.; fr. vinco, -cĕre, vīci, victum, 3rd trans., *to conquer, overcome, get the better of. Defeat, surpass, exceed, overmatch. Prove conclusively;* absol., *vanquish, prove victorious.* **amystide**, abl. (of means) s. fr. ămystis, -ĭdis, 3rd fem. (Gk.), *immoderate drinking. The emptying of a cup* at one draught.

831. **Desint**, 3rd plu. pres. conj. (hortative) fr. desum, -esse, -fui (-ee, as one syll. in poets), (de, 10; sum, 3) *to be away, be absent, fail, be wanting,* w. ab and abl. or dat., esp. *to fail, be wanting in one's duty* in aiding, assisting, etc. **epulis**, dat. plu. (incommodi) after desint; fr. ĕpŭlum, -i, 2nd neut., plu., heteroclite epulæ, -arum, 1st fem., *sumptuous food, dishes. Banquet, feast, splendid meal,* sing. usu. of a *religious festival* or *banquet to many persons.* **rosæ**, nom. plu. subj. of desint; fr. rosa (149).

832. **Vivax**, -ācis, adj.; nom. neut. s. ag. w. apium; (vivo, 731) *tenacious of life, long-lived.* Of things, *lasting, long, enduring, durable, lively, vigorous, vivacious,* here "*long remaining green.*" **ăpium**, -ii, 2nd neut., nom. s. jnd. by neu to rosæ; (aqua, 22), *parsley, mountain-parsley, celery.* The fragrant leaves of the water-parsley were used by the ancients for making chaplets. **breve**, nom. neut. s. ag. w. lilium; fr. brevis (143), here, *short-lived.* **lilium**, -ii, 2nd neut., nom. s. jnd. by neu to apium; *a lily.*

833. **Omnes**, nom. mas. plu. subj. of deponent; fr. omnis (43). **in** (81). **Damalin** (829), acc. (Gk.) gov. by in. **putres**, acc. mas. plu. ag. w. oculos; fr. pŭter or pŭtris, putre, adj.; (putro, *to moulder, rot*) prop. *stinking, fetid;* meton., *rotten, putrefying, decaying, putrid. Loose, crumbling, friable,* of earth, etc. *Languishing, melting, voluptuous* (here).

834. **Deponent**, 3rd plu. fut. ind. act. fr. dēpōno (642). **oculos**, acc. plu. gov. by deponent; fr. oculus (106). **nec** (19). **Damalis** (829) subj. of divelletur. **novo**, abl. mas. s. ag. w. adultero; fr. novus (42).

835. **Divelletur**, 3rd sing. fut. ind. pass. fr. divello (363). **adultero** (753), abl. (of separation) after divelletur: here ref. to Numida as displacing her other lovers.

836. **Lascivis**, abl. plu. fem. ag. w. hederis; fr. lascivus (495). **hederis**, abl. (of comparison) plu. after ambitiosior; fr. hedera (29). **ambitiosior**, nom. fem. sing. compar. adj. (as adverb. attribute) ag. w. Damalis; fr. ambĭtĭosus, -a, -um, adj.; (ambitio, *a going round*) *going round, surrounding.* Of plants, *entwining, clasping, close-clinging* (here). *Seeking for favour,*

CARMEN XXXVII.—AD SODALES.

837 NUNC est bibendum, nunc pede libero
838 Pulsanda tellus, nunc Saliaribus
839 Ornare pulvinar Deorum
840 Tempus erat dapibus, sodales.
841 Antehac nefas depromere Cæcubum
842 Cellis avitis, dum Capitolio

trying to ingratiate oneself. Of persons, *ambitious.* Of things, *vain, vain-glorious.* Pass., *willingly solicited, much sought, honoured* or *admired.*

CARMEN XXXVII. METRE.—*The Alcaic.* (Carmen ix.)

837. **Nunc** (21). **est** (19), w. bibendum; 3rd sing. ind. pres. of the periphrastic gerundival conjugation (664). **bibendum,** nom. neut. s. gerundive of bibo (518), "bibendum est," impers., *we must drink.* **pede** (135), instrum. **libero,** abl. mas. s. ag. w. pede; fr. līber, lībĕra, lībĕrum adj.; (orig., *doing as one pleases,* ak. to libet, 424). Of persons, *free, unrestricted, unshackled.* Socially, *free,* i.e., *not in slavery.* Politically, *not under a foreign ruler;* bad sense, *licentious.* Of things, *unconfined, unrestrained. Free* or *exempt from,* w. ab. Of things, *unrestrained, dissolute.*

838. **Pulsanda,** nom. fem. s. gerundive ag. w. tellus; fr. pulso (141); und. est; 3rd sing. ind. pres. of gerundival conj. **tellus** (551), subj. of pulsanda (est). **Săliāribus,** abl. plu. fem. ag. w. dapibus; fr. Săliāris, -e, adj.; (Salii, 828) *belonging to the Salii, worthy of the Salii,* i.e., *splendid, sumptuous,* from the sumptuousness of their banquets.

839. **Ornare,** pres. inf. (prolative), almost like a genit. case after tempus; fr. orno, -āre, -āvi, -atum, 1st trans., *to adorn, ornament, embellish,* lit. and fig. esp. *commend, praise. To show honour to, distinguish. To furnish, fit out, provide with necessaries* (class.), *equip, get ready.* **pulvinar,** acc. s. gov. by ornare; fr. pulvīnar, -āris, 3rd neut., *a couch* or *seat* made of cushions and spread over with splendid coverings. In the Lectisternium they were placed for the gods before their statues or altars. **Deorum** (261) after pulvinar.

840. **Tempus** (660), nom. s. subj. of erat. **erat** (98), impf. ref. to past thought, viz., when they began to make their preparations: see Laborabas (643). **dapibus** (741), abl. instrum. w. ornare. **sodales** (631).

841. **Antĕhac,** adv. of time, (ante, 687; hac=hæc) demonst., *before this present time, before now.* Relat., *before that time, formerly, previously* (rare). **nefas** (277), predic. **depromere,** pres. inf. act. subj. of est und.; fr. depromo (239). **Cæcubum** (517), gov. by depromere

842. **Cellis,** abl. of separation, plu. after depromere; fr. cella, -æ, 1st fem., (ak. to cēlo, *to conceal*) *a place for depositing grain* or *fruits,* or for the abode of animals, *granary, stall,* etc. *A small room* or *chamber, closet, cabinet.* **avitis,** abl. plu. fem. ag. w. cellis; fr. avitus (327), "cellis avitis," *i.e., old wine.* **dum** (53). **Capitolio,** dat. (incommodi) after (remote obj. of) parabat; fr. Căpĭtōlium, -ii, 2nd neut., (capitulum; fr. caput, 22) *the Capitol, i.e.,* the temple of Jupiter, at Rome, built on the summit of Mons Saturnius or Tarpeius, by the Tarquinii. More widely the whole hill (Clivus Capitolinus), separated fr. the Palatine hill by the Forum Romanum.

Regina dementes ruinas,
Funus et imperio parabat
Contaminato cum grege turpium
Morbo virorum, quidlibet impotens
Sperare fortunaque dulci
Ebria: sed minuit furorem
Vix una sospes navis ab ignibus,
Mentemque lymphatam Mareotico

843. **Regina** (701), *i.e.*, Cleopatra; nom. subj. of parabat. **dementes,** acc. plu. fem. ag. w. ruinas; fr. dēmens, -ntis, adj.; (de, 10; mens, 349) *out of one's mind* or *senses, beside oneself, mad, foolish;* here transferred from the person to the purpose (W.) **ruinas,** acc. plu. gov. by (direct obj. of) parabat; fr. ruīna, -æ, 1st fem., (ruo, 61) *rushing* or *tumbling down, fall, downfall, ruin, disaster, overthrow, destruction. That which has tumbled down, a building in ruins, ruin.*

844. **Funus,** acc. s. gov. by parabat; fr. funus (231). **et** (2), *also.* **imperio,** dat. s. (constr. as Capitolio) fr. imperium (62).

845. **Contaminato,** abl. s. mas. ag. w. grege; fr. contāmĭnatus, -a, -um, adj.; (cum, 31; tango, 224) *polluted,* fig., *morally polluted, stained with guilt, defiled, impure.* **cum** (31). **grege,** abl. s. gov. by cum; fr. grex (590). **turpium,** gen. plu. mas. ag. w. virorum; fr. turpis (727).

846. **Morbo,** abl. (of cause) s. w. turpium; fr. morbus, -i, 2nd mas., *a sickness, disease, disorder, illness, malady.* Morally, *fault, vice* of mind, *disturbance* of passion, etc. **virorum,** gen. plu. after grege; fr. vir (215). **quidlibet,** acc. s. gov. by sperare; fr. quilibet, quælibet, quodlibet (qui, 3; libet, 424), indef. pronoun, *any one whom you will, no matter who, any, all, the first that comes.* Subst., quidlibet, nom. and acc. s. exp. contempt, *no matter what.* **impŏtens,** -ntis, adj.; nom. fem. s. ag. w. regina, (in, neg.; potens, 89) *powerless, weak, feeble* (902). With gen., *having no power over, unable to control,* esp., *not master of himself,* i.e., *unbridled, headlong, violent, insolent, excessive, furious* of persons and things. Very rare w. inf. as here.; comp. and superl. regular.

847. **Sperare,** pres. inf. (prolative) after impotens; fr. spero (159). **fortuna,** abl. (of cause) s. w. ebria; fr. fortuna (847), "quidlibet impotens sperare," *i.e.*, with no restraint in her dreaming. **dulci** (443), ag. w. fortunâ.

848. **Ebria,** nom. fem. s. jnd. by -que to impotens; fr. ēbrius, -a, -um, adj.; *that has drunk enough, had his fill;* pregn., *drunk, intoxicated;* fig., *drenched, soaked, gorged;* here, *drunken with good fortune;* meton., *abundantly filled, full.* **sed** (591). **minuit,** 3rd s. pf. ind. act. fr. mĭnuo, -uĕre, -ui, -ūtum, 3rd trans. and intrans., (minor, 332) *to make small* or *less;* pass., *grow less. To reduce, diminish, lessen, lower,* lit. and fig. *To limit the power of To break into small pieces,* intrans. very rare. **furorem,** acc. s. gov. by minuit; fr. fŭror, -ōris, 3rd mas., *raging, raving* in sickness or passion, *rage, madness, fury.*

849. **Vix** (34), w. una. **una** (663), ag. w. navis. **sospes** (820), fem. ag. w. navis. **ab** (254), w sospes. **ignibus** (352), gov. by ab.

850. **Mentem** (426), gov. by redegit. **-que** (4), jns. this clause w. prec. **lymphatam,** acc. fem. s. pf. pass. partc ag. w. mentem; fr. lympho, -are, -avi, -atum, 1st trans., (lympha=nympha, 952, panic terrors being attributed

851 Redegit in veros timores
852 Cæsar ab Italia volantem
853 Remis adurgens, accipiter velut
854 Molles columbas aut leporem citus
855 Venator in campis nivalis
856 Hæmoniæ, daret ut catenis
857 Fatale monstrum : quæ generosius

to the agency of the nymphs) *to drive out of one's senses, distrac with fear;* intrans., *become crazy* (very rare). **Mareotico,** abl. (of means) s. fr. Mărĕōtĭcum, -i, 2nd neut., *Mareotic wine,* a sweet wine, prop. neut., (und. vinum) of Mărĕōtĭcus, -a, -um, adj., *of Mărĕa* or *Mărĕōtă,* a city and lake in Lower Egypt, near Alexandria.

851. **Redegit,** 3rd s. pf. ind. act. fr. rĕdĭgo, -ēgi, -ĭgĕrĕ, -actum, 3rd trans., *to drive, lead* or *bring back. To get together, call in, collect, raise* money or the like by selling, etc. *To bring, reduce to* any circumstance, condition, etc., *make* a thing so and so, w. in, sub, ad and acc. *To bring within* a certain number, extent, etc., *lessen, diminish, reduce.* **in,** w. acc. (76). **veros,** acc. plu. mas. ag. w. timores; fr. verus (663), opp. to the terrors of a disordered brain (lymphatam). **timores,** acc. plu. gov. by in; fr. tĭmor, -ōris, 3rd mas., *fear, dread, apprehension, alarm, anxiety, awe, reverence* (rare).

852. **Cæsar** (80), nom. subj. of redegit. **ab** (254), w. volantem. **Italia,** abl. s. gov. by ab; fr. Ītălia, -æ, 1st fem., *Italy.* **volantem,** acc. fem. s. pres. part. act. ag. w. eam (*her*) und., gov. by adurgens; fr. volo (70).

853. **Remis,** abl. (instrum.) plu. w. adurgens; fr. rēmus, -i, 2nd mas., *an oar.* **adurgens,** pres. part. act. nom. mas. s. ag. w. Cæsar; fr. adurgeo, -ēre, no pf., no sup., 2nd trans., (ad, 6; urgeo, 150) *to pursue after.* **accĭpiter,** -tris, 3rd mas.; nom. s. jnd. by velut to Cæsar; (ac, rt. of acus, *a needle,* Gk. πετ-, *to fly;* others der. fr. accipio), general name for *a bird of prey;* usu. *the sparrow hawk.* **velut** (329).

854. **Molles,** acc. fem. plu. ag. w. columbas; fr. mollis (203). **columbas,** acc. plu. gov. by adurgens und. w. accipiter; fr. columba (46). **aut** (131). **leporem,** acc. s. gov. by adurgens und. w. venator; fr. lĕpus, -ŏris, 3rd genly. mas., sts. fem., (leaping animal) *a hare.* **cĭtus,** -a, -um, adj.; nom. mas. s. ag. w. venator; (cieo, *to set in motion*) *put in motion, swift, rapid,* opp. to tardus.

855. **Venator** (26), jnd. by aut to accipiter. **in** (78). **campis** (553), gov. by in. **nĭvālis,** gen. s. fem. ag. w. Hæmoniæ; fr. nĭvālis, -e, adj.; (nivis, 37) *snowy, snow. e.g.,* dies.

856. **Hæmoniæ,** gen. after campis; fr. Hæmŏnia, -æ, 1st fem., poet. name of Thessaly; fr. Hæmon, father of Thessalus. **daret,** 3rd s. impf. (after adurgens, ref. to past time) subj. (in final clause) fr. do (65). **ut,** final (388). **catenis,** dat. plu. after (remote obj. of) daret; fr. catēna (689).

857. **Fatale,** acc. neut. s. ag. w. monstrum; fr. Fātālis, -e, adj.; (fatum, 335) *of* or *belonging to Fate, ordained by Fate, decreed, destined. Bad, dangerous, destructive, fatal* (poet. and post-Aug.). **monstrum,** acc. s. gov. by (direct obj. of) daret; fr. monstrum (42). **quæ** (46), nom. subj. to expavit; fem. s., ag. by the figure *synesis* w. reginam und. in monstrum. **generosius,** neut. s. as adv., *more nobly,* fr. generosior, compar. of generosus, -a, -um, adj.; (full of genus, 45). Of persons, *of good* or *noble birth,*

Perire quærens nec muliebriter
  Expavit ensem nec latentes
    Classe cita reparavit oras.
Ausa et jacentem visere regiam
Vultu sereno, fortis et asperas
  Tractare serpentes, ut atrum
    Corpore combiberet venenum,

good, eminent. Of animals, plants, etc., *of a good* and *noble species, superior, excellent;* fig., *noble-minded, excellent.*

858. **Perire,** pres. inf. (objective) after quærens; fr. pereo (58). **quærens** (562), nom. fem. s. ag. w. quæ. **nec** (19). **mŭlĭēbrĭter,** adv.; (muliebris, -e, adj., *womanly*) *in the manner of a woman, effeminately, in a womanly way.*

859. **Expavit,** 3rd s. pf. ind. act. fr. expăvesco, -scĕre, -vi, no sup., 3rd inceptive, not ante-Aug., (ex, 691; paveo, *to fear*) intrans., *to become greatly terrified, be very much afraid;* trans., *to be very much afraid of, be very terrified at.* **ensem,** acc. s. gov. by expavit; fr. ensis (430). **nec** (16). **latentes,** acc. plu. fem. ag. w. oras; fr. latens (454).

860. **Classe,** abl. (instrum.) s. fr. classis (418). **cita,** abl. fem. s. ag. w. classe; fr. citus (854). **reparavit,** 3rd s. pf. ind. act. fr. reparo (720); here, "sought not to take other shores in exchange for Egypt (M.). **oras,** acc. plu. fr. ora (289). The acc. of place, *whither,* is usually confined to towns and small islands, and to rus (*into the country*), domum (*home*), but in poetry it is used more extensively.

861. **Ausa,** nom. fem. s. pf. part. ag. w. quæ (857); fr. audeo, -ēre, ausus sum, a semi-deponenet vb., like gaudeo, soleo, *to venture* or *dare something,* or to do something. **et** (139), *also.* **jacentem,** acc. s. fem. ag. w. regiam; fr. jacens, pres. partc. of jăceo, -ēre, jăcui, jăcĭtum, 2nd intrans., (intr. of jacio, *to throw down*) *to be thrown* or *cast, lie, lie down. To be dead. To be situate. To lie low, be situated low To be level, calm, quiet. To be prostrate, afflicted* (here). **regiam,** acc. s. gov. by visere; fr. regia (1261).

862. **Vultu,** abl. (of manner) s. fr. vultus (76). **sereno,** abl. s. mas. ag. w. vultu; fr. sĕrēnus, -a, -um, adj.; *clear, fair, bright, serene.* Of a wind, *clearing the sky, bringing fair weather;* fig., *cheerful, glad, joyous, tranquil;* sĕrēnum, -i, 2nd neut., *a clear, bright, serene sky.* **fortis** (165), fem. ag. w. quæ (857). **et** (139). **asperas,** acc. fem. plu. ag. w. serpentes; fr. asper (154).

863. **Tractare,** pres. inf. (prolative, 570) after fortis; fr. tracto, -are, -avi, -atum, 1st trans., (intens. of traho, 130) *to draw violently, drag, tug, haul* (very rare). Without force, *to touch, take in hand, handle,* esp. *prepare* work, *get ready, e.g.,* lanam. *To manage, e.g.,* arms, so fig. pecuniam, casus, etc., *carry on, e.g.,* bellum; "partes, personam," etc., *to represent;* "me, te, se," *conduct* or *balance oneself* well or ill. *To investigate, discuss* anything mentally, orally, or in writing. **serpentes,** acc. plu. gov. by tractare; fr. serpens, -entis, (orig. partc. of serpo, *to creep*), 3rd fem. (und. bestia) mas., (und. draco) *a snake, serpent* (gen. pl. -tum and -tium). **ut,** final (388). **atrum,** acc. neut. s. ag. w. venenum; fr. ater (661).

864. **Corpore,** abl. (instrum.) s. fr. corpus (779). **combiberet,** 3rd s. impf. ind. act. fr. combĭbo, -bĭbere, -bĭbi, no sup., 3rd trans., (cum, 31; bibo, 518) *to drink together with* any one (rare). *To drink up wholly* or *entirely, drink a full draught of, swallow down;* meton., *absorb, imbibe, suck up.* **venenum,** acc. s. gov. by combiberet; fr. venenum (646).

Deliberata morte ferocior;
Sævis Liburnis scilicet invidens
Privata deduci superbo
Non humilis mulier triumpho.

CARMEN XXXVIII.—AD PUERUM.

PERSICOS odi, puer, apparatus,

865. **Deliberata,** abl. s. fem. pf. pass. partc. ag. w. morte; fr. dēlībĕro, -are, -avi, -atum, 1st trans., (de, 10; libro, *to weigh*) *to weigh well in one's mind, deliberate, take counsel about, advise upon.* *To resolve, determine on* after deliberation (here). **morte,** abl. absol. (88) fr. mors (105). **ferocior,** nom. fem. s. compar. ag. w. quæ (857); fr. ferox (167).

866. **Sævis** (306), ag. w. Liburnis. **Liburnis,** dat. (after invidens) pl. fr. Liburna, -æ, 1st fem., (orig. fem. of Liburnus, -a, -um, adj., und. navis) *a light, fast-sailing galley, brigantine.* The Liburni were an Illyrian people betw. Istria and Dalmatia (mod. Croatia). **scilicet,** adv.; (contr. for scire licet, wh. often used for scilicet in anct. lang.) *it is permitted to know, you may know,* confirms or completes the idea of what precedes. *It is evident, clear, manifest, of course, evidently, undoubtedly,* w. inf. in Sall., Plaut., Ter., Lucr. Then as a particle, esp. in answers, *of course, certainly,* esp. ironical *of course, to be sure, forsooth,* when the contrary is meant. Post-Aug., sts., explanatory, *namely, that is to say.* **invidens,** pres. partc. act. nom. fem. s. ag. w. quæ (837); fr. invideo (685).

867. **Privata,** nom. fem. s. ag. w. quæ; fr. prīvatus, -a, -um, adj.; *apart from the state, peculiar to oneself, of* or *belonging to an individual, private* (1273). It is here an adverbial attribute or apposite, *i.e.*, it agrees w. the noun, but is closely connected with the verb, *unqueened, uncrowned.* **deduci,** pres. inf. (prolative, here explanatory) pass. after invidens; fr. dēdūco, -cĕre, -xi, -ctum, 3rd trans., (de, 10; duco, 133) *to lead* or *bring away.* *To lead, fetch, bring* or *draw out;* milit., *to lead off* troops from one place to another. *To lead* to a place, *e.g.*, of conducting a colony to a place; nautical, *to launch* a ship. Of weavers, *to spin out, draw out* the thread, yarn. *To conduct, accompany* a person out of a house as a mark of respect. *To lead about* in a procession (here); mercant., *to subtract, deduct;* fig., *to lead away, withdraw, e.g.*, de sententiâ. **superbo,** abl. s. mas. ag. w. triumpho; fr. superbus (318).

868. **Non** (55). **hŭmĭlis,** -e, adj.; nom. fem. s. ag. w. mulier; (humus, *the ground*) *low, lowly, small, slight.* Of rank, birth, fortune, *base, mean, humble, poor, insignificant, e.g.*, agna (1352). Of language, *low, mean.* Of character, *mean, base, abject.* **mŭliĕr,** muliĕris, 3rd fem.; nom. s. in app to quæ, (ak. to mollis, 203) *a woman, fĕmale,* married or not, sts. *a wife* opp to a maid. **triumpho** (338), of manner.

CARMEN XXXVIII. METRE—*Lesser Sapphic.* (Carmen ii.)

869. **Persicos,** acc. plu. mas. ag. w. apparatus; fr. Persĭcus, -a, -um, adj.; *Persian, Persic. After the Persian manner.* The Persæ orig. people of the country of Persis, -is, aftwds. of the great kingdom of Persia. In 58, Persæ=Parthians. **odi,** collat. osus sum, inf. odisse; defective vb., 1st sing. pf. ind. act., *to hate;* meton., *to dislike, be displeased, vexed at*

870 Displicent nexæ philyra coronæ;
871 Mitte sectari, rosa quo locorum
872 Sera moretur.
873 Simplici myrto nihil allabores
874 Sedulus curo: neque te ministrum

Traces of pres. fms. in non-class. writers. **puer** (644). **apparatus,** acc. plu. gov. by odi; fr. appărātus, -us, 4th mas.; hardly in any class poet but here, (ad, 6; paro, 396) abstract, *a preparing, providing, getting ready;* concr., *tools, implements of war, baggage, engines, supplies; machines, e.g.,* for siege, *a magnificent preparation, magnificence, splendour, pomp.*

870. **Displicent,** 3rd plu. pres. ind. act. fr. displĭceo, -ēre, -ui, -ĭtum, 2nd intrans., (placeo, 263) *to displease,* esp. *to be displeased* or *dissatisfied w. oneself,* w. or without sibi. Dis-, di-, (διά) *apart, asunder,* implies *division, severance, difference, distinction, e.g.,* diduco, esp. of difference in argument, opinion, action, *e.g.,* disputŏ, dissero. In some words it has a neg. sense, *e.g.,* diffido, *to distrust* (so here), sts. intensive, *e.g.,* disperdo, *to destroy utterly.* **nexæ,** nom. fem. plu. pf. pass. part. ag. w. coronæ; fr. necto (619). **philyra,** abl. (instrum.) s. fr. phĭlўra, -æ or philura, -æ, 1st fem. (Gk. *the lime tree*), *the inner bark of the linden tree* of which bands for chaplets were made. **coronæ,** nom. plu. subj. of displicent; fr. corona (475).

871. **Mitte,** 2nd s. pres. imper. act. fr. mitto (38). **sectari,** pres. inf. (objective) after mitte; fr. sector, -ari (old, -arier), -atus sum, 1st depon. trans., (intens. of sequor, 402) *to follow continually;* good sense, *attend, accompany;* bad sense, *chase, pursue,* esp., *hunt* animals; fig., *pursue eagerly, e.g.,* voluptatem; here w. rel. clause. **rosa** (149), nom. s. subj. of moretur. **quo** (145). **lŏcorum,** gen. plu. after quo; fr. locus (543). The genitive of thing measured, loci, locorum, terrarum, gentium, etc., are used w. adverbs of place.

872. **Sera,** nom. fem. s. ag. w. rosa; fr. serus (81). **moretur,** 3rd s. pres. subj. fr. moror (293). The subj. in relat. dependent clause.

873. **Simplici,** dat. fem. s. ag. w. myrto; fr. simplex (153). **myrto,** dat. fem. s. after (indirect obj. of) allabores; fr. myrtus (137). **nihil** (660), gov. by (direct obj. of) allabores. **allabores,** 2nd s. subj. (ut being omitted) pres. (after curo) act. fr. allăbōro, -are, -avi, -atum, 1st traject. trans., (ad, 6; laboro, 235) *to toil much. To add to by labour. Trajective* is a name given to words that gov. a dat. case, viz. verbs or adjs. containing the notions of—(i.) proximity and remoteness; (ii.) demonstration and obscurity; (iii.) gratification and disfavour; (iv.) rule and subservience. This is the dat. of the remoter obj. Verbs which take such a dat. as well as an acc. of the direct or immediate obj. are trajective transitive: those which take this dat. only are trajective intransitive (Kennedy's Latin Grammar, §§ 133-4).

874. **Sēdŭlus,** -a, -um, adj.; nom. mas. s. adv. attribute (867) ag. w. tu und. in allăbōres; (sĕdeo, sēd- as in sĕdo, sēdes) *persisting in* some course of action; good sense, *busy, diligent, zealous, solicitous, assiduous;* bad sense, *officious, obtrusive.* **cūro,** -are, -avi, -atum, 1st trans. and intrans., (cura, 215) *to care for, take* or *have care of, be solicitous for, attend to.* With acc. and gerundive, *to cause* something *to be done, e.g.,* pontem faciendum. With inf. genly. w. negatives (1231). Very rare w. ut or ne or w. subj. alone as here. Polit., *to administer, take charge of, manage* state business; medic, *to heal, cure* a distemper. **neque** (32). **te** (83), gov. by dedecet. **ministrum,** acc. s. in app. to te; fr. mĭnister, -tri, 2nd mas., (manus, 474) *an attendant, waiter, servant. Official assistant. Aider, abettor, supporter.*

Dedecet myrtus, neque me sub arcta
Vite bibentem.

LIBER SECUNDUS.

CARMEN I.—AD ASINIUM POLLIONEM.

Motum ex Metello consule civicum
Belliqne causas et vitia et modos
Ludumque Fortunæ gravesque
Principum amicitias et arma

875. **Dedecet,** 3rd s. ind. pres. act. fr. dēdĕceo, only used in 3rd pers., -dĕcet, -dĕcēre, -dēcŭit, no sup., 2nd intrans., (de, 10; deceo, 134) *it is unseemly, unbecoming,* sts. w. subj. as here, sts. w. inf. (1181). **myrtus** (137), nom. s. subj. of dedecet. **me** (29), jnd. by neque to te. **sub** (21). **arcta,** abl. s. fem. ag. w. vite; fr. arctus, -a, -um, (artus) adj.; (rt. in Gk. *ἄρω joined, fitted, pressed) close, strait, confined;* fig., *straitened, sparing, scanty, small, e.g.,* vincula amoris. Of circumstances, *needy, indigent, e.g.,* arctæ res; here, "tied close over a trellis or otherwise so as to give shade" (W.).

876. **Vite** (477), gov. by sub. **bibentem,** acc. mas. s. pres. part. act. ag. w. me; fr. bibo (518).

BOOK II.

Carmen I.—Metre. *The Alcaic.* (Book I., Carmen ix.)

877. **Motum,** acc. s. gov. by tractas; fr. mōtus, -us, 4th mas., (moveo, 394) *a moving, motion* (class.). *Movement, gesture* of an orator, wrestler; fig., *motion, operation, impulse* of the mind, understanding (animi, ingenii). Of the heart or affections, *affection, passion,* esp. *agitation, disturbance, distress. Divine impulse, inspiration. Commotion, revolt, rising, change.* **ex** (691), here of time. **Metello,** abl. gov. by ex; fr. Mĕtellus, -i, 2nd mas., cognomen in the Gens Cæcilia; here Q. Cæcilius Metellus Celer, cos. B.C. 60. **consule,** abl. s. in app. to Metello; fr. consul, consŭlis, 3rd mas., usu. shrtnd. in s. and plu. cos., but coss. for plu. in 3rd and 4th centuries; *a consul,* one of the two chief magistrates in Rome. In abl. w. name of the cos. or coss. to designate the year, *e.g.,* Orgetorix, M. Messalâ et M. Pisone coss., etc. **civicum,** acc. mas s. ag. w. motum; fr. cīvĭcus, -a, -um, adj.; (civis, 57) *of or pertaining to citizens, civil, civic;* wholly poet. exc. in "civica corona," *the civic crown,* made of oak leaves, bestowed on him who had saved a fellow citizen [civilis in prose].

878. **Belli,** gen. s. after causas; fr. bellum (24). **causas,** acc. plu. jnd. by -que to motum; fr. causa (439). **vitia,** acc. plu. jnd. by et to causas; fr. vitium (59), *crimes* (W.). **modos,** acc. plu. jnd by et to vitia; fr. modus (422), *shifting phases,* now on land, now on sea.

879. **Ludum,** acc. s. jnd. by -que to modos; fr. ludus (73). **Fortunæ,** gen. s. after ludum; fr. Fortuna (209). **graves** (135), ag. w. amicitias.

880. **Principum,** gen. plu. after amicitias; fr. princeps, -cĭpis (86). **amicitias,** acc. plu jnd. by -que to ludum; fr. ămīcĭtia, -æ, 1st fem., *friendship;* in hist., *a league of unity* betw. difft. nations; meton. = amicus (here). **arma** (764), jnd. by et to amicitias.

881 Nondum expiatis uncta cruoribus,
882 Periculosæ plenum opus aleæ,
883 Tractas et incedis per ignes
884 Suppositos cineri doloso.
885 Paullum severæ Musa tragœdiæ
886 Desit theatris: mox ubi publicas

881. **Nondum** (55, 53), *not yet*. **expiatis**, abl. plu. mas. ag. w. cruoribus; fr. expĭātus, pf. pass. part. of expio (65). **uncta**, acc. neut. plu. ag. w. arma; fr. unctus (692). **cruoribus**, abl. (instrum.) plu. with uncta; fr. crŭor, -ōris, 3rd mas., (ak. to curro, *that which runs*) *blood* which flows from a wound, [sanguis, *blood in the veins* or *that is shed*] *the pouring out of blood, murder*; plural of quantity as 1257 (W.).

882. **Periculosæ**, gen. s. fem. ag. w. aleæ; fr. pĕrīcŭlōsus, -a, -um, adj., (periculum, *danger*) *full of danger, hazardous, perilous*. **plenum** (463), ag. w. opus. **opus**, acc. s. in app. to the accusatives in prec. clause; fr. ŏpus, ŏpĕris, 3rd neut., *work, labour, e.g.*, of military, agricultural labour. *Work; building* as the result of labour. *A book. A work of art. Workmanship, artistic skill. Deed, action, performance, business.* **aleæ**, gen. s. after plenum; fr. ālea, -æ, 1st fem., a *casting, playing of a game of hazard, gaming, gambling* w. tesseræ or tali; meton., *anything uncertain* or *doubtful; accident, change, hazard, venture, risk.* This is the gen. of abundance and want, which is of a partitive nature. Horace's object is not to discourage, but to exalt the difficulty of his task (W.).

883. **Tractas**, 2nd s. ind. pres. act. fr. tracto (863). **et** (2). **incedis**, 2nd s. ind. pres. act. fr. incēdo, -ĕre, -cessi, -cessum, 3rd intrans., (in, 76; cedo, 170) *to go in* or *along, proceed, advance*. *Move slowly* or w. *measured step and majestic gait*. Of abstract subjects, *to come to, happen to*. *To enter.* **per** (114) here, *across, over*. **ignes** (271), gov. by per.

884. **Suppositos**, acc. mas. plu. pf. pass. part. ag. w. ignes; fr. suppōno, -ĕre, -pŏsŭi, -pŏsĭtum, 3rd trans. traject., (sub, 21; pono, 104) *to place, put* or *set under*; "suppositus," *hidden under*. *To put in the place* of another, *substitute for* another, esp. falsely or fraudulently, *forge, falsify*. *To put at the end, subjoin.* **cineri**, dat. s. after suppositos; fr. cĭnis, cĭnĕris, 3rd mas. sts. fem. in sing., *ashes*, esp. of a buried corpse, in s. and plu. (1077). *Ruins* of a wasted city; fig., as in all languages, an emblem of destruction. **doloso**, dat. mas. s. ag. w. cineri; fr. dolosus (804).

885. **Paullum**, neut. s. as adv. fr. paullus, -a, um, (paulus) adj.; (ak. to paucus, 1145) *little, small, e.g.*, momentum; "paulo," adv., *by a little, a little, somewhat*. Of time, degree, etc., w. compar. adjs. and advs.; paullum = "paullisper," *for a little while*. **severæ**, gen. s. fem. ag. w. tragœdiæ; fr. severus (633), *solemn, stately*. **Musa**, -æ, 1st fem. (174); nom. s subj. of desit. **tragœdiæ**, gen. s. after musa; fr. trăgœdia, -æ (Gk), 1st fem., *tragedy*. *The tragic art.* Cic. uses it of *great commotion, disturbance*.

886. **Desit**, 3rd s. conj. (hortative) pres. fr. desum (831). **theatris**, dat. (incommodi) plu. after desit; fr. theatrum (511). "For a time cease to write tragedies." **mox** (17). **ubi** (553), here temporal. **publicas**, acc. fem. plu. ag. w. res; fr. publĭcus, -a, -um, adj.; (for pŏpulicus, fr. populus, 32) *of* or *belonging to the people, state* or *community, done for the sake* or *at the expense of the state, common*; "res publica," *commonwealth, state.*

887 Res ordinaris, grande munus
888 Cecropio repetes cothurno,
889 Insigne mæstis præsidium reis
890 Et consulenti, Pollio, curiæ;
891 Cui laurus æternos honores

887. **Res** (298), gov. by ordinaris. **ordinaris,** syncopated for ordinaveris, 2nd s. fut. pf. act. fr. ordĭno, -are, -avi, -atum, 1st trans., (ordo, *order, rank, row*) *to arrange, regulate, set in order, e.g.,* rempublicam. Of a narrative of events, *to draw up in order, narrate, describe* (here). *To reckon, count up. To command, appoint, ordain. To place in a row;* milit., *to draw up in rows or ranks. To appoint* to a civil office, dignity, etc.; see compulerit (590). **grande,** acc. neut. s. ag. w. munus; fr. grandis (173). **munus,** acc. s. gov. by repetes; fr. munus (483), here "*a calling.*"

888. **Cecropio,** abl. s. mas. predicative ag. w. cothurno; fr. Cĕcrŏpius, -a, -um, adj., *of* or *pertaining to Cecrops. Pertaining to Athens. Attic.* "Cecropio cothurno" *tragedy* native to Athens. Cĕcrops, Cecrŏpis, 3rd mas., the most ancient king of Athens. **repetes,** 2nd s. fut. ind. act. fr. repeto (252). **cothurno** abl. s. fr. cŏthurnus, -i, 2nd mas., (Gk.) a high Grecian hunting boot, bound up in front and covering the whole foot, esp. the boot similar in shape to this worn by Athenian actors in tragedy, having high soles [soccus the shoe of comedians], then, *an elevated style.* It is a kind of abl. absol. or emphatic abl. in which the adj. is predicative; subst. and adj. together constitute the circumstance which justifies or limits the main statement (W.).

889. **Insigne,** voc. neut. sing. ag. w. præsidium; fr. insignis (889). **mæstis,** dat. mas. plu. ag. w. reis; fr. mæstus, -a, -um, adj.; (mæreo, 984) *sad, sorrowful, afflicted, dejected, melancholy*=tristis. *Gloomy, severe* by nature. **præsidium,** voc. (2). **reis,** dat. plu. after presidium; fr. reus, rei, 2nd mas., and rea, reæ, 1st fem., *a party to an action;* either *plaintiff* or *defendant,* aftwds. only *the defendant.* More strictly, *one under obligation to do* or *pay anything, one answerable* or *responsible for;* rarely w. gen., *e.g.,* reus voti, *i.e.,* by any vow, *i.e.,* in having attained it. More com. w. gen. of crime, *one accused of;* w. gen. of punishment, *one condemned to.*

890. **Consulenti,** dat. s. fem. pres. part. act. ag. w. curiæ; fr consŭlo, -sŭlĕre, -sŭlui, -sultum, 3rd intrans. and trans., *to consider, reflect, deliberate, take counsel, consult;* w. in and acc., *to be thoughtful for;* with dat., *to care for, take care of, look to, have respect for,* "consulere aliquem," *to ask any one's advice,* "consulere aliquid," *to deliberate upon something, consider;* meton. (effect for cause) *to come to a conclusion, take a resolution, conclude, determine,* w. de aliquo or in aliquem, "boni consulere," *to take in good part, put a favourable construction upon;* here, *in its councils,* absol. (W.). **Pollio,** voc. s. fr. Pollio, -ōnis, 3rd mas., *Assinius Pollio,* friend of Augustus, and founder of the first library at Rome, author of a history of the war between Cæsar and Pompey. The final -o is short, never so in Verg. (M.). **curiæ,** dat. sing. jnd. by et to reis; fr. cūria, -æ, 1st fem., (ak. to Quiris, Quiritis, 7) a building in which the senate held its meetings, *the senate house,* then *the senate* (here).

891. **Cui** (578), mas. s. ag. w. Pollio; dat. after (remote obj. of) peperit. **laurus,** -us and -i, abl. -u (1059), nom. plu. -us, gen. -uum, 2nd and 4th fem.; nom. sing. subj. of peperit; *a laurel tree, laurel,* sacred to Apollo. Victorious generals wore wreaths of it.. *A laurel crown;* its leaves supposed to give poetic inspiration. **æternos,** acc. plu. mas. ag. w. honores; fr.

892 Dalmatico peperit triumpho.
893 Jam nunc minaci murmure cornuum
894 Perstringis aures, jam litui strepunt;
895 Jam fulgor armorum fugaces
896 Terret equos equitumque vultus.
897 Audire magnos jam videor duces
898 Non indecoro pulvere sordidos,
899 Et cuncta terrarum subacta.

æternus, -a, -um, adj.; (ævum, 329; -ternus as in sempiternus, hesternus) *eternal, everlasting* [sempiternus=*lasting during all time*, but measured by time; æternus, *above all time*]. **honores** (304), gov. by peperit.

892. **Dalmatico,** abl. mas. sing. ag. w. triumpho; fr. Dalmătĭcus, -a, -um, adj.; *of Dalmatia* on the east of the Hadriatic; Pollio gained victories over the Parthini, an Illyrian people (Dalmatæ). **peperit,** 3rd sing. pf. ind. act. fr. părio, părĕre, pĕpĕri, partum and parĭtum, 3rd trans., of women, animals, and birds, *bring forth, bear*. Of the earth, etc., *produce;* fig., *create, bring about, accomplish, devise, invent, acquire,* etc., *e.g.*, voluptatem. **triumpho** (338), abl. of manner.

893. **Jam** (37). **nunc** (21). **minaci** (266), neut. ag. w. murmure. **murmure,** abl. (of manner) s. fr. murmur, -ŭris, 3rd neut., *murmuring, muttering sound, any indistinct sound, roaring;* an onomatopœic word, *i.e.*, derived from the sound it expresses. **cornuum,** gen. plu. after murmure; fr. cornu (464).

894. **Perstringis,** 2nd sing. pres. ind. act. fr. perstringo, -ngĕre, -nxi, -nctum, 3rd trans., (per, 114; stringo, *tie, fasten*) *to bind, tie* or *fasten tightly;* fig., *fasten, seize,* of terror seizing a person. *To graze against;* fig., *wound, hurt, annoy. To touch lightly on, narrate briefly* in speaking. Of the ears, *to thrill, stun, deafen.* **aures,** acc. plu. gov. by perstringis; fr. auris (642). **jam** (37). **litui,** nom. plu. subj. of strepunt; fr. lituus (23). **strepunt,** 3rd plu. pres. ind. act. fr. strĕpo, -ĕre, -ui, -ĭtum, 3rd irreg. intrans., *to make a noise, rattle, rustle, rumble, hum, roar.*

895. **Jam,** a case of anaphora, *i.e.*, when instead of a sociative conjunction one or more words are repeated in each clause. **fulgor,** -ōris, 3rd mas. nom. s. subj. of terret; (fulgeo, 203) *lightning, a flash of lightning;* meton., *glitter, gleam, brightness;* fig., *splendour, glory, renown.* **armorum,** gen. after fulgor; fr. arma (226). **fugaces,** acc. plu. mas. ag. w. equos; fr. fŭgax, -ācis, adj., (fugio, 206) *apt to flee, flying swiftly, swift, fleet* (952). *Fleeing from wooers, coy* (1009); fig., *fleeting, transitory* (1233); predic., scares them till they would fain fly (W.).

896. **Terret** (267). **equos** (768), gov. by terret. **equitum,** gen. plu. after vultus; fr. eques (513). **vultus,** acc. plu. jnd. by -que to equos; fr. vultus (76).

897. **Audire,** pres. inf. (prolative) act. after videor; fr. audio (57). **magnos** (85), ag. w. duces. **jam** (37). **videor,** 1st s. pres. ind. pass. fr video (49). **duces,** acc. plu. gov. by audire; fr. dux (88), "audire duces," to hear you reading of, etc. (W.).

898. **Non** (55). **indecoro,** abl. s. mas. ag. w. pulvere; fr. indĕcōrus, -a, -um, adj.; (in, neg.; decorus, 259), *unbecoming, unseemly, shameful, unsightly.* **pulvere** (178), instrumental. **sordidos,** acc. plu. mas, predic. ag. w. duces; fr. sorditus (662).

899. **Cuncta,** acc. plu. neut. jnd. by et to duces; fr. cunctus, -a, -um,

900 Præter atrocem animum Catonis.
901 Juno et Deorum quisquis amicior
902 Afris inulta cesserat impotens
903 Tellure victorum nepotes
904 Rettulit inferias Jugurthæ
905 Quis non Latino sanguine pinguior
906 Campus sepulcris impia prœlia

adj.; (contr. for conjunctus) *all united into one, whole* [cuncti=omnes conjuncti et congregati]. **terrarum** (6), after cuncta. The gen. of the thing measured. **subacta,** acc. plu. neut. pf. pass. partc. predic. ag. w. cuncta; fr. subĭgo, -ĭgĕre, -ēgi, -actum, 3rd trans., (sub, 21; ago, 43) *to bring under, put under* any place. *To work, work up, knead. To press* or *rub down* by the hand. *To overcome, conquer, subdue. To turn up from beneath* the soil, etc., *i.e., dig, plough, cultivate. To urge, push on, e.g.,* a vessel, fig., *to incite, compel, force to* anything; und. "a Cæsare."

900. **Præter** (92). **atrocem,** acc. mas. s. ag. w. animum; fr. atrox (411), *stubborn.* **animum** (448), gov. by præter. **Catonis** (319), after animum.

901. **Juno** (192), nom. s. subj. of cesserat. **Deorum** (261), gen. of the thing distributed after quisquis. **quisquis** (10), nom. mas. s. joined by et, to Juno. **amicior,** nom. mas. s. comparat. adj., predic. ag. w. quisquis; fr. amicus, -a, -um, adj.; (208) *friendly.*

902. **Afris,** dat. plu. after traject. amicior; fr. Āfer, Afri, 2nd mas., the son of *the Lybian Hercules; Afri, Afrorum, the Africans.* "Afer" also as adj.=Hannibal (Hor.). In 1315=*Gœtulian.* **inulta,** abl. s. fem. ag. w. tellure; fr. inultus (87). **cesserat,** 3rd. sing. plpf. ind. act. fr. cedo (170). **impotens** (846), mas. ag. as adv. attribute w. quisquis, "*powerless to aid,*" (M.).

903. **Tellure** (213), abl. (of separation) s. after cesserat. **victorum,** gen. plu. after nepotes; fr. victor (166). **nepotes** (71), acc. direct obj. of rettulit.

904. **Rettulit,** 3rd sing. pf. ind. act. fr. refero (323). **inferias,** acc. plu. predic. in app. to nepotes; fr. infĕriæ, -ārum, 1st fem. plu., (inferi, *those in the nether world) sacrifices in honour of the dead.* On this predicative acc. or acc. of the oblique complement after factitive verbs, see 54. **Jugurthæ,** dat. (commodi) s. after (indirect obj. of) rettulit; fr. Jŭgurtha, -æ, 1st mas., successor of Micipsa, king of Numidia, conquered by Marius.

905. **Quis** (149), ag. w. campus. **non** (55). **Latino,** abl. s. mas. ag. w. sanguine; fr. Lătinus, -a, -um, adj.; *of* or *belonging to Latium.* **sanguine** (225), abl. of means w. pinguior. **pinguior,** nom. mas. s. compar. adj., ag. w. campus; fr. pinguis, -e, adj.; *fat,* opp. to miser; *rich, fertile, plump, in good condition. Thick, dense, e.g.,* coma. Of the mind, *dull, stupid, heavy; calm, quiet, still.*

906. **Campus** (195), subj. of testatur. **sepulcris,** abl. (instrum.) plu. w. testatur; fr. sĕpulcrum, -i, 2nd neut., (sepelio, *to bury) a burial place, grave, tomb, sepulchre.* **impia,** acc. neut. plu. ag. w. prœlia; fr. impius, -a, -um, adj.; (in, neg.; pius 273), *without reverence* or *respect for God, one's parents* or *country; irreverent, undutiful, unpatriotic; abandoned, wicked;* sts. of animals and abstr. things; no compar. **prœlia** (181), gov. by testatur.

Testatur auditumque Medis
Hesperiæ sonitum ruinæ?
Qui gurges aut quæ flumina lugubris
Ignara belli? quod mare Dauniæ
Non decoloravere cædes?
Quæ caret ora cruore nostro?
Sed ne relictis, Musa procax, jocis
Ceæ retractes munera neniæ:

907. **Testatur,** 3rd sing. ind. pres. fr. testor (660). **auditum,** acc. mas. s. pf. pass. part. ag. w. sonitum; fr. audio (57). **Medis,** dat. (of agent) plu. after auditum; fr. Medus (87).

908. **Hesperiæ,** gen. sing. after ruinæ; fr. Hespĕria, -æ, 1st fem., (prop. fem. of Hespĕrius, 674; und. terra). In the sense of the Gks. for *Italy* or as in 820, *Spain*. **sonitum,** acc. sing. jnd. by -que to prœlia; fr. sonitus (24). **ruinæ,** gen. s. after sonitum; fr. ruina (843).

909. **Qui,** interrog.=quis (65); nom. mas. s. ag. w. gurges; always adj.; quis is also a subst. **gurges,** -ĭtis, 3rd mas., nom. s. subj. of est und.; *a raging abyss, whirlpool, waters, sea.* **aut** (131). **quæ,** nom. plu. neut. ag. w. flumina; fr. qui interrog. **flumina** (236), subj. of sunt und. **lugubris,** gen. sing. neut. ag. w. belli; fr. lugubris (574).

910. **Ignara,** nom. neut. plu. predic. ag. w. flumina; fr. ignārus, -a, -um, adj.; (in, neg.; narus=gnarus, *knowing, acquainted with*) *ignorant of, not knowing* a thing, *unacquainted with. Inexperienced in. Exempt from.* Pass., *unknown* (not Cic.); ignara is predic. to gurges and flumina. In the case of a composite subj., the verb and attributes are often constructed with only one of the subjects and mentally supplied with the rest (zeugma); that one will be nearest to the predication and generally the most important. **belli** (878), gen. of matter after ignara. Adjs. of knowledge and ignorance take this gen. **quod,** acc. neut. s. ag. w. mare; fr. qui interrog. (910). **mare** (14), gov. by decoloravere. **Dauniæ,** nom. fem. plu. ag. w. cædes; fr. Daunius, -a, -um, adj.; (Daunias, 550), here *Roman.*

911. **Non** (55). **decoloravare,** 3rd plu. pf. ind. act. fr. decŏlōro, -are, -avi, -atum, 1st trans., (dēcŏlor, *deprived of colour*) *to discolour, deface, disfigure, soil.* **cædes,** nom. plu. subj. of decoloravere; fr. cædes (232).

912. **Quæ** (645), ag. w. ora. **caret,** 3rd sing. ind. pres. fr. carĕo (649). **ora** (289), nom. s. subj. of caret. **cruore,** abl. s. after caret; fr. cruor (881). **nostro,** abl. mas. sing. ag. w. cruore; fr. noster (83).

913. **Sed** (591). **ne,** final (231). **relictis,** abl. plu. mas. ag. w. jocis; fr. relictus (270). **Musa,** voc. s. fr. Musa (174). **prŏcax,** -ācis, adj.; voc. s. fem. ag. w. Musa; (prŏco, *to ask, beg*) *bold, shameless, impudent, insolent, forward, pert, wanton.* **jocis,** abl. absol. plu. fr. jocus (70).

914. **Ceæ,** gen. sing. fem. ag. w. neniæ; fr. Cēus (or Cius), -a, -um, adj. *Of Cea* or *Ceos,* one of the chief of the Cyclades, over against the promontory Sunium, birthplace of Simonides. **retractes,** 2nd sing. pres. subj. act. fr. retracto (in many MSS. -trecto), -are, -avi, -atum, 1st trans. and intrans., (re-, 659; tracto, 863) *to take hold, handle again, handle anew, undertake anew,* esp. mentally, *to reconsider, revise. To withdraw oneself from* an act, *refuse, decline, be reluctant* (class.), rarely w. acc.; here "take up the task which Simonides left unfinished" (W.). **munera** (483), gov. by retractes. **neniæ,** gen. s. after munera; fr. nēnia (næn-), -æ, 1st fem., *a*

Mecum Dionæo sub antro
    Quære modos leviore plectro.

CARMEN II.—AD C. SALLUSTIUM CRISPUM.

NULLUS argento color est avaris
Abdito terris, inimice lamnæ
Crispe Sallusti, nisi temperato
        Splendeat usu.

funeral song, song of lamentation, dirge, etc., recounting the praises of the deceased (1445). *A mournful song, elegy. Hymn of praise, incantation, common* or *ordinary song.*

915. **Mecum** (215). **Dionæo,** abl. s. neut. ag. w. antro; fr. Dionæus, -a, -um, adj.; (Dione, -es, 1st, Gk. *mother of Venus;* more com., *Venus*), *of Dione;* more com., *of Venus.* Dione's grotto, as the scene of love and love songs. **sub** (21). **antro,** abl. sing. gov. by sub; fr. antrum, -i, 2nd neut., (Gk.) *cave, cavern, grotto* (poet.).

916. **Quære,** 2nd sing. pres. imper. act. fr. quæro (245). **modos,** acc. plu. gov. by quære; fr. modus (422). **leviore,** abl. sing. neut. compar. adj., ag. w. plectro; fr. levis (31). **plectro** (623), abl. of quality, which always has an epithet.

CARMEN II. METRE.—*Lesser Sapphic.* (Bk. I., Carmen ii.)

917. **Nullus** (477), nom. mas. s. ag. w. colŏr. **argento,** dat. (acquisitive or possessive) s. after est; fr. argentum, -i, 2nd neut., (orig., *shining*) *silver;* meton., of things made of *silver, silver-plate, silver-work. Money coined from silver, silver coin* (the most current): hence *money* genly. **cŏlor,** -ōris, 3rd mas.; nom. s. subj. of est; *colour* of men, *complexion, hue, beauty. External quality, condition, position, outward appearance. A beautiful brilliant quality. Splendour, lustre;* (here) *general character, cast, colouring, style.* **est** (19). **avaris,** abl. fem. plu. ag. w. terris; fr. ăvārus, -a, -um, adj., (aveo, *to long for*) *eagerly desirous of* something, *avaricious, covetous, greedy of gain;* always except sts. in poetry in a bad sense [avidus, sts. in good sense].

918. **Abdito,** dat. neut. s. ag. w. argento; fr. abdĭtus, -a, -um, *hidden, concealed, secret;* pf. pass. partc., fr. abdo, -dĕre, -dĭdi, -dĭtum, 3rd trans., (ab, 254; do, 65), *to put away, remove;* abdere se, *to retire, withdraw oneself. To hide, conceal, secrete* **terris** (78), local. **inimice,** voc. s. mas. ag. w. Sallusti; fr. inimicus (306). **lamnæ,** dat. s. after traject. inimice; fr. lamna, -æ, (syncopated fr. lamina, -æ) 1st fem., any *thin piece of metal, wood,* etc., *e.g., a layer, plate, leaf,* esp. *thin blade* of a saw, of metal for torturing, etc.

919. **Crispe,** voc. mas. s. ag. w. Sallusti; fr. Crispus, a Roman cognomen. **Sallusti,** voc. s. fr. Sallustius, -ii, the grand-nephew of the Roman historian, died B.C. 20. **nisi** (265), here w. pres. subj. **temperato,** abl. mas. s. ag. w. usu; fr. tempĕrātus, -a, -um, (pf. pass. partc. fr. tempero, 223) *duly arranged* or *prepared* (rare). *Limited, moderate, temperate;* fig. of moral character, speech, etc., *sober, calm, steady,* w. ab (943).

920. **Splendeat,** 3rd s. pres. subj. (hypothetical) ag. w. lamna und.; fr. splendeo (498). **usu,** abl. (of manner) s. fr. usus (625).

921 Vivet extento Proculeius ævo,
922 Notus in fratres animi paterni;
923 Illum aget penna metuente solvi
924 Fama superstes.
925 Latius regnes avidum domando
926 Spiritum, quam si Libyam remotis
927 Gadibus jungas, et uterque Pœnus

921. **Vivet,** 3rd sing. fut. ind. act. fr. vivo (731). **extento,** abl. s. neut. ag. w. ævo; fr. extentus, -a, -um, adj.; *extensive, wide* (1263), pf. pass. part. of extendo, -dĕre, -di, -tum (-sum rare but class.), 3rd trans., (ex, 691; tendo, 34) *to stretch out, spread out, extend;* pass. reflex., *to spread oneself out, extend;* fig., *to extend, spread out, e.g.,* spem; famam. *To increase, enlarge.* Of time, *prolong, continue.* With iter, cursum, and words exp. the act of running, *to do* or *perform vigorously.* **Prŏcŭleius,** -ii, 2nd mas.; nom. s. subj. of vivet; a Roman knight, friend of Aug., who divided his property among his brothers when they had lost their patrimony in the civil war. **ævo** (329), abl. absol., "vivet extento ævo," *shall live beyond the term of life* (W.).

922. **Notus** (46), nom. mas. s. ag. w. Proculeius. **in,** used as in 750, w. animi. **fratres,** acc. plu. gov. by in; fr. frater (90). **animi,** gen. sing. w. notus; fr. animus (448). It is a Gk. gen. of respect. **paterni,** gen. mas. s. ag. w. animi; fr. paternus (513).

923. **Illum** (9), *i.e.,* Proculeius, gov. by agĕt. **aget** (536), *will upbear* (W.). **penna,** abl. (instrum.) s. fr. penna (123). **metuente,** abl. fem. s. ag. w. pennâ; fr. metuens (16). **solvi,** pres. inf. pass. after metuente; fr. solvo (129), metuens solvi, "*that dare not drop*" (W.).

924. **Fama** (330), subj. of aget. **superstes,** -stĭtis, adj.; nom. fem. s. ag. w. fama; (super, 237; sto, 233) *standing* or *remaining beyond* or *longer than;* hence, *remaining alive* after a given time, *surviving, outliving,* genly. w. dat.

925. **Latius,** compar. of late, adv. of latus (550). *In width. Widely, extensively, far and wide, in a widespread manner; among all men;* fig., *copiously, diffusively, at length, e.g.,* loqui. **regnes** (336), potential. **avidum,** acc. mas. s. ag. w. spiritum; fr avidus (487). **domando,** gerund (639) abl. (of manner) fr. domo (338).

926. **Spiritum,** acc. s. gov. by domando; fr. spīrĭtus, -us, 4th mas., (spiro, *to breathe*) *a breathing, blowing.* Concr. of wind or air, *a breath, breeze, exhalation, odour.* Of that which is breathed, *a breath, e.g.,* spiritum ducere. *The breath of life, life;* fig., *a haughty spirit, pride, arrogance. High spirit, courage. Inspiration,* esp. poetic (1318). **quam,** compar. (582) after latius. **si** (7), w. pres. subj. **Libyam,** acc. s. gov. by (direct obj. of) jungas; fr. Lĭbўa, -æ, 1st fem. collat., Gk., Lĭbўe, -es, 1st fem., *Libya.* **remotis,** dat. fem. plu. ag. w. Gadibus; fr. remotus, -a, -um, adj.; (656) *removed, far off, distant, remote, e.g.,* loca (946, 1393); fig., *disconnected, clear from,* only w. ab, *e.g.,* a memoriâ remotus.

927. **Gadibus,** dat. after (remote obj. of) jungas; fr. Gādes, -ium, 3rd plu. fem.; a Phœnician colony on an island of the same name in Hispania Bætica (1017), modern Cadiz. **jungas,** 2nd s. pres. subj. (in hypoth. clause) act. fr. jungo (134). **et,** *and so* (W.). **uterque,** -traque, -trumque, pron. adj.; nom. mas. s. ag. w. Pœnus; (uter, *which of two;* -que, 4) *both one and*

Serviat uni.
Crescit indulgens sibi dirus hydrops,
Nec sitim pellit, nisi causa morbi
Fugerit venis et aquosus albo
Corpore languor.
Redditum Cyri solio Phraaten
Dissidens plebi, numero beatorum

the other, both, each; with partit. gen. uterque nostrum; with plu. verb, *e.g.*, uterque insaniunt; plu. utrique, utræque, utraque used when there are several persons or things on each side, rarely of two single things or persons. **Pœnus** (322), nom. mas. s. subj. of serviat. This refers to Carthage in Africa and her colonies, esp. Nova Carthago in Spain.

928. **Serviat,** 3rd s. pres. subj. act. jnd. by et to jungas; fr. servio (690). **uni,** dat. s. mas. ag. w. tibi und. after serviat; fr. unus (189). Hor. refers to the latifundia or large estates, so common at the time.

929. **Crescit** (329). **indulgens,** pres. part. act. nom. mas. s. ag. w. hydrops; *indulgent, kind, tender to, fond of;* fr. indulgeo, -ēre, -si, -sum, 2nd intrans., *to be courteous, complaisant, kind, indulgent to. To humour, give way to, yield. To be addicted to, indulge in;* trans. w. acc., *to indulge, humour* (poet. and ante-class.). *To concede, allow, permit, e.g.*, usum alicui. **sibi,** dat. mas. s. after traject. indulgens; fr. sui (53). **dirus** (37), nom. mas. s. ag. w. hydrops. **hydrops,** -opis (Gk.) 3rd mas.; nom. s. subj. of crescit; *the dropsy.*

930. **Nec** (19). **sitim,** acc. s. gov. by pellit; fr. sĭtis, -is, 3rd fem., *thirst* only in sing. Of places, plants, etc., *dryness, drought, aridity;* fig., *ardent desire, eagerness, thirst.* **pellit,** 3rd s. pres. ind. act. jnd. by nec to crescit; fr. pello (215), *i.e.*, drinking does not lessen but increase the disease: the actions of the sick man are ascribed to the malady. It cannot quench the thirst till the malady is gone (W.). **nisi** (265), here w. fut. perf. **causa** (439), nom. s. subj. of fugerit. **morbi,** gen. s. after causa; fr. morbus (846).

931. **Fugerit** (283), see compulerit, 590. **venis,** abl. (of separation) pl. fr. vēna, -æ, 1st fem., *a blood vessel, vein,* esp. *an artery.* Of things similar, *e.g.*, *vein* in metal, *streak* in wood; fig., *innermost part* of anything, *innate quality, nature, innermost feelings. Natural bent, genius, disposition* (1362). **ăquōsus,** -a, -um, adj.; nom. mas. s. ag. w. languor; (ăqua, 22), *full of water, rainy, moist, humid, e.g.*, hiems; "languor," *the faintness caused by the water* (W.). **albo,** abl. neut. s. ag. w. corpore; fr. albus (199).

932. **Corpore** (864), abl. (of separation) after fugerit und. **languor,** -ōris, 3rd mas.; nom. s. subj. of fugerit und.; (langueo, *to be languid*) *weakness, faintness, languor, lassitude,* esp. fr. disease; fig., *inertness, apathy, illness, infirmity.*

933. **Redditum,** acc. mas. s. pf. pass. partc. ag. w. Phraaten; fr. reddo (95). **Cyri,** gen. after solio; fr. Cȳrus, -i, 2nd mas., founder of the Persian Empire, whose successors the Parthian Arsacidæ claimed to be. **solio,** dat. s. after redditum; fr. sŏlĭum, -ii, 2nd neut., (sedeo, *to sit*) *a seat,* esp. *chair of state, throne.* Poet., *rule, sway, dominion.* **Phraaten,** acc. s. gov. by eximit; fr. Phraates, -æ, 1st fem. (Gk.), name of several Parthian kings.

934. **Dissidens,** nom. fem. sing. pres. part. act. ag. w. virtus; fr. dissĭdeo,

Eximit Virtus populumque falsis
Dedocet uti
Vocibus, regnum et diadema tutum
Deferens uni propriamque laurum,
Quisquis ingentes oculo irretorto
Spectat acervos.

-ēre, -sēdi, -sessum, 3rd intrans., (dis, 870; sedeo, *to sit*) *to be remote from, divided, separated* (rare). *To disagree, think differently* w. dat. (rare). Of things, *to be unlike, dissimilar, different, be opposed to.* **plebi,** dat. s. after traject. dissidens; fr. plebs, plēbis, (anciently plebei and plebi) 3rd fem., *the multitude* or *the many* opp. to the few. Roman political term, the *common people, commons,* opp to Patricians, *i.e.*, senators and knights [populus, *collective people* including senate]. Poet. and post-Aug., *the lower classes, mass.* **numero** (649), abl. of separation after eximit. **beatorum,** gen. plu. mas. after numero; fr. beatus (142).

935. **Eximit,** 3rd s. pres. ind. act. fr. exĭmo, -ĭmĕre, -ēmi, -emptum, 3rd trans., (ex, 691; emo, *to buy*) *to take out, take away, remove. To free, deliver from, e.g.*, e vinculis, or abl. or dat., *e.g.*, morti. *To take away, banish, e.g.*, curas. Of time, *consume, waste.* **Virtus,** -ūtis, 3rd fem.; nom. s. subj. of eximit; (vir, 215) *manliness, manhood, i.e.*, all the corporeal and mental excellences of man, *strength, vigour, bravery; capacity, worth, excellence;* so of things, *worth, value, power. Moral perfection, virtuousness. Virtue* personified; here "*the judgment of a virtuous man.*" **populum,** acc. s. subj. of uti; fr. populus (32). **-que** (4), jns. this to prec. clause. **falsis,** abl. fem. plu. ag. w. vocibus; fr. falsus, -a, -um, adj.; (orig. pass. of fallo, 272) *deceptive, feigned, pretended, counterfeit, false.*

936. **Dedocet,** 3rd s. ind. pres. act. fr. dēdŏceo, -cēre, no pf , no sup., 2nd trans.; (de, 10; doceo, 29) *to cause to unlearn, unteach.* **uti,** pres. inf. after dedocet; fr. ūtor, ūti, ūsus sum, 3rd depon., *to use, make use of, avail oneself of, employ, practice, exercise,* w. abl. (instrumental).

937. **Vocibus,** abl. plu. after uti; fr. vox (259). **regnum** (318), gov. by (direct obj. of) deferens. **diadema,** acc. sing. jnd. by et to regnum; fr. diadēma, -ătis, (Gk.) neut., *a royal headdress, diadem.* **tutum** (453), predic. ag. w. diadema.

938. **Deferens,** pres. part. act. nom. fem. s. ag. w. virtus; fr. defĕro, -ferre, -tŭli, -lātum, irreg. trans., (de, 10; fero, 138) *to bear, bring away, carry, bring down,* w. in and acc. of place. *To bring over* and *give to one, transfer, deliver, e.g.*, aliquid ad aliquem or alicui (here). *To give an account of, report* by speech or writing. *To impeach* a man about something, *inform against* him. **propriam,** acc. fem. s. predic. ag. w. laurum; fr. proprius (9). **laurum,** acc. s. jnd. by -que to diadema; fr. laurus (891).

939. **Quisquis** (901), mas. s. ag. w. uni; nom. subj. to spectat. **ingentes,** acc. plu. mas. ag. w. acervos; fr. ingens (216). **oculo,** abl. (instrum.) s. fr. oculus (106). **irretorto,** abl. s. mas. ag. w. oculo; fr. irretortus, -a, -um, adj.; (in, neg.; re-, 659; torqueo, *to turn, twist*) *not turned back;* oculis irretortis, *without looking back again.*

940. **Spectat,** 3rd s. pres. ind. act. fr. specto, -are, -avi, -atum, 1st trans. and intrans., (intens. of -specio, which is only used in compds.) *to look at, gaze at, watch, observe,* esp. at a play, actor, etc. Of places, *to face, be situated towards. To examine, try, test;* fig., *look at, behold, see. To look to* a thing as a guide or pattern, *have in view, aim at, endeavour after. To*

CARMEN III.—AD DELLIUM.

941 ÆQUAM memento rebus in arduis
942 Servare mentem, non sĕcus in bonis
943 Ab insolenti temperatam
944 Lætitia, moriture Delli,
945 Seu mæstus omni tempore vixeris,
946 Seu te in remoto gramine per dies
947 Festos reclinatum bearis
948 Interiore nota Falerni.

pertain or *have regard to* a thing. *To judge, try, test.* **acervos**, acc. plu. gov. by spectat; fr. ăcervus, -i, 2nd mas., (rt. ac-, of a thing brought to a point) *a heap.*

CARMEN III. METRE.—*The Alcaic.* (Bk. I., Carmen ix.)

941. **Æquam**, acc. fem. s. ag. w. mentem; fr. æquus (141). **memento** (201). **rebus**, abl. plu. gov. by in; fr. res (62). **in** (78). **arduis**, abl. fem. plu. ag. w. rebus; fr. arduus (125).

942. **Servare**, pres. inf. (prolative) act. after memento; fr. servo (96). **mentem** (426), gov. by servare. **non** (55). **secus**, adv.; comp. sĕcius (sequor, 402), orig. *following*, then *later* than. *Otherwise, differently, not so.* With a neg. non, haud secus, *not otherwise, even so, just so.* **in** (941). **bonis**, abl. fem. plu. ag. w. rebus und.; fr. bonus (581).

943. **Ab** (254), w. temperatam. **insolenti**, abl. fem. s. ag. w. lætitiâ; fr. insolens (156). **temperatam**, acc. s. fem. ag. w. mentem; fr. temperatus (919).

944. **Lætitia**, abl. s. gov. by ab; fr. lætitia (625). **moriture**, voc. s. mas. ag. w. Delli; fr. moriturus (654). **Delli**, voc. s. fr. Dellius, -ii, 2nd mas.

945. **Seu** (27), depends on moriture. **mæstus** (889), nom. mas. s. ag. w. tu und. in vixeris. **omni**, abl. neut. s. ag. w. tempore; fr. omnis (43). **tempore**, abl. (of point of time) sing. fr. tempus (660). **vixeris**, 2nd sing. fut. pf. act. fr. vivo (731); see compulerit (590).

946. **Te** (83), gov. by bearis. **in** (78). **remoto**, abl. neut. s. ag. w. gramine; fr. remotus, (656) *retired, quiet.* **gramine**, abl. s. gov. by in; fr. gramen (414). **per** (114). **dies**, acc. plu. gov. by per; fr. dies (20).

947. **Festos**, acc. plu. mas. ag. w. dies; fr. festus, -a, -um, adj.; *of* or *belonging to holidays*, (opp. to working days) *solemn, festive.* **reclinatum**, pf. pass. part. acc. sing. mas. ag. w. te; fr. reclīno, -are, -avi, -atum, 1st trans., (re-, 659; -clino, whence declino) *to lean* or *bend backwards*, esp. w. acc. pers. pron. or pass. refl., *to bend oneself back*, i.e., *lean, recline. To rest, repose.* **bearis**, syncopated for beaveris, 2nd sing. fut. pf. act. fr. beo, -are, -avi, -atum, 1st trans., *to make happy, bless, gladden, refresh* any one. *To make happy with, enrich with, reward with* anything, *e.g.*, aliquem aliquâ re.

948. **Interiore**, abl. fem. s. ag. w. notâ; fr. intĕrior, -ius, gen. -ōris. Compar. adj.; (fr. obsol., interus, -a, -um) *inner, interior.* As a partitive attribute, *the inner part* of anything. *Nearer, closer to* any object (here to the wall). *More inland, more up the country;* fig., *more close* or *intimate*, *e.g.*, societas. *More hidden, secret.* **nota** (826), instrum. w. bearis; here

Quo pinus ingens albaque populus
Umbram hospitalem consociare amant
Ramis? Quid obliquo laborat
Lympha fugax trepidare rivo?
Huc vina et unguenta et nimium breves
Flores amœnæ ferre jube rosæ,
Dum res et ætas et Sororum

ref. to the name of the wine and the consul in whose year it was bottled, attached to the amphora (W.). **Falerni** (634), after nota.

949. **Quo,** adv. orig. abl. of qui; (i.) interrog., *whither? where?* (genly. w. loco, loci, etc.) *for which reason? wherefore? whence?* Of persons, *to whom? to what end* or *purpose? why?* here; (ii.) relat., *for which reason, wherefore, whence, because. To* or *in which place, whither;* (iii.) *to the end that, in order that;* final used for ut, esp. w. a comparative word; (iv.) eo...quo w. two comparatives, *the more...the more.* **pinus** (375), one member of composite subj. of amant. **ingens** (216), nom. fem. s. ag. w. pinus. **alba,** nom. fem. s. ag. w. populus; fr. albus (199). **pōpŭlus,** -i, 2nd fem.; nom. s. jnd. by -que to pinus; *poplar tree; populus alba, i.e., silver poplar.*

950. **Umbram,** acc. s. gov. by consociare; fr. umbra (205). **hospitalem,** acc. fem. s. ag. w. umbram; fr. hospĭtālis, -e, adj.; (hospes, 386) *relating to a guest* or *host; hospitable.* **consŏcĭare,** pres. inf. act. obj. after amant; fr. consŏcĭo, -are, -āvi, -atum, 1st trans., (cum, 31; socio, *to unite*) *to make common, share with* one. *To associate, join.* **amant,** 3rd plu. pres. ind. act. fr. amo (86).

951. **Ramis,** abl. (instrum.) plu. fr. rāmus, -i, 2nd mas., *a branch, bough, twig;* meton., *a tree.* **Quid** (229). The answer to this as well as to quo (949) is implied—"that we may make merry there." **obliquo,** abl. s. mas. ag. w. rivo; fr. oblīquus, -a, -um, adj.; *sidelong, slanting, awry,* "ab obliquo, ex obliquo," *from the side, sideways. Not straight.* **laborat,** 3rd s. ind. pres. act. fr. laboro (235).

952. **Lympha,** -æ, 1st fem.; nom. s. subj. of laborat; (=nympha, 31) *a water-nymph. Water* over which a nymph presides, *stream, river, fountain.* **fugax** (895), nom. fem. s. ag. w. lympha. **trepidare,** pres. inf. (prolative exp. purpose, 570) act. after laborat; fr. trĕpĭdo, -are, -avi, -atum, 1st intrans., *to hurry with alarm, bustle about anxiously, be confused* or *agitated.* Of flame, *flare, quiver.* Of mind (1397), trans., *to tremble at through fear.* **rivo,** abl. (of place) s. fr. rivus (198). "Frets in its haste to escape down its tortuous channel" (W.).

953. **Huc,** adv.; *to this place;* huc illuc, huc atque illuc, *hither and thither.* Meton., non-local, *to this point, so far.* Huccine? *hitherto? to this?* **vina** (282), gov. by ferre. **unguenta,** acc. plu. jnd. by et to vina; fr unguentum, -i, 2nd neut., (ungueo, 692) *ointment, unguent, perfume.* **nimium** (53), w. breves. **breves,** acc. plu. mas. ag. w. flores; fr. brevis (143), *short-lived, i.e.,* ere they be withered (W.).

954. **Flores** (619), jnd. by et to unguenta. **amœnæ,** gen. s. fem. ag. w rosæ; fr. amœnus (449). **ferre** (804), after jube. **jube,** 2nd s. pres. imper. act fr. jubeo (494). **rosæ,** gen. s. after flores; fr. rosa (149)

955. **Dum** (53). **res** (167), *i.e., property, fortune;* one member of compos. subj. of patiuntur. **ætas** (284), nom. s. jnd. by et to res **sororum,** gen. plu. after fila; fr. soror (578), *i.e.,* the Fates, Clotho, Lachesis, and Atropos.

956 Fila trium patiuntur atra.
957 Cedes coëmptis saltibus et domo
958 Villaque, flavus quam Tiberis lavit,
959 Cedes, et exstructis in altum
960 Divitiis potietur heres.
961 Divesne prisco natus ab Inacho,
962 Nil interest, an pauper et infima

956. **Fila,** nom. plu. jnd. by et to ætas; fr. fīlum, -i, 2nd neut., (old fm., hilum) *a thread* of anything woven; poet. of the *thread* of life spun by the Fates. Of things like a thread, *string, cord, filament, fibre, e.g.,* lyræ, *i.e.,* strings. *Outline, contour, shape, form, e.g.,* corporis, mulieris. Of speaking or writing, *texture, sort, quality, style.* **trium,** gen. plu. fem. ag. w. sororum; fr. tres, neut. tria; num. adj. card.; *three.* **patiuntur,** 3rd. plu. pres. ind. fr. patior (18). **atra,** nom. plu. neut. ag. w. fila; fr. ater (661).

957. **Cedes,** 2nd s. fut. ind. act. fr. cedo (170). **coëmptis,** abl. plu. mas. ag. w. saltibus; fr. coëmptus (697). **saltibus,** abl. (of separation) plu. after cedes; fr. saltus, -us, 4th mas., *a woody district* used for pasture, *woodland pasture,* esp. *a forest pass, a mountain pass.* **domo** (117), jnd. by et to saltibus, "the city house," opp. to villa.

958. **Villa,** abl. s. jnd. by -que to domo; fr. villa, -æ, 1st fem., (prob. dimin. of vīcus) *country-house, country-seat, farm.* **flavus** (49), nom. mas. s. ag. w. Tiberis. **quam** (70), fem. s. ag. w. villa; acc. gov. by lavit. **Tiberis** (958), nom. subj. of lavit. **lavit,** 3rd s. pres. ind. act. fr. lăvo, -are and -ĕre, lăvāvi and lāvi, lăvatum, lautum and lōtum, 1st and 3rd (always 3rd in Hor. Odes) trans. and intrans., *to wash, bathe, lave;* intrans. or pass. reflex., *to bathe oneself, bathe.* Of a river, *wash, flow against* or *close by.* Of tears, *to wet, moisten, bedew.* Of blood, etc., *to sprinkle, wet;* fig., *wash away, wash out.*

959. **Cedes** (957). **exstructis,** pf. pass. partc. abl. fem. plu. ag. w. divitiis; fr. exstruo, -struere, -struxi, -structum, 3rd trans., (ex, 691; struo, *to build*) *to pile* or *heap up thoroughly;* esp., *to build up, raise, rear, construct,* lit. and fig., *e.g.,* virtutem. **in** (76). **altum,** acc. sing. neut. gov. by in; fr. altus (43); "exstructus in altum," *piled up on high.*

960. **Divitiis,** abl. gov. by potietur; fr. dīvĭtĭæ, -ārum, 1st fem. plu., (dives, 270) *riches, wealth.* **potietur,** 3rd s. fut. ind. fr. pŏtior, pŏtīri, pŏtītus sum, 4th depon., *to become master of, get possession of, acquire* w. gen., acc., and abl. *To be master of, hold possession of.* **hēres,** herēdis, 3rd com.; nom. s. subj. of potietur; *an heir, heiress;* ex asse heres, *sole heir.*

961. **Dives** (270), nom. mas. s. ag. w. tu und. in moreris. **-nĕ,** enclitic interrog. particle. It asks indifferently [num expects a negative, nonne an affirmative answer]. Here folld. by an in a double question, *whether...or.* **prisco,** abl. mas. s. ag. w. Inacho; fr. priscus, -a, -um, adj.; (rt. in prior, 120) *of* or *belonging to former times, old, olden, ancient,* esp. w. a notion of what is *venerable,* having ref. to the earliest and best times. *Former, previous.* **natus** (679), nom. mas. s. ag. w. tu und. in moreris. **ab** (254). **Inacho,** abl. gov. by ab; fr. Inăchus (-os), -i, 2nd mas., the first king of Argos, here representing remote antiquity.

962. **Nil** (125), adv., as in 378. **interest,** 3rd s. pres. ind. fr. intersum (82), impers.; the clause "divesne...Inacho" being really the subject. **an** (317). **pauper** (781), jnd. by an to dives. **infima,** abl. fem. s. ag. w. gente; fr. infĭmus=imus (276). Of place, *the lowest, nethermost, last.* **As**

963 Dē gente sub divo moreris,
964 Victima nil miserantis Orci.
965 Omnes eodem cogimur, omnium
966 Versatur urna sērius ocius
967 Sors exitura et nos in æternum
968 Exilium impositura cymbæ.

a partitive attribute, *the lowest part of.* Meton., *meanest, basest* in quality or rank, *e.g.*, infimo loco natus.

963. **De** (10). **gente,** abl. s. gov. by de; fr. gens (41). **sub** (25). **divo,** abl. s. gov. by sub; fr. divum (89), *i.e., the heaven.* **moreris,** 2nd s. pres. subj. in indirect question (218), fr moror (293).

964. **Victima,** -æ, 1st fem.; nom. sing. in app. to tu und. in moreris; (vincio, 207) *a beast for sacrifice* adorned w. the fillet (vitta), fig., *a victim.* **nil** (125), adv. **miserantis,** pres. part. gen. mas. s. ag. w. Orci; fr. mĭsĕror, -ari, -atus sum, 1st depon. trans and intrans., (miser, 160) *to lament, deplore, bewail,* esp. of a lamenting speech. *To pity, compassionate,* w acc. **Orci,** gen. sing. after victima; fr. Orcus (658).

965. **Omnes** (833), ag. w. nos und. in cogimur. **eodem,** adv., (prop. abl. s. mas. fr. idem, 1132, ŭnd. loco) prop., *to the same place;* fig., *to the same position* or *degree, to the same matter, thereto.* **cogimur,** 1st plu. pres. ind. pass. fr. cogo (434), *we are driven.* **omnium,** gen. plu. mas. after sors; fr. omnis (43).

966. **Versatur,** 3rd s. pres. ind. pass. fr. verso, -are, -avi, -atum, 1st trans., (intens. of verto, 780), *to turn much* or *often, keep turning, turn frequently. To turn up* the soil w. spade, etc. *To drive about* cattle for pasture; here *to shake. To twist, bend, e.g.*, naturam (in good sense), *distort* (in bad sense). *To turn over* in the mind, *meditate upon. To vex, harass, e.g.*, spes versat mentes. Pass. reflex., *to turn* or *whirl round. To turn oneself about much in* a place, *dwell, remain in;* fig., *to be situated, circumstanced, e.g.*, in malis. *To occupy, busy oneself with, be engaged in,* w. in, circa, etc. **urna,** abl. (instrum.) s. fr. urna, -æ, 1st fem., *a water-pot, water-jar, wine-jar,* esp. vessel into which were thrown the voting tablets or lots, *voting urn. The urn* of fate, from which the lot of every one's destiny was drawn. *A cinerary urn.* **serius,** compar. of sero, (adv. of serus, 81) *at a late hour* of the day or night (rare but class.), *at a late period of time. Too late.* Superl. serissime. **ocius,** neut. of ocior (84), as adv., *more quickly;* superl., *very quickly;* "serius ocius," we say "sooner or later;" w. exitura.

967. **Sors,** sortis, 3rd fem.; nom. s. subj. of versatur; (sero) *a lot* (here of death). *Anything used to determine chance, a casting lots, decision by lot, oracular response* often written on a little tablet, *prophecy. Fate, destiny. Chance, condition. Share, part.* **exitura,** nom. fem. s. fut. partc. ag. w. sors; fr. exeo, -īre, -ĭi (rarely -īvi), -itum, irreg. intrans. and trans., (ex, 691; eo, 51), *to go out* or *forth, go away* w. ab, ex, de or abl. alone; milit., *to move out, march out;* fig., exire e or de vitâ, *to die.* Of time, *to run out, end, expire. To extend beyond* a limit or measure, with acc. *to pass beyond,* esp. *to avoid, evade, ward off, e.g.*, tela, vim. **nos** (143), direct obj. of impositura. **in,** of purpose (192). **æternum,** acc. neut. s. ag. w. exilium; fr. æternus (821).

968. **Exilium,** acc. sing. gov. by in; fr. exĭlĭum, -ĭi, 2nd neut., (exul, *an exile*) *a banishing from one's native shore;* meton., *place of exile, retreat.*

CARMEN IV.—AD XANTHIAM PHOCEUM.

969 Ne sit ancillæ tibi amor pudori,
970 Xanthia Phoceu! Prius insolentem
971 Serva Briseïs niveo colore
972 Movit Achillem;
973 Movit Ajacem Telamone natum
974 Forma captivæ dominum Tecmessæ;
975 Arsit Atrides medio in triumpho

impositura, nom. fem. s. fut. partc. act. jnd. by et to exitura; fr. impōno, -ĕre, -pŏsui, -pŏsĭtum, impostus syncop. for impŏsitus, 3rd trans. traject., (in, 76; pono, 104) *to put into; nautical, to put on board* a ship w. in and acc. *To put* or *lay on* or *upon*; fig., *to impose* or *inflict upon*. *To set, give* or *assign to*, esp., *to set over* as overseer, commander, etc. With dat. alone, *impose upon, deceive, cheat.* **cymbæ,** dat. after (remote obj. of) impositura; fr. cymba, -æ, 1st fem., *a boat, skiff,* esp. Charon's *boat,* in which sense "cumba," is said to be the form preferred (W.).

Carmen IV. Metre—*The Lesser Sapphic.* (Bk. I., Carmen ii.)

969. **Ne,** prohibitive w. pres. conj. (745). **sit** (245). **ancillæ,** gen. (objective) sing. after amor; fr. ancilla, -æ, 1st fem. (dimin. for anicula), *a maidservant, handmaid.* **tibi** (93), acquisitive after sit. **amor** (364), subj. of sit. **pudori,** dat. s. after sit; fr. pudor (173). The predicative dat. (462).

970. **Xanthia,** voc. s. fr. Xanthias (Gk.)=Flavius. **Phoceu,** voc. s. fr. Phoceus, (Gk.) *Phocian. Of Phocis.* **prius** (120), *i.e.,* before your time, *i.e.,* before now. **insolentem,** acc. mas. s. ag. w. Achillem; fr. insolens (156).

971. **Serva,** -æ, 1st fem.; nom. s. in app. to Briseïs; (ἐρύω, *one dragged away, taken captive*) *a female-slave; waiting woman;* servus, -i, 2nd mas., *a servant, serving-man.* **Brīsēis,** -ĭdos, 3rd fem.; nom. subj. of movit; Gk. fem. patronymic. Hippodamia dau. of Briseïs and slave of Achilles, from whom Agamemnon took her. **niveo,** abl. mas. s. ag. w. colore; fr. nĭveus, -a, -um, adj.; (nix, 37) *pertaining to snow, snowy, snow-white.* **colore,** abl. (of means) s. fr. color (917); niveo colore, *snow-white beauty.*

972. **Movit,** 3rd s. pf. ind. act. fr. moveo (394). **Achillem,** acc. s. gov. by movit; fr. Achilles (418).

973. **Movit** (972). **Ajacem** (403), gov. by movit. **Telamone,** abl. (of origin) after natum; fr. Tĕlămon or Tĕlămo, -ōnis (Gk.), 3rd mas., an Argonaut of Salamis, father of Ajax and Teucer. **natum,** acc. mas. s. ag. w. Ajacem; fr. natus (679).

974. **Forma** (755), nom. s. subj. of movit. **captivæ,** gen. s. fem. ag. w. Tecmessæ; fr. captīvus, -a, -um, adj.; (capio, 1388) *taken prisoner, captive, caught, taken.* Of things, *plundered, taken as booty, spoiled;* meton., *pertaining to captives, e.g.,* crines. **dominum,** acc. s. in app. to Ajacem; fr. dominus (6). **Tecmessæ,** gen. s. after forma; fr. Tecmessa, -æ, 1st fem., dau. of King Teuthras, mistress of Ajax.

975. **Arsit,** 3rd s. pf. ind. act. fr. ardeo, -ēre, arsi, arsum, 2nd intrans., (ak. to aridus, *dry*) *to be on fire, burn, blaze, e.g.,* tædæ. Of eyes, *to flash, sparkle, shine.* Of colours, *to glisten, glitter. To be inflamed* or *excited,*

976 Virgine rapta,
977 Barbaræ postquam cecidere turmæ
978 Thessalo victore et ademptus Hector
979 Tradidit fessis leviora tolli
980 Pergama Graiis.
981 Nescias, an te generum beati

strongly affected w. passion, love (here), etc. With inf., *to desire ardently* to do, etc. With acc., *to be violently in love with.* **Atrides** (269), *i.e.*, *Achilles;* nom. subj. of arsit. **medio**, abl. s. mas. ag. w. triumpho; fr. mĕdius, -a -um, adj.; *that is in the middle* or *midst, middle.* As a partitive attribute, *in the middle of. Middle,* i.e., *not extreme. Of a middle kind, middling, tolerable, moderate. Undetermined, undecided. Ambiguous, indefinite.* **in** (941). **triumpho** (338), gov. by in.

976. **Virgine**, abl. absol. s. fr. virgo (63). **rapta**, abl. fem. s. pf. pass. partc. ag. w. virgine; fr. rapio (489); here "taken captive by him." The abl. absol. here=a clause w. a causal conj.

977. **Barbaræ**, nom. fem. plu. ag. w. turmæ; fr. barbarus (626). **postquam**, temp. adv., also separated, post...quam, *after that, so soon as, when.* With ind. unless notion of *cause* is involved. **cĕcidĕre**, 3rd plu. pf. ind. act. fr. cădo, -ĕre, cĕcĭdi, cāsum, 3rd intrans., *to fall down, be precipitated, sink down* (genly. poet., in prose occĭdo, decĭdo, etc., used). *To fall dead, die. To be subjected to, belong to* anything. *To agree with. To fall to one's lot, happen to* any one. *To lose strength* or *value, perish, decay, die away, cease.* **turmæ**, nom. plu. subj. of cecidere; fr. turma, -æ, 1st fem., prop. a division of Roman cavalry, one-tenth of an ala, consisting first of thirty, then of thirty-two men. *Troop, squadron* of horse; meton., *crowd, throng, band, body.*

978. **Thessalo**, abl. s. mas. ag. w. victore; fr. Thessalus (188); here ref. to Achilles and his Myrmidons. **victore**, abl. absol. (88) s. fr. victor (166). **ademptus**, pf. pass. part. nom. mas. s. ag. w. Hector; fr. adimo (595). **Hector**, -ŏris, 3rd mas.; nom. subj. to tradidit; *Hector,* son of Priam and Hecuba.

979. **Tradidit**, 3rd s. pf. ind. act. fr. trado (614). **fessis**, dat. plu mas. ag. w. Graiis; fr. fessus, -a, -um, adj.; (usu. given as partc. of fatiscor. *to grow weary*) *weary, tired, fatigued, worn out, feeble;* here "in their weariness" (W.). **leviora**, acc. neut. plu. ag. w. Pergama; fr. levior (591). The predic. acc. after factitive tradidit (903). **tolli**, pres. inf. (prolative) pass. after leviora; fr. tollo (8).

980. **Pergama**, acc. direct obj. of tradidit; fr. Pergăma, -orum, 2nd neut., (s. Pergamon, -i, Gk.) *the citadel of Troy, Troy.* **Graiis**, dat. after (remote obj. of) tradidit; fr. Graii (1318).

981. **Nescias**, 2nd s. conj. (potential) act. fr. nescio, -īre, -īvi or -ĭi, -ītum, 4th trans., (ne-, 41; scio, 277) *not to know, to be ignorant.* With inf., *not to be aware that* something is taking place or *not to know how,* etc., *i.e., to be unable.* "Nescio quis, quid, quomodo, unde," etc., *I know not who, what, how, whence=some one, something, somehow,* etc., to express ignorance with regard to some particular or to indicate that it is trifling, unimportant. **an** (317), here in indirect quest. (218). **te** (83), gov. by decorent. **generum**, acc. s. in appos. to te; fr. gĕner, gĕnĕri, 2nd mas., *a daughter's,* sts. *a granddaughter's* or *great-granddaughter's husband; son-in-law.* **beati**, nom. mas. plu. ag. w. parentes; fr. beatus (142).

982 Phyllidis flavæ decorent parentes:
983 Regium certe genus et Penates
984 Mæret iniquos.
985 Crede non illam tibi de scelesta
986 Plebe dilectam, neque sic fidelem,
987 Sic lucro aversam potuisse nasci
988 Matre pudenda.

982. **Phyllidis**, gen. s. after parentes; fr. Phyllis, -ĭdis or -ĭdos, 3rd fem. (Gk.). **flavæ**, gen. s. fem. ag. w. Phyllidis; fr. flavus (49). **decorent**, 3rd plu. pres. subj. (in indirect quest.) fr. dĕcŏro, -are, -avi, -ātum, 1st trans., (decus, 2) *to adorn, embellish, grace, beautify*, lit. and fig. (1280). **parentes**, nom. plu. subj. of decorent; fr. parens (59).

983. **Regium**, acc. neut. s. ag. w. genus; fr. rēgĭus, -a, -um, adj.; (rex, 1) *of* or *belonging to a king, kingly, royal, regal*; fig., *splendid, magnificent, distinguished*; rēgia, -æ, 1st fem., (und. domus) *royal palace, castle, fortress, residence. The court. Royal tent* in a camp. *The court, i.e.*, king and his courtiers, (und. urbs) *a royal city, residence, capital.* **certe**, adv. of certus, *fixed, certain, with certainty, certainly, surely, of a truth* objectively [certo subjective, *e.g.*, certo scio, only in comic poets, and in Cic. chiefly in Epistles]. **genus** (71), gov. by mœret. **Penates**, acc. jnd. by et to genus; fr. Pĕnātes, -ium, 3rd mas. plu., (rt. PEN- in penetrare, penitus, exp. idea of *entering, interior*). *Deities of the interior*, old Latin guardian deities of the household and the state. *A dwelling, home.*

984. **Mæret**, 3rd s. pres. ind. act. fr. mæreo, -ēre, -ui, mœstum., (akin to miser, 160) 2nd intrans., *to be sad, mourn, grieve, lament*, trans., *to mourn over, bemoan, lament.* **iniquos**, acc. plu. mas. ag. w. Penates; fr. iniquus (83).

985. **Crede**, 2nd s. pres. imper. act. fr. credo (93). **non** (55). **illam**, acc. s. fem. subj. of esse und.; fr. ille (9) ref. to Phyllis. **tibi** (93), of agent after dilectam. **de** (10). **scelesta**, abl. s. fem. ag. w. plebe; fr. scĕlestus, -a, -um, adj.; (scelus, 65) *wicked, villanous, infamous, accursed, knavish, roguish.*

986. **Plebe**, abl. s. gov. by de; fr. plebs (934). **dilectam**, acc. fem. s. predic. ag. w. illam; fr. dilectus, -a, -um, *loved, beloved, dear*; pf. pass. part. of dīlĭgo, -lĭgĕre, -lexi, -lectum, 3rd trans., (dis, 870, exp. choice among several; lego, *to pick out*) *to value* or *esteem highly, love* (1009, 1431; of things, 1122) "de scelestâ plebe," goes closely w. dilectam, as an extension of its meaning, sts. called a tertiary predicate. "Believe that in her thou hast not loved one from the rabble crowd" (W.). **neque** (32). **sic** (89), w. fidelem. **fidelem**, acc. fem. s. ag. w. subj. (puellam or feminam) of potuisse; fr. fidelis (27).

987. **Lucro**, abl. (of separation) s. after aversam; fr. lucrum (246). **aversam**, acc. fem. s. (constr. as fidelem) fr. āversus, -a, -um, adj.; (ab, 254; verto, 780) *turned off* or *away. On the back side, behind, back*; fig., *disinclined to, alienated from, unfavourable, opposed*, w. ab, *e.g.*, a Musis aversus. **potuisse**, pf. inf. jnd. by neque to esse und. in prec. clause after crede; fr. possum (372). **nasci**, pres. inf. (prolative) after potuisse; fr. nascor, nasci, natus sum, 3rd depon. intrans., *to be born, spring, be descended from.* Of trees, *grow up, rise up*, Of abstract things, *arise, spring forth, be produced. To originate from, be produced by.*

988. **Matre** (421), abl. of origin (972) after nasci. **pudenda**, abl. s.

Brachia et vultum teretésque suras
Integer laudo; fuge suspicari,
Cujus octavum trepidavit ætas
    Claudere lustrum.

CARMEN V.—AD AMATOREM LALAGES.

Nondum subacta ferre jugum valet
Cervice, nondum munia comparis
    Æquare, nec tauri ruentis
        In Venerem tolerare pondus.

fem. ag. w. matre; fr. pŭdendus, -a, -um, (prop. gerundive of pudeo, 809) *of which one ought to be ashamed, shameful, scandalous, disgraceful.*

989. **Brachia** (227), acc. gov. by laudo. **vultum,** acc. s. jnd. by et to brachia; fr. vultus (76). **teretes** (28), ag. w. suras; *well-turned, shapely* (W.). **suras,** acc. plu. jnd. by -que to vultum; fr. sūra, -æ, 1st fem., *the calf of the leg.*

990. **Integer** (537), ag. w. ego und. in laudo. **laudo** (17), 1st s. pres. ind. act. **fuge** (245). **suspicari,** pres. inf. (objective) after fuge; fr. suspĭcor, -āri, -atus sum, 1st depon. trans., (suspicio, *suspicion*) *to mistrust, suspect,* rare. *To apprehend, surmise, suppose.*

991. **Cujus** (287), mas. s. ag. w. demonst. (Eng., *one,* i.e., *me*) und. after suspicari, gen. after ætas. **octavum,** acc. neut. s. ag. w. lustrum; fr. octāvus, -a, -um, adj.; (octo, *eight*) *the eighth.* **trepidavit,** 3rd s. pf. ind. act. fr. trepido (952), *hastens.* **ætas** (284), subj. of trepidavit.

992. **Claudere** (264), prolative (exp. purpose, 570) after trepidavit. **lustrum,** acc. s. gov. by claudere; fr. lustrum, -i, 2nd neut., (orig., *that which expiates*) *an expiatory offering* made by the censors for the people every five years, and in which a swine, a sheep and a bull (suovetaurilia) were offered: hence *a period of five years.*

Carmen V. Metre—*The Alcaic.* (Bk. I. Carmen ix.)

993. **Nondum** (881), w. valet. **subacta,** abl. s. fem. ag. w. cervice; fr subactus (899). **ferre** (804), prolative after valet. **jugum** (804), gov. by ferre. **valet** (772), ag. w. juvenca und. fr. follg.

994. **Cervice,** abl. (instrum.) s. fr. cervix (346). **nondum** (881). **munia,** acc. gov. by æquare; fr. mūnia, -orum, in class. age only in nom. and acc., *duties, functions;* esp., *official* or *professional duties.* **comparis,** gen. s. after munia; fr. compar, -ăris, abl. -i, gen. plu. -um, (cum, 31; par, 180) *like, equal to* another, sts. subst., *an equal, companion, comrade, colleague. Spouse, consort, mate, partner.*

995. **Æquare,** pres. inf. (prolative) act. after valet und. fr. prec. clause; fr. æquo, -avi, -atum, 1st trans., (æquus, 141) *to make even, lay smooth. To make equal to, equalize with,* w. cum or dat. *To place* a thing *on an equality with, compare to,* w. cum or dat. Intrans., *to become equal to, attain to, be equal with* w. acc. or dat. "Munia comparis æquare," *to match the labours of a yokefellow.* **nec** (19). **tauri,** gen. s. after pondus; fr. taurus, -i, 2nd mas., *a bull, bullock, steer.* **ruentis** (61), mas. ag. w. tauri.

996. **In** (192). **Venerem** (737), gov. by in. **tolerare,** pres. inf. act.

997 Circa virentes est animus tuæ
998 Campos juvencæ, nunc fluviis gravem
999 Solantis æstum, nunc in udo
1000 Ludere cum vitulis salicto
1001 Prægestientis. Tolle cupidinem
1002 Immitis uvæ : jam tibi lividos
1003 Distinguet Autumnus racemos

jnd. by nec to æquare; fr. tŏlĕro, -avi, -atum, 1st trans., (lengthened fm. of rt., tol-, whence tollo, 8) *to bear, support, endure, sustain, e.g.*, dolorem. *To support, nourish by food, wealth*, etc. **pondus,** acc. s. gov. by tolerare; fr. pondus, -ĕris, 3rd neut., *a weight* used in a scale. *Heaviness* of a body. *Heavy body, mighty mass;* fig., *load, burden, weight. Consequence, importance, consideration, influence, authority. Oppressive weight, burden*=ŏnus.

997. **Circa** (98), *i.e.*, engaged in. **virentes,** acc. mas. plu. ag. w. campos; fr. virens (249). **est** (19). **animus** (448), nom. s. subj. of est. **tuæ,** gen. s. fem. ag. w. juvencæ; fr. tuus (175).

998. **Campos,** acc. plu. gov. by circa; fr. campus (195). **juvencæ,** gen. s. after animus; fr. jŭvenca, 1st fem., *a young woman, girl. A young cow, heifer;* jŭvencus, -i, 2nd mas., *a young man* (1089), *a young bullock.* **nunc** (21), folld. by nunc, *at one time...at another time.* **fluviis** (525), instrum. w. solantis. **gravem** (169), ag. w. æstum.

999. **Solantis,** pres. part. gen. s. fem. ag. w. juvencæ; fr. sōlor, -ari, -ātus sum, 1st depon. trans., *to comfort, console, solace*, of persons. *To soothe, ease, lighten, assuage, mitigate*, of things [consolor is the more class. word]. **æstum,** acc. s. gov. by solantis; fr. æstus (466). **in** (78). **udo** (735), ag. w. salicto.

1000. **Ludere,** pres. inf. (prolative) after prægestientis; fr. ludo (730). **cum** (31). **vitulis,** abl. plu. gov. by cum; fr. vitulus (818). **salicto,** abl. s. gov. by in; fr. sălictum, -i, 2nd neut., (salix, *a willow*) *a plantation* or *thicket of willows.*

1001. **Prægestientis,** gen. s. fem. pres. part. act. ag. w. juvencæ; fr. prægestio, -īre, -īvi or -ĭi, -ītum, 4th trans., (præ, *beyond* others; gestio, *to delight*) *to desire greatly, delight.* **tolle,** 2nd s. pres. imper. act. fr. tollo (8). **cupidinem,** acc. s. gov. by tolle; fr. cupido (70).

1002. **Immitis** (746), ag. w. uvæ. **uvæ,** gen. (objective) s. after cupidinem; fr. uva (518). **jam** (37). **tibi** (93), commodi after distinguet. **lividos,** acc. plu. mas. ag. w. racemos; fr. lividus (226); here "*dull blue*" (W.).

1003. **Distinguet,** 3rd s. fut. ind. act. fr. distinguo, -guĕre, -xi, -ctum, 3rd trans., (dis-, 870; stinguo, *to prick*, orig. to *prick asunder, separate by points*) *to separate, divide, part* rare, mostly poet., *e.g.*, crimen. *To separate* things according to their differences, *i.e., distinguish, discriminate, e.g.*, vero falsum. *To ornament by pricking in different places*, hence, *to set off, adorn, decorate.* **Autumnus** (auctumnus), -i, 2nd mas.; nom. s. subj. of distinguet; (augeo, *to increase*) *the Autumn*, fr. Sept. 22nd (sun's entrance into Libra) to Dec. 22nd (setting of Pleiades); meton., *produce of autumn; harvest.* **racemos,** acc. plu. gov. by distinguet; fr. răcēmus, -i, 2nd mas., *stalk* of a cluster of grapes, etc. *Bunch of berries, cluster of grapes.*

1004 Purpureo varius colore.
1005 Jam te sequetur: currit enim ferox
1006 Ætas et illi, quos tibi dempserit,
1007 Apponet annos; jam proterva
1008 Fronte petet Lalage maritum:
1009 Dilecta, quantum non Pholoë fugax,
1010 Non Chloris albo sic humero nitens,
1011 Ut pura nocturno renidet
1012 Luna mari, Cnidiusve Gyges,

1004. **Purpureo,** abl. s. mas. ag. w. colore; fr. purpureus (788). **varius** (299), nom. mas. s. ag. w. Auctumnus, *motley coloured.* **colore** (971), of manner w. distinguet.

1005. **Jam** (37). **te** (83), gov. by sequetur. **sequetur,** 3rd s. fut. ind. fr. sequor (402). **currit,** 3rd s. ind. pres. act. fr. curro (684). **enim** (212). **ferox** (167), fem. ag. w. ætas (fero, 138, *bearing oneself along*); good sense, *impetuous, courageous, spirited*; bad sense, *wild, savage, headstrong, insolent*; here of time like "an unbroken horse."

1006. **Ætas** (284), subj. of currit. **et** (2). **illi** (91), fem. after (indirect obj. of) apponet. **quos** (3), mas. plu. ag. w. annos; acc. gov. by dempserit. **tibi** (93), incommodi after dempserit. **dempserit,** 3rd s. fut. pf. ag. w. ætas; fr. demo (20); see 590.

1007. **Apponet,** 3rd s. fut. ind. act. fr. appono (247). **annos,** acc. plu. gov. by (direct obj. of) apponet; fr. annus (722). **jam** (37). **proterva,** abl. s. fem. ag. w. fronte; fr. protervus (472).

1008. **Fronte** (749), instrumental. **petet,** 3rd s. fut. ind. act. fr. peto (126). **Lalage** (546), nom. subj. of petet. **maritum,** acc. s. gov. by petet; fr. maritus (455).

1009. **Dilecta,** nom. fem. s. ag. w. Lalage; fr. dilectus (524); und. a te, *by thee.* **quantum,** neut. s. fr. quantus (393), as adv., *as much as, so much as. As far as, so far as*; "quantum in aliquo" or "ad aliquem," *as far as concerns* one; meton., w. tantum or alone *as soon as*, sts. w. comparatives for quanto, *the more, in the greater degree.* **non** (55). **Pholoë** (833), subj. of dilecta est und. **fugax** (952), ag. w. Pholoë.

1010. **Non** (55). **Chlōris,** -ĭdis (Gk., *greenness*) 3rd fem.; subj. to dilecta est und. **albo,** abl s. mas. ag. w. humero; fr. albus (199). **sic,** correlative to ut (201). **humero,** abl. (instrum.) s. fr. humerus (67). **nitens** (383), nom. fem. s. ag. w. Chloris.

1011. **Ut,** comparative (199). **pura,** nom. fem. s. ag. w. luna; fr. purus, (498) *free from mist* (W.). **nocturno,** abl. neut. s. ag. w. mari; fr. nocturnus, -a, -um, adj.; (nox, 144) *of the night.* Of persons who do anything *at night* (poet. and post.-Aug.). **renidet,** 3rd s. pres. ind. act. fr. rĕnīdeo, -ēre, no pf., no sup., 2nd intrans., (re-, 659; niteo, 161) *to shine again* (here), *shine back, glitter, be bright* (1354), esp. *to shine* or *beam for joy, be glad, cheerful. To smile, laugh* (so conversely ridere used for splendere).

1012. **Luna** (133), nom. s. subj. of renidet. **mari** (424), of place whence, *from the sea.* **Cnidius** (Gn-), -a, -um, adj.; nom. mas. s. ag. w. Gyges; (Cnidos, 701) *of* or *belonging to Cnidos.* **-ve** (186). **Gȳges,** -is or -æ, 3rd mas.; nom. s. jnd. by -ve to luna, as subj. of renidet und.

1013 Quem si puellarum insereres choro,
1014 Mire sagaces falleret hospites
1015 Discrimen obscurum solutis
1016 Crinibus ambiguoque vultu.

CARMEN VI.—AD SEPTIMIUM.

1017 SEPTIMI, Gades aditure mecum et
1018 Cantabrum indoctum juga ferre nostra et
1019 Barbaras Syrtes, ubi Maura semper

1013. **Quem** (74), mas. s. ag. w. Gyges; acc. gov. by (direct obj. of) insereres. **si,** here w. impf. subj. in protasis and apodosis (sumptio ficti) the condition, exp. by protasis, is purely imaginary (Ken., p. 469). **puellarum,** gen. plu. after choro; fr. puella (254). **insereres,** 2nd s. impf. subj. act. fr. insero (85) in protasis. **choro,** dat. after (remote obj. of) insereres; fr. chorus (31).

1014. **Mire,** adv. of mirus (1225) w. falleret; *wonderfully, exceedingly;* mire quam, *wonderfully how,* i.e., *excessively, exceedingly.* **sagaces,** acc. plu. mas. ag. w. hospites; fr. săgax, -ācis, adj.; (sagio) *of quick perception, with acute senses;* chiefly *keen-scented;* fig. intellectually *quick, keen, acute, shrewd.* **falleret,** 3rd s. impf. subj. act. in apodosis; fr. fallo (272). **hospites,** acc. plu. gov. by falleret; fr. hospes, mas. of hospita (386), "*strangers who come in*" (W).

1015. **Discrimen,** -ĭnis, 3rd neut; nom. s. subj. of falleret; (dis-, 870; cri- in cerno, *to separate*) *intervening space, interval, distance, separation;* fig., *a distinction, difference. The point that decides a thing, critical point, turning point, crisis. Dangerous moment, risk, hazard.* **obscurum,** nom. neut. s. ag. w. discrimen; fr. obscurus (199). **solutis,** abl. mas. plu. pf. pass. part. ag. w. crinibus; fr. solvo (129).

1016. **Crinibus** (476), abl. (instrum.) w. falleret. **ambiguo,** abl. mas. s. ag. w. vultu; fr. ambiguus (213). **vultu** (862), jnd. by -que to crinibus.

CARMEN VI. METRE—*The Lesser Sapphic.* (Bk. I., Carmen ii.)

1017. **Septimi,** voc. s. fr. Septĭmĭus, -ii, 2nd mas., Septĭmĭa, -æ, 1st fem., the name of a Rom. gens; here Titus Septimus, a poet. **Gades,** acc. gov. by aditure; fr. Gades (927). **aditure,** voc. mas. s. fut. part. act. ag. w. Septimi; fr. adeo, -ire, -īvi or -ĭi, -ĭtum, irreg. trans. and intrans., (ad, 6; eo, 51) *to go to* or *approach* a person or thing w. ad, in, absol., etc. *To go to* or *up to* one for the purpose of asking, addressing him., etc. *To approach* in a hostile manner, *attack;* fig., *to undertake, enter upon* an employment. *To undergo, submit to, e.g.,* labores. **mecum** (215).

1018. **Cantabrum,** acc. sing. jnd. by et to Gades; fr. Cantăber, -bri, plu., Cantăbri, -ōrum, 2nd mas., *people of Cantabria,* a province of Hispania Tarraconensis, subjugated by Agrippa, A.U.C. 734; adj., Cantăbrĭcus, -a, -um. **indoctum,** acc. mas. s. ag. w. Cantabrum; fr. indoctus, -a, -um, adj.; (in, neg.; doceo, 29) *untaught, unlearned, unskilful.* **juga** (755), gov. by ferre. **ferre** (804), prolat. after indoctum. **nostra,** acc. neut. plu. ag. w. juga; fr. noster (83).

1019. **Barbaras,** acc. plu. fem. ag. w. Syrtes; fr. barbarus (626). **Syrtes** (541), jnd. by et to Cantabrum. **ubi** (553), relative. **Maura,** nom. fem. s. ag. w. unda; fr. Maurus (538). **semper** (158).

Æstuat unda;
Tibur Argeo positum colono
Sit meæ sedes utinam senectæ,
Sit modus lasso maris et viarum
Militiæque!
Unde si Parcæ prohibent iniquæ,
Dulce pellitis ovibus Galæsi
Flumen et regnata petam Laconi
Rura Phalanto.
Ille terrarum mihi præter omnes

1020. **Æstuat,** 3rd s. pres. ind. act. fr. æstuo, -āre, -avi, -atum, 1st intrans., (æstus, 466) *to be warm* or *hot, feel warm* or *hot.* Of the passions, *to be inflamed, excited, agitated.* Of the sea, *to rise in waves* or *billows, surge,* *To undulate, have a wave-like motion.* *To waver, vacillate, be uncertain.* **unda** (316), subj. of æstuat.

1021. **Tibur** (478), nom. s. subj. of sit. **Argeo,** dat. mas. s. ag. w. colono; fr. Argēus, -a, -um=Argīvus, *Argive* or *Grecian.* **positum,** pf. pass. part. nom. neut. s. ag. w. Tibur; fr. pono (104). **colono,** *i.e.*, Tiburnus, dat. (of agent) s. after positum; fr. colonus (782).

1022. **Sit** (245), optative. **meæ** (96), gen. s. fem. ag. w. senectæ; fr. meus (96). **sedes** (46), predic. after sit. **utinam,** w. pres. subj. (814). **senectæ,** gen. s. after sedes; fr. senecta (727).

1023. **Sit,** ag. w. Tibur, as in 1022. **modus** (573), predic. after sit. **lasso,** dat. mas. s. ag. w. mihi (acquisitive) und. after sit; fr. lassus, -a, -um, adj., (ak. to languidus, laxus) *faint, weary, tired;* fig., *exhausted, enfeebled, weak;* no comp., no sup. **maris** (164), a Gk. genit. after lasso (see 537, 922). **viarum,** gen. plu. jnd. by et to maris; fr. via (664).

1024. **Militiæ,** gen. s. jnd. by -que to viarum; fr. militia (481).

1025. **Unde** (291), relat. ref. to Tibur. **si,** w. pres. ind. (32). **Parcæ,** nom. plu. subj. of prohibent; fr. Parca, -æ, 1st fem., (paro, *to bring about*) *she who brings* or *assigns one's destiny.* Plu., the Fates, Nona, Decuma, Morta (Gk., Clotho, Lachesis, Atropos). **prohibent,** 3rd plu. pres. ind. act. fr. prohibeo (628). **iniquæ,** nom. fem. plu. ag. w. Parcæ; fr. iniquus (83).

1026. **Dulce,** acc. neut. s. ag. w. flumen; fr. dulcis (2). **pellitis,** dat. plu. mas. ag. w. ovibus; fr. pellītus, -a, -um, adj., (pellis, 1434) *covered* or *clad with skins;* here to protect the wool. **ovibus,** dat. plu. after traject. dulce; fr. ŏvis -is, acc. -im, abl. -i, 3rd fem. and mas., *a sheep.* **Galæsi,** gen. after ovibus; fr. Gălæsus, -i, 2nd mas., a river of Magna Græcia, near Tarentum (Galeso).

1027. **Flumen,** acc. s. gov. by petam; fr. flumen (236). **regnata,** pf. pass. partc. acc. neut. plu. ag. w. rura; fr. regno (336). The passive use of an intrans. verb is not common. **petam,** 1st s. fut. ind. act. fr. peto (126). **Laconi,** dat. mas. s. ag. w. Phalanto; fr. Lăco, -ōnis (Gk.), *Laconian, Lacedæmonian;* as subst., *a Lacedæmonian.*

1028. **Rura** (17), jnd. by et to flumen. **Phalanto,** dat. (of agent) after regnata; fr. Phălantus, -i, 2nd mas., a Spartan leader of the Parthenii, who founded Tarentum.

1029. **Ille** (337), ag. w. angulus. **terrarum** (6), gen. of the thing distri-

1030 Angulus ridet, ubi non Hymetto
1031 Mella decedunt viridique certat
1032 Bacca Venafro.
1033 Ver ubi longum tepidasque præbet
1034 Jupiter brumas, et amicus Aulon
1035 Fertili Baccho minimum Falernis
1036 Invidet uvis.

buted or measured, after angulus. **mihi** (277), dat. commodi, or ethical after ridet. **præter** (92) here=*beyond, more than.* **omnes** (217), ag. w. angulus und.

1030. **Angulus** (254), nom. s. subj. of ridet. **ridet,** 3rd s. pres. ind. act. fr. rideo (69). **ubi,** relat. (553). **non** (55). **Hymetto,** dat. s. after traject. decedunt; fr. Hȳmettus, -i, 2nd mas. and fem., a mountain near Athens, famed for honey and marble.

1031. **Mella,** nom. plu. subj. of decedunt; fr. mel, mellis, 3rd neut., (abl. s. melli, Plaut.; gen. and dat. plu. obsolete) *honey; fig., sweetness, agreeableness, e.g.,* in speech, etc. **decedunt,** 3rd plu. pres. ind. act. fr. dēcēdo, -cēdĕre, -cessi, -cessum, 3rd intrans., (de-, 10; cedo, 170) *to go away, depart.* Of heavenly bodies, *set.* Polit., *to retire from* one's province at the expiration of one's term of office; fig., of persons, *to die.* Of things, *to abate, cease, subside. To give up, resign, forego, yield, swerve from, e.g.,* one's opinion, right, etc. *To give up, yield to* another, *i.e.,* his will, superior advantages, etc., *to be second to,* very rare (here). **viridi,** dat. neut. s. ag. w. Venafro; fr. viridis (21). **-que** (4). **certat** (8).

1032. **Bacca,** -æ, 1st fem.; nom. s. subj. of certat; *a berry,* esp. of the olive; *any round fruit* growing upon a tree. *A pearl.* **Venafro,** dat. s. after traject. certat; fr. Vĕnafrum, -ī, 2nd neut., a very old Samnite town in the north of Campania, celebrated for olive oil.

1033. **Ver,** acc. s. gov. by præbet; fr. ver (129). **ubi** (553), local. **longum,** acc. neut. s. ag. w. ver; fr. longus (73). **tepidas,** acc. fem. plu. ag. w. brumas; fr tĕpĭdus, -a, -um, adj.; (tepeo, 148) *moderately warm, lukewarm.* Rarely opp. to heat, ardour, etc., *cooled, faint, languid.* **præbet,** 3rd s. pres. ind. act. fr. præbeo, -ēre, -ŭi, -ĭtum, 2nd trans., (præ, *before;* habeo, 641) *to hold forth, proffer, offer;* meton., *grant, furnish, supply, e.g.,* panem; fig., *render, e.g.,* operam reipublicæ; Præbere se, *to give up, surrender oneself,* and w. predic. acc., *to prove oneself something, exhibit oneself* as *something. To produce, originate, give rise to, e.g.,* gaudium, opinionem.

1034. **Jupiter** (66), subj. of præbet. **brumas,** acc. plu. jnd. by -que to ver; fr. brūma, -æ, 1st fem., (for brĕvĭma, fr. brevis, 142) *the shortest day* in the year; *winter solstice, winter-time.* **amicus** (613), adj.; nom. mas. s. ag. w. Aulon. **Aulon,** -ōnis, 3rd mas.; nom. s. subj. of invidet; a vine-bearing mountain and the valley near it in Calabria.

1035. **Fertili,** dat. mas. s. ag. w. Baccho; fr. fertĭlis, -e, adj.; *fruitful, fertile* (1268), fig., *productive;* act., *fertilizing, e.g.,* Nilus; here, "*giver of fertility.*" **Baccho,** dat. s. after trajective amicus; fr. Bacchus (482). **minimum** (284), within vidct. **Falernis,** dat. plu. fem. ag. w. uvis; fr Falernus (518).

1036. **Invidet,** 3rd sing. ind. pres. fr. invideo (685), *i.e.,* as being inferior. **uvis,** dat. plu. after traject. invidet; fr. uva (518).

Ille te mecum locus et beatæ
Postulant arces; ibi tu calentem
Debita sparges lacrima favillam
Vatis amici.

CARMEN VII.—AD POMPEIUM VARUM.

O SÆPE mecum tempus in ultimum
Deducte Bruto militiæ duce,
Quis te redonavit Quiritem

1037. **Ille** (337), ag. w. locus. **te** (83), gov. by postulant. **mecum** (215). **locus** (543), nom. sing., one member of composite subj. of postulant. **beatæ**, nom. fem. plu. ag. w. arces; fr. beatus (142), here=fortunatus.

1038. **Postulant**, 3rd plu. pres. ind. act. fr. postŭlo, -āre, -āvi, -ātum, 1st trans., (posco, 140) *to ask, command, require, request, desire,* aliquid ab aliquō or w. ut, ne and subj. Legal, *to summon before a court* or to *demand* a legal enquiry (quæstionem) from the prætor or other magistrate or one's opponents, etc. **arces**, nom. plu. jnd. by et to locus; fr. arx (39), here either of the hills behind Tarentum or the city itself, "*heights*" as a safe retreat (W.). **ibi**, adv. (fr. pron. rt. i-is). Of place, *in that place, there,* often correl. to ubi, unde, etc. Of time, *then, thereupon* (chiefly non-class.). Of other relations, *in that matter, on that occasion, in those things, circumstances,* etc. **tu** (69), subj. of sparges. **calentem**, acc. fem. s. pres. part. act. ag. w. favillam; fr. caleo (147).

1039. **Debita**, abl. s. fem. ag. w. lacrimā; fr. debitus (680). **sparges**, 2nd sing. fut. ind. act. fr. spargo, -gĕre, (Hor. has archaic spargier), -si, -sum, 3rd trans., *to scatter about here and there, throw here and there, strew,* esp. of weapons, *to hurl in all directions.* Of liquids, *sprinkle;* meton., *bestrew, e.g.,* humum foliis. *To bedew, wet, moisten;* "sparsus," *spotted, i.e.,* covered as if by sprinkling. *To disperse, scatter, divide, e.g.,* in fugam, fig., *distribute, e.g.,* animos in corpora. Of a report, etc., *to noise abroad, circulate.* **lacrima**, abl. (instrum.) s. fr. lacrĭma, -æ, (-cruma, -chryma, -cryma, old fm. dacrima) 1st fem., *a tear.* **favillam**, acc. sing. gov. by sparges; fr. făvilla, -æ, 1st fem., *hot cinders* or *ashes, embers,* esp. of the dead still glowing.

1040. **Vatis**, gen. sing. after favillam; fr. vates (35). **amici**, gen. s. in app. to vatis; fr. amicus (208) subst.

CARMEN VII. METRE.—*The Alcaic.* (Bk. I., Carmen ix.)

1041. **O** (2). **sæpe** (200). **mecum** (215). **tempus** (840), acc. gov. by in; here "*crisis,*" *i.e.*, time of special importance (W.). **ultimum**, acc. neut. s. ag. w. tempus; fr. ultimus (280), "to utmost peril" (W.).

1042. **Deducte**, voc. s. mas. pf. pass. part. ag. w. Pompei (1045); fr. deduco (867). **Bruto**, abl. absol. (824) fr. Brūtus, -i, Roman cognomen, here, M. Junius Brutus, son of Servilia (sister of Cato Uticensis) and M. Brutus, to whom Cicero dedicated several of his works. **militiæ** (1024), after duce. **duce** (88), in app. to Bruto.

1043. **Quis** (149), subj. of redonavit. **te** (83), gov. by redonavit. **redonavit**, 3rd sing. pf. ind. act. fr. rĕdōno, -āre, -avi, -atum, 1st trans., (re-,

1044 Dîs patriis Italoque cælo,
1045 Pompei meorum prime sodalium?
1046 Cum quo morantem sæpe diem mero
1047 Fregi coronatus nitentes
1048 Malobathro Syrio capillos.
1049 Tecum Philippos et celerem fugam
1050 Sensi relicta non bene parmula,
1051 Quum fracta virtus et minaces

659; dono, 726), only Hor., *to give back again, restore* (here). In Bk. III, iii. 33, *to forgive* a person for the sake of another. **Quiritem,** acc. s. in app. to te; fr. Quiris (7), either "a true Roman," *i.e.*, free fr. "deminutio capitis" as an exile, (or) "a man of peace," *i.e.*, no longer a soldier. This is merely a question of wonder=How came you here?

1044. **Dis** (30), commodi, remote obj. of redonavit. **patriis,** dat. mas. plu. ag. w. Dis; fr. patrius (11). **Italo,** dat. neut. sing. ag. w. cælo; fr. Ĭtălus, -a, -um, adj.; *Italian* (1044). **cælo,** dat. sing. jnd. by -que to Dis; fr. cælum (81).

1045. **Pompei,** voc. s. fr. Pompeius (trisyll. or ēius quadris.), -i, 2nd mas., name of a Roman general. This one unknown. **meorum,** gen. plu. mas. ag. w. sodalium; fr. meus (2). **prime,** voc. mas. s. ag. w. Pompei; fr. primus (100), either "*earliest*" or "*chiefest.*" **sodalium,** gen. of thing distributed after prime; fr. sodalis (611).

1046. **Cum** (31). **quo** (103), mas. s. ag. w. Pompei; abl. gov. by cum. **morantem** (293), ag. w. diem. **sæpe** (200). **diem** (284), gov. by fregi. **mero** (203), instrum.

1047. **Fregi,** 1st sing. pf. ind. act. fr. frango (570). **coronatus,** pf. pass. part. nom. mas. s. ag. w. ego und. in fregi; fr. cŏrōno, -āre. -āvi, -atum, 1st trans., (corona, 475) *to furnish with a garland* or *crown, crown, surround, enclose* something *in a circular form, wreathe.* **nitentes** (383), mas. ag. w. capillos.

1048. **Malobathro,** abl. (instrum.) s. fr. mălŏbăthrum, -i, 2nd neut. (Gk.) the name of an Indian or Syrian plant and of a costly oil procured from it. **Syrio,** abl. neut. s. ag. w. mălŏbathro; fr. Sȳrius, -a, -um, adj.; *of Syria.* **capillos,** acc. plu. after coronatus; fr. capillus (325). The acc. of the medial object (to be distinguished from the acc. of respect) which poetically follows pass. vbs. and partcps. used reflexively (like Gk. middle verb), *e.g.*, colligi (=colligere se) takes, as it were, a second accus. of the thing gathered up. Coronatus...capillos, with a garland on my hair glistening with Syrian perfume (W.).

1049. **Tecum** (705). **Philippos,** acc. gov. by sensi; fr. Philippi, -orum, 2nd mas.; a town where Octavius and Antony defeated Brutus and Cassius. **celerem** (402), fem. ag. w. fugam.

1050. **Sensi,** 1st sing. pf. ind. act. fr. sentio, -ire, sensi, sensum, 4th trans., *to discern by the senses, feel, hear, see, perceive, be sensible of. To feel the effects of, suffer, undergo. To observe, notice. To deem, judge, imagine, suppose.* **relicta,** abl. fem. s. ag. w. parmula; fr. relictus (270). **non** (55). **bene** (1130). **parmula,** abl. absol. s. fr. parmŭla, -æ. 1st fem., (diminutive of parma) *a little round shield, a small target.*

1051. **Quum** (43). **fracta,** nom. fem. s. pf. pass. partc. ag. w. virtus; w.

Turpe solum tetigere mento.
Sed me per hostes Mercurius celer
Denso paventem sustulit aëre;
Te rursus in bellum resorbens
Unda fretis tulit æstuosis.
Ergo obligatam redde Jovi dapem
Longaque fessum militia latus
Depone sub lauru mea nec

est und., 3rd sing. pf. ind. pass. fr. frango (570). **minaces,** nom. plu. mas. (as subst.) subj. of tetigere; fr. minax (266).

1052. **Turpe,** acc. neut. s. ag. w. solum; fr. turpis (727). **solum** (478), gov. by tetigere. **tetigere,** 3rd plu. pf. ind. act. fr. tango (224). **mento,** abl. (instrum.) s. fr. mentum, -i, 2nd neut., (mĭneo, *to project*) *the chin.* Some take this of the Pompeian soldiers begging for quarter after the battle of Pharsalia, others explain it as="bit the dust;" "turpe solum," the field of their shame (M.).

1053. **Sed** (591). **me** (29), gov. by sustulit. **per** (114). **hostes,** acc. plu. gov. by per; fr. hostis (76). **Mercurius** (590), subj. of sustulit. He was the guardian of poets. **celer** (294), nom. mas. s. ag. w. Mercurius.

1054. **Denso,** abl. mas. s. ag. w. āĕre; fr. densus (204). **paventem,** acc. mas. s. pres. partc. act. ag. w. me; fr. păveo, -ēre, -pāvi, no sup., 2nd intrans and trans., (pavio, *to beat, strike*) not in Cæs.; perh. not Cic., *to be struck with fear, dread* or *terror, be terrified;* trans., *to dread, be alarmed at.* **sustulit** (776). **aëre,** abl. (instrum.) s. fr. aër (122), *mist, cloud.*

1055. **Te** (83) gov. by tulit. **rursus** (class.) and rursum (ante-class.) adv.; (contr. for revorsus or revorsum; fr. reverto, 696) prop., *turned back* or *backwards,* opp. to prorsus. *On the contrary, on the other hand, in return, again*=retro, contra, invicem, of the reverse of something. *Back again, again, anew*=iterum, denuo, of repetition or return to a former action. **in** (81). **bellum** (533), gov. by in. **resorbens,** pres. part. act. nom. fem. s. ag. w. unda; fr. resorbeo, -ēre, no pf., no sup., 2nd trans., (re-. 659; sorbeo, *to suck*) *to suck back, swallow again.*

1056. **Unda** (316), subj. of tulit. **fretis** (759), instrum. **tulit** (326). **æstuosis,** abl. neut. plu. ag. w. fretis; fr. æstuosus (541).

1057. **Ergo** (577), *now, then* (W.). **obligatam,** acc. fem. s. pf. pass. part. ag. w. dapem; fr. oblĭgo, -are, -avi, -atum, 1st trans., (ob, 324; ligo, *to bind*) *to bind, tie* or *fasten round, put bands round* (rare). *To bind up, bandage, swathe,* of wounds etc.; fig., *to put under an obligation, make liable, e.g.,* sacramento; "obligatus," *to which one is bound, vowed. To render liable through guilt, make guilty* (1073). *To pledge, pawn, mortgage* a thing, *e.g.,* fratri prædia. **redde,** 2nd sing. pres. imper. act. fr. reddo (95). **Jovi** (524), after (indirect obj. of) redde. **dapem,** acc. s. gov. by (direct obj. of) redde; fr. daps (741).

1058. **Longa,** abl. s. fem. ag. w. militiâ; fr. longus (73), *i.e.,* from the death of Cæsar till the battle of Actium. **-que** (3). **fessum,** acc. neut. s. ag. w. latus; fr. fessus (979). **militia,** abl. (of cause) s. fr. militia (481). **latus** (368), gov. by depone.

1059. **Depone,** 2nd sing. pres. imper. act. fr. depono (834). **sub** (470),

1060 Parce cadis tibi destinatis.
1061 Oblivioso levia Massico
1062 Ciboria exple, funde capacibus
1063 Unguenta de conchis. Quis udo
1064 Deproperare apio coronas
1065 Curatve myrto? quem Venus arbitrum
1066 Dicet bibendi? Non ego sanius

lauru, abl. sing. gov. by sub; fr. laurus (891). **mea,** abl. fem. s. ag. w. lauru; fr. meus (2). **nec** (19).

1060. **Parce** (671). **cadis,** dat. plu. after traject. parce; fr. cadus (802). **tibi** (93), commodi after destinatis. **destinatis,** dat. plu. mas. pf. pass. part. ag. w. cadis; fr. destĭno, -are, -avi, -atum, 1st trans., (de, 10; stino, ak. to sto, 233) *to make to stand fast, make firm, e.g.,* rates; fig., *to establish, determine, design, appoint, elect, choose,* etc., w. inf. Of archers, etc., *to fix upon as a mark, aim at, e.g.,* locum; meton., sibi aliquid, *to fix upon for oneself, intend to buy* (comedy).

1061. **Oblivioso,** abl. neut. s. ag. w. Massico; fr. ōblīvĭōsus, -a, -um, adj.; (oblivio, *forgetfulness*) *that easily forgets, forgetful;* here, *fostering forgetfulness.* **levia,** acc. neut. plu. ag. w. ciboria; fr. lēvis (74). **Massico,** abl. (instrum.) fr. Massicum (19).

1062. **Cībōria,** acc. pl. gov. by exple; fr. cibōrium, -ii, 2nd neut. (Gk.), a drinking cup made in the shape of the pod of the Egyptian bean (ciboria, -æ, 1st fem.). **exple,** 2nd s. imper. pres. act. fr. expleo, -plēre, -plēvi, -plētum, 2nd trans., (syncopated fms. are expleris, explesse, explessent), (ex, 691; -pleo, *to fill*) *to fill up* or *full. To complete, furnish, e.g.,* beatam vitam. *To satisfy, glut, appease* a longing or one longing. With pers. pron. or pass. reflex., *to satiate oneself. To fulfil, discharge, perform, e.g.,* a duty. Of time, *to finish, bring to a close.* **funde,** 2nd s. pres. imper. act. fr. fundo (711). **capacibus,** abl. plu. fem. ag. w. conchis; fr. căpax, -ācis, adj.; (capio, 1388) *that can contain, hold, receive much, wide, large, roomy, spacious* (once only in Cic.); fig., *susceptible* or *capable of, able, fit for, ingenious.*

1063. **Unguenta** (953), gov. by funde. **de** (10). **conchis,** abl. plu. gov. by de; fr. concha, -æ, 1st fem., *a bivalve shell-fish, mussel, mussel-shell. An oil flask. Box for unguents. Salt cellar.* **quis** (149), subj. of curat. **udo** (735), ag. w. apio; "fresh gathered" (M.).

1064. **Deproperare,** pres. inf. (prolative) act. after curat; fr. dēprŏpēro, -āre, no pf., no sup., (de, 10; propero, 706) intr., *to make great haste,* trans., *accelerate greatly, hasten, make with speed.* **apio,** abl. (instrum.) s. fr. apium (832). **coronas,** acc. plu. gov. by deproperare; fr. corona (475).

1065. **Curat,** 3rd sing. ind. pres. act. fr. curo (874). **-ve** (186), notice its position; so -que (706, 1420). **myrto** (137), jnd. by -ve to apio. **quem** (61), gov. by dicet. **Venus** (133), subj. of dicet; here the "highest throw of the four tali," as "canis" was the worst. **arbitrum,** acc. s. dependent predicate (903) in app. to quem; fr. arbiter (103).

1066. **Dicet** (193). **bibendi,** gen. s. gerund (639) after arbitrum; fr. bĭbo (518). **non** (55). **ego** (445), subj. of bacchabor. **sanius,** comparative of sāne, (adv. of sanus, *sound, whole*) *soberly, sensibly, reasonably, discreetly* (here, but very rare, not Cic.); much more com. as an intensive particle=valde, *truly, surely.*

Bacchabor Edonis: recepto
Dulce mihi furere est amico.

CARMEN VIII.—AD BARINEN.

ULLA si juris tibi pejerati
Pœna, Barine, nocuisset unquam,
Dente si nigro fieres vel uno
Turpior ungui,

1067. **Bacchabor,** 1st s. fut. ind. fr. bacchor (603). **Edonis,** abl. comparative (103), after sanius; fr. Edoni, -orum, 2nd mas. plu., a people of South Thrace, near Mt. Pangæos, worshippers of Bacchus. **recepto,** abl. s. mas. pf. pass. partc. ag. w. amico; fr. recĭpio, -cĭpere, -cēpi, -ceptum, 3rd trans., (re, 659; capio, 1388) *to receive back, get back, retake, recover.* With acc. of pers. pron., *to betake oneself* somewhere, *withdraw, retire. To keep back, retain, reserve. To take to oneself, admit, accept. To take to* or *upon oneself, assume. To promise, warrant, pledge one's word, undertake.*

1068. **Dulce** (2), predic. ag. w. furere. **mihi** (277), after traject. dulce. **furere,** pres. inf. subj of est; fr. furo (355). **est** (19). **amico,** abl. absol. s. fr. amicus (208).

CARMEN VIII.—*The Lesser Sapphic.* (Bk. I., Carmen ii.).

1069. **Ulla,** nom. fem. s. ag. w. pœna; fr. ullus (580). **si** (7), w. plpf. subj. in protasis and impf. subj. in apodosis. **juris,** gen. s. after pœna; fr, jus (680), jūris, 3rd neut., (ak. to jungere, 134) orig. *that which binds* or *joins together;* hence *law* natural, human or divine, written or unwritten, in principle or practice; fig., *a right* or *title* to anything, *privilege, power. opportunity, means.* **tibi** (93), after traject. nocuisset. **pejerati,** gen. s. neut. pf. pass. part. ag. w juris; fr. pējĕro (orig. perjuro), -are, -avi, -atum, 1st intrans., (per, 114; juro, *to swear*), *to take an oath* by some deity, person, or thing, w. added notion of intended falsehood. *To swear falsely, forswear, perjure oneself.* In Plaut., *to lie;* pejeratus=(i.) *falsely uttered;* (ii.) of a god *sworn by falsely;* "jus pejeratum," *a broken oath,* on the analogy of "jus jurandum."

1070. **Pœna,** -æ, 1st fem.; nom. s. subj. of nocuisset, (pu- in punire, *to punish*) *that which purifies* or *acquits, indemnification, compensation, satisfaction, expiation, penalty. Hardship, torment, suffering* (post-Aug.). **Barine,** -es, 1st fem., (Gk.) voc. s.; name of a girl. **nocuisset,** 3rd s. plpf. subj. in protasis; fr. noceo (678). **unquam** (unquum), temp. adv., (contr. for unum, 189; quam, 284) *at any time, ever,* opp. to what *never* takes place, used in negative clauses, *i.e.,* w. nemo, neque, nihil, non, ne, and in interrogative and conditional clauses, but rarely alone or in affirmative clauses.

1071. **Dente** (356), abl. (of manner) w. turpior. **si,** w. impf. subj. in protasis and apodosis as in 1013. **nigro** (739), ag. w. dente. **fieres,** 2nd s. impf. subj. in protasis; fr. fio (447). **vel** (187). **uno** (467), ag. w. ungui.

1072. **Turpior,** nom. fem. s. compar.; predic. after fieres; fr. turpis (727). **ungui,** abl. s. jnd. by vel to dente; fr. unguis (182).

1073 Crederem. Sed tu, simul obligasti
1074 Perfidum votis caput, enitescis
1075 Pulchrior multo juvenumque prodis
1076 Publica cura.
1077 Expedit matris cineres opertos
1078 Fallere et toto taciturna noctis
1079 Signa cum cœlo gelidaque Divos
1080 Morte carentes.
1081 Ridet hoc, inquam, Venus ipsa, rident

1073. **Crederem,** 1st s. impf. ind. act. in apodosis; fr. credo (93). **sed** (591). **tu** (69), subj. of enitescis. **simul** (145). **obligasti,** syncopated for obligavisti, 2nd s. pf. ind. act. fr. obligo (1057).

1074. **Perfidum,** acc. neut. s. ag. w. caput; fr. perfidus (386). **votis,** abl. (instrum.) plu. w. obligasti; fr. vōtum, -i, 2nd neut., (vŏveo, *to vow*) *solemn promise made to* some deity, *vow* esp. in plu. *That which is vowed, thing solemnly promised, votive offering. Wish, desire, longing;* here *imprecations* on herself if her promises be not kept (W.). **cāput** (22), gov. by obligasti. **enitescis,** 2nd s. ind. pres. fr. ēnĭtesco, -scĕre, ēnĭtui, no sup., 3rd intrans, inceptive, (eniteo, *to shine out*) *to shine out* or *forth*; fig., *to become eminent, conspicuous, distinguished,* of virtue, eloquence; here *to become blooming* or *beautiful.*

1075. **Pulchrior** (421), nom. predic. after enitescis. **multo** (703), as adv.; *by far.* **juvenum** (667), gen. (subjective) after cura. **-que** (4). **prodis,** 2nd s. pres. ind. fr. prodeo, -īre, -ĭi, -ĭtum, intrans. irreg., (pro, *forward;* eo, 51) *to go* or *come forth, go abroad,* (class.). Of plants, *spring up, appear.* Of elevations, *stand out, project;* fig., *come forth, show itself, appear, e.g.,* of a custom. *To go forward, advance, proceed.*

1076. **Publica,** nom. fem. s. ag. w. cura; fr. publicus (886). **cura** (334), predic. in app. to tu.

1077. **Expedit,** 3rd s. ind. pres. act. fr. expedio (228), used impersonally; und. tibi. **matris,** gen. s. after cineres; fr. mater (24). **cineres,** acc. plu. gov. by fallere; fr. cinis (884). **opertos,** acc. plu. mas. ag. w. cineres; fr. ŏpertus, -a, -um, *hidden, concealed,* pf. pass. part. of ŏpĕrio, -īre, -ui, -ertum, 4th trans., *to cover, cover over;* meton., *to shut close, e.g.,* oculos; fig., *to hide, conceal, keep from observation;* here *bury. To load, overwhelm, e.g.,* contumeliis.

1078. **Fallere,** pres. inf. act. subj. of expedit; fr. fállo (272); here "*to swear falsely by.*" **toto,** abl. neut. s. ag. w. cælo; fr. totus (501). **taciturna,** acc. neut. plu. ag. w. signa; fr. taciturnus (1078). **noctis,** gen. s. after signa; fr. nox (144).

1079. **Signa,** acc. plu. jnd. by et to cineres; fr. signum (203). **cum** (31). **cælo** (199), gov. by cum. **gelida,** abl. fem. s. ag. w. morte; fr. gelidus (30). **Divos,** acc. plu. jnd. by -que to signa; fr. divus (61).

1080. **Morte** (865), after carentes. Abl. of plenty and want (540). **carentes,** acc. plu. mas. ag. w. Divos; fr. carens (649).

1081. **Ridet** (1030), here transitive. **hoc** (416), gov. by ridet. **inquam,** 1st sing. ind. pres.; an old and defective verb; ind. pres. sing. 2nd inquis, 3rd inquit, plu., inquimus, inquitis, inquiunt, pf. 2nd inquisti; fut. s.

1082 Simplices Nymphæ, ferus et Cupido
1083 Semper ardentes acuens sagittas
1084 Cote cruenta.
1085 Adde, quod pubes tibi crescit omnis,
1086 Servitus crescit nova; nec priores
1087 Impiæ tectum dominæ relinquunt
1088 Sæpe minati.
1089 Te suis matres metuunt juvencis,
1090 Te senes parci miseræque nuper

2nd inquies, 3rd inquiet, imperat. inque, inquito; *I say, says he, she*, etc., placed after one or more words, either in citing the words of another, or in emphatically stating one's own words or stating objections to one's own statements. **Venus** (133), subj. of ridet. **ipsa,** nom. fem. s. ag. w. Venus; fr. ipse (126). **rident,** 3rd plu. pres. ind. act. fr. rideo (69).

1082. **Simplices,** nom. fem. plu. ag. w. Nymphæ; fr. simplex (153). **Nymphæ** (706), subj. of rident. **ferus** (258), nom. mas. s. ag. w. Cupido. **Cupido** (70), jnd. by et to Nymphæ, as subj. of ridet.

1083. **Semper** (158). **ardentes,** acc. fem. plu. ag. w. sagittas; fr. ardens (136). **acuens,** pres. part. act. nom. mas. s. ag. w. Cupido; fr. acuo (57). **sagittas** (693), gov. by acuens.

1084. **Cote,** abl. (instrum.) s. fr. cōs, cōtis, 3rd fem., *a whetstone, hone, grindstone*; meton., *hard-stone, flint-stone.* **cruenta,** abl. s. fem. ag. w. cote; fr. cruentus (75), epith. of the whetstone as sharpening the weapons by which deadly wounds are inflicted (M.).

1085. **Adde,** 2nd sing. pres. imper. act. fr. addo (433). **quod** (35), introduces a substantival sentence which stands as object to adde. **pubes** (609), subj. of crescit. **tibi** (93), commodi after crescit. **crescit** (329). **omnis** (148), ag. w. pubes.

1086. **Servitus,** -ūtis, 3rd fem.; nom. sing. subj. of crescit; *condition* of a servus (*slave*), *serfdom, slavery, service; fig., servitude, subjection;* here= servi, abstract for concrete. **nova** (118), ag. w. servitus. **nec** (19). **priores,** nom. mas. plu. subj. of relinquent; fr. prior, neut. prius, gen. prioris, (pre- in primus, pridie) *former, previous.* Of time, to be rendered *first*, an adverbial attribute. "Priores," *forefathers, ancients* (poet. and post-Aug.). *Better, preferable, more excellent* (not Cic. nor Cæs.).

1087. **Impiæ,** gen. sing. fem. ag. w. dominæ; fr. impius (111). **tectum,** acc. s. gov. by relinquunt; fr. tectum, -i, 2nd neut., (tego, 177) *a roof. Roofed dwelling, abode, cover, shelter, quarters.* **dominæ,** gen. s. after tectum; fr. domina (782). **relinquunt,** 3rd plu. pres. ind. act. fr. relinquo (270).

1088. **Sæpe** (200). **minati,** pf. partc. (concessive) nom. mas. plu. ag. with priores; fr. mĭnor, -āri, -ātus sum, 1st depon. trans. and intrans., (akin to mineo, *to project*) *to jut forth, project. To rise high, on high;* meton., *threaten, menace*, w. acc. of thing, dat. of person. *To promise boastfully* (rare).

1089. **Te** (83), gov. by metuunt. **suis,** dat. mas. plu. ag. w. juvencis; fr. suus (17). **matres** (787), subj. of metuunt. **metuunt** (456). **juvencis,** dat. (incommodi) plu. w. metuunt; fr. juvencus (998).

1090. **Te,** anaphora (895). **senes,** nom. plu. subj. of metuunt und.; fr.

1091 Virgines nuptæ, tua ne retardet
1092 Aura maritos.

CARMEN IX.—AD C. VALGIUM.

1093 NON semper imbres nubibus hispidos
1094 Manant in agros aut mare Caspium,
1095 Vexant inæquales procellæ
1096 Usque, nec Armeniis in oris,

senex (667). **parci,** nom. mas. plu. ag. w. senes; fr. parcus (761). **miseræ,** nom. fem. plu. ag. w. virgines; fr. miser (160). **nuper** (381), w. nuptæ.

1091. **Virgines** (63) jnd. by -que to senes. **nuptæ,** nom. fem. plu. pf. pass. partc. ag. w. virgines; fr. nūbo, -ĕre, nupsi, nuptum, 3rd trans. and intrans., (rt. in nubes, 67) *to cover* (very rare). Of a bride w. ellipse of se or pass. reflexive, *to cover* or *veil oneself for the bridegroom,* i.e., *marry* or *wed* a man. *To be married* or *wedded to* a man. **tua,** nom. fem. s. ag. w. aura; fr. tuus (175). **ne** (41). **retardet,** 3rd sing. pres. subj. act. fr. retardo, -are, -avi, -atum, 1st trans., (re-, 659; tardo, 1545) *to keep back. hinder, delay, detain, impede;* intrans., *tarry, remain behind.* Pres. after pres. metuunt, subjunct. after ne. Verbs of *fearing* have the same construction as words expressing purpose.

1092. **Aura** (84), subj. of retardet. Marshall takes it here as "*sheen,*" "*glitter.*" Orelli understands it, as suggested by "juvencis," to be an expression properly applicable to animals. **maritos,** acc. plu. gov. by retardet; fr. maritus (455).

CARMEN IX. METRE.—*The Alcaic.* (Bk. I., Carmen ix.)

1093. **Non** (55). **semper** (158). **imbres,** nom. plu. subj. of manant; fr. imber (200). **nubibus,** abl. (instrum.) plu. fr. nubes (1093). **hispidos,** acc. plu. mas. predic. ag. w. agros; from hispĭdus, -a, -um, adj. *rough, shaggy, bristly, prickly;* here, *dirty, foul* with rain.

1094. **Manant,** 3rd plu. pres. ind. act. fr. mano (463). **in,** local (81). **agros** (12), gov. by in. **aut** (131). **mare** (14), gov. by vexant. **Caspium,** acc. neut. s. ag. w. mare; fr. Caspius, -a, -um, adj.; *Caspian.*

1095. **Vexant,** 3rd plu. pres. ind. act. fr. vexo, -are, -avi, -atum, 1st trans., (intens. of veho, prop. *to carry much* or *frequently*) *to move violently, shake, agitate* (rare); meton., physically *to injure, damage. To molest, annoy, maltreat, disquiet, torment, attack, harass, e.g.,* contumeliis. **inæquales,** nom. fem. plu. ag. w. procellæ; fr. inæqualis, -e, adj.; (in, neg.; æqualis, 222), *not of corresponding size, of different-size.* Of surface, *uneven;* meton., of things, *unlike, dissimilar, not corresponding,* compared with another object or not. Of persons, *inconsistent, fickle.* Act., *that makes uneven* or *unequal, e.g.,* tonsor, *i.e.,* that cuts unevenly (Hor.). Of a storm, *roughening, making rough.* Others take it here "*changeful, gusty.*" **procellæ,** nom. plu. subj. of vexant; fr. procella (1118).

1096. **Usque** (452). **nec** (19). **Armeniis,** abl. fem. plu. ag. w. oris; fr. Armenius. **in** (78). **oris** (289), gov. by in.

1097 Amice Valgi, stat glacies iners
1098 Menses per omnes aut Aquilonibus
1099 Querceta Gargani laborant
1100 Et foliis viduantur orni:
1101 Tu semper urges flebilibus modis
1102 Mysten ademptum, nec tibi Vespero
1103 Surgente decedunt amores
1104 Nec rapidum fugiente Solem.

1097. **Amice,** voc. s. mas. ag w. Valgi; fr. amicus (208). **Valgi,** voc. s. fr. Valgius, -ii, name of a Roman general; here C. Valgius Rufus, who wrote elegies. **stat,** 3rd s. ind. pres. fr. sto (233). **glăcĭes,** -ei, 5th fem.; nom. s. subj. of stat; *ice;* meton., *hardness.* **iners,** -ertis, adj.; nom. fem. s. ag. w. glacies; (in, neg.; ars, 293) *unskilled, without skill, unskilful;* meton., *inactive, idle, indolent, sluggish.* Of food, *without flavour, insipid.* Act. in poets, *that renders idle* or *inactive.*

1098. **Menses,** acc. plu. gov. by per; fr. mensis, -is, 3rd mas., gen. plu. mensium and (rarely) mensum; (ak. to metiri, *to measure*) *a month* as a measure of time. **per** (946). **omnes** (297), ag. w. menses. **aut** (131). **Aquilonibus** (101), causal w. laborant.

1099. **Querceta,** nom. plu. subj. of laborant; fr. quercētum, -i, 2nd neut., (quercus, 296) *oak wood, oak forest.* **Gargani,** gen. s. after quercita; fr. Gargānus, -i, 2nd mas., a mountain ridge in Apulia, reaching into the Adriatic. **laborant,** 3rd plu. pres. ind. act. fr. laboro (235), *are tossed* (M.).

1100. **Foliis** (566), abl of separation (*i.e.*, abl. propĕr), after viduantur. **viduantur,** 3rd plu. pres. ind. pass. fr. vĭdŭo, -āre, -avi, -atum, 1st trans., (viduus, 267) *to deprive, bereave of* anything; esp. pf. pass. part. fem., viduata, -æ, 1st fem., *widowed, i.e.,* bereft of a husband. **orni** (244), subj. of viduantur.

1101. **Tu** (69), subj. of urges. **semper** (158). **urges,** 2nd s. pres. ind. act. fr. urgeo (150). **flebĭlĭbus,** abl. plu. mas. ag. w. modis; fr. flebilis (581). **modis,** abl. (instrum.) plu. fr. modus (422).

1102. **Mysten,** acc. s. gov. by urges; fr. Mystes, -æ, 1st mas. (Gk.). **ademptum,** acc. mas. s. ag. w. Mysten; fr. ademptus (978). **nec** (19). **tibi** (93), dat. (commodi) after decedunt. **Vespero,** abl. absol. s. fr. Vesper, -ĕris and -ĕri, acc. Vesperum, abl. Vespere, or adv. Vesperi, (these forms most com. in class. prose; mas. and neut. forms are ante-class.) *the evening star, even, eventide. The West.*

1103. **Surgente,** abl. s. mas. pres. partc. (temporal) act. ag. w. Vesperi; fr. surgo, -gĕre, surrexi, surrectum, 3rd trans., (sub, 21; rego, 91) *to lift, raise, erect, lift up;* pass., *to lift oneself up, rise* (very rare after Aug. age, the uncontracted fms., subrigo, subrigit, etc., being so used to distinguish it from class. age); intrans., *to arise, stand, get up.* Of things, *to mount up, ascend. To get up* from bed or sleep. *To rise in growth, grow;* fig., *to rise, e.g.,* animo sententia surgit. **decedunt** (1031). **amores,** nom. plu. subj. of decedunt; fr. amor (247).

1104. **Nec** (19). **rapidum,** acc. mas. s. ag. w. Solem; fr. rapidus (293), *striding* (W.). **fugiente,** pres. part. act. abl. mas. s. jnd. by nec to surgente; fr. fugio (206). **Solem,** acc. s. gov. by fugiente; fr. Sol (220).

1105 At non ter ævo functus amabilem
1106 Ploravit omnes Antilochum senex
1107 Annos, nec impubem parentes
1108 Troïlon aut Phrygiæ sorores
1109 Flevere semper. Desine mollium
1110 Tandem querelarum, et potius nova
1111 Cantemus Augusti tropæa
1112 Cæsaris et rigidum Niphaten,

1105. **At** (483). **non** (55). **ter** (361). **ævo** (329), after functus. This abl. as w. frui, uti, vesci, potiri, though construed like an object, is properly instrumental, as these words were originally reflexive. **functus,** pf. partc. nom. mas. s. ag. w. senex; fr. fungor, -ngi, -nctus sum, 3rd depon., *to busy oneself with, be engaged in, perform, administer, discharge, do,* w. abl. rarely acc. or absol. (1390); here, *who had lived through.* With acc. in class. prose chiefly in partc. fut.; hence gerundive fungendus used; "fungi pro," *to serve for,* esp. *perform, discharge, contribute, pay* anything due for one, *e.g.,* sumptu; "ter ævo functus," *who had lived life three times over* (W.), ref. to Nestor. **amabilem** (159), mas. ag. w. Antilochum.

1106. **Ploravit,** 3rd s. pf. ind. act. fr. plōro, -āre, -āvi, -ātum, 1st trans. and intrans., (fluo, orig. *to make to flow;* hence w. accessory idea of noise) *to wail, lament, weep aloud;* trans., *to weep over* anything, *bewail.* **omnes** (217), ag. w. annos. **Antilochum,** acc. s. gov. by ploravere; fr. Antilŏchus, -i, 2nd mas., a son of Nestor, slain by Hector before Troy. **senex** (667), nom. s. subj. of ploravit.

1107. **Annos** (1007), acc. of duration of time. **nec** (19). **impubem,** acc. mas. s. ag. w. Troïlon; fr. impūbes, -puberis and -pubis, latter poet. and post-Aug. (in, neg.; pubes, 609). Of persons, *not having attained to manhood, under age, youthful.* **parentes** (982), subj. of flevere.

1108. **Troïlon,** acc. s. gov. by flevere; fr. Troïlos (-us), -i (Gk.), a son of Priam, slain by Achilles. **aut** (131). **Phrygiæ,** nom. fem. plu., ag. w. sorores; fr. Phrўgius, -a, -um, adj.; *Phrygian;* meton., *Trojan.* **sorores,** nom. plu. jnd. by aut to parentes; fr. soror (578).

1109. **Flevere,** 3rd plu. pf. ind. act. fr. fleo (154). **semper** (158) **desine** (571). **mollium,** gen. plu. fem. ag. w. querelarum; fr. mollis (203).

1110. **Tandem** (66). **querelarum,** gen. plu. after desine; fr. quĕrēla, -æ, 1st fem., (queror, 42) *a complaining, complaint. Plaintive sound* or *note* of animals or instruments, *e.g.,* frogs. This is a Greek use of the gen.; see 1230. **et** (2). **potius** (85). **nova** (42), ag. w. tropæa.

1111. **Cantemus,** 1st plu. pres. conj. (optative) act. fr. canto (183). **Augusti,** gen. mas. s. ag. w. Cæsaris; fr. Augustus, -i, 2nd mas., *majesty* or *imperial majesty,* a cognomen of Octavius Cæsar, after he attained to undivided authority, and after him of all Roman emperors. **tropæa,** acc. plu. gov. by cantemus; fr. trŏpæum, -i, 2nd neut., (Gk.) *a sign and memorial of victory,* orig. the trunk of a tree on which were fixed the arms, shields, etc., taken from the enemy, afterwards made of stone and similarly ornamented; meton., *a victory. A token, sign, monument, memorial, e.g.,* hospitii, ingenii.

1112. **Cæsaris** (80), after tropæa. **rigidum,** acc. mas. s. ag. w. Niphaten; fr. rĭgĭdus, -a, -um, adj.; (rĭgeo, *to be stiff*) *stiff, hard, inflexible, rigid,*

Medumque flumen gentibus additum
Victis minores volvere vertices,
Intraque præscriptum Gelonos
Exiguis equitare campis.

CARMEN X.—AD LICINIUM.

Rectius vives, Licini, neque altum
Semper urgendo neque, dum procellas

fr. cold, etc. Of a mountain, *hard, rocky; fig., stern, rigid, rough, e.g.*, vox, Mars, mores. **Niphaten,** acc. s. jnd. by et to tropæa; fr. Nĭphātes, -æ, 1st mas. (Gk.), a part of Mt. Taurus. Later poets took it for a river; then rigidum=*stiff frozen.*

1113. **Medum,** acc. neut. s. ag. w. flumen; fr. Medus (629). **flumen** (1027), subj. of volvere; "Medum flumen"=*the Euphrates*, ref. to the recovery of the captured standards of Crassus (M.). **gentibus** (116), after traject. additum. **additum,** pf. pass. part. acc. neut. s. ag. w. flumen; fr. addo (433).

1114. **Victis,** dat. plu. fem. pf. pass. part. ag. w. gentibus; fr. vinco (830). **minores** (332), ag. w. vertices. **volvere,** pres. inf. act. jnd. by -que to Niphaten, after cantemus; fr. volvo, -ĕre, volvi, vŏlutum, 3rd trans., *to roll, turn about, turn round, tumble; fig., to roll along, undergo, go through successively. Revolve in the mind, reflect on.* **vertices,** acc. plu. gov. by volvere; fr. vertex (36).

1115. **Intra,** adv.; *on the inside, within. Towards the inside.* Prep. of space, *within, inside.* With verbs of motion, *into, within. To the inside of.* Of time, *within the space of, in the course of, before the expiration of,* etc.; intra se, *within one's self, secretly, within one's own breast.* **præscriptum,** acc. s. gov. by intra; fr. præscriptum, -i, 2nd neut., (præscribo, *to write beforehand*) *that which is written before* or *first* (from writing a form for children). *That which is traced out, a boundary line. That which is ordered, a precept, rule;* "intra præscriptum," *within the bounds that we have put them* (W.). **Gelonos,** acc. subj. of equitare; fr. Gēlōni, -ōrum, 2nd mas. plu., *a Scythian people in the Borysthenes* (1443).

1116. **Exiguis,** abl. plu. mas. predic. ag. w. campis; fr. exiguus (486); "and find them too narrow" (W.). **equitare** (87), jnd. by -que to volvere. **campis** (553), local.

Carmen X.—Metre.—*The Lesser Sapphic.* (Bk. I., Carmen ii.)

1117. **Rectius,** compar. of recte, (adv. of rectus) prop. *in a straight line,* perpendicular or horizontal (rare); fig., *rightly, correctly, properly, duly, suitably, well.* It strengthens the meaning of adjs., *right, well, thoroughly.* Colloquially, *quite well, right excellently,* w. an ellipsis. Courteously evasive, *all's well, it's all right, there's nothing the matter.* **vives,** 2nd s. fut. ind. act. fr. vivo (731). **Licini,** voc. s. fr. Licinius, -a, -um, adj.; name of a Roman gens. This was Murena, brother of Terentia (Mæcenas' wife) and Proculeius (921), put to death on a charge of conspiracy, B.C. 22. **neque** (32). **altum** (959), gov. by urgendo.

1118. **Semper** (158). **urgendo,** abl. gerund (639) of means; fr. urgeo (150); altum urgendo, *steering on and on into the open sea.* **neque** (32).

1119 Cautus horrescis, nimium premendo
1120 Litus iniquum.
1121 Auream quisquis mediocritatem
1122 Diligit, tutus caret obsoleti
1123 Sordibus tecti, caret invidenda
1124 Sobrius aula.
1125 Sæpius ventis agitatur ingens

dum (53). **procellas,** acc. plu. gov. by horrescis; fr. prŏcella, -æ, 1st fem., (pro, *forward;* obsol. cello, *to strike* or *dash*) *a violent wind which prostrated things, storm, hurricane, tempest;* fig., *storm, tumult, commotion, violence;* milit., *charge, onset, sudden attack,* of cavalry.

1119. **Cautus** (226), nom. mas. s. ag. as adv. attribute with tu und. in horrescis. **horrescis,** 2nd s. ind. pres. fr. horresco, -escĕre, horrui, no sup., 2nd intrans. and trans., (inceptive of horreo). Of the hair, *to rise on end, bristle up;* meton., *to grow rough,* esp. *to begin to shake, shudder* or *tremble* for fear, *become terrified;* here *to be frightened at,* w. acc. **nimium** (53), w. premendo. **premendo,** abl. gerund. jnd. by neque to urgendo; fr. premo (144); "nimium...iniquum," *hugging too close the dangerous shore* (W.).

1120. **Litus** (651), gov. by premendo. **iniquum** (83), neut. ag. w. litus.

1121. **Auream,** acc. fem. s. ag. w. mediocritatem; fr. aureus (157). **quisquis** (901), subj. of diligit. **mediocritatem,** acc. s. gov. by diligit; fr. mĕdiocrĭtas, -atis, 3rd fem., (*state* or *condition* of the mediocris) *a middle state between two extremes, medium, mean, moderation.* Of ability, style, etc., *absence of anything remarkable, mediocrity.* Of mental affections, *moderate state, amount* or *degree;* meton., *meanness, insignificance, inferiority;* here "the mean state and the moderation of mind which is content with it" (W.).

1122. **Diligit,** 3rd s. ind. pres. act. fr. diligo (524). **tutus** (453), nom. mas. s. ag. w. subj. (quisquis) of caret. **caret** (912). **obsoleti,** gen. neut. s. ag. w. tecti; fr. obsŏlētus, -a, -um, adj.; (obsoleo, *to wear out, grow old*), *worn out, decayed, old.* Of words, *gone out of use.* Of persons, *meanly clad, poor, common.* Of things, *everyday, common, vulgar. That has ceased to be of value, valueless, e.g.,* gaudia. Of language, *ordinary, low.*

1123. **Sordibus,** abl. plu. after caret; fr. sordes, sordis, 3rd fem., (sordeo, *to be mean* or *dirty*) esp. frequ. in fig. sense and in plu., *dirt, filth, nastiness, uncleanness, squalor;* fig., *meanness of rank* or *condition. Baseness of behaviour* or disposition. *Stinginess, niggardliness. A mourning garment,* usu. sordid or dirty. *Mourning. Dregs* of the people, *mob, rabble.* **tecti,** gen. s. after sordibus; fr. tectum (1087). **invidenda,** abl. s. fem. ag. w. aulâ; fr. invidendus, -a, -um, gerundive (639) of invideo (685).

1124. **Sobrius,** -a, -um, adj.; nom. mas. s. ag. w. subj. (quisquis) of caret; (se-, 120, 370; ebrius, *drunken*). Of persons, *not drunk, sober,* opp. to vinolentus; fig. of things. In poets, *sober, moderate, continent;* fig. of mind and things, *sober-minded, clever, sensible, prudent, reasonable, cautious.* **aula** (691), after caret.

1125. **Sæpius,** compar. of sæpe (200). **ventis** (155), instrum w. agitatur. **agitatur,** 3rd s. pres. ind. pass. fr. agito (244). **ingens** (216), nom. fem. s. ag. w. pinus.

1126 Pinus, et celsæ graviore casu
1127 Decidunt turres, feriuntque summos
1128 Fulgura montes.
1129 Sperat infestis, metuit secundis
1130 Alteram sortem bene præparatum
1131 Pectus. Informes hiemes reducit
1132 Jupiter, idem

1126. **Pinus** (375), subj. of agitatur **celsæ,** nom. fem. plu. ag. w. turres; fr. celsus, -a, -um, adj.; (orig., *driven to a high place;* cello=*to impel, urge,* seen in antecello) *raised high, extending upwards, high, lofty. Elevated, above the common, noble, eminent.* **graviore,** abl. mas. s. compar. adj. ag. w. casu; fr. gravis (41) **casu,** abl. (of manner) s. fr. casus, -us, 4th mas., (cado, 977) *a falling down, fall, overthrow. That which happens unexpectedly, accident, event*

1127. **Decidunt,** 3rd plu. pres. ind. act. fr. decĭdo, -cĭdere, -cĭdi, no sup., 3rd intrans., (de, 10; cado, 977) *to fall down. To fall down from* or *off*, esp. *to sink down dying, die,* (genly poet.) fig., *to fall from* hope, etc. **turres,** nom. plu. subj. of decidunt; fr. turris (142). **feriunt,** 3rd plu. pres. ind. act. fr. ferio (36). **-que** (4). **summos,** acc. plu. mas. ag. as partitive attribute w. montes; fr. summus (45)

1128. **Fulgura,** nom. plu. subj. of feriunt; fr. fulgur, -ŭris, 3rd neut., (fulgeo, 203) *a flash of lightning* [fulmen, *a thunderbolt*]. Perhaps not class. =fulmen, *lightning that strikes.* Very rare, *brightness, splendour*=fulgor. **montes** (44), gov. by feriunt.

1129. **Sperat** (159). **infestis,** abl. neut. plu. (as subst.) fr. infestus, -a, -um, adj.; (in, *against;* festus for fenstus, fr. fendo, whence defendo, infensus, etc.) *made unsafe, disturbed, molested, insecure, unsafe* (class.). Act., *that renders unsafe, acts in a hostile manner, inimical, dangerous.* **metuit,** 3rd sing. pres. ind. act. fr. metuo (16). **secundis,** abl. plu. neut. (as subst.) fr. secundus (302), "infestis," "secundis," abl. absol., (824) "*in evil fortune*" "*in good fortune.*"

1130. **Alteram,** acc. fem. s. ag. w. sortem; fr. alter (413). **sortem,** acc. s. gov. by metuit; fr. sors (967); "alteram sortem," *a change of fortune.* **bĕnĕ,** adv. of bonus (581). Compar. mĕlius; superl. optĭme, *well, beautifully, ably, honourably, favourably, prosperously* of every kind of excellence. It enhances the idea of adjs. and advs., *very, rightly, extremely,* genly. before, only in poets, separated or after (1179). **præparatum,** nom. neut. s. ag. w. pectus; fr. præpărātus, -a, -um, *prepared, provided with* anything; pf. pass. part. of præpăro, -āre, -avi, -atum, 1st trans., (præ, *before;* păro, *to prepare*) *to make ready beforehand,* esp. w. pers. pron., *to make oneself ready.* With acc., *to make preparations for, get ready for* eating, drinking, etc.

1131. **Pectus** (98), nom. s. subj. of sperat, metuit, etc. **informes,** acc. plu. fem. ag. w. hiemes; fr. informis, -e, adj., (in, neg.; forma, 755) *without form* or *without a proper form, unformed, unshaped, shapeless;* meton., *ill-shaped, deformed, hideous.* **hiemes** (280), gov. by reducit. **reducit,** 3rd sing. pres. ind. act. fr. reduco (465).

1132. **Jupiter** (66), subj. of reducit. **idem,** ĕadem, ĭdem, gen. ejusdem; nom. mas. s. ag. w. subj. (Jupiter) of summovet; the definitive pronoun (I-pronom. rt., and -dem). If the predicates are of the same kind, *the same, likewise, also, at the same time.* When the predicates differ or are opposite,

1133 Summovet. Non, si male nunc, et olim
1134 Sic erit. Quondam cithara tacentem
1135 Suscitat musam neque semper arcum
1136 Tendit Apollo.
1137 Rebus angustis animosus atque
1138 Fortis appare; sapienter idem

it expresses contrast, *e.g.*, *but yet;* here, *he also.* It is connected with, or corresponds to, ego, tu, hic, ille, iste, qui or unus, *e.g.*, idem dixisti, *you also said it.* Followed by et, ac, -que, ut, hic, it is used as a word of comparison, *the same ..as; the same...with.* Hor. uses it w. dat., idem facit occidenti, "*he does the same as the man who kills;*" alter idem=*a second self.* Adverbial cases "eadem," *the same way* (rare, but class.) "eodem," *to the same place, position, degree, matter,* etc.

1133, **Summovet,** 3rd s. ind. pres. act. fr. summŏveo (subm.), -mŏvēre, -mōvi, -mōtum, 2nd trans., (sub, 21; moveo, 394) *to move from beneath.* Of persons, *to send* or *drive away, remove* (1373), esp. of a lictor *to clear away* the people; fig.; *to keep away, withhold, withdraw, e.g.*, aliquem a republicâ. *To clear away, disperse* (1290). **non** (55). **si** (7), w. ellipse of est (19), *i.e.*, verb in pres. ind. in protasis, w. fut. ind. in apodosis. **male** (256), predic. The subject to est und. is indefinite, *fortune*, etc. **nunc** (21). **et** (2). **olim** (265); here, *hereafter.*

1134. **Sic** (89). **erit** (279), in apodosis, the subject being indefinite. **quondam** (quum, 43; -dem, demonst. term.), temp. adv.; (i.) *at a certain time, at one time, once, heretofore, formerly;* (ii.) *at certain times, at times, sometimes,* here; (iii.) of the future, *one day, some day.* **cithara** (399), instrum. w. suscitat. **tacentem,** acc. fem. s. pres. partc. act. ag. w. musam; fr. tăceo, -ēre, -ŭi, -ĭtum, 2nd intrans. and trans. Of persons, *to be silent, not to speak, say nothing, hold one's peace* [silere more extended, *to make no noise*]; meton., of animals, *e.g.*, a dog, or things, *e.g.*, night, *to be still, noiseless, quiet*=sĭlēre; trans., *to pass over in silence, be silent about, e.g.*, dicenda tacendaque.

1135. **Suscitat,** 3rd s. pres. ind. act. fr. suscĭto, -are, -avi, -atum, (sus=subs, 21; cĭto, *to stir up*) *to move violently from beneath. To lift up, elevate* (only poet.). Of clods, *to throw up, cast up. To build, erect* (ante and post-class.). *To stir up, rouse up, awaken, set in motion, encourage, incite.* Of persons and things at rest or quiet. **musam,** acc. s. gov. by suscitat; fr. musa (174). **neque** (32). **semper** (158). **arcum,** acc. s. gov. by tendit; fr. arcus (538), *i.e.*, the bow with which he inflicts death, plague, etc.

1136. **Tendit,** 3rd s. pres. ind. act. fr. tendo (34). **Apollo** (68), subj. of tendit.

1137. **Rebus** (941), absolute. **angustis,** abl. pl. fem. ag. w. rebus; fr. angustus, -a, -um, adj.; (ango, Gk., *to choke*) *draw together, close* (rare). Of places, *narrow, strait, contracted;* fig., *confined, within narrow limits.* Of duration, *short, brief.* Of means, *needy, pinching, stinting;* here *critical, difficult.* Of mind and character, *narrow, base, low, mean, e.g.*, animus; "rebus angustis," *in straits of fortune.* **animosus** (503), nom. mas. s. predic. after appare. **atque** (37).

1138. **Fortis** (165), jnd. by atque to animosus. **appare,** 2nd s. pres. imper. act. fr. appāreo, -ēre, -ŭi, -ĭtum, 2nd intrans., (ad, 6; pareo, *to appear*) *to appear* in some place, *come in sight, make one's appearance,* esp. *to be evident, apparent, show oneself* (here) or *itself, be in public;* res apparet,

1139 Contrahes vento nimium secundo
1140 Turgida vela.

CARMEN XI.—AD QUINTIUM.

1141 QUID bellicosus Cantaber et Scythes,
1142 Hirpine Quinti, cogitet, Hadria
1143 Divisus objecto, remittas

more com. apparet is impers. w. acc. and. inf., or relat clause, *the thing* or *it is evident, clear, manifest* of objective certainty [videtur is subjective]. With predic. adj. or subst., *to be evidently*, etc. **sapienter,** adv.; (sapiens, 201) *sensibly, discreetly, prudently, wisely, judiciously.* **idem** (1132), *at the same time;* ag. w. tu und. in contrahes.

1139. **Contrahes,** 2nd sing. fut. ind. act. fr. contrăho, -hĕrĕ, -xi, -ctum, 3rd trans., (cum, 31; traho, 130) *to draw together, collect, assemble,* esp. *to shorten* (here) or *diminish by drawing together, contract, abridge;* fig., *to bring about, draw on, occasion, cause, produce, make, e.g.*, iram, bellum; fig., *to check, restrain;* contrahere cum, *to do business with, associate with, make a bargain with.* **vento** (604), of cause w. turgida. **nimium** (53), w. secundo, "dangerously favourable" (W.). **secundo** (335), ag. w. vento.

1140. **Turgida,** acc. neut. plu. ag. w. vela; fr. turgidus (107). **vela** (764), gov. by contrahes.

CARMEN XI. METRE.—*The Alcaic.* (Bk. I., Carmen ix.)

1141. **Quid** (297), gov. by cogitet. **bellicosus,** -a, -um, adj.; nom. mas. s. ag. w. Cantaber; (bellum, 24) *warlike, martial, valorous.* **Cantaber** (1018), nom. sing. subj. of cogitet. **Scythes** (502), nom. sing. jnd. by et to Cantaber.

1142. **Hirpine,** voc. mas. s. ag. w. Quinti; fr. Hirpīnus, -a, -um, adj.; perh. a local name. *The Hirpini* were a Samnite tribe of which Beneventum was the capital (W.). **Quinti,** voc. mas. s. fr. Quintius, -a, -um, name of a Roman gens. **cōgĭtet,** 3rd sing. pres. subj. act. fr. cōgĭto, -are, -avi, -ātum, 1st trans., (cum, 31; agito, 244) *to weigh thoroughly* in the mind, *consider on all points, ponder well, weigh, reflect, think upon. To have something in the mind, meditate upon,* of a work to be undertaken or a conclusion to be made; subj. in indirect quest. after quærere. **Hadria,** abl. (instrum.) s. after divisus; fr. Hadria (103).

1143. **Divisus,** pf. pass. part. nom. mas. sing. ag. w. Cantaber; fr. dīvĭdo, -vĭdĕre, -vīsi, -vīsum, 3rd trans., (dis-, 870; -vid, rt., *to separate*) *to part asunder, divide;* meton.=distribuere, *to divide among* several, *distribute,* w. acc., and in w. acc., or dat. *To part from, remove from; fig., to separate, distinguish,* w. ab. **objecto,** pf. pass. part. abl. mas. sing. ag. w. Hadria; fr. objĭcĭo, -jĭcĕre, -jēci, -jectum, 3rd trans., (ob, 329; jăcio, *to throw*) *to throw, cast* or *put before; throw towards,* esp. *to present, hold* or *present to, place before, expose to. To put before* as a defence. *To bring before, suggest. To expose, deliver up, abandon to, e.g.*, death. *To bring upon* one, *cause, occasion to;* pass., *to be occasioned, befal, occur. To throw out against, reproach, upbraid* one with. **remittas,** 2nd sing. conj. (hortative) fr. rĕmitto, -mittere, -mīsi, -missum, 3rd trans., (re, 659; mitto, 38) *to suffer to go back;* hence *loosen, slacken* anything; so fig., *relax, abate. To let*

1144 Quærere nec trepides in usum
1145 Poscentis ævi pauca. Fugit retro
1146 Levis juventas et decor, arida
1147 Pellente lascivos amores
1148 Canitie facilemque somnum.
1149 Non semper idem floribus est honor
1150 Vernis neque uno Luna rubens nitet
1151 Vultu. Quid æternis minorem
1152 Consiliis animum fatigas ?

sink or *fall down*, of parts of the body. *To leave off, forbear, omit to* do anything, w. inf. (here; not Cic. nor Cæs.). Of mind, *to relieve, refresh. To free* a person *from* anything. *To give up, grant, yield, resign, surrender, sacrifice*=concedere, condonare, aliquid alicui; intrans., *to decrease, abate. To send back, cause to go back. To return, restore, resign, e.g.*, provinciam. *To refer* a matter *to*, w. ad.

1144. **Quærere** (245), objective (see 871) after remittas. **nec** (19). **trepides,** 2nd sing. pres. conj. act. jnd. by nec to remittas; fr. trĕpĭdo (952, 991). **in** (76), of purpose as in 192. **usum** (625), gov. by in.

1145. **Poscentis,** gen. neut. s. pres. part. act. ag. w. ævi; fr posco (140). **ævi,** gen. s. after usum; fr. ævum (329). **pauca,** acc. neut. plu. gov. by poscentis; fr. paucus, -a, -um, adj. In sing. rare, *small, little*, i.e., *slight, trifling*. Of number, *few*; plu., *few, little*; neut. plu. esp. used as subst.= *a few words* (und. verba). "Trepides pauca," *worry thyself about provision for life which needs but little* (W.) **fugit** (548). **retro** (801). The years of those who have passed the flower of youth are "racedentes" no longer "venientes" (W.).

1146. **Levis** (74), nom. fem. s. ag. w. juventas, *unwrinkled*. **juventas,** -ātis, 3rd fem.; nom. s. subj. of fugit; *age of a juvenis, youthful age*, also of animals. Personified (707), the Goddess of Youth, *i.e.*, Hebe. **dĕcor,** -ōris, 3rd mas.; nom. s. jnd. by et to juventas; (decet, 134) *what is becoming, decorum, comeliness, elegance*, esp. *personal charms, beauty*. **arida,** abl. s. fem. ag. w. canitie; fr. aridus (352).

1147. **Pellente,** pres. part. act. abl. fem. s. ag. w. canitie; fr. pello (215). **lascivos,** acc. plu. mas. ag. w. amores; fr. lascivus (495). **amores** (247), gov. by pellente.

1148. **Canitie,** abl. absol. s. fr. canities (249). **facilem,** acc. mas. s. ag. w. somnum; fr. facilis (597). **somnum,** acc. jnd. by -que to amores, fr somnus (595).

1149. **Non** (55). **semper** (158). **idem** (1132), ag. w. honor **floribus,** dat. acquisitive (of possessor) after est; fr. flos (138). **est** (19). **honor** (8), nom. s. subj. of est; "*pride of beauty*" (W.).

1150. **Vernis,** dat. mas. plu. ag. w. floribus; fr. vernus, -a, -um, (ver, 129) *of* or *belonging to spring*. **neque** (32). **uno** (467), ag. w. vultu **Luna** (332), subj. of nitet. **rubens** (38), nom. fem. s. ag. w. Luna, here *to shine* or *glitter* (M.). **nitet,** 3rd sing. ind. pres. act. fr. niteo (161)

1151. **Vultu** (862), instrum. w. nitet or rubens. **quid** (229). **æternis,** abl. neut. plu. ag. w. consiliis; fr. æternus (891). **minorem,** acc. mas. s. ag. w. animum; fr. minor (63, 332).

1152. **Consiliis,** abl. plu. after minorem; fr. consĭlĭum, -ii, 2nd neut.

1153 Cur non sub alta vel platano vel hac
1154 Pinu jacentes sic temere et rosa
1155 Canos odorati capillos,
1156 Dum licet, Assyriaque nardo
1157 Potamus uncti? Dissipat Evius
1158 Curas edaces. Quis puer ocius
1159 Restinguet ardentis Falerni

(consulo, 890) *deliberation, consultation, counsel. Conclusion made with deliberation, determination, resolution, plan, purpose. Counsel, advice* to a person. *Aptness to deliberate, discretion, prudence. Any deliberate assembly, council* of war, etc. [This last is the orig. meaning of concilium]. This is the compar. abl.; "consiliis minor" = *less than, i.e.*, overtasked by, a Græcism. "Æterna consilia," *plans for a life that is not to end* (W.). **animum** (448), gov. by fatigas. **fatigas,** 2nd s. ind. pres. act. fr. fatigo (62).

1153. **Cur** (218). **non** (55). **sub** (21). **alta** (233), ag. w. platano. **vel vel** (187), *either..or.* **platano,** abl. s. gov. by sub; fr. plătănus, -i, 2nd fem., *the Greek* or *Oriental plane tree*, called cælebs (1264), because, unlike the elm, it did not support vines. **hac,** abl. fem. s. ag. w. pinu; fr. hic (7).

1154. **Pinu,** abl. s. jnd. by vel to platano; fr. pinus (375). **jacentes,** nom. mas. plu. ag. w. nos und. in potamus; fr. jacens (861). **sic** (89), *as we are* (W.). **temere** (291), *with no preparation* (W.), "just thrown at careless ease" (Con.). **rosa** (149), instrum. w. odorati.

1155. **Canos,** acc. plu. mas. ag. w. capillos; fr. canus (132). **odorati,** nom. mas. plu. jnd. by et to jacentes; fr. ŏdōrātus, -a, -um, *that emits an odour*, esp., *sweet smelling, fragrant*, pf. pass. part. of ŏdoro, -āre, -avi, -atum, 1st trans., (odor, 150) *to give a smell* or *fragrance to, perfume* a thing. **capillos** (1048), acc. of medial object (1048) w. odorati; "rosa odorati capillos," = *crowned with sweet smelling roses.*

1156. **Dum** (53). **licet,** 3rd sing. (impers.) ind. pres. fr. liceo (683), und. as subject potare, fr. potamus. **Assyria,** abl. fem. s. ag. w. nardo; fr. Assȳrĭus, -a, -um, adj.; *of Assyria* in Asia, betw. Media, Mesopotamia and Babylon. **nardo,** abl. s. jnd. by -que to rosâ; fr. nardus, -i, (the herb) 2nd fem., and nardum, -i, (the product) 2nd neut., *spikenard*; meton., *balsam, nard-oil.*

1157. **Potamus,** 1st plu. pres. ind. act. fr. poto (509). **uncti,** nom. mas. plu. ag. w. nos und. in potamus; fr. unctus (692). **dissipat,** 3rd sing. pres. ind. act. fr. dissĭpo, -are, -avi, -atum, 1st trans., (dis, 870; supo = jacio) *to spread abroad, scatter, disperse.* In pass. part. plu. dissipati; reflex., *having scattered themselves. To disperse, scatter*; pregn., *to demolish, destroy, squander, e.g.*, rem familiarem, fig., *spread abroad, disseminate, e.g.*, famam; here *to dismiss, dissipate.* **Evius** (485), -ii, acc. Evion, voc. Evie, 2nd mas.; nom. s. subj. of dissipat; a surname of Bacchus.

1158. **Curas** (215), gov. by dissipat. **edaces,** acc. fem. plu. ag. w. curas; fr. ĕdax, -ācis, adj.; abl. edaci, (edo, *to eat*) *voracious, gluttonous.* Of things, *devouring, gnawing, destroying.* **Quis puer** (149), subj. of restinguet. **ocius** (966).

1159. **Restinguet,** 3rd s. fut. ind. act. fr. restinguo, -guĕre, -xi, -ctum, 3rd trans., (re-, 659; stinguo, *to quench*) *to put out, extinguish* (class.); fig., *exterminate, annihilate. To assuage, slake, allay, e.g.*, sitim. Of wine, *to*

1160 Pocula prætereunte lympha?
1161 Quis devium scortum eliciet domo
1162 Lyden? Eburna, dic age, cum lyra
1163 Maturet in comptum Lacænæ
1164 More comas religata nodum.

CARMEN XII.—AD MÆCENATEM.

1165 Nolis longa feræ bella Numantiæ

temper, i.e., mix with water. Of poison, *to make ineffectual, counteract.* **ardentis,** gen. s. neut. ag. w. Falerni; fr. ardens (136). **Falerni** (634), after pocula.

1160. **Pocula** (19), gov. by restinguet. **prætereunte,** pres. part. abl. fem. s. ag. w. lympha; fr. prætereo, -īre, -īvi, more frequ. -ĭi, -ĭtum, irreg. intrans. and trans., (præter, 92; eo, 51) *to go by* or *past, pass by,* "præterit me," w. subjective clause or nom., *a thing escapes me* or *is unperceived by me. To pass over, omit, not mention, exclude, neglect* in reading, writing, legacies, invitations, etc. *To neglect to do* a thing. **lympha,** abl. (instrum.) s. fr. lympha (952).

1161. **Quis** (149), subst., subj. of eliciet. **devium,** acc. neut. s. ag. w. scortum; fr. devius (454), predic. "*entice to our retreat*" (W.). **scortum,** acc. s. in app. to Lyden; fr. scortum, -i, 2nd neut., (sibilated collat. fm. of corium) *a skin, hide,* (only once post-class.) *a harlot.* **eliciet,** 3rd sing. fut. ind. act. fr. ēlĭcĭo, -lĭcĕre, -lĭcui and -lexi, -lectum, 3rd trans., (e, 691; -lacio, *to draw*). Of living objects, *to entice forth, bring out.* Relig., *call forth* or *down* a god, *e.g.*, Jovem, by religious rites. *To conjure up* a departed spirit by incantations; fig., *to entice forth, elicit, e.g.*, misericordiam.

1162. **Lyden,** acc. s. gov. by eliciet; fr. Lȳde, -es, 1st fem. (Gk.). **eburna,** abl. fem. s. ag. w. lyra; fr. ĕburnus, -a, -um, adj.; (ebur, 714) *of ivory. White as ivory* [eburneus is prose word]. **dic** (217). **age** (641). **cum** (31). **lyra** (285), gov. by cum.

1163. **Maturet,** 3rd sing. pres. subj. act. after dic (ut being omitted); fr. mātūro, -are, -āvi, -ātum, 1st trans. and intrans. Of fruits, etc., *to make ripe, bring to maturity;* pass. reflex., *to become ripe;* meton., *to do early* or *betimes, hasten, quicken, accelerate* a thing. With inf., *to hasten* to do a thing, sts. *to be precipitate* in doing; intrans., of fruits, *to grow ripe;* meton., *to make haste* (rare but class.). **in,** w. acc. (76). **comptum,** acc. mas. s. ag. w. nodum; fr. comptus, -a, -um, *adorned, ornamented,* pf. pass. part. of como, cômĕre, compsi, comptum, 3rd trans., (cum, 31; emo, *to buy*) *to take* or *gather together,* genly. of the hair, *to comb, braid, dress. To ornament, deck,* often of rhetorical embellishment. Others read "incomptum," *unadorned,* for in comptum. **Lacænæ,** gen. s. after more; fr. Lăcæna, -æ, 1st fem., (prop. fem. adj. und. mulier) *a Lacedæmonian* or *Spartan woman,*

1164. **More** (260), here adv.=*like.* **comas,** acc. of medial obj. (1048) plu. w. religata; fr. coma (152). **religata,** nom. fem. s. pf. pass. part. ag. w. subj. (Lyde) of maturet; fr. religo (152). **nodum,** acc. s. gov. by in; fr. nodu. (297). If "incomptum" be read, this must be a cogn. accus. w. religata.

Carmen XII. Metre.—*The Third Asclepiadean.* (Bk. I., Carmen vi.)

1165. **Nolis,** 2nd sing. pres. conj. (hortative) fr. nōlo, nolle, nōlui, irreg. intrans., (non, volo, 104) *to not wish, be unwilling.* Imper. w. inf. used in a

Nec dirum Hannibalem nec Siculum mare
Pœno purpureum sanguine mollibus
    Aptari citharæ modis,
Nec sævos Lapithas et nimium mero
Hylæum domitosque Herculea manu
Telluris juvenes, unde periculum
    Fulgens contremuit domus
Saturni veteris; tuque pedestribus

neg. command, *e.g.*, noli irasci, "*don't be angry.*" **longa,** acc. neut. plu. ag. w. bella; fr. longus (73). **feræ,** gen. sing. fem. ag. w. Numantiæ; fr. ferus (258). **bella** (24), subj. of aptari. **Numantiæ,** gen. after bella; fr. Numantia, 1st fem., a city in Hispania Tarraconensis, destroyed by Scipio Africanus the younger.

1166. **Nec** (19). **dirum,** acc. mas. s. ag. w. Hannibalem; fr. dirus (37). **Hannibalem,** acc. s. jnd. by nec to bella; fr. Hannibal, -ălis, a Punic surname, here the most celebrated, the leader of the Carthaginians in the second Punic war. **Siculum,** acc. neut. s. ag. w. mare; fr. Sĭcŭlus, -a, -um, adj.; *of* or *belonging to the Siculi, Sicilian.* **mare** (14), jnd. by nec to Hannibalem. "Siculum mare," in Hor. the sea between the north coast of Sicily and Italy.

1167. **Pœno** (322), adj., mas. ag. w. sanguine. **purpureum,** acc. neut. s. ag. w. mare; fr. purpureus (788). **sanguine** (225), instrum. w. purpureum. **mollibus,** dat. mas. plu. ag. w. modis; fr. mollis (203).

1168. **Aptari,** pres. inf. pass. after nolis; fr. apto, -āre, -avi, -atum, 1st trans., (aptus, 193; intens. of obsol. apio or apo, *to seize, hold, fasten*) *to join on, adapt, fit, apply, adjust, accommodate,* w. dat. or ad. *To get ready, prepare, fashion.* With se, etc., *to get oneself ready.* **citharæ,** gen. s. after modis; fr. cithara (399). **modis,** dat. plu. after traject. aptari; fr. modus (422).

1169. **Sævos,** acc. plu. mas. ag. w. Lapithas; fr. sævus (172). **Lapithas,** acc. jnd. by nec to mare; fr. Lapithæ (484). **nimium,** acc. mas. s. ag. w. Hylæum; fr. nimius (53). **mero** (203), of manner w. nimium, which genly. takes the gen., *e.g.*, nimius sermonis (M.); nimius mero, "*overcharged with wine*" (W.).

1170. **Hylæum,** acc. s. jnd. by et to Lapithas; fr. Hȳlæus, -i, 2nd mas., a centaur shot by Atalanta, to whom he offered violence. **domitos** (338), ag. w. juvenes. **Herculea,** abl. fem. s. ag. w. manu; fr. Herculeus (124). **manu** (794), instrum. w. domitos.

1171. **Telluris,** gen. s. after juvenes; fr. tellus (213). **juvenes** (182), jnd. by -que to Hylæum. **unde** (676)=a quibus, *from whom.* **periculum,** acc. s. gov. by contremuit; fr. pĕrīcŭlum, -i (pĕriclum, -i, comic poet.), 2nd neut., (perior, *to try,* whence peritus, experior) *a trial, experiment, attempt, proof, essay* (class.). *Risk, hazard, danger,* which accompanies an attempt. *Trial, action, suit at law. A writ of judgment, sentence.*

1172. **Fulgens** (203), nom. fem. s. ag. w. domus. **contremuit,** 3rd s. pf. ind. act. fr. contrĕmisco, -iscĕre, -trĕmui, no sup., 3rd inceptive, (cum, 31; tremo, 43) intrans., *to tremble all over, quake;* trans., *to tremble at something very much.* **domus** (145), subj. of contremuit.

1173. **Saturni,** gen. s. after domus; fr. Saturnus (334). **veteris** (19), mas. ag. w. Saturni. **tu** (69), subj. of dices. **-que,** exp. contrast, *while* (M.).

1174 Dices historiis prœlia Cæsaris,
1175 Mæcenas, melius ductaque per vias
1176 Regum colla minacium.
1177 Me dulces dominæ Musa Licymniæ
1178 Cantus, me voluit dicere lucidum
1179 Fulgentes oculos et bene mutuis
1180 Fidum pectus amoribus;
1181 Quam nec ferre pedem dedecuit choris
1182 Nec certare joco nec dare brachia

pedestribus, abl. fem. plu. ag. w. historiis; fr. **pĕdester, -tris, -tre,** adj.; (pes, 135) *on foot, that goes, is done,* etc., *on foot. Belonging to or representing one on foot.* Of style, *not elevated, written in prose, plain, common, without poetic flights, prosaic. By land, on land.*

1174. **Dices** (467). **historiis,** abl. (of manner) plu. fr. **histŏria, -æ,** 1st fem., prop. *a narrative of past events, history;* meton., *narrative, account, tale, story.* **prœlia** (181), gov. by dices. **Cæsaris** (80), after prœlia.

1175. **Mæcenas** (1). **melius** (58), w. dices. **ducta,** acc. neut. plu. pf. pass. part. ag. w. colla; fr. duco (133). **-que** (4). **per** (114). **vias,** acc. plu. gov. by per; fr. via (664), *i.e.*, the streets of Rome (W.).

1176. **Regum** (142), after colla. **colla,** acc. plu. jnd. by -que to prœlia; fr. collum, -i, 2nd neut., collat. collus, -i, 2nd mas., (ak. to collis, *a hill*) *the neck* of men and animals, often as symbol of *life* or *servitude.* **minacium,** gen. mas. plu. ag. w. regum; fr. minax (266); "*that just now threatened so high*" (W.).

1177. **Me** (29), subj. of dicere. **dulces** (247), ag. w. cantus. **dominæ** (1087), in app. to Licymniæ, *i.e.*, your mistress (W.). **Musa** (174), subj. of voluit. **Licymniæ,** gen. (objective) s. after cantus; fr. Licymnia, -æ, 1st fem.

1178. **Cantus** (575), gov. by dicere. **voluit,** 3rd s. pf. ind. fr. volo (104). **dicere** (169), prolat. after voluit. **lucidum,** acc. neut. s. as adv. w. fulgentes; fr. lucidus (90).

1179. **Fulgentes,** acc. mas. plu. ag. w. oculos; fr. fulgens (203). **oculos** (834), gov. by dicere. **et** (2). **bene** (1050), *wisely* or=valde (W.); intensifies fidum. **mutuis,** dat. mas. plu. ag. w. amoribus; fr. **mūtuus, -a, -um,** adj.; (muto, 77) *in return, in exchange, mutual, reciprocal;* **mutuum, -i,** 2nd neut., *a mutual* or *reciprocal thing, like for like, a return;* meton., of money, etc., *lent* or *borrowed.*

1180. **Fidum,** acc. neut. s. ag. w. pectus; fr. **fīdus, -a, -um,** adj.; (fido, 379) *that may be relied on, trusty, faithful, reliable, sure.* Of things, *sure, certain, safe.* **pectus** (98), jnd. by et to oculos. **amoribus** (496), after traject. fidum.

1181. **Quam** (70), fem. s. ag. w. Licymniæ, acc. subj. of ferre. **nec,** folld. by nec (349). **ferre** (804), subj. of dedecuit. **pedem,** acc. s. gov. by ferre; fr. pes (135). **dedecuit,** 3rd sing. pf. ind. fr. dedecet (875). **choris,** dat. plu. after (indirect obj. of) ferre; fr. chorus (31).

1182. **Certare,** pres. inf. act. jnd. by nec to ferre; fr. certo (8). **joco** (756), abl. of manner w. certare. **dare** (673), jnd. by nec to certare. **brachia,** acc. plu. gov. by (direct obj. of) dare; fr. **brăchium, -ii,** 2nd neut.,

1183 Ludentem nitidis virginibus sacro
1184 Dianæ celebris die.
1185 Num tu, quæ tenuit dives Achæmenes,
1186 Aut pinguis Phrygiæ Mygdonias opes
1187 Permutare velis crine Licymniæ,
1188 Plenas aut Arabum domos ?—
1189 Dum flagrantia detorquet ad oscula

(Gk.) *an arm, i.e.*, the whole arm from shoulders to fingers, esp. the lower part; "brachia circumdare" or "injicere," *to throw the arms around*, w. dat. Also of the *claws* of fish, *branches* of trees, etc.

1183. **Ludentem,** acc. fem. s. pres. part. act. ag. w. quam; fr. ludo (730). **nitidis,** dat. fem. plu. ag. w. virginibus; fr. nĭtĭdus, -a, -um, adj.; (nĭteo, 161) *shining, glittering, bright, polished, clear.* Of persons, *well-conditioned, healthy, beautiful, neat, spruce, trim,* "*in holiday dress*" (W.). Of plants, etc., *blooming, luxurious, flourishing.* Of speech, *polished, cultivated, refined.* **virginibus,** dat. plu. after dare; fr. virgo (63). **sacro,** abl. s. mas. ag. w. die; fr. sacer (22).

1184. **Dianæ,** gen. s. after die; fr. Diana (521). **celebris,** gen. s. fem. ag. w. Dianæ; fr. cĕlĕber (sts. -bris), -brĭs, -bre, adj.; (acc. to some, collat. of creber, acc. to others akin to cluo, calo). Of places, *much frequented* or *resorted to, crowded. That exists in abundance* or *happens often* (creber and frequens more com. in this sense). *Renowned, distinguished, famous,* of a god whose temple is thronged (here). **die** (20), temporal, "*the sacred day that fills Diana's temple*" (W.).

1185. **Num,** interrog. adv. used genly. where a neg. answ. is expected; (i.) direct, no corresp. Eng., *e.g.*, numquid me vis? Do you wish anything further? Is there anything else? sts. jnd. to -nam or -ne. (ii.) indirect, *whether.* **tu** (69), subj. of velis. **quæ** (359), neut. plu. ag. w. demonst. (ea) und. after permutare; acc. gov. by tenuit. **tenuit,** 3rd s. pf. ind. act. fr. teneo (204). **dives** (270), ag. w. Achæmenes. **Achæmĕnes,** -is, 3rd mas., nom. s., subj. of tenuit; first king of Persia, ancestor of the Achæmenidæ, grandfather of Cyrus. "Quæ...Achæmenes,"=*Asiatic wealth.*

1186. **Aut** (131). **pinguis,** gen. s. fem. ag. w. Phrygiæ; fr. pinguis (905). **Phrygiæ,** gen. s. after opes; fr. Phrȳgia, 1st fem., the country *Phrygia* (418). **Mygdonias,** acc. plu. fem. ag. w. opes; fr. Mygdŏnĭus, -a, -um, adj.; *Phrygian,* the Mygdones being a people of Thrace, who aftwds. took possession of part of Phrygia. **opes,** acc. plu. jnd. by aut to antecedent of quæ; fr. opis (179).

1187. **Permutare,** pres. inf. (prolative) act. after velis; fr. permūto, -are, -avi, -atum, 1st trans., (per, 114; muto, 77) *to move* or *turn completely. To change* or *alter completely. To change between* two parties, hence *exchange, interchange* one thing for another. *To buy,* with abl. of price. **velis,** 2nd s. pres. conj. (potential) fr. volo (104). **crine,** abl. (of price w. permutare) fr. crinis, -is, 3rd mas., (cresco, 329) *the hair,* also the *tail* of a comet. **Licymniæ** (1177), after crine.

1188. **Plenas,** acc. fem. plu. ag. w. domos; fr. plenus (463). **aut** (131). **Arabum** (685), after domos. **domos** (420), jnd. by aut to opes.

1189. **Dum** (53). **flagrantia,** acc. neut. plu. ag. w. oscula; fr. flagrans (605). **detorquet,** 3rd s. ind. pres. act. fr. dētorqueo, -ēre, -torsi, -tortum or -torsum, 2nd trans., (de, 10; torqueo, *to twist, turn*) *to turn* or *bend aside*

1190 Cervicem aut facili sævitia negat,
1191 Quæ poscente magis gaudeat eripi,
1192 Interdum rapere occupat.

CARMEN XIII.

IN ARBOREM, CUJUS CASU IN AGRO SABINO PÆNE OPPRESSUS EST.

1193 Ille et nefasto te posuit die,
1194 Quicunque primum, et sacrilega manu
1195 Produxit, arbos, in nepotum

turn off or *away*. *To twist out of shape, distort*; fig., *turn away* or *aside, divert, distort, misrepresent*. **ad** (6). **oscula** (359), gov. by ad.

1190. **Cervicem** (346), gov. by detorquet. **aut** (131). **facili**, abl. fem. s. ag. w. sævitiâ; fr. facilis (597), "*that yields easily*" (W.). **sævitia**, abl. (of manner) s. fr. sævĭtĭa, -æ, 1st fem., (sævus, 172) of animals, *a raging, fierceness, ferocity*; meton., *any violent excitement, fierceness, cruelty, severity*. **negat**, 3rd s. pres. ind. act. fr. nego (694).

1191. **Quæ** (46), fem. s. ag. w. Licymniæ; nom. to gaudet. **poscente**, pres. part. act. abl. mas. s. ag. w. te und.; fr. posco (140). The abl. is compar. after magis, "*more than you ask them*" (W.). **magis** (603). **gaudeat** (610), subj. giving the reason of the epithet facili (W.). **eripi**, pres. inf. pass. after gaudeat; fr. ēripĭo, -rĭpĕre, -rĭpui, -reptum, 3rd trans., (e, 691; rapio, 489) *to snatch, tear, pull out, tear away*. *To deliver, set free, remove, deprive of*. Its subject is oscula. Others take magis w. gaudeat in the sense, "*which she would have you snatch, not beg*" (M.).

1192. **Interdum**, temp. adv.; (inter, 330; dum, 53) *sometimes, occasionally, now and then*; meton., *in the meanwhile*. **rapere**, pres. inf. (prolative, 570) act. after occupat; fr. rapio (489). **occupat**, 3rd s. pres. ind. act. fr. occupo (303), "rapere occupat," *is the first to snatch* (W.). Constr. same as gaudeat. The obj. of rapere is the same as the subj. of eripi.

Carmen XIII. Metre.—*The Alcaic*. (Bk. I., Carmen ix.)

1193. **Ille** (337), subj. of posuit. **et** (2). **nefasto**, abl. s. mas. ag. w. die; fr. nefastus (811), "*of ill-omen*" (W.). **te** (83), gov. by posuit. **posuit**, 3rd sing. pf. ind. act. fr. pono (104). **die** (20), temporal.

1194. **Quicunque** (167), mas. s. ag. w. ille; nom. to posuit und. **primum** (733), w. posuit und. **sacrilĕga**, abl. sing. fem. ag. w. manu; fr. săcrĭlĕgus, -a, -um, adj.; (sacer, 22; lego, *to gather, collect*) *that robs a temple, sacrilegious*; meton., *one that violates* or *profanes sacred things, impious*. **manu** (794), instrum.

1195. **Produxit**, 3rd s. pf. ind. act. fr. prōdūco, -cĕre, -xi, -ctum, 3rd trans., (pro, *forward*; duco, 133) *to lead forth, bring forward*. Of an actor, *to represent, perform*. Of a father, *to beget*. Of a mother, *to bear*. Of trees, *to produce*; fig., *to bring forward* to distinction, *raise, advance, promote*. *To educate, rear*. *To lengthen out, protract, prolong, e.g.*, vitam, cœnam. **arbos** (329), voc. s. **in**, of purpose (192). **nepotum**, gen. plu. after perniciem; fr. nepos (71).

1196 Perniciem opprobriumque pagi;
1197 Illum et parentis crediderim sui
1198 Fregisse cervicem et penetralia
1199 Sparsisse nocturno cruore
1200 Hospitis; ille venena Colcha
1201 Et quidquid usquam concipitur nefas
1202 Tractavit, agro qui statuit meo

1196. **Perniciem,** acc. s. gov. by in; fr. pernĭcĭes, -ei, old gen. -nĭcii or -nĭci; dat. pernicie rare; 5th fem., (perneco, *to kill thoroughly*) *a killing utterly, destruction* by violence, slaughter, etc.; meton., *ruin, overthrow, disaster, calamity.* Abstract for concrete of a thing, *ruinous* or *baneful, ruin, pest, e.g.,* Verres, Clodius, etc. **opprobrium,** acc. s. jnd. by -que to perniciem; fr. opprobrium (448). **pagi,** gen. s. after opprobrium; fr. pāgus, -i, 2nd mas., (ak. to pango, *to fix, what is fixed, settled*) *a district, canton, province;* meton., *the country=country-people* (Hor.).

1197. **Illum** (9), subj. of fregisse. **parentis** (297), after cervicem. **crediderim,** 1st s. pf. conj. act. fr. credo (93). This tense as well as fut. pf. is used to convey opinion or assertion moderately. **sui,** gen. mas. s. ag. w. parentis; fr. suus (17).

1198. **Fregisse,** pf. ind. act. after crediderim; fr. frango (570). **cervicem** (345), gov. by fregisse. **penetralia,** acc. neut. plu. gov. by sparsisse; fr. pĕnĕtrālis, -e, adj., (penetro, *to penetrate*) *piercing, penetrating* (ante-class.). *Inward, inner, interior, innermost;* penetrālia, -um, 3rd neut. plu., (und. loca) rarely sing., penetrale, -is, and penetral, -ālis, 3rd neut., *the inner part* of anything, esp. a building. *Inner room* or *space. Sanctuary,* esp. of Penates, *a chapel.*

1199. **Sparsisse,** pf. ind. act. jnd. by et to fregisse; fr. spargo (1039). **nocturno** (1011), ag. w. cruore. **cruore** (912), instrum.

1200. **Hospitis,** gen. s. after cruore; fr. hospes (386). **ille** (337), subj. of tractavit. **venena,** acc. plu. gov. by tractavit; fr. venenum (646). **Colcha,** acc. neut. plu. ag. w. venena; fr. Colchus, -a, -um, adj.; *of Colchis,* province of Asia Minor, E. of the Black Sea, celebrated on account of the golden fleece and Medea.

1201. **Et** (2), unites this relat. (substantival) sentence to venena, as obj. of tractavit. **quidquid** (10), neut. sing. ag. w. nefas; nom. to concipitur, **usquam,** adv. like uspiam, (akin to que) *at* or *in any place* or *anywhere,* usu. in neg. or quasi-neg. clauses, *e.g.,* hypoth. clauses, questions of surprise, etc. [uspiam in affirm. sentences]. Of other relations, *in anything, anywhere.* **concipitur,** 3rd s. pres. ind. pass. fr. concĭpio, -cĭpĕre, -cēpi, -ceptum, 3rd trans., (cum, 31; capio, 1388), *to take* or *lay hold of on all sides,* or (as it were) *with both hands, take to oneself, receive,* esp. *to become pregnant.* Of the mind, *to imagine, conceive,* esp. *understand, comprehend. To adopt, harbour, give place to* any state of mind, passion, etc., *undertake, commit, e.g.,* vitia, furores, amorem. *To draw up, express in words, compose, e.g.,* a treaty, oath, etc. *To declare in solemn form* or *words* a festival, auspices, etc. **nefas** (277), would prop. be in acc., but being in the relative clause, it is attracted into the case of the relative.

1202. **Tractavit,** 3rd sing. pf. ind. act. fr. tracto (863). **agro,** abl. (local) sing. fr. ager (12). **qui** (19), sing. mas. ag. w. ille; nom. to statuit.

1203 Te, triste lignum, te caducum
1204 In domini caput immerentis.
1205 Quid quisque vitet, nunquam homini satis
1206 Cautum est in horas: navita Bosporum
1207 Pœnus perhorrescit neque ultra
1208 Cæca timet aliunde fata,
1209 Miles sagittas et celerem fugam
1210 Parthi, catenas Parthus et Italum

statuit, 3rd sing. pf. ind. act, fr. statuo (692). **meo,** abl. mas. s. ag. w. agro; fr. meus (2).

1203. **Te** (83), gov. by statuit. **triste,** acc. neut. s. ag. w. lignum; fr. tristis (102). **lignum,** acc. in app. to te; fr. lignum (237). **te** (83), in app. to prec. te. **caducum,** acc. neut. s. ag. w. te; fr. cădūcus, -a, -um, adj.; (cado, 977) *that falls* or *has fallen, falling. Destined to fall, that easily falls;* fig., *failing, fleeting, perishable.*

1204. **In** (81), w. caducum. **domini,** gen. s. after caput; fr. dominus (6). **caput** (22), gov. by in. **immerentis,** gen. s. mas. ag. w. domini; fr. immĕrens, -ntis, adj.; (in, neg.; mereo, *to deserve*) *undeserving, not meriting, innocent.*

1205. **Quid** (297), gov. by vitet. **quisque,** quæque, quodque and as subst. quicque, quidque. Indef. pron., *each, every.* Of persons, *each person, every one.* Of things, *each thing, everything.* With superlatives exp. universality, "doctissimus quisque," *all the most learned.* With ordinal numerals it exp. universality, generality, "quinto quoque anno," *every five years.* Often jnd. w. plu. verb, and very com. w. se, suus, *e.g.*, pro se quisque. **vitet,** 3rd s. pres. subj. (in depend. quest.) act. fr. vito (226). **nunquam** (13). **homini** (123), of agent after cautum est. **satis** (37).

1206. **Cautum,** nom. sing. neut. predic. ag. w. clause quid...vitet; fr. cautus (226). **est** (19), w. cautum; combinate pf. pass. 3rd sing. ind. of caveo (380). **horas,** acc. pl. gov. by in; fr. hora (252). **in,** of time (730). **navita** (378), subj. of perhorrescit. **Bosporum,** acc. s. gov. by perhorrescit; fr. Bospŏrus (Bosphorus), -i, 2nd mas. (Gk.), *Heifer's Ford, i.e.*, the Thracian Bosphorus (Straits of Constantinople), so called from Io's passage here as a heifer.

1207. **Pœnus** (927), adj.; ag. w. navita. **perhorrescit,** 3rd s. ind. pres. act. fr. perhorresco, -scĕre, -horrŭi, no sup., (per, 114; horreo, *to dread, shudder*) 3rd inceptive intrans., *to tremble* or *shudder greatly,* trans., *to shudder greatly at* or *have a great horror of.* **neque** (32). **ultra** (546).

1208. **Cæca,** acc. neut. plu. ag. w. fata; fr. cæcus (490), *hidden, unseen.* **timet** (224). **aliunde,** adv.; (alius, 92; unde, 291) *from another person, place* or *thing, from elsewhere.* With verbs which take ab, ex, etc., *e.g.*, pendēre, mutuare, sumere, etc. With kindred words, *e.g.*, alius, alio, aliter, an abbreviated way of speaking, *e.g.*, "aliis aliunde est periculum," *danger comes to some from one quarter, to others from another.* **fata** (389), gov. by timet.

1209. **Miles** (168), subj. of timet und. **sagittas** (693), gov. by timet und. **celerem fugam** (1049), jnd. by et to sagittas.

1210. **Parthi,** gen. s. after fugam; fr. Parthus (504). **catenas** (689),

1211 Robur; sed improvisa leti
1212 Vis rapuit rapietque gentes.
1213 Quam pæne furvæ regna Proserpinæ
1214 Et judicantem vidimus Æacum,
1215 Sedesque discretas piorum, et
1216 Æoliis fidibus querentem
1217 Sappho puellis de popularibus,

gov. by timet und. **Parthus** (504), nom. s. subj. of timet und. **Italum,** acc. neut. s. ag. w. robur; fr. Italus (1044).

1211. **Robur,** acc. s. jnd. by et to catenas; fr. robur (97). Here the Tullianum or lower dungeon of the Mamertine prison, near the Capitol (W.). **sed** (591). **improvisa,** nom. fem. sing. ag. w. vis; fr. imprōvīsus, -a, -um, adj.; (in, neg.; provideo, *to foresee*) *not foreseen, unexpected;* "de" or "ex improviso," *unexpectedly.* **leti** (121), after vis.

1212. **Vis** (436), nom. s. subj. of rapuit. **rapuit,** 3rd s. pf. ind. act. fr. rapio (489). **rapiet,** 3rd s. fut. ind. act. **gentes** (41), gov. by rapiet; here "*mankind*" (W.).

1213. **Quam** (352), w. adv. **pæne,** adv.; *nearly, almost* (class.). **furvæ,** gen. s. fem. ag. w. Proserpinæ; fr. furvus, -a, -um, adj.; (akin to uro, *to burn*) *dark, dusky, gloomy, swarthy, black.* **regna** (146), gov. by vidimus. **Proserpinæ,** gen. after regna; fr. Prōserpina (668).

1214. **Judicantem,** acc. mas. s. pres. part. act. ag. w. Æacum; fr. jūdĭco, -are, -avi, -atum, 1st trans., (jus, 680; dico, 86) *to declare what is law, be* or *act as judge. To investigate* a case *judically,* w. accessory notion of pronouncing legal sentence; intrans., *to pass judgment, determine, decide.* With things as objs., *to pass judgment about* a matter, *determine. To pronounce sentence against* one of being guilty of a crime, w. acc. of crime and dat. pers.; fig., *to pass an opinion, pronounce judgment,* w. acc. of that about which. *To resolve, determine in one's mind.* With two accs., *to pronounce, declare* a person *to be* something. *To deem, consider, suppose, think, imagine. To settle, decide.* **vidimus** (49). **Æacum,** acc. s. jnd. by et to regna; fr. Æăcus, -i, 2nd mas., (Gk.) acc. Æacon. Son of Jupiter by Europa, king of Ægina, father of Peleus and Telamon, grandfather of Achilles and Ajax; on account of his justice made judge in the lower world with Rhadamanthus.

1215. **Sedes,** acc. plu. jnd. by -que to Æacum; fr. sedes (46). **discretas,** pf. pass. part. acc. fem. plu. ag. w. sedes; fr. discerno (487); *separate.* Elysium was separate fr. Tartarus. **piorum,** gen. plu. mas. after sedes; fr. pius (273).

1216. **Æoliis,** abl. fem. plu. ag. w. fidibus; fr. Æŏlius, -a, -um, -adj.; here *of Æolia.* Sappho being a Lesbian woman; "Æolium carmen" = *a Sapphic* or *Lesbian ode.* **fidibus** (295), instrum. w. querentem. **querentem,** acc. fem. s. pres. part. ag. w. Sappho; fr. queror (53).

1217. **Sappho,** acc. s. jnd. by et to sedes; fr. Sapphō, -ūs, fem. (Gk.), a poetess of Mitylene, who, on account of her hopeless love for Phaon, threw herself fr. the Leucadian rock into the sea. **puellis,** abl. plu. gov. by de; fr. puella (254). **de** (10). **popularibus,** abl. plu. fem. ag. w. puellis; fr. pŏpŭlāris, -e, adj.; (populus, 32) *proceeding from, belonging to* or *designed for the people, agreeable to the people, popular. Of* or *belonging to the same people* or *country, indigenous, native;* genly as subst., pŏpŭlāris, -is, 3rd mas., (und. homo) *a fellow-countryman,* so of animals, plants. *Companion,*

1218 Et te sonantem plenius aureo,
1219 Alcæe, plectro dura navis,
1220 Dura fugæ mala, dura belli!
1221 Utrumque sacro digna silentio
1222 Mirantur Umbræ dicere; sed magis
1223 Pugnas et exactos tyrannos
1224 Densum humeris bibit aure vulgus.
1225 Quid mirum, ubi illis carminibus stupens

partner, comrade, associate in the same trade, occupation, etc. *Devoted to the people*, opp. to the nobility, *democratic;* pŏpŭlāres, -ium, 3rd mas., *the people's party*, opp. to optimates or aristocrats.

1218. **Te** (83), jnd. by et to Sappho. **sonantem,** acc. mas. s. pres. part. act. ag. w. te; fr. sono (200), here trans. **plenius,** neut. s. of plenus (463), compar. of adv. plene; *fully, wholly, completely, thoroughly, largely;* superl., plenissime. **aureo,** abl. neut. s. ag. w. plectro; fr. aureus (157).

1219. **Alcæe,** voc. s. fr. Alcæus, -i, 2nd mas., celebrated lyric poet of Mitylene, contemporary of Sappho, inventor of the Alcaic verse. **plectro** (623), w. sonantem. **dura** (479), gov. by sonantem. **navis,** gen. s. after dura; fr. navis (93).

1220. **Dura** (479), ag. w. mala. **fugæ,** gen. s. after mala; fr. fŭga, -æ, 1st fem., *a fleeing, flight, running away. Exile, expatriation* (here). *Swift course* or *motion, speed. An avoiding, trying to escape, flying from.* **mala,** acc. neut. plu. as subst. gov. by sonantem; fr. malus (116). **dura,** anaphora (895). **belli** (878), after dura.

1221. **Utrumque,** acc. mas. s. subj. of dicere; fr. uterque (927). **sacro,** abl. neut. s. ag. w. silentio; fr. sacer (22). **digna,** acc. plu. neut. gov. by dicere; fr. dignus (644). **silentio,** abl. s. after digna; fr. silentium, -ii, 2nd neut., (sileo, 305) *noiselessness, stillness, silence* of night, etc. *Standing still*, opp. to motion or activity, *cessation, inaction* (class.); "sacro silentio," the silence with which divine rights are received (W.).

1222. **Mirantur,** 3rd plu. pres. ind. fr. miror (147). **umbræ,** nom. plu. subj. of mirantur; fr. umbra (205). **dicere** (169), objective after mirantur. **sed** (591). **magis** (603), w. bibit.

1223. **Pugnas** (59), gov. by bibit. **exactos,** acc. plu. mas. pf. pass. part. ag. w. tyrannos; fr. exĭgo, -ĭgĕre, -ēgi, -actum, 3rd trans., (ex, 691; ago, 43) *to drive out* or *forth, get out. To demand, require, enforce, exact* payment, etc. *To claim. To lead, spend, pass* time. *To weigh accurately, ponder, consider. To treat, consult, deliberate.* **tyrannos,** acc. plu. jnd. by et to pugnas; fr. tyrannus (788).

1224. **Densum,** nom. neut. s. ag. w. vulgus; fr. densus (204). **humeris,** abl. (instrum.) plu. w. densum; fr. humerus (67). "Densum humeris," *pressing shoulder to shoulder* (W.). **bibit,** 3rd s. ind. pres. act. fr. bibo (518). **aure,** abl. (instrum.) w. bibit; fr. auris (642). **vulgus** (801), subj. of bibit. "Sed magis...vulgus," they crowd more thickly and drink the words more greedily where Alcæus is singing (W.).

1225. **Quid** (245), subj. of est und. **mirum,** nom. neut. s. ag. w. quid; fr. mirus, -a, -um, adj.; (miror, 147) *wonderful, marvellous, astonishing;* comp. mirior ante-class. **ubi** (553), here=*considering that.* **illis,** abl. neut. plu. ag. w. carminibus; fr. ille (9). **carminibus,** abl. causal plu.

1226 Demittit atras bellua centiceps
1227   Aures et intorti capillis
1228   Eumenidum recreantur angues ?
1229 Quin et Prometheus et Pelopis parens
1230 Dulci laborum decipitur sono;
1231   Nec curat Orion leones
1232   Aut timidos agitare lyncas

CARMEN XIV.—AD POSTUMUM.

1233 Eheu fugaces, Postume, Postume,

w. stupens; fr. carmen (64). **stupens,** nom. fem. s. pres. part. act. ag. w bellua; fr. stŭpeo (495).

1226. **Demittit,** 3rd s. pres. ind. act. fr. demitto (659). **atras,** acc. plu. fem. ag. w. aures; fr. ater (661). **bellua** (307), nom. s. subj. of demittit, *i.e., Cerberus* **centiceps,** -cĭpĭtis, adj.; nom. fem. s. ag. w. bellua; (centum, 1258; caput, 22) *hundred-headed.*

1227. **Aures** (894), gov. by demittit. **intorti,** pf. pass. part. nom. mas. plu. ag. w. angues; fr. intorqueo, -ēre, -si, -tum, 2nd trans. irreg., (in, 76; tŏrqueo, *to turn, twist*) *to twine, turn round.* Pass. reflex., *to turn, bend oneself round. To whirl* or *twirl round rapidly* or *violently. To wind, twine, wrap.* Of face, eyes, features, *to turn round fiercely, distort.* Of hair, *to curl;* here *to entwine, wind about.* Of weapons, *to brandish, hurl,* so fig. of reproaches, etc., w. in and acc. or absol. *To make by twisting, e.g.,* funes. **capillis,** dat. plu. after traject. intorti; fr. capillus (325).

1228. **Eumenidum,** gen. after capillis; fr. Eumĕnĭdes, 3rd fem. plu. *The benevolent, gracious ones,* euphonic for the Furies, rare in the sing. **recreantur,** 3rd plu. pres. ind. pass. fr. recreo (554), *take rest* (W.). **angues,** nom. plu. subj. of recreantur; fr. anguis, -is, 3rd fem. and mas., abl. reg. angue, also angui, *a serpent, snake.*

1229. **Quin et** (269). **Prometheus** (433), subj. of decipitur. **Pelopis** (172), after parens. **parens** (59), *i.e.,* Tantalus; nom. s. jnd. by et to Prometheus.

1230. **Dulci,** abl. s. mas. ag. w. sono; fr. dulcis (2). **laborum** (742), after decipitur. This is the Gk. gen. of relation. Others read laborem, acc. of respect. **decipitur,** 3rd sing. pres. ind. pass. fr. dēcĭpĭo, -cĭpĕre, -cēpi, -ceptum, 3rd trans., (de, 10; capio, 1388) *to catch, ensnare, entangle, beguile, deceive, cheat;* "laborum decipitur," *is beguiled of his sufferings, i.e.,* forgets his sufferings, being charmed by the melody. **sono,** abl. (instrum.) s. fr. sŏnus, -i, 2nd mas., *a noise, sound.*

1231. **Nec** (19). **curat** (1065). **Orion** (669), nom. sing. subj. of curat. **leones,** acc. plu. gov. by agitare; fr. leo (435).

1232. **Aut** (131). **timidos,** acc. plu. mas. ag. w. lyncas; fr. timidus (378). **agitare,** pres. inf. prolat. after curat; fr. agito (244). **lyncas,** acc. plu. jnd. by aut to leones; fr. lynx, lyncis, (Gk.) *a lynx,* mas. and fem.

Carmen XIV. Metre—*The Alcaic.* (Bk. I., Carmen ix.)

1233. **Eheu** (809). **fugaces,** nom. mas. plu. ag. w. anni; fr. fugax (895). **Postume,** voc. s. fr. Postumus, -a, Rom. cognomen.

1234 Labuntur anni nec pietas moram
1235 Rugis et instanti senectæ
1236 Afferet indomitæque morti;
1237 Non, si trecenis, quotquot eunt dies,
1238 Amice, places illacrimabilem
1239 Plutona tauris, qui ter amplum
1240 Geryonen Tityonque tristi

1234. **Labuntur,** 3rd plu. pres. ind. fr. labor (55). **anni,** nom. plu. subj. of labuntur; fr. annus (722). **nec** (19). **pietas** (461), subj. of afferet. **moram,** acc. s. gov. by (direct obj. of) afferet; fr. mora (683).

1235. **Rugis,** dat. plu. after (indirect obj. of) afferet; fr. rūga, -æ, 1st fem., *a crease* in the face, *wrinkle. Creases, corrugations* in garments, etc., post-Aug. **instanti,** dat. fem. s. ag. w. senectæ; fr. instans, -ntis, *present. Impending, menacing, threatening. Pressing, urgent, vehement, e.g.*, bellum; prop. pres. part. of insto (in, 534; sto, 233). **senectæ,** dat. s. jnd. by et to rugis; fr. senecta (727).

1236. **Afferet,** 3rd s. fut. ind. act. fr. affero, afferre, attŭli, allātum, irreg. trans. traj., (ad, 6; fero, 138) *to bring, take, carry, convey* a thing *to* or *up to* a place, etc., *bring up,* of things "afferre manus"=*to assist* or *to assail.* With pers. pron. or pass. reflex., *to betake oneself, go* or *come to* a place. *To bring news about, announce, tell. To cause, occasion, e.g.*, illness to any one. *To assign, allege,* etc., as a reason; "afferre aliquid" ad or w. dat., *to contribute towards.* **indomitæ,** dat. s. fem. ag. w. morti; fr. indŏmĭtus, -a, -um, adj.; (in, neg.; domo, 338) *untamed, not broken in. That cannot be checked* or *tamed, wild, unbridled, uncurbed, ungovernable.* **morti** (661), jnd. by -que to senectæ.

1237. **Non** (55). The apodosis must be here understood, "You could not delay old age and death." **si,** w. pres. subj. in protasis (357). **trecenis,** abl. plu. mas. ag. w. tauris; fr. trĕcēni (sts. terceni), -æ, -a, adj. Numeral distributive adj.; (ter, 361; centum, 1258) *three hundred each, three hundred distributively;* here of an indef. large number. **quotquot,** indecl. adj.; *as many soever, as many soever as,* "quotquot...dies," *daily.* **eunt,** 3rd plu. pres. ind. fr. eo (51). **dies,** nom. plu. subj. of eunt; fr. dies (20).

1238. **Amice** (1097), as subst. **places,** 2nd s. pres. subj. in protasis; fr. placo (818). The pres. exp. "*try to appease.*" **illacrimabilem,** acc. mas. s. ag. w. Plutona; fr. illăcrĭmābĭlis, -e, adj.; (in, neg.; lacrimabilis, *to be wept*) *unwept, unlamented. That is not* or *cannot be moved by tears.*

1239. **Plutona,** acc. (Gk.) s. gov. by places; fr. Pluto or Pluton (145). **tauris,** abl. (instr.) plu. fr. taurus (995), w. places. **qui** (19), mas. s. ag. w. Plutona; nom. to compescit. **ter** (361), w. amplum. **amplum,** acc. mas. s. ag. w. Geryonen; fr. amplus, -a, -um, adj.; (amb, *around,* see ambiguus, 213; pleo, *to fill*) *of large extent, great, ample, spacious, roomy. Comprising much, abundant, great, full, copious;* fig., *extensive, strong, great, violent, mighty,* ref. to internal power or force. Of external circumstances, *magnificent, splendid, glorious.* With ref. to the opinion of others, *illustrious, renowned, distinguished;* amplissimus, epith. of high state officers. "Ter amplum," *with three bodies.*

1240. **Geryonen,** acc. gov. by compescit; fr. Gĕryon, -ŏnis, 3rd mas., and Gĕryŏnes, -æ, 1st fem. (Gk.), a mythic king of Sparta with three bodies, whose oxen were carried off by Hercules. **Tityon,** acc. s. jnd. by -que to

1241 Compescit unda, scilicet omnibus,
1242 Quicunque terræ munere vescimur,
1243 Enaviganda, sive reges
1244 Sive inopes erimus coloni.
1245 Frustra cruento Marte carebimus
1246 Fractisque rauci fluctibus Hadriæ,
1247 Frustra per autumnos nocentem
1248 Corporibus metuemus Austrum:

Gerўonen; fr. Tĭtўos, Titўi, Gk. mas.; a giant, son of Jupiter, slain by Apollo, attempted Latona's chastity; a vulture preyed on his liver in the infernal regions, where he lay stretched over nine jugera. **tristi,** abl. fem. s. ag. w. undâ; fr. tristis (102).

1241. **Compescit,** 3rd sing. pres. ind. act. fr. compesco (442). **unda,** abl. s. instrum. fr. unda (50). **scilicet** (866). **omnibus,** dat. mas. plu. ag. w. nobis und., the agent (524), after gerundive enavigandâ; fr. omnis (43).

1242. **Quicunque,** mas. plu. 1st pers. ag. w. nobis und.; nom. subj. of vescimur; fr. quicunque (167). **terræ** (649), after munere. **munere,** abl. s. after vescimur; fr. munus (483); see fruimur, 725. **vescimur,** 1st plu. pres. ind. fr. vescor, vesci, no pf., no sup., 3rd depon., (esca, *food*) *to fill oneself with food, take food, eat. To enjoy, make use of. Have*=frui, uti, trans. w. acc., *to take* something *as food, feed upon, eat.*

1243. **Enāvĭganda,** abl. s. fem. gerundive ag. w. undâ; fr. ēnāvĭgo, -are, -āvi, -atum, 1st intrans., (ex, 691, exp. completeness; nāvĭgo, *to sail*) *to sail from, sail away*; trans., *traverse by sailing, sail over.* **sive** (69), folld. by sive, *whether...or.* **reges,** nom. plu. predic. after erimus; fr. rex (1).

1244. **Inopes,** nom. mas. plu. ag. w. coloni; fr. ĭnops, -ŏpis, adj.; (in, neg.; ops, 179) physically, *without strength, weak.* Mentally w. inf., *unable to* do. *Without means* or *resources, poor, needy.* Of an orator or style, *meagre, jejune, barren in ideas, devoid of words* or *expression. Poor, pitiful, wretched, miserable, e.g.,* senecta. With genitive, *destitute, devoid of* anything. **erimus,** 1st s. fut. ind. fr. sum (3). **coloni,** nom. plu. jnd. by sive to reges; fr. colonus (782).

1245. **Frustra** (583), w. carebimus. **cruento,** abl. mas. s. ag. w. Marte; fr. cruentus (881). **Marte** (471), of plenty or want (540), after carebimus. **carebimus,** 1st plu. fut. ind. act. fr. careo (649), here, *to abstain from, shun.*

1246. **Fractis,** abl. plu. mas. ag. w. fluctibus; fr. fractus (1051). **rauci,** gen. sing. mas. ag. w. Hadriæ; fr. raucus, -a, -um, adj.; *hoarse* of living beings. Of inanimate things, *hollow, deep-sounding, harsh.* **fluctibus,** abl. jnd. by -que to Marte; fr. fluctus (15). **Hadriæ** (103), after fluctibus.

1247. **Frustra** (583), w. metuemus. **per,** of time (946). **autumnos,** acc. plu. gov. by per; fr. autumnus (1003). **nocentem,** acc. mas. s. pres. part. act. ag. w. Austrum; fr. noceo (678).

1248. **Corporibus,** dat. plu. (commodi or incommodi, w. metuemus) fr. corpus (779). **metuemus,** 1st plu. fut. ind. act. fr. metuo (16). **Austrum,** acc. s. gov. by metuemus; fr. Auster, -tri, 2nd mas., a dry, hot south wind, opp. to Aquilo. *The South.*

1249 Visendus ater flumine languido
1250 Cocytos errans et Danai genus
1251 Infame damnatusque longi
1252 Sisyphus Æolides laboris.
1253 Linquenda tellus et domus et placens
1254 Uxor, neque harum, quas colis, arborum

1249. **Visendus,** nom. mas. s. gerundive predic. ag. w. Cocytos; fr. viso (44). With est und. 3rd s. ind. pres. of the gerundive conjugation (664). **ater** (661), nom. mas. s. ag. w. Cocytos. **flumine,** abl. (instrum.) s. w. errans; fr. flumen (236). **languido,** abl. neut. s. ag. w. flumine; fr. languĭdus, -a, -um, adj.; (langueo, *to be languid*) *weak, feeble, faint,* lit. and fig.; mentally, *enervated, listless, apathetic. Destitute of energy, relaxed in efforts.* Of countenance, *dull, heavy, inanimate.* Of water, *dull, sluggish.*

1250. **Cōcȳtos** (-us) -i, 3rd mas., subj. of est und.; (Gk., *river of Lamentation*) a mythic river in the lower world. **errans,** pres. part. act. nom. mas. s. ag. w. Cōcȳtos; fr. erro (763). **Danaï,** gen. s. after genus; fr. Dănaus, 2nd mas., son of Belus, brother of Ægyptus, founded Argos, the father of fifty daughters (Dănăides, -um, 3rd fem. plu.), who, except Hypermnestra, murdered their husbands at their father's command. **genus** (45), jnd. by et to Cōcȳtos.

1251. **Infame,** nom. neut. s. ag. w. genus; fr. infamis (108). **damnatus,** nom. mas. s. pf. pass. part. ag. w. Sisyphus; fr. damno, -are, -avi, -atum, 1st trans., *to bring damage* or *loss to, occasion harm* or *damage to.* Legal, *to sentence to* a punishment or *declare guilty* of a crime, with acc. of person and gen. of punishment or crime; also w. abl. or de w. abl. *To bind, oblige* by last will, with ut and subj., sts. inf. (Hor.). Non-legal, *to censure, condemn, disapprove.* Of things, *to condemn, reject.* **longi,** gen. mas. s. ag. w. laboris; fr. longus (73).

1252. **Sisyphus,** -i, 2nd mas., jnd. by -que to genus. The king of Corinth, celebrated for cunning and robberies, who was killed by Theseus, and whose punishment in the lower world was to roll a stone uphill, which was constantly rolling backwards. **Æolides,** -æ, mas. (Gk., patronymic) nom. s. in app. to Sisyphus; *son of Æolus.* **laboris,** gen. s. w. damnatus; fr. labor (124). This gen. approaches nearest to that of value and price (signifies the equivalent at which the crime is assessed, W.) and is a particular instance of the gen. of quality.

1253. **Linquenda,** nom. fem. s. predic. ag. w. tellus, gerundive, und. est (1249); fr. linquo (681). **tellus** (551), subj. to est und. **domus** (145), jnd. by et to tellus. **placens,** pres. part. nom. fem. s. ag. w. uxor; fr. placeo (263).

1254. **Uxor** (455), nom. s. jnd. by et to domus. **neque** (32). **harum,** gen. plu. fem. ag. w. arborum; fr. hic (7). **quas** (429), fem. plu. ag. w arborum, acc. gov. by colis. **colis,** 2nd s. pres. ind. act. fr. colo (797). **arborum,** gen. of thing distributed, after ulla; fr. arbor (329). The plu. gen. of the thing distributed is a divisible whole, and depends on partitive words indicating that one or more parts (or no part) of such whole are taken. It depends on substs. exp. partition, *e.g.,* pars, portio; pronominals alius, alter, etc.; numerals and comparat. and superl. adjs.

1255 Te præter invisas cupressos
1256 Ulla brevem dominum sequetur.
1257 Absumet heres Cæcuba dignior
1258 Servata centum clavibus et mero
1259 Tinget pavimentum superbo,
1260 Pontificum potiore cœnis.

CARMEN XV.—IN SUI SECULI LUXURIAM

1261 JAM pauca aratro jugera regiæ

1255. **Te** (83), gov. by sequetur. **præter** (92) **invisas,** acc. plu. fem. ag. w. cupressos; fr. invisus (770). **cupressos,** acc. plu. gov. by præter; fr. cupressus (243); used to ornament the funeral pile.

1256. **Ulla** (1069), ag. w. arbor und. fr. arborum. **brevem,** acc. mas. s. ag. w. dominum; fr. brevis (143); "*master on a short tenure*" (W.). **dominum** (974), gov. by sequetur. **sequetur** (1005).

1257. **Absumet,** 3rd s. fut. ind. act. fr. absūmo, -ĕre, -sumpsi, -sumptum, 3rd trans., (ab, 254; sumo, *to take*) *to devour, consume*, lit. and fig., esp. of persons. Pass., *to be lost* or *undone*, of persons. *To waste away*, of disease, care, etc. *To destroy wholly, consume* things. *To kill, carry off* persons. **heres** (960), subj. of absumet. **Cæcuba,** acc. plu. gov. by absumet; fr. Cæcubum (517); plu. of quantity. **dignior,** nom. mas. s. compar. ag. w. heres; fr. dignus (644).

1258. **Servata,** pf. pass. part. act. neut. plu. ag. w. Cæcuba; fr. servo (96). **centum,** num. adj. card. indeclin., *a hundred*; also used of any undefined large number. **clavibus,** abl. (instrum.) plu. fr. clāvis, -is, acc. -em, sts. -im, abl. -i, sts. -e; 3rd fem., *a key*. **mero** (203), w. tinget.

1259. **Tinget,** 3rd s. fut. ind. act. fr. tingo (1316). **pavimentum,** acc. s. gov. by tinget; fr. păvīmentum, -i, 2nd neut., (pavo *to beat, strike*) prop., *a floor* composed of small stones, earth or lime, beaten down with a rammer, *a hard floor*. This means, "he will use it lavishly and wastefully." **superbo** (868), neut. ag. w. mero.

1260. **Pontificum,** gen. plu. after cœnis; fr. pŏntĭfex, -fĭcis, 3rd mas., (ak. to purifico, *he who purifies* or *purges with religious rites*) a Roman *high priest, pontiff*, then *Chief Priest*. **potiore,** abl. neut. s. ag. w. mero; fr. pŏtior, neut. -ius, prop., *more powerful*; meton., *to be preferred, that may* or *can be preferred*. Positive, pŏtis, (rarely neut. pote) *ruling*; hence, *powerful*; *mighty* (rare). *Able, capable, possible, e.g.*, "potis est"=potest, *he, she* or *it is able*. Superl. potissimus, -a, -um, adj.; *the chief, principal, most prominent*, of persons and things. **cœnis,** abl. (of comparison) plu. after potiore; fr. cœna, -æ, 1st fem. (cæna, cēna). The principal Rom. meal taken in early times about midday, aftwds. about three o'clock. The "prandium" was taken at mid-day.

CARMEN XV. METRE—*The Alcaic* (Bk. I., Carmen ix.)

1261. **Jam** (37). **pauca** (1145), ag. w. jugera. **aratro,** dat. (commodi) s. after relinquent; fr. aratrum (441). **jugera,** acc. plu. gov. by relinquent; fr. jūgĕrum, -i, 2nd neut.; plu. of 3rd decl., jūgĕra, -um, (abl. s. jugere, found once). Dat. and abl. plu. jugeris, once or twice. *A juger* of land.

1262 Moles relinquent, undique latius
1263 Extenta visentur Lucrino
1264 Stagna lacu platanusque cælebs
1265 Evincet ulmos. Tum violaria et
1266 Myrtus et omnis copia narium
1267 Spargent olivetis odorem
1268 Fertilibus domino priori;

28,800 squ. feet (240 long, 140 broad). Eng. acre is 43,560 squ. feet. **regiæ,** nom. plu. fem. ag. w. moles; fr. regius (983); in poetry sts. as here=regalis, *princely, splendid, magnificent.*

1262. **Moles,** nom. plu. subj. of relinquent; fr. mōles, gen. molis, 3rd fem., *a huge* or *vast mass, heap, pile, bulk. An immense building, mole, dam, pier. A vast number, immense crowd. Greatness, vastness. Power, might. Difficulty, labour.* **relinquent,** 3rd plu. fut. ind. act. fr. relinquo (270). **undique** (191). **latius** (925), w. extenta.

1263. **Extenta,** nom. neut. plu. ag. w. stagna; fr. extentus (921). **visentur,** 3rd plu. fut. ind. pass. fr. viso (44), *i.e.*, they will be sights to see (W.) **Lucrino,** abl. mas. s. ag. w. lacu; fr. Lucrīnus, -a, -um, adj., (with or without lacus). *The Lucrine Lake* on the coast of Campania, near Baiæ (Lago Lucrino).

1264. **Stagna,** nom. plu. subj. of visentur; fr. stagnum, -i, 2nd neut., (sto, 233) *a piece of standing water* permanent or caused by the overflowing of a stream, *pool, pond, swamp. Waters* (genly.); here of *fish ponds.* **lacu,** abl. (of comparison) s. after latius, fr. lăcus, -us, 4th mas., (anything hollowed out) *tank, vat,* for liquids. *Reservoir, public cistern;* meton., a large body of water in a natural hollow or artificial excavation which does not flow nor become stagnant, *a lake* (opp. to stagnum). *Pool, deep* in a river **platanus** (1153), subj. of evincet. **cælebs,** cælĭbis, adj.; nom. fem. s. ag. w. platanus; *unmarried, single.* Of trees, *near which no vine is planted.*

1265. **Evincet,** 3rd s. fut. ind. act. fr. ēvinco, -ĕre, -vīci, -victum, 3rd trans. and intrans., (ex, 691; vinco, 830) *to conquer completely, vanquish utterly;* fig., *to completely conquer* or *get the better of;* here "*will supplant.*" Legal, *to win, gain, recover one's property by judicial means. To carry one's point, succeed in doing* something, etc. **ulmos,** acc. plu. gov. by evincet; fr. ulmus (45). **tum** (349) **violaria,** nom. plu. subj. of spargent; fr. vĭŏlārium, -ii, 2nd neut., *a bed* or *bank of violets.*

1266. **Myrtus** (875), jnd. by et to violaria. **omnis** (148), ag. w. copia. **copia** (462), jnd. by et to myrtus. **narium,** gen. plu. after copia; fr. naris, -is, 3rd fem., (akin to nasus) *a nostril;* plu., *the nostrils, nose;* meton. sing., (by synecdoche) *the nose.* Plu., *what is inhaled by the nose, scent,* rare (here); or "narium copia," =*all the fulness of the nostrils=the fulness of all that pleases the nostrils,* the gen. expressing that for the gratification of which the abundance exists (W.).

1267. **Spargent,** 3rd plu. fut. ind. act. fr. spargo (1039). **olivetis,** abl. (local) plu. fr. ŏlīvētum, -i, 2nd neut., *a place planted with olive trees, olive-yard.* **odorem,** acc. s. gov. by spargent; fr. odor (150).

1268. **Fertilibus,** abl. plu. neut. ag. w. olivetis; fr. fertilis (1035). **domino,** dat. (commodi w. fertilibus) fr. dominus (6). **priori,** dat. mas. s. ag. w. domino; fr. prior (1086).

Tum spissa ramis laurea fervidos
Excludet ictus. Non ita Romuli
  Præscriptum et intonsi Catonis
    Auspiciis veterumque norma.
Privatus illis census erat brevis,
Commune magnum; nulla decempedis
  Metata privatis opacam

1269. **Tum** (349). **spissa,** nom. fem. s. ag. w. laurea; fr. spissus, -a, -um, adj.; *thick, crowded, close.* Of time, *slow, tardy, late*; fig., *difficult, hard* (very rare but class.). **ramis** (951), abl. of manner w. spissa. **laurea,** -æ, 1st fem.; nom. s. subj. of excludet; *a bay tree,* much more com. *a bay crown*; proply. fem. of laureus, -a, -um, adj.; (laurus, 891) *pertaining to bay.* **fervidos,** acc. plu. mas. ag. w. ictus; fr. fervidus (4).

1270. **Excludet,** 3rd s. fut. ind. act. fr. exclūdo, -dĕre, -clūsi, -clusum, 3rd trans., (ex, 691; claudo, *to shut*) *to shut out, cut off, remove, separate from* anything; fig., *except, remove, hinder, prevent.* Of birds, *to hatch* young. **ictus,** acc. plu. gov. by excludet; fr. ictus (594). **non** (55). **ita** (583), w. præscriptum. **Romuli,** gen. s. after auspiciis; fr. Romulus (317).

1271. **Præscriptum** nom. neut. s. predic. fr. præscriptus (1115). With est und. 3rd s. pf. ind. pass. fr. præscribo. **et** (2), folld. by -que, *both. and.* **intonsi,** gen. mas. s. ag. w. Catonis; fr intonsus (522)=*antique.* **Catonis** (319), jnd. by et to Romuli.

1272. **Auspiciis,** abl. (of manner) plu. fr. auspĭcĭum, -ii, 2nd neut., (auspex, 211) *the observation of birds bred for auspices, augury from birds, auspices*; meton., *sign, omen, divine premonition* or *token. Command, guidance, authority*; milit. of a commander in chief. *Right, power, inclination, will*; here, *example* (W.). **veterum,** gen. plu. after normâ; fr. vetus (19). **norma,** abl. s. jnd. by -que to auspiciis; fr. norma, -æ, 1st fem., *a square* used by carpenters, masons, etc., for making right angles. Fig., *a rule, pattern, precept.*

1273. **Privatus** (867), nom. mas. s. ag. w. census. **illis,** dat. (possessive or acquisitive) plu. after erat; fr. ille (9), ref. to veterum. **census,** -us, 4th mas., nom. s. subj. of erat; (censeo) *a regulating* and *rating of the property of Roman citizens. The register of the census, censor's lists. Registered property* of Rom. citizens. "Census equester," 400,000 sesterces. *Wealth, property, possessions.* **erat** (98). **brevis** (143), nom. mas. s. predic. ag. w. census.

1274. **Commune,** nom. neut. s. (as subst.) subj. of erat und.; fr. commūnis, -e, adj., (cum, 31; munus, 483, *serving together*) *common, ordinary, general,* opp. to proprius (*belonging to one*); commune, -is, 3rd neut., *commonalty, state*; here, *the common stock, public treasury* (W.). *Easy in intercourse with* any one, *courteous, condescending, affable.* **magnum,** nom. neut. s. predic. ag. w. commune; fr. magnus (85). **nulla** (553), ag. w. porticus. **decempedis,** abl. (instrum. w. metata) plu. fr. decempĕda, -æ, 1st fem., (decem, *ten*; pes, 135) *a ten-foot measuring rod.*

1275. **Metata,** pf. pass. part. nom. fem. s. ag. w. porticus; fr. mēto, -are, -avi, -atum, 1st trans., (akin to metior, *to measure*) *to measure out.* **privatis,** abl. plu. fem. ag. w. decempedis; fr. privatus (867). **opacam,** acc. fem. s. ag. w. Arcton; fr. ŏpācus, -a, -um, adj.; *in the shade, shaded*; opa-

1276 Porticus excipiebat Arcton;
1277 Nec fortuitum spernere cespitem
1278 Leges sinebant, oppida publico
1279 Sumptu jubentes et Deorum
1280 Templa novo decorare saxo.

CARMEN XVI.—AD POMPEIUM GROSPHUM.

1281 Otium Divos rogat in patenti

cum, -i, 2nd neut., *a shade*, plu. ŏpāca, -orum, *shady places. Darkened, dark, obscure. That gives* or *casts a shade, e.g.*, nemus.

1276. **Portĭcus,** -us, 4th fem.; nom. s. subj. of excipiebat; (porta, *a gate*) *a walk covered by a roof supported on columns, colonnades, piazza; arcade, gallery,* here *a colonnade* facing North to avoid the sun in summer. **excipiebat,** 3rd s. impf. ind. act. fr. excĭpĭo, -cĭpĕre, -cēpi, -ceptum, 3rd trans., (ex, 691; capio, 1388) *to take* or *draw out, e.g.*, e mari, or dat. *To withdraw, rescue, e.g.*, from slavery. *To make an exception of, i.e.*, take from a whole anything as not belonging to it, often in pf. pass. *To take* anything *from* anywhere *to oneself* (in good and bad sense) *catch, capture, take, receive. To come next to, succeed* a thing, *follow after*, in time or order of succession; fig., *to catch up, intercept, incur, e.g.*, invidiam, laudem. *To catch in the ear, listen eagerly to.* **Arcton,** acc. s. gov. by excipiebat; fr. Arctos (615); "excipiebat Arcton," *faced the North.*

1277. **Nec** (19). **fortuitum,** acc. mas. s. ag. w. cespitem; fr. fortŭĭtus, -a, -um, adj.; (forte, 246; analogous to gratuitus) *that takes place by chance* or *by hazard, casual, accidental;* here "*chance cut*" (W.). **spernere,** pres. inf. act. after sinebant; fr. sperno (21). **cespitem** (505), gov. by spernere.

1278. **Leges,** nom. plu. subj. of sinebant; fr. lex, lēgis, 3rd fem., (lego, *to read*) *a proposition* or *motion* read to the people with a view to their passing it into law, *a bill. A bill passed, law, enactment. A precept, regulation, rule. Terms, conditions* of a treaty, agreement of sale, etc. **sinebant,** 3rd plu. impf. ind. act. fr. sino (87). **oppida,** acc. plu. gov. by decorare; fr. oppidum (16). **publico,** abl. mas. s. ag. w. sumptu; fr. publicus (1076).

1279. **Sumptu,** abl. (of manner) s. fr. sumptus, -us, 4th mas., (sumo, *to take*) *expense, cost, charge.* **jubentes,** nom. fem. plu. pres. part. act. ag. w. leges; fr. jubeo (494). **Deorum** (261), after templa.

1280. **Templa** (52), jnd. by et to oppida. **novo** (834), neut. ag. w. saxo; here almost=exquisito, *hewn on purpose* (W.). **decorare,** pres. inf. act. after jubentes; fr. decoro (982). **saxo,** abl. (instrum.) s. fr. saxum (313).

Carmen XVI. Metre—*The Lesser Sapphic.* (Bk. I., Carmen ii.)

1281. **Otium** (16), gov. by rogat as internal or contained obj.; see 584. **Divos** (1079), external or attained object after rogat. **rogat,** 3rd s. pres. ind. act. fr. rŏgo, -āre, -āvi, -atum, 1st trans., *to ask, interrogate, question* any one about a thing, aliquem aliquid; "legem rogare," *to propose a law; meton., to ask, beg, request, solicit* one *for* a thing=aliquem aliquid, ab aliquo, also ut or ne w. subj., sts. subj. alone. **in** (78). **patenti,** abl. neut. s. pres.

1282 Prensus Ægæo, simul atra nubes
1283 Condidit Lunam neque certa fulgent
1284 Sidera nautis;
1285 Otium bello furiosa Thrace,
1286 Otium Medi pharetra decori,
1287 Grosphe, non gemmis neque purpura ve-
1288 nale neque auro.
1289 Non enim gazæ neque consularis
1290 Summovet lictor miseros tumultus

part. ag. w. Ægæo; fr. păteo, -ēre, -ui, no sup., 2nd intrans., *to stand* or *lie open, be open.* Of roads, etc., *to be open, passable.* Of plains, etc., *to stretch out, extend. To be free, attainable, accessible, obtainable. To be exposed to.*

1282. **Prensus,** pf. pass. part. nom. mas. s. (as subst.) subj. of rogat; fr. prĕhendo, syncopated prendo, -dĕre, -di, -sum, 3rd trans., (præ, *before;* obsolete, hendo) *to lay hold of firmly, seize, catch, grasp, snatch,* esp. *to detain* one in order to speak with him. *To seize, take by surprise, catch* (here); prob. "prensus," technical for "*caught in a storm.*" **Ægæo,** abl. s. gov. by in; fr. Ægæum, -i, 2nd neut., *The Ægean Sea;* prop. neut. (und. mare); fr. Ægæus, -a, -um. **simul** (145). **atra** (67), nom. fem. s. ag. w. nubes; fr. ater (661). **nubes** (67), nom. s. subj. of condidit.

1283. **Condidit,** 3rd s. pf. ind. act. fr. condo (264). **Lunam,** acc. s. gov. by condidit; fr. Luna (133). **neque** (32). **certa,** nom. neut. plu. ag. w. sidera; fr. certus (212); "certa," *on which to rely* (W.). **fulgent,** 3rd plu. pres. ind. act. fr. fulgeo (203).

1284. **Sidera** (90), subj. of fulgent. **nautis** (311), commodi after fulgent.

1285. **Otium** (16), gov. by rogat und. fr. 1281. **bello** (734), of manner w. furiosa. **furiosa,** nom. fem. s. ag. w. Thrace; fr. fŭriōsus, -a, -um, adj.; (furiæ, 665) *full of madness* or *rage, mad, furious.* **Thrace,** -es, 1st fem.; nom. to rogat und.=Threce, Thracia, *Thrace.*

1286. **Otium** (895), anaphora. **Medi** (87), nom. subj. of rogant und. **pharetra** (267), instrum. w. decori. **decori,** nom. mas. plu. ag. w. Medi; fr. decorus (259).

1287. **Grosphe,** voc. s. fr. Grosphus, -i (Rom. cognomen), a wealthy man, whose property was in Sicily. **non** (55). **gemmis,** abl. (of price) plu. w. venale; fr. gemma, -æ, 1st fem., (rt. in gero, 168) *a bud, eye* or *germ* in a plant. *A precious stone,* esp. one already cut, *a jewel, gem.* Of things made of precious stones, *goblets, seals, rings,* etc. **purpura,** abl. s. jnd. by neque to gemmis; fr. purpŭra, -æ, 1st fem., prop. *the purple fish;* meton., *purple cloth, purple. Purple cloth,* as a valuable thing (here); sts. *lofty station, high dignity.* **venale,** acc. neut. s. ag. w. otium; fr. vēnālis, -e, adj.; (venus, *sale,* found only in dat. and acc.) *relating to selling, to be sold, for sale,* w. abl. pretii; meton., *that can be bought for bribes* or *presents, venal.*

1288. **Auro,** abl. s. jnd. by neque (32) to purpurâ; fr. aurum (714).

1289. **Enim** (212). **gazæ,** nom. plu. fr. gaza (686). **consularis,** -e, adj.; nom. mas. s. ag. w. lictor; (consul, 877) *of* or *pertaining to a consul;* consŭlāris, -is, 3rd mas., *one who has been consul.*

1290. **Summovet** (1133), on sing. see 98, 555. **lictor,** -ōris, 3rd mas.;

1291 Mentis et curas laqueata circum
1292 Tecta volantes.
1293 Vivitur parvo bene, cui paternum
1294 Splendet in mensa tenui salinum,
1295 Nec leves somnos timor aut cupido
1296 Sordidus aufert.

nom. s. jnd. by neque to gazæ; (ligo, *to bind*) *he who binds* or *ties* the rods or culprits. They were granted to magistrates who had "imperium cum potestate." They bore a bundle of sticks from which an axe projected. They walked before the magistrate in a line, calling upon the people to clear the way (summovere turbam), and reminding them to pay their respects to him (animadvertere). They also executed judicial sentences. **miseros,** acc. plu. mas. ag. w. tumultus; fr. miser (160). **tumultus,** acc. plu. gov. by summovet; fr. tumultus (432).

1291. **Mentis,** gen. s. after tumultus; fr. mens (349). **curas** (215), jnd. by et to tumultus. **laqueata,** acc. neut. plu. pf. pass. part. ag. w. tecta; fr. lăqueo, -are, -avi, -atum, 1st trans., (lacus, 1264; cf. coc- in coquus) *to make a lacus* or *hollow place* in a casting. *To make* or *form panels* in a ceiling, *panel, adorn with fretwork,* genly. in pf. part. *fretted. To adorn with anything like panels.* **circum** (70).

1292. **Tecta,** acc. plu. gov. by circum; fr. tectum (1087). **volantes,** acc. pl. fem. ag. w. curas; fr. volans (852).

1293. **Vivitur,** 3rd s. pres. ind. pass. fr. vivo (731). Intrans. vbs. can be used in the pass. only impersonally. The persons may be expressed by a or ab with abl., *e.g.*, luditer a me, a nobis, *I, we play;* or the verb is usually rendered as expressing the 1st or 3rd pers., the case being understood, *we* or *they play.* **parvo,** abl. (of means) neut. s. as adv., *on a little;* fr. parvus, -a, -um, adj. Compar mĭnor. Superl. mĭnĭmus. Of size or space, *small.* Of time, *short, brief;* parvo post, *a little after.* Of persons, *little, youthful, young.* Of degree, extent, etc., *slight, little.* Of value, consideration, etc., *low, slight;* parvo, *at a low price;* also used of what is *humble, of little ability, small* in quantity, measure, degree, etc. Comparat. often=*too small* or *little;* minores, *descendants* or *younger ones;* minoris (und. pretii), *at a less rate, of less account* or *importance.* Superl., quam minimum, *as little as possible;* non minimum, *chiefly, particularly;* minimo (und. pretio), *at a very low sum.* **bene** (1050), w. vivitur. **cui** (575), *i.e.*, ab illo, cui; mas. s. ag. w. demonst. illo und. after vivitur; dat. commodi w. splendet. The dat. thus used is often equivalent to a possessive gen. as here cui=cujus, after salinum. **paternum,** nom. neut. s. ag. w. salinum; fr. paternus (513).

1294. **Splendet,** 3rd s. pres. ind. act. fr. splendeo (498). **in** (78). **mensa,** abl. s. gov. by in; fr. mensa, -æ, 1st fem., (rt. in mineo, *to project*) *a table* of any kind, *dinner table. That which is put on the table, food, e.g.,* secunda mensa, *the second course.* **salīnum,** -i, 2nd neut.; nom. s. subj. of splendet; (sal, *salt*) *a salt-cellar.*

1295. **Nec** (19). **leves,** acc. plu. mas. ag. w. somnos; fr. levis (31), *untroubled* (W.). **somnos** (595), gov. by aufert. **timor** (851), nom. s. subj. of aufert. **aut** (131). **cupido** (70), jnd. by aut to timor.

1296. **Sordidus** (662), ag. w. cupido (wh. is always mas. in Hor.). **aufert,** 3rd s. pres. ind. act. fr. aufero, auferre, abstŭli, ablātum, irreg. trans., (ab, 254; fero, 138) *to take, bear away* or *off, carry off, remove by bearing* or *carrying;*

Quid brevi fortes jaculamur ævo
Multa? quid terras alio calentes
Sole mutamus? Patriæ quis exsul
    Se quoque fugit?
Scandit æratas vitiosa naves
Cura nec turmas equitum relinquit,
Ocior cervis et agente nimbos
    Ocior Euro.
Lætus in præsens animus, quod ultra est,

auferre se, *to retire, go away. To take away violently, rob, steal. To destroy by taking away, annihilate, kill, slay. To bear off*, as the fruit of one's labour, *gain, procure, acquire*; so fig., *gain, get, receive. To carry away* the knowledge of anything from some one, *learn, understand. To cease from, lay aside, omit, e.g.*, jurgium, lacrimas.

1297. **Quid** (229). **brevi** (282), neut. ag. w. ævo. **fortes**, nom. plu. mas. ag. w. nos und. in jaculamur; fr. fortis (165), *undaunted.* **jaculamur,** 1st plu. pres. ind. fr. jaculor (39). **ævo** (329), temporal.

1298. **Multa** (821), gov. by jaculamur. **terras** (111), gov. by mutamus. **alio** (824), ag. w. sole. **calentes,** acc. plu. fem. ag. w. terras; fr. calens (1038).

1299. **Sole,** abl. (of cause) s. w. calentes; fr. sol (220). **mutamus,** 1st plu. pres. ind. act. fr. muto (77); here=*to take in exchange*, w. acc. The thing given in exchange (one's own land), which would be abl. (of price), is not expressed. **patriæ,** gen. s. after exsul; fr. patria (11), *one's native land.* The abl. would be more usu. in Lat.; the gen. is a Græcism. **quis** (149), ag. w. exsul. **exsul** (exul), -ŭlis, 3rd com.; nom. s. subj. of fugit; (ex, *out;* solum, 478) *one who quits* or *is banished from his native soil, an exile.*

1300. **Se** (53), gov. by fugit; ref. to exsul. **quoque** (310). **fugit** (548).

1301. **Scandit,** 3rd s. pres. ind. act. fr. scando, -dĕre, -di, -sum, 3rd trans. and intrans., *to climb, mount, clamber, ascend*, here; fig. intrans., *to mount, rise, arise.* **æratas,** acc. plu. fem. ag. w. naves; fr. ærātus, -a, -um, adj.; (æro, obsol.), *furnished* or *covered with brass, copper* or *bronze.* **vitiosa,** nom. fem. s. ag. w. cura; (vitium, 59) *full of faults* or *defects, bad, corrupt, morbid.* **naves,** acc. plu. gov. by scandit; fr. navis (93).

1302. **Cura** (334), subj. of scandit. **nec** (19). **turmas,** acc. plu. gov. by relinquit; fr. turma (977). **equitum** (896), after turmas. **relinquit,** 3rd s. pres. ind. act. fr. relinquo (270).

1303. **Ocior** (84), ag. w. cura. **cervis,** abl. (of comparison) plu. after ocior; fr. cervŭs (413). **agente,** pres. part. act. abl. mas. s. ag. w. Euro; fr. ago (43). **nimbos,** acc. plu. gov. by agente; fr. nimbus, -i, 2nd mas., *a violent* or *powerful rain, rain-cloud, thunder-cloud,* esp. *the bright cloud* which surrounded the gods when they appeared on earth. *Cloud* of smoke, dust. *A multitude.*

1304. **Ocior,** jnd. by et to ocior in prec. line. **Euro,** abl. (of comparison) s. after ocior; fr. Eurus (673).

1305. **Lætus** (82), ag. w. animus. **in** (76), of time as in 730. **præsens,** acc. neut. s. gov. by in; fr. præsens (778). **animus** (997), subj. of oderit. **quod** (730), neut. s. ag. w. demonst. und. after curare; nom. subj. to est. **ultra** (546), predic. after est. **est** (19). "Quod ultra est," *the future.*

1306 Oderit curare et amara lento
1307 Temperet risu. Nihil est ab omni
1308 Parte beatum.
1309 Abstulit clarum cita mors Achillem,
1310 Longa Tithonum minuit senectus,
1311 Et mihi forsan, tibi quod negarit
1312 Porriget hora.
1313 Te greges centum Siculæque circum
1314 Mugiunt vaccæ, tibi tollit hinnitum

1306. **Oderit** (220), here conj. (hortative) **curare,** pres. inf. (objective) gov. by oderit; fr. curo (874). **amara,** acc. neut. plu. gov. by temperet; fr. ămārus, -a, -um, adj.; *bitter* in flavour (opp. to dulcis); fig., *calamitous, unpleasant, sad.* Subst., ămāra, -orum, 2nd neut., *bitter things, bitterness. Bitter, biting, acrimonious, sarcastic, caustic, morose, sour.* **lento,** abl. s. mas. ag. w. risu; fr. lentus (352), *easy*

1307. **Temperet,** 3rd s. pres. conj. (hortative) act. jnd. by et to oderit; fr. tempĕro (223). **risu,** abl. (of manner) s. fr. risus (254). **nihil** (125), here as nom. subj. of est. **est** (19). **ab** (254), here=*on.* **omni,** abl fem. s. ag. w. parte; fr. omnis (43).

1308. **Parte** (360), gov. by ab. **beatum,** nom. neut. s. predic. ag. w. nihil; fr. beatus (142).

1309. **Abstulit,** 3rd s. pf. ind. act. fr. aufero (1296). **clarum,** acc. mas. s. ag. w. Achillem; fr. clarus (185). **cita,** nom. fem. s. ag. w mors; fr. citus (854). **mors** (141), subj. of abstulit. **Achillem** (972), gov. by abstulit.

1310. **Longa** (683), ag. w. senectus. **Tithonum,** acc. sing gov. by minuit; fr. Tithonus (656). **minuit** (848). **sĕnectus,** -ūtis, 3rd fem.; nom. s. subj. of minuit. Of living beings, *old age, extreme old age, senility* (class. only sing.). In poetry and very rare of inanimate things=vetustas. *The old skin, slough,* cast off yearly by serpents, etc.

1311. **Et** (2). **mihi** (277), dat. (commodi) after (remote obj of) porriget. **forsan,** concessive particle, *perhaps, peradventure* (poet. and post-Aug.). Prob. elliptical for fors sit an; fors (246), used adverbially, *it is a chance, perchance,* w. ind. or subj. **tibi** (93), dat. incommodi; after negarit. **quod** (510), neut. s. ag. w. demonst. und. after porriget; acc. gov. by negarit. **negarit,** syncopated for negaverit; 3rd s. fut. pf. fr. nego (694), see 590.

1312. **Porriget,** 3rd s. fut. ind. act. fr. porrĭgo, -rĭgĕre, -rexi, -rectum, 3rd trans. traj., (por=pro, *forward;* rego, 91) *to stretch* or *spread out before oneself, put forth, reach out, extend.* Pass. reflex., *to stretch* or *spread oneself out, extend,* so of localities, etc. *To lay at full length, stretch on the ground. To hold out* or *forth, offer, present, e.g.,* manum; fig., *to grant* a thing (here). **hora** (252), nom. s. subj. of porriget; here=*time* (rare).

1313. **Te** (83), gov. by circum. **greges,** nom. plu. subj. of mugiunt; fr. grex (590). **centum** (1258), w. greges. **Siculæ,** nom. fem. plu. ag. w. greges (1166). **circum** (70).

1314. **Mugiunt,** 3rd plu. pres. ind. act. fr. mūgio, -īre, -īvi or -ĭi, -ītum, 4th intrans. Of cattle, *to low, bellow, moo.* Of a trumpet, *bray.* Of a

1315 Apta quadrigis equa, te bis Afro
1316 Murice tinctæ
1317 Vestiunt lanæ : mihi parva rura et
1318 Spiritum Graiæ tenuem Camenæ
1319 Parca non mendax dedit et malignum
1320 Spernere vulgus.

mast, *groan.* Of an earthquake, *rumble;* here, as applied to greges; it is a case of zeugma, a species of ellipsis, by which one word is connected w. two words or clauses, to both of which it does not equally apply, so that for one of them, another word (to be gathered from the sense of the passage) must be mentally supplied. **vaccæ,** nom. plu. jnd. by -que to greges; fr. vacca, -æ, 1st fem., (ak. to veho, *to carry*) *a cow,* orig. a beast of burden. **tibi** (93), commodi after tollit. **tollit,** 3rd s. pres. ind. act. fr. tollo (8). **hinnitum,** acc. s. gov. by tollit; fr. hinnītus, -us, 4th mas., (hinnio, *to neigh*), *a neighing.*

1315. **Apta,** nom. fem. s. ag. w. equa; fr. aptus (193). **quadrigis,** dat. after traject. apta; fr. quādrigæ, -arum, 1st fem. plu., contr. for quadrijugæ, (quatuor, *four;* jugum, 755) of animals, *a set* or *team of four,* of the four-horse team used in races or of the sun., rare in sing; metón., *a chariot drawn by four horses.* **ĕqua,** -æ, 1st fem.; nom. s. subj. of tollit; dat. and abl. plu. equis, also ĕquābus, *a mare.* **te** (83), gov. by vestiunt. **bis** (71), w. tinctæ. **Afro,** abl. mas. s. ag. w. murice; fr. Āfer, Afra, Afrum, adj.; *of* or *belonging to the Afri, African.*

1316. **Murice,** abl. (instrum) s. fr. mūrex, -ĭcis, 3rd mas., (ak. to murus, 440, *that which wards off*). *The purple fish, i.e.,* a fish, armed with sharp prickles and a kind of long beak, from which a purple dye was obtained. *The purple dye* made from it. Of bodies shaped like it, *a pointed rock* (Verg.). **tinctæ,** pf. pass. part. nom. fem. plu. ag. w. lanæ; fr. tingo (-guo), -ngĕre, -nxi, -nctum, 3rd trans., *to wet, bathe* w. any liquid. *To soak in colour, dye, tinge;* fig., *to tincture, imbrue, furnish with,* etc.

1317. **Vestiunt,** 3rd plu. pres. ind. act. fr. vestio, -īre, -īvi, or -ĭi, -ītum, 4th trans., (vestis, 476) *to cover with a garment, dress, clothe;* pass., (reflex.) *to clothe oneself, dress.* Of inanimate things, *to cover, surround, adorn.* With pers. pron. (reflex.), *to cover, deck oneself;* fig., of words, etc., *to dress, clothe,* etc. **lanæ,** nom. plu. subj. of vestiunt; fr. lāna, -æ, 1st fem., (Gk.) *wool. Anything made of wool, a woollen article. Wool-like hair* of animals. *Down* of birds. **mihi** (277), remote obj. of dedit. **parva,** acc. plu. neut. ag. w. rura; fr. parvus (1293). **rura** (17), direct obj. of dedit.

1318. **Spiritum** (926), jnd. by et to rura; here, *inspiration.* **Graiæ,** gen. s. fem. ag. w. Camenæ; fr. Graius, -a, -um, adj.; *of* or *belonging to the Greeks;* "Graii" less frequ. and more poet. form for "Græci." **tenuem,** acc. mas. s. ag. w. spiritum; fr. tenuis (173), exp. fineness and delicacy. **Camenæ,** gen. s. after spiritum; fr. Camena (323).

1319. **Parca** (1025), nom. s. subj. of dedit. **non** (55), w. mendax. **mendax,** -ācis, adj.; nom. fem. s. ag. w. Parca; (mentior, *to lie*) *given* or *prone to lying;* subst., *a liar.* Of things, *deceptive,* here, "*not yielding expected fruits;*" fig., *feigned, fictitious, not real, e.g.,* loss, etc.; non mendax, *not deceptive.* She assigned me that lot and has kept her word. (W.). **dedit** (576). **malignum,** acc. neut. s. ag. w. vulgus; fr. malignus (671); prob. ref. to the envy which his fortune and rising fame excited.

1320. **Spernere** (1277), objective jnd. by et to spiritum. **vulgus,** acc. s. gov. by spernere; fr. vulgus (801).

CARMEN XVII.—AD MÆCENATEM.

1321 Cur me querelis exanimas tuis?
1322 Nec Dîs amicum est nec mihi te prius
1323 Obire, Mæcenas, mearum
1324 Grande decus columenque rerum.
1325 Ah te meæ si partem animæ rapit
1326 Maturior vis, quid moror altera,
1327 Nec carus æque nec superstes
1328 Integer? Ille dies utramque

Carmen XVII. Metre.—*The Alcaic.* (Bk. I., Carmen ix.)

1321. **Cur** (218). **me** (29), gov. by exanimas. **querelis,** abl. (causal) plu. fr. querela (1110). **exanimas,** 2nd s. pres. ind. act. fr. exănĭmo, -āre, -avi, -atum, 1st trans., (ex, 691; anima, 96) *to deprive of life, kill;* meton. pass., *to be deprived of strength, weakened, exhausted;* fig., *to deprive of life* or *spirit, alarm* or *terrify greatly, trouble, discourage, put out of one's senses*=conturbare. **tuis,** abl. plu. fem. ag. w. querelis; fr. tuus (175).

1322. **Nec** (19). **Dis** (30), after traject. amicum. **amicum,** nom. neut. s. predic. ag. w. obire; fr. amicus (208). **est** (19). **mihi** (277), jnd. by nec to Dis. **te** (83), subj. of obire. **prius** (120), w. obire; und. quam me.

1323. **Obire,** pres. inf. subj. of est; fr. obeo, -īre, -īvi or -ii, -ĭtum, trans. and intrans. irreg., (ob, 329; eo, 51) *to go* or *come to* or *towards, go to meet, go against.* Of sun, etc., *to go down, set;* pregn., *to die;* trans., *to go* or *come towards* a thing or place, esp. *travel over* or *through, wander through, traverse, visit. To apply oneself to, engage in, attend to* any business. **Mæcenas** (1). **mearum,** gen. fem. plu. ag. w. rerum; fr. meus (2).

1324. **Grande,** voc. s. neut. ag. w. decus; fr. grandis (173). **decus** (2), in app. to Mæcenas. **columen**=columna (790), voc. s. jnd. by -que to decus. **rerum,** gen. plu. after columen; fr. res (167).

1325. **Ah** (642). **te** (83), gov. by rapit. **meæ** (96), ag. w. animæ. **si** (7), w. pres. und. in protasis and a question in apodosis. **partem** (20), in app. to te. **animæ** (96), after partem. **rapit,** 3rd s. pres. ind. act. fr. rapio (489).

1326. **Maturior,** nom. fem. s. compar. ag. w. vis; fr. mātūrus, -a, -um, adj. Of fruits, *ripe, mature, arrived at full growth,* so fig., esp. *arrived at a proper age* or *time for,* w. dat. With gen. or abl., *mature, ripe in;* meton., *full, powerful, e.g.,* soles. *Of good old age, ripe in years. Seasonable, timely, at the fit time, e.g.,* tempus. *That is* or *takes place early. Speedy, quick.* Superl., maturissimus (maturrimus, fr. obsol. matur, not com.). **vis** (1212), subj. of rapuit. **quid** (229). **moror** (293), 1st sing. pres. ind. act. **altera,** nom. fem. s. ag. w. pars und. in app. to ego und. in moror; fr. alter (413).

1327. **Nec** (19). **carus** (721), ag. w. ego und. in moror; *i.e.,* to myself. **æque** (427), w. carus. **superstes** (924), mas.; jnd. by nec to carus.

1328. **Integer** (537), predic. after superstes, which partakes of the nature

1329 Ducet ruinam. Non ego perfidum
1330 Dixi sacramentum: ibimus, ibimus,
1331 Utcunque præcedes, supremum
1332 Carpere iter comites parati.
1333 Me nec Chimæræ spiritus igneæ,
1334 Nec si resurgat centimanus Gyas,
1335 Divellet unquam: sic potenti
1336 Justitiæ placitumque Parcis.

of a participle. **ille** (337), ag. w. dies. **dies** (826), subj. of ducet. **utramque,** acc. fem. s. ag. w. ruinam; fr. uterque (927).

1329. **Ducet,** 3rd sing. fut. ind. act. fr. duco (133). **ruinam,** acc. s. gov. by ducet; fr. ruina (843); "utramque ducet ruinam," *will cause both to fall at once* (W.). **non** (55). **ego** (445), subj. of dixi. **perfidum** (1074), ag. w. sacramentum.

1330. **Dixi,** 1st sing. pf. ind. act. fr. dico (86). **sacramentum,** acc. s. gov. by dixi; fr. săcrāmentum, -i, 2nd neut., (sacro, 623) *that which sets apart* and *devotes* to military service, etc., *i.e.*, the preliminary engagement entered into by newly enlisted troops (folld. by the proper military oath) wh. was at first voluntary, but after the second Punic War demanded by the military tribune; then="jus jurandum," *the military oath of allegiance. A solemn engagement* or *obligation*; "non perfidum dixi sacramentum." *I have taken a soldier's oath and will not break it* (W.). **ibimus** (219).

1331. **Utcunque** (-cumque), adv.; (ut, 13; -cunque, 743) *in what way soever, howsoever.* Rarely=quandocunque, *whenever, at whatever time.* **præcedes,** 2nd s. fut. ind. act. fr. præcēdo, -cedĕre, -cessi, -cessum, 3rd trans. and intrans., (præ, *before*; cedo, 170) *to go before, precede*; fig., *surpass, outstrip, outdo.* **supremum,** acc. neut. s. ag. w. iter.; fr. supremus (364).

1332. **Carpere,** pres. inf. (prolat. after parati) act. fr. carpo (284). **iter** (541), gov. by carpere. **comites,** nom. plu. predic. after parati; fr. comes (210). **parati,** nom. mas. plu. ag. w. nos und. in ibimus; fr. paratus (725).

1333. **Me** (29), gov. by divellet. **nec** (19). **Chimæræ,** gen. s. after spiritus; fr. Chimæra (648). **spiritus** (926), nom. s. subj. of divellet. **igneæ,** gen. s. fem. ag. w. Chimæræ; fr. igneus (450).

1334. **Si** (7), w. pres. subj. in protasis, fut. ind. in apodosis. **resurgat,** 3rd s. pres. subj. (in protasis) act. fr. resurgo, -surgĕre, -surrexi, -surrectum, 3rd intrans., (re, 659; surgo, 1103) *to rise* or *raise oneself again, appear again.* **centimanus,** -a, -um, adj.; nom. mas. s. ag. w. Gyas; (centum, 1258; manus, 474) *with a hundred hands.* **Gyas,** -æ, 1st mas., (Gk.) nom. subj. of resurgat; a giant.

1335. **Divellet,** 3rd s. fut. ind. act. fr. divello (363). **unquam** (1070). **sic** (89). **potenti** (163), fem. ag. w. justitiæ.

1336. **Justitiæ,** dat. s. after traject. placitum; fr. Justitia (578). **placitum,** nom. neut. s. pf. part.; w. est und. 3rd s. pf. ind.=placuit; fr. placeo (263); here impersonally. The pf. of pass. and deponent vbs. is a combinate tense made up of sum and the past partc.; so plpf. is made up of eram and past partc., the pf. inf. of esse and past partc. **Parcis,** dat. plu. jnd. by -que to Justitiæ; fr. Parca (1025).

1337 Seu Libra seu me Scorpios adspicit
1338 Formidolosus, pars violentior
1339 Natalis horæ, seu tyrannus
1340 Hesperiæ Capricornus undæ,
1341 Utrumque nostrum incredibili modo
1342 Consentit astrum. Te Jovis impio
1343 Tutela Saturno refulgens

1337. **Seu** (27). **Libra,** -æ, 1st fem.; nom. s. subj. of adspicit; the constellation Libra or the Scales. **me** (29), gov. by adspicit. **Scorpios** or Scorpius, or Scorpĭo, -ōnis, 3rd mas.; nom. s. jnd. by seu to Libra; *a scorpion,* one of the signs of the zodiac. **adspicit,** 3rd s. pres. ind. act. fr. adspĭcio, -cĕre, -spexi, -spectum, 3rd trans., (ad, 6; -spocio only in comp., *to behold) to look upon* something. *To consider, survey, inspect;* fig. mentally, *to reflect upon, weigh, consider, ponder,* esp. aspice, *see, behold!* Of a place, *to lie in the direction of, face. To obtain a view of, descry;* the pres. is used because the influence of the star continues through life.

1338. **Formīdŏlosus,** -a, -um, adj.; nom. mas. s. ag. w. Scorpios; (formido, *fear*) *full of fear, fearful;* act., *producing fear, dreadful;* pass., *experiencing fear, afraid, timid.* **pars** (20), nom. s. subj. in app. to Scorpios. **violentior,** nom. fem. s. compar. ag. w. pars; fr. vĭolens, -ntis, adj.; (vis, 436) *impetuous, vehement, furious* (poet. and post-Aug.), violentus is class.

1339. **Natalis,** gen. s. fem. ag. w. horæ; fr. natalis (530). **horæ,** gen. s. after pars; fr. hora (252); pars...horæ, *more stormy influence in the hour of birth*" (W.). **seu** (27). **tyrannus** (788), nom. s. in app. to Capricornus.

1340. **Hesperiæ** (908), ag. w. undæ. **Caprĭcornus,** -i, 2nd mas.; (caper, *a goat;* cornu, 464) a sign of the zodiac which the sun enters at the winter solstice (opp. to Cancer, in which the sun is found in the summer solstice). **undæ,** gen. s. after tyrannus; fr. unda (50).

1341. **Utrumque,** nom. neut. s. ag. w. astrum; fr. uterque (927). **nostrum,** gen. plu. after utrumque astrum; fr. noster (83). The genitives nostrum, vestrum (old Lat., nostrorum, vestrorum), are used in partitive construction of the thing distributed (1254), while mei, tui, nostri, vestri, are used quantitatively or objectively. **incredibili,** abl. s. mas. ag. w. modo; fr. incrēdĭbilis, -e, adj.; (in, neg.; credo, 93), *that can't be believed, extraordinary, incredible, unparalleled* (class.). **modo,** abl. (of manner) s. fr. modus (422).

1342. **Consentit,** 3rd s. pres. ind. act. fr. consentio, -sentīre, -sensi, -sensum, 4th irreg. intrans. and trans., (cum, 31; sentio, 1050). Of persons, *to agree, accord with* any person or thing, *assert, determine, decree* something, w. cum or the dat.; "sibi ipse consentit," *he is consistent with himself.* In bad sense, *to agree, combine* for any wrong purpose, *plot together, conspire.* Of things, *to accord, agree, harmonize with, fit, suit.* **astrum,** -i, 2nd neut.; nom. s. subj. of consentit; *a star, constellation, any luminous celestial body;* symbol for height, heaven, glory, etc. **Te** (83), gov. by eripuit. **Jovis** (261), after tutela. **impio,** dat. mas. s. ag. w. Saturno; fr. impius (111); here ref. to crimes of the mythological Saturn, as well as the bad influence of the planet (W.).

1343. **Tutela,** -æ, 1st fem.; nom. s. subj. of eripuit; *a defence, protection.* Legal, *office of guardian, wardship, tutelage* of minors, insane, etc. Abstr.

1344 Eripuit volucrisque Fati
1345 Tardavit alas, quum populus frequens
1346 Lætum theatris ter crepuit sonum:
1347 Me truncus illapsus cerebro
1348 Sustulerat, nisi Faunus ictum
1349 Dextra levasset, Mercurialium
1350 Custos virorum. Reddere victimas

for concrete, *watch, keeper, warder, protector* (poet.). Pass., *a charge, care, i.e.,* that which is guarded or protected. **Saturno,** dat. s. after trajective refulgens; fr. Saturnus (334). **refulgens,** pres. part. act. nom. fem. s. ag. w. tutela; fr. refulgeo (312); here, *shining against, i.e.,* to counteract its influence.

1344. **Eripuit,** 3rd s. pf. ind. act. fr. eripio (1191). **volucris,** gen. neut. s. ag. w. Fati; fr. volucris (768). **Fati,** gen. s. after alas; fr. Fatum (335).

1345. **Tardavit,** 3rd s. pf. ind. act. fr. tardo, -are, -avi, -atum, 1st trans. and intrans., (tardus, 120) *to make slow, hinder, delay, retard, impede, prevent*; intrans., *to tarry, linger, loiter* (very rare). **alas,** acc. plu. gov. by tardavit; fr. āla, -æ, 1st fem., *a wing;* fig. of *sails* and *oars,* as remi is used of wings. *The* upper and under part of a man's arm where it unites with the shoulder, *an armpit. A side apartment* in a building. *Wing* of an army. **populus frequens** (790), subj. of eripuit.

1346. **Lætum,** acc. mas. s. ag. w. sonum; fr. lætus (82). **theatris,** abl. (local) plu. fr. theatrum (511); plu. generalises, "the people in crowded theatres" (W.). **ter** (361), of an indefinite number of times. **crepuit,** 3rd s. pf. ind. act. fr. crepo (481). It is trans. here, but in a diff. sense fr. that in 481. **sonum,** acc. s. after crepuit; fr. sonus (1230). The contained acc. or acc. of internal object or cognate acc.

1347. **Me** (29), gov. by sustulerat. **truncus,** -i, 2nd mas.; nom. sing. subj. of sustulerat; *the stem, stock, bole* or *trunk* of a tree without branches; so of a human *body* without limbs. **illapsus,** pf. part. nom. mas. s. ag. w. truncus; fr. illābor, -lābi, -lapsus sum, 3rd depon., (in, 76; *against;* labor, 55) *to fall, slip, slide, glide,* or *flow into. To fall down, sink down;* here, *to fall upon.* **cerebro,** abl. s. after illapsus; fr. cĕrĕbrum, -i, 2nd neut., *the brain;* fig., *understanding. Anger, choler* (Hor.).

1348. **Sustulerat,** 3rd s. plpf. ind. act. fr. tollo (8). The ind. in apodosis w. plpf. in protasis, is a rhetorical exaggeration. *I was a dead man, had not* (W.). **nisi** (265). **Faunus** (450), subj. of levasset. **ictum,** acc. s. gov. by levasset; fr. ictus (594).

1349. **Dextra**=dexterâ (29), instrum. w. levasset. **levasset,** syncopated for levavisset; 3rd s. plpf. subj. act. fr. lĕvo, -are, -avi, -atum, 1st trans., (levis, 31) *to make light* by removing weight, etc., *ease, relieve, raise, lift up. To lift up and take away. Lighten, lessen, diminish, allay, abate. To alleviate, mitigate, free from* anything. **Mercurialium,** gen. mas. plu. ag. w. virorum; fr. Mercŭrĭālis, -e, adj.; (Mercŭrĭus, 257) *of* or *belonging to Mercury,* applied to traders or poets, learned men, etc.

1350. **Custos** (333), in app. to Faunus. **virorum** (846), after custos. **reddere** (496), prolat. after memento. **victimas,** acc. plu. gov. by reddere; fr. victima (964).

1351 Ædemque votivam memento:
1352 Nos humilem feriemus agnam.

CARMEN XVIII.

DE CONTINENTIA QUA PAUPERTATEM SUAM DIVITIIS PRÆFERT.

1353 Non ebur neque aureum
1354 Mea renidet in domo lacunar,
1355 Non trabes Hymettiæ
1356 Premunt columnas ultima recisas
1357 Africa, neque Attali
1358 Ignotus heres regiam occupavi,

1351. **Ædem** (704), jnd. by -que to victimas. **votivam,** acc. fem. s. ag. w. ædem; fr. votivus (162). **memento** (201).
1352. **Nos** (169), subj. of feriemus. **humilem,** acc. fem. s. ag. w. agnam; fr. humilis (868). **feriemus,** 1st plu. fut. ind. act. fr. ferio (36). **agnam,** acc. s. gov. by feriemus; fr. agna (140).

Carmen XVIII.—*Trochaic* (the only instance in Horace).

1st. A dimeter trochaic catalectic – ⏑ | – ⏑ | – ⏑ | ⏓

2nd. A trimeter iambic catalectic ⏓ | ⏑ – | ⏓ – | ⏑ – | ⏓ – | ⏓

1353. **Non** (55). **ebur** (714), nom. s. subj. of renidet; here it may refer to "*ivory furniture*" or an "*ivory roof.*" **neque** (32). **aureum,** nom. neut. s. ag. w. lacunar; fr. aureus (157).
1354. **Mea** (1059), ag. w. domo. **renidet** (1011). **in** (78). **domo** (117), gov. by in. **lăcūnar,** -āris, 3rd neut.; nom. s. jnd. by neque to ebur; (lăcūna, *a cavity*) *a panelled* or *fretted ceiling, i.e.,* with indented or panelled apartments.
1355. **Trabes** (13), nom. plu. subj. of premunt; fr. trabs (13). **Hymettiæ,** nom. fem. plu. ag. w. trabes; fr. Hȳmettius, -a, -um, adj.; (Hȳmettus, 1030) *of* or *from Hymettus, i.e.,* slabs of white Hymettian marble for the architrave.
1356. **Premunt,** 3rd plu. pres. ind. act. fr. premo (144). **columnas,** acc. plu. gov. by premunt; fr. columna (790). **ultima** (820), ag. w. Africâ. **recisas,** pf. pass. part. acc. fem. plu. ag. w. columnas; fr. recīdo, -dĕre, -cīdi, -cīsum, 3rd trans., (re, 659; cædo, *to cut*) *to cut away, cut down, cut off;* here *to hew out;* fig. (borrowed fr. agriculture) *to lop off, cut short, retrench, abridge.*
1357. **Africa,** abl. (local) s. fr. Afrĭca, -æ, 1st fem., *the land of Afer* (1315), son of the Libyan Hercules. *Africa.* **Attali,** gen. s. after regiam; fr. Attălus, -i, 2nd mas., the name of several kings of Pergamos, the most noted of whom both for wealth and for discovering the art of weaving cloth of gold, was Attalus III., who made the Roman people his heir.
1358. **Ignotus,** -a, -um, adj.; nom. mas. s. ag. w. heres; (in, neg.; -gnotus=notus, 46) *unknown, strange, i.e.,* to the testator, and so enriched

1359 Nec Laconicas mihi
1360 Trahunt honestæ purpuras clientæ.
1361 At fides et ingenî
1362 Benigna vena est, pauperemque dives
1363 Me petit: nihil supra
1364 Deos lacesso, nec potentem amicum
1365 Largiora flagito,
1366 Satis beatus unicis Sabinis.

by chance (M). **heres** (960), in app. to ego und. in occupavi. **regiam** (861), gov. by occupavi. **occupavi**, 1st s. pf. ind. act. fr. occupo (303), *i.e.*, nor has any rich stranger left me a palace (W.).

1359. **Laconicas**, acc. pl. fem. ag. w. purpuras; fr. Lăcōnĭcus, -a, -um, adj.; *Lacedæmonian, Spartan.* **mihi** (277), commodi after trahunt.

1360. **Trahunt** (130), *spin.* **honestæ**, nom. fem. plu. ag. w. clientæ; fr. hŏnestus, -a, -um, adj.; (honos=honor, 8) *full of honour. Regarded with honour, enjoying respect* or *consideration, distinguished, noble, well born* (here). *Bringing* or *deserving of honour, respectable, worthy, virtuous, decent, proper;* meton., *noble, fine, handsome.* **purpuras**, acc. plu. gov. by trahunt; fr. purpura (1287). **clientæ**, nom. plu. subj. of trahunt; fr. clienta, -æ, 1st fem., (cliens, 1377) a *protégé, female client.*

1361. **At** (483). **fides** (492), subj. of est; *honesty* (W.). **ingeni** (176), after vena.

1362. **Benigna**, *full, teeming,* nom. fem. s. ag. w. vena; fr. benignus (238). **vena** (931), nom. s. subj. of est. **est** (19); und. possessive dat. mihi. **pauperem**, acc. s. in app. to me; fr. pauper (141). **dives** (270), subj. of petit.

1363. **Me** (29), gov. by petit. **petit**, 3rd s. pres. ind. act. fr. peto (126), *seeks my friendship* (W.). **nihil** (660), contained acc. gov. by lacesso; see 584. **sŭpra** (orig. sŭpĕra), adverb. Of place, *on the upper side, on the top,* opp. to subter, infra. Of time, *before, formerly, previously.* Of number or measure, *above, beyond, over, more* (here); folld. by quam or quod, *above* or *beyond what, more than.* Prepos. w. acc. of place, *above, over.* Geographically, *above, beyond.* Of time, *before* (rare). Of number, quantity, degree or ability, *over, beyond, above.* Suprafundo and suprascendo, are the only undoubted compounds.

1364. **Deos**, acc. of attained obj., gov. by lacesso. **lacesso** (783), 1st s. pres. ind. act.; here "*weary with prayers.*" **nec** (19). **potentem**, acc. mas. s. ag. w. amicum; fr. potens (89). **amicum**, acc. (attained) s. gov. by flagito; fr. amicus (208).

1365. **Largiora**, acc. neut. plu. compar. contained obj. of flagito; fr. largus, -a, -um, adj. Of size, *large, long, great* (rare). Of quantity, *abundant, copious, plentiful, much.* With gen., *abounding in;* fig., *giving abundantly* or *much, bountiful, profuse, liberal.* **flāgito**, -are, -avi, -atum, 1st trans. and intrans., (flag-, whence flagro, 605) *to demand* anything *hotly, fiercely, violently*=flagranter posco, rogo, exigo (the strongest of such words). With acc. pers., *to press earnestly, importune, dun.*

1366. **Satis** (37), adv. w. beatus. **beatus** (635), ag. w. ego und. in flagito. **unicis**, abl. plu. neut. ag. w. Sabinis; fr. ūnĭcus, -a, -um, adj.; (unus, 189) of number, *one and no more, only, sole, single* (here); fig. in good sense,

1367 Truditur dies die,
1368 Novæque pergunt interire Lunæ.
1369 Tu secanda marmora
1370 Locas sub ipsum funus, et sepulcri
1371 Immemor struis domos
1372 Marisque Baiis obstrepentis urges

alone of its kind, singular, unparalleled, rarely in bad sense. **Sabinis,** abl. (causal) plu. w. beatus; fr. Săbīnum, -i, 2nd neut., (prop. neut. adj.; und. prædium) *the Sabine estate.*

1367. **Truditur,** 3rd s. pres. ind. pass. fr. trūdo, -ĕre, trūsi, trūsum, 3rd trans., *to thrust, push; shove,* or *shove forward, press on, impel* (class.); fig., *to come close upon* (here). Of growth, *to put forth, send forth* (often in Georgics). **dies** (826), subj. of truditur. **die** (20), instrumental, "*day treads on the heel of day*" (W.).

1368. **Novæ,** nom. fem. plu. ag. w. lunæ; fr. novus (42). **pergunt,** 3rd plu. pres. ind. act. fr. pergo, -ĕre, perrexi, perrectum, 3rd trans., (per, 114; intensive, rego, 91) *to proceed* or *go on with, continue with* w. acc.; in Cic. w. inf. only; intrans., *to proceed,* i.e., *go* or *come* (most usu.), esp. *to proceed to speak.* **interire,** pres. inf. prolative (570) after pergunt; fr. intĕrĕo, -ire, -ĭi, -itum, irreg. intrans., (inter, 330; eo, 51) *to go among things so as to be no longer perceived, mingle, commingle with, be lost among;* meton., *perish, go to ruin* or *decay, die;* fig., *perish, be undone.* Interii, *I am ruined.* **lunæ,** nom. plu. subj. of pergunt; fr. luna (133).

1369. **Tu** (69), subj. of locas; ref. to an imaginary person representing a class. **secanda,** acc. plu. predicate ag. w. marmora; fr. secandus, gerundive of seco (14), probably ref. to cutting the marble into slabs for the pavement. **marmora,** acc. plu. gov. by locas; fr. marmor (498).

1370. **Locas,** 2nd s. pres. ind. act. fr. lŏco, -are, -avi, -atum, 1st trans., (locus, 543) *to place, put, lay, set, dispose, arrange. To let, lease* or *farm out, give out on contract, contract for* a thing to be done, esp. w. gerundive, *e.g.,* locare aliquid faciendum. Of money, *to put* or *lend out on interest;* fig., *to place, put, set.* **sub** (230), of time. **ipsum** (126), ag. w. funus. **funus** (844), gov. by sub. **sepulcri,** gen. s. after immemor; fr. sepulcrum (906), see 910.

1371. **Immemor** (26), ag. w. tu. **struis,** 2nd s. pres. ind. act. fr. struo, struĕre, struxi, structum, 3rd trans., (ak. to sterno, 22) *to place* one thing *by* or *upon* another *in regular order, pile up,* etc. *To make by joining together, build, erect, arrange, compound, compose. To prepare* something detrimental, *e.g.,* insidias. *To cause, occasion, devise, contrive, instigate. To dispose, arrange, regulate.* **domos** (420), gov. by struis.

1372. **Maris** (164), after litora. **Baiis,** dat. after obstrepentis; fr. Baiæ, -arum, 1st plu. fem., a town on the coast of Campania betw. Cumæ and Puteoli, a favourite resort of the Romans on account of its climate and warm baths. **obstrepentis,** gen. neut. s. pres. part. act. ag. w. maris; fr. obstrĕpo, -ĕre, -ŭi, -ĭtum, 3rd intrans. and trans., (ob, 329; strepo, 894) *to make a noise against* or *at, roar against* or *at, dash against with a roaring noise;* fig., *to raise a clamour* or *outcry against, try to clamour down. To exclaim against, annoy, molest, be troublesome to. To make a great noise* or *din.* **urges** (1101).

1373 Summovere litora,
1374 Parum locuples continente ripa.
1375 Quid, quod usque proximos
1376 Revellis agri terminos et ultra
1377 Limites clientium
1378 Salis avarus? Pellitur paternos
1379 In sinu ferens Deos

1373. **Summovere,** pres. inf. act. objective after urges; fr. summoveo (1133). **litora,** acc. plu. gov. by summovere; fr. litus (50).

1374. **Parum** (343), w. locuples. **lŏcŭples,** ētis, adj.; gen. plu. locupletum and locupletium; nom. mas. s. ag. w. tu; (locus, 543; pleo, *to fill*) prop., *rich in lands;* meton., *rich, wealthy, opulent* of persons and things. With gen. or abl., *rich, abounding in.* Of language, composition, etc., *rich, copious, rich in language.* With ad and gerund, *richly provided for* any purpose. *Sufficient, credible, satisfactory, e.g.,* auctor, oraculum. **continente,** abl. fem. s. ag. w. ripa; fr. contĭnens, -ntis, adj.; (contineo, *to hold together*) *that restrains his passions, moderate, temperate.* Of space, *bordering upon, neighbouring, adjoining* (some take it so here). *Hanging together, cohering in itself, connected,* of space or time. "Terra continens," *main land* or *continent.* Subst. continens, -ntis, 3rd neut., *a bordering* or *neighbouring place;* fem., *the main land* or *continent.* **ripa** (55), abl. of means w. locuples; here of the seashore.

1375. **Quid** (229). **quod** (35). There is an ellipse of dicam. Quid quod is an expression used to introduce some stronger argument or charge (W.) here=*nay worse.* **usque** (452), of time. **proximos,** acc. mas. plu. ag. w. terminos; fr. proxĭmus, -a, -um, adj.; superl. of propior. Positive only in prope (651). Of place, *the nearest, next.* With ab, *nearest to, next to;* neut. as subst., *of the immediate neighbourhood;* mas. as subst., *a neighbour, attendant, bystander.* Of time, *next,* either preceding or following, *the last* or *the next following* or *ensuing;* so of succession, estimation, worth, etc., *the next.* Of value or quality, *most nearly approaching, most similar.* Of relationship, etc., *most nearly related* or *connected, next of kin.*

1376. **Revellis,** 2nd s. pres. ind. act. fr. rĕvello, -velli, -vulsum, 3rd trans., (re, 659; vello, *to pluck*) *to pluck* or *pull away, pull* or *tear out. Tear off* or *away; remove.* **agri,** gen. s. after terminos; fr. ager (12). **terminos,** acc. plu. gov. by revellis; fr. terminus (547). **ultra** (546).

1377. **Limites,** acc. plu. gov. by ultra; fr. līmes, -ĭtis, 3rd mas., (ak. to limen, 596) *a connecting path between two paths, cross-path. Boundary. limit, i.e.,* stone or balk between two fields. *A fortified boundary line, boundary-wall;* genly. *path, passage, road, way. Track* of a comet; fig., *path, way.* **clientium,** gen. plu. after limites; fr. cliens, -ntis; gen. plu., also -tum; 3rd com., (for cluens, fr. clueo, *to hear*) *a dependant, protégé* in relation to his protector (patronus), *a client.* Poet., *a favourite.*

1378. **Salis,** 2nd s. ind. pres. act. fr. sălio, -īre, sălui, saltum, 4th irreg. intrans. and trans., *to leap, spring, jump, hop.* **avarus** (917), nom. mas. s. ag. w. tu und. in salis. **pellitur,** 3rd s. pres. ind. pass. ag. w. uxor; fr. pello (215). **paternos,** acc. mas. plu. ag. w. Deos; fr. paternus (513).

1379. **Sinu,** abl. s. gov. by in (78), fr. sinus (760). **ferens,** pres. part. act. nom. fem. s. ag. w uxor; fr. fero (138). **Deos** (6), gov. by ferens.

Et uxor et vir sordidosque natos.
Nulla certior tamen
Rapacis Orci fine destinata
Aula divitem manet
Herum. Quid ultra tendis? Æque tellus
Pauperi recluditur
Regumque pueris, nec satelles Orci
Callidum Promethea
Revexit auro captus. His superbum

1380. **Et...et** (2). **uxor** (1254), subj. of pellitur. **vir** (215), jnd. by et to uxor. **sordidos** (898), ag. w. natos. **natos,** acc. plu. jnd. by -que to Deos; fr. natus (679), subst.

1381. **Nulla** (553), ag. w. aula. **certior,** nom. fem. s. compar., ag. as adv. attribute (867) w. aula; fr. certus (212). **tamen** (111).

1382. **Rapacis,** gen. mas. s. ag. w. Orci; fr. rapax (774). **Orci** (964), after fine. **fine** (486), abl. of instrument w. destinatâ. **destinata,** abl. fem. s. ag. w. abl. aula und.; fr. destinatus (1060). Others make "destinatâ" ag. w. fine as the abl. of comparison after certior; "*than the destined end of Orcus,*" but finis fem. is unusual.

1383. **Aula** (691), nom. s. subj. of manet. **divitem,** acc. mas. s. ag. w. herum; fr. dives (270). **manet** (25).

1384. **Herum,** acc. s. gov. by manet; fr. hĕrus, -i, 2nd mas., *the master of a house* or *family* in respect of servants. Of men, *a master, lord, owner, proprietor.* **quid** (229). **ultra** (546). **tendis** (700), *i.e.*, death has set the limit, why do you try to overpass it? (W.). **æque** (427), w. recluditur. **tellus** (551), subj. of recluditur.

1385. **Pauperi,** dat. (incommodi) s. after recluditur; fr. pauper (781). **recluditur,** 3rd s. pres. ind. pass. fr. recludo (589), *opens.*

1386. **Regum** (142), after pueris. **pueris,** dat. plu. jnd. by -que to pauperi; fr. puer (149). **nec** (19). **sătelles,** -ĭtis, 3rd com.; nom. s. subj. of revexit; prop. *an attendant* upon a distinguished person, esp. a prince, *life-guard;* plur., *attendants, retinue, train, escort;* meton., here of Charon; fig., *an attendant* in a good sense, or *accomplice, partner, abettor* in crime in a bad sense. **Orci** (964), after satelles.

1387. **Callidum** (263), ag. w. Promethea. **Promethea,** acc. s. gov. by revexit; fr. Prometheus (433).

1388. **Revexit,** 3rd s. pf. ind. act. fr. rĕvĕho, -hĕre, -xi, -ctum, 3rd trans., (re, 659; veho, *to carry*) *to carry* or *bring back, convey back* (class.). Pass., *to return* on foot, horse, ship, etc.; fig. act., *to bring back*; pass., *go back,* of age, etc. **auro** (1288), instrum. w. captus. **captus,** pf. pass. part. nom. mas. s. ag. w. satelles; fr. căpio, căpĕre, cēpi, captum, 3rd trans., *to take, lay hold of, seize. To take prisoner, capture. To choose, elect, i.e.,* take for a definite purpose or as something. Of things, *to receive, hold, contain, have space for. To reach* a place. *To gain, participate in, e.g.,* revenues, inheritance, etc.; fig., *to seize, e.g.,* occasionem. Pass., *to be deprived* of powers, *weakened, e.g.,* pedibus; so fig. w. mente, etc. *To captivate, ensnare, mislead, seduce. To take a thing into the mind in all its details. To undertake, enter upon*=suscipio. As a man may admit emotions, passions, etc., or they may seize him, we may say capio odium, satietatem, etc., or odium,

1389 Tantalum atque Tantali
1390 Genus coërcet; hic levare functum
1391 Pauperem laboribus
1392 Vocatus atque non vocatus audit.

CARMEN XIX.—AD LIBERUM PATREM.

1393 BACCHUM in remotis carmina rupibus
1394 Vidi docentem, credite posteri,
1395 Nymphasque discentes et aures
1396 Capripedum Satyrorum acutas.

satietas, etc., capit me. **hic** (533), *i.e.*, Orcus, sub. of coërcet. **superbum**, acc. mas. s. ag. w. Tantalum; fr. superbus (318).

1389. **Tantalum**, acc. s. gov. by coërcet; fr. Tantălus, -i, 2nd mas., a king of Phrygia, son of Jupiter, and father of Pelops and Niobe; for disclosing the secrets of the gods, after being admitted to their banquets, he was made to stand in the infernal regions, up to his chin in water, under an overhanging fruit-tree, both of which retreated when he tried to satisfy his hunger and thirst; a rock also hung over him threatening to fall. **atque** (37). **Tantali**, gen. s. after genus.

1390. **Genus** (71), gov. by coërcet. **coërcet**, 3rd s. pres. ind. act. fr. coërceo (274). **hic** (1388), subj. of audit. **levare**, pres. inf. (prolative) after audit or vocatus; fr. levo (1349). **functum**, acc. mas. s. ag. w. pauperem; fr. functus (1105).

1391. **Pauperem** (1362), gov. by levare. **laboribus**, abl. plu. after functum; fr. labor (124).

1392. **Vocatus**, pf. pass. part. nom. mas. s. ag. w. hic; fr. voco (61). **atque** (37). **non** (55), w. vocatus. **audit**, 3rd s. pres. ind. act. fr. audio (57).

CARMEN XIX. METRE.—*The Alcaic* (Bk. I., Carmen ix.)

1393. **Bacchum** (657), gov. by vidi. **in** (78). **remotis** (926), abl. fem. ag. w. rupibus. "Far away from the ways of men" (W.). **carmina** (64), gov. by docentem. **rupibus**, abl. plu. gov. by in; fr. rupes (162).

1394. **Vidi**, 1st sing. pf. ind. act. fr. video (49). **docentem**, pres. part. act. acc. s. mas. ag. w. Bacchum; fr. doceo (29). **credite**, 2nd plu. pres. imper. act. fr. credo (93). **posteri**, voc. plu. mas. fr. posterus (284).

1395. **Nymphas**, acc. plu. jnd. by -que to Bacchum; fr. nympha (31). **discentes**, pres. part. act. acc. fem. plu. ag. w. nymphas; fr. disco, -ĕre, dĭdĭci, no sup., 3rd trans., (dic-, rt. in dico, 86; -sco, inceptive termination) *to come to know, come to be acquainted with, learn.* **aures** (894), jnd. by et to nymphas.

1396. **Capripedum**, gen. mas. plu. ag. w. Satyrorum; fr. Caprĭpes, -pĕdis, adj.; (caper, *goat;* pes, 135) *goat-footed*, poet. epith. of rural deities. **Satyrorum**, gen. plu. after aures; fr. Satyrus (31). **acutas**, acc. fem. plu. predic. ag. w. aures; fr. acutas (236), *i.e., pricked up*. Others take it as a mere epith., *sharp pointed.*

1397 Euœ, recenti mens trepidat metu,
1398 Plenoque Bacchi pectore turbidum
1399 Lætatur. Euœ, parce Liber,
1400 Parce, gravi metuende thyrso.
1401 Fas pervicaces est mihi Thyiadas
1402 Vinique fontem, lactis et uberes
1403 Cantare rivos atque truncis
1404 Lapsa cavis iterare mella,
1405 Fas et beatæ conjugis additum

1397. **Euœ** (disyll.) onomatopœic interj., a joyous sound at the festival of Bacchus. **recenti,** abl. s. mas. ag. w. metu; fr. recens (258). **mens** (349), subj. of trepidat. **trepidat,** 3rd s. pres. ind. act. fr. trepido (952). **metu** (564), abl. of cause w. trepidat.

1398. **Pleno,** abl. neut. s. ag. w. pectore; fr. plenus (463). **Bacchi,** gen. s. of abundance (882), after pleno; fr. Bacchus (482). **pectore,** abl. (824) absol. fr. pectus (98). **turbidum,** neut. s. as adv.; fr. turbĭdus, -a, -um, adj.; (turba, 7) *full of confusion* or *disorder, wild, confused;* esp. of fluids, *thick, muddy, turbid;* fig., *troubled, disturbed, perplexed;* neut. s. as adv., *in a confused* or *troubled manner. Boisterous, vehement, violent. Mutinous, seditious,* of persons. Of circumstances, *perilous, disturbed, e.g.,* res.

1399. **Lætatur,** 3rd s. pres. ind. fr. lætor, -ari, -atus sum, 1st depon. intrans., *to feel joy, rejoice, be very glad* or *joyous, exult.* **Euœ** (1399). **parce** (671). **Liber** (306).

1400. **Gravi** (342), ag. w. thyrso. **metuende** (307), ag. w. Tiber. **thyrso,** abl. (of cause) s. fr. thyrsus, -i, 2nd mas. (Gk.), a staff twined round with ivy and vine shoots, borne by Bacchus and the Bacchantes, *the Bacchic staff. A thorn, goad.*

1401. **Fas** (486), nom. predic. after est. **pervicaces,** acc. fem. plu. ag. w. Thyiadas; fr. pervĭcax, -cācis, adj.; (pervinco, *to conquer thoroughly*) *maintaining* or *upholding one's views, firm, determined;* genly. in a bad sense, *stubborn, headstrong, obstinate,* rarely good, *firm, steadfast, untiring.* **est** (19). **mihi** (277), after traject. fas. **Thyiadas,** acc. plu. gov. by cantare; fr. Thȳias or Thȳas, -ădis, 3rd fem., *a Bacchante,* genly. in plu.

1402. **Vini** (146), after fontem. **fontem,** acc. s. jnd. by -que to Thyiadas; fr. fons (618). **lactis,** gen. s. after rivos; fr. lac, 3rd neut., *milk.* **uberes,** acc. plu. mas. ag. w. rivos; fr. ūber, ūbĕris, adj. Of the soil, *rich, fruitful, fertile;* meton., *productive.* With abl. or gen., *abounding in, rich in. Copious, plentiful, abundant, e.g.,* crop, etc.; fig., *rich, fertile, fruitful, e.g.,* an orator, etc. Of hope, etc., *abundant, plentiful, copious.*

1403. **Cantare,** pres. inf. act. subj. of est; fr. canto (183). **rivos** (695), gov. by cantare. **atque** (37) **truncis,** abl. (of separation) plu. after lapsa; fr. truncus (1347).

1404. **Lapsa,** pf. part. acc. plu. neut. ag. w. mella; fr. labor (55). **cavis,** abl. mas. plu. ag. w. truncis; fr. căvus, -a, -um, adj.; *hollow, excavated, concave,* sts. used of a cloud or darkness enveloping as a cloud. **iterare** (764), jnd. by atque to cantare; *to sing of repeatedly.* **mella** (1031), acc. gov. by iterare.

1405. **Fas** (1401), predic. to cantare und. as subj. **et** (2), *also.* **beatæ,**

1406 Stellis honorem, tectaque Pentheï
1407 Disjecta non leni ruina,
1408 Thracis et exitium Lycurgi.
1409 Tu flectis amnes, tu mare barbarum,
1410 Tu separatis uvidus in jugis
1411 Nodo coërces viperino
1412 Bistonidum sine fraude crines:
1413 Tu, quum parentis regna per arduum
1414 Cohors Gigantum scanderet impia,

gen. s. fem. predic. ag. w. conjugis; fr. beatus (142). **conjugis** (26), *i.e.*, *Ariadne*, after honorem. **additum** (1113), mas. ag. w. honorem.

1406. **Stellis**, dat. plu. after traject. additum; fr. stella (312). **honorem** (192), *her ornament*, *i.e.*, her crown; gov. by cantare und. **tecta** (1292), jnd. by -que to honorem. **Pentheï**, gen. s. after tecta; fr. Pentheus, gen. -ĕi and -ĕos (Gk.), mas., son of Echion and Agave, grandson of Cadmus, king of Thebes. His mother and sisters, influenced by Bacchus, tore him in pieces for treating with contempt the rites of that god.

1407. **Disjecta**, pf. pass. part. acc. neut. plu. ag. w. tecta; fr. disjĭcio, -jĭcere, -jēci, -jectum, 3rd trans., (dis, 870; jăcio, *to throw, cast, hurl*) *to rend apart, cleave, tear asunder. To dash to pieces, destroy. To disperse, scatter, drive hither and thither.* **non** (55). **leni**, abl. fem. s. ag. w. ruinâ; fr. lenis (22). **ruina**, abl. (of manner) s. fr. ruina (843).

1408. **Thracis**, gen. mas. sing. ag. w. Lycurgi; fr. Thrax (626), adj. **exitium** (405), jnd. by et to tecta. **Lycurgi**, gen. after exitium; fr. Lўcurgus, -i, 2nd mas., son of Dryas, king of the Edones, who prohibited the worship of Bacchus to his subjects, and ordered all the vines to be destroyed.

1409. **Tu** (69), subj. of flectis. **flectis**, 2nd s. pres. ind. act. fr. flecto, -ĕre, flexi, flexum, 3rd trans., (ak. to plico, plecto) *to bend, bow, curve, turn, turn round. To turn, direct. To move, persuade, prevail upon, overcome.* **amnes**, acc. plu. gov. by flectis; fr. amnis (56). **mare** (14), gov. by flectis und., a case of zeugma. **barbarum** (636), neut. ag. w. mare, *i.e.*, *the Indian Ocean.*

1410. **Separatis**, pf. pass. part. abl. neut. plu. ag. w. jugis; fr. sēpăro, -are, -avi, -atum, 1st trans., (se, 120; paro, 396) *to put asunder, disjoin, sever, part, separate;* fig., *to treat* or *consider separately, distinguish, except.* **uvidus** (162), nom. mas. s. ag. w. tu. **jugis**, abl. plu. gov. by in; fr. jugum (755).

1411. **Nodo**, abl. instrum. s. fr. nodus (1164). **coërces** (274). **viperino** (225), ag. w. nodo.

1412. **Bistonidum**, gen. plu. after crines; fr. Bistŏnis, -ĭdis, fem. adj.; *Thracian*, as subst. *a Thracian woman;* here plu., *the Bacchantes.* The Bistones were a Thracian people, who lived S. of Mt. Rhodope, near Abdera. **sine** (370). **fraude** (116), gov. by sine; "sine fraude," *harmlessly*, *i.e.*, without injury to thyself or them. **crines** (404), gov. by coërces.

1413. **Tu**, subj. of retorsisti. **quum** (206), w. impf subj. **parentis** (297), after regna. **regna** (146), gov by scanderet **per** (114), local. **arduum**, acc. neut. s. gov. by per; fr. arduus (125).

1414. **Cohors** (119), subj. of scanderet. **Gigantum**, gen. after cohors;

Rhœtum retorsisti leonis
Unguibus horribilique mala;
Quamquam choreis aptior et jocis
Ludoque dictus non sat idoneus
Pugnæ ferebaris: sed idem
Pacis eras mediusque belli.
Te vidit insons Cerberus aureo

fr. gigantes, -um (Gk.). *The giants*, sons of Earth and Tartarus, who stormed the heavens, but were smitten by Jupiter with lightning and buried under Mt. Ætna. **scanderet**, 3rd s. impf. subj. act. fr. scando (1301) after quum. **impia**, nom. fem. s. ag. w. cohors; fr. impius (111).

1415. **Rhœtum**, acc. s. gov. by retorsisti; fr. Rhœtus, -i, 2nd mas., a giant. **retorsisti**, 2nd s. pf. ind. act. fr. retorqueo (49). **leonis** (435), after unguibus.

1416. **Unguibus** (182), instrum. w. retorsisti. **horribili** (688), fem. ag. w. mala. **mala**, abl. s. jnd. by -que to unguibus; fr. māla, -æ, 1st fem., (mando, *to chew*, cf. scala with scando) *the cheek-bone, jaw*, more strictly the bones of the face between the eyes, nose and mouth, in which the teeth are fixed, usu. in the plu.; meton., *the cheek, i.e.*, corresponding external part of the face (plu.).

1417. **Quamquam** (683), qualifying what precedes, "*and yet*" (W.). **choreis**, dat. plu. after trajective aptior; fr. chorea (248). **aptior**, nom. mas. s. predic. after dictus, compar. fr. aptus (193). **jocis**, dat. plu. jnd. by et to choreis; fr. jocus (70).

1418. **Ludo**, dat. s. jnd. by -que to jocis; fr. ludus (73). **dictus**, pf. pass. part. (concessive) ag. w. tu und. in ferebaris; fr. dico (86). **non** (55), w. ferebaris. **sat**=satis (37), adv. w. idoneus. **idōnĕus**, -a, -um, adj.; nom. mas. s. predic. ag. w. tu und. in ferebaris; *fit for* something, esp. for doing something, *meet, proper, suitable, able, capable, convenient, sufficient*, of persons and things, w. ad, qui, or relat. adv., or dat. or absolute. Hor. uses it w. inf., which is rare.

1419. **Pugnæ**, dat. s. after traject. idoneus; fr. pugna (59). **ferebaris**, 2nd s. impf. ind. pass. fr. fero (138). **sed** (591). **idem** (1132), ag. w. tu und. in eras; here=*for all that, notwithstanding*.

1420. **Păcis**, gen. s. after medius; fr. pax, 3rd fem., (rt. pac-, in paciscor, *to covenant*) prop. *peace* concluded between parties at variance; fig., *peace, tranquillity*. Personified, *the goddess of peace, grace, favour, assistance* of the gods; "pace tua, alicujus," *with your* or *any one's good leave* or *permission*; "pax," interj.; *peace, silence, enough*. **eras**, 2nd s. impf. ind. fr. sum (3). **medius** (975), nom. mas. s. predic. after eras; as subst., *an arbitrator*. **-que** (4), misplaced as in 706, 1424. **belli** (878), jnd. by -que to pacis. If "medius" is the main predicate, "*Thou wast equally adapted for peace or war;*" if idem, "*thou wast the same, i.e., equally vigorous and successful in the midst of peace and in the midst of war*" (W.).

1421. **Te** (83), gov. by vidit. **vidit** (107). **insons**, -ntis, adj.; nom. mas. s. ag. as adv. attribute w. Cerberus; (in, neg.; sons, *hurtful*) *guiltless, innocent, e.g.*, culpæ (not Cic. nor Cæs.); meton., *that does no hurt* or *harm, commits no injury, gives no offence*. **Cerbĕrus**, -i, 2nd mas.; nom. s. subj. of videt; the monster who guarded Hades, represented sometimes with three, sometimes with one hundred heads. **aureo** (1218), ag. w. cornu.

1422 Cornu decorum, leniter atterens
1423 Caudam et recedentis trilingui
1424 Ore pedes tetigitque crura.

CARMEN XX.—AD MÆCENATEM.

1425 Non usitata nec tenui ferar
1426 Penna biformis per liquidum æthera
1427 Vates, neque in terris morabor

1422. **Cornu** (464), instrum. w. decorum. **decorum,** acc. mas. s. predic. ag. w. te; fr. decorus (259). **leniter,** adv.; (lenis, 22) *moderately, gently, not violently.* Of anything rising to a point *gradually.* Of pace or motion, *gently, softly, not rapidly;* fig., esp. of speech, *mildly, calmly.* **atterens,** pres. part. act. nom. mas. s. ag. w. Cerberus; fr. attĕro, -tĕrĕre, -trīvi, rare -tĕrŭi, -trītum, 3rd trans., (ad, 6; tero, *to rub*) *to rub* one thing *against* another; here *against* Bacchus, or *moving it from side to side* on the ground (W.). Of the effects of this rubbing, *to wear away, destroy, injure,* etc.; fig., *to destroy, waste, weaken, e.g.,* opes, Germanos.

1423. **Caudam,** acc. s. gov. by atterens; fr. cauda, -æ, 1st fem., (also cōda, cf. codex, plostrum), (rt. perh. κυθ-, cut-, is *that which covers, hides*) *the tail* of animals. **recedentis,** gen. mas. s. pres. part. act. ag. w. tui und. after pedes; fr. rĕcēdo, -ĕre, -cessi, -cessum, 3rd intrans., (re, 659; cedo, 170) *to go back, give ground, retire, recede, withdraw.* Of places, *recede, stand back,* and of places seeming to recede from people going away from them. Of figures in a picture, *to stand back, be behind. To go away, depart from* a place=discedo. Of a thing, *to be separated from* that with which it was connected; fig., *to depart from, e.g.,* ab exemplo, e vitâ, etc. **trilingui,** abl. neut. s. ag. w. ore; fr. trĭlinguis, -e, adj.; (tres, 956; lingua, *a tongue*) *three-tongued;* post-class., *speaking three languages.* "Ore trilingui," *i.e.,* the tongue of each of his three mouths (W.).

1424. **Ore,** abl. (instrum.) s. fr. os (223). **pedes,** acc. plu. gov. by tetigit; fr. pes (135). **tetigit,** 3rd s. pf. ind. act. fr. tango (224). **crura,** acc. plu. jnd. by -que to pedes; fr. crus, crūris, 3rd neut., (ak. to curro, *that which goes*) *the leg.*

Carmen XX. Metre. *The Alcaic.* (Bk. I., Carmen ix.)

1425. **Non** (55). **usitata,** abl. fem. s. ag. w. pennâ; fr. ūsĭtātus, -a, -um, adj.; *usual, wonted, customary, common, ordinary, familiar.* Cic. has compar. and superl. regular. The verb usitor, *to use often,* is intensive of utor, *to use,* only found a few times in Gellius. **nec** (19). **tenui** (749), jnd. by nec to usitatâ. **ferar,** 1st s. fut. ind. pass. fr. fero (138).

1426. **Penna** (923), instrum. w. ferar. **biformis,** -e, adj.; nom. mas. s. ag. w. vates; (bis, *twice;* forma, 755) *double* or *two-formed, two-shaped;* here of a poet as a man and a swan. **per** (114), local. **liquidum,** acc. mas. s. ag. w. æthera; fr. liquidus (150). **æthera,** acc. s. gov. by per; fr. æther, æthĕris or -os (Gk.), 3rd mas., *the upper, pure air, clear air. Heaven. Air* generally [aĕr, *the lower atmosphere*].

1427. **Vates** (710), in app. to ego und. in ferar. **neque** (32). **terris,** gov. by in (78). **morabor,** 1st s. fut. ind. fr. moror (293).

1428 Longius invidiaque major
1429 Urbes relinquam. Non ego pauperum
1430 Sanguis parentum, non ego, quem vocas,
1431 Dilecte, Mæcenas, obibo,
1432 Nec Stygia cohibebor unda.
1433 Jam jam residunt cruribus asperæ
1434 Pelles et album mutor in alitem
1435 Superne, nascunturque leves

1428. **Longius,** adv. w. morabor; compar. of longe, (adv. of longus, 73) *in length. Far off, a long way off,* w. ab and abl., *at a distance from,* esp. "longe esse or abesse," *to be far off* or *away,* i.e., *to be of no aid, avail, assistance. To a distance far off, far away. From a distance off, from a long way.* Of time, *for a long time.* Of speeches, compositions, etc., *at length, long, copiously. Widely, greatly, much, by much, exceedingly.* **invidia,** abl. (of comparison) s. after major; fr. invĭdia, -æ, 1st fem., (invidus, 283) act., *envy, jealousy, grudge, ill-will* which one person has towards another. Pass., *ill-will, odium,* esp. public, in which a person or thing is held, w. object. gen. of that against whom or which it is felt; sts. *an object of hatred* or *ill-will,* or *a cause, source, origin* of public *hatred.* **-que,** adversative after a neg. clause; see 640, 1173. **major** (104), ag. w. ego und. in relinquam; invidiâ major, *above the range of envy* (W.).

1429. **Urbes,** acc. plu. gov. by relinquam; fr. urbs (40). **relinquam,** 1st s. fut. ind. act. fr. relinquo (270). **non** (55). **ego** (445), subj. of obibo. **pauperum** (141), ag. w. parentum.

1430. **Sanguis** (587), in app. to ego; here *scion, offspring.* **parentum** (59), after sanguis. **quem** (74), mas. s. ag. w. ego; acc. gov. by vocas. **vocas,** 2nd s. ind. pres. act. fr. voco (61).

1431. **Dilecte,** voc. s. mas. fr. dilectus (524). The voc. here is in the place of a dependent predicate or oblique complement; "*whom thou stylest Beloved.*" **Mæcenas** (1), others join "dilecte" w. Mæcenas, and then vocas, = "*invitest* to thy table." **obibo,** 1st s. fut. ind. fr. obeo (1323).

1432. **Nec** (19). **Stygia,** abl. fem. s. ag. w. undâ; fr. Stȳgĭus, -a, -um, adj.; see Styx (770). **cohibebor,** 1st s. fut. ind. pass. fr. cohibeo (1432). **unda** (1241), instrum. w. cohibebor.

1433. **Jam** (37). **residunt,** 3rd plu. pres. ind. act. fr. resīdo, -sīdĕre, -sēdi, no sup., 3rd trans., (re-, 659; sido, ak. to sedeo, *to sit*) *to sit down, settle* anywhere. Of feathers, *to settle, gather* on the body, etc. Of things, *to sink down, subside,* w. in and acc. (cf. consido, desido); fig., *settle down, abate, grow calm.* **cruribus,** dat. plu. after traject. residunt; fr. crus (1424). **asperæ,** nom. fem. plu. ag. w. pelles; fr. asper (154).

1434. **Pelles,** nom. plu. subj. of residunt; fr. pellis, -is, 3rd fem., (perh. akin to vello, *to pluck*) *the skin* or *hide* of animals stripped off the body, or of human beings and animals on the body, as that which may be pulled off. Of a *shoe, garment,* etc., made of skins. A soldier's *tent* covered w. skins, hence "sub pellibus, *in the camp.* **album,** acc. mas. s. ag. w. alitem; fr. albus (311). **mutor,** 1st s. pres. ind. pass. fr. muto (77). **alitem,** acc. s. gov. by in; fr. ales (78).

1435. **Sŭpernĕ,** adv.; (supernus, adj.) *from above, above, upward.* **nascuntur,** 3rd plu. pres. ind. fr. nascor (679). **leves** (74), ag. w. plumæ.

1436 Per digitos humerosque plumæ.
1437 Jam Dædaleo ocior Icaro
1438 Visam gementis litora Bospori
1439 Syrtesque Gætulas canorus
1440 Ales Hyperboreosque campos.
1441 Me Colchus et qui dissimulat metum
1442 Marsæ cohortis Dacus et ultimi
1443 Noscent Geloni, me peritus
1444 Discet Iber Rhodanique potor.

1436. **Per** (114). **digitos,** acc. plu. gov. by per; fr. digitus (256). **humeros** (67), jnd. by -que to digitos. **plumæ,** nom. plu. subj. of nascuntur; fr. plūma, -æ, 1st fem., *a small soft feather*, next the skin and under the larger feathers; plu., *down*, esp. for stuffing pillows, etc.; an emblem of lightness, frivolity, etc.

1437. **Jam** (37). **Dædaleo,** abl. mas. s. ag. w. Icaro; fr. Dædălēus, -a, -um, adj.; *of* or *belonging to Dædalus* (122), *i.e.*, who had Dædalus to make wings for him (W.): **ocior** (84), mas. ag. w. ego und. in visam. Some read "notior," *more known*. **Icaro,** abl. (of comparison) s. after ocior; fr. Icarus (see Icarius, 15).

1438. **Visam,** 1st s. fut. ind. act. fr. viso (44). **gementis,** gen. s. mas. pres. part. act. ag. w. Bospori; fr. gemo (370). **litora** (1373), gov. by visam. **Bospori,** gen. s. after litora; fr. Bosporus (1206).

1439. **Syrtes** (541), jnd. by -que to litora. **Gætulas,** acc. fem. plu. ag. w. Syrtes; fr. Gætulus (570). **canorus** (295), nom. mas. s. ag. w. ales.

1440. **Ales** (78), in app. to ego und. in visam; here "*a swan*." **Hyperboreos,** acc. mas. plu. ag. w. campos; fr. Hўpérbŏreus, -a, -um, adj.; *Northern*; the Hyperboreans being a fictitious people at the extreme north. **campos** (998), jnd. by -que to Syrtes.

1441. **Me** (29), gov. by noscent. **Colchus** (1200), nom. mas. sing. as subst. one member in composite subj. of noscent. **qui** (19), mas. s. ag. w. Dacus; nom. subj. to dissimulat. **dissimulat,** 3rd s. pres. ind. act. fr. dissĭmŭlo, -are, -avi, -atum, 1st trans., (dis, 870; simulo, *to pretend*) *to represent* a thing *unlike* or *different from* itself, *to feign* that a thing *is not* that which it is, *dissemble, disguise, hide, conceal, keep secret*. **metum,** acc. s. gov. by dissimulat; fr. metus (564). "Qui dissimulat metum," *i.e.*, fears, though he tries to hide his fear.

1442. **Marsæ,** gen. s. fem. ag. w. cohortis; fr. Marsus (28). **cohortis,** gen. (objective) s. after metum; fr. cohors (119). **Dacus** (785), jnd. by et (1441) to Colchus. **ultimi,** nom. mas. plu. ag. w. Geloni; fr. ultimus (280).

1443. **Noscent,** 3rd plu. fut. ind. act. fr. nosco (411). **Geloni** (1115), nom. jnd. by et to Dacus as composite subj. of noscent. **me** (29), gov. by discet. **peritus,** -a, -um, adj.; nom. mas. s. ag. w. Iber; (perior, whence periculum and experior) *experienced, practised, practically acquainted*, w. gen. or abl. of thing and inf. (poet.); here proleptically used, *i.e.*, it is not so much an epith. of Iber as it expresses the effect of the verb discet.

1444. **Discet,** 3rd s. fut. ind. act. fr. disco (1395). **Iber,** nom. subj. of discet; genly. plu. Ibēres (Gk.) = *Spaniards*; here sing. used collectively.

1445 Absint inani funere·neniæ
1446 Luctusque turpes et querimoniæ;
1447 Compesce clamorem ac sepulcri
1449 Mitte supervacuos honores.

Rhodani, gen. s. after potor; fr. Rhŏdănus, -i, 2nd mas., *the Rhone,* a river in Gaul. **pōtor,** -ōris, 3rd mas.; nom. s. jnd. by -que to Iber; (poto, 509) *a hard drinker, drunkard, sot;* here, *a drinker, dweller by.*

1445. **Absint,** 3rd plu. pres. conj. (optative); fr. absum (796). **inani,** abl. s. neut. ag. w. funere; fr. ĭnānis, -e, adj.; physically, *empty, void, without contents,* opp. to plenus (463). *Poor, without money;* subst. inane, -is, 3rd neut., *an empty space, void;* meton., *poor, worthless. Void of meaning* or *value, frivolous, e.g.,* vox, verba. *Vain, useless, unprofitable* of hopes, threats, etc. Of time, *unoccupied, at leisure.* Of men, *vain, arrogant, haughty, boastful;* inane, -is, 3rd neut., *what is empty* or *vain* (Hor.). **funere,** abl. (of separation) s. after absint; fr. funus (231). **neniæ,** nom. plu. subj. of absint; fr. nenia (914).

1446. **Luctus,** nom. plu. jnd. by -que to neniæ; fr. luctus, -us, 4th mas., (lugeo, *to mourn*) *sorrow, bewailing, lamentation,* esp. for the dead, also of external signs of mourning for the dead, exiled or accused. *Mourning apparel, weeds;* rarely *a source of grief.* **turpes,** nom. mas. plu. ag. w. luctus; fr. turpis (727). **querimoniæ,** nom. plu. jnd. by et to luctus; fr. querimonia (363).

1447. **Compesce** (442). **clamorem** (631), gov. by compesce. **sepulcri** (1370), gen. (objective) after honores.

1448. **Mitte** (871). **supervacuos,** acc. plu. mas. ag. w. honores; fr. supervăcuus, -a, -um, adj.; (super, 237; vacuus, 122) *exceedingly empty;* hence *useless, needless, unmeaning, unnecessary, superfluous, redundant* (not ante-Aug.); [supervăcāneus is classical]; here not general in meaning, but ref. only to Horace. **honores** (304), gov. by mitte.

Note.—W. or Wick., in the above notes refers to Wickham's Horace; **M.** to Marshall's.

THE

ODES OF HORACE.

BOOK FIRST.

ODE I. To Mæcenas.

Mæcenas, descended from regal ancestors, O both my protection and fond pride; there are *some* whom it delights to collect the Olympic dust in the chariot-course, and *whom* the pillar cleared by the glowing wheels and the ennobling palm exalt to the gods, lords of the earth. This *man it delights* if a crowd of fickle Romans strives to extol *him* with triple honours; that *man*, if he has hoarded in his own barn whatever is swept from Lybian threshing-floors. *The man* who delights to cleave with a hoe his paternal fields, you can never induce, *even* for terms such-as-Attalus-could-propose, to cut, as a timid sailor, the Myrtoan sea in a Cyprian bark. The trader, dreading a South-wester struggling with the Icarian billows, eulogizes repose and the rural-scenes of his native town; soon, he repairs his shattered ships, untaught to endure poverty. There is *many a one* who refuses neither cups of old Massic-wine, nor to take away a portion from the substantial day, at one time with his limbs stretched under the green arbute, at another time by the smooth source of *some* hallowed stream. The camp and the sound of the trumpet confused with *that of* the clarion, and wars, execrated by mothers, delight many. The huntsman, thoughtless of his tender wife, abides under the cold sky, if either a hind has been seen by his faithful hounds or if a Marsian boar has burst *his* well-wrought nets. Me do ivy-chaplets, the rewards of learned brows associate with the gods above; me do the cool grove and the lively bands of Nymphs with Satyrs separate from the populace, if (*i.e.*, as long as) neither Euterpe withholds her pipes nor Polyhymnia refuses to stretch her lyre. But if thou wilt rank me with lyric bards, I shall strike (*i.e.*, reach to) the stars with my towering head.

ODE II. To Augustus Cæsar.

Already has the Sire sent on the world enough of snow and dismal hail, and having struck the sacred summits, with *his* red right-hand he alarmed the city, he alarmed the nations, lest the terrible age of Pyrrha, complaining of strange prodigies, should return, when Proteus drove all *his* flock to visit high mountains, and the fishy race stuck on the top of the elm, which had been a well-known roost for pigeons, and the timid deer swam in the overwhelming flood. We have seen the yellow-sanded Tibur, *his* waves being forced back from the Tuscan shore, go to throw down the memorials of the King, and Vesta's temple; while to Ilia excessively complaining, he exhibits himself as an avenger, and the wife-doting river-god, deviating-from-his-course, overflows on the left bank, Jupiter not approving. *Our* youth, thinned by the crime of their forefathers, will hear that citizens have whetted the sword by which the formidable Persians would have better perished, it will hear of battles. Whom of the gods shall the people invoke *in behalf of* the concerns of a tottering empire? With what prayer shall the sacred virgins importune Vesta *now* less attentive to their hymns? To whom shall Jupiter assign the duty of atoning for our guilt? At length come, we beseech *thee*, prophetic Apollo, having thy glistening shoulders enveloped in a cloud; or, if thou preferrest, smiling goddess-of-Eryx, around whom hover Mirth and Love, or if thou, O its founder, regardest thy abandoned race and descendants, glutted with thy sport, alas, too long *continued*, whom the war-shout and polished helmets delight, and the fierce look of the Moorish foot-soldier *gazing* on his blood-weltering foe; or if, thy form being changed, *thou* winged son of bounteous Maia, assumest-the-form-of a youth, deigning to be called Cæsar's avenger; late mayest thou return to heaven, and long mayest thou graciously be among the people of Quirinus, nor may an untimely blast carry thee away displeased with our vices. Here, rather, mayest thou love mighty triumphs, here to be styled Father and Prince, nor suffer, O Cæsar, whilst thou art our leader, the Medes to ride-up-and-down unpunished.

ODE III.

To the Ship on which Vergil Sailed to Athens.

So may the goddess who rules over Cyprus direct thee; so may the brilliant constellations, brothers of Helen, and the fathers of the winds, all others being confined except

Iapyx *direct thee,* O ship, which owest Vergil entrusted to thy care, that thou mayest deliver him safe on the Athenian shores, I pray, and preserve the half of my soul. He had (*lit.* there was to him) oak and triple brass around his breast who first committed a frail bark to the cruel deep, nor dreaded the swooping South-wester battling with the North-eastern blasts, nor the gloomy Hyades, nor the fury of the south wind, than whom there is not a more powerful master of the Adriatic, whether he wishes to excite or to calm its friths. What approach of death did he fear who with tearless eyes gazed on floating monsters, who *gazed on* the swelling sea and on Acroceraunia, ill-famed rocks? In vain did a foreseeing Deity sever lands by the intercourse-barring ocean, if notwithstanding, god-defying ships bound over waters that ought not to be touched. The human race, daring to endure all things, hurries through forbidden wickedness. The daring offspring of Japetus, with mischievous deceit, introduced fire among the nations. After fire had been stolen from *its* ethereal abode consumption and an unusual throng of fevers brooded over the earth, and the formerly slow doom of distant death accelerated *its* pace. Dædalus essayed the impalpable air on wings not given to man. Hercules' energy burst through Acheron. There is nothing *too* difficult for man. Heaven itself do we seek in our folly, nor by reason of our wickedness suffer we Jupiter to lay aside his wrathful thunderbolts.

ODE IV. To L. Sestius.

Sharp winter is relaxing beneath the pleasing change of spring and the western-breeze, and engines are launching the dry vessels, and neither now do the cattle like *their* shelters nor the ploughman his fire-side; nor are the meadows white with hoar frost. Now Venus, goddess of Cythera, leads *her* choirs beneath the overhanging moon, and the comely Graces, joined with the Nymphs, shake the earth with alternate foot, whilst glowing Vulcan is heating the laborious forges of the Cyclops. Now is it befitting to wreath the glossy head either with the green myrtle or with the flower which the unfettered lands produce. Now is it befitting also to offer-sacrifice to Faunus in shady groves whether he requires *us to do so* with a lamb or prefers *it* with a kid. Pale Death beats with impartial foot at the cottages of the poor and the castles of princes. O blest Sestius, the short span of life forbids us to broach lengthened hope. Soon shall night and folklore Ghosts and Pluto's shadowy abode overpower thee, whither as soon as thou shalt arrive, thou wilt neither obtain by lot the sovereignty of wine, nor wilt admire youthful Lycidas, by whom all the youth are now fired, and *of whom* maidens will soon be enamoured.

ODE V. To Pyrrha.

What slender youth *crowned* with many a rose *and* bedewed with liquid perfumes courts thee, Pyrrha, in the pleasant grotto? For whom dost thou bind back thy auburn hair, plain in thy neat-habiliments? Alas! how often will he lament thy perfidy (*lit.* altered faith) and the gods, *appealed to by thee,* changed *towards him,* and, unaccustomed *to such usage,* will be amazed at the waters roughened by the blackening winds, who now confidingly enjoys thee, *as though* all-perfect (*lit.* golden); who, ignorant of *thy* deceitful fickleness, hopes *to find thee* always disengaged, always charming. Wretched *are they* for whom thou, untried, exhibitest thy beauty. The sacred wall *of a temple* with a votive tablet makes-known that I have hung up my wet garments *as offerings to* the God, the monarch of the sea.

ODE VI. To Agrippa.

Thou shalt be described as brave and conqueror of *thy* foes by Varius, a bird of Mæonian verse, for whatever exploit the brave soldier shall have performed, either in naval or cavalry-engagements, under thy leadership. We, Agrippa, attempt neither to sing of these things nor the destructive wrath of Peleus' son, incapable of yielding, nor the voyages of wily Ulysses, nor the murderous house of Pelops, of humble ability *as we are to sing of such* lofty *themes,* whilst modesty and *my* muse, having power *only* over the unwarlike lyre, forbid *me* to diminish by lack of genius, the praises of illustrious Cæsar and thine own. Who can adequately describe Mars clad in a coat of adamant? Or Meriones begrimed with Trojan dust? Or Tydeus' son, *who was,* by the aid of Pallas, a match for the gods? We, *whether we be* free-from-love or are somewhat inflamed, with our usual frivolity (*lit.* light not beyond usual) sing of banquets. We *sing of* the fights of maidens with *their* cut nails sharp towards (*i.e.,* sharply attacking) youths.

ODE VII. To L. Munatius Plancus.

Some will praise bright Rhodes or Mytilene or Ephesus or the walls of Corinth, situated-between-two-seas, or Thebes rendered-illustrious, from Bacchus or Delphi from Apollo or Thessalian Tempe. There are *some* whose sole employment is to celebrate in *an* unbroken song the city of the chaste Minerva, to place on *their* brow an olive plucked from every quarter. Many a one, in honour of Juno, will sing of Argos, adapted *for rearing* horses and of opulent Mycænæ. Neither has hardy Lacedæmon smitten me, nor the plain of rich Larissa, so much as the home of resounding Albunea, and headlong Anio and the grove of Tiburnus, and orchards watered by running rills. As the clearing South-wind often sweeps the clouds from the dark sky, nor produces incessant showers, so do thou wisely remember to put an end to melancholy and toils of life with mellow wine, O Plancus, whether the camp glittering with banners *now* detain thee, or the thick shade of thy Tibur shall *hereafter* detain thee. When Teucer was going an exile from Salamis and his father, yet he is reported to have wreathed with a chaplet of poplar his temples drenched with wine, thus addressing his sorrowful friends: "Whithersoever fortune, kinder than *my* sire, shall lead us, we will go, O associates and comrades! Nothing is to be despaired of under the guidance and auspices of Teucer, for unerring Apollo has promised that there shall be a second (*lit.* causing doubt) Salamis in a foreign land. O brave men and who have often with me suffered greater *hardships*, banish now cares with wine: to-morrow we will traverse-again the mighty deep."

ODE VIII. To Lydia.

Lydia, tell me, I pray thee by all the gods, why by thy love dost thou hasten to ruin Sybaris; why does he hate the sunny plain, *once* able-to-endure the dust and the sun's heat? Why, neither like-a-soldier does he ride among his compeers, nor with jagged bits does he curb the mouths *of* Gallic *steeds*? Why does he dread to touch the yellow-sanded Tiber? Why does he shun the *wrestler's* oil more cautiously than a viper's blood, nor now carries his arms discoloured by military weapons, *formerly* distinguished often by flinging *his* quoit, often *his* javelin, beyond the mark? Why does he hide himself, as they say that the son of the sea-goddess Thetis *did* on the eve of the mournful slaughter of Troy, lest *his* man's attire should hurry him to carnage and *against* the Lycian troops?

ODE IX. To Thaliarchus.

Thou seest how Soracte stands white with deep snow, nor now can the overburdened woods sustain the weight *of snow,* and the rivers stand-still by *reason of* the keen frost. Dispel the cold, by piling logs abundantly on the hearth, and more plentifully bring forth four-year-old wine from the Sabine jar, O Thaliarchus. Leave the rest to the gods, for as soon as they have calmed the winds battling with the boiling sea, neither the cypresses nor the old ash trees are shaken. Avoid inquiring what will be the morrow, and whatever day fate should give thee, set down as gain, nor while *still* young, disdain either sweet love or the dance, so long as peevish old age is absent from thee *still* blooming. Now let both the plain and the promenades and soft whispers at the approach of night be repeated at the appointed hour, now also let the pleasing laughter, betrayer of the lurking maid, *be repeated* from the inner-nook, and the forfeit snatched from her arms or her faintly resisting finger.

ODE X. To Mæcenas.

Mercury, eloquent grandson of Atlas, who didst wisely fashion the savage manners of the early race of men by *the-gift-of* language and by the institution of the graceful palæstra, thee will I sing, the messenger of mighty Jove and of the gods, and the parent of the curved lyre, cunning in concealing whatever it hath pleased thee by a sportive theft. While Apollo was formerly frightening thee when a child in threatening language unless thou didst restore *his* oxen, by craft removed, he smiled *at being also* bereft of his quiver. Nay more, under thy guidance, Priam, laden with gold, having left Ilium, eluded the haughty sons of Atreus, and the Thessalian watch-fires, and the camp hostile to Troy. Thou replacest sainted souls in blissful abodes, and with thy golden wand restrainest the disembodied throng, a favourite with the upper and the nether gods.

ODE XI. To Leuconoe.

Do not thou inquire, it is an impiety *to try* to know, what term-of-existence the gods may have assigned to me, what to thee, Leuconoe, nor try Babylonian calculations. How much better to submit to whatever it be! whether Jupiter gives more winters, or *this as* the last, which now is breaking-the-force-of the Tuscan sea against the pumiceous-rocks opposing *it*. Be wise, filter thy wines, and because of the brief span *of life*, curtail lengthened hope While we are speaking, jealous time has sped away. Enjoy the *present* day, trusting as little as possible to the morrow.

ODE XII. To Augustus.

What living or departed hero dost thou, Clio, take to celebrate on the lyre or shrill pipe? What god? Whose name shall sportive echo resound either amid the shady borders of Helicon, or on Pindus, or on cool Hæmus, whence the woods followed the tuneful Orpheus in-wild-confusion, who-checked the rapid currents of rivers by his maternal art, and the swift winds, *so* enchanting *as* even to lead the listening oaks by his melodious lays? What shall I sing before the usual praises of the Sire, who rules the affairs of men and of the gods, who *regulates* the sea and the land and the universe with *its* changing seasons? from whom nothing is produced greater than himself, nor springs there anything like him or second-in-degree; Pallas however has received honours next to him. Nor will I pass in silence thee, O Bacchus, brave in fights, and thee, O virgin, deadly to savage beasts, nor thee, Phœbus, to be dreaded for thine unerring arrow. I will sing also of Hercules and the sons of Leda, one celebrated for equestrian-feats, the other for pugilistic-encounters, whose *sky*-clearing constellation no sooner reappears to the mariners than the troubled water flows down from the rocks, the winds are lulled, and the clouds disappear, and the threatening flood, for they so will it, subsides again on the sea. I am in doubt whether after these I shall first commemorate Romulus, or the peaceful reign of Pompilius, or the splendid monarchy of Tarquin, or Cato's noble death. Regulus and the Scauri and Paullus, lavish of his mighty soul, when the Carthaginian (*i.e.*, Hannibal) was-conquering, and Fabricius will I eulogize in fame-conferring verse. Him and Curius with untrimmed locks, and Camillus did stern poverty, and an hereditary estate with a suitable dwelling, rear up serviceable for war. The fame of Marcellus grows, like a tree, the time of *its actual growth* being concealed, the Julian constellation sparkles among all *others*, just as the moon among the smaller fires. O son of Saturn, father and guardian of the human race, to thee the charge of mighty Cæsar has been by the fates assigned; do thou reign, Cæsar being next *to thee*. He, whether he has led along and subdued in a just triumph the Parthians, hovering over Latium, or the Chinese and Indians, lying along the margin of the East, inferior to thee *alone*, will impartially rule the wide world; thou wilt, in thy ponderous chariot, shake Olympus; thou wilt discharge the hostile thunderbolts upon *our* polluted groves.

ODE XIII. To Lydia.

When thou, Lydia, praisest the rosy neck of Telephus, the waxen (*i.e.*, smooth and glossy) arms of Telephus, alas! my burning heart swells with irrepressible jealousy. Then, neither my mind nor colour remains in an unaltered state, the tear also stealthily glides on my cheek, proving how thoroughly I am wasted by slow-consuming fires. I burn-with-rage, if ever brawls made-immoderate by wine, have soiled thy fair shoulders, or if ever the raving youth hath with *his* tooth imprinted a lasting mark on thy lips. Thou must not expect, if thou fully listenest to me, that he will be constant *in his attachment*, who barbarously wounds those sweet lips, which Venus has imbued with the fifth part of *all* her nectar. Thrice happy, and more than that, *are they* whom an indissoluble union holds, and whom love unsevered by provoking complaints, will not untie sooner than the last day *of their existence.*

ODE XIV. To the Republic.

O ship! new billows will bear thee back to the deep! O what art thou doing? Courageously occupy the harbour. Dost thou not see how bare thy side is of oars and thy mast is shattered by the rapid South-wester, and thy sail-yards groan, and thy hull without cables [to undergird it] scarcely can hold out against the unusually-boisterous ocean? Thy sails are not whole, nor *hast thou* gods, whom thou mayest again invoke *when* overpowered by ill. Though *made of* Pontic pine, the daughter of a famous forest, thou boastest both of *thy* lineage and unavailing fame; the timid mariner trusts not-at-all to pictured ships. Unless thou art doomed to be the sport of the winds, beware. Thou who *wert* lately a source of wearying disquietude to me, and now *art* an object of fond-desire and strong apprehension, avoid the waters spread between the glittering Cyclades.

ODE XV.

Nereus' Prediction of the Fall of Troy.

When the treacherous shepherd was forcibly bearing away over the seas his hostess, Helen, in ships made of Ida's timber, Nereus, that he might foretell their cruel destinies, hushed the swift winds in an unwelcome calm. Under an evil omen thou takest home *her*, whom Greece will re-demand, with a numerous army, bound-by-a-common-oath to sever thy nuptials, and *to destroy* the ancient kingdom of Priam. Alas! Alas! What sweat is at hand for steeds, what for men! What carnage art thou originating for the Dardan race! Already Pallas is preparing *her* helmet and *her* shield and *her* chariot, and *is kindling her* martial fury. In vain, exulting in the protection of Venus, wilt thou dress thy hair, and sing-and-play (*lit.* divide) on the peaceful lyre songs pleasing to women; in vain in thy bedchamber wilt thou avoid the ponderous spears, and the points of the Cretan arrow, and the din-of-war, and Ajax swift to follow; *though* late *in the conflict,* still thou, alas! wilt begrime an adulterer's hair in the dust. Dost thou not consider (*or,* see behind thee) Laertes' son, the ruin of thy race, no, nor Nestor of Pylos? Teucer of Salamis and Stheneleus, skilled in battle, or if there be need to control steeds, no inactive charioteer, are undauntedly closing on thee. Meriones too shalt thou know. Lo! Tydeus' fierce son, braver than his sire, is-mad to catch thee; whom, as a stag, regardless of his pasture, *flees from* a wolf seen *by it* on the opposite side of a valley, thou, as a coward, shalt flee from, with deep pantings, not having promised this to thy *mistress.* The angry fleet of Achilles shall protract the day of destruction for Ilium and the Phrygian matrons; after a destined number of years (*lit.* winters) Grecian fire shall burn Ilian houses.

ODE XVI. To a Mistress.

O daughter, fairer than *thy* fair mother, put whatever end thou pleasest to my defamatory iambics, whether *thou* choosest by the fire or in the Hadriatic sea. Neither Dindymene, nor the dweller of the Pythian temple agitates the soul of *his* priests in *his* inmost shrines, not

Bacchus, nor do the Corybantes tinkle their shrill sounding cymbals, so much as gloomy anger *rages* which neither the Noric sword checks, nor the ship-wrecking sea, nor the cruel lightning, nor Jupiter himself, rushing *down* in dreadful commotion. Prometheus is said to have been compelled to add to the original clay a part taken from every-quarter (*i.e.*, every animal) and to have superadded to our breast the violence of a raving lion. Angry-contentions overthrew Thyestes in a terrible ruin, and have proved the primary (*lit.* final or chief) cause to lofty cities *as the reason* why they were utterly razed, and the haughty army drove the hostile plough across *their* walls. Restrain thy passion; the boiling-rage of *my* bosom tempted me also in sweet youth, and sent *me* madlike to *resort to* rapid iambics. Now I am seeking to exchange bitter for soothing *strains*, provided that, if I recant my defamatory-expressions, thou wilt become friendly to me and restore *my* peace-of-mind (*or thy* affection).

ODE XVII. To Tyndaris.

Swift Faunus often exchanges Lycæus for pleasant Lucretilis and ever wards off the fiery heat and the rainy winds from my pet-goats. With security through the protected grove do the wives of the fetid sire, as they wander, seek for arbutes lying-hid, and thyme, nor do they fear green-coloured lizards. Nor do they fear savage wolves of Hædilia, whenever, Tyndaris, the valleys and smooth rocks of sloping Ustica have echoed with *thy* melodious lute. The gods protect me; my devotion and my muse are agreeable to the gods. Here rich store of rural honours shall flow abundantly for thee from the bounteous horn *of fortune*. Here, in a secluded valley, thou shalt escape the heat of the Dog-days, and on the Teian lyre wilt sing of Penelope and the glassy Circe, striving for one and the same hero. Here thou shalt quaff goblets of unintoxicating Lesbian wine beneath the shade, nor will Bacchus, offspring of Semele, mingle his brawls with *those* of Mars, nor shalt thou, though an object-of-jealous-suspicion, fear the rude Cyrus lest he should lay rash hands *on thee*, ill-fitted-to-contend-with *him*, and tear the chaplet clinging to *thy* tresses and thy innocent dress.

ODE XVIII. To Quintilius Varus.

O Varus, plant no tree in preference to the sacred vine about the genial soil of Tivoli and the walls of Catilius, for to total-abstainers, the god *of wine* has ordained all hardships, nor do gnawing cares by any other means disperse. Who, after wine-drinking, complains of severe military-service or of poverty? Who does not rather talk of thee, father Bacchus, and of thee, graceful Venus? But that no one should exceed the gifts of moderate Bacchus, the Centaurs' quarrel with the Lapithæ, fought over their wine, warns us; *so* does Evius warn *us*, unpropitious to the Sithonians, when, eager-for-the-gratification-of-their-passion, they distinguish right and wrong *only* by a narrow boundary. I will not disturb thee against thy will, O Bacchus ever blooming, nor will I hurry into open day the *things* concealed under various leaves. Cease the shrill-sounding cymbals, with the Berecynthian horn, whom closely follow blind self-love and vain-glory, lifting up its empty head far too high (*lit.* more than very much), and faith that is lavish of a secret and more transparent than glass.

ODE XIX. To Glycera.

The cruel mother of the Loves, and the son of Theban Semele, and sportive wantonness, prompt me to restore *my* affection to *once* abandoned amours. The brilliant beauty of Glycera, dazzling more brightly than Parian marble, burns me; *her* pleasant coquetry burns *me*, and *her* countenance, too bewitching (*lit.* slippery) to be gazed upon *with safety*. Venus, rushing on me with-all-her-strength, has forsaken Cyprus, nor suffers *me* to sing of the Scythian, nor the Parthian, courageous on *his* retreating steeds, nor *of things* that in no wise concern *her*. Here put the verdant turf for me, O boys, here vervains and incense with a goblet of two-year-old wine. More gently will she come, after a sacrifice has been offered.

ODE XX. To Mæcenas.

Thou shalt drink in small goblets common (*or,* cheap) Sabine wine which I myself stored and sealed in a Grecian jar, when applause was given to thee in the theatre, beloved knight Mæcenas, so that the banks of thy paternal river, and likewise the sportive echo of the Vatican mount reverberated thy praises. Thou wilt drink [at home] Cæcuban wine and the juice-of-the-grape crushed in the press of Cales. Neither Falernian grapes nor *those* of the Formian hills season my cups.

ODE XXI. To Diana and Apollo.

Sing Diana, youthful virgins; sing, ye boys, Apollo ever-young, and Latona deeply beloved by supreme Jupiter. Do ye *maidens sing her* who-takes-delight in rivers and the foliage of groves such-as-that-which overhangs either cold Algidus, or the dark woods of Erymanthus, or of green Cragus. Exalt ye Tempe with equal praise, O boys, and Delos the native *isle* of Apollo, and the shoulder graced both by a quiver and *his* brother's lyre. He, moved by your prayer, will drive away tear-fraught war, he *will drive away* wretched famine and pestilence from the people and the Prince Cæsar to the Persians and the Britons.

ODE XXII. To Aristius Fuscus.

The man of upright life and free from crime needs not Moorish javelins, nor a bow, nor a quiver loaded with poisoned arrows, O Fuscus, whether he is about to take a journey through the burning sands of Africa, or through the inhospitable Caucasus, or the places which the storied Hydaspes laves. For me did a wolf in the Sabine wood flee from, though *I was* unarmed, while I was singing my Lalage and was roving, with *all* my cares dispelled, beyond the boundary; such a monster as neither the soldier-furnishing Daunia rears in its spacious mast-oak-thickets, nor Juba's land, the parched nurse of lions, produces. Put me in those barren plains where no tree is invigorated by the summer breeze, a quarter of the world which clouds and an inclement sky beset: put me under the chariot of the too neighbouring Sun in a land bereft of houses, I will *still* love *my* sweetly smiling, sweetly prattling Lalage.

ODE XXIII. To Chloe.

You shun me, Chloe, like a pet-fawn seeking its timid dam on the lonely mountains, not without a vague dread of the breezes and of the wood, for if either the arrival of the spring has rustled in the fluttering leaves, or if the green lizards have stirred (*lit.* have moved aside) the bramble-bush, she trembles both in heart and knees. I am not, however, hunting *you* to tear *you* in-pieces, as a rough tiger or Gætulian lion. Cease at length to *follow your* mother *being* of-seasonable-age for a husband.

ODE XXIV. To Vergil.

What shame can *be attached,* or *what* limit put, to *our* regret-for-the-loss of so dear a one? Teach me mournful strains, Melpomene, to whom *thy* father hath given a clear voice with the lyre. So then eternal sleep overwhelms Quintilius, to whom when will Modesty and unsullied Honour, the sister of Justice, and undisguised Truth find any one a match? He died, wept by many men-of-worth, by none more wept than by thee, Vergil. Thou, alas! devotional in vain, demandest Quintilius of the gods not thus consigned *to their protection.* Nay, though thou shouldest tune thy harp, listened to by trees, more winningly than the Thracian Orpheus, the blood would not return to the unsubstantial shade, which once, with *his* dread-inspiring wand, Mercury, not gentle *enough* to change the-order-of the Fates at thy entreaties, has driven among the sable flock. 'Tis hard : but whatever it is contrary-to-heaven's-decree to amend becomes lighter by patience (*or* submission).

ODE XXV. To Lydia.

Wanton youths do *now* more sparingly beat at *thy* fastened windows with frequent taps, nor do they take away thy slumbers, and *thy* door clings to *its* threshhold, which formerly most easily moved its hinges. Thou hearest less and less now *the serenade,* "While I thy lover am pining through the long nights, sleepest thou, O Lydia?" *Now* a hag, in poverty, thou wilt by-way-of-retribution bewail haughty suitors in some lonely alley, while the Thracian wind is raving more-and-more during the moon's absence, when burning love and passion, which is wont to infuriate brood-mares, will rankle around thy gangrened liver, not without complaining because joyous youth is more pleased with verdant ivy and the dark myrtle, and consigns withered leaves *like thee* to Hebrus, winter's companion.

ODE XXVI. To the Muse on Ælius Lama.

A friend to the Muses, I will consign melancholy and fears to the blustering winds, to waft to the Cretan sea, singularly careless *of such matters as,* by whom the king, of a cold region under the North is feared, *or* what frightens Tiridates. O thou which delightest in pure fountains, entwine the sunny flowers, entwine a chaplet for my Lamia; O sweet Muse of Pimplea, my honours profit *me* nothing without thee; him it is befitting for thee and thy sisters to immortalize in new strains, him, *I say*, on the Lesbian lyre.

ODE XXVII. To my Comrades.

To fight over cups made for joyous purposes is *characteristic* of Thracians; away with a barbarous custom and shield moderately-inclined Bacchus from bloody brawls. It is amazing how much the dagger *of* the Parthian is at variance with nocturnal banquets; hush the unhallowed noise, and remain with the elbow pressing *on the couch*, my comrades. Would you have me also to take a share of strong Falernian-wine? Let the brother of Megilla of Opus tell us by what wound he *is* blessed, by what arrow he is dying. Dost thou refuse (*lit.* does thy inclination hesitate)? On no other condition will I drink. Whoever the fair-one *is that* sways thee, she inflames thee with fires that-need-not-cause-a-blush, for thou always indulgest (*lit.* sinnest) in honourable love. Whatever thou hast, come, entrust to safe ears. Ah wretch, in what a whirlpool didst thou flounder, O boy, worthy of a better flame! What witch, what magician, by Thessalian drugs, what god will be able to disenchant thee? Scarce will Pegasus extricate thee, entangled *as thou art*, from *this* three shaped Chimæra.

ODE XXVIII. The Mariner and Archytas.

M.—Thee, O Archytas, the measurer of the sea and land and of the sand which is without number, does the scanty present of a little dust, *denied to thy remains*, confine near the shore of Matinum, nor does it profit thee at all to have essayed the ethereal abodes, and to have traversed in thought the round world, since thou wert doomed to die. *A.*—Pelops' sire died also *though he had been* a guest of the gods, and Tithonus removed to the sky, and Minos, admitted to the secrets of Jove; and Tartarus contains Panthus' son, sent a second time to Orcus, although he, in thy judgment no mean authority on physical and moral truth, had given up to gloomy death,—as he called the Trojan times to witness by taking down the shield,—nothing but sinews and skin. But the same night awaits all, and the path of death must once be trod *by all.* Some the Furies give as spectacles to grim-visaged War; the greedy ocean is the destruction of mariners; the intermingled funerals of old and young are crowded together; stern Proserpine passes off from no soul. Me too did the South Wind, rapid companion of setting Orion, overwhelm in Illyrian waters. But do not thou, sailor, unkindly refuse to bestow a small-portion of shifting sand on my bones and unburied head. So, whatever the South-East-Wind may threaten to the western waves, may the Venusian woods be lashed *by it,* thou being safe, and may abundant gain flow to thee, from whom it can come, *even* from just Jove and Neptune, tutelary-guardian of sacred Tarentum. Dost thou make light of committing a crime which will prove injurious to thy unoffending posterity? Perhaps both a well-merited punishment and a haughty retribution may be awaiting thee thyself. I shall not be left with my prayers unavenged, and thee shall no expiations absolve. Though thou hastenest, there is no long delay: thou mayest run on, after having thrice cast dust *on my remains.*

ODE XXIX. To Iccius.

Iccius, now dost thou envy the blessed (*ironically*) riches of the Arabians, and dost thou prepare an energetic campaign against the kings of Sabæa never conquered before, and dost thou forge chains for the formidable Parthian? What barbarian virgin, *her* betrothed slain, shall serve thee? What royal page shall stand (*lit.* be stationed) as thy cup-bearer with anointed locks, skilled in aiming Eastern arrows with his paternal bow? Who will deny that the downward rivers can glide back to the lofty mountains, and that the Tiber can return *in his course*, when thou intendest to exchange for Spanish corselets books of celebrated Panætius, bought from every *quarter*, and *the writings of* the Socratic school, though thou hadst avowed better things.

ODE XXX. To Venus.

O Venus, queen of Cnidos and of Paphos, disregard thy loved Cyprus and betake thyself to the graceful shrine of Glycera, *now* invoking *thee* with abundant frankincense. With thee let *thy* glowing child *Cupid*, and the Graces with *their* girdles loose, and the Nymphs, hasten, and the Goddess-of-youth, little able to please without thee, and Mercury.

ODE XXXI. To Apollo.

What does the bard ask of Apollo on-the-dedication-of-his-temple? What does he pray for when pouring new wine from the goblet? Not for the fruitful corn-fields of rich Sardinia, not for the pleasing herds of sunny Calabria, not for gold nor Indian ivory, not for the rural-lands, which Liris, a noiseless river, is eating-away with its still stream. Let those to whom Fortune has given the vine of Cales prune *it* with the hook; and let the wealthy merchant drain from golden cups wine bartered for Syrian wares, dear to the very gods, inasmuch as he revisits the Atlantic Ocean without harm three or four times in the year. Olives, endives and light mallows feed me. I pray that thou, son of Latona, wouldst enable me both in health and with unimpaired mind to enjoy what-I-have, and not to spend an old age gloomy and without the harp.

ODE XXXII. To his Lyre.

We are called upon *for an ode.* If, when at leisure under the shade, we have ever composed anything playfully with thee, which may last both for this year and more, come dictate a Latin ode, my Lyre, formerly attuned by a Lesbian citizen, who, though bold in war, still amidst arms, or if he had moored his tempest-tossed ship on the sea-beaten shore, used to sing of Bacchus, and the Muses, and Venus, and the boy that ever cleaves to her, and Lycus graced with dark eyes and dark hair. O pride of Phœbus, harp welcomed even at the banquets of supreme Jove, O sweet sedative of toil, be propitious to me whenever I duly invoke thee.

ODE XXXIII. To Albius Tibullus.

Albius, do not grieve overmuch, thinking of the cruel Glycera, nor be always singing doleful elegies, because, in violation of her-plighted-fidelity, a younger man outshines thee *in her favour.* The love of Cyrus inflames

Lycoris remarkable for her low forehead; Cyrus inclines from *her* to rough Pholoe; but sooner will goats be united to Apulian wolves than Pholoe sin with *such a* disgraceful libertine. So it seemed good to Venus, whose pleasure it is to send unequal forms and minds under *her* iron yoke with a cruel joke. Myself, when a better love assailed me, Myrtale, the slave-born, more impetuous than the waves of the Hadriatic, indenting-with-bays the coast of Calabria, held in the pleasing chain *of love.*

ODE XXXIV. To Himself.

Once a niggardly and unfrequent worshipper of the gods, whilst I was going-astray, skilled in an unwise system of philosophy, now I am compelled to turn my sails and retrace the tracts which I had abandoned, for the Father-of-light, cleaving the clouds with his flashing lightning, drove his thundering steeds and swift chariot through a cloudless sky, whereby the unconscious earth and meandering rivers, whereby Styx and the dreadful seat of odious Tænarus, and Atlas, limit of the world, was shaken. The Deity is able to convert the highest to the lowest *degree*, and he lowers the distinguished, bringing-to-prominence the obscure; from one, sweeping Fortune with shrill whizzing takes off the tiara (*or*, diadem); on another she delights to put *it*.

ODE XXXV. To Fortune.

O Goddess, who rulest pleasing Antium, ready to exalt mortal man either from the lowest state or to convert haughty triumphs to funeral-processions; the poor occupant of the country supplicates thee with anxious prayer, thee as queen of the ocean does he *supplicate*, whoever plies the Carpathian sea in a Bithynian bark. Thee the savage Dacian, thee the roving Scythians, and cities and nations, and warlike Latium, and the mothers of barbarous kings, and purple-clad tyrants dread, lest with destructive foot thou overthrow the standing pillar (*i.e.*, public security), or lest the thronging populace arouse the inactive "to arms!" "to arms!" and destroy the government (*or*, public repose). Thee dire Necessity ever precedes, carrying in her iron hand spike-nails and wedges, nor is the unyielding clamp and melted lead absent. Thee, Hope and rare Fidelity, arrayed in white attire, attend, nor refuse *to be thy* companions, even when, as an enemy with changed dress, thou leavest the home of the powerful. But the false rabble and forsworn courtezan draw back: friends flee-away-in-different-directions, when the casks are drained to the dregs, *too* faithless to bear in common *with* us the yoke-of-adversity. Mayest thou keep Cæsar purposing-to-go against the Britons, remotest-inhabitants of the world, and the recent levy of youthful warriors to be dreaded by Eastern lands and the Red Sea (*or*, Indian Ocean). Alas! *I* am ashamed of *our* scars and of *our* guilt and of brothers slain—What, *in fine*, have we, a hardened age, avoided? What have we in our impiety left undesecrated? From what has our youth restrained its hand through fear of the gods? What altars has it spared? O mayest thou forge again on a new anvil our blunted swords *to be wielded* against the Massagetæ and Arabs.

ODE XXXVI. In honour of Plotius Numidas.

With both incense and the lyre, and the blood of a steer due-to-the-fulfilment-of-our-vow it delights *us* to appease the gods, guardians of Numidas, who now, returning-in-safety from the farthest Spain, distributes many kisses to his loved companions, to none, however, more than to *his* pet Lamias, remembering his childhood spent under the same preceptor, and his toga changed at the same time. Let not this bright day (*or,* season) be without a white mark, nor *let there be any* restriction on the jar brought forth, nor rest of feet after the manner of the Salii, nor let hard-drinking Damalis surpass Bassus in-tossing-off-the-wine-cup after-the-Thracian-fashion, nor let roses be wanting to our banquets, nor long-verdant parsley, nor the short-lived lily. All will rest their languishing eyes on Damalis, nor will Damalis be severed from *his* new paramour, clinging to *him* more closely than wanton ivy.

ODE XXXVII. To his Companions.

Now should we drink, now should the ground be beaten with unfettered foot, now is it time to bedeck the couch of the gods with a Salian banquet, *my* comrades. Hithertofore *it would have been* profanity to bring forth from the cellars filled-by-our-forefathers Cæcuban wine, while the Queen was preparing madly-conceived ruin and destruction for the Capitol and the empire with a polluted herd of men, foul with diseases, weak enough to hope for anything, and intoxicated with *her* prosperous fortune: but scarcely a single ship, saved from the fire, diminished her frenzy, and her soul inflamed-to-madness with Mareotic wine did Cæsar reduce to unfeigned terrors, pursuing her with oars, as she fled from Italy just-as a hawk *pursues* gentle doves, or the swift huntsman the hare in the plains of snowy Hæmonia, that he might clap in chains the fated monster; but she, seeking to perish more nobly, neither dreaded the sword effeminately, nor repaired to (*lit.*, procured in exchange) hidden shores with *her* swift fleet. She dared both to visit with a placid countenance her dejected palace, brave enough even to handle exasperated serpents, that she might suck into her body *their* dark poison, *becoming* more fierce, after having determined to die (*lit.*, death being deliberately planned), disdaining, when-divested-of-her-power, to be led away forsooth in the hostile galleys-of-the-Liburnians, to a proud triumph, *being* no mean woman.

ODE XXXVIII. To his Page.

My page, I hate the festal-preparations of the Persians. Chaplets bound with the inner-bark-of-the-lime-tree displease me. Give over searching in what place the late rose lingers. I am particularly anxious *that* thou shouldest not toil-to-add anything to the simple myrtle, nor does the myrtle ill become thee *my* attendant, nor me while I drink under the shady vine.

BOOK SECOND.

ODE I. To Asinius Pollio.

The civil commotion since the consulship of Metellus, and the causes of the war, and *its* blunders and operations, and the sport of fortune, and the grievous confederacies of the chiefs, and arms stained with blood not yet atoned for—an undertaking full of danger and hazard—thou treatest of, and art walking over fires placed under deceitful ashes. Let the Muse of stern tragedy be absent for a while from our theatres: soon, when thou hast completed-the-history of our public affairs, thou wilt resume *thy* great work (*viz.*, the composition of Tragedies) with the Cecropian buskin, Pollio, distinguished source-of-aid to distressed defendants and to a deliberating Senate, for whom the laurel has won immortal honours by the triumph over Dalmatia. Even now thou stunnest my ears with the threatening blast of trumpets, now the clarions resound; now the flashing of arms frightens the flying-steeds and *spreads-alarm-over* the countenances of *their* riders. Already methinks I hear the shout of mighty leaders, stained with no inglorious dust, and all the world subdued, except the invincible soul of Cato. Juno, and whichever of the gods more friendly to the Africans had helplessly quitted the land unavenged, in-their-turn-offered the grandsons of the conquerors *as* a sacrifice-to-the-manes of Jugurtha. What plain, enriched by Latin blood, does not, by *its* graves, bear-witness-to *our* unnatural wars, and the uproar of Italy's ruin heard by the Medes? What sea or what rivers *are* unacquainted with the mournful war? What sea has Roman blood not discoloured? What coast is free from our blood? But do not, wayward Muse, abandon sportive-themes and resume the task of the Cæan dirge; with me, in a grotto sacred-to-Venus, seek for lays of a lighter strain.

ODE II. To C. Sallustius Crispus.

Silver has no brilliancy when hidden in the greedy earth, O Crispus Sallust, thou foe to wealth (*lit.*, gold or silver plate), unless it shine by moderate use. Proculeius, known for his fatherly disposition to his brothers, will live to a distant age; him will lasting fame waft on an unrelaxing pinion (*lit.*, fearing to be loosened). Thou wouldest rule over a wider domain by curbing thy greedy spirit, than if thou wert to unite Africa to remote Gades, and both Carthages served *thee* alone. The direful dropsy increases by self-indulgence, and does not drive away the thirst, unless the cause of the disease has escaped from the veins, and the watery torpor from the pale body. Virtue, dissenting from the commonalty, exempts Phraates, though restored to Cyrus' throne, from the number of the happy, and unteaches the people to use false names *for things*, conferring independent-rule, and a safe diadem, and an enduring laurel on *him* alone whoever *he be that* gazes with unconcerned eye on huge heaps of gold.

ODE III. To Dellius.

Remember to preserve a composed mind in adversity, as well as *one* restrained from immoderate joy in prosperity, O Dellius! doomed to die, whether thou hast lived in sorrow all thy life-time, or, reclining in a secluded meadow, thou hast, during the holy-days enjoyed thyself with old Falernian wine (*lit.*, the innermost marked wine). To what purpose are the huge pine and white poplar wont to unite-in-forming a sheltering shade with their boughs? Why does the running water strive to ripple in the winding stream? Hither bid *them* bring wines and perfumes and the too short-lived blossoms of the lovely rose, while circumstances, and youth, and the black threads of the three Sisters permit. Thou must quit thy woodlands bought-from-every-quarter, and *thy* mansion and *thy* farm, which the yellow Tiber laves, and *thine* heir shall enjoy *thy* riches piled on high. It matters not whether thou dwellest beneath the-light-of-heaven, rich and descended from old Inachus, or poor and of the lowest birth, the victim of unrelenting Orcus. We are all driven to the same place. The lots of all are shaken in the urn, destined sooner or later to come forth and place us in the bark (Charon's) for an everlasting exile.

ODE IV. To Xanthias Phoceus.

Let not the love of a servant-maid be a source-of-shame to thee, Xanthias Phoceus. Formerly Briseïs of snowy complexion, *though* a slave, roused the haughty Achilles. The beauty of the captive Tecmessa roused *her* master Ajax, Telamon's son. Atreus' son, in the midst of his conquest, fired *with rage* for the ravished virgin, after the barbarous bands fell, the Thessalian *being* conqueror, and Hector's death rendered Troy easier to be destroyed by the weary Greeks. Possibly (*lit.*, you may not know whether) the noble parents of auburn-haired Phyllis may be an honour to thee, *their* son-in-law; no doubt she mourns her royal race and *her* unpropitious gods (*i.e.*, her fate). Believe that she, beloved by thee, is not of the wicked rabble, nor that *one* so faithful, so averse to lucre could ever have sprung from a disreputable mother. *Her* arms and countenance and tapering ankles I disinterestedly commend; avoid being jealous of one whose age is hastening to close its eighth period-of-five-years.

ODE V. To Lalage's Lover.

Nor yet is she able to bear the yoke on *her* tamed neck, not yet to be equal to the duties of a partner, nor to submit to the weight of the bull rushing on to enjoyment. The affection of thy heifer is around green plains, at one time assuaging the burning-heat in streams, at another delighting to play with calves on the green willow-bed. Put away *thy* passion for *the* unripe grape: soon will changing autumn tinge for thee the livid clusters with a purple hue. Soon she will follow thee, for stubborn age is hastening and will add to her the years which it has taken away from thee: soon shall Lalage seek her mate with wanton forehead. Loved more than ever shy Pholoe *was;* more than Chloris, shining as *brightly* with her fair shoulder as the unclouded moon glistens upon the midnight sea, or Gyges of Cnidos, whom if thou hadst placed among a bevy of maidens, he would wonderfully mislead sharp-sighted guests, an imperceptible distinction through his flowing hair and doubtful countenance.

ODE VI. To Septimius.

Septimius, ready-to-go with me to Gades and the Cantabrian, untaught *as yet* to endure our yoke, and to the barbarous Syrtes, where the Moorish water is ever seething: may Tibur, founded by the Argive colonist be the resting-seat of my old age; may it be to me weary of the sea and of journeys and campaigning, the termination *of them.* From it, if the rigorous Fates exclude *me,* I will repair to the river pleasing to skin-covered sheep of Galæsus, and the rural-scenes reigned-over by the Lacedæmonian Phalantus. That nook has charms for me above *all* others of the earth, where the honey yields not to *that of* Hymettus, and the olive vies with *the produce of* the verdant Venafrum, where Jupiter grants a long spring and mild winters, and Aulon, favourable to fertile Bacchus, does not in the least envy Falernian grapes. That spot and *those* happy hills demand thee in-company-with-me: there thou shalt scatter the hot ashes of thy poet friend with a tear due-to-his-memory.

ODE VII. To Pompeius Varus.

O thou who wast often led with me into the utmost danger under Brutus, the leader of *our* warfare, who has restored thee, *as* a Roman-citizen, to thy country's gods and the air of Italy, O Pompey, foremost of my companions? with whom I have often spent the long-lived day over wine having my locks wreathed and shining with Syrian perfume. With thee I experienced Philippi's-battle and the rapid flight, *my* shield being ingloriously abandoned, when heroism *itself* was vanquished, and threatening *warriors* touched the gore-bespattered ground with *their* chin. But me, terror-struck, did Mercury rapidly carry off in a thick mist through the enemy: *but* thee did the receding swell carry away a second time to war on *its* boiling billows. Therefore pay to Jupiter thy votive sacrifice, and lay down *thy* side weary with a long campaigning beneath my laurel, nor spare casks intended for thee. Fill polished drinking-cups with care-dispelling Massic wine; pour perfumes from capacious shells. Who takes-the-charge of quickly-making chaplets of the moist parsley or of the myrtle? Whom will the dice declare the captain of our drinking-bout? I will revel as wildly as the Thracians. It is pleasant for me to-play-the-madman on the recovery of a friend.

ODE VIII. To Barine.

If, Barine, any penalty for perjury had at any time injured thee, if thou hadst become more ugly by a black tooth or one nail, I should believe *the popular superstition.* But thou, as soon as thou hast bound under vows thy treacherous head, shinest forth much more beautiful *than before,* and struttest forth the common object-of-concern of our youths. It is to-thy-advantage to-violate-thine oath-made-by the buried ashes of *thy* mother, and by the silent stars of night with the whole heaven, and by the gods that are free from cold death. At this, I say, Venus herself smiles, the good-natured Nymphs smile, and fierce Cupid, always sharpening *his* fiery arrows on a bloody whetstone. Add *the fact* that all the youth is growing up for thee, a new throng of slaves is growing: nor do former *suitors*, though they have often threatened *to do so*, leave the roof of *their* perjured mistress. Mothers dread thee on account of their young-sons, thee do niggardly old men *dread*, and young-ladies lately married, *being* wretched lest thy attraction should alienate-the-affections of *their* husbands.

ODE IX. To C. Valgius.

Showers do not always flow from the clouds into the rough fields, nor do varying blasts for ever disturb the Caspian sea, nor, *my* friend Valgius, does the motionless ice remain on Armenia's borders during all the months *of the year*, nor do the oak-groves of Garganus struggle with the northern-blasts. *Yet* thou art always in mournful strains lamenting *thy* lost Mystes, nor does affectionate sorrow leave thee, *either* when the Evening Star arises, or when she flees away from the rapid sun. But the aged man, who had lived three generations, did not mourn the love-inspiring Autilochus all the years *of his life*, nor did *his* parents, or the Phrygian sisters, mourn for ever the youthful Troilus. Cease, at length, unmanly complaints, and rather let us sing of the new triumphs of Augustus Cæsar, and of ice-bound Niphates, and how the river of the Medes, added to *our* conquered nations, is rolling humbler waves, and how the Geloni ride-up and down, within the limits prescribed to them, in *their* diminished plains.

ODE X. To Licinius.

Thou wilt live, Licinius, more suitably, by neither always plying the deep, nor, while thou cautiously dreadest the tempests, by keeping too-closely to the rock-indented (*or* perilous) shore. Every one who loves the golden mean keeps at a safe distance from the shabbiness of a decayed building, *and* prudently avoids a hall exciting envy. The tall pine is more frequently tossed by the winds *than low ones,* and lofty towers fall with a heavier crash, and the lightning strikes the tops of mountains. A well-regulated breast in adversity hopes for a changed condition, in prosperity dreads *it.* Jupiter periodically-brings hideous winters, he-likewise removes *them.* Though *it is* bad now, it will not continue to be so hereafter. At times, Apollo awakes the silent muse with *his* lyre, nor does he always bend *his* bow. In adversity show thyself *spirited* and firm : *and* thou shouldest also reef *thy* sails when swollen with too favourable a gale.

ODE XI. To Quintius.

Cease to inquire, Herpinus Quintius, what the warlike Cantabrian and the Scythian may be meditating, separated *from us* by the intervening Hadriatic, and be not solicitous about the wants of a life that requires *but* few things *for its support.* Beardless youth, and beauty pass away, seared hoariness driving away playful loves and gentle sleep. There is not for-ever the same loveliness to vernal flowers, nor does the blushing moon shine with unvarying appearance. Why dost thou weary with unending designs *thy* soul unequal-*to-the task?* Why do we not drink, while *we* may, thus at-ease lying either beneath the tall plane-tree or this pine, and having our grey hairs scented by the rose and anointed with Assyrian spikenard. Bacchus dispels gnawing cares. What boy will most quickly cool cups of hot Falernian wine with the water that runneth by *us?* Who will draw out of *her* house the roving wench Lyde? Come, bid her hasten with her ivory lyre, having her hair tied into a graceful knot, after the fashion of a Spartan maid.

ODE XII. To Mæcenas.

Be unwilling that the long wars of fierce Numantia, or cursed Hannibal, or the Sicilian sea empurpled with Carthaginian blood, be adapted to the soft measures of the lyre, or the savage Lapithæ, and Hylæus too-much-given to wine, and Earth's sons subdued by Hercules' hand, from whom the bright mansion of old Saturn dreaded danger; and thou, Mæcenas, wilt better relate in prose narratives the battles of Cæsar, and the necks of defiant kings dragged through the streets. The Muse has willed me to sing the sweet vocal-powers of *thy* mistress Licymnia, *her* bright shining eyes, and breast most faithful to reciprocated loves; whom it neither ill-befits to raise the foot in the dance, nor to vie in sportive-mirth, nor, while playing, to throw her arms around gay virgins on Diana's sacred day. Thou wouldest not wish, wouldest thou, to exchange for a lock of Licymnia's hair, *the wealth* which rich Achæmenes possessed, or the Mygdonian opulence of rich Phrygia, or the full houses of the Arabs, while she turns her neck towards *thy* ardent kisses, or with goodnatured cruelty denies, what she is more pleased should be snatched than at thy asking for *them, and* is sometimes *herself* the first to snatch them.

ODE XIII. To the Tree by whose Fall on his Sabine Farm he was nearly Killed.

He, whosoever first *did so,* both planted thee on an unlucky day and with an unholy hand reared *thee up,* O tree, for the ruin of *his* descendants and the disgrace of *thy* village. I could believe that he had even broken the neck of his own parent, and had bespattered the innermost-part-of-his-dwelling with the night-committed bloodshed of a guest-friend. He has handled Colchian poisons and *perpetrated* every wickedness which is anywhere conceived (*i.e.*, every conceivable wickedness) who set thee in my field, unlucky log, ready-to-fall on the head of *thy* owner undeserving *such treatment.* Man is never sufficiently on his guard against what each-one should avoid from hour-to-hour; the Carthaginian mariner greatly dreads the Bosporus, but does not fear unforeseen fates from some-other-quarter; the soldier *fears only* the arrows and rapid retreat of the Parthian, *while* the Parthian fears chains and Italian prowess; but the unforeseen force of death carries off, and will carry off, people. How nearly did we see the realms of sable Proserpine, and Æacus dispensing-justice, and the separated abodes of the pious, and with *her* Æolian lyre Sappho complaining of her young countrywomen, and thee, Alcæus, sounding forth in-deeper-strains with thy golden quill the hardships of ocean, the cruel hardships of exile, the hardships of war! The shades listen-with-admiration to each, as they pour forth strains worthy *of being heard* in holy silence; but the crowd, pressing with *their* shoulders *to hear,* drinks in with more delight *the narrative of* conflicts, and of tyrants driven *from their thrones.* What wonder, when, astounded at those strains, the hundred-headed beast hangs down his black ears, and snakes, entwined in the hair of the Furies, are refreshed. Nay more, both Prometheus and the father of Pelops, by the sweet melody, are lulled into-a-forgetfulness of their sufferings, nor cares Orion to hunt lions or timid jackals.

ODE XIV. To Postumus.

Alas! Postumus, Postumus, the fleet years glide away, nor will devotion bring a check to wrinkles and impending old age and unconquered death; no, not, my friend, if thou attemptest-to-appease with three hundred bulls, for every day that passes, the inexorable Pluto, who confines the triple-bodied Geryon, and Tityos by the dreary flood, which must assuredly be sailed over by all *of us* who live on the bounty of the earth, whether *we be* lords or poor peasants. In vain shall we keep aloof from bloody war and the broken waves of the hoarse Hadriatic; in vain during autumns shall we shun the South-Wind injurious to our bodies: dark Cocytos meandering with its sluggish stream must be visited, and the infamous offspring of Danaus and Sisyphus, the son of Æolus, condemned to eternal toil. The world, and thy mansion, and pleasing wife, must be left behind, nor of these trees which thou art cultivating will any accompany *thee, their* short-lived owner, except the odious cypresses. Thine heir more worthy, will consume thy Cæcuban-wines, guarded with a hundred keys, and will dye thy mosaic floor with costly undiluted-wine, better than *that which is quaffed* at the banquets of the pontiffs.

ODE XV. Against the Luxury of his own Age.

Soon will palatial structures leave *but* few acres for the plough. Ponds, extended more widely than the Lucrine lake, will be seen on every side, and the unwedded plane-tree shall take the place of the elms. Then beds-of-violets and myrtle, and every abundance of scented-flowers, will shed perfume over olive-beds *which were* productive to their former owner. Then the laurel, thick with branches, will exclude the burning rays. It was not so ordained under the directions of Romulus, and unshorn Cato, and the regulation of the ancients. Their private fortunes were small, the public income large: no portico, measured for private individuals by rods-ten-feet-in-length, received the cool Northern breeze, nor did the laws, while they ordered them to adorn *their* towns at the public charge, and the temples of the gods with new stone, permit them [*in rearing their simple abodes*] to reject chance turf.

ODE XVI. To Pompeius Grosphus.

One overtaken-by-a-storm in the wide Ægean-sea prays the gods for repose, as soon as a dark cloud has overshadowed the moon, and the sure-guiding stars shine not for the mariners: Thrace, furious in war, *prays for* repose; for repose, the Medes graced with a quiver, O Grosphus, which cannot be purchased with gems, or purple, or gold. For neither riches, nor the consular lictor, removes the wretched disorders of the mind, and cares hovering around fretted ceilings. That man lives happily, on scanty means, whose paternal salt-cellar glitters on *his* frugal board, and neither fear nor mean avarice takes away *his* light slumbers. Why do we, with life *so* brief, venturously project many *plans ?* Why do we change our own for lands hot beneath another sun? What exile from his country escapes *also* from himself? Corroding cares climb the brazen-headed galleys, nor leaves squadrons of horsemen, swifter than the hinds, and the East-Wind driving the clouds. Let the mind that is contented with the present dislike to be anxious about what is beyond, and sweeten bitter *mishaps* with a placid smile. Nothing is in every respect of a happy-turn. Quick death carried off the illustrious Achilles, protracted old age wasted away Tithonus, and for me perhaps the passing-hour will grant what it has denied to thee. Around thee a hundred herds and Sicilian cows are lowing; for thee the mare fit for the chariot-of-four raises *her* neighing, woollen-vestments twice dipped in African purple clothe *thee*: to me, Fate, not disappointing *my hopes*, has given a small rural-estate, and a slight inspiration of the Grecian Muse, and *the position* to despise the spiteful rabble.

ODE XVII. To Mæcenas.

Why dost thou kill me with thy complaints? It is agreeable neither to the gods nor to me that thou shouldest die before me, O Mæcenas, noble source-of-my-honour and support of my fortune. Ah! if the untimely force of *death* hurries thee away, the one-half of my soul, why do I, the other *part*, linger-behind, neither equally dear *to myself*, nor surviving entire? That day will bring destruction to us both. I have not uttered *as* a false oath "we will go, we will go, whenever *thou* precedest, ready to take the last journey as companions." Neither the breath of fire-emitting Chimæra, nor if the hundred-handed Gyas were to rise to life-again, shall ever sever *thee from me*: so has it been ordained by powerful Justice and the Fates. Whether Libra or formidable Scorpio, as the more influential part of the hour of my birth, presides over-my-existence (*lit.* looks to me), or Capricorn, the monarch of the Western wave, our respective horoscopes agree in a wonderful manner. The guardianship of Jupiter, shining-in-opposition-to impious Saturn, rescued thee and slackened the wings of rapidly-coming Fate, when, in the theatre, a crowded audience thrice raised a shout-of-joy: a tree, falling on my head, would have cut me off, had not Faunus, guardian of men of letters, warded off the blow with *his* right hand. Remember to offer victims and a votive shrine *in discharge of thy vow*; we will sacrifice a humble ewe-lamb.

ODE XVIII. On the Contentment with which he Prefers his Poverty to Riches.

Neither ivory nor gold-fretted ceiling glitters in my house. Slabs of Hymettian marble do not press upon pillars hewn from the remotest part of Africa. Nor have I, as an unrecognized heir, seized upon the palace of an Attalus, nor do female-dependants of-noble-birth spin for me Laconian purple-robes. But I have integrity and a liberal vein of talent, and the rich court me, a poor man. I worry the gods for nothing beyond, nor do I importune my powerful friend for larger gifts, being abundantly satisfied with my single Sabine farm. Day is pushed on by day, and the new moons hasten to wane away. Thou, on the verge of death, art contracting for the cutting of marble, and unmindful of the grave, art building houses, and art impatient to remove the shores of the sea that echoes round Baiæ, not rich enough with the shore of the mainland. What *shall I say,* in that thou art ever removing the neighbouring landmarks, and, through avarice, art leaping over the boundaries of thy dependants. The wife and the husband, bearing in their bosom their paternal gods and squalid children, are evicted. Yet no home awaits the rich master with greater certainty than *that* destined by the limit of rapacious Orcus. Why strivest thou for more? The earth impartially opens to the poor and the children of princes, nor did Orcus' guardsman carry back the cunning Prometheus, bribed by gold. He confines haughty Tantalus and the race of Tantalus: he *whether* invoked, or not, to relieve the poor discharged of his toils, attends *to him.*

ODE XIX. To Father Bacchus.

I saw Bacchus dictating strains amid rocks far-distant *from the haunts of men,* believe *me* posterity, and the Nymphs learning *them,* and the attentively listening ears of the goat-footed Satyrs. Evoë! *my* mind trembles with recent dread, and my bosom, filled with *the inspiration of* Bacchus, is agitated with troubled joy. Evoë! forbear,

Bacchus, forbear, *thou* that art to be dreaded for thy heavy thyrsus. It is allowed me to sing of the stubbornly-raging Bacchantes, and of the fountain of wine, and abundant rivulets of milk, and to tell-again-and-again-of honey flowing from hollow trunks. It is allowed *me* also *to sing of* the ornament of *thy* blessed spouse added to the stars, and the palace of Pentheus thrown down with no gentle ruin, and the destruction of the Thracian Lycurgus. Thou turnest back rivers, thou *swayest* the Indian sea, thou, on the lonely mountain-tops, moist-with-wine, confinest, without harm *to them*, the locks of the Bacchantes with a knot of vipers. Thou, when the impious throng of Giants was climbing the realms of *thy* Sire over the height, didst hurl back Rhœtus with the claws and hideous jaw of a lion, though said *to be* fitter for dances and festive mirth and sport, thou wast reported not *to be* equally well suited for the fight; yet thou, the same *deity*, didst become the arbiter of peace and war. Thee, graced with *thy* golden horn, did Cerberus behold without-offering-any-harm, gently wagging his tail, and the feet and legs *of thee* withdrawing he licked with his triple-tongued mouth.

ODE XX. To Mæcenas.

A bard of double-form, I shall be borne through the liquid air on no common, no feeble pinion, nor shall I linger *much* longer on the earth, and, beyond-the-reach-of detraction, I shall leave this *world's* cities, I, the offspring of poor parents shall not, I, whom thou Mæcenas called "darling," shall not die, neither shall I be confined by the water of the Styx. Now, *even* now, the rough skin is settling on my legs, and I am being transformed to a white swan in my-upper-parts, and the downy plumage is forming on my fingers and shoulders. Soon, swifter than Dædalian Icarus, I shall visit the shores of the roaring Bosporus, and the Gætulian Syrtes, and the farthest plains of the North, a melodious bird. Me shall the Colchian and the Dacian, who dissembles *his* fear of the Marsic soldiery, and the remote Geloni know, me the literary Spaniard and he who drinks of the Rhone shall learn. Let dirges, and unbecoming mournings and lamentations be away from *my* useless funeral-ceremony; check *thy* cry, and abandon the superfluous honour of my burial.